VOLUME II

ASPECTS *of* WESTERN CIVILIZATION

Problems and Sources in History

Sixth Edition

Edited by
PERRY M. ROGERS

Upper Saddle River, New Jersey 07458

For Ann, Elisa, Kit, and Tyler

Library of Congress Cataloging-in-Publication Data

Aspects of Western civilization: problems and sources in history / edited by Perry M. Rogers.— 6th ed.
p. cm.
Includes bibliographical references and index.
ISBN-13: 978–0–13–241402–9 (alk. paper)
ISBN-10: 0–13–241402–3 (alk. paper)
1. Civilization, Western—History. 2. Civilization, Western—History—Sources. I. Rogers, Perry McAdow.
CB245.A86 2008
909'.09821—dc22

2007011774

Editorial Director: Charlyce Jones Owen
Executive Editor: Charles Cavaliere
Editorial Assistant: Maureen Diana
Associate Marketing Manager: Sasha Anderson-Smith
Sr. Managing Editor: Joanne Riker
Production Liaison: Fran Russello
Manufacturing Buyer: Ben Smith
Creative Director: Jayne Conte
Cover Design: Bruce Kenselaar
Cover Illustration/Photo: Ichikawa Hoin Ga, "The Picture of the Procession of the foreigners in Okohama, c. 1855" Courtesy, Library of Congress
Director, Image Resource Center: Melinda Patelli
Manager, Rights and Permissions: Zina Arabia
Manager, Visual Research: Beth Brenzel
Manager, Cover Visual Research & Permissions: Rita Wenning
Image Permission Coordinator: Fran Toepfer
Composition/Full-Service Project Management: Karpagam Jagadeesan/GGS Book Services
Printer/Binder: R.R. Donnelley & Sons Company

Pearson Education LTD. London
Pearson Education Singapore, Pte. Ltd
Pearson Education, Canada, Ltd
Pearson Education–Japan
Pearson Education Australia PTY, Limited
Pearson Education North Asia Ltd
Pearson Educación de Mexico, S.A. de C.V.
Pearson Education Malaysia, Pte. Ltd
Pearson Education, Upper Saddle River, New Jersey

10 9 8 7 6 5 4 3 2 1
ISBN-13: 978-0-13-205049-4
ISBN-10: 0-13-205049-8

Brief Contents

VOLUME I
The Ancient World Through the Reformation

VOLUME II

THE AGE OF THE RENAISSANCE THROUGH THE CONTEMPORARY WORLD

Contents

11 THE RUSSIAN REVOLUTION AND THE DEVELOPMENT OF THE SOVIET STATE (1917–1939) 308

PREFACE

The Roman orator Cicero once remarked, "History is the witness of the times, the torch of truth, the life of memory, the teacher of life, the messenger of antiquity." In spite of these noble words, historians have often labored under the burden of justifying the value of studying events that are over and done. Humankind is practical, more concerned with its present and future than with its past. And yet the study of history provides us with unique opportunities for self-knowledge. It teaches us what we have done and therefore helps define what we are. On a less abstract level, the study of history enables us to judge present circumstance by drawing on the laboratory of the past. Those who have lived and died, through their recorded attitudes, actions, and ideas, have left a legacy of experience.

One of the best ways to travel through time and space and perceive the very humanness that lies at the root of history is through the study of primary sources. These are the documents, coins, letters, inscriptions, art, music, architecture, and monuments of past ages. The task of historians is to evaluate this evidence with a critical eye and then construct a narrative that is consistent with the "facts" as they have established them. Such interpretations are inherently subjective and therefore open to dispute. History is thus filled with controversy as historians argue their way toward the so-called truth. The only way to work toward an understanding of the past is through personal examination of the primary sources.

Yet, for the beginning student, this poses some difficulties. Such inquiry casts the student adrift from the security of accepting the "truth" as revealed in a textbook. In fact, history is too often presented in a deceptively objective manner; one learns facts and dates in an effort to obtain the "right" answers for multiple-choice tests. But the student who has wrestled with primary sources and has experienced voices from the past on a more intimate level accepts the responsibility of evaluation and judgment. He or she understands that history does not easily lend itself to "right" answers but demands reflection on the problems that have confronted past societies and are at play even in our contemporary world. Cicero was right in viewing history as the "life of memory." But human memory is fragile and the records of the past can be destroyed or distorted. Without the past, people have nothing with which to judge what they are told in the present. Truth then becomes the preserve of the ruler or government, no longer relative, but absolute. The study of history, and primary sources in particular, goes far in making people aware of the continuity of humankind and the progress of civilization.

Aspects of Western Civilization offers the student an opportunity to evaluate the primary sources of the past and to do so in a structured and organized format. The documents provided are diverse and include state papers, secret dispatches, letters, diary accounts, poems, newspaper articles, papal encyclicals, propaganda flyers, and even wall graffiti. Occasionally, the assessments of modern historians are included to lend perspective. All give testimony to human endeavor in Western societies. Yet this two-volume book has been conceived as more than a simple compilation of primary sources. The subtitle of the work, *Problems and Sources in History*, gives true indication of the nature of its premise. It is meant to provide the student with thoughtful and engaging material focused around individual units that encompass time periods, specific events, and historical questions. Students learn from the past most effectively when posed with problems that have meaning for their own lives. In evaluating the material from *Aspects of Western Civilization*, the student will discover that issues are not nearly as simple as they may appear at first glance. Historical sources often contradict each other, and truth then depends on logic and one's own experience and outlook on life. Throughout these volumes, the student is confronted with basic questions regarding historical development, human nature, moral action, and practical necessity. The text is therefore broad in its scope and incorporates a wide variety of political, social, economic, religious, intellectual, and scientific issues. It is internally organized around **seven major themes** that provide direction and cohesion to the text while allowing for originality of thought in both written and oral analysis:

1. ***The Power Structure:*** What are the institutions of authority in Western societies, and how have they been structured to achieve political, social and economic stability? This theme seeks to introduce the student to the various systems of rule that have shaped Western civilization: classical democracy, representative democracy (republican government), oligarchy, constitutional monarchy, divine-right monarchy, theocracy, and dictatorship (especially fascism and totalitarian rule). What are the advantages and drawbacks to each? This rubric also includes the concepts of balance of power and containment, principles of succession, geopolitics, and social and economic theories such as capitalism, communism, and socialism.
2. ***The Institution and the Individual:*** What is the relationship between personal, creative expression in society and the governing political, religious, and social institutions of the age? How have writers, artists, and poets variously been employed through patronage systems to enhance political authority, perpetuate myths, and create heroes who embody the values of the age? What is the role of the rebel, the free thinker, who works against the grain and threatens the status quo by exploring new dimensions of thought or creative expression?
3. ***Social and Spiritual Values:*** The Judeo-Christian and Islamic heritage of Western civilization form the basis of this theme. How have religious values and moral attitudes affected the course of Western history? Is there a natural competition between church and state as two controlling units in society? Which is more influential, which legacy more enduring? How has religion been used as a means of securing political power or of instituting social change? To what extent have spiritual reform movements resulted in a change of political or social policy, or artistic style? Are ideas more potent than any army? Why have so many people died fighting for religions that abhor violence? Does every society need a spiritual foundation? How do art, architecture, and literature reflect the dominant values of an era?
4. ***Imperialism:*** How has imperialism been justified throughout Western history, and what are the moral implications of gaining and maintaining empire? Is defensive imperialism a practical foreign policy option? Is containment essentially a defensive or offensive policy? This theme is often juxtaposed with subtopics of nationalism, war, altruism, and human nature.
5. ***Revolution and Historical Transition:*** This theme seeks to define and examine the varieties of revolution: political, intellectual, economic, social, and artistic. What are the underlying and precipitating causes of political revolution? How essential is the intellectual foundation? Do technological and economic revolutions have a direct correlation to political or social revolutions? Does an artistic revolution stem from political change or a shifting of social realities? This theme focuses on transition through historical or artistic periods.
6. ***The Varieties of Truth:*** What is the role of propaganda in history? Many sections

examine the use and abuse of information, often in connection with absolute government, revolution, imperialism, or genocide. What roles do art, architecture, poetry, and literature play in the "creation of belief" and in the successful consolidation of power? This theme emphasizes the relativity of truth and stresses the responsibility of the individual to assess the validity of evidence.

7. ***Women in History:*** The text intends to help remedy the widespread omission of women from the history of Western society and to develop an appreciation for their contributions to the intellectual and political framework of Western civilization. At issue is how women have been viewed—or rendered invisible—throughout history and how individually and collectively their presence is inextricably linked with the development and progress of civilization. This inclusive approach stresses the importance of achieving a perspective that lends value and practical application to history.

STRUCTURE OF THE BOOK

The main strength of the text lies in its structure and the direction given to the student through introductions to each primary source. Study questions promote analysis and evoke critical response. Each chapter follows the same format:

- ***Timeline Chronological Overview:*** These brief timelines are designed to give students a visual perspective of the main events, movements, and personalities discussed in the chapter.
- ***Quotations:*** These are statements from various historians, artists, philosophers, diplomats, literary figures, and religious spokespersons who offer insight and give perspective on the subject matter of the chapter.
- ***Chapter Themes:*** Each chapter is framed by several questions that direct the reader to broader issues and comparative perspectives found in the ideas and events of other chapters. This feature acknowledges the changing perspectives of different eras while linking historical problems that emphasize the continuity of history.
- ***General Introduction:*** A general introduction then provides a brief historical background and focuses the themes or questions to be discussed in the chapter.
- ***Headnotes:*** These are extensive introductions that explain in detail the historical or biographical background of each primary source. They also focus themes and discuss interrelationships with other relevant primary sources.
- ***Primary Sources:*** The sources provided are diverse and include excerpts from drama and literature, short stories, speeches, letters, diary accounts, poems, newspaper articles, philosophical tracts, propaganda flyers, and works of art and architecture.
- ***Study Questions:*** A series of study questions conclude each source or chapter section and present a basis for oral discussion or written analysis. The study questions do not seek mere regurgitation of information but demand a more thoughtful response that is based on reflective analysis of the primary sources.

FEATURES AND INTEGRATED FORMAT

The study of history is necessarily an integrative experience. *Aspects of Western Civilization* provides insight into the interrelationships among art, music, literature, poetry, and architecture during various historical periods. Students are linked to relevant historical events, broader artistic movements, and styles through **four unique features** included in each chapter:

1. ***The Artistic Vision:*** This feature emphasizes the creative processes and vision of an artist who embodies a dominant style of the period or expresses the social or spiritual values of the age.
2. ***Against the Grain:*** This feature focuses on those who don't fit or are in conflict with their societies but embody the edge of creative

change and set new artistic or historical parameters: the outsider, the radical mind, the free thinker. What impact does the individual have on the historical landscape? To what extent does progress depend on those who threaten the status quo and seek new directions outside the mainstream?

3. ***The Architectural Foundation:*** This feature emphasizes architecture as an expression of culture. Most often, this section includes a visual analysis of floor plans, religious shrines, theaters, or other monuments that are important cultural expressions of a particular society.
4. ***The Reflection in the Mirror:*** This feature offers an analysis of a focused moral or philosophical problem within a culture. It emphasizes the more abstract themes of progress and decline, arrogance and power, salvation, the impact of war and disease, the conflict between science and religion, the relationship between divinity and humanity, and the importance of human memory and creativity when juxtaposed with technological progress. This feature promotes thoughtful reflection at critical moments of change.

USE OF THE BOOK

Aspects of Western Civilization offers the instructor a wide variety of didactic applications. The chapters fit into a more or less standard lecture format and are **ordered chronologically**. An entire chapter may be assigned for oral discussion, or sections from each chapter may satisfy particular interests or requirements. Some of the chapters provide extensive treatment of a broad historical topic ("The Sword of Faith: The High Middle Ages"; "'I Am the State'": The Development of Absolutism in England and France"; "The Enlightenment and the Revolution of the Mind"; "'Liberty, Equality, Fraternity!': The French Revolution"). To make them manageable and effective, I have grouped them into topical sections that can be utilized separately, if so desired.

The chapters may also be assigned for **written analysis**. One of the most important concerns of both instructor and student in an introductory class is the written assignment. *Aspects of Western Civilization* has been designed to provide self-contained topics that are problem oriented, promote reflection and analysis, and encourage responsible citation of particular primary sources. The study questions for each chapter should generally produce an eight- to ten-page paper or a two- to three-page comparative analysis.

ACKNOWLEDGMENTS

I would particularly like to thank friends and colleagues who contributed their expertise and enthusiasm to this book. Susan Altan lent her perspective and sensitive awareness of women's issues at critical moments when new avenues of thought were most needed. Daniel Hall and Thomas Tappan advised me on several scientific and technological matters that broadened the scope of the text immeasurably. Linda Swarlis and Mary Ann Leonard offered their unique perspectives regarding ethical issues, which often caused me to pause and certainly forced the introduction of new questions into the discussion. Marsha Ryan provided me with material and literary insight that added greatly to the accuracy of the text, and Jack Guy read drafts of some chapters, offering sterling commentary throughout. Thanks also to the students of Columbus School for Girls, who continue to test the chapters in this book with their typical diligence and hard work; the final product has benefited greatly from their suggestions and ideas. I would like to thank the following reviewers: George J. Marcopoulos, Tufts University, and Robert Bucholz, Loyola University. Finally, I owe an immeasurable debt to my wife, Ann, who suffered all the outrageous fortune and disruption that goes into writing a book of this kind over a period of years—she did it with me.

P. M. R.

Part I

Foundations of the Modern World

The Age of Renaissance and Reformation

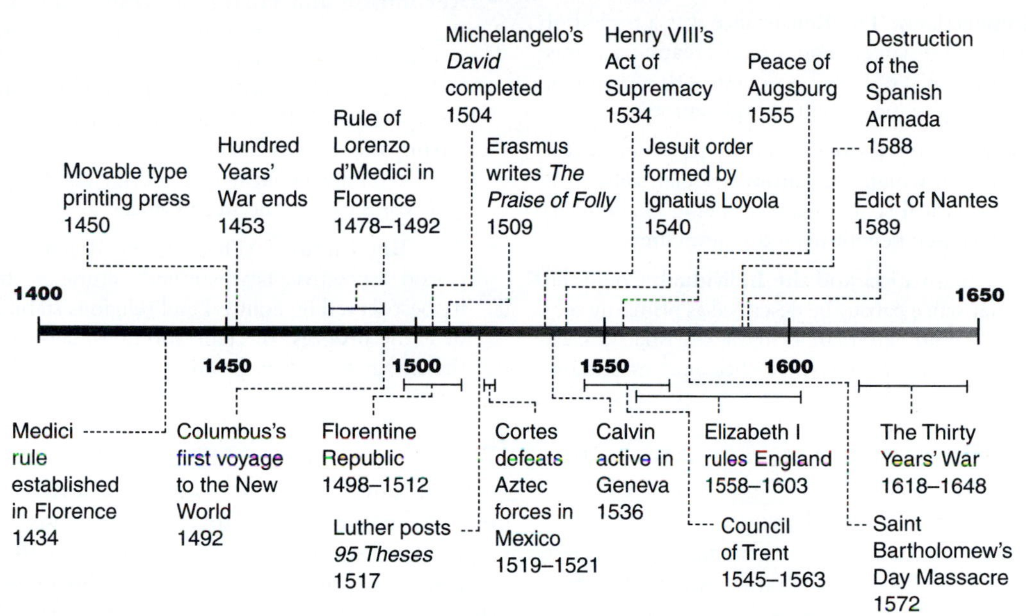

SECTION I: THE AGE OF THE RENAISSANCE

Learning is the only thing the mind never exhausts, never fears and never regrets.

—Leonardo da Vinci

What a piece of work is man, how noble in reason, how infinite in faculty; in form and moving, how express and admirable, in action how like an angel, in apprehension how like a god: a beauty of the world, the paragon of animals!

—William Shakespeare, Hamlet

Apart from man, no being wonders at his own existence.

—Arthur Schopenhauer

Man is the measure of all things.

—Protagoras

Man—a creature made at the end of the week's work when God was tired.

—Mark Twain

SECTION THEMES

- **The Power Structure:** How did the Medici family control Florence? Was their influence based on their "power" or on their "authority"? How could this be compared to the rule of the Roman emperor Augustus? Could the government of Savonarola legitimately be described as a theocracy?
- **Imperialism:** The Renaissance was a period of personal discovery and artistic creativity. It was also a period of brutal conquest of the Americas. Must exploration result in exploitation?
- **Women in History:** The Renaissance was a period in which conventional social, religious, and political structures were being challenged. Did women benefit from this new climate?
- **The Institution and the Individual:** Could the Renaissance papacy be described as primarily secular and not spiritual? Had the Christian church during the Renaissance become essentially another secular institution in order to compete with European monarchs? Were the Renaissance popes secular rulers?
- **Social and Spiritual Values:** What were the fundamental tenets of humanism, and why were they considered radical, especially to the church?
- **Revolution and Historical Transition:** The Renaissance has been seen as a period of transition between the "static" Middle Ages and the "vibrant" modern world. Is this a reasonable interpretation? How was progress measured during the Renaissance, and what drawbacks were evident? What debt does our contemporary world owe to the Renaissance?
- **The Big Picture:** Why was the Renaissance period so creative? Is artistic and cultural creativity best served by political and religious stability, or is the progress of civilization best served by the energy that chaos promotes?

The Late Middle Ages, from about 1300 to 1450, was a time of great struggle and calamity in western Europe. The fabric of medieval civilization was gradually torn apart by a plenitude of simultaneous catastrophes that oppressed the spirit and augured the decline of an age of faith.

The great political debacle of the period was the Hundred Years' War, which began in 1337 over English claims to the French throne and did not end until 1453. Although battles were fought only intermittently during this period, the war sapped the economic resources of the developing nation-states and directed the energy of Europe onto a path of self-destruction. No longer were Europeans united in some foreign crusade against the enemies of God; they now tore each other apart in rather mindless confusion. But wars are made by people, and at least they have some foreknowledge of the destruction that inevitably ensues. No one, however, could have predicted the devastating effects of the Black Death. From 1347 to 1351, it raged throughout Europe, destroying a third to a half of the population. Apart from the physical agony of the disease, the mental terror of an unseen, unknown enemy was enough to divert the energy of life into a dance of death. No one was exempt from the potential of its destruction. God seemed to forsake his flock, and the church was hard-pressed to explain or prevail against the "grim reaper." But the church's credibility as the instrument of God had already been called into question by corruption and disunity. In 1309, the papacy was transferred from its traditional seat in Rome to the city of Avignon, France. This "Babylonian Captivity," as it was called, deprived the papacy of authority and contributed to its loss of respect as prelates became known for their licentiousness and corruption. In 1378, the papacy was transferred back to Rome. But political maneuvering resulted in a "schism" that split Western Christianity into two camps, led by two popes, one in Rome and one in Avignon. This spiritual calamity was finally resolved by a series of councils of the church that were empowered to pass judgments on the papacy itself. In effect, they declared their superiority over the pope in spiritual affairs. The reformist zeal of these councils, however, did little but underscore the need for widespread change in the church. The papacy continued to degenerate: Pope Alexander VI fathered several children and Pope Julius II, bedecked in full armor, led papal armies against the French.

These political, social, and spiritual calamities sapped the energy of medieval civilization and destroyed the spiritual foundation that had inspired people to build the cathedrals and to resist the barbarism that came close on the heels of Rome's decline. The focus of Western Civilization was shifting from a dutiful devotion to God to an emphasis on the worth and importance of humanity. This transformation was centered, at the outset, in Italy, and began during the calamitous fourteenth century. By 1450, the Renaissance was in full bloom.

The term *renaissance* means "rebirth"; it was coined by scholars in the fifteenth and sixteenth centuries who felt a new inspiration. They viewed the medieval world as one of mindless chanting and uncreative introspection. According to Renaissance man, the preceding centuries were "Middle Ages" between the brilliance of the ancient Greeks and Romans and the reflection of that light in the culture of fifteenth-century Italy. The Middle Ages became synonymous with the "Dark Ages." For the scholars of the Renaissance, the hope of Western Civilization lay in a cultivation of the classical works of antiquity. The masters of thought and erudition were figures like Cicero, Aristotle, Plato, Virgil, and Thucydides. They became models and authorities for argument, insight, and eloquence. No longer was it enough to be able to read Cicero: one was now expected to imitate his Latin style. A cult of the classics developed as people admired the ancient monuments of Roman civilization and sought copies of the ancient texts. The Renaissance movement was primarily a scholarly pursuit of the ideals and values of classical civilization.

Chief among those values was the emphasis on man; this led to the movement known as humanism. The Renaissance emphasized the most positive aspects of humanity. Rational thought and creative instinct were prized. Man was composed of two natures: the brutal force of the animal and some of the divine qualities of God. Most important, he had the free will to pursue his own path. The course of his life was determined not by God but by his own ambition, talent, or deceit. The glory of humanity was portrayed in the poetry and astoundingly rich art of the period. The names of Leonardo, Raphael, and Michelangelo evoke mastery of technique and perfection of style. But perhaps the most transparent assessment of reality was made by Niccolò Machiavelli. For him, power and control were the watchwords of existence. This was man, stripped of his embellishment and conscious of the political realities of life. *The Prince* was Machiavelli's manual on practical survival in a chaotic age. Glory could also be attained by strong, competent rule.

Machiavelli made people aware of the realities of power politics, and in doing so he was fulfilling a need in society. For Italy was not a united kingdom, but rather a disjointed chaotic grouping of city-states, led variously by despots, oligarchs, and republicans. It is a curious paradox that societal chaos seems to breed creativity; Michelangelo painted the Sistine Chapel while Rome was in peril of being taken by French armies. The relationship between chaos and creativity is a question worth pursuing, for it precedes discussion of a wider issue: the progress of civilization. Why was the Renaissance such a creative period, artistically, technologically, and politically?

Is creativity truly an ingredient of progress, or is the progress of civilization best served by solid administration and continuity, as we found during the height of the Roman Empire? This chapter investigates some of the ideas and attitudes that influenced European Renaissance society and continue to influence our lives today.

The Humanist Movement

Oration on the Dignity of Man (1486)

PICO DELLA MIRANDOLA

Perhaps the supreme statement of the Renaissance idolization of man is an extended essay by Pico della Mirandola, a linguist and philosopher who lived from 1463 to 1494. Note Pico's conception of man's relationship to God in this excerpt from the *Oration on the Dignity of Man.*

At last I understand why man is the most fortunate of creatures and therefore worthy of all admiration and given the highest rank in the universal chain of Being—a rank envied not only by those who are disreputable, but even by the stars and by minds beyond this world. This is a wonderful vision, and even a matter past faith. And why shouldn't it be? For, it is because of this that man has been rightly described as a great miracle and wondrous creature indeed. . . . God the Father, the supreme Architect, had already built his cosmic home that we see all around us, that most sacred temple of His divinity, by the laws of His mysterious wisdom. The region above the heavens He had adorned with wise minds, the heavenly spheres He had refreshed with eternal souls, and the . . . filthy parts of the lower world He had filled with many animals of every kind. But, when the work was finished, the Craftsman kept wishing that there were someone to consider and appreciate the plan of so great a work, to love its beauty, and to wonder at its profundity. Therefore, when everything was done, God finally decided to create man. But he had no model—nor was there any treasure that he might give to His son as an inheritance, nor did any place exist where His new son might contemplate the universe. All was now finished and everything had been assigned to the highest, the middle, and the lowest orders. . . . At last the best of artisans . . . took man as a creature whose nature was not fully determined and, assigning him a place in the middle of the world, addressed him like this: "The nature of all other beings is limited and constrained within the bounds of laws prescribed by Us. You, however, are constrained by no limits, and in accordance with your own free will . . . , shall determine for yourself the limits of your nature. We have placed you at the world's center so that from here, you may more easily observe all that composes the world. We have made you neither of heaven nor of earth, neither mortal nor immortal, so that endowed with freedom of choice and with honor, as though you create and control your own life, you may fashion yourself in whatever way you decide. You shall have the power to

"Oration on the Dignity of Man" is from *A Platonic Discourse on Love*, edited by Edmund G. Gardner (Boston: The Merrymount Press, 1914). Based on the translation of Thomas Stanley, 1651. Translation modernized by the editor.

degenerate into the lower forms of life, which are savage. And you shall have the power, through reflection of your soul, to be reborn into the higher forms, which are divine." What supreme generosity of God the Father! What most wonderful happiness for man! God has granted you the power to have whatever you want, to be whatever you will.

The Soul of Man (1474)

MARSILIO FICINO

The ideas of the Greek philosopher Plato were revived during the Renaissance by Neoplatonists who applied his theory on transmigration of the soul to Christian concepts of resurrection. The leading exponent of this philosophy was Marsilio Ficino. Some of his ideas on God and man follow.

Man is really the vicar of God, since he inhabits and cultivates all elements and is present on earth without being absent from the ether. He uses not only the elements, but also all the animals which belong to the elements, the animals of the earth, of the water, and of the air, for food, convenience, and pleasure, and the higher celestial beings for knowledge and the miracles of magic. Not only does he make use of the animals, he also rules them. It is true, with the weapons received from nature some animals may at times attack man or escape his control. But with the weapons he has invented himself man avoids the attacks of wild animals, puts them to flight and tames them. Who has ever seen any human beings kept under the control of animals, in such a way as we see everywhere herds of both wild and domesticated animals obeying men throughout their lives? Man not only rules the animals by force, he also governs, keeps and teaches them. Universal providence belongs to God, who is the universal cause. Hence man who provides generally for all things, both living and lifeless, is a kind of god. Certainly he is the god of the animals, for he makes use of them all, and instructs many of them. It is also obvious that he is the god of the elements for he inhabits and cultivates all of them. Finally, he is the god of all materials for he handles, changes and shapes all of them. He who governs the body in so many and so important ways, and is the vicar of the immortal God, he is no doubt immortal. . . .

Individual animals are hardly capable of taking care of themselves or their young. Man alone abounds in such a perfection that he first rules himself, something that no animals do, and thereafter rules the family, administers the state, governs nations and rules the whole world. . . .

We have shown that our soul in all its acts is trying with all its power to attain the first gift of God, that is, the possession of all truth and all goodness. Does it also seek His second attribute? Does not the soul try to become everything just as God is everything? It does in a wonderful way; for the soul lives the life of a plant when it serves the body in feeding it; the life of an animal, when it flatters the senses; the life of a man, when it deliberates through reason on human affairs; the life of the heroes, when it investigates natural things; the life of the angels, when it enquires into the divine mysteries; the life of God, when it does everything for God's sake. Every man's soul experiences all these things in itself in some way, although souls do it in different ways, and thus the human species strives to become all things

"The Soul of Man" is from Josephine L. Burroughs, trans., "Marsilio Ficino's Platonic Theology," *Journal of the History of Ideas* 5 (1944), pp. 234–236. Reprinted by permission of the *Journal of the History of Ideas*.

by living the lives of all things. . . . Man is a great miracle, a living creature worthy of reverence and adoration, for he transforms himself into God as if he were God himself.

CONSIDER THIS:

- How would you define "humanism"? Give examples of its most important tenets from the many sources offered in the section entitled "The Humanist Movement." According to Pico della Mirandola, what is man's relationship to God?
- The humanists were criticized by the church for their secular interest at the expense of devotion to God. Do you agree with this criticism? Were the humanists disrespectful of God and irreligious? Note especially Marsilio Ficino on this point. In his opinion, what is man's position with respect to God?

The Political Life of Florence

The Rule of Cosimo d'Medici

VESPASIANO

Florence was perhaps the city most representative of Renaissance activity and inspiration. This was the home of the statesman Leonardo Bruni, the sculptor Michelangelo, the political scientist Machiavelli, and the greatest literary figure of the age, Dante. But during this era, Florence truly belonged to one family—the Medici. They were led by Cosimo d'Medici, who developed the family's financial interests, and they eventually became the bankers of the papacy. Cosimo and his son Lorenzo (the Magnificent) wrote poetry, discussed philosophy, and heavily patronized the great artists of Florence. They were truly humanists in their own right. Although Florence was ostensibly a republic, it was in fact dominated by the Medici family. In their reign, they applied a valuable lesson of "controlled freedom" from the Roman emperor Augustus. In many ways Florence owed its greatness to their efforts. The portrait of Cosimo presented here is by the Renaissance biographer Vespasiano.

Cosimo di Giovanni dé Medici was of most honorable descent, a very prominent citizen and one of great weight in the republic. . . .

He had a knowledge of Latin which would scarcely have been looked for in one occupying the station of a leading citizen engrossed with affairs. He was grave in temperament, prone to associate with men of high station who disliked frivolity, and averse from all buffoons and actors and those who spent time unprofitably. He had a great liking for men of letters and sought their society. His natural bent was to discuss matters of importance; and, although at this time the city was full of men of distinction, his worth was recognized on account of his praiseworthy qualities, and he began to find employment in affairs of every kind. By his twenty-fifth year he had gained great reputation in the city. . . . Cosimo and his party took every step to strengthen their own position. . . . Cosimo found that he must be careful to keep their support by temporizing and making believe that [they would] enjoy power equal to his own. Meantime he kept concealed the source of his influence in the city as well as he could. . . .

"The Rule of Cosimo d'Medici" is from Vespasiano da Bisticci, Lives of Illustrious Men of the XV Century, trans. W. George and E. Waters (London: Routledge and Kegan Paul, Ltd., 1926), pp. 213, 217, 222–224.

I once heard Cosimo say that the great mistake of his life was that he did not begin to spend his wealth ten years earlier; because, knowing well the disposition of his fellow-citizens, he was sure that, in the lapse of fifty years, no memory would remain of his personality or of his house save the few fabrics he might have built. He went on, "I know that after my death my children will be in worse case than those of any other Florentine who has died for many years past; moreover, I know I shall not wear the crown of laurel more than any other citizen." He spake thus because he knew the difficulty of ruling a state as he had ruled Florence, through the opposition of influential citizens who rated themselves his equals in former times. He acted privately with the greatest discretion in order to safeguard himself, and whenever he sought to attain an object he contrived to let it appear that the matter had been set in motion by some one other than himself and thus he escaped envy and unpopularity. His manner was admirable; he never spoke ill of anyone, and it angered him greatly to hear slander spoken by others. He was kind and patient to all who sought speech with him: he was more a man of deeds than of words: he always performed what he promised, and when this had been done he sent to let the petitioner know that his wishes had been granted. His replies were brief and sometimes obscure, so that they might be made to bear a double sense. . . .

So great was his knowledge of all things, that he could find some matter of discussion with men of all sorts, he would talk literature with a man of letters and theology with a theologian, being well versed therein through his natural liking, and for the reading of the Holy Scripture. With philosophy it was just the same. . . . He took kindly notice of all musicians, and delighted greatly in their art. He had dealings with painters and sculptors and had in his house works of diverse masters. He was especially inclined towards sculpture and showed great favor to all worthy craftsmen, being a good friend to Donatello and all sculptors and painters; and because in his time the sculptors found scanty employment, Cosimo, in order that Donatello's chisel might not be idle, commissioned him to make the pulpits of bronze in St. Lorenzo and the doors of the sacristy. He ordered the bank to pay every week enough money to Donatello for his work and for that of his four assistants. . . . He had a good knowledge of architecture, as may be seen from the buildings he left, none of which were built without consulting him; moreover, all those who were about to build would go to him for advice.

Precepts of Power: *"Everyone Sees What You Appear to Be, Few Perceive What You Are"*

NICCOLÒ MACHIAVELLI

Over the centuries, the name of Machiavelli has become synonymous with evil. The adjective "Machiavellian" still evokes images of deceit and political backstabbing. Machiavelli's ideas were condemned by the church as immoral and inspired by Satan himself. In reality, Niccolò Machiavelli (1469–1527) was a loyal citizen of Florence who had been schooled in the classics and had chosen a career in public service. He disliked the rule of the Medici and was a great advocate of republicanism. After Savonarola's fall from power in 1498, his theocracy was replaced by a true

"Precepts of Power" is from *The Historical, Political and Diplomatic Writings of Niccolò Machiavelli*, translated by C. E. Detmold (Boston, 1882), pp. 51–52; 54–59 (Chapters 8, 17 and 18). Translation modernized by the editor.

republic, led by elected officials of the people. Machiavelli became ambassador to France, and this duty served as a laboratory for the science of politics where he could observe men and governments in action. The Florentine republic was successful until 1512, when a Spanish mercenary army defeated Machiavelli's personally trained Florentine militia. They reinstalled Medici rule, and Machiavelli was tortured on the rack and thrown into prison for a time. He retired to the country and wrote a little book entitled *The Prince*. In it, Machiavelli gives the wisdom of his experience in politics. It is a manual of power: how to obtain it, maintain it, and lose it. In his analysis, Machiavelli is brutally realistic about the nature of human beings and the world of power politics: Learn the rules and you may survive and prosper. In the political chaos of Renaissance Italy, where alliances shifted frequently and distrust prevailed, such a guide proved useful and popular. Some of Machiavelli's most important ideas from *The Prince* are excerpted here.

On Those Who Have Become Princes by Crime

It should be noted at this point that in securing a state by force, its conqueror should consider carefully all the harmful things he must do and do them all at once so he does not to have to repeat them daily. By avoiding such constant brutality, men will begin to feel secure and the prince will gain their loyalty with the benefits he bestows on them. Any ruler who does otherwise, either because he is timid and hesitant, or because he listens to poor advice, must always keep his dagger in his hand. He can never count on the support of his subjects because their continual wounds are always fresh and they will never feel secure with him. The prince, therefore, should inflict all injuries at the same time, for the less often they are imposed, the less they offend. Benefits, on the other hand, should be distributed in small amounts, but continually so that they may be fully appreciated. And a prince should most importantly live with his subjects and be so aware of their attitudes that no unexpected event, whether good or bad, forces him to change his plans. For when emergencies arise, you will not have time to get your subjects to respond through cruelty, and what good you might do will help you little, since they will think that circumstances forced your hand and you will derive no thanks from it whatsoever.

On Cruelty and Mercy

A prince must always be cautious in believing too deeply or in acting too overtly. But he also must never seem timid and hesitant. He should temper his actions with an eye to prudence and a human touch so that too much trust doesn't result in foolish risk, or too little trust make him intolerable. From this arises the question as to whether it is better to be loved than to be feared, or the opposite. I reply that the prince should be both, but since it is difficult to combine them, it is much safer to be feared than to be loved when one must choose. For it is true about men that they are ungrateful and unfaithful, deceitful and two-faced—bootlicking cowards, who nevertheless are always greedy for their own gain. And while you shower them with benefits, they are all yours and will give you their blood, their property, their lives, and their children—so long as danger is remote. But when danger approaches, they turn away. And that prince who relies exclusively on their empty words, rather than on finding other ways to protect himself, will surely be destroyed. For any friendships that are purchased rather than founded on greatness and nobility of character, are never truly owned—and you can never cash them in at the crucial time.

Besides, men don't mind harming someone who makes himself loved than one who makes himself feared because love is held together by a bond of obligation which, since men are basically a dismal bunch, is broken whenever their own self-interest is threatened. But fear always holds the bond tightly because the dread of punishment never leaves them.

A prince, however, must make himself feared in such a way that, even if he has not won the affection of his people, he has avoided their hatred. For being feared yet not hated is a good combination, if the prince keeps his hands off the property and the women of his subjects. And if he must execute someone, then be sure to do so only when there is manifest cause and proper justification for it. But above all, he should avoid taking the property of others, for men will sooner forget the death of their fathers than the loss of their inheritance. Moreover, there will never be any lack of reason for taking people's property. And a prince who begins to live by stealing will always find a excuses for confiscating property. On the other hand, it is not as easy to find reasons for taking a life, and these justifications dissipate more quickly. . . . To come back now

FIGURE 1.1 Niccolò Machiavelli: "Let a prince therefore act to seize and to maintain the state; his methods will always be judged honorable and will be praised by all; for ordinary people are always deceived by appearances and by the outcome of a thing; and in the world there is nothing but ordinary people." (*Alinari Art Resource, NY*)

to the question of whether it is better to be loved or feared, I conclude that since men love at their own pleasure and fear at the pleasure of the prince, a wise prince should always rely on himself, and not on the will of others. But, above all, he should strive only to avoid hatred, as I have already noted.

How a Prince Should Keep His Word

It must be evident to everyone that it is more commendable for a prince to keep his word at all times and practice integrity rather than live by deceit. And yet, the experience of our own times has shown that the princes who have achieved great things have not cared much for keeping promises but have been expert at manipulating the minds of others. In the end, they have surpassed those rulers whose actions were dictated by loyalty and honesty.

Therefore, you must know that there are two ways of fighting: one according to the laws, the other by force; men practice the first way, and animals the second. But because the first is often insufficient, it becomes necessary to resort to the second. A prince, then, must know how to use both the natures of the beast and of man. . . .

Since it is necessary for a prince to know how to make good use of the nature of the beast, he should choose from among animals the fox and the lion; for the lion cannot defend itself from traps and the fox cannot protect itself from wolves. A prince should be a fox in order to recognize the traps laid for him and a lion in order to frighten the wolves. Those who simply employ the nature of the lion do not understand their business. A wise ruler, therefore, cannot and should not keep his word when it is to his disadvantage or when the reasons that made him promise no longer exist. And if men were all good, this rule would be wrong; but since men are basically bad and will not keep their promises to you, you likewise need not keep yours to them. A prince never lacks legitimate reasons to break his promises. I could offer an infinite number of modern examples that demonstrate this and show how many peace treaties, how many promises have been made null and void by the infidelity of princes. And the ruler who knows best how to play the fox has always been the most successful. But the prince must also know how to disguise this nature well and to be a great hypocrite and a bold liar. For men are so simple and so controlled by their immediate needs that the deceiver will always find a dupe who will allow himself to be deceived. . . .

It is not necessary for a ruler to possess all the qualities mentioned above, but it is essential that he should at least seem to have them. . . . A prince, therefore, must appear to be all mercy, all faithfulness, all integrity, all kindness, all religion. And it is most necessary for the prince to seem to possess this last quality, since men in general judge more by what they see and hear, than by what they feel. Everyone sees what you appear to be, few perceive what you are, and those few do not dare to contradict the opinion of the many who are protected by the majesty of the state. For the actions of all men, and especially those of princes where there is no other arbiter, are judged by the final result. A prince, therefore, should boldly seize and maintain the state. His methods will always be judged honorable and will be praised by everyone; for ordinary people are always deceived by appearances and by results—and in the world, there is nothing but ordinary people. . . .

CONSIDER THIS:

- Niccolò Machiavelli has been called "the disciple of the devil." After reading the excerpts from *The Prince*, why do you think this view has prevailed? Is it better for a prince to be loved or feared? Why kill all enemies or potential enemies when you come into power through crime? Interpret the phrase "the ends justify the means." How does Machiavelli's view of human nature compare with that of other Renaissance humanists? Do you see Machiavelli as moral, immoral, or amoral? Why did he write *The Prince*?

SECTION II: THE REFORMATION ERA

I am more afraid of my own heart than of the pope and all his cardinals. I have within me the great pope—Self.

—MARTIN LUTHER

Whatever your heart clings to and confides in, that is really your God.

—MARTIN LUTHER

All religions must be tolerated for every man must get to heaven his own way.

—FREDERICK THE GREAT

SECTION THEMES

- **Social and Spiritual Values:** Why did the Reformation occur? What led Martin Luther to challenge the belief system of the church? To what extent can faith and personal commitment to a religion change the course of history? Is faith a more powerful force than any army?
- **Revolution and Historical Transition:** Was the Protestant Reformation a spiritual revolution that consequently altered the political and economic institutions of Europe? Or was it a spiritually based reform movement that sought limited change in religious matters? Was Luther a revolutionary who was just as influential as Robespierre, Napoleon, or Lenin?
- **The Power Structure:** How did secular rulers benefit from the division of Christianity during the Reformation era? Which monarchs became "defenders of the church" and which ones aided the reformers? Why? How did King Henry VIII of England solve the competition between church and state? Were his actions based on a sincere spirituality or on pure political expediency?
- **The Individual and the Institution:** Would the Protestant Reformation have occurred without Martin Luther? To what extent can an individual change the course of history? Was the printing press more essential to the success of this transitional movement than was Luther?
- **The Big Picture:** Was the Protestant Reformation ultimately the best thing that could have happened to the Christian church in the West? Do you expect another splinter movement in the contemporary Roman Catholic church, and if so, what would be the ramifications?

During the Middle Ages, the church was the focal point of society. One's life was inextricably bound to the dictates of religion from the baptism that followed birth to the last rites that accompanied death. But by the sixteenth century, the omnipotence of the church, both in a spiritual sense and in the political realm, had been called into question. The church had lost much of the authority that had allowed it, in the eleventh through the thirteenth centuries, to claim superiority in the ongoing struggle between church and state. Crises such as the Babylonian Captivity (1309–1377) and the Great Schism (1378–1417) had strained the loyalty of the faithful and devastated the unity of the church for over a century. By the middle of the fifteenth century, the papacy was occupied with finding new sources of income that would help it fend off political challenges to its territory and increase its influence in the secular realm. The Renaissance papacy became infamous in its corruption and succumbed to the sensual delights of the world, as well as to the more traditional abuses of simony (the selling of church offices) and pluralism (allowing an individual to hold more than one position). Pope Julius II (1503–1513) was a glaring example of the age as, bedecked in armor, he personally led his armies into battle.

These actions resulted in a plenitude of criticism from within the church and especially from Christian humanists such as Desiderius Erasmus. Perhaps the most controversial practice of the church was the sale of indulgences. An indulgence was a piece of paper, signed by the pope that remitted punishment in purgatory because of sin. It was based on the theory that all humans are by nature sinful and after death will have to undergo a purgation of sin before being allowed to enter the kingdom of heaven. The pope, however, controlled an infinite "treasury of grace" that could be dispensed to mortals, thus removing the taint of sin and freeing the soul from purgatory. By the late fifteenth century, the remission of sin was extended to both the living and the dead, and one could therefore liberate the soul of a relative "trapped" in purgatory by purchasing an indulgence. The sale of indulgences became a routine affair of peddling forgiveness of purgatorial punishment, and the papacy came to rely on it as a necessary source of income. In 1507, Pope Julius II issued a plenary indulgence to obtain funds for the construction of Saint Peter's Basilica in Rome. Leo X renewed the indulgence in 1513, and subcommissioners actively began selling to the faithful. It was in response to this sale that a young monk named Martin Luther protested and nailed his *Ninety-five Theses* to the door of the Wittenberg church.

It is important to note that although Luther called into question the sale of indulgences, the main issue was salvation. Salvation, he reasoned, was cheap indeed if it could be purchased. Luther was tortured by the demands of God for perfection and worried that his own righteousness was insufficient for salvation in the sight of God. The church taught that in addition to winning grace through faith, one could also merit God's grace through good works or the remission of sin by indulgence. In fact, the purchase of an indulgence was considered a good work. But to Luther's mind, salvation required more, much more, and it had nothing to do with deeds. While studying Saint Paul's Epistle to the Romans (1:17), Luther achieved a breakthrough that freed him from his torment: By the grace of God alone one could be saved, and this salvation was obtained only through faith in Christ. Neither good works nor indulgences could have anything to do with salvation. This stand called into question the very foundation of established Christian belief. Was the pope the true vicar of Christ who spoke the words of God? If so, why did he advocate indulgences as a means of salvation? Was he in fact infallible on such matters of faith? The corruption of the papacy was also troubling, yet Luther's objective was not to overthrow the church but to reform it from within.

The church replied to such a challenge with what it considered swift and appropriate action. Luther was excommunicated and his writings were condemned as heretical. It became evident to Luther that his desire to reform the church could be achieved only by defying the authority of the pope and starting a new church. Supported by the Holy Roman Emperor Charles V, the church sought to eliminate the root of the controversy. However, Luther was hidden, protected by the secular princes in Germany who, because of their location and traditional independence, were willing to defy their emperor and promote a religion that to them served a secular purpose. Yet Luther's movement was spiritual in nature, and he decried such political connections even as he sought the aid of the princes and nobility.

This section explores the spiritual and political foundations of the Reformation and the Protestant movement, from its inception by Martin Luther through its development under John Calvin to its royal imposition in England under Henry VIII and Elizabeth I. The Reformation era must also be viewed in its proper context, noting that during this period the Catholic church made significant strides toward reform in its own right. The themes presented in this chapter include the role of the individual in changing history and the impact of religion on the political framework and social fabric of the times. The Reformation era was one of transition and instability that eventually led to war and bloodshed as nations fought during the sixteenth and seventeenth centuries in support of a singular conception of the "true religion." This bloody future was far from Martin Luther's mind when he nailed his *Ninety-five Theses* on the Wittenberg church door in 1517 and thus started a movement that shook the spiritual foundations of Christendom and altered the political face of Europe for centuries to come.

The Lutheran Reformation

"How Many Sins Are Committed in a Single Day?" (1517)

JOHANN TETZEL

The controversy over the sale of indulgences was the spark that set the Reformation in motion. In 1515, Pope Leo X made an agreement with Archbishop Albert to sell indulgences in Mainz and other areas of northern Germany, with half the proceeds going to support Leo's construction of Saint Peter's Basilica in Rome and half going to pay for the debts that Albert had incurred in securing his church offices. In the first selection, Archbishop Albert gives instructions to those subcommissioners who actually sold the indulgences in 1517. One of the most successful subcommissioners was Johann Tetzel, prior of the Dominican monastery at Leipzig. His oratorical ability is evident in the second passage.

Venerable Sir, I pray you that in your utterances you may be pleased to make use of such words as shall serve to open the eyes of the mind and cause your hearers to consider how great a grace and gift they have had and now have at their very doors. Blessed eyes indeed, which see what they see, because already they possess letters of safe conduct by which they are able to lead their souls through that valley of tears, through that sea of the mad world, where storms and tempests and dangers lie in wait, to the blessed land of Paradise. Know that the life of man upon earth is a constant struggle. We have to fight against the flesh, the world and the devil, who are always seeking to destroy the soul. In sin we are conceived,—alas! what bonds of sin encompass us, and how difficult and almost impossible it is to attain to the gate of salvation without divine aid; since He causes us to be saved, not by virtue of the good works which we accomplish, but through His divine mercy, it is necessary then to put on the armor of God.

You may obtain letters of safe conduct from the vicar of our Lord Jesus Christ, by means of which you are able to liberate your soul from the hands of the enemy, and convey it by means of contrition and confession, safe and secure from all pains of Purgatory, into the happy kingdom. For know that in these letters are stamped and engraven all the merits of Christ's passion there laid bare. Consider, that for each and every mortal sin it is necessary to undergo seven years of penitence after confession and contrition, either in this life or in Purgatory.

"'How Many Sins Are Committed in a Single Day?'" is from James H. Robinson, ed., *Translations and Reprints from the Original Sources of European History*, vol. 2, no. 6 (Philadelphia: University of Pennsylvania, 1902), pp. 9–10.

Johannes Tezelius Dominicaner Münch/mit seinen Römischen Ablaßkram/welchen er im Jahr Christi 1517. in Deutschenlanden zu marckt gebracht/wie er in der Kirchen zu Pirn in seinem Vaterland abgemahlet ist.

O ihr deutschen mercket mich recht/
Des heiligen Vaters Papstes Knecht/
Bin ich/vnd br ing euch jtzt allein/
Zehn tausent vnd neun hundert carein/
Gnad vnd Ablaß von einer Sünd/
Vor euch/ewer Eltern/Weib vnd Kind/
Sol ein jeder gewehret sein
So viel ihr leget ins Kästelein/
So bald der Gülden im Becken klingt/
Im huy die Seel im Himel springt/

Als Babst Leo der zehend genandt/
Nu mehr fast vnmüglich befand/
Das er das Römisch Jubel Jahr
Erlebet/hat er die faule wahr/
Des Ablaßkrams in Deutschenland/
Durch seine Kramknecht ausgesandt/
Dazu sich denn ohn all verdrieß/
Johann Tetzel gebrauchen ließ/
Der was jtzt kaum dem Hencker entlauffen/
Als er wegen Ehebruchs solt ersauffen/
Wo nicht der from Fürst Friederich/
Seiner het angenommen sich/
Vnd beim Keyser Maximilian/
Ein gnedigste Fürbit gethan/
Hierbey es aber so nicht blieb/
Aus eim Ehebrecher wurd ein Dieb/
Welcher durch vermeint gewalt vnd macht/
Viel Gelds vnd Guts zu weg gebracht/

Als er die blinde Welt beredt/
Das er den Himel feil tragen thet/
Wenn man nu Gelt gnug gebe dar/
Hets mit den Menschen kein gefahr/
So bald der Grosch im Kasten klingt/
So bald die Seel in Himel sich schwingt/
Durch diesen Teuffelischen Tandt/
Hat er betrogen sein Vaterland/
Biß jhn Gott hat ins Spiel gesehen/
Durch Doctor Luthern seligen/
Welcher jhm seinen Krämertisch/
Gewaltiglich zu Boden stieß/
Daher/Gott lob/biß auff die zeit/
Der Ablaßkram zerstrewet leit/
So bleibet nun Christi verdienst/
Einig allein vnser Gewinst/
Des Tezels Kram vnd Bapsts Betrug/
Findet bey vns kein recht noch fug.

FIGURE 1.2 Caricature of Johann Tetzel, the indulgence preacher who spurred Luther to publish his *Ninety-five Theses.* The last line of the caption reads: "As soon as gold in the basin rings, right then the soul to heaven springs."
(*Staatliche Lutherhalle, Wittenberg/Courtesy of the Library of Congress*)

How many mortal sins are committed in a day, how many in a week, how many in a month, how many in a year, how many in the whole course of life! They are well-nigh numberless, and those that commit them must needs suffer endless punishment in the burning pains of Purgatory.

But with these confessional letters you will be able at any time in life to obtain full indulgence for all penalties imposed upon you, in all cases except the four reserved to the Apostolic See. Therefore throughout your whole life, whenever you wish to make confession, you may receive the same remission, except in cases reserved to the Pope, and afterwards, at the hour of death, a full indulgence as to all penalties and sins, and your share of all spiritual blessings that exist in the church militant and all its members.

Do you not know that when it is necessary for anyone to go to Rome, or undertake any other dangerous journey, he takes his money to a broker and gives a certain percent—five or six or ten—in order that at Rome or elsewhere he may receive again his funds intact, by means of the letter of this same broker? Are you not willing, then, for the fourth part of a florin, to obtain these letters, by virtue of which you may bring, not your money but your divine and immortal soul safe and sound into the land of Paradise?

CONSIDER THIS:

- Why were indulgences so detested by critics of the church? Can you construct a logical argument in support of indulgences with which the church could have satisfactorily defended itself against criticism? Is the principle of indulgences at issue here or just the manner in which they were sold?

Salvation Through Faith Alone

MARTIN LUTHER

Martin Luther's transformation from monk to reformer was not a preconceived act; it developed gradually not only as a result of corruption around him but especially because of a spiritual awakening. Luther struggled with the need to imitate the perfection of Christ, which was important in the eyes of the church for salvation. Luther realized that because of his nature as a human, he was too sinful, and no amount of prayer or good works could help him achieve the kingdom of Heaven. After much study and pain, he concluded that salvation was a free gift of God and that a person was saved by faith in Christ alone. In the first selection, Luther explains his enlightenment. The second document is his answer to the indulgences being sold by Johann Tetzel. When Luther posted the *Ninety-five Theses* on the church in Wittenberg, the Reformation began in earnest.

I, Martin Luther, entered the monastery against the will of my father and lost favor with him, for he saw through the knavery of the monks very well. On the day on which I sang my first mass he said to me, "Son, don't you know that you ought to honor your father?" . . . Later when I stood there during the mass and began the canon, I was so frightened that I would have fled if I hadn't been admonished by the prior. . . .

When I was a monk I was unwilling to omit any of the prayers, but when I was busy

"Salvation Through Faith Alone" is from Theodore Tappert and H. Lehmann, eds., *Luther's Works, vol. 54: Table Talk* (Philadelphia: Fortress Press, 1965), pp. 85, 193–194, 234, 264–265.

with public lecturing and writing I often accumulated my appointed prayers for a whole week, or even two or three weeks. Then I would take a Saturday off, or shut myself in for as long as three days without food and drink, until I had said the prescribed prayers. This made my head split, and as a consequence I couldn't close my eyes for five nights, lay sick unto death, and went out of my senses. Even after I had quickly recovered and I tried again to read, my head went 'round and 'round. Thus our Lord God drew me, as if by force, from that torment of prayers. . . .

The words "righteous" and "righteousness of God" struck my conscience like lightning. When I heard them I was exceedingly terrified. If God is righteous [I thought], he must punish. But when by God's grace I pondered, in the tower and heated room of this building, over the words, "He who through faith is righteous shall live" [Rom. 1:17] and "the righteousness of God" [Rom. 3:21], I soon came to the conclusion that if we, as righteous men, ought to live from faith and if the righteousness of God should contribute to the salvation of all who believe, then salvation won't be our merit but God's mercy. My spirit was thereby cheered. For it's by the righteousness of God that we're justified and saved through Christ. These words [which had before terrified me] now became more pleasing to me. The Holy Spirit unveiled the Scriptures for me in this tower.

God led us away from all this in a wonderful way; without my quite being aware of it he took me away from that game more than twenty years ago. How difficult it was at first when we journeyed toward Kemberg after All Saints' Day in the year 1517, when I first made up my mind to write against the crass errors of indulgences! Jerome Schurff advised against this: "You wish to write against the pope? hat are you trying to do? It won't be tolerated!" I replied, "And if they have to tolerate it?" Presently Sylvester, master of the sacred palace, entered the arena, fulminating against me with this syllogism: "Whoever questions what the Roman church says and does is heretical. Luther questions what the Roman church says and does, and therefore [he is a heretic]." So it all began.

The Ninety-five Theses (1517)

MARTIN LUTHER

In the desire and with the purpose of elucidating the truth, a disputation will be held on the underwritten propositions at Wittenberg, under the presidency of the Reverend Father Martin Luther, Monk of the Order of St. Augustine, Master of Arts and of Sacred Theology, and ordinary Reader of the same in that place. He therefore asks those who cannot be present and discuss the subject with us orally, to do so by letter in their absence. In the name of our Lord Jesus Christ, Amen. . . .

5. The Pope has neither the will nor the power to remit any penalties except those which he has imposed by his own authority, or by that of the canons.
6. The Pope has no power to remit any guilt, except by declaring and warranting it to have been remitted by God; or at most by remitting cases reserved for himself; in which cases, if his power were [disregarded], guilt would certainly remain. . . .

"The Ninety-five Theses" by Martin Luther is from H. Wace and C. A. Buchheim, eds., *First Principles of the Reformation* (London: John Murray, 1883), pp. 6–13.

20. Therefore the Pope, when he speaks of the plenary remission of all penalties, does not really mean of all, but only of those imposed by himself.
21. Thus those preachers of indulgences are in error who say that by the indulgences of the Pope a man is freed and saved from all punishment.
22. For in fact he remits to souls in Purgatory no penalty which they would have had to pay in this life according to the canons.
23. If any entire remission of all penalties can be granted to any one it is certain that it is granted to none but the most perfect, that is to very few.
24. Hence, the greater part of the people must needs be deceived by his indiscriminate and high-sounding promise of release from penalties.
25. Such power over Purgatory as the Pope has in general, such has every bishop in his own diocese, and every parish priest in his own parish. . . .
27. They are wrong who say that the soul flies out of Purgatory as soon as the money thrown into the chest rattles.
28. It is certain that, when money rattles in the chest, avarice and gain may be increased, but the effect of the intercession of the Church depends on the will of God alone. . . .
32. Those who believe that, through letters of pardon, they are made sure of their own salvation will be eternally damned along with their teachers.
33. We must especially beware of those who say that these pardons from the Pope are that inestimable gift of God by which man is reconciled to God. . . .
35. They preach no Christian doctrine who teach that contrition is not necessary for those who buy souls (out of Purgatory) or buy confessional licenses.
37. Every true Christian, whether living or dead, has a share in all the benefits of Christ and of the Church, given by God, even without letters of pardon.
42. Christians should be taught that it is not the wish of the Pope that buying of pardons should be in any way compared to works of mercy.
43. Christians should be taught that he who gives to a poor man, or lends to a needy man, does better than if he bought pardons.
45. Christians should be taught that he who sees any one in need, and, passing him by, gives money for pardons, is not purchasing for himself the indulgences of the Pope but the anger of God. . . .
50. Christians should be taught that, if the Pope were acquainted with the exactions of the Preachers of pardons, he would prefer that the Basilica of St. Peter should be burnt to ashes rather than that it should be built up with the skin, flesh, and bones of his sheep. . . .
62. The true treasure of the Church is the Holy Gospel of the glory and grace of God.
66. The treasures of indulgences are nets, wherewith they now fish for the riches of men.
86. Again; why does not the Pope, whose riches are at this day more ample than those of the wealthiest of the wealthy, build the Basilica of St. Peter with his own money rather than with that of poor believers. . . .
94. Christians should be exhorted to strive to follow Christ their head through pains, deaths, and hells.
95. And thus not trust to enter heaven through many tribulations, rather than in the security of peace.

Consider This:

- What would you identify as the underlying causes for the Reformation, and what was the spark that set things in motion? To what extent was Martin Luther's action directed against abuses within the church?

"Here I Stand": Address at the Diet of Worms (1521)

MARTIN LUTHER

After his excommunication by Leo X in June 1520, Luther was summoned to appear before a diet (assembly) of prelates and officials of the Holy Roman Empire in the city of Worms to answer questions about his heretical writings. His safe conduct to the meeting was guaranteed by the Holy Roman Emperor Charles V, who presided over the diet. Accompanied by his secular protector, Frederick the Wise, elector of Saxony, Luther appeared on April 17, 1521. When asked whether he wished to defend all his writings or retract some, Luther delivered this famous speech. On April 23, Luther secretly left Worms and was hidden by friends at Wartburg castle. Charles V's edict against Luther is the second selection.

"Most serene emperor, most illustrious princes, most clement lords, obedient to the time set for me yesterday evening, I appear before you, beseeching you, by the mercy of God, that your most serene majesty and your most illustrious lordships may deign to listen graciously to this my cause—which is, as I hope, a cause of justice and truth. If through my inexperience I have either not given the proper titles to some, or have offended in some manner against court customs and etiquette, I beseech you to kindly pardon me, as a man accustomed not to courts but to the cells of monks. I can bear no other witness about myself but that I have taught and written up to this time with simplicity of heart, as I had in view only the glory of God and the sound instruction of Christ's faithful. . . .

"[A] group of my books attacks the papacy and the affairs of the papists as those who both by their doctrines and very wicked examples have laid waste the Christian world with evil that affects the spirit and the body. For no one can deny or conceal this fact, when the experience of all and the complaints of everyone witness that through the decrees of the pope and the doctrines of men the consciences of the faithful have been most miserably entangled, tortured, and torn to pieces. Also, property and possessions, especially in this illustrious nation of Germany, have been devoured by an unbelievable tyranny and are being devoured to this time without letup and by unworthy means. [Yet the papists] by their own decrees . . . warn that the papal laws and doctrines which are contrary to the gospel or the opinions of the fathers are to be regarded as erroneous and reprehensible. If, therefore, I should have retracted these writings, I should have done nothing other than to give strength to this [papal] tyranny and I should have opened not only windows but doors to such great godlessness. It would rage further and more freely than ever it has dared up to this time. Yes, from the proof of such a revocation on my part, their wholly lawless and unrestrained kingdom of wickedness would become still more intolerable for the already wretched people; and their rule would be further strengthened and established, especially if it should be reported that this evil deed had been done by me by virtue of the authority of your most serene majesty and the whole Roman Empire. Good God! What a cover for wickedness and tyranny I should have then become.

"'Here I Stand': Address at the Diet of Worms" is from J. Pelikan, ed., *Luther's Works, vol. 2: Career of the Reformer* (Saint Louis: Concordia Publishing House, 1958), pp. 109–112.

FIGURE 1.3 Martin Luther by Lucas Cranach the Elder (1521). This picture of Luther was painted in the same year that he defied the pope and the Holy Roman Emperor at the Diet of Worms. His complete break with Rome ushered in an age of religious reform. (*Lucas Cranach, "Martin Luther," Firenze, Galleria degli Uffizi*)

"I have written a third sort of book against some private and (as they say) distinguished individuals—those, namely, who strive to preserve the Roman tyranny and to destroy the godliness taught by me. Against these I confess I have been more violent than my religion or profession demands. But then, I do not set myself up as a saint; neither am I disputing about my life, but about the teachings of Christ. It is not proper for me to retract these works, because by this retraction it would again happen that tyranny and godlessness would, with my patronage, rule and rage among the people of God more violently than ever before.

"However, because I am a man and not God, I am not able to shield my books with any other protection than that which my Lord Jesus Christ himself offered for his teaching. When questioned before Annas about his teaching and struck by a servant, he said: 'If I have spoken wrongly, bear witness to the wrong' [John 18:19–23]. If the Lord himself, who knew that he could not err, did not refuse to hear testimony against his teaching, even from the lowliest servant, how much more ought I, who am the lowest scum and able to do nothing except err, desire and expect that somebody should want to offer testimony against my teaching! Therefore, I ask by the mercy of God, may your most serene majesty, most illustrious lordships, or anyone at all who is able, either high or low, bear witness, expose my errors, overthrowing them by the writings of the prophets and the evangelists. Once I have been taught I shall be quite ready to renounce every error, and I shall be the first to cast my books into the fire.

"From these remarks I think it is clear that I have sufficiently considered and weighed the hazards and dangers, as well as the excitement and dissensions aroused in the world as a result of my teachings, things about which I was gravely and forcefully warned yesterday. To see excitement and dissension arise because of the Word of God is to me clearly the most joyful aspect of all in these matters. For this is the way, the opportunity, and the result of the Word of God, just as He [Christ] said, 'I have not come to bring peace, but a sword. For I have come to set a man against his father, etc.' [Matt. 10:34–35]. . . . Therefore we must fear God. I do not say these things because there is a need of either my teachings or my warnings for such leaders as you, but because I must not withhold the allegiance which I owe my Germany. With these words I commend myself to your most serene majesty and to your lordships, humbly asking that I not be allowed through the agitation of my enemies, without cause, to be made hateful to you. I have finished."

When I had finished, the speaker for the emperor said, as if in reproach that I had not answered the question, that I ought not call into question those things which had been condemned and defined in councils; therefore what was sought from me was not a horned response, but a simple one, whether or not I wished to retract.

Here I answered:

"Since then your serene majesty and your lordships seek a simple answer, I will give it in this manner, neither horned nor toothed: Unless I am convinced by the testimony of the Scriptures or by clear reason (for I do not trust either in the pope or in councils alone, since it is well known that they have often errored and contradicted themselves), I am bound by the Scriptures I have quoted and my conscience is captive to the Word of God. I cannot and I will not retract anything, since it is neither safe nor right to go against conscience.

"I cannot do otherwise, here I stand, may God help me, Amen."

The Edict of Worms (1521)

EMPEROR CHARLES V

In view of the fact that Martin Luther still persists obstinately and perversely in maintaining his heretical opinions, and consequently all pious and God-fearing persons abominate and abhor him as one mad or possessed by a demon . . . we have declared and made known that the said Martin Luther shall hereafter be held and esteemed by each and all of us as a limb cut off from the Church of God, an obstinate schismatic and manifest heretic. . . .

And we publicly attest by these letters that we order and command each and all of you, as you owe fidelity to us and the Holy Empire, and would escape the penalties of the crime of treason, and the ban and over-ban of the Empire, and the forfeiture of all regalia, fiefs, privileges, and immunities, which up to this time you have in any way obtained from our predecessors, ourself, and the Holy Roman Empire—commanding, we say, in the name of the Roman and imperial majesty, we strictly order that immediately after the expiration of the appointed twenty days, terminating on the fourteenth day of May, you shall refuse to give the aforesaid Martin Luther hospitality, lodging, food, or drink; neither shall any one, by word or deed, secretly or openly, succor or assist him by counsel or help; but in whatever place you meet him, you shall proceed against him; if you have sufficient force, you shall take him prisoner and keep him in close custody; you shall deliver him, or cause him to be delivered, to us or at least let us know where he may be captured. In the meanwhile you shall keep him closely imprisoned until you receive notice from us what further to do, according to the direction of the laws. And for such holy and pious work we will indemnify you for your trouble and expense. . . .

And in order that all this may be done and credit given to this document we have sealed it with our imperial seal, which has been affixed in our imperial city of Worms, on the eighth day of May, after the birth of Christ 1521, in the second year of our reign over the Roman Empire, and over our other lands the sixth.

By our lord the emperor's own command.

CONSIDER THIS:

- Edward Bulwer-Lytton once said, "A reform is a correction of abuses; a revolution is a transfer of power." Under this definition, would you consider the Protestant Reformation to be a revolution?

In the Wake of Luther

John Calvin and the Genevan Reformation

Although Lutheranism formed the basis of the Reformation. By the mid-sixteenth century it had lost much of its energy and was confined to Germany and Scandinavia. The movement was spread throughout Europe by other reformers, the most influential of whom was John Calvin (1509–1564).

"The Edict of Worms" is from James H. Robinson, ed., *Readings in European History*, vol. 2 (Boston: Ginn and Company, 1906), pp. 87–88.

A trained lawyer and classical scholar, Calvin had been a convert to Luther's ideas and was forced to leave France, eventually settling in Geneva in the 1530s. There in the 1540s, he established a very structured society that can best be described as a theocracy. Calvin's strict adherence to biblical authority and his singular strength of personality can be seen in his treatise, *On the Necessity of Reforming the Church*. In it he defines the church as "a society of all the saints, a society spread over the whole world, and existing in all ages, yet bound together by the one doctrine and the one Spirit of Christ." In the words of Saint Cyprian, which Calvin often quoted, "We cannot have God for our Father without having the Church for our mother." The importance of this idea cannot be overestimated in Calvin's understanding of doctrine and of the reform of the church. In the following excerpt from his famous treatise, which was addressed to the Holy Roman Emperor Charles V in 1544. Calvin expressed disgust that the church had become divorced from the society of saints it was supposed to serve. The continuity of the church as a universal embodiment of all believers had to be reestablished through clerical reform and a reconceptualization of Spirit.

On the Necessity of Reforming the Church (1544)

JOHN CALVIN

In the present condition of the empire, your Imperial Majesty, and you, Most Illustrious Princes, necessarily involved in various cares, and distracted by a multiplicity of business, are agitated, and in a manner tempest-tossed. . . . I feel what nerve, what earnestness, what urgency, what ardor, the treatment of this subject requires. . . . First, call to mind the fearful calamities of the Church, which might move to pity even minds of iron. Nay, set before your eyes her squalid and unsightly form, and the sad devastation which is everywhere beheld. How long, pray, will you allow the spouse of Christ, the mother of you all, to lie thus protracted and afflicted–thus, too, when she is imploring your protection, and when the means of relief are at hand? Next, consider how much worse calamities impend. Final destruction cannot be far off, unless you interpose with the utmost speed. Christ will, indeed, in the way which to him seems good, preserve his Church miraculously, and beyond human expectation; but this I say, that the consequence of a little longer delay on your part will be, that in Germany we shall not have even the form of a Church. Look round, and see how many indications threaten that ruin which it is your duty to prevent, and announce that it is actually at hand. These things speak loud enough, though I were silent. . . .

Divine worship being corrupted by so many false opinions, and perverted by so many impious and foul superstitions, the sacred Majesty of God is insulted with atrocious contempt, his holy name profaned, his glory only not trampled under foot. Nay, while the whole Christian world is openly polluted with idolatry, men adore, instead of Him, their own fictions. A thousand superstitions reign, superstitions which are just so many open insults to Him. The power of Christ is almost obliterated from the minds of men, the hope of salvation is transferred from him to empty, frivolous, and insignificant ceremonies, while there is a

"On the Necessity of Reforming the Church" is from John Calvin, *Tracts and Treatises on the Reformation of the Church*, trans. by Henry Beveridge (Edinburgh: Calvin Translation Society, 1844), vol. 1, pp. 231–234.

pollution of the Sacraments not less to be execrated. Baptism is deformed by numerous additions, the Holy Supper [communion] is prostituted to all kinds of ignominy, religion throughout has degenerated into an entirely different form. . . .

In the future, therefore, as often as you shall hear the croaking note–"The business of reforming the Church must be delayed for the present"–"there will be time enough to accomplish it after other matters are transacted"–remember, Most Invincible Emperor, that the matter on which you are to deliberate is, whether you are to leave to your posterity some empire or none. Yet, why do I speak of posterity? Even now, while your own eyes behold, it is half bent, and totters to its final ruin. . . .

But be the issue what it may, we will never repent of having begun, and of having proceeded thus far. The Holy Spirit is a faithful and unerring witness to our doctrine. We know, I say, that it is the eternal truth of God that we preach. We are, indeed, desirous, as we ought to be, that our ministry may prove salutary to the world; but to give it this effect belongs to God, not to us. If, to punish, partly the ingratitude, and partly the stubbornness of those to whom we desire to do good, success must prove desperate, and all things go to worse, I will say what it befits a Christian man to say, and what all who are true to this holy profession will subscribe: We will die, but in death even be conquerors, not only because through it we shall have a sure passage to a better life, but because we know that our blood will be as seed to propagate the Divine truth which men now despise.

CONSIDER THIS:

- In the treatise *On the Necessity of Reforming the Church*, what is John Calvin's primary message to the Holy Roman Emperor Charles V? Do you think Calvin was exaggerating when he reminded the Emperor that "the matter on which you are to deliberate is, whether you are to leave to your posterity some empire or none"?

Predestination: Institutes of the Christian Religion (1536)

JOHN CALVIN

Calvin's doctrines were primarily Lutheran in nature, but Calvin went a step beyond and stressed the doctrine of predestination: One's salvation had already been determined by God, and those elect who had been "chosen" gave evidence of their calling by living exemplary lives. Calvinism became popular in the Netherlands and Scotland and it formed the core of the Puritan belief that was to be so influential in the colonization of America. The following excerpts reveal Calvin's justification for reform, his concept of predestination, and his strict regulation of lives and beliefs in Geneva.

The covenant of life is not preached equally to all, and among those to whom it is preached, does not always meet with the same reception. This diversity displays the unsearchable depth of the divine judgment, and is without doubt subordinate to God's purpose of eternal election. But it is plainly owing to the mere pleasure of God that salvation is spontaneously offered to some, while others have no access to it, great and difficult questions immediately

"Predestination" is from John Calvin, *Institutes of the Christian Religion*, vol. 2, trans. Henry Beveridge (Edinburgh: Calvin Translation Society, 1845), pp. 529, 534, 540.

arise, questions which are inexplicable, when just views are not entertained concerning election and predestination. . . .

By predestination we mean the eternal decree of God, by which he determined with himself whatever he wished to happen with regard to every man. All are not created on equal terms, but some are preordained to eternal life, others to eternal damnation; and, accordingly, as each has been created for one or other of these ends, we say that he has been predestined to life or to death. . . .

We say, then, that Scripture clearly proves this much, that God by his eternal and immutable counsel determined once for all those whom it was his pleasure one day to admit to salvation, and those whom, on the other hand, it was his pleasure to doom to destruction. We maintain that this counsel, as regards the elect, is founded on his free mercy, without any respect to human worth, while those whom he dooms to destruction are excluded from access to life by a just and blameless, but at the same time incomprehensible judgment. In regard to the elect, we regard calling as the evidence of election, and justification as another symbol of its manifestation, until it is fully accomplished by the attainment of glory. But as the Lord seals his elect by calling and justification, so by excluding the reprobate either from the knowledge of his name or the sanctification of his Spirit, he by these marks in a manner discloses the judgment which awaits them. I will here omit many of the fictions which foolish men have devised to overthrow predestination. There is no need of refuting objections which the moment they are produced abundantly betray their hollowness. I will dwell only on those points which either form the subject of dispute among the learned, or may occasion any difficulty to the simple. . . .

CONSIDER THIS:

- How would you define the concept of predestination and why is it so efficient as a device for controlling a congregation? What is the basis for the success of the Calvinist movement?

The English Reformation

The Protestant Reformation has often been viewed as essentially a spiritual movement that had a fundamental political and social impact throughout Europe. But the motives of some reformers were not purely spiritual, and they sought a more expedient premise. As the Reformation spread to Switzerland, northern Germany, and Scandinavia, it met with little organized opposition. But England, it seemed, was prepared to resist any incursion. Its monarch, Henry VIII, was a gregarious and dynamic king who had grown up amidst political intrigue and international power plays in the court of his father, Henry Tudor (VII). Henry VIII knew how to handle himself politically and sought to maintain domestic tranquility by promoting secure alliances abroad.

Henry VIII had himself been a pawn in his father's political accommodations. In order to preserve an alliance with Spain, Henry had been allowed to marry his brother's widow, Catherine of Aragon, through a special papal dispensation. For a time, this arrangement seemed to work all around. Henry VIII had proved a dutiful son of the church by writing a religious tract supporting the pope that earned him the title "Defender of the Faith." But Henry became concerned when Catherine suffered a series of miscarriages and was unable to provide a male heir to the Tudor throne. Although she bore Henry a daughter named Mary, this did not conciliate the English king. To secure the succession, he needed a male heir, so he turned to a young favorite at court named Anne Boleyn. When Henry wanted an annulment of his marriage to Catherine on the grounds that his union with his brother's widow was incestuous and accursed by God, the pope could not renege on his earlier dispensation. The pathway to a workable solution seemed closed. Henry became increasingly consumed with the need to stabilize the future of England with a male heir. He finally decided to break with Rome and found the Church of England with himself as head. He granted himself a divorce from Catherine and married Anne in 1533. He was excommunicated by the pope "with the sword of eternal damnation" that same year. Henry did not buckle. The Protestant Reformation had come to England, although through political expediency rather than through spiritual commitment.

The following sources are essential in understanding the English Reformation. The first is the Act of Supremacy (1534), which recognized Henry VIII as the supreme head of the Church of England. He had already extorted from the English bishops, abbots, and priests written declaration that the pope had no more authority in England than any other foreign bishop. The next source is an excerpt from "The Act of Succession" (1534), which declared his marriage with Catherine void and also provided for the royal succession: Anne Boleyn's daughter, the princess Elizabeth, would succeed unless Anne should have sons by the king. Note the harsh provisions should anyone not accept the arrangement. Anne, indeed, failed to produce a son and paid for it with her life as Henry accused her of adultery and moved on to more fertile pastures. Elizabeth was then bumped down the succession ladder.

The Supremacy Act (1534): "The Only Supreme Head of the Church of England"

Albeit the king's majesty firstly and rightfully is and ought to be the supreme head of the Church of England, and so is recognized by the clergy of this realm in their Convocations. . . ; be it enacted by authority of this present Parliament, that the king our sovereign lord, his heirs and successors, kings of this realm, shall be taken, accepted, and reputed the only supreme head in earth of the Church of England . . . and shall have and enjoy, annexed and united to the imperial crown of this realm, as well the title and style thereof, as all honors, dignities, pre-eminences, jurisdictions, privileges, authorities, immunities, profits, and commodities to the said dignity of supreme head of the same Church . . . ; and that our said sovereign lord, his heirs and successors, kings of this realm, shall have full power and authority from time to time to visit, repress, redress, reform, order, correct, restrain, and amend all such errors, heresies, abuses, offenses, contempts, and enormities, whatsoever they be . . . to the pleasure of Almighty God, the increase of virtue in Christ's religion, and for the conservation of the peace, unity, and tranquility of this realm . . .

"The Supremacy Act" is from *Statutes of the Realm*, vol. 3, no. 492, in Henry Gee and W. J. Hardy, eds., *Documents Illustrative of English Church History* (London: Macmillan and Co., Ltd., 1896), pp. 243–244.

The Act of Succession (1534)

If any person or persons, of what estate, dignity, or condition whosoever they be, maliciously, by writing, print, deed, or act, procure or do any thing or things to the prejudice, slander, or derogation of the said lawful matrimony solemnized between your Majesty and the said Queen Anne, or to the peril or slander of any of the heirs of your Highness, being limited by this act to inherit the crown of this realm, every such person and persons, and their aiders and abettors, shall be adjudged high traitors, and every such offense shall be adjudged high treason, and the offenders . . . shall suffer pain of death, as in cases of high treason.

All are to be sworn truly, firmly, and constantly, without fraud or guile, to observe, fulfill, maintain, and keep, . . . to the utmost of their powers, the whole effects and contents of this present act.

The Enforcement of the Elizabethan Settlement (1593): "Divine Service According to Her Majesty's Laws"

After the unsettling reign of Mary Tudor, Henry VIII's daughter by Anne Boleyn came to the throne as Elizabeth I (1558–1603). A talented and diligent queen, she became one of the greatest of all English monarchs, and her reign established England as the most formidable political power of its age. Her religious solution to the struggle between Catholicism and Protestantism was a compromise: The Church of England would be Protestant in doctrine and Catholic in ritual. This "Anglican Settlement" would endure, though Catholic dissent and Protestant attempts at "purifying" or purging Catholic elements from the Church of England would not be settled for nearly two centuries. The following selection demonstrates Elizabeth's commitment to enforcing her religious compromise by demanding Catholic allegiance to the authority of the English crown. Other statutes demanding Puritan obeisance were likewise initiated.

For the better discovering and avoiding of all such traitorous and most dangerous conspiracies and attempts as are daily devised and practiced against our most gracious sovereign lady the queen's majesty and the happy estate of this commonweal, by sundry wicked and seditious persons, who, terming themselves Catholics, and being indeed spies and intelligencers, not only for her majesty's foreign enemies, but also for rebellious and traitorous subjects born within her highness's realms and dominions, and hiding their most detestable and devilish purposes under a false pretext of religion and conscience, do secretly wander and shift from place to place within this realm, to corrupt and seduce her majesty's subjects, and to stir them to sedition and rebellion: Be it ordained and enacted by our sovereign lady the queen's majesty, and the Lords spiritual and temporal, and the Commons, in this present Parliament assembled, and by the authority of the same, that every person above the age of sixteen years, born within any of the queen's majesty's realms and dominions . . .

"The Act of Succession" is from *Statutes of the Realm*, vol. 3, no. 471, in Henry Gee and W. J. Hardy, eds., *Documents Illustrative of English Church History* (London: Macmillan and Co., Ltd., 1896), p. 240.

"The Enforcement of the Elizabethan Settlement" is from Statutes of the Realm, vol. 4, part 2, p. 843, in Henry Gee and W. J. Hardy, eds., *Documents Illustrative of English Church History* (London: Macmillan and Co., Ltd., 1896), pp. 499, 506.

shall come to some parish church on some Sunday or other festival day, and then and there hear divine service, and make public and open submission and declaration of his and their conformity to her majesty's laws and statutes. . . .

Consider This:

- Did the English Reformation involve personal conscience or political expediency? How was the religious authority of the monarch achieved?

The Catholic Reformation

Spiritual Exercises (1548)

IGNATIUS LOYOLA

During the Protestant movement, the Catholic church was active in its own efforts to reform from within. The Society of Jesus (Jesuits) was a religious order founded by Ignatius Loyola in 1540. Loyola (1491–1556) was a soldier who had turned to religion while recovering from wounds. Under Loyola's firm leadership, the Jesuits became a disciplined organization that was dedicated to serving the pope with unquestioned loyalty. The next selection from the famous *Spiritual Exercises* of Loyola demonstrate the purity and determination of these Catholic reformers.

1. Always to be ready to obey with mind and heart, setting aside all judgement of one's own, the true spouse of Jesus Christ, our holy mother our infallible and orthodox mistress, the Catholic Church, whose authority is exercised over us by the hierarchy.
2. To commend the confession of sins to a priest as it is practiced in the Church; the reception of the Holy Eucharist once a year, or better still every week, or at least every month, with the necessary preparation.
4. To have a great esteem for the religious orders, and to give the preference to celibacy or virginity over the married state.
5. To approve of the religious vows of chastity, poverty, perpetual obedience, as well as the other works of perfection and supererogation. Let us remark in passing, that we must never engage by vow to take a state (such e.g. as marriage) that would be an impediment to one more perfect. . . .
6. To praise relics, the veneration and invocation of Saints: also the stations, and pious pilgrimages, indulgences, jubilees, the custom of lighting candles in the churches, and other such aids to piety and devotion.
9. To uphold especially all the precepts of the Church, and not censure them in any manner; but, on the contrary, to defend them promptly, with reasons drawn from all sources, against those who criticize them.
10. To be eager to commend the decrees, mandates, traditions, rites and conduct; although there may not always be the uprightness of conduct that there ought to be, yet to attack or revile them in

"*Spiritual Exercises*" is from Henry Bettenson, ed., *Documents of the Christian Church*, 2nd ed. (London: Oxford University Press, 1963), pp. 364–365. Reprinted by permission of the publisher.

private or in public tends to scandal and disorder. Such attacks set the people against their princes and pastors; we must avoid such reproaches and never attack superiors before inferiors. The best course is to make private approach to those who have power to remedy the evil.

The Council of Trent: Profession of Faith

The Council of Trent was an involved effort by the Catholic church to clarify its doctrine and bring about internal reform. The Church sought to make its own stand in the face of the Protestant threat, and thus its traditional doctrinal views are set forth with firmness and confidence, as the first excerpt indicates. One of the most significant actions of Trent was its reorganization and codification of laws concerning censorship and the prohibition of books. The last selection, published after the Council closed, sets out some of the restrictions. These general rules were in force until they were replaced with new decrees in 1897.

I profess that true God is offered in the Mass, a proper and propitiatory sacrifice for the living and the dead, and that in the most Holy Eucharist there are truly, really and substantially the body and blood together with the soul and divinity of Our Lord Jesus Christ, and that a conversion is made of the whole substance of bread into his body and of the whole substance of wine into his blood, which conversion the Catholic Church calls transubstantiation. I also confess that the whole and entire Christ and the true sacrament is taken under the one species alone.

I hold unswervingly that there is a purgatory and that the souls there detained are helped by the intercessions of the faithful; likewise also that the Saints who reign with Christ are to be venerated and invoked; that they offer prayers to God for us and that their relics are to be venerated. I firmly assert that the images of Christ and of the ever-Virgin Mother of God, as also those of the older Saints, are to be kept and retained, and that due honor and veneration is to be accorded them; and I affirm that the power of indulgences has been left by Christ in the Church, and that their use is very salutary for Christian people.

I recognize the Holy Catholic and Apostolic Roman Church as the Mother and mistress of all churches; and I vow and swear true obedience to the Roman Pontiff, the successor of blessed Peter, the chief of the Apostles and the representative [vicar] of Jesus Christ.

I accept and profess, without doubting the traditions, definitions and declarations of the sacred Canons and Ecumenical Councils and especially those of the holy Council of Trent . . .

CONSIDER THIS:

- Read carefully the selections on the Society of Jesus and the Council of Trent. What specifically do Loyola and the Council of Trent demand from the Catholic faithful? Does the closing oration at the Council of Trent seem to be progressive in its message? Why then does the Tridentine Index of Books seem so repressive? Can faith be enforced in this manner?

- Some historians have called the Catholic reform movement the "Counter Reformation." Do you think a reformation of the church would have occurred without Martin Luther? How important was Luther in changing history?

"The Profession of Faith" is from Henry Bettenson, ed., *Documents of the Christian Church*, 2nd ed. (London: Oxford University Press, 1963), pp. 364–365. Reprinted by permission of the publisher.

The Tridentine Index of Books (1564)

The holy council in the second session, celebrated under our most holy Lord, Pius IV, commissioned some fathers to consider what ought to be done concerning various censures and books either suspected or pernicious and to report to this holy council. . . .

1. All books which have been condemned either by the supreme pontiffs or by ecumenical councils before the year 1515 and are not contained in this list, shall be considered condemned in the same manner as they were formerly condemned.
2. The books of those heresiarchs, who after the aforesaid year originated or revived heresies, as well as those who are or have been the heads or leaders of heretics, as Luther, Zwingli, Calvin, Balthasar Friedberg, Schwenkfeld, and others like these, whatever may be their name, title or nature or their heresy, are absolutely forbidden. The books of other heretics, moreover, which deal professedly with religion are absolutely condemned. Those on the other hand, which do not deal with religion and have by order of the bishops and inquisitors been examined by Catholic theologians and approved by them, are permitted. Likewise, Catholic books written by those who afterward fell into heresy, as well as by those who after their fall returned to the bosom of the Church, may be permitted if they have been approved by the theological faculty of a Catholic university or by the general inquisition.
3. The translations of writers, also ecclesiastical, which have till now been edited by condemned authors, are permitted provided they contain nothing contrary to sound doctrine. Translations of the books of the Old Testament may in the judgment of the bishop be permitted to learned and pious men only. . . . Translations of the New Testament made by authors of the first class of this list shall be permitted to no one, since great danger and little usefulness usually results to readers from their perusal. . . .
4. Since it is clear from experience that if the Sacred Books are permitted everywhere and without discrimination in the vernacular, there will by reason of the boldness of men arise therefrom more harm than good, the matter is in this respect left to the judgment of the bishop or inquisitor, who may with the advice of the pastor or confessor permit the reading of the Sacred Books translated into the vernacular by Catholic authors to those who they know will derive from such reading no harm but rather an increase of faith and piety, which permission they must have in writing. Those, however, who presume to read or possess them without such permission may not receive absolution from their sins until they have handed them over to the authorities. . . .
5. Those books which sometimes produce the works of heretical authors, in which these add little or nothing of their own but rather collect therein the sayings of others, as lexicons, concordances, apothegms, parables, tables of contents and such like, are permitted if whatever needs to be eliminated in the additions is removed and corrected in accordance with the suggestions of the bishop, the inquisitor and Catholic theologians.

"The Tridentine Index of Books" is from J. Barry Colman, ed., *Readings in Church History*, rev. ed., vol. 2 (Westminster, Md.: Christian Classics, Inc., 1985), pp. 705–706, 708.

7. Books which professedly deal with, narrate or teach things lascivious or obscene are absolutely prohibited, since not only the matter of faith but also that of morals, which are usually easily corrupted through the reading of such books, must be taken into consideration, and those who possess them are to be severely punished by the bishops. Ancient books written by heathens may by reason of their elegance and quality of style be permitted, but may by no means be read to children.
8. Books whose chief contents are good but in which things have incidentally been inserted which have reference to heresy, ungodliness, divination or superstition, may be permitted if by the authority of the general inquisition they have been purged by Catholic theologians. . . . Finally, all the faithful are commanded not to presume to read or possess any books contrary to the prescriptions of these rules or the prohibition of this list. And if anyone should read or possess books by heretics or writings by any author condemned and prohibited by reason of heresy or suspicion of false teaching, he incurs immediately the sentence of excommunication. . . .

CONSIDER THIS:

- A critical issue of the Reformation era centered on the diverse means of attaining salvation. How is this issue reflected in the sources? According to Luther, Calvin, Loyola, and the Catholic church, how is one saved? Be specific in your documentation.

- One of the most important questions of this period that separated the reformers from the church centered on religious authority. In spiritual matters, did religious authority rest in the church (as dictated by the pope), in church councils (such as Trent), in scripture, or in individual conscience? How is this problem reflected in the sources?

"I Am the State": The Development of Absolutism in England and France

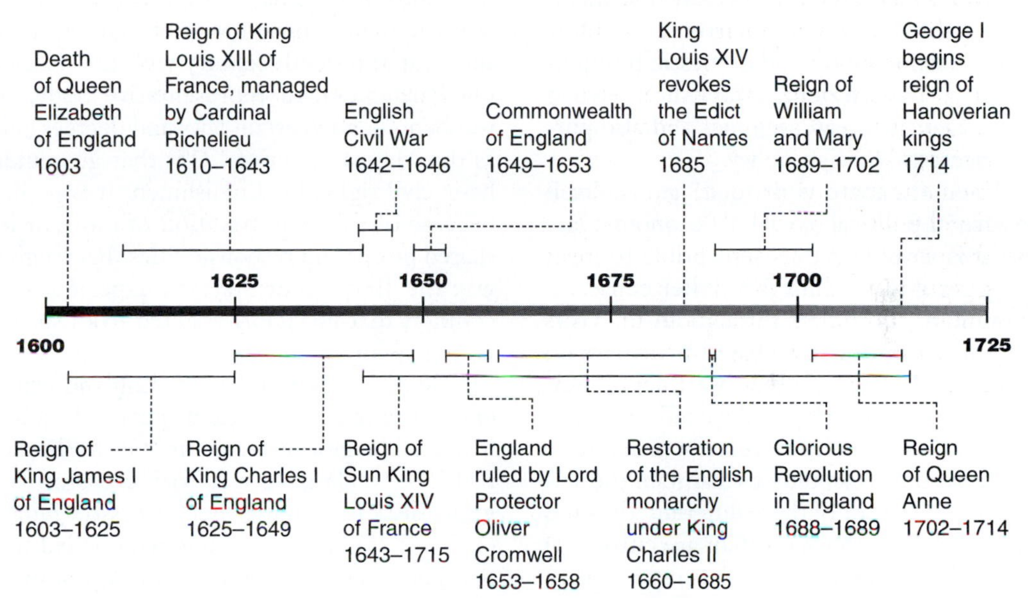

CHAPTER THEMES

- **The Power Structure:** How would you define the term *absolute monarchy*? Is it the most efficient form of government? Can an absolute monarch be compared to a dictator? What is the difference between the two? Was Oliver Cromwell as Lord Protector of England a democrat or a dictator?
- **The Varieties of Truth:** How did Louis XIV use court painters and historians, as well as the Palace of Versailles, to create an image that would benefit him politically? Does it follow that the image of government is more important than the substance of government?
- **The Individual and the Institution:** How would you best define the phrase *divine-right monarchy*? Did Louis XIV really consider himself divine, and how did this connection serve to strengthen his political authority? Can one be an absolute monarch without being a divine-right monarch?
- **Revolution and Historical Transition:** It has been asserted that the seeds of the French Revolution of 1789 were sown during the monarchies of Louis XIV and his immediate successors. For all his glory and prestige, was Louis XIV's reign disastrous for France economically

and militarily? Do revolutions depend on contemporary precipitating causes, or do revolutions have broadly based underlying causes without which political and social change could not be possible?

- **The Big Picture:** Are societies that have a large gap between an elite class and the poor doomed to fail eventually? How important is the presence of a strong middle class? Does the authority of a state's leader increase the more removed the person is from the people he or she rules? Or can governments maintain control over citizens through image alone? Does modern technology change the equation in any way?

It has often been said that the primary purpose of government is to create and maintain a stable domestic environment. Only through such stability and domestic tranquility can a government establish a strong defense against threatening foes and also pursue a successful foreign policy.

When the state is divided against itself into several political, social, or economic factions, it is weak and thus susceptible to invasion or revolution. This is a rather conservative opinion, and others throughout the years have argued that a state based primarily on efficiency and security does not tolerate new ideas or respond quickly to the needs of its citizens; in essence, such a state is not progressive in outlook, but seeks only to maintain the status quo. At the root of these different ideas lies a basic problem: To what extent are citizens of a state able to rule themselves? Is democracy a "noble experiment" that errs by ascribing extraordinary possibilities to ordinary people? Indeed, is progress best served when a citizen body is directed and controlled by a monarch or even a dictator who uses all the resources of the state to achieve his goals? These questions form the basis of political theory in the Western world. How best should humans organize society to provide stability, security, and happiness?

During the fifteenth through the eighteenth centuries, these questions were fundamentally important. As the Middle Ages blended into the Renaissance, decentralized feudalism gave way to more structured monarchies in France, England, and Spain. The modern state was forming under the control of kings who had relatively few restrictions on their authority. The major exception to this was England, whose monarch had coexisted since the thirteenth century with the developing Parliament, or representative body, and was beholden to certain laws and decrees (such as the Magna Carta of 1215) that guaranteed basic civil rights for Englishmen. It is perhaps because of this long tradition of more or less shared power and responsibilities that England was the first major state to experience the conflicts that inevitably resulted from such an arrangement.

Between 1603 and 1715, England experienced the most tumultuous years of its long history. The glorious reign of Queen Elizabeth I (1558–1603) gave way to increasing religious dissension under her successor, James I (1603–1625). The new king, who hailed from Scotland, lacked tact and was ignorant of English institutions. More seriously, he advocated absolute, divine-right monarchy. According to this theory, the authority of a king was unlimited and could not be challenged because it was sanctioned by God. The reign of James I began a breach between the monarchy and Parliament that was eventually to result in a civil war (1642–1646) between supporters of the Parliament (Roundheads) and those of the king (Cavaliers). The victory of Parliament was crowned with the beheading of King Charles I (1649), an act without precedent in English history. After this, the government was controlled first by Parliament alone and then under the direction of Oliver Cromwell, who was determined to give England efficient rule as Lord Protector (1653–1658). On Cromwell's death, the monarchy was restored under Charles II (1660–1685), but it was conciliatory to the will of Parliament. The final breach occurred when King James II (1685–1688) once again tried to assert authority as an absolute monarch. Parliament deposed him, banned his Catholic relatives from succession, and invited the popular Dutch Protestant leader William of Orange and his wife Mary to rule as monarchs (1688). This so-called Glorious Revolution was bloodless and resulted in a Bill of Rights that limited the powers of the monarchy; henceforward the king would rule with the consent of Parliament.

Seventeenth-century France, in contrast to England, saw representative government crushed by the success of absolute monarchy. It was Henry IV (1589–1610) who began the process of establishing a strong centralized state by curtailing the privileges of the nobility and restricting provincial governors and regional councils called *parlements*. Henry and his finance minister, the Duke of Sully (1560–1641), also sought to control the economy of France by establishing government monopolies on gunpowder, mines, and salt. When Henry IV was assassinated in 1610, he was succeeded by his son, Louis XIII (1610–1643). Because Louis was only nine years old at the time of his father's death, France was ruled by his mother, Marie de Medici, who sought internal security by promoting Cardinal Richelieu (1585–1642) as chief adviser to the king. Richelieu, an efficient and shrewd counselor, sought to make France the dominant European power by consolidating the domestic authority of the king. There was to be but one law—that of the king. To this end, Richelieu imprisoned and executed recalcitrant nobles; indeed, the French nobility eventually became docile in their subservience at court. Richelieu was succeeded in 1642 by another cardinal named Mazarin (1602–1661), who acted as regent for the young monarch, Louis XIV. It is because of the strict policies of Richelieu and Mazarin that Louis XIV inherited a basic foundation for absolute rule.

The reign of Louis XIV (1643–1715) was fundamentally important for the establishment of France both as the supreme political power on the Continent and as the dominant cultural influence throughout Europe. The sun shone brightly on the fortunes of France in the seventeenth and eighteenth centuries, and Louis, or the Sun King as he was called, became the model of stable, secure rule. His control over his subjects was absolute, subject to no authority except that of God. God had appointed Louis, and God alone could judge his actions. Thus, all political, social, economic, and military decisions were made by the king and his various advisers without interference or input from the people of France. Collectively, his subjects were Louis's children and as such were expected to follow the policies of their "father." Louis's famous comment, "I am the state," was the essence of French divine-right monarchy.

This period of history, however, was not in any sense tranquil. For over half a century before Louis's accession, France had been disrupted by religious wars between Catholics, whom the French monarchy supported, and the Huguenots or French Protestants. The wars had secured certain political and military privileges for the Huguenots that were scarcely compatible with the ideal of a strong, centralized monarchy. When Louis assumed control of the government in 1661 after his eighteen-year minority, the Huguenots were still an independent religious group, officially tolerated by the crown but an embarrassment nonetheless. Finally, in 1685 Louis demanded conformity to Catholic doctrine and revoked the Edict of Nantes (1598), which had granted religious toleration to the Huguenots.

Another major threat to the tranquility of the state and the supremacy of royal power came from the nobility. During the minority of Louis XIV, France had lapsed into civil war, fomented by nobles who were jealous of the increasing power of the monarchy and particularly its close financial support from an active middle class. To many, the chaos of such disturbances was a greater fear than the existence of a strong, centralized monarchy that could ensure domestic tranquility and external security. This fear of chaos and desire for order probably lay behind popular support of Louis's divine-right monarchy. The longevity and relative harmony of his reign demonstrates Louis's successful disarming of the nobility. His magnificent palace at Versailles, testimony to his pursuit of order, not only was an enduring artistic legacy of his reign but also served a practical purpose: Louis could house all his important nobles at the palace and thus maintain close control over their activities. Louis reserved high government positions for handpicked members of the aristocracy and aspiring middle class, who thus owed their success to him; this in turn assured their loyalty.

In the late seventeenth and early eighteenth centuries, France was the envy and terror of Europe, its most powerful state and cultural center. Other monarchs imitated Louis's court at Versailles and even the palace itself. His army was perhaps the best trained and best supplied military force of its day, and his diplomatic service proved to be a model of excellence. The French language became accepted as the common tongue among diplomats. French dominance of European affairs was cultural as well as political.

This chapter examines the theory and practice of absolute rule, especially as it was applied in France under Louis XIV. Is absolute monarchy a natural form of government, in keeping with the human desire to follow and be enveloped in the security of political stability? Or do you resist this idea? To what extent is absolutism, whether justified by God or by force of arms, different from tyranny? Is a competent, even enlightened despot more attractive than divisive democracy? Charles I, Oliver Cromwell, and Louis XIV were all assertive rulers who struggled to define and maintain their dominant positions. Indeed, Louis sought glory in foreign wars and domestic stability under the motto "one King, one law, one faith." The formula is simplistic, yet the policy was effective. To his admirers, Louis represented the quintessential monarch. Yet, the Sun King was certainly not without his critics. And Oliver Cromwell, in the fluid political environment of seventeenth-century England, can be seen variously as the "caretaker of democracy," as well as the "scourge of freedom." Each would have you believe his actions were in accordance with the preference of his particular political community and required by the necessities of state. But voices of dissent must also be heard for a balanced assessment of absolutism.

The English Revolution (1649–1689)

It is atheism and blasphemy to dispute what God can do; so it is presumption and contempt to dispute what a king can do, or say that a king cannot do this or that.

—JAMES I

Every subject's duty is the king's, but every subject's soul is his own.

—WILLIAM SHAKESPEARE

William and Mary, George and Anne/Four such children had never a man:
They put their father to flight and shame/And called their brother a shocking bad name.

—ENGLISH NURSERY RHYME

The Origins of Confrontation (1603–1625)

When Queen Elizabeth died in 1603, she was succeeded by her nephew, James I (1603–1625), who was already King of Scotland. He was a leader of ability and assertive personality who inherited an ambiguous political position in England. It was never very clear to James, who had no experience with parliamentary institutions in Scotland, just where the authority of the king left off and where that of the Parliament began. Because England had no written constitution, the country was governed through traditions and laws that had developed since Magna Carta in 1215. During the sixteenth century, Parliament grew into a powerful representative institution, fully confirmed in its authority to offer advice to the monarch on questions of policy and especially in its control over taxation. James thus looked to rule England with the kind of dominant authority he had exercised in Scotland while members of the English Parliament adopted an aggressive attitude designed to uphold their traditional rights and privileges.

Charles I and the Limitations of Royal Authority (1625–1628)

Although James I succeeded in avoiding a sharp break with Parliament over the limits of royal authority and the supremacy of the Anglican church, events moved to a crisis under his son, Charles I (1625–1649). Charles seemed to have none of the qualifications of a successful ruler. In 1624, he advised his dying father into a war with Spain and then one with France. Both ventures fared poorly, and although at peace again by 1630, the monarchy was in severe financial straits. When Parliament failed to grant him customary revenues, Charles collected them anyway through "forced loans" from the people, imprisoning those who refused to pay. In addition, royal troops in transit to war zones were often quartered in private English homes. Politically, the king's authoritarianism was blatant and alienated many of those who could have helped him.

Religiously, tensions also increased under Charles. He was a devout Anglican, who looked to maintain the Church of England as the moderate and stable force that had been so ably directed by his predecessor, Elizabeth I. But the Church of England was in turmoil, split by two basic factions. The Puritans wanted to modify the rites and doctrines of the Anglican church in accordance with the Calvinist creed of predestination and by instituting preaching as an integral part of worship. The other faction, known as the Arminians, emphasized human free will and a conservative definition of the sacraments and rituals of the church. Charles had difficulty maintaining his political position in the realm because his enemies in Parliament denounced him as an Arminian and accused him of even being a "papist" in support of Catholicism and the supremacy of the pope. Although Charles was quite willing to tolerate Catholics, these charges were untrue. Nevertheless, Charles was saddled with a majority in the House of Commons who actively pursued their own policies in religious and foreign affairs by withholding the appropriation of taxes. As a result, Charles was forced to negotiate and compromise by signing the Petition of Right in 1628 that compelled the king, according to the provisions of Magna Carta, to stop collecting "forced loans" and imprisoning his subjects without due process of law.

Confrontation and the Drift to Civil War (1628–1642)

Although it is true that Charles accepted the Petition of Right, he did not intend to deprive himself of income that could be obtained through reviving ancient rights of the crown that had fallen into disuse. After a serious parliamentary attempt to limit royal prerogative in 1629, Charles dismissed Parliament and did not call it into session for eleven years. To conserve his limited resources, Charles and his ministers instituted a policy called *thorough*, whereby strict efficiency and administrative centralization would contribute to the king's ability to operate independently of Parliament. Charles handled the finances of the country by enforcing neglected laws and relying on impositions such as "Ship Money" (1634) that the courts determined could be garnered as personal income without the approval of Parliament. These issues were disputed throughout the decade, but because Parliament could not be called into session by anyone but the king, there was no official confrontation.

The situation changed in 1640 when Charles was compelled to summon Parliament to provide funds to quell a rebellion in Scotland that had been provoked when Charles imposed an episcopal system and an Anglican prayer book on the Calvinist Scots. The Parliament reacted quickly by passing a series of acts that were designed to curtail royal power: Parliament in the future was to meet at least every three years; the king's chief minister, the Earl of Stafford, was accused of high treason and executed; Parliament resolved that it could not be dissolved without its own consent, and abolished the king's personally controlled court (Star Chamber) and the "ship money" tax, which the king had used for financial support in lieu of parliamentary taxation. Because Charles was faced with the crisis of a Scottish rebellion, he signed all of these acts, thus making them valid statutes.

The English Civil War (1642–1649)

Although royal authority had thus been limited by large majorities in Parliament, Charles refused to assent to Parliament's assertion of authority. Relations between the king and Parliament deteriorated quickly and in June 1642, Charles raised an army in recognition of "an urgent and inevitable necessity of putting our subjects into a posture of defense for the safeguard both of our person and people." In response, Parliament a month later raised an army "for the safety of the King's person, defense of both Houses of Parliament, and those who have obeyed their orders and commands, and preserving of the true religion, the laws, the liberty and peace of the kingdom." A bloody civil war ensued that ended in the defeat of the royal forces (Cavaliers) and Scots, with whom the king had allied in 1647. But in 1648, Parliament was divided between a majority who wanted to negotiate with the king for the reestablishment of the monarchy (although with limited powers) and the Roundhead faction that sought the death of the king. Under the direction of Oliver Cromwell, a fiery member of Parliament and primary architect of the New Model Army that was responsible for the Roundhead victory over the king, the Parliament was purged of all members opposed to the army's policies. The surviving remnant called the "Rump Parliament" declared their supremacy and established a High Court of Justice to try the king on charges of high treason. This act was passed by the Commons, but not by the Lords.

The Struggle for Constitutional Government (1650–1660)

The radicalized Rump Parliament asserted that the king had violated the rights and liberties of the people of England "out of a wicked design to erect and uphold in himself an unlimited and tyrannical power" and had "traitorously and maliciously levied war against Parliament and the people therein represented." A death warrant was issued for the king on order of the High Court, whose legitimacy he had called into question. On the scaffold, Charles gave a last defense of his reign and declared himself a "martyr of the people."

After the execution of Charles I on January 29, 1649, Parliament immediately established its supremacy in the new political environment by passing a series of acts that abolished the office of king (March 17, 1649) and the House of Lords (March 19, 1649) and instituted the Commonwealth of England "for the good of the people." The crime of high treason was thus appropriately defined to bolster and protect the new regime as the next document attests.

Treason and the Commonwealth (July 17, 1650)

Whereas the Parliament has abolished the kingly office in England and Ireland, and in the dominions and territories thereunto belonging; and having resolved and declared, that the people shall for the future be governed by its own Representatives or national meetings in Council, chosen and entrusted by them for that purpose, has settled the Government in the way of a Commonwealth and Free State, without King or House of Lords: be it enacted by this present Parliament, and by the authority of the same, that if any person shall maliciously or advisedly publish, by writing, printing, or openly declaring, that the said Government is tyrannical, usurped, or unlawful; or that the Commons in Parliament assembled are not the supreme authority of this nation; or shall plot, contrive, or endeavour to stir up, or raise force against the present Government, or for the subversion or alteration of the same, and shall declare the same by any open deed, that then every such offence shall be taken, deemed, and adjudged by authority of this Parliament to be high treason.

And whereas the Keepers of the liberty of England, and the Council of State, constituted by authority of Parliament, are to be under the said representatives in Parliament entrusted for the maintenance of the said Government with several powers and authorities limited, given, and appointed unto them by the Parliament: be it likewise enacted by the authority aforesaid, that if any person shall maliciously and advisedly plot or endeavour the subversion of the said Keepers of the liberty of England, or the Council of State, . . . then every such offence and offenses shall be taken, deemed, and declared to be high treason.

"Treason and the Commonwealth" is from G. Adams and H. Stephens, *Select Documents of English Constitutional History* (New York: The Macmillan Company, 1916), pp. 400–401.

"The Mortal God": Leviathan (1651)

THOMAS HOBBES

The establishment of a Commonwealth without a king was uncharted political territory for England. The institution of monarchy could arguably trace its national origins to the ninth-century warrior king, Alfred the Great, and its consolidation under the Norman king, William the Conqueror, in 1066. Rule by Parliament without prescribed executive leadership beyond a Council of State contributed to a fluid political environment with factional infighting and corruption. Some doubted the benefits of "unregulated" democracy.

Thomas Hobbes was one of the great political philosophers of the seventeenth century. His major work, entitled *Leviathan,* was published in 1651 and reflects the insecurity and fear of the English Revolution that had resulted in civil war (1642–1646) and had just seen the decapitation of a sovereign monarch in 1649. Hobbes himself, because of his aristocratic associations, had been forced to flee England. Not surprisingly, *Leviathan* is a treatise that advocates political absolutism. Its theme is power, and it justifies absolute rule as necessary to subdue a violent human nature and promote a reasonable existence. For Hobbes, the authority of the absolute monarch did not lie in hereditary right or in divine sanction, but only in his ability to achieve power and maintain it. In this sense, Hobbes borrowed much from the Renaissance political philosopher Niccolò Machiavelli. But Hobbes went much further by providing an integrated social and political philosophy of government.

Nature has made men so equal, in the faculties of the body and mind; as that though there be found one man sometimes manifestly stronger in body, or of quicker mind than another; yet when all is reckoned together, the differences between man and man, is not so considerable . . . For as to the strength of body, the weakest has strength enough to kill the strongest, either by secret machination, or by confederacy with others, that are in the same danger with himself. And as to the faculties of the mind . . . I find yet a greater equality among men, than that of strength. . . . Such is the nature of men, that howsoever they may acknowledge many others to be more witty, or more eloquent, or more learned; yet they will hardly believe there are many so wise as themselves; for they see their own wit at hand, and other men's at a distance. . . .

From this equality of ability, arises equality of hope in the attaining of our ends. And therefore if any two men desire the same thing, which nevertheless they cannot both enjoy, they become enemies; and in the way to their end, which is principally their own conservation . . . endeavour to destroy, or subdue one another. And from hence it comes to pass, that . . . an invader has no more to fear than another man's single power; if one plant, sow, build, and possess a convenient seat, others may probably be expected to come prepared with forces united, to dispossess, and deprive him, not only of the fruit of his labour, but also of his life, or liberty. And the invader again is in the like danger of another. . . .

[Thus], men have no pleasure, but on the contrary a great deal of grief, in keeping company, where there is no power able to overawe them all. . . .

"The Mortal God: *Leviathan*" is from W. Molesworth, ed., *The English Works of Thomas Hobbes*, vol. 3 (London: John Bohn, 1839), from chapters 13 and 17, pp. 110–113, 153, 157–158. Text modernized by the editor.

FIGURE 2.1 This illustration from the title page to *Leviathan* captures the essence of Thomas Hobbes's philosophy: The ruler is embodied by individuals who consent to his dominance for the general welfare. All look to him and in the process lose their individual authority, but gain stability and security. The Latin quotation reads, "Upon the earth, there is not his like." *(Library of Congress)*

So that in the nature of man, we find three principal causes of quarrel. First, competition; secondly, insecurity; thirdly, glory.

The first, makes men invade for gain; the second, for safety; and the third, for reputation. The first use violence, to make themselves master of other men's persons, wives, children, and cattle; the second, to defend them; the third, for trifles, as a word, a smile, a different opinion, and any other sign of undervalue, either direct in their persons, or by reflection in their kindred, their friends, their nation, their profession, or their name.

[Therefore, it is clear] that during the time men live without a common power to keep them all in awe, they are in that condition which is called war; and such a war is of every man, against every man. . . . In such condition, there is no place for industry; because the fruit thereof is uncertain: and consequently no culture of the earth; no navigation, nor use of the commodities that may be imported by sea; no commodious building; no instruments of moving, and removing, such things as require much force; no knowledge of the face of the earth; no account of time; no arts; no letters; no society; and which is worst of all, continual fear, and danger of violent death; and the life of man, solitary, poor, nasty, brutish, and short. . . .

The final cause, end, or design of men, who naturally love liberty, and dominion over others, [is] the introduction of that restraint upon themselves, [by] which we see them live in commonwealths. . . . The only way to erect such a common power, as may be able to defend them from the invasion of foreigners, and the injuries of one another, and thereby to secure them in such sort, as that by their own industry, and by the fruits of the earth, they may nourish themselves and live contentedly; is, to confer all their power and strength upon one man, or upon one assembly of men, that may reduce all their wills, by plurality of voices, unto one will. . . . [All men shall] submit their wills . . . to his will, and their judgments, to his judgment. This is more than consent, or concord; it is a real unity of them all, in one and the same person, made by covenant of every man with every man, in such manner, as if every man should say to every man, I authorize and give up my right of governing myself, to this man, or to this assembly of men, on this condition, that you give up your right to him, and authorize all his actions in like manner. This done, the multitude so united in one person, is called a COMMONWEALTH. . . . This is the generation of that great LEVIATHAN, or rather, to speak more reverently, of that mortal god, to which we own under the immortal God, our peace and defense. For by this authority, given him by every particular man in the commonwealth, he hath the use of so much power and strength conferred on him, that by terror thereof, he is enabled to perform the wills of them all, to peace at home, and mutual aid against their enemies abroad. And in him consists the essence of the commonwealth; which, to define it, is one person of whose acts a great multitude, by mutual covenants one with another, have made themselves every one the author, to the end he may use the strength and means of them all, as he shall think expedient, for their peace and common defense.

And this person is called SOVEREIGN, and said to have sovereign power; and every one besides, his SUBJECT.

CONSIDER THIS:

- Discuss the ideas of Thomas Hobbes. What was his view of human nature, and how does he justify absolute monarchy? Be specific in your assessment. How does Hobbes's *Leviathan* reflect the uncertainty of the time?

Cromwell's Dismissal of the "Rump Parliament" (April 22, 1653)

EDMUND LUDLOW

The central figure in the period from the English civil wars to the end of the Commonwealth in 1660 was Oliver Cromwell. He was born in 1599 to a family of solid, although not distinguished reputation. In 1628, he became a member of Parliament and played an active, if not a leading role in the controversies of the time. Presumably he voted for the Grand Remonstrance, for he once declared that he would have sold all his possessions and left the country if it had not been passed. When war came, he was the primary architect of the "New Model Army" that rebounded to defeat the king's forces at Marsten Moor (1644) and at Naseby (1645). Cromwell's military skill and political talents assured him a position of prominence, although he was never supreme commander of the parliamentary forces during the wars.

"Cromwell's Dismissal of the 'Rump Parliament'" is from C. H. Firth, *The Memoirs of Edmund Ludlow* (Oxford: Oxford University Press, 1894), vol. 1, pp. 352–354.

When the Commonwealth was established in 1649, Cromwell was sent to reconquer and pacify Ireland, which had broken away from English control during the civil wars. His brutality in reducing the Irish shocked even his contemporaries, but Cromwell in a letter of 1649 noted that their destruction was "a righteous judgment of God" and that extreme measures "tend to prevent the effusion of blood for the future, which are satisfactory grounds to such actions."

When Charles II, son of the executed monarch, landed in Scotland in 1650, Cromwell was dispatched to deal with this threat to the new Commonwealth. After two smashing victories, Cromwell entered London in triumph and was granted an annual income and the royal palace of Hampton Court as a residence. When the Rump Parliament seemed on the verge of making itself perpetual in April 1653, Cromwell felt constrained to dismiss it, so disillusioned was he with the moral fabric of its membership. His strict Puritan standards are evident in the following account.

Calling to Major-General Harrison, who was on the other side of the House, to come to him, [Cromwell] told him, that he judged the Parliament ripe for a dissolution, and this to be the time of doing it. The Major-General answered, . . . " Sir, the work is very great and dangerous, therefore I desire you seriously to consider of it before you engage in it." "You say well," replied General [Cromwell], and thereupon sat still for about a quarter of an hour; and then . . . he said again to Major-General Harrison, "this is the time I must do it"; and suddenly standing up, made a speech, wherein he loaded the Parliament with the vilest reproaches, charging them not to have a heart to do any thing for the public good, to have espoused the corrupt interest of . . . lawyers who were the supporters of tyranny and oppression, accusing them of an intention to perpetuate themselves in power, . . . and thereupon told them, that the Lord had done with them, and had chosen other instruments for the carrying on his work that were more worthy. This he spoke with so much passion and discomposure of mind, as if he had been distracted.

Sir Peter Wentworth stood up to answer him, and said, that this was the first time that ever he had heard such unbecoming language given to the Parliament, and that it was the more horrid in that it came from their servant . . . whom they had so highly trusted and obliged: but as he was going on, the General stepped into the midst of the House, where continuing his distracted language, he said, "Come, come, I will put an end to your prating"; then walking up and down the House like a madman, and kicking the ground with his feet, he cried out, "You are no Parliament, I say you are no Parliament; I will put an end to your sitting; call them in"; whereupon the sergeant attending the Parliament opened the doors, and two files of musketeers entered the House; which Sir Henry Vane observing from his place, said aloud, "This is not honest, yea it is against morality and common honesty." Then Cromwell fell a railing at him, crying out with a loud voice, "O Sir Henry Vane, Sir Henry Vane, the lord deliver me from Sir Henry Vane." Then looking upon one of the members, he said, "There sits a drunkard"; and giving much reviling language to others, he commanded the mace [symbolic of Parliament's authority] to be taken away, saying "What shall we do with this bauble here, take it away." Having brought all into this disorder, Major-General Harrison went to the Speaker [of the House] as he sat in the chair, and told him, that seeing things were reduced to this pass, it would not be convenient for him to remain there. The Speaker answered, that he would not come down unless he were forced. "Sir," said Harrison,

"I will lend you my hand"; and thereupon putting his hand within his, the Speaker came down. Then Cromwell applied himself to the members of the House, who were in number between 80 and 100, and said to them, "It's you that have forced me to this, for I have sought the Lord night and day, that he would rather slay me than put me upon the doing of this work."

CONSIDER THIS:

- Why did Oliver Cromwell dismiss the Rump Parliament in 1653? By dismissing Parliament, was Cromwell guilty of restricting the democratic bases of Parliament that had been so threatened by Charles I and so heartily promoted by Cromwell himself? On what principles did Cromwell justify his actions?

The Instrument of Government (December 16, 1653)

In December 1653, Cromwell finalized his political solution for the stability of the Commonwealth. The Instrument of Government established Cromwell as Lord Protector of the Commonwealth, a misleading title that some have suggested was created to mask his military despotism. In a speech dated 1657, a year before his death, Cromwell denied the crown that would have formalized his position as king of England.

The government of the Commonwealth of England, Scotland, and Ireland, and the dominions thereunto belonging:

1. That the supreme legislative authority of the Commonwealth of England, Scotland, and Ireland, shall be and reside in one person, and the people assembled in Parliament; the style of which person shall be the Lord Protector of the Commonwealth of England, or Ireland.
2. That the exercise of the chief magistracy and the administration of the government over the said countries and the dominions, and the people thereof, shall be in the Lord Protector, assisted with a council. . . .
4. That the Lord Protector, the Parliament sitting, shall dispose and order the militia and forces, both by sea and land, for the peace and good of the three nations, by consent of the Parliament.
6. That the laws shall not be altered, suspended, abrogated, or repealed, nor any new law made, nor any tax, charge, or imposition laid upon the people, but by common consent in Parliament. . . .
24. That all Bills agreed unto by the Parliament, shall be presented to the Lord Protector for his consent; and in case he shall not give his consent thereto within twenty days after they shall be presented to him, then such Bills shall pass into and become laws, although he shall not give his consent thereunto.
32. That the office of Lord Protector over these nations shall be elective and not hereditary; and upon the death of the Lord Protector, another fit person shall be forthwith elected to succeed him in the Government; which election shall be by the Council. . . .
33. That Oliver Cromwell, Captain-General of the forces of England, Scotland and Ireland, shall be, and is hereby declared to be, Lord Protector of the Commonwealth. . . .
51. That every successive Lord Protector over these nations shall take and subscribe a solemn oath . . . that he will seek the peace, quiet and welfare of these nations, cause law and justice to be equally administered, and . . . will govern these nations according to the laws, statutes and customs thereof.

"The Instrument of Government" is from George Adams and H. Stephens, *Select Documents of English Constitutional History* (New York: The Macmillan Company), pp. 407–416.

Cromwell Denies the Crown (May 8, 1657)

OLIVER CROMWELL

Mr. Speaker,

I have, the best I can, resolved the whole business in my thoughts. . . . I think [this] is a government that, in the aims of it, seeks the settling the nation on a good foot, in relation to civil rights and liberties, which are the rights of the nation. And I hope I shall never be found to be one of them that go about to rob the nation of those rights, but shall ever be found to serve them, what I can, to the attaining of them. It is also exceeding well provided there for the safety and security of honest men, in the great, natural, and religious liberty, which is liberty of conscience. These are the great fundamentals; and I must bear my testimony to them . . . so long as God lets me live in this world, that the intentions of the thing are very honorable and honest, and the product worthy of a Parliament.

I have only had the unhappiness . . . not to be convinced of the necessity of that thing, that has been so often insisted on by you, to wit, the title of King, as in itself so necessary, as it seems to apprehended by yourselves. . . . And, while you are granting others liberties, surely you will not deny me this? It being not only a liberty, but a duty to examine mine own heart, and thoughts, and judgment, in every work which I am to set my hand to, or to appear in, or for I have truly thought, and do still think, that if I should at the best do anything on this account, to answer your expectation, at the best I should do it doubtingly. And certainly what is so done, is not of faith—is sin to him that does it. I should not be an honest man if I should not tell you, that I cannot accept of the government, nor undertake the trouble and charge of it. . . . I say, I am persuaded therefore to return this answer to you, that I cannot undertake this government with that title of King. And that is my answer to this great weighty business.

Consider This:

- How would you define the position of Lord Protector as created by the "Instrument of Government" (1653)? Was he an absolute monarch? A constitutional monarch? Or simply the leader of a free Commonwealth? Did the English Parliament substitute one king (Charles I) for another (Oliver Cromwell)? Why, then, did Cromwell refuse the title of "king"?
- In Cromwell's letter refusing to accept the crown and the position of king of England (1657), he stated that he hoped he would never be found guilty of robbing the nation of civil rights and liberties, "but shall ever be found to serve them . . . to the attaining of them." He hoped to provide for security for the "great, natural and religious liberty, which is the liberty of conscience." After reading the documents entitled "Treason and the Commonwealth" (1650) and the "Instrument of Government" (1653), do you think he succeeded? Is freedom of speech central to freedom of conscience, or do the requirements of establishing political order preclude religious tolerance and open expression?

"Cromwell Denies the Crown" is from Charles Stainer, *Speeches of Oliver Cromwell* (London: Henry Frowde, 1901), pp. 350–353.

THEME: THE VARIETIES OF TRUTH

The Reflection in the Mirror

Oliver Cromwell: The Lord Protector

Oliver Cromwell, like many other individuals who have played a major role in the determination of historical events, was a complex and controversial figure. The two accounts of his career that follow were written from very different perspectives separated by fifty years.

John Milton (1608–1674) has achieved a place of literary distinction as one of the greatest poets of the English language. Concerned with the Puritan cause, Milton spent much of the years from 1641 to 1660 pamphleteering for civil and religious liberty and serving as the secretary for foreign languages in the Cromwell government. After the restoration of the Stuart monarchy in 1660, he was arrested but soon released.

Edward Hyde (1609–1674), in contrast, championed Parliament's cause in judiciously limiting the royal prerogative, but he remained a close adviser to Charles I and even served as guardian to his son, Charles II, and later chancellor. His strict morality and acerbic temper eventually led to exile in France, where he finished a history of the civil wars.

Keep in Mind . . .

- The following excerpts are from these two important and influential ministers of state, nearly the same age, writing about the most dramatic and controversial personality of their time.

"To You Our Country Owes Its Liberties"

JOHN MILTON

The whole surface of the British empire has been the scene of [Cromwell's] exploits, and the theatre of his triumphs. . . . He collected an army as numerous and as well equipped as any one ever did in so short a time; which was uniformly obedient to his orders, and dear to the affections of the citizens; which was formidable to the enemy in the field, but never cruel to those who laid down their arms; which committed no lawless ravages on the persons or the property of the inhabitants; who, when they compared their conduct with the turbulence, the intemperance, the impiety and the debauchery of the royalists, were wont to salute them as friends and to consider them as guests. They were a stay to the good, a terror to the evil, and the warmest advocates for every exertion of piety and virtue.

[Here Milton addresses himself directly to Cromwell regarding the dismissal of the Rump Parliament]

But when you saw that the business [of governing the realm] was artfully procrastinated, that every one was more intent on his own selfish interest than on the public good, that the people complained of the disappointments which they had experienced, and the fallacious promises by which they had been gulled, that they were the dupes of a few overbearing individuals, you put an end to their domination.

"To You Our Country Owes Its Liberty" is from John Milton, *Second Defense of the People of England* (1654).

FIGURE 2.2 Portrait of the Lord Protector, Oliver Cromwell: Did England owe its liberty to Cromwell, or was he guilty of crimes "for which hell fire is prepared"? (*Library of Congress*)

In this state of desolation to which we were reduced, you, O Cromwell! alone remained to conduct the government and to save the country. We all willingly yield the palm of sovereignty to your unrivalled ability and virtue, except the few among us who, either ambitious of honors which they have not the capacity to sustain, or who envy those which are conferred on one more worthy than themselves, or else who do not know that nothing in the world is more pleasing to God, more agreeable to reason, more politically just, or more generally useful, than that the supreme power should be vested in the best and the wisest of men. Such, O Cromwell, all acknowledge you to be. . . . Other names you neither have nor could endure; and you deservedly reject that pomp of title which attracts the gaze and admiration of the multitude.

"Nothing in the world is more pleasing to God, more agreeable to reason, more politically just, or more generally useful, than that the supreme power should be vested in the best and the wisest of men."

—JOHN MILTON

Do you then, sir, continue your course with the same unrivalled magnanimity; it sits well upon you;—to you our country owes its liberties. . . . And, after having endured so many sufferings and encountered so many perils for the sake of liberty, do not suffer it, now it is obtained, either to be violated by yourself, or in any one instance impaired by others. You cannot be truly free unless we are free too; for such is the nature of things, that he who entrenches on the liberty of others is the first to lose his own and become a slave.

But if you, who have hitherto been the patron and tutelary genius of liberty, if you, who are exceeded by no one in justice, in piety and goodness, should hereafter invade that liberty which you have defended, your conduct must be fatally operative, not only against the cause of liberty, but the general interests of piety and virtue. Your integrity and virtue will appear to have evaporated, your faith in religion to have been small; your character with posterity will dwindle into insignificance, by which a most destructive blow will be levelled against the happiness of mankind.

At once wisely and discreetly to hold the scepter over three powerful nations, to persuade people to relinquish inveterate and corrupt for new and more beneficial maxims and institutions, to penetrate into the remotest parts of the country, to have the mind present and operative in every quarter, to watch against surprise, to provide against danger, to reject the blandishments of pleasure and pomp of power—these are exertions compared with which the labor of war is mere pastime; which will require every energy and employ ever faculty that you possess; which demand a man supported from above and almost instructed by immediate inspiration.

"Guilty of Crimes for Which Hell-Fire Is Prepared"

EDWARD HYDE, EARL OF CLARENDON

He was one of those men [whom his very enemies could not condemn without commending him at the same time], for he could never have done half that mischief without great parts of courage, industry and judgment. He must have had a wonderful understanding in the natures and humors of men, and as great a dexterity in applying them,

"Guilty of Crimes for Which Hell-Fire Is Prepared" is from Edward Hyde, *The True Historical Narrative of the Rebellion and the Civil Wars in England*, vol. 3 (1704), pp. 862–864.

who, from a private and obscure birth (though of a good family) without interest or estate, alliance or friendship, could raise himself to such a height and compound and knead such opposite and contradictory tempers, humors and interests into a consistence that contributed to his designs and to their own destruction. Without doubt, no man with more wickedness ever attempted anything, or brought to pass what he desired more wickedly, more in the face and contempt of religion and moral honesty; yet wickedness as great as his could never have accomplished those designs without the assistance of a great spirit, an admirable circumspection and sagacity, and a most magnanimous resolution. . . .

After he was confirmed and invested Protector, he consulted with very few upon any action of importance. . . . What he once resolved, in which he was not rash, he would not be dissuaded from, nor endure any contradiction of his power and authority; but extorted obedience from them who were not willing to yield it. . . .

To conclude his character, Cromwell was not so far a man of blood as to follow Machiavelli's method, which prescribes upon a total alteration of government, as a thing absolutely necessary, to cut off all the heads of those, and extirpate their families, who are friends to the old one. It was confidently reported that in the Council of Officers it was more than once proposed that there might be a general massacre of all the royal party, as the only expedient to secure the government, but that Cromwell would never consent to it; it may be, out of too much contempt of his enemies. In a work, as he was guilty of many crimes against which damnation is denounced and for which hell-fire is prepared, so he had some good qualities, which have caused the memory of some men in all ages to be celebrated; and he will be looked upon by posterity as a brave wicked man.

> "Cromwell will be looked upon by posterity as a brave wicked man."
> —EDWARD HYDE

COMPARE AND CONTRAST:

- Compare the two evaluations of the character and career of Oliver Cromwell by John Milton and Edward Hyde, Earl of Clarendon. Identify the elements of propaganda and overstatement in each. Which account do you find more in keeping with the evidence of the sources?
- What appears to be Milton's purpose in writing his account in 1654? Why was Edward Hyde's opinion published fifty years later than Milton's?

The Restoration and the Glorious Revolution (1660–1689)

Oliver Cromwell died in 1658 and his son, Richard, was elected Lord Protector. He was simply not able to accumulate the support or achieve the authority that had maintained his father in power. The army soon seized control, and some of its leaders promoted the restoration of the Stuart monarchy as the only way to end the chronic political turbulence. The Rump Parliament was called back into session by one of the commanders, and it summoned Charles Stuart from exile and installed him as Charles II. After the bloodshed of a civil war, the execution of a king, and the struggle of creating the Commonwealth, the Stuart monarchy was restored to power.

England had been politically changed in the process of revolution. The Restoration of 1660 left Parliament essentially supreme but allowed the king to lead the nation with authority. What really undid the later Stuart monarchs was their inability to handle the Catholic problem. Charles II ruled an officially Anglican nation but personally harbored a sympathy for Catholicism. Because he left no legitimate children, the crown passed to his brother James II (1685–1688). James was an avowed Catholic, and when he fathered a son by his Catholic second wife, Parliament was threatened with the reality of a Catholic heir to the throne. Some of the parliamentary leadership opened negotiations with William of Orange, a Protestant leader who had made his reputation on the Continent as the container of Catholic France. He accepted the invitation to take the English crown and ruled jointly with his wife (a Protestant daughter of James II) as William III and Mary II. After an initial attempt to rally support, James II fled to France, giving William a nearly bloodless victory.

In the first selection, William of Orange offers justification for his invasion of England. Note that blame is focused on the "evil counsellors" of James II rather than on the king himself. Parliament quickly enacted a Bill of Rights in 1689 that laid down the principles of parliamentary supremacy that had been in dispute since the Petition of Right in 1628.

"A Force Sufficient to Defend Us from the Violence of Those Evil Counsellors"

WILLIAM OF ORANGE

It is both certain and evident to all men, that the public peace and happiness of any state or kingdom cannot be preserved where the laws, liberties, and customs established by the lawful authority in it are openly transgressed and annulled: more especially where the alteration of religion is endeavored, and that a religion, which is contrary to law, is endeavored to be introduced. . . .

Upon these grounds it is that we can't any longer forbear to declare that, to our great regret, we see that those counsellors, who have now the chief credit with the King, have overturned the religion, laws, and liberties of these realms, and subjected them, in all things relating to their consciences, liberties, and properties, to arbitrary government, and that not only by secret and indirect ways, but in an open and undisguised manner. . . .

They have also, by putting the administration of civil justice in the hands of Papists [Catholics], brought all the matters of civil justice into great uncertainty. . . . The king's evil counsellors have not only armed the Papists, but have likewise raised them up to the greatest military trust, both by sea and land, and that strangers as well as natives, and Irish as well as English, that so by those means, having rendered themselves as masters both of the affairs of the church, of the government of the nation, and of the courts of justice, and subjected them all to a despotic and arbitrary power, they might be in a capacity to maintain and execute their wicked designs by the assistance of the army, and thereby to enslave the nation. . . .

Therefore it is, that we have thought fit to go over to England, and to carry over with us a force sufficient, by the blessing of God, to defend us from the violence of those evil counsellors. And we, being desirous that our intention in this might be rightly understood, have for this end prepared this declaration, in which, as we have hitherto given a true account of the reasons inducing us to it, so we now think fit to declare, that this our expedition is intended for no other design, but to have a free

"A Force Sufficient to Defend Us" is from James Harvey Robinson, *Readings in Modern European History*, Vol. 1 (Boston: Ginn & Co., 1908), pp. 28–31.

and lawful Parliament assembled, as soon as possible, and that the members shall meet and sit in full freedom. . . .

And we will endeavor, by all possible means, to procure such an establishment in all the three kingdoms [England, Scotland, Ireland] that they may all live in a happy union and correspondence together; and that the Protestant Religion, and the peace, honor, and happiness of those nations may be established upon lasting foundations.

Given under Our Hand and Seal at Our Court in the Hague, the 10th Day of October, in the Year of Our Lord 1688

WILLIAM HENRY, *Prince of Orange*

The Bill of Rights (1689)

Whereas the said late King James II having abdicated the government, and the throne being thereby vacant, his Highness the prince of Orange (whom it has pleased Almighty God to make the glorious instrument of delivering this kingdom from popery and arbitrary power) did cause letters to be written for the choosing of such persons to represent them, as were of right to be sent to parliament being now assembled in a full and free representative of this nation . . . do in the first place . . . for the vindicating and asserting their ancient rights and liberties, declare:

1. That the pretended power of suspending of laws, or the execution of laws, by regal authority, without the consent of parliament, is illegal.
2. That the pretended power of dispensing with laws, or the execution of laws, by regal authority, as it has been assumed and exercised of late [by James II], is illegal.
4. That levying of money for or to the use of the crown . . . without the grant of parliament . . . is illegal.
5. That it is the right of the subjects to petition the king. . . .
6. That the raising or keeping of a standing army within the kingdom in time of peace, unless it be with the consent of parliament is against the law.
8. That election of members of parliament ought to be free.
9. That the freedom of speech, and debates or proceedings in parliament, ought not to be impeached or questioned in any court or place out of parliament.
10. That excessive bail ought not to be required, nor excessive fines imposed; nor cruel and unusual punishments inflicted.
13. And that for redress of all grievances, and for the amending, strengthening, and preserving of the laws, parliament ought to be held frequently. . . .

Consider This:

- How did William of Orange justify his invasion of England and the overthrow of the monarch James II? Why did he blame the "evil counsellors" of the king?

Compare and Contrast:

- The Bill of Rights was formulated in 1689 after nearly seventy-five years of confrontation and accommodation between king and Parliament. Compare the principles stated in that document with those enunciated by James I in his speech to Parliament in 1610. How far had the English come in establishing constitutional rule and a restricted monarchy?

"The Bill of Rights" is from *Statutes of the Realm*, 6:142.

The Absolutism of Louis XIV

It is atheism and blasphemy to dispute what God can do; so it is presumption and contempt to dispute what a king can do, or say that a king cannot do this or that.

—JAMES I

It is in my person alone that ultimate power resides. It is from me alone that my courts derive their authority. It is to me alone that the power to make law belongs, without any dependence and without any division. The whole public order comes from me, and the rights and interests of the nation are necessarily joined with mine and rest only in my hands.

—LOUIS XIV

Resistance on the part of people to the supreme legislative power of the state is never legitimate; it is the duty of the people to bear any abuse of the supreme power.

—IMMANUEL KANT

The Theory of Divine-Right Monarchy

The stable monarchy that Louis XIV inherited was largely the product of two master political craftsmen, cardinals Richelieu and Mazarin. These statesmen actually ran the day-to-day affairs of the French state under Louis XIII and during Louis XIV's minority, respectively. Under their strict control, the French nobility was subdued and made to realize that the king was absolute in his authority and would tolerate no defiance. It was under their direction, from 1610 to 1661, that absolutism was advanced out of the realm of theory and made a part of the political life of France.

The practical rule of any government must be justified through some doctrine, whether it be a devotion to the principles of democracy or to the more blatant dictum "might makes right." Louis XIV justified his absolutism through the belief that God so willed it. Such a "divine-right" monarch ruled with the authority of God and was beholden to no power except that of God. For his part, the king was accountable to God and was expected to rule with the best interests of his people at heart.

The following selections explain the theoretical basis of Louis's absolutism. The first is by Jean Domat (1624–1696), one of the most renowned jurists and legal scholars of his age. He was responsible for a codification of French law that was sponsored by the king himself. The selection presented is from his treatment of French public law and may be regarded as the official statement of divine-right absolutism. The second excerpt is from a treatise by Jacques Bénigne Bossuet (1627–1704), bishop and tutor to Louis XIV's heir. An eloquent political writer, Bossuet justified divine-right monarchy by basing his support on direct evidence from the Bible. The treatise, entitled *Politics Drawn from the Very Words of Scripture*, was directed specifically at Louis's son and successor, the dauphin.

The Ideal Absolute State (1697)

JEAN DOMAT

All men being equal by nature because of the humanity that is their essence, nature does not cause some to be inferior to others. But in this natural equality, they are separated by other principles that render their conditions unequal and give rise to relationships and dependencies that determine their varying duties toward others and render government necessary. . . .

The first distinction that subjects some persons to others is that which birth introduces between parents and children. . . . The second distinction among persons is that which requires different employments in society and unites all in the body of which each is a member. . . . And it is these varying occupations and dependencies that create the ties that form society among men, as those of its members form a body. This renders it necessary that a head coerce and rule the body of society and maintain order among those who should give the public the benefit of the different contributions that their stations require of them. . . .

Since government is necessary for the common good and God himself established it, it follows that those who are its subjects must be submissive and obedient. For otherwise they would resist God, and the government which should be the source of the peace and unity that make possible the public good would suffer from dissension and trouble that would destroy it. . . .

As obedience is necessary to preserve the order and peace that unite the head and members of the body of the state, it is the universal obligation of all subjects in all cases to obey the ruler's orders without assuming the liberty of judging them. For otherwise each man would be master because of his right to examine what might be just or unjust, and this liberty would favor sedition. Thus every man owes obedience even to unjust laws and orders, provided that he may execute and obey them without injustice. And the only exception that may exempt him from this obligation is limited to cases in which he may not obey without violating divine law. . . .

According to these principles, which are the natural foundations of the authority of those who govern, their power should have two essential attributes: first, to cause justice to rule without exception and, second, to be as absolute as the rule of justice, that is, as absolute as the rule of God Himself who is justice, rules according to its principles, and desires rulers to do likewise. . . .

Since the power of princes comes to them from God and is placed in their hands as an instrument of his providence and his guidance of the states that He commits to their rule, it is clear that princes should use their power in proportion to the objectives that providence and divine guidance seek . . . and that power is confided to them to this end. This is without doubt the foundation and first principle of all the duties of sovereigns that consist of causing God Himself to rule, that is, regulating all things according to His will, which is nothing more than justice. The rule of justice should be the glory of the rule of princes. . . .

The power of sovereigns includes the authority to exercise the functions of government and to use the force that is necessary to their ministry. For authority without force would be despised and almost useless, while force without legitimate authority would be mere tyranny. . . .

There are two uses of sovereign power that are necessary to the public tranquillity. One

"The Ideal Absolute State" is from William F. Church, ed. and trans., *The Impact of Absolutism in France: National Experience under Richelieu, Mazarin and Louis XIV* (New York: John Wiley & Sons, 1969), pp. 377–381.

consists of constraining the subjects to obey and repressing violence and injustice, the other of defending the state against the aggressions of its enemies. Power should be accompanied by the force that is required for these two functions.

The use of force for the maintenance of public tranquillity within the state includes all that is required to protect the sovereign himself from rebellions that would be frequent if authority and force were not united, and all that is required to keep order among the subjects, repress violence against individuals and the general public, execute the orders of the sovereign, and effect all that is required for the administration of justice. Since the use of force and the occasions that require it are never-ending, the government of the sovereign must maintain the force that is needed for the rule of justice. This requires officials and ministers in various functions and the use of arms whenever necessary. . . .

One should include among the rights that the law gives the sovereign that of acquiring all the evidences of grandeur and majesty that are needed to bring renown to the authority and dignity of such great power and to instill awe in the minds of the subjects. For although the latter should view royal power as from God and submit to it regardless of tangible indications of grandeur, God accompanies his own power with a visible majesty that extends over land and sea. . . . When He wishes to exercise his August power as lawgiver, He proclaims his laws with prodigies that inspire reverence and unspeakable terror. He is therefore willing that sovereigns enhance the dignity of their power . . . in such manner as to win the respect of the people. . . .

The general duties . . . of those who have sovereign authority include all that concern the administration of justice, the general polity of the state, public order, tranquillity of the subjects, security of families, attention to all that may contribute to the general good, the choice of skillful ministers who love justice and truth . . . discrimination between justice and clemency whenever justice might suffer from relaxation of its rigor, wise distribution of benefits, rewards, exemptions, privileges and other concessions, wise administration of the public funds, prudence regarding foreigners, and all that may render government agreeable to the good, terrible to the wicked, and entirely worthy of the divine function of ruling men by wielding power that comes only from God and is a participation in his own.

As the final duty of the sovereign, one may add the following which stems from the administration of justice and includes all others. Although his power seems to place him above the law, since no man has the right to call him to account for his conduct, he should observe the laws that concern himself not only because he should be an example to his subjects and render their duty pleasant but because he is not dispensed from his own duty by his sovereign power. On the contrary, his rank obliges him to subordinate his personal interests to the general good of the state, which it is his glory to regard as his own.

Politics and Scripture (1679)

JACQUES BÉNIGNE BOSSUET

Monarchy Is the Best Form of Government: Monarchy is the most natural, the most enduring, and therefore the strongest form of government. It is also the best defense against political instability, which is the deadliest disease of states, and the most certain cause of their destruction: "Every kingdom divided against itself is brought to desolation; and

"Politics and Scripture" is from J. B. Bossuet, *Politique tirée des propres paroles de l'Écriture Sainte*, Book I (Paris, 1870).

every city or house divided against itself shall not stand" [Matt. 12:25].

The purpose of the creation of a state is political unity, and there is no greater unity than the rule of a single individual. . . .

Kings Should Respect Their Powers and Use Them Only for the General Good: Since the power of kings is derived from God, they must realize that they are not supreme masters and therefore cannot use it however they please. They should employ their power with restraint, since it has been conferred on them by God, who will judge their actions: "Hear therefore, O ye Kings, and understand; learn, ye that be judges of the ends of the earth. Give ear, ye that rule the people, and glory in the multitude of nations. For power is given you of the Lord, and sovereignty from the Highest, who shall try your works and search out your counsels. Because, being ministers of His kingdom, ye have not judged aright, not kept the law, nor walked after the counsel of God. Horribly and speedily shall He come upon you: for a sharp judgment shall be to them that are in high places . . . " [Ws. 6].

Kings should therefore tremble to exercise the power that God has granted to them, and they should remember that it is a terrible sacrilege to abuse this authority derived from God.

We have seen kings occupy the throne of the Lord and hold in their hand the sword that He has entrusted to them. What blasphemy and arrogance for an unjust ruler to occupy the throne of God and issue judgments that are against His law! What presumption it is to oppress and destroy God's children with the very sword that He has placed in the hands of the king!

The Judgment of the King Is Supreme: Kings are gods, and are endowed with at least some of the independence of God: "I have said, Ye are gods; and all of you are children of the most High" [Pss. 82:6].

Therefore, it is evident that whoever refuses to obey the king cannot appeal to some other judge, but will be condemned to death without appeal as an enemy of the public peace and of humanity. The king can always correct himself whenever he realizes that he has made a mistake, but his authority is absolute and there can be no appeal unless it derives from his own will.

Kings Are Not Above the Law: Kings, just like anybody else, are subject to the equity of the laws. Not only are they required by God to act justly, but also because they owe it to their people to set a fair example. But even though they are subject to the law, they are not liable to the penalties of the law. In other words, kings are subject to laws only in their direction, but not in their coercion.

The Definition of Majesty: Nothing is more majestic than pure goodness. And there is nothing that debases majesty than the misery that a king brings down upon his people. God is the quintessence of holiness, goodness, power, reason. These are the components of divine majesty and in their reflection is the majesty of the king.

So great is this majesty that its source could never reside in the king. Rather, it is borrowed from God, who entrusts it to the king for the good of his people. It is proper that God should so restrain this power. . . .

Therefore, kings should be bold in exercising this authority, for it is divine and benefits all people. But kings must wield power with humility, since it is conferred from above. In the end, such awesome power leaves the king weak and mortal, still a sinner and with a greater responsibility to God.

On Arbitrary Government: It is one thing for a government to be absolute, and quite another for it to be arbitrary. It is absolute only in that no human authority can constrain it. But it does not follow that the government should be arbitrary. Besides the fact that the king is subject to the judgment of God, the king must also act within the boundaries of the law or all action is null and void in a legal sense. Moreover, there is always an opportunity for appeal, so each man remains the legitimate owner of his property. This is in fact the definition of legitimate government, and by its very nature, it is the opposite of arbitrary government.

CONSIDER THIS:

- Louis XIV was a divine-right monarch. What does this mean, and how did Louis use religion to strengthen his political position in the state?
- How compelling in support of absolutism are the arguments of Jean Domat on "The Ideal Absolute State" and Jacques Bénigne Bossuet in "Politics and Scripture"? What are the responsibilities of the king and the political advantages of absolute rule?

THE BROADER PERSPECTIVE:

- What is the difference between tyranny and the absolutism of Louis XIV's monarchy? What were the advantages and disadvantages of absolute rule for the different classes of French society? Who profited the most?

The Sun King and the Practice of Absolute Rule

"Vanity Was His Ruin"

THE DUKE OF SAINT-SIMON

The Duke of Saint-Simon (1675–1755) was a rather indifferent soldier and diplomat, but he was a passionate observer of affairs at Louis's court and has provided us with our most vivid account of the king and his activities. Saint-Simon was typical of the feudal nobility that Louis was trying to control, and thus this account, from his memoirs, was by no means free from prejudice.

Portrait of the King

Louis XIV was made for a brilliant Court. In the midst of other men, his figure, his courage, his grace, his beauty, his grand mien, even the tone of his voice and the majestic and natural charm of all his person, distinguished him till his death as the King Bee, and showed that if he had only been born a simple private gentleman, he would equally have excelled in fetes, pleasures, and gallantry, and would have had the greatest success in love. . . . Vanity, this unmeasured and unreasonable love of admiration, was his ruin. His ministers, his generals, his mistresses, his courtiers, soon perceived his weakness. They praised him with emulation and spoiled him. Praises, or to say the truth, flattery, pleased him to such an extent, that the coarsest was well received, the vilest even better relished. It was the sole means by which you could approach him. Those whom he liked owed his affection for them, to their untiring flatteries. This is what gave his ministers so much authority, and the opportunities they had for adulating him, of attributing everything to him, and of pretending to learn everything from him. Suppleness, meanness, an admiring, dependent, cringing manner—above all, an air of nothingness—were the sole means of pleasing him. . . .

Though his intellect, as I have said, was beneath mediocrity, it was capable of being

"'Vanity Was His Ruin'" is from Bayle St. John, ed., *The Memoirs of the Duke of Saint-Simon*, vol. 2 (New York: James Pott and Co., 1901), pp. 202–203, 214–219, 226–227, 231–232, 273–276.

formed. He loved glory, was fond of order and regularity; was by disposition prudent, moderate, discreet, master of his movements and his tongue. Will it be believed? He was also by disposition good and just! God had sufficiently gifted him to enable him to be a good King; perhaps even a tolerably great King! All the evil came to him from elsewhere. His early education was so neglected that nobody dared approach his apartment. He has often been heard to speak of those times with bitterness, and even to relate that, one evening he was found in the basin of the Palais Royale garden fountain, into which he had fallen! He was scarcely taught how to read or write, and remained so ignorant, that the most familiar historical and other facts were utterly unknown to him! He fell, accordingly, and sometimes even in public, into the grossest absurdities. . . .

Louis XIV took great pains to be well informed of all that passed everywhere; in the public places, in the private homes, in society and familiar intercourse. His spies and telltales were infinite. He had them of all species; many who were ignorant that their information reached him; others who knew it; others who wrote to him direct, sending their letters through channels he indicated; and all these letters were seen by him alone, and always before everything else; others who sometimes spoke to him secretly in his cabinet, entering by the back stairs. These unknown means ruined an infinite number of people of all classes, who never could discover the cause; often ruined them very unjustly; for the King, once prejudiced, never altered his opinion, or so rarely, that nothing was more rare. He had, too, another fault, very dangerous for others and often for himself, since it deprived him of good subjects. He had an excellent memory; in this way, that if he saw a man who, twenty years before, perhaps, had in some manner offended him, he did not forget the man, though he might forget the offence. This was enough, however, to exclude the person from all favour. The representations of a minister, of a general, of his confessor even, could not move the King. He would not yield.

The most cruel means by which the King was informed of what was passing—for many years before anybody knew it—was that of opening letters. The promptitude and dexterity with which they were opened passes understanding. He saw extracts from all the letters in which there were passages that the chiefs of the post-office, and then the minister who governed it, thought ought to go before him; entire letters, too, were sent to him, when their contents seemed to justify the sending. Thus the chiefs of the post, nay, the principal clerks were in a position to suppose what they pleased and against whom they pleased. A word of contempt against the King or the government, a joke, a detached phrase, was enough. It is incredible how many people, justly or unjustly, were more or less ruined, always without resource, without trial, and without knowing why. The secret was impenetrable; for nothing ever cost the King less than profound silence and dissimulation. . . .

The King loved air and exercise very much, as long as he could make use of them. He had excelled in dancing, and at tennis and mall. On horseback he was admirable, even at a late age. He liked to see everything done with grace and address. To acquit yourself well or ill before him was a merit or fault. He said that with things not necessary it was best not to meddle, unless they were done well. He was fond of shooting, and there was not a better or more graceful shot than he. . . .

He liked splendour, magnificence, and profusion in everything: you pleased him if you shone through the brilliancy of your houses, your clothes, your table, your equipages. Thus a taste for extravagance and luxury was disseminated through all classes of society; causing infinite harm, and leading to general confusion of rank and to ruin.

The King's Day

At eight o'clock the chief valet de chambre on duty, who alone had slept in the royal chamber, and who had dressed himself, awoke the King. The chief physician, the chief surgeon, and the nurse (as long as she lived), entered at the same time. The latter kissed the King; the others rubbed and often changed his shirt, because he was in the habit of sweating a great deal. At the quarter, the grand chamberlain was called (or, in the absence, the first gentleman of the chamber), and those who had what was called the grandes entrées. The chamberlain (or chief gentleman) drew back the curtains which had been closed again, and presented the holy-water from the vase, at the head of the bed.... Then all passed into the cabinet of the council. A very short religious service being over, the King called, they reentered. The same officer gave him his dressing-gown; immediately after, other privileged courtiers entered, and then everybody, in time to find the King putting on his shoes and stockings, for he did almost everything himself and with address and grace. Every other day we saw him shave himself; and he had a little short wig in which he always appeared, even in bed, and on medicine days. He often spoke of the chase, and sometimes said a word to somebody. No toilette table was near him; he had simply a mirror held before him.

As soon as he was dressed, he prayed to God, at the side of his bed, where all the clergy present knelt, the cardinals without cushions, all the laity remaining standing; and the captain of the guards came to the balustrade during the prayer, after which the King passed into his cabinet.

He found there, or was followed by all who had the *entrée*, a very numerous company, for it included everybody in any office. He gave orders to each for the day; thus within a half a quarter of an hour it was known what he meant to do; and then all this crowd left directly. The bastards, a few favorites, and the valets alone were left. It was then a good opportunity for talking with the King; for example, about plans of gardens and buildings; and conversation lasted more or less according to the person engaged in it....

On Sunday, and often on Monday, there was a council of state; on Tuesday a finance council; on Wednesday council of state; on Saturday finance council. Rarely were two held in one day or any on Thursday or Friday. Once or twice a month there was a council of despatches on Monday morning....

The dinner was always *au petit couvert*, that is the King ate by himself in his chamber upon a square table in front of the middle window. It was more or less abundant, for he ordered in the morning whether it was to be "a little," or "very little" service. But even at this last, there were always many dishes, and three courses without counting the fruit.

The King's Diet

As during the last year of his life the King became more and more costive, Fagon [the court physician] made him eat at the commencement of his repasts many iced fruits, that is to say, mulberries, melons, and figs rotten from ripeness; and at his dessert many other fruits, finishing with a surprising quantity of sweetmeats. All the year round he ate at supper a prodigious quantity of salad. His soups, several of which he partook of morning and evening, were full of gravy, and were of exceeding strength, and everything that was served to him was full of spice, to double the usual extent, and very strong also....

This summer he redoubled his regime of fruits and drinks. At last the former clogged his stomach, taken after soup, weakened the digestive organs and took away his appetite, which until then had never failed him all his life, though however late dinner might be delayed he never was hungry or wanted to eat. But after the first spoonfuls of soup, his appetite came, as I have several times heard him say, and he ate so prodigiously and so solidly morning and evening that no one could get accustomed to see it. So much water and so much fruit unconnected by anything spirituous, turned his blood into gangrene; while those forced night sweats diminished its strength and impoverished it; and thus his death was caused, as was seen by the opening of his body. The organs were found in such good and healthy condition that there is reason to believe he would have lived beyond his hundredth year. His stomach above all astonished, and also his bowels by their volume and extent, double that of the ordinary, whence it came that he was such a great yet uniform eater.

The King's Death

Friday, August the 30th, was a bad day preceded by a bad night. The King continually lost his reason. About five o'clock in the evening Madame de Maintenon left him, gave away her furniture to the domestics, and went to Saint-Cyr never to leave it.

On Saturday, the 31st of August, everything went from bad to worse. The gangrene had reached the knee and all the thigh. Towards eleven o'clock at night the King was found to be so ill that the prayers for the dying were said. This restored him to himself. He repeated the prayers in a voice so strong that it rose above all the other voices. At the end he recognised Cardinal de Rohan, and said to him, "These are the last favours of the Church." This was the last man to whom he spoke. He repeated several times, *Nunc et in hora mortis* [Now and in the hour of death], then said, "Oh, my God, come to my aid: hasten to succour me."

These were his last words. All the night he was without consciousness and in a long agony, which finished on Sunday, the 1st September, 1715, at a quarter past eight in the morning, three days before he had accomplished his seventy-seventh year, and in the seventy-second of his reign. He had survived all his sons and grandsons, except the King of Spain. Europe never saw so long a reign or France a King so old.

Compare and Contrast:

- Was Louis XIV a responsible monarch? From the accounts in his own memoirs and those of the Duke of Saint-Simon, do you think that Louis worked hard at his job? How did he view his duties as king? Do the criticisms of Pierre Jurieu in *The Sighs of Enslaved France* seem valid to you? Why should a historian be somewhat careful in the judgments drawn from this evidence?

Letters to His Heirs: "Allow Good Sense to Act"

KING LOUIS XIV

In this selection, drawn from Louis's memoirs, the king himself gives practical advice to his heirs concerning the demands and duties of absolute monarchy.

Two things without doubt were absolutely necessary: very hard work on my part, and a wise choice of persons capable of seconding it.

As for work, it may be, my son, that you will begin to read these Memoirs at an age when one is far more in the habit of dreading than loving it, only too happy to have escaped subjection to tutors and to have your hours regulated no longer, nor lengthy and prescribed study laid down for you.

On this heading I will not warn you solely that it is none the less toil *by which* one reigns,

"Letters to His Heirs" is from Jean Longnon, ed., *A King's Lessons in Statecraft: Louis XIV*, trans. H. Wilson (London: T. Fisher Unwin Ltd., 1924), pp. 48–53, 149.

and *for which* one reigns, and that the conditions of royalty, which may seem to you sometimes hard and vexatious in so lofty a position, would appear pleasant and easy if there was any doubt of your reaching it.

There is something more, my son, and I hope that your own experience will never teach it to you: nothing could be more laborious to you than a great amount of idleness if you were to have the misfortune to fall into it through beginning by being disgusted with public affairs, then with pleasure, then with idleness itself, seeking everywhere fruitlessly for what can never be found, that is to say, the sweetness of repose and leisure without having the preceding fatigue and occupation.

I laid a rule on myself to work regularly twice every day, and for two or three hours each time with different persons, without counting the hours which I passed privately and alone, nor the time which I was able to give on particular occasions to any special affairs that might arise. There was no moment when I did not permit people to talk to me about them, provided that they were urgent; with the exception of foreign ministers who sometimes find too favourable moments in the familiarity allowed to them, either to obtain or to discover something, and whom one should not hear without being previously prepared.

I cannot tell you what fruit I gathered immediately I had taken this resolution. I felt myself, as it were, uplifted in thought and courage; I found myself quite another man, and with joy reproached myself for having been too long unaware of it. This first timidity, which a little self-judgment always produces and which at the beginning gave me pain, especially on occasions when I had to speak in public, disappeared in less than no time. The only thing I felt then was that I was King, and born to be one. I experienced next a delicious feeling, hard to express, and which you will not know yourself except by tasting it as I have done. For you must not imagine, my son, that the affairs of State are like some obscure and thorny path of learning which may possibly have already wearied you, wherein the mind strives to raise itself with effort above its purview, more often to arrive at no conclusion, and whose utility or apparent utility is repugnant to us as much as its difficulty. The function of Kings consists principally in allowing good sense to act, which always acts naturally and without effort. What we apply ourselves to is sometimes less difficult than what we do only for our amusement. Its usefulness always follows. A King, however skillful and enlightened be his ministers, cannot put his own hand to the work without its effects being seen. Success, which is agreeable in everything, even in the smallest matters, gratifies us in these as well as in the greatest, and there is no satisfaction to equal that of noting every day some progress in glorious and lofty enterprises, and in the happiness of the people which has been planned and thought out by oneself. All that is most necessary to this work is at the same time agreeable, for; in a word, my son, it is to have one's eyes open to the whole earth; to learn each hour the news concerning every province and every nation, the secrets of every court, the mood and the weaknesses of each Prince and of every foreign minister; to be well-informed on an infinite number of matters about which we are supposed to know nothing; to elicit from our subjects what they hide from us with the greatest care; to discover the most remote opinions of our own courtiers and the most hidden interests of those who come to us with quite contrary professions. I do not know of any other pleasure we would not renounce for that, even if curiosity alone gave us the opportunity. . . .

I gave orders to the four Secretaries of State no longer to sign anything whatsoever without speaking to me; likewise to the Controller, and that he should authorise nothing as regards finance without its being registered in a book which must remain with me, and being noted

FIGURE 2.3 Portrait bust of King Louis XIV, the Sun King by GianlorenzoBernini (1665). (*Caisse Nationale des Monuments Historique et des Sites*)

down in a very abridged abstract form in which at any moment, and at a glance, I could see the state of the funds, and past and future expenditure. . . .

Regarding the persons whose duty it was to second my labours, I resolved at all costs to have no prime minister; and if you will believe me, my son, and all your successors after you, the name shall be banished for ever from France, for there is nothing more undignified than to see all the administration on one side, and on the other, the mere title of King.

To effect this, it was necessary to divide my confidence and the execution of my orders without giving it entirely to one single person, applying these different people to different spheres according to their diverse talents, which is perhaps the first and greatest gift that Princes can possess.

I also made a resolution on a further matter. With a view the better to unite in myself alone all the authority of a master, although there must be in all affairs a certain amount of detail to which our occupations and also our dignity do not permit us to descend as a rule, I conceived the plan, after I should have made choice of my ministers, of entering sometimes into matters with each one of them, and when they least expected it, in order that they might understand that I could do the same upon other subjects and at any moment. Besides, a knowledge of some small detail acquired only occasionally, and for amusement rather than as a regular rule, is instructive little by little and without fatigue, on a thousand things which are not without their use in general resolutions, and which we ought to know and do ourselves were it possible that a single man could know and do everything.

I have never failed, when an occasion has presented itself, to impress upon you the great respect we should have for religion, and the deference we should show to its ministers in matters specially connected with their mission, that is to say, with the celebration of the Sacred Mysteries and the preaching of the doctrine of the Gospels. But because people connected with the Church are liable to presume a little too much on the advantages attaching to their profession, and are willing sometimes to make use of them in order to whittle down their most rightful duties, I feel obliged to explain to you certain points on this question which may be of importance.

The first is that Kings are absolute *seigneurs* [Lords], and from their nature have full and free disposal of all property both secular and ecclesiastical, to use it as wise dispensers, that is to say, in accordance with the requirements of their State. . . .

CONSIDER THIS:

- What was the most important advice that Louis gave to his heirs? What does this reveal about the character of Louis XIV? What was important to him?

"A Frightful Plot": The Revocation of the Edict of Nantes (1685)

THE DUKE OF SAINT-SIMON

On October 22, 1685, Louis XIV annulled the Edict of Nantes, which had provided political and religious freedom for the French Protestants, or Huguenots, since 1598. Louis was determined to control a nation that was unified politically under his rule and religiously under his faith; Catholicism was to be the only accepted religion for the French people. The revocation was hailed by Catholics but was not without its critics even at court, as reflected in the opinion of the Duke of Saint-Simon, which follows the text of the treaty.

The revocation of the Edict of Nantes, without the slightest pretext of necessity, and the various proscriptions that followed it, were the fruits of a frightful plot, in which the new spouse was one of the chief conspirators, and which depopulated a quarter of the realm; ruined its commerce; weakened it in every direction; gave it up for a long time to the public and avowed pillage of the dragoons; authorized torments and punishments by which many innocent people of both sexes were killed by thousands; ruined a numerous class; tore in pieces a world of families; armed relatives against relatives, so as to seize their

"The Revocation of the Edict of Nantes" is from James H. Robinson, ed., *Readings in European History*, vol. 2 (Boston: Ginn and Company, 1906), pp. 288–291.

property and leave them to die in hunger; banished our manufactures to foreign lands; made those lands flourish and overflow at the expense of France, and enabled them to build new cities; gave to the world the spectacle of a prodigious population proscribed without crime, stripped, fugitive, wandering, and seeking shelter far from their country; sent to the galleys nobles, rich old men, people carefully nurtured, weak, and delicate;—and all solely on account of religion. . . .

The king congratulated himself on his power and his piety. He believed himself to have brought back the days of the apostles, and attributed to himself all the honor. The bishops wrote panegyrics of him; the Jesuits made the pulpit resound with his praise. All France was filled with horror and confusion; and yet there was never such triumph and joy, such boundless laudation of the king.

Consider This:

- What was the Edict of Nantes? Why was it invoked in 1598 and why did Louis XIV revoke it? Was this a wise move politically? Are you persuaded by the Duke of Saint-Simon's criticism? If you accept his criticism as valid, then how would you characterize the absolute rule of Louis XIV? Was he a tyrant—or a wise monarch?

The Sighs of Enslaved France (1690)

PIERRE JURIEU

As a result of the revocation of the Edict of Nantes, the persecution of Huguenots began in earnest. The author of the following memoirs cannot be positively identified, but they are probably from the pen of Pierre Jurieu, a Calvinist pastor who had fled to Holland. Louis endured much criticism from such dissidents in exile. Jurieu's memoirs are among the most provocative because they characterize Louis's absolutism as oppressive and responsible for many of the ills of France.

The oppression of the people is caused primarily by the prodigious number of taxes and excessive levies of money that are everywhere taken in France. Taxes and finance are a science today, and one must be skilled to speak knowledgeably of them, but it suffices for us to relate what we all feel and what the people know of the matter. There are the personal and [land taxes]. There are taxes on salt, wine, merchandise, principal, and revenue. This miserable century has produced a flood of names [of taxes], most of which were unknown to our ancestors or, if some were known, they were not odious because of the moderation with which they were imposed and levied. . . . It does not serve my purpose to acquaint you with the details of these taxes so that you may feel their weight and injustice. It will suffice to enable you to understand the horrible oppression of these taxes by showing (1) the immense sums that are collected, (2) the violence and abuses that are committed in levying them, (3) the bad use that is made of them, and (4) the misery to which the people are reduced.

First, dear unfortunate compatriots, you should realize that the taxes that are taken from you comprise a sum perhaps greater than that which all the other princes of Europe together draw from their states. One thing is certain, that France pays two hundred million in taxes of which about three-fourths go into the coffers of the king and the rest to expenses

"*The Sighs of Enslaved France*" is from William F. Church, ed. and trans., *The Impact of Absolutism in France: National Experience under Richelieu, Mazarin and Louis XIV* (New York: John Wiley & Sons, 1969), pp. 102–105.

of collection, tax-farmers, officials, keepers, receivers, the profits of financiers, and new fortunes that are created in almost a single day. For the collection of the salt tax alone, there is a great army of officers and constables. . . .

If tyranny is clear and evident in the immense sums that are levied in France, it is not less so in the manner of collecting them. Kings were established by the people to preserve their persons, lives, liberty, and properties. But the government of France has risen to such excessive tyranny that the prince today regards everything as belonging to him alone. He imposes taxes at will without consulting the people, the nobles, the Estates, or the Parlements. I shall tell you something that is true and that thousands know but most Frenchmen do not. During Colbert's ministry [supervisor of the royal finances] it was discussed whether the king should take immediate possession of all real and personal property in France and reduce it to royal domain, to be used and assigned to whomever the court judged appropriate without regard for former possession, heredity, or other rights. . . .

How much abuse and violence is committed in the collection of taxes? The meanest agent is a sacred person who has absolute power over gentlemen, the judiciary, and all the people. A single blow is capable of ruining the most powerful subject. They confiscate houses, furnishings, cattle, money, grain, wine, and everything in sight. The prisons are full of wretches who are responsible for sums that they impose upon other wretches who cannot pay what is demanded of them. Is there anything more harsh and cruel than the salt tax? They make you buy for ten or twelve sous per pound something that nature, the sun, and the sea provide for nothing and may be had for two farthings. Under pretext of exercising this royal right, the realm is flooded with a great army of scoundrels called constables of the *gabelle* [salt tax] who enter houses, penetrate the most secret places with impunity, and do not fail to find unauthorized salt wherever they think there is money. They condemn wretches to pay huge fines, cause them to rot in prison, and ruin families. They force salt upon people everywhere and give each family more than three times as much as they can consume. In the provinces by the sea, they will not permit a poor peasant to bring home salt water; they break jugs, beat people, and imprison them. In a word, every abuse is committed in levying this and other taxes which is done with horrible expense, seizures, imprisonments, and legal cases before the collectors and courts with costs far above the sums involved. . . .

This is how all of France is reduced to the greatest poverty. In earlier reigns, that is, during the ministries of Cardinal Richelieu and Cardinal Mazarin, France was already burdened with heavy taxes. But the manner of collecting them, although not entirely just, nevertheless exhausted the realm much less than the way in which they are collected today. . . . The government of today has changed all of this. M. de Colbert made a plan to reform the finances and applied it to the letter. But what was this reformation? It was not the diminution of taxes in order to relieve the people. . . . He increased the king's revenue by one half. . . .

After this, if we examine the use that is made of these immense sums that are collected with such abuses and extortion, we shall find all the characteristics of oppression and tyranny. It sometimes happens that princes and sovereigns exact levies that appear excessive and greatly inconvenience individuals, but are required by what are called the needs and necessities of the state. In France there is no such thing. There are neither needs nor state. As for the state, earlier it entered into everything; one spoke only of the interests of the state, the needs of the state, the preservation of the state, and the service of the state. To speak this way today would literally be a crime of lese majesty [treason]. The king has taken the place of the state. It is the service of the king, the interest of the king, the preservation of the provinces and wealth of the king. Therefore the king is all and the state nothing. And these are no mere figures of speech but realities. At the French court, no interest is considered but the personal interest of the king, that is, his grandeur and glory. He is the idol to which are sacrificed princes, great men and small, families, provinces, cities, finances and generally everything. Therefore, it is not for the good of the state that these horrible exactions are made, since there is no more state. . . .

This money is used solely to nourish and serve the greatest self-pride and arrogance that ever existed. It is so deep an abyss that it would have swallowed not only the wealth of the whole realm but that of all other states if the king had been able to take possession of it as he attempted to do. The king has caused himself to receive more false flattery than all the pagan demi-gods did with true flattery. Never before was flattery pushed to this point. Never has man loved praise and vainglory to the extent that this prince has sought them. In his court and around himself he supports a multitude of flatterers who constantly seek to outdo each other. He not only permits the erection of statues to himself, on which are inscribed blasphemies in his honor and below which all the nations of the earth are shown in chains; he causes himself to be represented in gold, silver, bronze, copper, marble, silk, in paintings, arches of triumph, and inscriptions. He fills all Paris, all his palaces, and the whole realm with his name and his exploits, as though he far surpasses the Alexanders, the Caesars, and all the heroes of antiquity.

Consider This:

- What were some of Pierre Jurieu's criticisms concerning Louis's reign? In his opinion, how was France "reduced to the greatest poverty"?

THEME: THE POWER STRUCTURE

The Architectural Foundation

The Palace of Versailles

In 1661, Louis XIV began construction of his famous palace at Versailles, about 20 miles from Paris. By 1668, two shifts of laborers were working constantly, and by 1682, enough of the palace had been completed to warrant Louis's move from Paris. Amid the construction that continued until 1710, Louis lived, along with most of the French aristocracy, entertaining lavishly and administering the affairs of state.

The expense of the palace was indeed a concern, especially to Jean Colbert, who supervised the royal finances. Still, in 1665, Colbert did not doubt that such a venture was an essential component of Louis's monarchy. In the second selection, Louis himself reveals the necessity of a palace on such a scale as Versailles.

"A Celebration of Greatness"

JEAN COLBERT

If Your Majesty desires to discover where in Versailles are the more than 500,000 ecus spent there in two years, he will have great difficulty in finding them. Will he also deign to reflect that the Accounts of the Royal Buildings will always record the evidence that, during the

"'A Celebration of Greatness'" is from Gilette Ziegler, ed., *The Court of Versailles in the Reign of Louis XIV*, trans. Simon Watson Taylor (London: George Allen and Unwin, Ltd., 1966), p. 26. Reprinted by permission of the publisher.

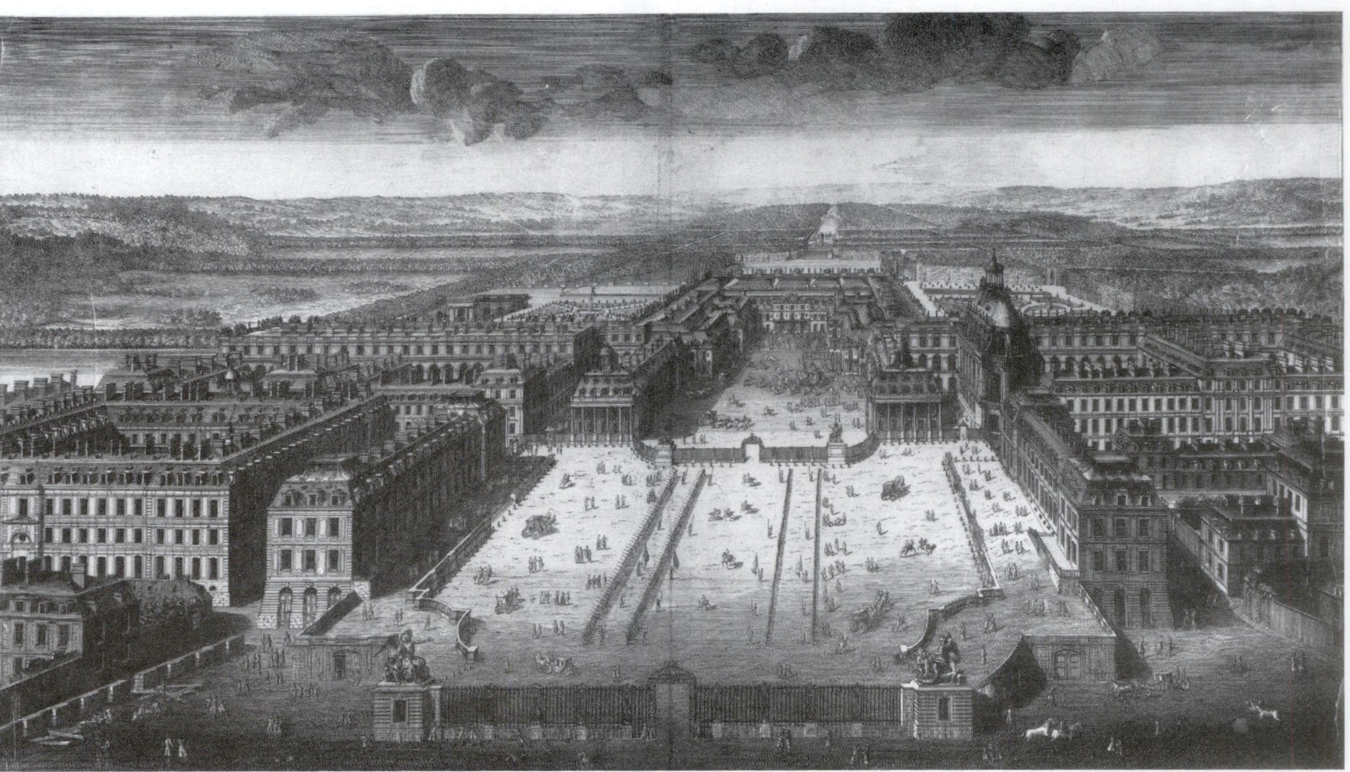

FIGURE 2.4 The facade of Versailles as it appeared after its expansion from a hunting lodge to the royal residence and seat of government (ca. 1682). A center of culture, the palace also served as propaganda, being symbolic of the absolute authority of the Sun King. (*French Government Tourist Office*)

FIGURE 2.5 The Hall of Mirrors in the palace of Versailles. (*French Government Tourist Office*)

time he has lavished such vast sums on this mansion, he has neglected the Louvre, which is assuredly the most superb palace in the world and the one worthiest of Your Majesty's greatness. . . . And God forbid that those many occasions which may impel him to go to war, and thus deprive him of the financial means to complete this superb building, should give him lasting occasion for regret at having lost the time and opportunity.

Your Majesty knows that, apart from glorious actions of war, nothing celebrates so advantageously the greatness and genius of princes than buildings, and all posterity measures them by the yardstick of these superb edifices which they have erected during their life. O what pity were the greatest and most virtuous of kings, of that real virtue which makes the greatest princes, to be measured by the scale of Versailles!

Visible Majesty

KING LOUIS XIV

Those who imagine that these are merely matters of ceremony are gravely mistaken. The peoples over whom we reign, being able to apprehend the basic reality of things, usually derive their opinion from that they can see with their eyes.

"Visible Majesty" is from Gilette Ziegler, ed., *The Court of Versailles in the Reign of Louis XIV*, trans. Simon Watson Taylor (London: George Allen and Unwin, Ltd., 1966), p. 26. Reprinted by permission of the publisher.

CONSIDER THIS:

- Look closely at the picture of Louis's palace at Versailles. In what ways did this structure reflect the character of Louis's monarchy? According to the preceding comments about Versailles, was the palace an effective propaganda medium? Why?

THE BROADER PERSPECTIVE:

- What was the difference between English absolutist government under Charles I and French absolutism under Louis XIV? Why were the English so unwilling to tolerate the personal rule of Charles I and the French so willing to serve Louis XIV? Note that the English fought a civil war from 1642 to 1649 over this issue. The French monarchy collapsed in violence in 1789 at the outset of the French Revolution. What advantages did the English obtain in their competition with France by undergoing their domestic chaos earlier?

- To what extent do you think absolute rule is a so-called natural form of government, generally acceptable to most people, especially if it is benign or even enlightened so that the best interests of citizens are promoted? Do people want a government that provides for their security and happiness but prevents the participation and personal responsibility that a democracy demands? What are your own opinions on the subject?

FIGURE 2.6 View of Versailles from the Gardens: "Those who imagine that these are merely matters of ceremony are gravely mistaken. The peoples over whom we reign, being able to apprehend the basic reality of things, usually derive their opinion from that they can see with their eyes." (*Perry M. Rogers*)

"DARE TO KNOW!": THE SCIENTIFIC REVOLUTION

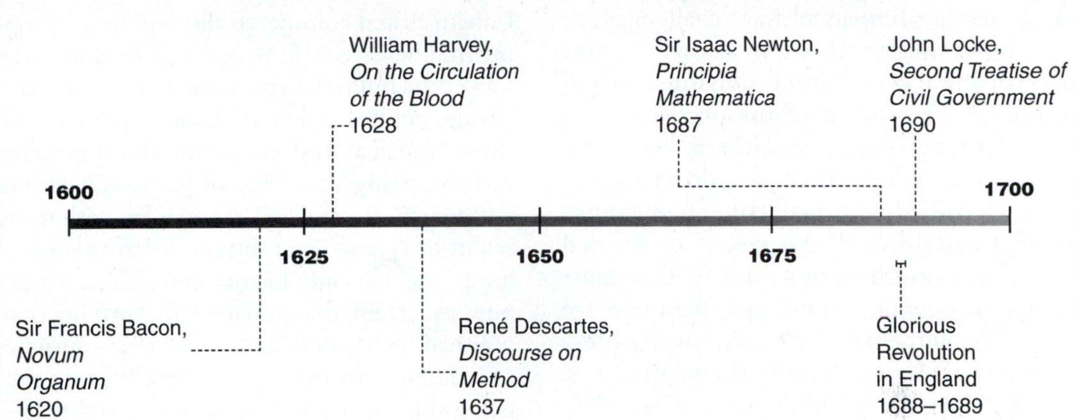

Reason is the greatest enemy that faith has. It never comes to the aid of spiritual things, but struggles against the divine Word, treating with contempt all that emanates from God.

—MARTIN LUTHER

All nature and nature's law lay hid in night / God said let Newton be and all was light.

—ALEXANDER POPE

The real and legitimate goal of the sciences, is the endowment of human life with new inventions and riches.

—FRANCIS BACON

Science has done more for the development of western civilization in one hundred years than Christianity has done in eighteen hundred years.

—JOHN BURROUGHS

CHAPTER THEMES

- **Social and Spiritual Values:** The advancements of the Scientific Revolution were the result of a spirit of rational inquiry and confidence in the ability of human beings to understand and improve their world. Do the demands of science necessarily preclude the validity of religion? Can science and religion coexist with mutual respect and even admiration?

- **Revolution and Historical Transition:** Why do certain eras of history seem to explode with creativity and intellectual risk whereas others stagnate? What do the Scientific Revolution and the Enlightenment have in common with the spirit of fifth-century Athens or the Renaissance era? Do we live in an age of intellectual enlightenment or stagnation?

- **The Big Picture:** Why must one "dare to know"? Does intellectual inquiry require risk and even courage, or are these matters confined to political and military concerns? Is human progress more dependent on the mind than on the sword?

When the great eighteenth-century thinker Immanuel Kant challenged his contemporaries to "Dare to know!" he was also voicing a classic intellectual defiance of authority. The origin of the phrase can be traced to the Roman poet Horace, but nearly every era has possessed those individuals who are not satisfied with maintaining adherence to the "established doctrine" as defined by those in positions of authority. One must be bold in seeking knowledge, for there are many impediments to its attainment. Ideas have power. If successfully transmitted and accepted by the general population, they threaten the status quo, whatever its nature. This makes the pursuit of ideas a risky business that requires an intangible confidence, a willingness to gamble on the potential of an uncertain future. Curiosity and determination, therefore, coupled with a measure of defiance, are the essential components of progress.

Just as the individual in our modern society struggles to define and seek personal knowledge to make rational judgments independent of advertisers, politicians, and television preachers, so too did individuals in the seventeenth and eighteenth centuries struggle against similar constraints imposed on them by secular and spiritual institutions. Despite the condemnation of the Catholic Church and the intimidation of the Inquisition, people gradually changed the way they viewed the world around them. The long religious wars between Catholics and Protestants had ended by 1648, leaving people disillusioned and repulsed. Their belief had been shaken by the mindless fighting of the Thirty Years' War. Instead, many invested their confidence in a new association between Protestantism and monarchy. The compatibility between the Calvinists and commerce allowed the developing middle class to seek godly profit and at the same time build the economic foundations of a strong, centralized state. Contemporary with these political and economic developments was the rising influence of philosophers and writers whose primary concern lay within the realm of science and letters. With the aid of hindsight that only history can afford, we can now ascertain that most of the intellectual, political, economic, and social characteristics associated with the modern world came into being during the seventeenth and eighteenth centuries.

Indeed, juxtaposed with the chaos of religious warfare and its attendant human destruction during the seventeenth century was an intellectual attempt to foster progress in the realm of science. Sweeping changes took place in humanity's conception of the universe and of one's place in it. Although the movement has been called the Scientific Revolution, the changes were not rapid, nor did they involve large numbers of people. On the contrary, the revolution evolved slowly, through experimentation, often in makeshift laboratories. Yet great thinkers such as Sir Isaac Newton, René Descartes, and Francis Bacon attempted to discover the physical and natural laws of the universe and to organize and criticize that diverse body of knowledge. Thus did Descartes champion the principles of deduction and invent analytical geometry; so too did Newton seek to explain motion in the universe through observation, experimentation, and induction. Others, like John Locke, even endeavored to explain human relationships through such rational thought.

Although the study of ideas does not easily lend itself to chronological arrangement as does political history, it is still possible to see intellectual development over time. The Enlightenment movement of the eighteenth century drew confidence from the scientific worldview that had developed as a result of the efforts and sacrifices of the pioneers of modern science.

Science and the Church

One of the most important and fundamental areas of investigation during the Scientific Revolution was astronomy. For centuries, humans had subscribed to a geocentric theory that placed Earth at the center of the universe with all the planets orbiting around it. This theory, ascribed to the Egyptian astronomer Ptolemy (fl. 150 C.E.) and supported by Aristotelian physics, maintained that the earth had to be the center of the universe because of its heaviness and that the stars and other planets existed in surrounding crystalline spheres. Beyond these crystalline spheres lay the realm of God and the angels. This view was supported by the Catholic Church, which saw humanity as the central focus of God's creation and therefore at the epicenter of all existence. Biblical support for the geocentric theory included Psalm 104: "Thou didst set the earth on its foundation, so that it should never be shaken." Still, mathematical problems were associated with this theory. For one, it was difficult to explain the motion of the planets, which seemed to be moving in noncircular patterns around the earth. At times the planets actually appeared to be going backward. This was explained by epicycles. Ptolemy maintained that planets make a second revolution in an orbit tangent to the first. It was therefore difficult to predict the location of a planet at any given time. A Polish astronomer named Nicolaus Copernicus (1473–1543) attempted to eliminate many of the mathematical inconsistencies by proposing that the sun, not the earth, was the center of the universe. In most other ways, including the acceptance of epicycles and the circular orbit of planets, Copernicus's system was still Ptolemaic. Yet Copernicus freed scientists from a rigid conception of cosmic structure and in essence proposed the empirical evidence of mathematics as the cornerstone of scientific thought.

The first selection is the simple statement by Copernicus proposing the heliocentric theory; it is excerpted from a letter entitled *Commentariolus,* written sometime after 1520. In 1543, Copernicus published *On the Revolutions of the Heavenly Spheres.* The second excerpt is from the preface of that work and was addressed to Pope Paul III. In it, Copernicus explains why he questioned the geocentric theory.

The Heliocentric Statement (ca. 1520)

NICOLAUS COPERNICUS

What appears to us as motions of the sun arise not from its motion but from the motion of the earth and our sphere, with which we revolve about the sun like any other planet. The earth has, then, more than one motion.

"The Heliocentric Statement" is from Copernicus, *De Revolutionibus Orbium Caelestium* (1543), trans. John F. Dobson and Selig Brodetsky, published in Occasional Notes of the Royal Astronomical Society, vol. 2, no. 1 (London: Royal Astronomical Society, 1947), excerpts from the preface and Book I.

On the Movement of the Earth (1543)

NICOLAUS COPERNICUS

I may well presume, most Holy Father, that certain people, as soon as they hear that in this book about the Revolutions of the Spheres of the Universe I ascribe movement to the earthly globe, will cry out that, holding such views, I should at once be hissed off the stage. . . .

So I should like your Holiness to know that I was induced to think of a method of computing the motions of the spheres by nothing else than the knowledge that the mathematicians [who had previously considered the problem] are inconsistent in these investigations.

For, first, the mathematicians are so unsure of the movements of the Sun and Moon that they cannot even explain or observe the constant length of the seasonal year. Secondly, in determining the motions of these and of the other five planets, they use neither the same principles and hypotheses nor the same demonstrations of the apparent motions and revolutions. . . . Nor have they been able thereby to discern or deduce the principal thing—namely the shape of the Universe and the unchangeable symmetry of its parts. . . .

I pondered long upon this uncertainty of mathematical tradition in establishing the motions of the system of the spheres. At last I began to chafe that philosophers could by no means agree on any one certain theory of the mechanism of the Universe, wrought for us by a supremely good and orderly Creator. . . . I therefore took pains to read again the works of all the philosophers on whom I could lay hand to seek out whether any of them had even supposed that the motions of the spheres were other than those demanded by the [Ptolemaic] mathematical schools. I found first in Cicero that Hicetas [of Syracuse, fifth century B.C.E.] had realized that the Earth moved. Afterwards I found in Plutarch that certain others had held the like opinion. . . .

Thus assuming motions, which in my work I ascribe to the Earth, by long and frequent observations I have at last discovered that, if the motions of the rest of the planets be brought into relation with the circulation of the Earth and be reckoned in proportion to the circles of each planet, . . . the orders and magnitudes of all stars and spheres, nay the heavens themselves, become so bound together that nothing in any part thereof could be moved from its place without producing confusion of all the other parts of the Universe as a whole.

CONSIDER THIS:

- What reasons does Copernicus give for supporting the heliocentric theory? Is he convincing? Why is it significant that Copernicus refers to ancient authors like Cicero and Plutarch?

Science and the Bible: "They Would Have Us Abandon Reason" (1615)

GALILEO GALILEI

After Copernicus, the quest for rational truth was continued by Tycho Brahe, who compiled accurate tables of astronomical observations, and Johannes Kepler, who analyzed these tables and posited the elliptical orbits of planets. And yet this

"On the Movement of the Earth" is from Copernicus, *De Revolutionibus Orbium Caelestium* (1543), trans. John F. Dobson and Selig Brodetsky, published in Occasional Notes of the Royal Astronomical Society, vol. 2, no. 1 (London: Royal Astronomical Society, 1947), excerpts from the preface and Book I.

"Science and the Bible" is from *Discoveries and Opinions of Galileo by Galileo Galilei*, pp. 175, 177–179, 181–184, 189–190, 194–195.

progress in scientific thought was to encounter various roadblocks beyond the difficulties of gathering and interpreting data. For the Catholic church, the question was not one of empirical evidence and rational inquiry but rather of faith and authority.

During the sixteenth century, the church established an organization that was designed to maintain purity of doctrine and authority over the faithful. The Inquisition, as it came to be called, was administered by Dominican friars, whose responsibilities had always involved the explanation of doctrine to those who had strayed from the path. Now they actively sought out those whose deeds and ideas seemed to contradict established Catholic doctrine. The Inquisition became a vehicle for reform through coercion, with allegiance being obtained through argument, intimidation, and torture if necessary.

During the seventeenth century, the church found itself embroiled in events that again threatened its established authority. The attack was now centered on the new scientific theories that challenged Catholic doctrine and were being pursued and advocated independently of church control. At the forefront of the controversy was one of the most influential scientists in history—Galileo Galilei.

Galileo was born in Pisa, Italy, in the year of Shakespeare's birth and Michelangelo's death (1564). He had much in common with these great men because he played the lute, painted, wrote poetry, and enjoyed polemics and satire. In 1592, Galileo was appointed professor of mathematics at the University of Padua, and he remained in this position for eighteen years, supporting a mistress, two daughters, a son, and a widowed mother on a small income supplemented by tutoring. During this time, Galileo came to doubt the teachings of Aristotle and other ancient philosophers and scientists, which were accepted by the church as being consistent with Catholic doctrine. Galileo had admired the mathematical aesthetics of the Copernican theory and became even more confirmed in his support of this thesis after viewing the heavens through a new instrument that he had recently improved—the telescope. Galileo considered himself a devout and obedient son of the church, but he believed that the Bible conveyed truth figuratively as well as literally. He argued that scientific facts must first be discovered, then interpreted according to observation. As Galileo noted, "The Bible shows the way to go to Heaven, not the way the heavens go." No one, not even the pope, could alter the facts.

Galileo's response to charges that the ideas of Copernicus contradicted the Bible is contained in the following letter to the Grand Duchess of Tuscany in 1615. Nevertheless, the next year the heliocentric theory was condemned as formally heretical. For his impertinence and continuing adherence to the Copernican theory, Galileo was twice ordered to appear before the Inquisition, although he was a frail man of seventy. Under threat of torture, he finally recanted his position. Only in 1992 was Galileo formally absolved from his sin by Pope John Paul II.

Some years ago, as Your Serene Highness well knows, I discovered in the heavens many things that had not been seen before our own age. The novelty of these things, as well as some consequences which followed from them in contradiction to the physical notions commonly held among academic philosophers, stirred up against me no small number of professors—as if I had placed these things in the sky with my own hands in order to upset nature and overturn the sciences. . . .

Showing a greater fondness for their own opinions than for truth, they sought to deny and disprove the new things which, if they had

FIGURE 3.1 Portrait of Galileo Galilei by Justus Sustermans (*CORBIS*).

cared to look for themselves, their own senses would have demonstrated to them. To this end they hurled various charges and published numerous writings filled with vain arguments, and they made the grave mistake of sprinkling these with passages taken from places in the Bible which they had failed to understand properly, and which were ill suited to their purposes. . . .

Persisting in their original resolve to destroy me and everything mine by any means they can think of, these men . . . know that as to the arrangement of the parts of the universe, I hold the sun to be situated motionless in the center of the revolution of the celestial orbs while the earth rotates on its axis and revolves about the sun. They know also that I support this position not only by refuting the arguments of Ptolemy and Aristotle, but by producing many counter-arguments; in particular, some which relate to physical effects whose causes can perhaps be assigned in no other way. In addition there are astronomical arguments derived from many things in my new celestial discoveries that plainly confute the Ptolemaic system while admirably agreeing with and confirming the contrary hypothesis. . . . These men have resolved to fabricate a shield for their fallacies out of the mantle of pretended religion and the authority of the Bible. These they apply, with little judgment, to the refutation of arguments that they do not understand and have not even listened to.

First they have endeavored to spread the opinion that such propositions in general are contrary to the Bible and are consequently damnable and heretical. . . . Next, becoming bolder, and hoping (though vainly) that this seed which first took root in their hypocritical minds would send out branches and ascend to heaven, they began scattering rumors among the people that before long this doctrine would be condemned by the supreme authority. . . .

They go about invoking the Bible, which they would have minister to their deceitful purposes. Contrary to the sense of the Bible and the intention of the holy Fathers, if I am not mistaken, they would extend such authorities until even in purely physical matters—where faith is not involved—they would have us altogether abandon reason and the evidence of our senses in favor of some biblical passage, though under the surface meaning of its words this passage may contain a different sense. . . .

I think in the first place that it is very pious to say and prudent to affirm that the holy Bible can never speak untruth—whenever its true meaning is understood. But I believe nobody will deny that it is often very abstruse, and may say things which are quite different from what its bare words signify. . . .

This being granted, I think that in discussion of physical problems we ought to begin not from the authority of scriptural passages, but from sense-experiences and necessary demonstrations; for the holy Bible and the phenomena of nature proceed alike from the divine Word, the former as the dictate of the Holy Ghost and the latter as the observant executrix of God's commands. It is necessary for the Bible, in order to be accommodated to the understanding of every man, to speak many things which appear to differ from the absolute truth so far as the bare meaning of the words is concerned. But Nature, on the other hand, is inexorable and immutable; she never transgresses the laws imposed upon her, or cares a whit whether her abstruse reasons and methods of operation are understandable to men. For that reason it appears that nothing physical which sense-experience sets before our eyes, or which necessary demonstrations prove to us, ought to be called in question (much less condemned) upon the testimony of biblical passages which may have some different meaning beneath their words. For the Bible is not chained in every expression to conditions as strict as those which govern all physical effects; nor is God any less excellently revealed in Nature's actions than in the sacred statements of the Bible. . . .

From this I do not mean to infer that we need not have an extraordinary esteem for the passages of holy Scripture. On the contrary, having arrived at any certainties in physics, we ought to utilize these as the most appropriate aids in the true exposition of the Bible and in the investigation of those meanings which are necessarily contained therein for these must be concordant with demonstrated truths. I should judge the authority of the Bible was designed to persuade men of those articles and propositions which, surpassing all human reasoning, could not be made credible by science, or by any other means than through the very mouth of the Holy Spirit. . . .

But I do not feel obliged to believe that the same God who had endowed us with senses, reason, and intellect has intended to forgo their use and by some other means to give us knowledge which we can attain by them.

Consider This:

- What were Galileo's specific ideas regarding the relationship between science and the Bible? Be particular in your analysis. Why did the Inquisition consider Galileo's ideas dangerous? Did the Inquisition do the church more harm than good?

■ Consider the words of Martin Luther quoted at the beginning of this chapter: "Reason is the greatest enemy that faith has. It never comes to the aid of spiritual things, but . . . struggles against the divine Word, treating with contempt all that emanates from God." Does it surprise you that this statement comes from the leader of the Protestant Reformation? Discuss the compatibility of science and religion in light of this quotation.

THEME: THE INDIVIDUAL AND THE INSTITUTION

THE REFLECTION IN THE MIRROR

Galileo Absolved: The Resolution

"Science and Faith Are Both Gifts from God"

POPE JOHN PAUL II

The papacy, which played such a fundamental role in the Middle Ages, declined in international authority after the Protestant Reformation. However, with the emergence of twentieth-century leaders such as John XXIII, Paul VI, and John Paul II, the papacy has played an important role in international affairs apart from the 800 million Catholics it represents. For example, John Paul II (1978–2005) was a formidable figure in defying Soviet threats to invade his native Poland in 1980; his knowledge of languages and frequent travel made him a vital force, especially in developing countries. The following address of John Paul II to the international scientific community discusses the relationship between science and faith, which he believed could be mutually supportive. This relationship had been strained since the sixteenth century when Galileo was condemned by the church as a heretic for his scientific theories. This concession of the pope indicates a new tolerance between rational scientific methods and the realm of faith.

KEEP IN MIND . . .

■ In this statement, why does Pope John Paul II believe that science and faith are compatible and mutually supportive?

From the beginning of my pontificate I have taken pains to emphasize that the dialogue between science and faith is not merely possible, but essential. I have been committed to removing the obstacles which could still impair its constant development. In that regard it seemed important to resolve, once and for all, some perennial controversies which unfortunately have undermined the good understanding between the Church and the scientific community. I am referring, in particular, to regrettable past events of history, such as the "Galileo case." On November 19, 1979, in an address to the Pontifical Academy of Sciences on the occasion of the commemorations marking the centenary of the birth of Albert Einstein, I suggested an objective review of the Copernican-Ptolemaic controversy of the 17th century. On that occasion I said: "I give all my support to this task which could do

"Science and Faith Are Both Gifts from God" is from Pope John Paul II's address delivered to the international scientific community at the Ettore Maiorana Research Centre on May 8, 1993, contained in *The Pope Speaks*, vol. 38 (1993), pp. 296–300.

honor to the truth of the faith and of science and open the doors for future collaboration." I wanted to emphasize the same urgency in a message for the 300th anniversary of Isaac Newton's publication of the *Philosophiae Naturalis Principia Mathematica*, recalling that science and religion are at the service of the human community, and expressing the wish for a common search based on critical frankness and an exchange that will not only continue but also grow in quality and scope. . . . However, what direction will the dialogue between science and faith take in the future? My reflection takes its cue from the bronze inscription unveiled here today: "Science and faith are both gifts of God."

This terse statement not only excludes the idea that science and faith must view one another with mutual suspicion, but also shows the deepest reason calling them to establish a constructive and cordial relationship: God, the common foundation of both; God, the ultimate reason for the logic of creation which science explores, and the source of the Revelation by which He freely gives himself to man, calling him to faith, in order to make him a son instead of a creature, and opening to him the gates of intimacy with Him. The light of reason, which makes science possible, and the light of Revelation, which makes faith possible, emanate from a single source. They are two distinct, autonomous trajectories, but by their very nature they are never on a collision course. Whenever some type of friction is noted, it is the symptom of an unfortunate pathological condition. . . .

> "The light of reason, which makes science possible, and the light of Revelation, which makes faith possible, emanate from a single source."
>
> —POPE JOHN PAUL II

In what sense is science a "gift" of God? Such a statement could seem ambiguous, even provocative, to a person without faith if it were to be understood as playing down the natural capacity of the mind to grasp reality by means of a rigorous logical and cognitive procedure. Such a sense, however, is quite far from the thinking of the Church, which even in the realm of faith rejects a blind "fideism." There is even greater reason to acknowledge the human mind's natural capacity to obtain truth in its own areas of experience and knowledge of the world.

The dialogue between science and faith, each respecting the other's areas, is doubly necessary in the domain of applied science. . . . If human life is at enormous risk today, it is not because of the truth discovered through scientific research but because of the deadly applications made of it on the technological level. . . . Both of them, however, must take on a precise ethical responsibility in regard to their relationships and applications. The stakes are too high to be taken lightly. . . .

In recent years we have witnessed rapid and surprising social transformation. Among these, how can we fail to mention overcoming the rigid division of the world into opposite ideological, political and military blocs? It is because of this event that the threat of the "nuclear holocaust" has been removed, at least to a large degree. In this same span of time, however, other emergencies of a planetary nature have reached levels of extreme danger, making us see the risk of a type of "environmental holocaust" due to the careless destruction of vital ecological resources and the increase of ever more insidious attacks on the defense of and respect for human life. The unbridled race by the few and privileged to hoard and exploit the earth's resources is laying the foundations of another form of cold war, this time between the planet's North and South, between the highly industrialized countries and the poor nations, which cannot be ignored by those who take the world's fate to heart. Threatening clouds are once again gathering on mankind's horizon. . . .

Whenever scientific activity has a positive effect on respect for and protection of human dignity, it contributes significantly to building peace. Therefore it is necessary to be tireless in promoting a scientific culture capable of looking always at "the whole person" and at "the whole of peoples," serving the universal good and solidarity. In this regard, great importance is attached to making progress in the dialogue between science and faith. We must work together to reestablish the connection between truth and values, between science and ethical commitment. We must all be truly convinced that progress is really such if it is at the service of the true and total well-being of individuals and of the whole human family. I am therefore compelled to emphasize once again what I have stressed more than once, namely, that although science's main task is to seek the truth in the free and legitimate liberty belonging to it, scientists are nevertheless not permitted to prescind from the ethical implications concerning the means of their research and the use of the truths they discover. Ethical goodness is simply another name for truth sought by the practical intellect.

CONSIDER THIS:

- What are some of the current areas of tension between science and religion? In our quest for knowledge and understanding about the world around us and our place in it, must one choose between the mind and the spirit? What did Pope John Paul II say about this?

THE BROADER PERSPECTIVE:

- Is morality constantly undergoing revision because of the advances of technology? The cloning of animals or humans, for example, poses new ethical questions that certainly did not exist in the seventeenth century. Must we adapt to new ethical parameters established by technology, or does an absolute morality exist regarding the sanctity of life that finds its greatest defenders in the confines of religion and law and does not bend to the will of science?

The Foundations of Modern Science

The Advancement of Learning (1605)

SIR FRANCIS BACON

Sir Francis Bacon (1561–1626) was born in London. Educated at Cambridge in law and science, he was an Englishman of almost universal accomplishment. He rose quickly as a lawyer during the reign of Queen Elizabeth I and was knighted in 1603 before being named Lord Chancellor by King James I in 1618. His career took a tragic turn in 1621 when he was charged with financial corruption, expelled from Parliament, and briefly imprisoned before his death in 1626. Throughout his career as a royal official, he wrote histories, moral essays, and philosophical treatises. But he never lost his interest in scientific studies, and, although not a scientist except in an amateur sense, he has traditionally been regarded as the father of scientific

"The Advancement of Learning" is from James H. Robinson and Charles A. Beard, eds., *Readings in Modern European History*, vol. 1 (Boston: Ginn and Company, 1908), p. 176.

empiricism, the doctrine that all knowledge is derived from sense experience, observation, and experimentation. In books such as *The Advancement of Learning (1605)* and *Novum Organum (1620),* he set the tone for a new standard of scientific inquiry and attacked the medieval Scholastic belief that most truth had already been discovered by calling into question the traditional reverence for the authority of the ancient authors. Bacon urged his contemporaries to have confidence in their own abilities and see change as desirable.

Lastly, some are weakly afraid lest a deeper search into nature should transgress the permitted limits of sober-mindedness, wrongfully wresting and transferring what is said in Holy Writ against those who pry into sacred mysteries to the hidden things of nature, which are barred by no prohibition. Others, with more subtlety, surmise and reflect that if the secondary causes are unknown, everything can be more readily referred to divine hand and rod—a point in which they think religion greatly concerned; which is, in fact, nothing else but to seek to gratify God with a lie. Others fear from past example that movements and changes in philosophy will end in assaults on religion; and others again appear apprehensive that in the investigation of nature something may be found to subvert, or at least shake, the authority of religion, especially with the unlearned.

But these two last fears seem to me to savor utterly of carnal wisdom; as if men in the recesses and secret thoughts of their hearts doubted and distrusted the strength of religion, and the empire of faith over the senses, and therefore feared that the investigation of truth in nature might be dangerous to them. But if the matter be truly considered, natural philosophy is, after the word of God, at once the surest medicine against superstition and the most approved nourishment for faith; and therefore she is rightly given to religion as her most faithful handmaid, since the one displays the will of God, the other his power.

Consider This:

- What did Sir Francis Bacon contribute to the Scientific Revolution? What specific ideas did he offer regarding the authority of religion and the "nourishment of faith"?

"I Think, Therefore I Am": Discourse on Method (1637)

RENÉ DESCARTES

René Descartes (1596–1650) was born in western France but lived primarily in Holland for the last twenty years of his life. He attended Jesuit schools and graduated in law from the university in Poitiers. He was not attracted to a legal career, however, and became a soldier in the German wars of the time. It was while he was billeted in a German town that he had an intellectual revelation akin, as he later maintained, to a religious conversion. He had a vision of the great potential for progress if mathematical method were to be applied to all fields of knowledge. He thus pursued a career devoted to the propagation of a strict method, best exemplified by his invention of analytical geometry. Descartes believed that human beings were endowed by God with the ability to reason and that God served as the

"'I Think, Therefore I Am'" is from René Descartes, *The Discourse on Method and Metaphysical Meditations*, trans. G. B. Rawlings (London: Walter Scott, 1901), pp. 32–35, 60–61, 75–76.

guarantor of the correctness of clear ideas. The material world could thus be understood through adherence to mathematical laws and methods of inquiry. Descartes championed the process of deductive reasoning whereby specific information could be logically deduced from general information. His method was influential well into the eighteenth century when it was supplanted by the method of scientific induction, whereby generalizations could be drawn from the observation of specific data.

The following selection is drawn from Descartes's most famous work, *Discourse on the Method of Rightly Conducting the Reason (1637).*

As a multitude of laws often furnishes excuses for vice, so that a state is much better governed when it has but few, and those few strictly observed, so in place of the great number of precepts of which logic is composed, I believed that I should find the following four sufficient, provided that I made a firm and constant resolve not once to omit to observe them.

The first was, never to accept anything as true when I did not recognize it clearly to be so, that is to say, to carefully avoid precipitation and prejudice, and to include in my opinions nothing beyond that which should present itself so clearly and so distinctly to my mind that I might have no occasion to doubt it.

The second was, to divide each of the difficulties which I should examine into as many parts as were possible, and as should be required for its better solution.

The third was, to conduct my thoughts in order, by beginning with the simplest objects, and those most easy to know, so as to mount little by little, as if by steps, to the most complex knowledge, and even assuming an order among those which do not naturally precede one another.

And the last was, to make everywhere enumerations so complete, and reviews so wide, that I should be sure of omitting nothing. . . .

I had long remarked that, in conduct, it is sometimes necessary to follow opinions known to be very uncertain, just as if they were indisputable, as has been said above; but then, because I desired to devote myself only to the research of truth, I thought it necessary to do exactly the contrary, and reject as absolutely false all in which I could conceive the least doubt, in order to see if afterwards there did not remain in my belief something which was entirely indisputable. Thus, because our senses sometimes deceive us, I wanted to suppose that nothing is such as they make us imagine it; and because some men err in reasoning . . . and judging that I was as liable to fail as any other, I rejected as false all the reasons which I had formerly accepted as [true]; . . . I resolved that everything which had ever entered into my mind was no more true than the illusions of my dreams. But immediately afterwards I observed that while I thus desired everything to be false, I, who thought, must of necessity [exist]; and remarking that this truth, I think, therefore I am, was so firm and so assured that all the most extravagant suppositions of the skeptics were unable to shake it, I judged that I could unhesitatingly accept it as the first principle of the philosophy I was seeking. . . .

After this, and reflecting upon the fact that I doubted, and that in consequence my being was not quite perfect (for I saw clearly that to know was a greater perfection than to doubt), I [wondered where] I had learned to think of something more perfect than I; and I knew for certain that it must be from some nature which was in reality more perfect. [And I clearly recognized that] this idea . . . had been put in me by a nature truly more perfect than I, which had in itself all perfections of which I could have any idea; that is, to explain myself in one word, God. . . .

Finally, whether awake or asleep, we ought never to allow ourselves to be persuaded of the truth of anything unless on the evidence of our Reason. And it must be noted that I say of our Reason, and not of our imagination or of our senses: thus, for example, although we very clearly see the sun, we ought not therefore to determine that it is only of the size which our sense of sight presents; and we may very distinctly imagine the head of a lion joined to the body of a goat, without being therefore shut up to the conclusion that a chimaera exists; for it is not a dictate of Reason that what we thus see or imagine is in reality existent; but it plainly tells us that all our ideas or notions contain in them some truth; for otherwise it could not be that God, who is wholly perfect and veracious, should have placed them in us.

CONSIDER THIS:

- What are some of Descartes's ideas on the scientific method? Why is it so important to establish a method of inquiry to explore the dimensions of science? What did Descartes mean by the phrase "I think, therefore I am"? Why was this statement so fundamental to his method?
- Reconstruct Descartes's logic for the existence of God. Do you find it compelling?

THEME: THE INSTITUTION AND THE INDIVIDUAL

AGAINST THE GRAIN

On the Circulation of the Blood

"A Motion, As It Were, in a Circle!"

WILLIAM HARVEY

William Harvey has been termed the father of modern physiology. He was heir to a legacy of interest in the internal workings of the human body that had been most recently in evidence among artists during the Renaissance. But whereas Michelangelo studied the body to better represent the human form, Harvey sought to discover the internal workings on their own scientific merit. In this, he was more closely akin to the earlier scientific studies of Leonardo da Vinci. Harvey built on the work of the Greek physician Galen (fl. 150 C.E.), who demonstrated that the arteries carried blood instead of air. Harvey's exacting methods set the pattern of scientific research for generations. In the following selection, which was an address to the Royal College of Physicians in 1628, he gave the results of his methodical dissections and experiments.

KEEP IN MIND . . .

- Note how Harvey methodically proves, through dissection and observation, that the blood circulates through the body.

As this book alone declares the blood to course and revolve by a new route, very different from the ancient and beaten pathway trodden for so many ages, and illustrated by such a host of learned and distinguished men, I was greatly afraid lest I might be charged with presumption did I lay my work before the public at home, or send it beyond seas for impression, unless I had first proposed its subject to you, had confirmed its conclusions by ocular demonstrations in

"'A Motion, As It Were, in a Circle'" is from R. Willis, trans., *The Works of William Harvey* (London: Sydenham Society, 1847), pp. 5–7, 31–32, 45–47.

your presence, had replied to your doubts and objections, and secured the assent and support of our distinguished President. For I was most intimately persuaded, that if I could make good my proposition before you and our College, I had less to fear from others. . . . For true philosophers, who are only eager for truth and knowledge, never regard themselves as already so thoroughly informed, but that they welcome further information from whomsoever and from whencesoever it may come; nor are they so narrow-minded as to imagine any of the arts or sciences transmitted to us by the ancients, in such a state of forwardness or completeness, that nothing is left for the ingenuity and industry of others. . . . Neither do they swear such fealty to their mistress Antiquity, that they openly, and in sight of all, deny and desert their friend Truth. . . .

My dear colleagues, I profess both to learn and to teach anatomy, not from books, but from dissections; not from the positions of philosophers, but from the fabric of nature. . . . From these and other observations of the like kind, I am persuaded it will be found that the motion of the heart is as follows:

First of all, the auricle contracts, and in the course of its contraction throws the blood, (which it contains in ample quantity as the head of the veins, the store-house and cistern of the blood,) into the ventricle, which being filled, the heart raises itself straightway, makes all its fibers tense, contracts the ventricles, and performs a beat, by which beat it immediately sends the blood

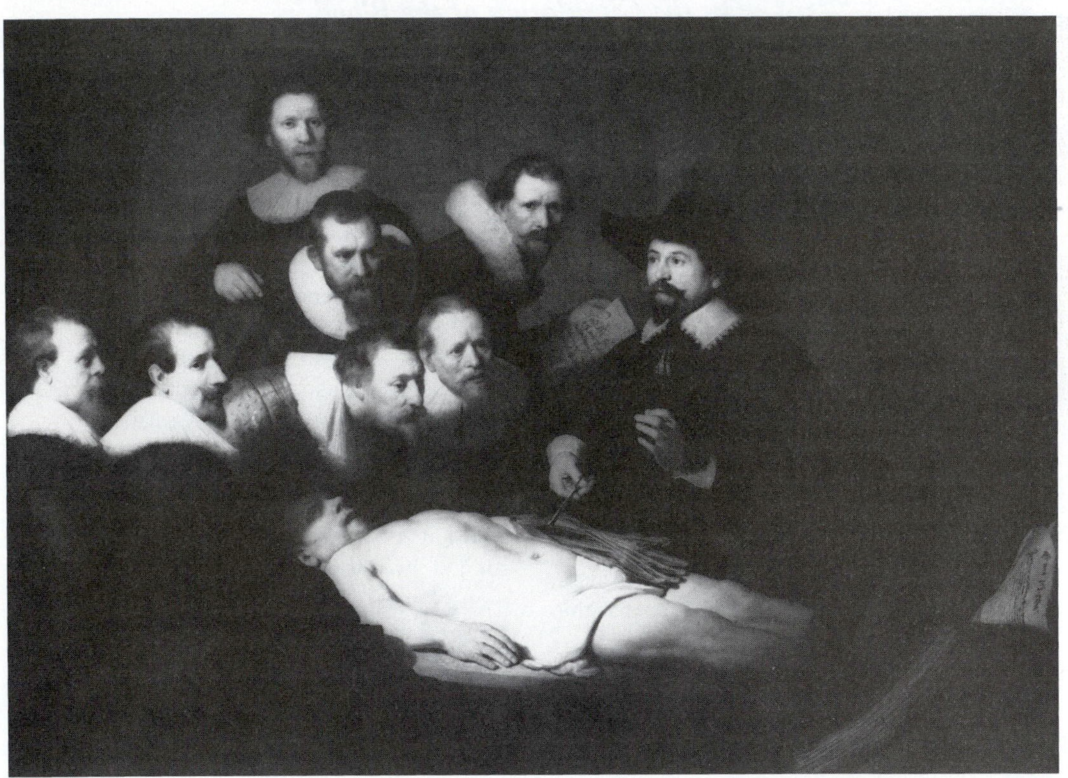

FIGURE 3.2 *The Anatomy Lesson of Dr. Tulp* by Rembrandt van Rijn (Dutch, 1660–1669). [Oil on canvas, 169.5 × 216.5 cm] (*Mauritshuis, The Hague*)

supplied to it by the auricle into the arteries; the right ventricle sending its charge into the lungs by the vessel which is called *vena arteriosi*, but which, in structure and function, and all things else, is an artery; the left ventricle sending its charge into the aorta, and through this by the arteries to the body at large. . . .

Thus far I have spoken of the passage of the blood from the veins into the arteries, and of the manner in which it is transmitted and distributed by the action of the heart. . . . But what remains to be said upon the quantity and source of the blood which thus passes, is of so novel and unheard-of character, that I not only fear injury to myself from the envy of a few, but I tremble lest I have mankind at large for my enemies. . . . Still, the die is cast, and my trust is in my love of truth, and the candor that inheres in cultivated minds. And when I surveyed my mass of evidence, I revolved in my mind, what might be the quantity of blood which was transmitted, in how short a time its passage might be effected, and the like; . . . I began to think whether there might not be A MOTION, AS IT WERE, IN A CIRCLE. Now this I afterwards found to be true; and I finally saw that the blood, forced by the action of the left ventricle into the arteries, was distributed to the body at large, impelled by the right ventricle through the veins, and so round to the left ventricle in the manner already indicated. . . .

The heart, consequently, is the beginning of life; the sun of the microcosm, even as the sun in his turn might well be designated the heart of the world; for it is the heart by whose virtue and pulse the blood is moved, perfected, made apt to nourish, and is preserved from corruption and coagulation; it is the household divinity which, discharging its function, nourishes, cherishes, quickens the whole body, and is indeed the foundation of life, the source of all action.

CONSIDER THIS:

- Why did William Harvey want to present his findings in an address before the Royal College of Physicians? What was he afraid of? Why were his discoveries about the heart and circulation of blood so important and perhaps so threatening?
- Harvey also argued that scientists never "swear fealty to their mistress Antiquity. . . and deny or desert their friend Truth." What did he mean, and can you apply this idea to our contemporary society? What does it mean to learn and teach "from the fabric of Nature"?

THE BROADER PERSPECTIVE:

- Harvey noted that true philosophers (or scientists in this case) "are only eager for truth and knowledge" and welcome information and opinions from others. Why is this sharing of ideas so important in the process of scientific discovery?
- In contrast, consider this quote from the American humorist, Mark Twain: "Discovery! To know that you are walking where no others have walked; that you are beholding what the human eye has not seen before; to give birth to an idea, to discover a great thought. To be the first—that is the idea!" Isn't it as important in the scientific world for a researcher to claim primacy in the discovery of a cure for cancer as it is for explorers in the physical world to conquer a mountain or discover a lost civilization? Must the personal desire for primacy, to be the first in discovery, necessarily be moderated by the demands of cooperation in order to achieve success?
- Dutch artist Rembrandt van Rijn's painting entitled *The Anatomy Lesson of Dr. Tulp* was finished in 1632, four years after Harvey wrote on the circulation of the blood. Dissection at the time was still condemned by the Catholic church. Why do you think Rembrandt felt secure enough to paint such a procedure when the great mathematician and scientist, Galileo, was on trial at the same time in Rome for supporting the heretical sun-centered, or heliocentric, theory of the rotation of the planets proposed by Copernicus?

Principles of Analysis—Induction and God: Optics (1704)

SIR ISAAC NEWTON

Sir Isaac Newton (1642–1727) was perhaps the most brilliant scientist in an age of genius. He drew on the work of his predecessors and his own vast mental abilities to devise a system of physical laws that have endured for more than 250 years. Newton reasoned that the planets and all other material objects in the universe moved in an orderly regimen, dictated by the principles of gravity and mutual attraction. Newton made no attempt to explain the nature of gravity itself, but he did demonstrate the principles mathematically. He adopted the methods of empirical observation established by Francis Bacon a half century earlier and championed inductive reasoning as the primary method for scientific inquiry. With the work of Newton, the immense universe became rational and knowable, a realm of regularity, subject to immutable laws. Humankind no longer lived in a haphazard and chaotic universe, dependent on the intervention of spirits and angels for its regulation. And yet, Newton was no atheist. The new universe simply demanded a new conception of God. For Newton, science and faith could not only be reconciled but were mutually dependent. The following selection from his *Optics (1704) gives evidence of this important concept.*

All these things being considered, it seems probable to me, that God in the Beginning formed Matter in solid, massy, hard, impenetrable, moveable Particles, of such Sizes and Figures, and with such other Properties, and in such Proportion to Space, as most conduced to the End for which he formed them; and that these primitive Particles being Solids, are incomparably harder than any porous Bodies compounded of them; even so very hard, as never to wear or break in pieces; no ordinary Power being able to divide what God himself made one in the first Creation. . . .

To derive two or three general Principles of Motion from Phaenomena, and afterwards to tell us how the Properties and Actions of all corporeal Things follow from those manifest Principles, would be a very great step in Philosophy, though the Causes of those Principles were not yet discovered: And therefore, I scruple not to propose the Principles of Motion . . . and leave their Causes to be found out.

Now by the help of these Principles, all material Things seem to have been composed of the hard and solid Particles above-mentioned, variously associated in the first Creation by the Counsel of an intelligent Agent. For it became him who created them to set them in order. And if he did so, it's unphilosophical to seek for any other Origin of the World, or to pretend that it might arise out of a Chaos by the mere Laws of Nature; though being once formed, it may continue by those Laws for many Ages. For while Comets move in very eccentric orbits in all manner of Positions, blind Fate could never make all the Planets move one and the same way in concentric orbits, some inconsiderable Irregularities excepted, which may have risen from the mutual Actions of Comets and Planets upon one another, and which will be apt to increase, till this System wants a Reformation. Such a wonderful Uniformity in the Planetary System must be allowed the Effect of Choice. And so must the Uniformity in the Bodies of Animals, they having generally

"Principles of Analysis" is from Sir Isaac Newton, *Optics* (London: W. & J. Innys, 1721), pp. 344–345, 375–381. Text modernized by the editor.

a right and a left side shaped alike, and on either side of their Bodies two Legs behind, and either two Arms, or two legs, or two Wings before upon their Shoulders, and between their Shoulders a Neck running down into a Back-bone, and a Head upon it; and in the Head two Ears, two Eyes, a Nose, a Mouth, and a Tongue, alike situated . . . and the Instinct of Brutes and Insects, can be the effect of nothing else than the Wisdom and Skill of a powerful ever-living Agent, who being in all Places, is more able by his Will to move the Bodies within his boundless uniform Sensorium, and thereby to form and reform the Parts of the Universe, than we are by our Will to move the Parts of our own Bodies. And yet we are not to consider the World as the Body of God, or the several Parts thereof, as the Parts of God. He is a uniform Being, void of Organs, Members or Parts, and they are his Creatures subordinate to him, and subservient to his Will. . . .

And since Space is divisible in infinitum, and Matter is not necessarily in all places, it may be also allowed that God is able to create Particles of Matter of several Sizes and Figures, and in several Proportions to Space, and perhaps of different Densities and Forces, and thereby to vary the Laws of Nature, and make Worlds of several sorts in several Parts of the Universe. At least, I see nothing of Contradiction in all this.

As in Mathematics, so in Natural Philosophy, the Investigation of difficult Things by the Method of Analysis, ought ever to precede the Method of Composition. This Analysis consists in making Experiments and Observations, and in drawing general Conclusions from them by Induction, and admitting of no Objections against the Conclusions, but such as are taken from Experiments, or other certain Truths. For Hypotheses are not to be regarded in experimental Philosophy. And although the arguing from Experiments and Observations by Induction be no Demonstration of general Conclusions; yet it is the best way of arguing which the Nature of Things admits of. . . . By this way of Analysis, we may proceed from Compounds to Ingredients, and from Motions to the Forces producing them; and in general, from Effects to their Causes, and from particular Causes to more general ones, till the Argument end in the most general. This is the Method of Analysis: And the Synthesis consists in assuming the Causes discovered, and established as Principles, and by them explaining the Phaenomena proceeding from them, and proving the Explanations.

Compare and Contrast:

- How would you define the process of induction as championed by Sir Isaac Newton? How did he specifically demonstrate this principle in his work on *Optics*? If Newton was such a methodical scientist, why did he accept the compatibility of science and God in the pursuit of empirical truth? What does Sir Francis Bacon say about this compatibility in the selection from *The Advancement of Learning* (1605)? Compare this with Pope John Paul II's views on the links between science and religion.

The Broader Perspective:

- Where does "greatness" lie? In the conquests of men like Julius Caesar or Alexander the Great, the political leadership of Augustus or Oliver Cromwell, or in the intellectual influence of Isaac Newton? Is knowledge the most powerful force in the secular world?

The Enlightenment and the Revolution of the Mind

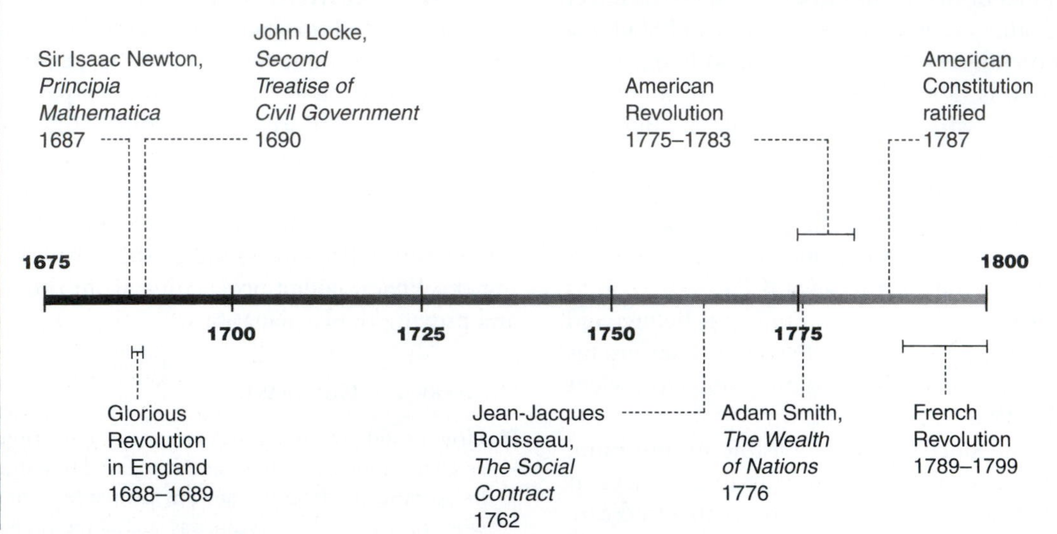

Intellect does not attain its full force unless it attacks power.

—Madame de Staël

I respect faith, but doubt is what gets you an education.

—Wilson Mizner

He who desires to have understanding must be free in mind.

—Alcinous

CHAPTER THEMES

- **Social and Spiritual Values:** Was the Enlightenment a secular age that was devoid of spirituality and belief? Had the Catholic church become irrelevant in the face of scientific inquiry? Or did the deist philosophy simply offer the spiritual nourishment and intellectual consolation that institutionalized religion could or would not offer? What is the difference between philosophy and religion?
- **Women in History:** How important were the contributions of women to the enlightened thought of the eighteenth century? What were salons, and how did they allow women to compete with men on an equal intellectual footing?
- **Revolution and Historical Transition:** Why do certain eras of history seem to explode with

creativity and intellectual risk whereas others stagnate? What do the Scientific Revolution and the Enlightenment have in common with the spirit of fifth-century Athens or the Renaissance era? Was the Enlightenment an age in which human beings broke free of the confines of religion and delighted in the wonder of human achievement? Do we live in an age of intellectual enlightenment or stagnation?

- **The Big Picture:** Why did the Enlightenment occur? To what extent did the Enlightenment depend on the advances of the Scientific Revolution?

The eighteenth century in Europe has been called the Age of Reason, or the Enlightenment. This was a dynamic era in which the human experience was indeed transformed. In the salons of Paris, in the coffeehouses of London, the talk was of machines and the heavens, of natural laws and moral responsibility, of education and the purpose of religion. The ideals of reform captured the imagination and directed the energy of many writers, who exported great advancements in science and political thought throughout the world. The writers and thinkers of this time, following precedents set in the preceding century, were convinced that natural laws governed the universe and that a human, essentially a rational creature, could further discover and apply those laws in the world. These intellectuals, called *philosophes*, examined and challenged the economic theories and political and religious assumptions of the day. The philosophes were diverse in their thought and often contended among themselves, but they were united by the conviction that one had natural rights (defined by political philosopher John Locke as life, liberty, and property) and that one must control one's own destiny for the sole purpose of a better life on earth. Thus the political divine-right absolutism of King Louis XIV (1643–1715), although providing security, could not be tolerated by many philosophes because it curtailed individual liberty. Similarly, the philosophes were generally opposed to the accepted economic theory of mercantilism, which sought complete government control of the national economy and especially promoted the establishment of foreign trading monopolies. Under mercantilism, the production and distribution of goods in colonial markets were therefore regulated for the benefit of the mother country. The theory of capitalism was born as a reaction to this strict economic regulation by the state. Adam Smith, in his treatise *The Wealth of Nations* (1776), argued that such a rigid monopolistic policy restricted individual initiative and the natural pursuit of profit. In spiritual matters as well, the philosophes regarded religion, especially Christianity, as fantasy that drew humanity away from the rational world into a realm of hope and belief in a nonexistent life beyond. The spiritual world was not subject to reason or proof and therefore drew scorn from the philosophes. Indeed, they contended that organized religion sought to control thought and was therefore anathema to true intellectual freedom.

But the rationalists of the Enlightenment were also adamant that knowledge must have practical purpose and inquiry must yield useful knowledge. Voltaire, perhaps the best known and most influential philosophe of them all, exclaimed, "What light has burst over Europe within the last few years! It is the light of common sense." Reason was synonymous with common sense. To the intellectuals of the time, anyone who could rid the mind of the chains of thought and social constraints established by the political and religious institutions of the day could possess reason.

Yet a certain naïveté in this relationship between reason and common sense also characterized the philosophes. This naïveté appears most clearly in their conception of "progress." They professed a profound faith in the future and some even predicted a united era of peace and prosperity by the dawn of the twenty-first century. When one compares George Orwell's dire predictions in his novel *1984*, the contrast between the cockiness of the Age of Reason and the brutal realities of the twentieth century is staggering. The philosophes had none of the fear and distrust of human nature and technology that has been reflected in our experience with poisonous gas and nuclear destruction. For the enlightened thinker, education in the simple laws of nature, technological progress, and increased production could only bring increased happiness. And for the eighteenth century, that was enough. Humankind was breaking its medieval chains, discarding archaic attitudes, and taking the risks requisite of a new era where religion was but a personal choice, and monarchs seemingly embodied Plato's ideal of philosopher-kings. It was therefore reasonable to think that happiness was in the offing.

This chapter introduces some of the most important personalities, ideas, and attitudes of this remarkable period. In so many ways, by "daring to know," the scientists and philosophers of the seventeenth and eighteenth centuries picked up the gauntlet laid down by the thinkers of the Renaissance and provided the intellectual challenge for future generations.

Thoughts on the Human Condition and Human Progress

The Blank Slate of the Mind: An Essay Concerning Human Understanding (1690)

JOHN LOCKE

John Locke (1632–1704) was one of the most important figures of this period of scientific discovery and reason. He initiated the Age of Enlightenment in England and France, was an inspirer of the U.S. Constitution, and remains a powerful influence on the life and thought of Western Civilization. Locke was educated at Oxford, where he was fascinated with experimental science. He became a physician but was particularly attracted to human relationships concerning how people learn, and how they are best governed. Well known in the academic circles of England and France, his political philosophy was to provide a confirmation of the Glorious Revolution of 1688 and a framework for the American and French revolutions of 1776 and 1789.

The following selection from one of his primary works investigates a seminal question debated in the Enlightenment: Are children born with any innate ideas that have been inherited from parents, or are all ideas products of associations within society? This work extended empirical investigation into the realm of the human mind and reveals Locke's inquiring nature and intellectual depth.

It is established opinion among some men, that there are in the understanding certain innate principles; some primary notions, characters, as it were stamped upon the mind of man, which the soul receives in its very first being, and brings into the world with it. It would be sufficient to convince unprejudiced readers of the falseness of this supposition, if I should only show . . . how men, barely by the use of their natural faculties, may attain to all the knowledge they have, without the help of any innate impressions; and may arrive at certainty, without any such original notions or principles. . . .

"The Blank Slate of the Mind" is from John Locke, *An Essay Concerning Human Understanding*, ed. A. D. Fraser (Oxford: Clarendon Press, 1894), vol. 1, pp. 37–38, 121–124.

Let us then suppose the mind to be, as we say, white paper, void of all characters, without any ideas:—How comes it to be furnished? Whence comes it by that vast store which the busy and boundless fancy of man has painted on it with an almost endless variety? Whence has it all the materials of reason and knowledge? To this I answer, in one word, EXPERIENCE. In that all our knowledge is founded; and from that it ultimately derives itself. Our observation employed either, about external sensible objects, or about the internal operations of our minds perceived and reflected on by ourselves, is that which supplies our understandings with all the materials of thinking. These two are the fountains of knowledge, from whence all the ideas we have, or can naturally have, do spring. . . .

The understanding seems to me not to have the least glimmering of any ideas which it does not receive from [sensation or reflection]. External objects furnish the mind with the ideas of sensible qualities, which are all those different perceptions they produce in us; and the mind furnishes the understanding with ideas of its own operations.

He that attentively considers the state of a child at his first coming into the world, will have little reason to think him stored with plenty of ideas that are to be the matter of his future knowledge. It is by degrees [that] he comes to be furnished with them. . . . But all that are born into the world being surrounded with bodies that perpetually and diversely affect them, variety of ideas, whether care be taken about it or not, are imprinted on the minds of children. Light and colors are busy at hand everywhere when the eye is but open; sounds and some tangible qualities fail not to solicit their proper senses; but yet I think it will be granted easily, that if a child were kept in a place where he never saw any other but black and white till he were a man, he would have no more ideas of scarlet or green than he that from his childhood never tasted an oyster or a pineapple has of those particular relishes. . . .

Consider This:

- Do you find Locke's assertion that the mind is a blank slate at birth and that there are no innate ideas to be a compelling argument? This still remains a disputed issue in modern psychology: Can you solve it? What notions and actions are instinctive to human beings and what is learned through experience?

THEME: THE INSTITUTION AND THE INDIVIDUAL

Against the Grain

On Crimes and Punishments (1764)

"The Greatest Happiness of the Greatest Number"

CESARE BECCARIA

Cesare Beccaria was the son of a Milanese aristocrat of modest means. He was educated initially at a Jesuit school, an experience that he later described as "fanatical" and stifling to "the development of human feelings." At age twenty-six, he became an international celebrity with the publication of his work on criminal law in 1764. Translated into several languages, it enjoyed a remarkable success in France, where it went through seven editions in six months. In it, Beccaria lashed out against

"'The Greatest Happiness of the Greatest Number'" is from Cesare Beccaria, *An Essay on Crimes and Punishments*, trans. E. D. Ingraham (Philadelphia: H. Nicklin, 1819), pp. xii, 18–19, 47, 59–60, 93–94, 104–105, 148–149.

the barbarities of the day, including the torture of prisoners to induce confession, the corruption of judges, and degrading and brutal punishments. Penalties, he concluded, should be scaled to the offense. Beccaria was the first modern writer to advocate the complete abolition of capital punishment, and his treatise remains the most important and influential volume written on criminal justice.

KEEP IN MIND . . .

- What is the logic behind Beccaria's argument to eliminate torture and have the penalty fit the crime?

If we look into history, we shall find that laws, which are, or ought to be, conventions between men in a state of freedom, have been, for the most part the work of the passions of a few, or the consequences of a fortuitous or temporary necessity; not dictated by a cool examiner of human nature, who knew how to collect in one point the actions of a multitude, and had only this end in view, the greatest happiness of the greatest number. . . .

> "Punishments . . . and such a mode of inflicting them ought to be chosen, as will make the strongest and most lasting impressions on the minds of others, with the least torment to the body of the criminal."
> —CESARE BECCARIA

Observe that by justice I understand nothing more than that bond which is necessary to keep the interest of individuals united, without which men would return to their original state of barbarity. All punishments which exceed the necessity of preserving this bond are in their nature unjust. . . .

The end of punishment, therefore, is no other than to prevent the criminal from doing further injury to society, and to prevent others from committing the like offence. Such punishments, therefore, and such a mode of inflicting them ought to be chosen, as will make the strongest and most lasting impressions on the minds of others, with the least torment to the body of the criminal.

The torture of a criminal during the course of his trial is a cruelty consecrated by custom in most nations. It is used with an intent either to make him confess his crime, or to explain some contradiction into which he had been led during his examination, or discover his accomplices, or for some kind of metaphysical and incomprehensible purgation of infamy, or, finally, in order to discover other crimes of which he is not accused, but of which he may be guilty.

No man can be judged a criminal until he be found guilty; nor can society take from him the public protection until it have been proved that he has violated the conditions on which it was granted. What right, then, but that of power, can authorize the punishment of a citizen so long as there remains any doubt of his guilt? This dilemma is frequent. Either he is guilty, or not guilty. If guilty, he should only suffer the punishment ordained by the laws, and torture becomes useless, as his confession is unnecessary. If he be not guilty, you torture the innocent; for in the eye of the law, every man is innocent whose crime has not been proved. . . .

> "Crimes are more effectually prevented by the certainty than by the severity of punishment."
> —CESARE BECCARIA

Crimes are more effectually prevented by the certainty than by the severity of punishment. . . . In proportion as punishments become more cruel, the minds of men, as a fluid rises to the same height with that which surrounds it, grow hardened and insensible; and the force of the passions still continuing, in the space of an hundred years the wheel [torture device] terrifies no more than formerly the prison. That a punishment may produce the effect required, it is sufficient that the evil it occasions should exceed the good expected from the crime, including in the calculation the certainty of the punishment, and the privation of the expected advantage. All severity beyond this is superfluous, and therefore tyrannical.

The punishment of death is pernicious to society, from the example of barbarity it affords. If the passions, or the necessity of war, have taught men to shed the blood of their fellow creatures, the laws, which are intended to moderate the ferocity of mankind, should not increase it by examples of barbarity, them more horrible as this punishment is usually attended with formal pageantry. Is it not absurd, that the laws, which detest and punish homicide, should, in order to prevent murder, publicly commit murder themselves? . . .

It is better to prevent crimes than to punish them. This is the fundamental principle of good legislation, which is the art of conducting men to the maximum of happiness, and to the minimum of misery, if we may apply this mathematical expression to the good and evil of life. . . .

Would you prevent crimes? Let the laws be clear and simple, let the entire force of the nation be united in their defense, let them be intended rather to favor every individual than any particular classes of men; let the laws be feared, and the laws only. The fear of the laws is salutary, but the fear of men is a fruitful and fatal source of crimes.

Consider This:

- What mathematical equation did Cesare Beccaria apply to "the good and evil of life"? Would the sentence of "an eye for an eye" be a just punishment in Beccaria's view? How do you think he might have reacted to our modern concern over capital punishment? Ultimately, how does a society prevent crime?

The Broader Perspective:

- The torture of prisoners by American military forces at Guantanamo Bay or by CIA officials in so-called Black Camps located in Eastern European countries has been a controversial product of the "war on terror." Although decrying extreme abuse as was evidenced at the Abu Ghraib prison in Iraq, the Bush administration has defended the use of torture in principle as essential in extracting information that may make the United States more secure against future attacks. How does this square with Beccaria's vision of just laws equitably and inevitably enforced? Must Beccaria's principles apply only to domestic laws over citizens? Has the world changed so much that Enlightenment principles no longer apply?

What Is Enlightenment? (1784)

IMMANUEL KANT

Immanuel Kant (1724–1804) was a German philosopher whose comprehensive and systematic work in the theory of knowledge, ethics, and aesthetics greatly influenced subsequent philosophy. Kant's entire life was spent in Königsberg, where he

"What Is Enlightenment?" is from Immanuel Kant, *Foundations of the Metaphysics of Morals, What is Enlightenment?*, 2nd ed., trans. and ed. Lewis White Beck (New York: Macmillan Publishing Company), pp. 83–85, 88.

was educated and served as a popular teacher and lecturer at the local university. In his writings, he hoped to avoid the confusion of earlier thinkers by examining the possibilities and limitations of applied reason. He sought to accept the rationalism of the Enlightenment while still preserving a belief in human freedom, immortality, and the existence of God. In fact, Kant found the world open to pure reason to be quite limited and postulated a sphere of moral reality known only by "practical reason and conscience." Although he hoped to raise philosophy to the level of a science, he believed that all things could not be proved by discursive reasoning—God and eternal life among them.

In the following selection, Kant seeks to define the Enlightenment by empowering the individual to break away from a somnolent dependence, toward an active intellectual existence. Only through such personal initiative could one attain true enlightenment.

Enlightenment is man's release from his self-incurred tutelage. Tutelage is man's inability to make use of his understanding without direction from another. Self-incurred is this tutelage when its cause lies not in lack of reason but in lack of resolution and courage to use it without direction from another. Dare to Know! Have courage to use your own reason!—that is the motto of enlightenment.

Laziness and cowardice are the reasons why so great a portion of mankind, after nature has long since discharged them from external direction, nevertheless remains under lifelong tutelage, and why it is so easy for others to set themselves up as their guardians. It is so easy not to be of age. If I have a book which understands for me, a pastor who has a conscience for me, a physician who decides my diet, and so forth, I need not trouble myself. I need not think, if I can only pay—others will readily undertake the irksome work for me.

That the step to competence is held to be very dangerous by the far greater portion of mankind (and by the entire fair sex)—quite apart from its being arduous—is seen to by those guardians who have so kindly assumed superintendence over them. After the guardians have first made their domestic cattle dumb and have made sure that these placid creatures will not dare take a single step without the harness of the cart to which they are confined, the guardians then show them the danger which threatens if they try to go alone. Actually, however, this danger is not so great, for by falling a few times they would finally learn to walk alone. But an example of this failure makes them timid and ordinarily frightens them away from all further trials.

For any single individual to work himself out of the life under tutelage which has become almost his nature is very difficult. He has come to be fond of this state, and he is for the present really incapable of making use of his reason, for no one has ever let him try it out. Statutes and formulas, those mechanical tools of the rational employment or rather misemployment of his natural gifts, are the fetters of an everlasting tutelage. Whoever throws them off makes only an uncertain leap over the narrowest ditch because he is not accustomed to that kind of free motion. Therefore, there are only few who have succeeded by their own exercise of mind both in freeing themselves from incompetence and in achieving a steady pace.

But that the public should enlighten itself is more possible; indeed, if only freedom is granted, enlightenment is almost sure to follow. For there will always be some independent thinkers, even among the established guardians of the great masses, who, after throwing off the yoke of tutelage from their own shoulders, will disseminate the spirit of the rational appreciation of both their own worth and every man's vocation for thinking for himself. . . .

For this enlightenment, however, nothing is required but freedom, and indeed the most harmless among all the things to which this term can properly be applied. It is the freedom to make public use of one's reason at every point. But I hear on all sides, "Do not argue!" The officer says: "Do not argue but drill!" The tax collector: "Do not argue but pay!" The cleric: "Do not argue but believe!" Only one prince in the world [Frederick the Great of Prussia] says, "Argue as much as you will, and about what you will, but obey!" Everywhere there is restriction on freedom. . . .

If we are asked, "Do we now live in an enlightened age?" the answer is, "No," but we do live in an age of enlightenment. As things now stand, much is lacking which prevents men from being, or easily becoming, capable of correctly using their own reason in religious matters with assurance and free from outside direction. But, on the other hand, we have clear indications that the field has now been opened wherein men may freely deal with these things and that the obstacles to general enlightenment or the release from self-imposed tutelage are gradually being reduced. In this respect, this is the age of enlightenment, or the century of Frederick.

Consider This:

- How does Immanuel Kant answer the question "What is Enlightenment?" In what ways do you see his views on freedom and risk in evidence throughout this chapter? Select four other thinkers and demonstrate specifically how Kant's attitude applies to the tenor of their writings.

Thoughts on Religion

God—"A Cause Contradicted by Its Effects": Common Sense (1770)

BARON D'HOLBACH

Paul-Henri Dietrich, Baron d'Holbach (1723–1789), was a naturalized French citizen who was best known for his radical atheism. Some of the most esteemed and even the more radicalized of the philosophes, including d'Alembert and Rousseau, reportedly withdrew from his gatherings, frightened by the audacity of their speculations. A major contributor of over 375 articles on chemistry and related topics to Diderot's *Encyclopedia*, Holbach held views on atheism that represent an extreme in the critical analysis of the Age of Reason.

Morality and virtue are totally incompatible with the idea of a God, whose ministers and interpreters have painted him in all countries as the most fantastic, the most unjust, and the most cruel of tyrants, whose pretended wishes are to serve as rules and laws for the inhabitants of the earth. To discover the true principles of morality, men have no need of theology, of revelation, or of Gods; they need but common sense; they have only to look within themselves, to reflect upon their own nature, to consult their obvious interests, to consider the object of society and of each of the members who compose it, and they will easily understand that virtue is an advantage, and that vice is an injury to beings of their species.

By metaphysics, God is made a pure spirit, but has modern theology advanced one step

"God—'A Cause Contradicted by Its Effects'" is from Baron d'Holbach, *Common Sense*, trans. Anna Knoop (New York: Miss A. Knoop, 1884), pp. 43, 55–56, 63–65, 69–70.

further than the theology of the barbarians? They recognized a grand spirit as master of the world. The barbarians, like all ignorant men, attribute to spirits all the effects of which their inexperience prevents them from discovering the true causes. Ask a barbarian what causes your watch to move, he will answer, "a spirit!" Ask our philosophers what moves the universe, they will tell you "it is a spirit."

Is it not more natural and more intelligible to deduce all which exists, from the bosom of matter, whose existence is demonstrated by all our senses, whose effects we feel at every moment, which we see act, move, communicate, motion, and constantly bring living beings into existence, than to attribute the formation of things to an unknown force, to a spiritual being, who cannot draw from his ground that which he has not himself, and who, by the spiritual essence claimed for him, is incapable of making anything, and of putting anything in motion?

We are assured that the wonders of nature are sufficient to a belief in the existence of a God, and to convince us fully of this important truth. . . . The unprejudiced philosopher sees nothing in the wonders of nature but permanent and invariable law; nothing but the necessary effects of different combinations of diversified substance.

Whence comes man? What is his origin? Is he the result of the fortuitous meeting of atoms? Was the first man formed of the dust of the earth? I do not know! Man appears to me to be a production of nature like all others she embraces. I should be just as much embarrassed to tell you whence came the first stones, the first trees, the first elephants, the first ants, the first acorns, as to explain the origin of the human species. Recognize, we are told, the hand of God, of an infinitely intelligent and powerful workman, in a work so wonderful as the human machine. I would admit without question that the human machine appears to me surprising; but since man exists in nature, I do not believe it right to say that his formation is beyond the forces of nature. . . . I see that this admirable machine is subject to derangement; that at that time this wonderful intelligence is disordered, and sometimes totally disappears; from this I conclude that human intelligence depends upon a certain disposition of the material organs of the body, and that, because man is an intelligent being, it is not well to conclude that God must be an intelligent being, any more than because man is material, we are compelled to conclude that God is material. The intelligence of man no more proves the intelligence of God than the malice of men proves the malice of this God, of whom they pretend that man is the work. In whatever way theology is taken, God will always be a cause contradicted by its effects, or of whom it is impossible to judge by His works. We shall always see evil, imperfections, and follies resulting from a cause claimed to be full of goodness, or perfections, and of wisdom.

CONSIDER THIS:

- After carefully scrutinizing the arguments of Baron d'Holbach, does his atheism seem well supported by his argument? What does he mean by denoting God as "a cause contradicted by its effects"?

On Universal Toleration

VOLTAIRE

The Enlightenment is often characterized as an era of empirical reasoning and critical thought, of doubt and skepticism, of individual assertion at the expense of formal

"On Universal Toleration," is from Tobias Smollett, ed., *The Works of Voltaire* (London: E. R. DuMont, 1901), vol. 4, pp. 272–273, 275–276, 278. Text modernized by the editor.

control by the state or church. For the most part, this is a fair assessment. God, if he existed, was prone to be antiseptic, the "great clock-winder," who created the universe and then sat back, uninvolved in the lives of his creations. This philosophy, called *deism*, generally prevailed among the philosophes. It did not deny the existence of God, but it gave virtually no support to organized religion. The deists particularly denounced the mysteries of the Christian religion, such as the Trinity, and miracles like the Virgin Birth and the Eucharist. Because God was disinterested in the affairs of the world, formal prayers were useless. Deism enabled many of the philosophes to effect a reconciliation between a perfect God and an imperfect world.

Voltaire was the quintessential personality of the Enlightenment. An author of dramas, histories, and scathing satires, his wit and intellectual power dominated the age. Voltaire adamantly opposed organized religion, but he enthusiastically advocated religious toleration and the deist viewpoint. The first selection is from his famous *Treatise on Toleration*. In the letter that follows, Voltaire argues for the logic and necessity of a supreme deity. His ideas are generally representative of the enlightened thinkers of the age.

It does not require any great art or studied elocution to prove that Christians ought to tolerate one another. Nay, I shall go still farther and say that we ought to look upon all men as our brethren. How! Call a Turk, a Jew, and a Siamese, my brother? Yes, doubtless; for are we not all children of the same parent, and the creatures of the same Creator?

But these people hold us in contempt, and call us idolaters! Well, then, I should tell them that they were to blame. And I fancy that I could stagger the headstrong pride of an imam, or a talapoin [religious leaders], were I to address them in the following manner:

"This little globe, which is no more than a point, rolls, together with many other globes, in that immensity of space in which we are all alike confounded. Man, who is an animal, about five feet high, is certainly a very inconsiderable part of the creation; but one of those hardly visible beings says to others of the same kind inhabiting another spot of the globe: Hearken to me, for the God of all these worlds has enlightened me. There are about nine hundred millions of us little insects who inhabit the earth, but my ant-hill is alone cherished by God, who holds all the rest in horror and detestation; those who live with me upon my spot will alone be happy, and all the rest eternally wretched."

They would here stop me short and ask, "What madman could have made so ridiculous a speech?" I should then be obliged to answer them, "It is yourselves." . . .

O you different worshiper of a God of mercy! If you have cruel hearts, if, while you adore that Deity who has placed the whole of His law in these few words, "Love god and you neighbor," you have loaded that pure and holy law with sophistical and unintelligible disputes, if you have lighted the flames of discord sometimes for a new word, and at others for a single letter only; if you have annexed eternal punishment to the omission of some few words, or of certain ceremonies which other people cannot comprehend, I must say to you with tears of compassion for mankind: "Transport yourselves with me to that great instant in which all men are to receive judgment from the hand of God, who will then do unto every one according to their works, and with me behold all the dead of past ages appearing in His presence. Are you very sure that our heavenly Father and Creator will say to the wise and virtuous Confucius, to the great legislator Solon, to Pythagoras, Socrates, Plato, the divine Antoninus, the good Trajan, to Titus, the delight of humankind, and to may others who have been the models of humankind: 'Depart from me, wretches! into torments that know neither alleviation nor end; but are, like Himself, everlasting.'"

I think I see you start with horror at these words. . . .

May all men remember that they are brethren! May they alike abhor that tyranny which seeks to subject the freedom of the will, as they do the rapine which tears from the arms of industry the fruits of its peaceful labors! And if the scourge of war is not to be avoided, let us not mutually hate and destroy each other in the midst of peace; but rather make use of the few moments of our existence to join in praising, in a thousand different languages, from one extremity of the world to the other, Thy goodness, O all-merciful Creator, to whom we are indebted for that existence!

"If God Did Not Exist, He Would Have to Be Invented"

VOLTAIRE

To Frederick William, Prince of Prussia:

Monseigneur, the royal family of Prussia has excellent reasons for not wishing the annihilation of the soul. It has more right than anyone to immortality.

It is very true that we do not know any too well what the soul is: no one has ever seen it. All that we do know is that the eternal Lord of nature has given us the power of thinking, and of distinguishing virtue. It is not proved that this faculty survives our death: but the contrary is not proved either. It is possible, doubtless, that God has given thought to a particle to which, after we are no more, He will still give the power of thought: there is no inconsistency in this idea.

In the midst of all the doubts which we have discussed for four thousand years in four thousand ways, the safest course is to do nothing against one's conscience. With this secret, we can enjoy life and have nothing to fear from death.

There are some charlatans who admit no doubts. We know nothing of first principles. It is surely very presumptuous to define God, the angels, spirits, and to pretend to know precisely why God made the world, when we do not know why we can move our arms at our pleasure. Doubt is not a pleasant condition, but certainty is an absurd one.

What is most repellent in the System of Nature [by the Baron d'Holbach] . . . is the audacity with which it decides that there is no God, without even having tried to prove the impossibility. There is some eloquence in the book: but much more rant, and no sort of proof. It is a pernicious work, alike for princes and people: "Si Dieu n'existait pas, il faudrait l'inventer." [If God did not exist, he would have to be invented].

But all nature cries aloud that He does exist: that there is a supreme intelligence, an immense power, an admirable order, and everything teaches us our own dependence on it.

From the depth of our profound ignorance, let us do our best: this is what I think, and what I have always thought, amid all the misery and follies inseparable from seventy-seven years of life. . . . I am, with deep respect, Voltaire

COMPARE AND CONTRAST:

- Why was toleration so important to Voltaire? Do you regard him as a religious person? Why is deism a comfortable philosophy? Are you persuaded by Voltaire's arguments in opposition to the Baron d'Holbach as expressed in his letter to Frederick William of Prussia?

"'If God Did Not Exist, He Would Have to Be Invented,'" is from S. G. Tallentyre, trans., *Voltaire in His Letters* (New York: G. P. Putnam's Sons, 1919).

Thoughts on Education

Introduction to the Encyclopedia (1751)

JEAN LE ROND D'ALEMBERT

One of the most ambitious and dramatic accomplishments of the Enlightenment was the publication of the *Encyclopedia*, a work of twenty-one volumes of text, twelve of plates illustrating the trades and mechanical arts, and two of index. The aim of the work was to provide a summary of human knowledge—a task that had been attempted before on a smaller scale but with uneven and disappointing results.

The mind-set and guiding influence behind the *Encyclopedia* was a young little known journalist named Denis Diderot (1713–1784). Together with the renowned mathematician Jean Le Rond d'Alembert, he directed the project from the publication of the first volume in 1745 to its completion thirty-five years later in 1780. Diderot solicited the most accomplished scholars of the age to contribute articles on their research and to offer theories and opinions on a wide variety of topics. The task of distillation and compilation was formidable, and Diderot was constantly engaged in disputes with scholars, publishers, and the Catholic church in bringing the project to its remarkable conclusion. Apart from the impressive body of knowledge contained in the *Encyclopedia*, it stands as the quintessential expression of the ideals and attitudes of the Enlightenment. The first excerpt is from the introduction to the first volume. The second passage recounts the dedication of Diderot in overcoming opposition to his grand project.

The *Encyclopedia* is, as its title proclaims, the work of a company of men of letters. Were we not one of them, we might venture to claim that they have, or are worthy of having, a good reputation. But without wishing to anticipate a judgment which scholars alone may form, it is at least our duty to set aside, before everything else, the objection most capable of prejudicing the success of such a vast enterprise. We declare, therefore, that we have by no means had the temerity to take upon ourselves alone a burden so far beyond our capabilities, and that our role as editors consists principally in putting in order materials of which the greater part was supplied to us. . . .

The work which we are beginning (and wish to complete) has two aims: as an encyclopedia, its purpose is to set forth, as well as possible, the order and continuity of human knowledge; as an analytical dictionary of the arts, the sciences, and the professions, its purpose is to contain, for each science and each art, whether liberal or mechanical, the general principles on which it is based and the most essential details which make up its body and substance. These two points of view, of encyclopedia and of analytical dictionary, will therefore dictate the outline and the division of this preliminary discourse. We will consider them, pursue them one after the other, and report on the means by which we have attempted to satisfy this double aim.

If one has ever reflected at all on the connections between discoveries, it is easy to realize that the arts and sciences lend each other mutual assistance that there is consequently a chain which joins them. But it is often difficult to reduce to a small number of rules or general

"Introduction to the Encyclopedia" is from Nina B. Gunzenhauser, trans., in *Major Crises in Western Civilization*, vol. 2 (New York: Harcourt Brace and World, 1965), pp. 13–14.

ideas each particular science or art; it is no less difficult to enclose in a unified system the infinitely varied branches of human knowledge.

The first step we have to take in this research is to examine . . . the genealogy of our knowledge and the relationships within it, the causes which must have led to its birth and the nature that distinguishes it—in brief, to go back to the origin and generation of our ideas. Aside from the benefits we will reap from examining this encyclopedic enumeration of the arts and sciences, this will not be out of place at the head of an analytical dictionary of human knowledge.

We can divide all our knowledge into direct knowledge and reasoned knowledge. Direct knowledge is that which we receive immediately without an operation of our will, which finding open . . . all of the doors of our soul, enters it without resistance and without effort. Reasoned knowledge is that which the mind acquires in operating on direct knowledge, in uniting and combining it.

All of our direct knowledge can be reduced to that which we receive through the senses; from which it follows that we owe all our ideas to our sensations. The system of innate ideas, tempting in many respects . . . after having reigned for a long time [still] has some partisans; with such difficulty does truth [gain] its place. . . . At last, quite recently, there has been almost universal consensus that [innate ideas do not exist].

"We Did Not Live Entirely in Vain" (1764)

DENIS DIDEROT

The public has judged the first seven volumes; we ask for the current batch only the same indulgence. . . . From the point where we started to the point we have reached the distance was tremendous. . . . Thanks to our labor, those who come after us will be able to go further. Without declaring what they have yet to do, we will turn over to them at least the best book on tools and machines that ever existed . . . and an infinite number of precious morsels concerning all the sciences. O compatriots and contemporaries! With whatever severity you judge this work, remember that it was undertaken, continued, completed by a small number of isolated men, thwarted in their views, shown in the worst light, slandered and insulted in the most atrocious manner, having no other encouragement than the love of the good, no other support than several commendations, no other help but that which they found in the confidence of three or four tradesmen!

Our main purpose was to collect the discoveries of preceding centuries. . . . Should a revolution, the germ of which is forming perhaps in some unknown canton of the earth or incubating secretly in the very center of the civilized world, break out in time, destroy the cities, scatter the nations once again, and bring back ignorance and darkness; if one single complete set of this work survives, all will not be lost.

At least it cannot be contested, I think, that our work is on a level with our century, and that is something. The most enlightened man will find in it ideas that were unfamiliar to him and facts he did not know. If only general education could advance at such a rapid rate that twenty years from now there would be, out of a thousand of our pages, scarcely a single line that was not popular knowledge! It is up to the rulers of the world to hasten that happy revolution; it is they who expand or contract

" 'We Did Not Live Entirely in Vain' " is from Nina B. Gunzenhauser, trans., in *Major Crises in Western Civilization*, vol. 2 (New York: Harcourt Brace and World, 1965), pp. 35–37.

the sphere of enlightenment. Happy the time when they will all have understood that their security consists in commanding educated men! The major crimes have never been attempted by any except blinded fanatics. . . . [We hope that] we led our fellow men to love each other, to tolerate each other and to recognize at last the superiority of universal ethics over all the particular morals that inspire hatred and disorder and that break or relax the general and common bond. Such was our aim throughout. . . .

If one adds to the years of our life that had passed at the time we planned this work those we have given to its accomplishment, one will easily realize that we have lived more years than we have left. But we shall have received the compensation that we look for from our contemporaries and our descendants if we make them say one day that we did not live entirely in vain.

CONSIDER THIS:

- Why did Denis Diderot think his *Encyclopedia* necessary and reflective of the age of Enlightenment? What was the method that Diderot employed in obtaining articles for the *Encyclopedia*? According to d'Alembert, what were the aims of the *Encyclopedia*? What is the difference between reasoned knowledge and direct knowledge?

- In the selection "We Did Not Live Entirely in Vain," Diderot expressed some of the general attitudes of the Enlightenment. He mentions the topics of toleration, education, progress, and ethics. Choose the specific writers and documents from this chapter that best represent Diderot's generalized comments. Defend your choices.

Thoughts on Government: The Political Framework

Second Treatise of Civil Government (1690)

JOHN LOCKE

The following selection presents a theoretical foundation for the political structure of human society and presents a justification for the elimination of absolute monarchy. John Locke (1632–1704) was an English political philosopher whose *Second Treatise of Civil Government* (1690) later influenced both the French and American revolutions. It is also the first philosophical statement of liberalism, a doctrine that sought the limitation of the arbitrary power of government and the establishment of legal equality, religious toleration, and freedom of the press.

Political power, then, I take to be a right of making laws with penalties of death, and consequently all less penalties, for the regulating and preserving of property, and of employing the force of the community, in the execution of such laws, and in the defence of the commonwealth from foreign injury; and all this only for the public good.

Chapter II: Of the State of Nature

To understand political power right, and derive it from its original, we must consider what state all men are naturally in, and that is, a state of perfect freedom to order their actions and dispose of their possessions and persons, as they think fit, within the bounds of the law of

"*Second Treatise of Civil Government*" is from John Locke, *The Treatises of Government* (London, 1694).

nature; without asking leave, or depending upon the will of any other man.

A state also of equality, wherein all the power and jurisdiction is reciprocal, no one having more than another; there being nothing more evident, than that creatures of the same species and rank, promiscuously born to all the same advantages of nature, and the use of the same faculties, should also be equal one amongst another without subordination or subjection; unless the lord and master of them all should, by any manifest declaration of his will, set one above another, and confer on him, by an evident and clear appointment, an undoubted right to dominion and sovereignty. . . .

But though this be a state of liberty, yet it is not a state of license: though man in that state has an uncontrollable liberty to dispose of his person or possessions, yet he has not liberty to destroy himself, or so much as any creature in his possession, but where some nobler use than its bare preservation call for it. The state of nature has a law of nature to govern it, which obliges every one: and reason, which is that law, teaches all mankind, who will but consult it, that being equal and independent, no one ought to harm another in his life, health, liberty, or possessions: for men being all the workmanship of one omnipotent and infinitely wise Maker; all the servants of one sovereign master, sent into the world by his order, and about his business; they are his property, whose workmanship they are, made to last during his, not another's pleasure: and being furnished with like faculties, sharing all in one community of nature, there cannot be supposed any such subordination among us, that may authorize us to destroy another, as if we were made for one another's uses, as the inferior ranks of creatures are for ours. Every one, as he is bound to preserve himself, . . . ought he, as much as he can, to preserve the rest of mankind, and may not, unless it be to do justice to an offender, take away or impair the life, or what tends to the preservation of life, the liberty, health, limb, or goods of another.

And that all men may be restrained from invading others's rights, and from doing hurt to one another, and the law of nature be observed, which willeth the peace and preservation of all mankind, the execution of the law of nature is, in that state, put into every man's hands, whereby every one has a right to punish the transgressors of that law to such a degree as may hinder its violation: for the law of nature would, as all other laws that concern men in this world, be in vain, if there were nobody that in the state of nature had a power to execute the law, and thereby preserve the innocent and restrain offenders. . . . And thus, in the state of nature, "one man comes by a power over another"; but yet this is not an absolute or arbitrary power. . . .

Chapter III: Of the State of War

[It is reasonable and just that . . .] I should have a right to destroy that which threatens me with destruction; for, by the fundamental law of nature, man being to be preserved as much as possible, when all cannot be preserved, the safety of the innocent is to be preferred: and one may destroy a man who makes war upon him, or has discovered an enmity to his being, for the same reason that he may kill a wolf or a lion; because such men are not under the ties of the common law of reason, have no other rule, than that of force and violence, and so may be treated as beasts of prey, those dangerous and noxious creatures, that will be sure to destroy him whenever he falls into their power.

And hence it is, that he who attempts to get another man into his absolute power, does thereby put himself into a state of war with him; it being to be understood as a declaration of a design upon his life: for I have reason to conclude, that he who would get me into his power without my consent, would use me as he pleased when he got me there, and destroy me too when he had a fancy to it; for nobody can desire to have me in his absolute power, unless it be to compel me by force to that which is against the right of my freedom, i.e., make me a slave. To be free from such force is the only security of my preservation; and reason bids me look on him, as an enemy to my preservation, who would take away that freedom which is the fence to it; so that he who makes an attempt to enslave me, thereby puts himself into a state of war with me. He that, in the state of nature, would take away the freedom that belongs to any one in that state, must necessarily be supposed to have a design to take away everything else, that freedom being the foundation of all the rest; as he that, in the state of society, would take away the freedom belonging to those of that society or commonwealth, must be supposed to design to take away from them every thing else, and so be looked on as in a state of war. . . .

Chapter IV: Of Slavery

The natural liberty of man is to be free from any superior power on earth, and not to be under the will or legislative authority of man, but to have only the law of nature for his rule. The liberty of man, in society, is to be under no other legislative power, but that established, by consent, in the commonwealth; nor under the dominion of any will, or restraint of any law, but what that legislative shall enact, according to the trust put in it. Freedom then is not what Sir Robert Filmer tells us, "a liberty for every one to do what he lists, to live as he pleases, and not to be tied by any laws": but freedom of men under government is, to have a standing rule to live by, common to every one of that society, and made by the legislative power erected in it; a liberty to follow my own will in all things, where the rule prescribes not; and not to be subject to the inconstant, uncertain, unknown, arbitrary will of another man: as freedom of nature is, to be under any other restraint but the law of nature.

This freedom from absolute, arbitrary power, is so necessary to, and closely joined with a man's preservation, that he cannot part with it, but by what forfeits his preservation and life together.

Chapter VIII: Of the Beginning of Political Societies

Men being, as has been said by nature, all free, equal, and independent, no one can be put out of this estate, and subjected to the political power of another, without his own consent. The only way, whereby any one divests himself of his natural liberty, and puts on the bonds of civil society, is by agreeing with other men to join and unite into a community, for their comfortable, safe, and peaceable living one amongst another, in a secure enjoyment of their properties, and a greater security against any, that are not of it. This any number of men may do, because it injures not the freedom of the rest; they are left as they were in the liberty of the state of nature. When any number of men have so consented to make one community or government they are thereby presently incorporated, and make one body politic, wherein the majority have a right to act and conclude the rest. . . .

And thus every man, by consenting with others to make one body politic under one government, puts himself under an obligation, to every one of that society, to submit to the determination of the majority, and to be concluded by it; or else this original compact, whereby he with others incorporate into one society, would signify nothing, and be no compact, if he be left free, and under no other ties than he was in before in the state of nature.

Chapter XV: Of Despotical Power

Despotical power is an absolute, arbitrary power one man has over another, to take away his life whenever he pleases; and this is a power which neither Nature gives, for it has made no such distinction between one man and another, nor compact can convey. . . . For having quitted reason, which God has given to be the rule betwixt man and man, and the peaceable ways which that teaches, and made use of force to compass his unjust ends upon another where he has no right, he renders himself liable to be destroyed by his adversary whenever he can, as any other noxious and brutish creature that is destructive to his being. . . .

Chapter XIX: Of the Dissolution of Government

The reason why men enter into society, is the preservation of their property; and the end why they choose and authorize a legislative, is, that there may be laws made, and rules set, as guards and fences to the properties of all the members of the society: to limit the power, and moderate the dominion, of every part and member of the society: for since it can never be supposed to be the will of the society, that the legislative should have a power to destroy that which every one designs to secure by entering into society, and for which the people submitted themselves to legislators of their own making; whenever the legislators endeavour to take away and destroy the property of the people, or to reduce them to slavery under arbitrary power, they put themselves into a state of war with the people, who are thereupon absolved from any farther obedience, and are left to the common refuge, which God hath provided for all men, against force and violence. Whensoever therefore the legislative shall transgress this fundamental rule of society; and either by ambition, fear, folly or corruption, endeavour to grasp themselves, or put into the hands of any other, an absolute power over the lives, liberties, and estates of the people, by this breach of trust they forfeit the power the people had put into their hands for quite contrary ends, and it devolves to the people, who have a right to resume their original liberty, and, by the establishment of a new legislative, (such as they shall think fit) provide for their own safety and security, which is the end for which they are in society. What I have said here, concerning the legislative in general holds true also concerning the supreme executor, who having a double trust put in him, both to have a part in the legislative, and the supreme execution of the law, acts against both, when he goes about to set up his own arbitrary will as the law of the society. . . .

Whosoever uses force without right, as every one does in society, who does it without law, puts himself into a state of war with those against whom he so used it; and in that state all former ties are cancelled, all other rights cease, and every one has a right to defend himself, and to resist the aggressor.

CONSIDER THIS:

- How does Locke define a "state of equality"? Why is the state of liberty not a state of license? What principle governs the natural world and allows human beings to live together?
- According to Locke, under what circumstances is it legitimate for members of society to dissolve the contract that binds citizens to their government?

COMPARE AND CONTRAST:

- Compare John Locke's conception of the equality of human beings in a "state of nature" with that of Thomas Hobbes in *Leviathan* (1651). What was Hobbes's solution to controlling human excesses?
- Both Hobbes and Locke believed that human beings are equal in their original freedom, but Hobbes saw storm clouds and Locke saw light. Why were their visions so different?

THE BROADER PERSPECTIVE:

- To what extent did Thomas Jefferson employ John Locke's arguments in justifying American rebellion against British authority in the Declaration of Independence (1776)?

The Spirit of the Laws (1748)

BARON DE MONTESQUIEU

Baron de Montesquieu (1689–1755) was one of the most penetrating political analysts of his age. This selection from *The Spirit of the Laws* was published in 1748, about forty years before the French Revolution broke out.

When the legislative and executive powers are united in the same person, or in the same body of magistrates, there can be no liberty; because apprehensions may arise lest the same monarch or senate should enact tyrannical laws to execute them in a tyrannical manner.

Again there is no liberty if the power of judging be not separated from the legislative and executive powers. Were it joined with the legislature, the life and liberty of the subject would be exposed to arbitrary control; for the judge would be then the legislator. Were it joined to the executive power, the judge might behave with all the violence of an oppressor.

There would be an end of everything were the same man or the same body, whether of the nobles or of the people, to exercise those three powers, that of enacting the laws, that of executing the public resolutions, and that of judging the crimes or differences of individuals.

Most kingdoms of Europe enjoy a moderate government because the prince who is invested with the two first powers leaves the third to his subjects. In Turkey, where these three powers are united in the sultan's person, the subjects groan under the weight of the most frightful oppression.

In the republics of Italy, where these three powers are united, there is less liberty than in our monarchies. Hence their government is obliged to have recourse to as violent methods for its support as even that of the Turks; witness the state inquisitors (at Venice), and the lion's mouth into which every informer may at all hours throw his written accusations.

What a situation must the poor subjects be in, under those republics! The same body of magistrates are possessed, as executors of the laws, of the whole power they have given themselves in quality of legislators. They may plunder the state by their general determination, and as they have likewise the judiciary power in their hands, every private citizen may be ruined by their particular decisions.

The whole power is here united in one body; and though there is no external pomp that indicates a despotic sway, yet the people feel the effects of it every moment.

Hence it is that many of the princes of Europe, whose aim has been levelled at arbitrary power, have constantly set out with uniting in their own persons all the branches of magistracy, and all the great offices of the state.

Consider This:

- Montesquieu harbored a great fear of "arbitrary power" through which political leaders "may plunder the state." How did he propose to solve this problem through the structure of government?

The Broader Perspective:

- How did Montesquieu's ideas influence the structure of the Constitution of the United States?

"*The Spirit of the Laws*" is from Baron de Montesquieu (Charles de Secondat), *The Spirit of the Laws*, 2 vols. (London, 1758), pp. 216–217.

The Social Contract (1762)

JEAN-JACQUES ROUSSEAU

The last selection in this section is from *The Social Contract* (1762) by Jean-Jacques Rousseau (1712–1778). Although Rousseau spent much of his life in intimate contact with the philosophes, he rejected their attitude that the human being is a rational creature whose confidence in reason would result in liberty and equality. Rousseau advocated the elimination of political despotism and the introduction of a new social order in which only the authority of the "general will" of the governed placed limits on individual freedom. His ideas provided the most inspirational justification for revolutionary action during the eighteenth century.

We will suppose that men in a state of nature are arrived at that crisis when the strength of each individual is insufficient to defend him from the attacks he is subject to. This primitive state can therefore subsist no longer; and the human race must perish, unless they change their manner of life.

As men cannot create for themselves new forces, but merely unite and direct those which already exist, the only means they can employ for the preservation is to form by aggregation an assemblage of forces that may be able to resist all assaults, be put in motion as one body, and act in concert upon all occasions.

This assemblage of forces must be produced by the concurrence of many: as the force and the liberty of a man are the chief instruments of his preservation, how can he engage them without danger, and without neglecting the care which is due to himself? This doubt, which leads directly to my subject, may be expressed in these words:

Where shall we find a form of association which will defend and protect with the whole aggregate force the person and the property of each individual; and by which every person, while united with ALL, shall obey only HIMSELF, and remain as free as before the union? Such is the fundamental problem, of which the Social Contract gives the solution.

The articles of this contract are so unalterably fixed by the nature of the act, that the least modification renders them vain and of no effect. They are the same everywhere, and are everywhere understood and admitted, even though they may never have been formally announced: so that, when once the social pact is violated in any instance, all obligations it created cease; and each individual is restored to his original rights, and resumes native liberty, as the consequence of losing that conventional liberty for which he exchanged them.

All the articles of the social contract will, when clearly understood, be found reducible to this single point—THE TOTAL ALIENATION OF EACH ASSOCIATE, AND ALL HIS RIGHTS, TO THE WHOLE COMMUNITY. For every individual gives himself up entirely—the condition of every person is alike; and being so, it would not be the interest of anyone to render himself offensive to others.

Moreover, the alienation is made without any reserve; the union is as complete as it can be, and no associate has a claim to anything; for if any individual was to retain rights not enjoyed in general by all, as there would be no common superior to decide between him and the public, each person being in some points his own proper judge, would soon pretend to be so in everything; and thus would the state of nature be revived, and the association become tyrannical or be annihilated.

Finally, each person gives himself to ALL, but not to any INDIVIDUAL: and as there is

"*The Social Contract*" is from Jean-Jacques Rousseau, *An Inquiry into the Nature of the Social Contract* (London, 1791), pp. 33–49.

FIGURE 4.1 Jean-Jacques Rousseau brilliantly challenged the established thought of his day and even alienated several *philosophes*. He outlined a political structure that he hoped would nurture human virtue. (*Library of Congress*)

no one associate over whom the same right is not acquired which is ceded to him by others, each gains an equivalent for what he loses, and finds his force increased for preserving that which he possesses.

If, therefore, we exclude from the social compact all that is not essentially necessary, we shall find it reduced to the following terms:

"We each of us place, in common, his person, and all his power, under the supreme direction of the general will; and we receive into the body each member as an indivisible part of the whole."

From that moment, instead of so many separate persons as there are contractors, this act of association produces a moral collective body, composed of as many members as there are voices in the assembly; which from this act receives its unity, its common self, its life, and its will. This public person, which is thus formed by the union of all the private persons, took formerly the name of city, and now takes that of republic or body politic. It is called by its members state when it is passive, and sovereign when in activity: and whenever it is spoken of with other bodies of a similar kind, it is denominated power. The associates take collectively the name of people, and separately that of citizens, as participating in the sovereign authority: they are also styled subjects, because they are subjected to the laws. But these terms are frequently confounded, and used one for the other; and a man must understand them well to distinguish when they are properly employed. . . .

In fact, each individual may, as a man, have a private will, dissimilar contrary to the general will which he has as a citizen. His own particular interest may dictate to him very differently from the common interest; his mind, naturally and absolutely independent, may regard what he owes to the common cause as a gratuitous contribution, the omission of which would be less injurious to others than the payment would be burdensome to himself; and considering the moral person which constitutes the state as a creature of the imagination, because it is not a man, he may wish to enjoy the rights of a citizen, without being disposed to fulfill the duties of a subject: an injustice which would in its progress cause the ruin of the body politic.

In order therefore to prevent the social compact from becoming an empty formula, it tacitly includes this premise, which alone can give effect to the others—That whoever refuses to obey the general will, shall be compelled to it by the whole body, which is in fact only forcing him to be free; for this is the condition which guarantees his absolute personal independence to every citizen of the country: a condition which gives motion and effect to the political machine; which alone renders all civil engagements legal; and without which they would be absurd, tyrannical, and subject to the most enormous abuses.

CONSIDER THIS:

- What are the arguments used by Locke, Montesquieu, and Rousseau to justify revolution? Who or what is the "sovereign power" Rousseau mentions? Comment in particular on Rousseau's belief that "whoever refuses to obey the general will shall be compelled to it by the whole body." Isn't this a form of tyranny?

THE BROADER PERSPECTIVE:

- To be enduring, must revolutions have an intellectual foundation that inspires and legitimatizes radical, even violent action? Must they have some philosophical justification or is the spark or precipitating act that sets a revolution in motion enough to sustain the movement?

THEME: THE INDIVIDUAL AND THE INSTITUTION

THE REFLECTION IN THE MIRROR

The African Slave Trade

"A Whole Scene of Horror Almost Inconceivable"

OLAUDAH EQUIANO

Olaudah Equiano (1745?–1797) was captured at age eleven from his home in the southern Benin region of Nigeria. He was taken to Barbados in 1756 and sold to a British naval officer in Virginia who took him to England as his servant. In his remarkable life, Equiano was sold again to West Indies slavers and finally bought by Robert King, a Quaker merchant from Philadelphia, who allowed Equiano to engage in petty trade while he served as an assistant to one of his captains in the Caribbean. Equiano finally purchased his freedom in 1766.

In these memoirs written in 1789, Equiano describes the brutal "middle passage" across the Atlantic and the auction itself in Barbados. Equiano was actively engaged in the antislavery movement in England and petitioned Queen Victoria to bring the slave trade to an end.

"A Whole Scene of Horror Almost Inconceivable" is from Olaudah Equiano, *The Interesting Narrative of Olaudah Equiano, or Gustavus Vasa, the African*, 2 volumes (London, 1789), pp. 50–57.

The first object which saluted my eyes when I arrived on the coast was the sea, and a slave ship, which was then riding at anchor, and waiting for its cargo. These filled me with astonishment, which was soon converted into terror, which I am yet at a loss to describe. . . . When I was carried on board, I was immediately handled, and tossed up, to see if I were sound, by some of the crew; and I was persuaded that I had got into a world of bad spirits, and that they were going to kill me. Their complexions also differing so much from ours, their long hair, and the language they spoke, which was very different from any I had ever heard, united to confirm me in this belief. Indeed, such were the horrors of my views and fears at the moment, that, if ten thousand worlds had been my own, I would have freely parted with them all to have exchanged my condition with that of the meanest slave in my own country. When I looked round the ship too, and saw a large furnace or copper boiling, and a multitude of black people of every description chained together, every one of their countenances expressing dejection and sorrow, I no longer doubted of my fate; and, quite overpowered with horror and anguish, I fell motionless on the deck and fainted. . . .

Soon after this, the blacks who brought me on board went off, and left me abandoned to despair. I now saw myself deprived of all chance of returning to my native country, or even the least glimpse of hope of gaining the shore, which I now considered as friendly; and I even wished for my former slavery, in preference to my present situation, which was filled with horrors of every kind, still heightened by my ignorance of what I was to undergo. I was

FIGURE 4.2 "A Slave Coffle" in the West Indies (*Library of Congress*).

not long suffered to indulge my grief; I was soon put down under the decks, and there I received such a salutation in my nostrils as I had never experienced in my life; so that, with the loathsomeness of the stench, and crying together, I became so sick and low that I was not able to eat, nor had I the least desire to taste anything. I now wished for the last friend, Death, to relieve me. . . .

In a little time after, amongst the poor chained men, I found some of my own nation, which in a small degree gave ease to my mind. I inquired of them what was to be done with us? They gave me to understand we were to be carried to these white people's country to work for them. I then was a little revived, and thought, if it were no worse than working, my situation was not so desperate: but still I feared I should be put to death, the white people looked and acted, as I thought, in so savage a manner; for I had never seen among any people such instances of brutal cruelty; and this not only shown towards us blacks, but also to some of the whites themselves. One white man in particular I saw, when we were permitted to be on deck, flogged so unmercifully with a large rope near the foremast, that he died in consequence of it; and they tossed him over the side as they would have done a brute. This made me fear these people the more; and I expected nothing less than to be treated in the same manner. . . .

"The closeness of the place, and the heat of the climate, added to the number in the ship, which was so crowded that each had scarcely room to turn himself, almost suffocated us."
—OLAUDAH EQUIANO

The stench of the hold while we were on the coast was so intolerably loathsome that it was dangerous to remain there for any time, and some of us had been permitted to stay on the deck for the fresh air; but now that the whole ship's cargo were confined together, it became absolutely pestilential. The closeness of the place, and the heat of the climate, added to the number in the ship, which was so crowded that each had scarcely room to turn himself, almost suffocated us. This produced copious perspiration, so that the air soon became unfit for respiration, from a variety of loathsome smells, and brought on a sickness among the slaves, of which many died, thus falling victims to the improvident avarice, as I may call it, of their purchasers. This wretched situation was again aggravated by the galling of the chains, now become insupportable; and the filth of the necessary tubs, into which the children often fell, and were almost suffocated. The shrieks of the women, and the groans of the dying, rendered the whole a scene of horror almost inconceivable. . . .

At last, we came in sight of the island of Barbados, at which the whites on board gave a great shout, and made many signs of joy to us. We did not know what to think of this; but, as the vessel drew nearer, we plainly saw the harbor, and other ships of different kinds and sizes: and we soon anchored among them off Bridgetown. . . . We were conducted immediately to a merchant's yard, where we were all penned up together like so many sheep in a fold, without regard to sex or age. As every object was new to me, everything I saw filled me with surprise. What struck me first was, that the houses were built with bricks, in stories, and in every other respect different from those I have seen in Africa: but I was still more astonished on seeing people on horseback. I did not know what this could mean; and indeed I though these people were full of nothing but magical arts. . . .

We were not many days in the merchant's custody, before we were sold after their usual manner, which is this: on a signal given (as the beat of a drum), the buyers rush at once into the yard where the slaves are confined, and make choice of the parcel they like best. . . . In this manner, without scruple, are relations and friends separated, most of them never to see each other again.

> "O, ye nominal Christians! Might not an African ask you, learned you this from your God who says unto you, do unto all men as you would men should do unto you?"
> —Oladuah Equinao

O, ye nominal Christians! Might not an African ask you, learned you this from your God who says unto you, do unto all men as you would men should do unto you? Is it not enough that we are torn from our country and friends to toil for your luxury and lust of gain? Must every tender feeling be likewise sacrificed to your avarice? Are the dearest friends and relations, now rendered more dear by their separation from their kindred, still to be parted from each other, and thus preventing from cheering the gloom of slavery with the small comfort of being together, and mingling their sufferings and sorrows? Why are parents to love their children, brothers their sisters, or husbands their wives? Surely this is a new refinement in cruelty, which, while it has no advantage to atone for it, thus aggravates distress, and adds fresh horrors even to the wretchedness of slavery.

Consider This:

- Analyze Olaudah Equiano's account of the transatlantic passage from Africa to Barbados. What were some of the common fears of slaves?
- According to Equiano, how was the slave auction conducted? Analyze the last paragraph of this selection. What were some of the tragedies and hypocrisies concerning the slave trade that Equiano emphasized?

The Broader Perspective:

- Enlightenment thinkers like John Locke and Jean-Jacques Rousseau emphasized the "social contract" between the institution of government and the individual that guaranteed natural rights of life, liberty, and property to every human being by simple virtue of birth. It would take centuries for this progressive theory to become a reality in many societies with revolutions, civil wars, and civil rights movements necessary stepping-stones in the struggle to obtain equal human rights. Why has the process taken so long and cost so many lives over the years? And why is there so much yet to accomplish?
- Were the philosophes wrong about the perfectibility of human beings? Does our desire to be special and to hold control over others truly reflect the limitations of our human nature? Is the world, therefore, a maze of power relationships, of political control and imperialism, of sexual primacy of men over women, of racial priority? How do we achieve Enlightenment goals in the real world?

Thoughts on Women: The Social Framework

Woman: "Especially Constituted to Please Man"

JEAN-JACQUES ROUSSEAU

Jean-Jacques Rousseau's radical stance on nature and the establishment of the civil state was viewed as dangerous by many philosophes. Voltaire, in a horrified state of mind, wrote to him, "Never has anyone employed so much genius to make us into

"Woman: 'Especially Constituted to Please Man'" is from W. H. Payne, ed., Rousseau's *Émile* (New York: D. Appleton and Co., 1895), pp. 260–263, 281, 303.

beasts. When one reads your book, one is seized at once with a desire to go down on all fours." Indeed, under Rousseau, the social contract theory was limited in its application. Both Thomas Hobbes and John Locke advocated a government predicated on equality of human rights. Although Rousseau never mentioned women in his treatise *The Social Contract*, his many other works defined more exactly the particular role he assigned them in society. Rousseau's woman knew her place. He urged that women be "trained to bear the yoke from the first, so that they may not feel it." The following selection is from *Émile* (1762), his treatise on education.

A perfect man and a perfect woman ought no more to resemble each other in mind than in features. . . . In the union of the sexes each contributes equally toward the common end, but not in the same way. Hence arises the first assignable difference among their moral relations. One must be active and strong, the other passive and weak. One must needs have power and will, while it suffices that the other have little power of resistance.

This principle once established, it follows that woman is especially constituted to please man. If man ought to please her in turn, the necessity for it is less direct. His merit lies in his power; he pleases simply because he is strong. I grant that this is not the law of love, but it is the law of Nature, which is anterior even to love. . . .

The moment it is demonstrated that man and woman are not and ought not to be constituted in the same way, either in character or in constitution, it follows that they ought not to have the same education. In following the directions of Nature they ought to act in concert, but they ought not to do the same things; their duties have a common end, but the duties themselves are different, and consequently the tastes which direct them. After having tried to form the natural man, let us also see, in order not to leave our work incomplete, how the woman is to be formed who is befitting to this man. . . .

Woman is worth more as a woman, but less as a man; wherever she improves her rights she has the advantage, and wherever she attempts to usurp ours she remains inferior to us. Only exceptional cases can be urged against this general truth—the usual mode of argument adopted by the gallant partisans of the fair sex. . . .

Does it follow that she ought to be brought up in complete ignorance, and restricted solely to the duties of the household? . . . No, doubtless. . . . They ought to learn multitudes of things, but only those which it becomes them to know. . . . The whole education of women ought to be relative to men. To please them, to be useful to them, to make themselves loved and honored by them, to educate them when young, to care for them when grown, to counsel them, to console them, and to make life agreeable and sweet to them—these are the duties of women at all times, and what should be taught them from their infancy. . . .

The search for abstract and speculative truths, principles, and scientific axioms, whatever tends to generalize ideas, does not fall within the compass of women; all their studies ought to have reference to the practical; it is for them to make the application of the principles which man has discovered. . . . She must therefore make a profound study of the mind of man, not the mind of man in general, through abstraction, but the mind of the men who surround her, the mind of the men to whom she is subject, either by law or by opinion. She must learn to penetrate their feelings through their conversation, their actions, their looks, and their gestures. Through her conversations, her actions, her looks, and her gestures she must know how to give them the feelings which are pleasing to her, without even seeming to think of them. . . .

A woman of wit is the scourge of her husband, her children, her friends, her servants, of everybody. . . . If all the men in the world were sensible, every girl of letters would remain unmarried all her life.

A Vindication of the Rights of Women (1792)

MARY WOLLSTONECRAFT

The events of 1789 were to bring into focus many of the philosophical arguments concerning natural rights presented in the previous section. But the emphasis was on the rights of male citizens. Many accepted the views of Rousseau that women were not rational creatures and lacked the capacity for understanding the abstract tenets of the Enlightenment. Mary Wollstonecraft, an English writer and early disciple of Rousseau's political views, nevertheless took him to task. In her work *A Vindication of the Rights of Women* (1792), she extended the call for political liberty into the social realm. Her arguments gave justification to a different kind of revolution between the sexes.

But what have women to do in society? . . . Women might certainly study the art of healing, and be physicians as well as nurses. . . . They might also study politics, and settle their benevolence on the broadest basis. . . . Business of various kinds, they might likewise pursue, if they were educated in a more orderly manner, which might save many from common and legal prostitution. Women would not then marry for a support . . . nor would an attempt to earn their own subsistence . . . sink them almost to the level of those poor abandoned creatures who live by prostitution. . . . The few employments open to women, so far from being liberal, are menial; and when a superior education enables them to take charge of the education of children as governesses, they are not treated like the tutors of sons. . . . But as women educated like gentlewomen, are never designed for the humiliating situation which necessity sometimes forces them to fill; these situations are considered in the light of a degradation; and they know little of the human heart, who need to be told, that nothing so painfully sharpens sensibility as such a fall in life.

How many women thus waste life away the prey of discontent, who might have practised as physicians, regulated a farm, managed a shop, and stood erect, supported by their own industry, instead of hanging their heads surcharged with the dew of sensibility, that consumes the beauty to which it at first gave lustre; nay, I . . . have seldom seen much compassion excited by the helplessness of females unless they were fair; then, perhaps pity was the soft handmaid of love, or the harbinger of lust. How much more respectable is the woman who earns her own bread by fulfilling any duty, than the most accomplished beauty!

Proud of their weakness, however, [some women believe] they must always be protected, guarded from care, and all the rough toils that dignify the mind. If this be the fiat of fate, if they will make themselves insignificant and contemptible, sweetly to waste "life away," let them not expect to be valued when their beauty fades, for it is the fate of the fairest flowers to be admired and pulled to pieces by the careless hand that plucked them. In how many ways do I wish, from the purest benevolence, to impress this truth on my sex; yet I fear that they will not listen to a truth that dear bought experience has brought home to many an agitated bosom, nor willingly resign the privileges of rank and sex for the privileges of humanity, to which those have no claim who do not discharge its duties. . . .

Would men but generously snap our chains, and be content with rational fellowship

"*A Vindication of the Rights of Women*" is from Mary Wollstonecraft, *A Vindication of the Rights of Women*, 2nd ed. (London: J. Johnson, 1792), chapter 9.

instead of slavish obedience, they would find us more observant daughters, more affectionate sisters, more faithful wives, more reasonable mothers—in a word, better citizens. We should then love them with true affection, because we should learn to respect ourselves; and the peace of mind of a worthy man would not be interrupted by the idle vanity of his wife, nor the babes sent to nestle in a strange bosom, having never found a home in their mother's. . . .

It is time to effect a revolution in female manners—time to restore to them, as a part of the human species, labour by reforming themselves to reform the world. It is time to separate unchangeable morals from local manners. . . .

I wish to sum up what I have said in a few words, for I here throw down my gauntlet, and deny the existence of sexual virtues, not excepting modesty. For man and woman, truth, if I understand the meaning of the word, must be the same; yet the fanciful female character, so prettily drawn by poets and novelists, demanding the sacrifice of truth and sincerity, virtue becomes a relative idea, having no other foundation than utility, and of that utility men pretend arbitrarily to judge, shaping it to their own convenience.

Women, I allow, may have different duties to fulfill; but they are human duties, and the principles that should regulate the discharge of them, I sturdily maintain, must be the same.

To become respectable, the exercise of their understanding is necessary, there is no other foundation for independence of character; I mean explicitly to say that they must only bow to the authority of reason, instead of being the modest slaves of opinion.

In the superior ranks of life how seldom do we meet with a man of superior abilities, or even common acquirements? The reason appears to me clear: the state they are born in was an unnatural one. The human character has ever been formed by the employments the individual or class pursues; and if the faculties are not sharpened by necessity, they must remain obtuse. The argument may fairly be extended to women; for, seldom occupied by serious business, the pursuit of pleasure gives that insignificancy to their character which renders the society of the great so insipid. . . . Such are the blessings of civil governments, as they are at present organized, that wealth and female softness equally tend to debase mankind, and are produced by the same cause; but allowing women to be rational creatures, they should be incited to acquire virtues which they may call their own, for how can a rational being be ennobled by anything that is not obtained by its own exertions? . . .

There must be more equality established in society, or morality will never gain ground, and this virtuous equality will not rest firmly even when founded on a rock, if one half of mankind be chained to its bottom by fate, for they will be continually undermining it through ignorance or pride.

COMPARE AND CONTRAST:

- Compare the views of Rousseau and Mary Wollstonecraft on the education and abilities of women. In what ways do Wollstonecraft's arguments mirror the ideals of the Enlightenment? In this regard, does Rousseau appear somewhat hypocritical? Or can one rationalize his arguments?

The Parisian Salon of an "Indispensable Woman"

The Parisian salons during the Enlightenment brought writers together for elegant, stylized conversation. It was in the salon, a rather formal reception room of a private home, where the intellectual elite congregated to spend the evening engaged in

"The Parisian Salon of an 'Indispensable Woman'" is from Katherine P. Wormley, trans., *Letters of Julie de Lespinasse* (Boston: Hardy, Pratt and Co., 1903), pp. 34–35, 75.

disputation, storytelling, timely debate over the latest issues of the day, or relaxed musing about the potentials of the future. Good conversation flourished under the guidance of an elegant hostess, who often directed the debate, smoothed ruffled feathers, and generally maintained an atmosphere conducive to discovery and pleasant conversation. It was in this setting that women not only competed with men on an equal intellectual footing but assumed a leading role by organizing and conducting the proceedings. In the process, women often became the arbiters of good taste and the dispensers of merit.

The following selection gives testimony to one of the most remarkable women of the Age of Reason, Julie de Lespinasse. Note carefully why others regarded her as an indispensable woman.

From Memoir of Baron de Grimm

Her circle met daily from five o'clock until nine in the evening. There we were sure to find choice men of all orders in the State, the Church, the Court,—military men, foreigners, and the most distinguished men of letters. Every one agrees that though the name of M. d'Alembert may have drawn them, it was she alone who kept them there. Devoted wholly to the care of preserving that society, of which she was the soul and the charm, she subordinated to this purpose all her tastes and all her personal intimacies. She seldom went to the theatre or into the country, and when she did make an exception to this rule it was an event of which all Paris was notified in advance. . . . Politics, religion, philosophy, anecdotes, news, nothing was excluded from the conversation, and, thanks to her care, the most trivial little narrative gained, as naturally as possible, the place and notice it deserved. News of all kinds was gathered there in its first freshness.

From Memoir of Marmontel

The circle was formed of persons who were not bound together. She had taken them here and there in society, but so well assorted were they that once there they fell into harmony like the strings of an instrument touched by an able hand. Following out that comparison, I may say that she played the instrument with an art that came of genius; she seemed to know what tone each string would yield before she touched it; I mean to lay that our minds and our natures were so well known to her that in order to bring them into play she had but to say a word. Nowhere was conversation more lively, more brilliant, or better regulated than at her house. It was a rare phenomenon indeed, the degree of tempered, equable heat which she knew so well how to maintain, sometimes by moderating it, sometimes by quickening it. The continual activity of her soul was communicated to our souls, but measurably; her imagination was the mainspring, her reason the regulator. Remark that the brains she stirred at will were neither feeble nor frivolous: the Coudillacs and Turgots were among them; d'Alembert was like a simple, docile child beside her. Her talent for casting out a thought and giving it for discussion to men of that class, her own talent in discussing it with precision, sometimes with eloquence, her talent for bringing forward new ideas and varying the topic—always with the facility and ease of a fairy, who, with one touch of her wand, can change the scene of her enchantment—these talents, I say, were not those of an ordinary woman. It was not with the follies of fashion and vanity that daily, during four hours of conversation, without languor and without vacuum, she knew how to make herself interesting to a wide circle of strong minds.

FIGURE 4.3 The Parisian salons were presided over by fashionable, intelligent women who engaged the intellectual elite in stimulating debate concerning the issues of the day. (*Getty Images, Inc.—Liason*)

CONSIDER THIS:

- What talents did Julie de Lespinasse possess that made her indispensable to the success of her salon? How did women of her social class and education contribute to the progress of this age? Do you think that hers was an important function, or would this type of social/intellectual discussion have taken place without hostesses of such talent and ability? What does this say about the role of women during the Enlightenment?

Thoughts on Commerce: The Economic Framework

Mercantilist Regulation: "The Maxim of All Polite Nations"

SIR WILLIAM KEITH

Since the Renaissance, Europeans had sought new economic horizons. The commercial revolution of the sixteenth century and the exploration of the Americas had

"Mercantilist Regulation" is from Sir William Keith, *A Collection of Papers and Other Tracts, Written Occasionally on Various Subjects* (London: J. Mechell, 1740), pp. 169–170, 173–175.

resulted in the establishment of colonies that engendered competition among imperial powers. Dominance and success in this commercial rivalry required that nations such as Spain, France, Great Britain, and the Netherlands become efficient producers and resourceful traders. To this end, governments focused their domestic economies and strictly regulated their foreign colonies to produce profit at each turn. This was especially important because these powers were constantly at war with each other in the eighteenth century, often squandering the precious wealth that they had accumulated.

To the extent that any formal economic theory was behind this process of accumulating wealth, it was called *mercantilism,* which gradually became a structured economic system based on the notion that the world was an arena of scarce resources. Because gold, silver, and other products were limited, governments had to regulate trade with protective tariffs, navigation laws that restricted trade with rivals, and domestic monopolies on salt and gunpowder. Mercantilist statesmen believed that their economies could grow only at the expense of others.

Although this economic system developed in the seventeenth century, it became more pronounced in the eighteenth as the wars in Europe and North America forced each country to become even more heavy-handed. The following selection by Sir William Keith encapsulates the tenets of mercantilism. But there were also critics, and the reaction to this economic regulation reached a climax in the late eighteenth century with the ideas of Adam Smith.

When either by conquest or increase of people, foreign provinces are possessed, and colonies planted abroad, it is convenient, and often necessary, to substitute little dependant provincial governments, whose people being enfranchised, and made partakers of the liberties and privileges belonging to the original Mother State, are justly bound by its laws, and become subservient to its interests, as the true end of their incorporation.

Every act of a dependant provincial government therefore ought to terminate in the advantage of the Mother State, unto whom it woes its being, and by whom it is protected in all its valuable privileges: hence it follows, that all advantageous projects, or commercial gains in any colony, which are truly prejudicial to, and inconsistent with the interest of the Mother State, must be understood to be illegal, and the practice of them unwarrantable, because they contradict the end for which the colony had a being, and are incompatible with the terms on which the people claim both privilege and protection. . . .

It has ever been the Maxim of all polite nations, to regulate their government to the best advantage of their trading interest. . . . By this short view of trade in general we may plainly understand that those colonies can be very beneficially employed both for Great Britain and themselves, without interfering with any of the staple manufactures in England.

But in order to set this point yet in a clearer light, we will proceed to consider some of the obvious regulations on the American trade, for rendering the colonies truly serviceable to Great Britain.

1. That all the product of the colonies, for which the manufacture and trade of Britain has a constant demand, be enumerated among the goods which by law must be first transported to Britain, before they can be carried to any other market.
2. That all kinds of woollen manufactures for which the colonies have a demand, shall continue to be brought from Britain only, and linens from Great Britain and Ireland.

3. All other European commodities to be carried to the colonies, (salt excepted) entry thereof to be first made in Britain, before they can be transported to any of the English colonies.
4. The colonies to be absolutely restrained in their several governments from laying any manner of duties on shipping or trade from Europe, or upon European goods transported from one colony to another.

Supposing these things to be done, it will evidently follow in that the more extensive the trade of the colonies is, the greater will be the advantages accruing to Great Britain therefrom; and consequently, that the enlargement of the colonies, and the increase of their people, would still be an addition to the national strength. . . .

From what has been said of the nature of colonies, and the restriction that ought to be laid on their trade, it is plain that none of the English plantation in America can with any reason or good sense pretend to claim an absolute legislative power with themselves; so that let their several Constitutions be founded by Charters, Royal Patents, . . . or what other legal authority you please; yet still they cannot be possessed of any rightful capacity to contradict, or evade the true intent and force of any Act of Parliament, wherewith the wisdom of Great Britain may think fit to affect them from time to time.

CONSIDER THIS:

- What are the primary tenets of mercantilism as noted by Sir William Keith in the selection "The Maxim of All Polite Nations"? As the ruler of a state, would you find his arguments impressive?

The Wealth of Nations (1776)

ADAM SMITH

Adam Smith can rightly be considered one of the most influential thinkers of the Enlightenment. He studied moral philosophy at Oxford and in his mid-twenties conceived of an economic philosophy of "the obvious and simple system of natural liberty," which the world would come to know as capitalism. In response to the restrictive emphasis of mercantilism, Smith conceived of an expansive universe, full of opportunity for the individual or nation to exercise initiative, accumulate wealth, and serve others in the process.

The following selection is an excerpt from his major work, *The Wealth of Nations*. It focuses on Smith's view of human nature and the "invisible hand" of competition as a guide to an economic system based on individual self-interest. If one views the Industrial Revolution of the early nineteenth century and the birth of Marxism in 1848 as being directly influenced by Smith's theories, then his impact on the history of the twentieth century is immeasurable.

Human Nature and the Division of Labor

This division of labour, from which so many advantages are derived, is not originally the effect of any human wisdom, which foresees and intends that general opulence to which it gives occasion. It is the necessary, though very slow and gradual, consequence of a certain propensity in human nature which has in view

"The Wealth of Nations" is from Adam Smith, *An Inquiry into the Nature and Causes of the Wealth of Nations*, ed. Edwin A. Seligman (London: J. M. Dent, 1901), pp. 12–15, 400–401, 436–437.

no such extensive utility; the propensity to truck, barter, and exchange one thing for another.

Whether this propensity be one of those original principles in human nature, of which no further account can be given; or whether, as seems more probable, it be the necessary consequence of the faculties of reason and speech, it belongs not to our present subject to enquire. It is common to all men, and to be found in no other race of animals, which seem to know neither this nor any other species of contracts. . . . In civilized society, [man] stands at all times in need of the cooperation and assistance of great multitudes, while his whole life is scarce sufficient to gain the friendship of a few persons. In almost every other race of animals each individual, when it is grown up to maturity, is entirely independent, and in its natural state has occasion for the assistance of no other living creature. But man has almost constant occasion for the help of his brethren, and it is in vain for him to expect it from their benevolence only. He will be more likely to prevail if he can interest their self-love in his favour, and show them that it is for their own advantage to do for him what he requires of them. Whoever offers to another a bargain of any kind, proposes to do this. Give me that which I want, and you shall have this which you want, is the meaning of every such offer; and it is in this manner that we obtain from one another the far greater part of those good offices which we stand in need of. It is not from the benevolence of the butcher, the brewer, or the baker, that we expect our dinner, but from their regard to their own interest. We address ourselves, not to their humanity but to their self-love, and never talk to them of our own necessities but of their advantages. . . .

The difference of natural talents in different men is, in reality, much less than we are aware of; and the very different genius which appears to distinguish men of different professions, when grown up to maturity, is not upon many occasions so much the cause, as the effect of the division of labour. The difference between the most dissimilar characters, between a philosopher and a common street porter, for example, seems to arise not so much from nature, as from habit, custom, and education. When they came into the world, and for the first six or eight years of their existence, they were, perhaps, very much alike, and neither their parents nor playfellows could perceive any remarkable difference. About that age, or soon after, they come to be employed in very different occupations. The difference of talents comes then to be taken notice of, and widens by degrees, till at last the vanity of the philosopher is willing to acknowledge scarce any resemblance. . . . By nature a philosopher is not in genius and disposition half so different from a street porter, as a mastiff is from a greyhound, or a greyhound from a spaniel, or this last from a shepherd's dog. . . . Among men, on the contrary, the most dissimilar geniuses are of use to one another; the different produces of their respective talents, by the general disposition to truck, barter, and exchange, being brought, as it were, into a common stock, where every man may purchase whatever part of the produce of other men's talents he has occasion for. . . .

The Invisible Hand

As every individual, therefore, endeavors as much as he can both to employ his capital in the support of domestic industry, and so to direct that industry that its produce may be of the greatest value; every individual necessarily labours to render the annual revenue of the society as great as he can. He generally, indeed, neither intends to promote the public interest, nor knows how much he is promoting it. . . . He intends only his own security; and by directing that industry in such a manner as its produce may be of the greatest value, he intends only his own gain, and he is in this, as in many other cases, led by an invisible hand to promote an end which was no part of his intention. Nor is it always the worse for the society that it was no part of it. By pursuing his own interest he frequently promotes that of the society more effectually than when he really intends to promote it. I have never known much good done by those who affected to trade for the public good. . . . The statesman, who should attempt to direct private people in what manner they ought to employ their capitals, would not only load himself with a most unnecessary attention, but assume an authority which could safely be trusted, not only to no single person, but to no council or senate whatever, and which would nowhere be so dangerous as in the hands of a man who had folly and presumption enough to fancy himself fit to exercise it.

Unreasonableness of Restraints

Each nation has been made to look with an invidious eye upon the prosperity of all nations with which it trades, and to consider their gain as its own loss. Commerce, which ought naturally to be, among nations, as among individuals, a bond of union and friendship, has become the most fertile source of discord and animosity. . . . The violence and injustice of the rulers of mankind is an ancient evil, for which, I am afraid, the nature of human affairs can scarce admit of a remedy. But the mean rapacity, the monopolising spirit of merchants and manufacturers, who neither are, nor ought to be, the rulers of mankind, though it cannot perhaps be corrected, may very easily be prevented from disturbing the tranquility of anybody but themselves.

That it was the spirit of monopoly which originally both invented and propagated this doctrine cannot be doubted; and they who first taught it were by no means such fools as they who believed it. In every country it always is and must be the interest of the great body of the people to buy whatever they want of those who sell it cheapest. The proposition is so very manifest that it seems ridiculous to take any pains to prove it; nor could it have ever been called in question had not the interested sophistry of merchants and manufacturers confounded the common sense of mankind. Their interest is, in this respect, directly opposite to that of the great body of the people. As it is the interest of the freemen of a [guild] to hinder the rest of the inhabitants from employing any workmen but themselves, so it is the interest of the merchants and manufacturers of every country to secure to themselves the monopoly of the home market. Hence in Great Britain, and in most other European countries, the extraordinary duties upon almost all goods imported by alien merchants. Hence the high duties and prohibitions upon all those foreign manufactures which can come into competition with our own. Hence, too, the extraordinary restraints upon the importation of almost all sorts of goods from those countries . . . whom national animosity happens to be most violently inflamed. . . . This very competition, however, is advantageous to the great body of the people, who profit greatly besides by the good market which the great expense of such a nation affords them in every other way. . . .

CONSIDER THIS:

- What was Adam Smith's view of human nature as expounded in the selection from *The Wealth of Nations*? Do you find his thoughts on self-interest to be compelling? Does his belief negate the sincerity of altruism? What are the primary ingredients of success in the world?

- How do you define the principle of the "invisible hand"? How do you interpret his phrase "I have never known much good done by those who affected to trade for the public good"? Smith foresaw a "mean rapacity" of merchants and manufacturers that "cannot perhaps be corrected." Why was he so sure that it could "very easily be prevented from disturbing the tranquility of anybody but themselves"

Part II

The Era of Revolution

"Liberty, Equality, Fraternity!": The French Revolution

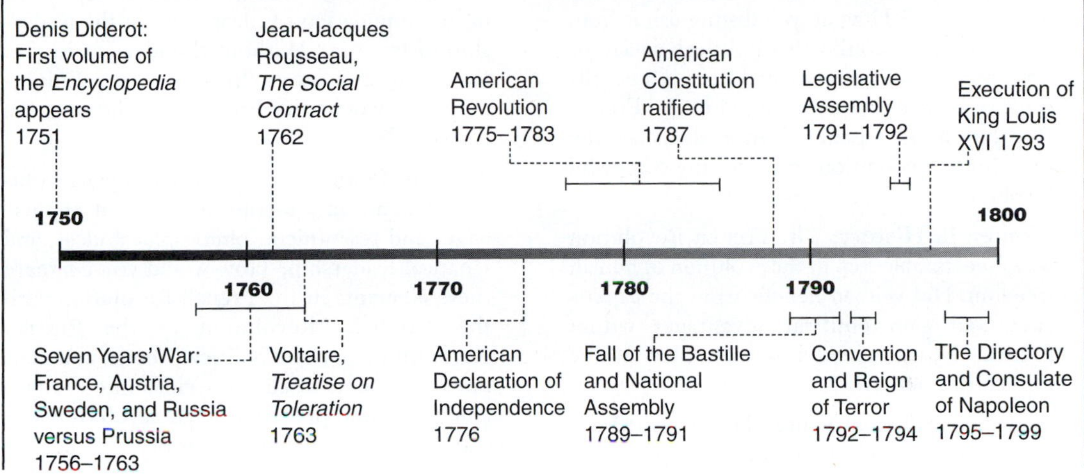

A time of revolution is not the season of true liberty. Alas! The obstinacy and perversion of men is such that she is too often obliged to borrow the very arms of despotism to overthrow him, and in order to reign in peace must establish herself by violence.

—William Wordsworth

The greatest dangers to liberty lurk in insidious encroachment by men of zeal—well-meaning, but without understanding.

—Justice Louis D. Brandeis

Extremism in the defense of liberty is no vice. And . . . moderation in the pursuit of justice is no virtue.

—Barry Goldwater

True tragedy arises when the idea of "justice" appears to be leading to the destruction of higher values.

—Max Scheler

Marriage is the tomb of trust and love. I offer a foolproof way to elevate the soul of women; it is to join them to all the activities of man.

—Olympe de Gouges

CHAPTER THEMES

- **The Power Structure:** Did the French Revolution establish a republic committed to Enlightenment principles of "natural rights" and equality of opportunity? Or was it crippled by the chaotic nature of democratic rule that was at once its greatest benefit and greatest defect?
- **Revolution and Historical Transition:** What is a revolution? How do you distinguish it from a riot or a rebellion? What political, social, or economic conditions existed in eighteenth-century France that contributed to the French Revolution? In a general sense, do you think that difficult conditions precede any successful revolution?
- **Women in History:** The French Revolution was a measurable step in the evolution of human freedom. Did women benefit from the experience and gain political advantages within France? What role did women play in the French Revolution?
- **Social and Spiritual Values:** How did the leaders of the French Revolution suppress the Catholic church and then use religion to their advantage? Does a revolution produce its own pantheon of gods, which when syncretized with the political leadership renders a church-and-state relationship unnecessary?
- **The Individual and the Institution:** To what extent is a successful revolution more dependent on the foundation of ideas than on the leadership of fanatics? Without the ideas of Locke, Rousseau, and other thinkers of the Enlightenment, would the French Revolution have succeeded?
- **The Big Picture:** To what extent does revolution depend on a fortuitous blend of popular anger and resentment, philosophical ideas, and fanatical leadership? How would you compare these elements in the French Revolution with the American Revolution or the Russian Revolution? Are the political, social, and economic elements of all revolutions interchangeable? Can one predict when a revolution will occur? What is the value of history?

One of the most exciting periods of change and development in Western civilization occurred during the seventeenth and eighteenth centuries. The attitudes and ideas that flourished during this time have formed the intellectual and political bases of our modern Western world.

Although the writers and thinkers of this period, often called *philosophes*, generally advocated intellectual freedom and political equality, it should be added that the eighteenth-century Enlightenment was not initially a concerted effort but took shape in individual minds over several generations; it did not become a conscious movement until about 1750. Yet the ideas of such important figures as John Locke, the Baron de Montesquieu, Voltaire, Denis Diderot, and Jean-Jacques Rousseau were to be influential apart from the theoretical and abstract world of thought. They were to give philosophical justification to the notion that it was proper and desirable to remove a monarch who was incompetent or inattentive to the needs of the people. Revolution often requires philosophical inspiration to succeed; without the underlying attitude that revolution can be a proper and progressive act, perhaps the French middle class would not have been motivated to lead a revolt against the established order.

And yet the French Revolution in 1789 did not simply happen as a result of intellectual commitment to abstract principles. In fact, there existed more tangible evidence that revolution could succeed and produce desired results. The precedents were clear. In 1649, the English executed their monarch Charles I for his autocratic behavior, and in 1688, Parliament established itself as the supreme depository of law and the "popular will" by restricting monarchical authority. It should be remembered, however, that the English had a long tradition of representative government and monarchical limitation dating back most importantly to the Magna Carta in 1215. The French lacked this tradition, and their representative institution, the Estates-General, had not met in 175 years. More recent precedent for French revolutionary action existed in the American example. In 1776, the American colonies declared their independence from Britain and were supported in this venture by the French government itself.

There were also economic problems that moved France toward revolution. The wars and extravagance of Louis XIV had sent France to the brink of bankruptcy by 1715—and Louis was a competent and diligent administrator. His heirs, in contrast, were not particularly dedicated to the governance of France. Louis XV (1715–1774) was poorly educated and preferred to allow his mistresses (one of whom had been a Parisian prostitute) to control the politics of state. Louis XVI (1774–1792) was well educated but more interested in hunting than in administration. From 1715 to 1789, the French economy spiraled into chaos. With the nobility and church exempt from taxation, the burden fell on the Third Estate.

The French Revolution drew much of its support from the Third Estate, a conglomeration of middle-class professionals, artisans, and peasants. As a group, the middle class, or bourgeoisie, was ambitious, educated, and competent. Could they be expected to sit idly by while the nobility held offices that should have been theirs? Inspired by philosophical ideals as well as by potential economic and social advantages, they provided the leadership for the revolution. Lower members of the Third Estate, the artisans and peasants, generally could not read and were not concerned with philosophical justifications. It was the peasantry that labored under intolerable taxes, rents, and *corvées* (feudal services), which they were forced to undertake by the nobility without payment. What were their demands in 1789? Did their needs justify revolution?

This chapter explores some of the ideological and social origins of the French Revolution, as well as some of its most important events, such as the storming of the Bastille, the execution of Louis XVI, and the Terror. The French Revolution presents historians with complex problems of great importance. The many themes—the social and economic components of revolution, the intellectual foundation, the influence of the individual or the crowd on events, the relationship between power and progress—all assume importance in understanding the process of revolution and the complexities of historical change. At issue is this fundamental question: Did the French Revolution succeed in realizing its ideals of liberty, equality, and fraternity?

Conditions of Society on the Eve of Revolution

French society in the eighteenth century was composed of three main classes that were divided on the basis of occupation and ancient privilege. The First Estate consisted of the clergy, the Second Estate of the nobility, and the Third Estate of everyone else. Within the estates themselves there were also social divisions. The following selections relate many of the problems and criticisms of the time.

Corruption of the French Court

MARQUIS D'ARGENSON

Marquis d'Argenson was minister of foreign affairs under Louis XV. He claimed he "loved both royalty and the people."

The court! The court! In that single word lies all the nation's misfortune. . . . It is the court that corrupts the morals of the nation by its luxury, its extravagance, its artificial manners, its ignorance, and its intrigue in place of emulation. All places, positions, and grades in the army go to the courtiers through favoritism; hence there is no longer any attempt to rise by merit.

In the finances everything is sold; all the money of the provinces goes to Paris never to return; all the people go there to make fortunes by intrigue. . . .

Justice cannot be administered with integrity; the judges fear the grandees, and base their hopes only upon favor. In short, the king no longer reigns, and disregards even the virtues that he has.

Those are the fruits of the establishment by Louis XIV of a capital at Versailles expressly for the court. He was still powerful and gave authority to his ministers. But these are not supported under Louis XV, who distrusts them and prefers his courtiers and favorites. There is, as a result, anarchy and an oligarchy of satraps. Favor means influence, and the possession of favor is more important than the rights of authority.

"Ancient Oaks Mutilated by Time"

MARQUIS DE BOUILLE

Marquis de Bouille was a noble, general, governor, and trusted adviser to Louis XVI.

The nobility had undergone still greater changes; it had lost, not only its ancient splendor, but almost its existence, and had entirely decayed. There had been in France nearly eighty thousand noble families. . . . Included in this numerous nobility were about a thousand families whose origin dated from the earliest times of the monarchy. Among these there were scarcely two or three hundred who had escaped poverty and misfortune. There could still be found at court a few great names which brought to mind the noted personages who had made them illustrious, but which too often were brought into disrepute by the vices of those who had inherited them. There were a few families in the provinces who had continued to exist and command respect. . . . The remainder of this ancient nobility languished in poverty, and resembled those ancient oaks mutilated by time, where nothing remains except the ravaged trunks. No longer convoked either for military service or for the

"The Corruption of the French Court" is from E. L. Higgins, ed., *The French Revolution as Told by Contemporaries* (Boston: Houghton Mifflin, 1966), p. 10.

"'Ancient Oaks Mutilated by Time'" is from E. L. Higgins, ed., *The French Revolution as Told by Contemporaries* (Boston: Houghton Mifflin, 1966), p. 19.

provincial or national assemblies, they had lost their ancient hierarchy. If honorary titles remained to some illustrious or ancient families, they were also held by a multitude of newly created nobles who had acquired by their riches the right to assume them arbitrarily. . . . The nobility, in short, were not distinguishable from the other classes of citizens, except by the arbitrary favors of the court, and by the exemptions from imposts, less useful to them than onerous to the state and shocking to the people. They had conserved nothing of their ancient dignity and consideration; they retained only the hate and jealousy of the plebeians. Such was the situation of the nobility of the kingdom.

Consider This:

- What were the main criticisms leveled at the French nobility as noted in the preceding selections? Why were they scorned and held up to ridicule by people from their own class?

Beggars, Rags, and Misery

ARTHUR YOUNG

Arthur Young was an English writer on agricultural subjects who traveled through France before and during the revolution.

1787

The same wretched country continues to La Loge; the fields are scenes of pitiable management, as the houses are of misery. Yet all this country is highly improvable, if they knew what to do with it: the property, perhaps, of some of those glittering beings, who figured in the procession the other day at Versailles. Heaven grant me patience while I see a country thus neglected—and forgive me the oaths I swear at the absence and ignorance of the possessors. . . .

Pass Payrac, and meet many beggars, which we had not done before. All the country, girls and women, are without shoes or stockings; and the ploughmen at their work have neither sabots nor feet to their stockings. This is a poverty, that strikes at the root of national prosperity; a large consumption among the poor being of more consequence than among the rich the wealth of a nation lies in its circulation and consumption; and the case of poor people abstaining from the use of manufacturers of leather and wool ought to be considered as an evil of the first magnitude. It reminded me of the misery of Ireland.

1788

To Montauban. The poor people seem poor indeed; the children terribly ragged, if possible worse clad than if with no clothes at all; as to shoes and stockings they are luxuries. A beautiful girl of six or seven years playing with a stick, and smiling under such a bundle of rags as made my heart ache to see her: they did not beg and when I gave them any thing seemed more surprised than obliged. One third of what I have seen of this province seems uncultivated, and nearly all of it in misery. What have kings, and ministers, and parliaments, and states, to answer for their prejudices, seeing millions of hands that would be industrious, idle and starving, through the execrable maxims of despotism, or the equally detestable prejudices of a feudal nobility. . . .

"Beggars, Rags, and Misery" is from Arthur Young, *Travels in France During the Years 1781, 1788, 1789*, 3rd ed. (London: George Bell and Sons, 1889), pp. 19, 27.

THE BROADER PERSPECTIVE:

- Note the wide chasm between the extreme poverty of the rural population and the extravagance of life at court among the nobility. Given this disparity, was a revolution inevitable? Or does a revolution require more motivating factors than poverty and hunger? Was this a revolution to eliminate poverty?

The Outbreak of Revolution (1789–1791)

"What Is the Third Estate?" (January 1789)

THE ABBÉ SIEYÈS

By August 1788, Louis XVI had decided to summon the Estates-General, a convocation of the three estates, which had not met since 1614, to solve the government's financial problems. Louis was in debt, and he wanted the Estates-General to raise new taxes. This pamphlet by the Abbé Sieyès (1748–1836) was issued in January 1789 before the Estates-General met. It was intended to unite the various interests within the Third Estate toward a common cause: reform of the unequal voting procedure that gave advantage to the first two estates.

What Does the Third Estate Demand? To Become Something

The true petitions of this order may be appreciated only through the authentic claims directed to the government by the large municipalities of the kingdom. What is indicated therein? That the people wishes to be something, and, in truth, the very least that is possible. It wishes to have real representatives in the Estates General, that is to say, deputies drawn from its order, who are competent to be interpreters of its will and defenders of its interests. But what will it avail it to be present at the Estates General if the predominating interest there is contrary to its own! Its presence would only consecrate the oppression of which it would be the external victim. Thus, it is indeed certain that it cannot come to vote at the Estates General unless it is to have in that body an influence at least equal to that of the privileged classes; and it demands a number of representatives equal to that of the first two orders together. Finally, this equality of representation would become completely illusory if every chamber voted separately. The third estate demands, then, that votes be taken by head and not by order. This is the essence of those claims so alarming to the privileged classes, because they believed that thereby the reform of abuses would become inevitable. The real intention of the third estate is to have an influence in the Estates General equal to that of the privileged classes. I repeat, can it ask less?

What Remains to Be Done: Development of Some Principles

The time is past when the three orders, thinking only of defending themselves from ministerial despotism, were ready to unite against the common enemy. . . .

The third estate awaits, to no purpose, the meeting of all classes, the restitution of its political rights, and the plenitude of its civil rights; the fear of seeing abuses reformed alarms the first two orders far more than the desire for liberty inspires them. Between liberty and some odious privileges, they have chosen the latter. Their soul is identified with the favors of servitude. Today they dread this Estates General which but lately they invoked so ardently. All is well with them; they no longer complain, except of the spirit of innovation. They no longer lack anything; fear has given them a constitution.

The third estate must perceive in the trend of opinions and circumstances that it can hope for nothing except from its own enlightenment and courage. Reason and justice are in its favor; . . . there is no longer time to work for the conciliation of parties. What accord can be anticipated between the energy of the oppressed and the rage of the oppressors?

They have dared pronounce the word secession. They have menaced the King and the people. Well! Good God! How fortunate for the nation if this desirable secession might be made permanently! How easy it would be to dispense with the privileged classes! How difficult to induce them to be citizens!

In vain would they close their eyes to the revolution which time and force of circumstances have effected; it is none the less real. Formerly the third estate was serf, the noble order everything. Today the third estate is everything, the nobility but a word. . . .

In such a state of affairs, what must the third estate do if it wishes to gain possession of its political rights in a manner beneficial to the nation? There are two ways of attaining this objective. In following the first, the third estate must assemble apart: it will not meet with the nobility and the clergy at all; it will not remain with them, either by order or by head. I pray that they will keep in mind the enormous difference between the assembly of the third estate and that of the other two orders. The first represents 25,000,000 men, and deliberates concerning the interests of the nation. The two others, were they to unite, have the powers of only about 200,000 individuals, and think only of their privileges. The third estate alone, they say, cannot constitute the Estates General. Well! So much the better! It will form a National Assembly.

Consider This:

- What were the specific demands of the Third Estate? Do they seem reasonable to you? Why was no assembly called for the elimination of poverty among rural subjects of the king?
- Why did the middle class assume leadership of the coming revolution?

Women of the Third Estate (January 1789)

Juxtaposed with the famous document just presented is the little known petition from the women of the Third Estate. The petitioners were women of humble origin who sought not political equality but dignity and the opportunity to improve themselves. Note that they did not conceive of themselves as part of the political process but appealed directly to the king to improve the conditions of their lives.

Sire,

At a time when the various orders of the state are busy with their interests, when everyone is trying to assert his titles and his rights, when some people are worrying about recalling centuries of servitude and anarchy, when others

"Women of the Third Estate" is from *Women in Revolutionary Paris 1789–1795. Selected Documents Translated with Notes and Commentary.* Translated with notes and commentary by Darline Gay Levy, Harriet Branson Applewhite, and Mary Durham Johnson (Urbana: University of Illinois Press, 1979), pp. 18–20.

are making every effort to shake off the last links which still bind them to the imperious remains of the feudal system, women—continual objects of the admiration and scorn of men—women, wouldn't it be possible for them also to make their voice heard amidst this general agitation?

Excluded from the national assemblies by laws too well consolidated for them to hope to break, they do not ask, Sire, for your permission to send their deputies to the Estates General. . . . We prefer, Sire, to place our cause at your feet; not wishing to obtain anything except from your heart, we address our complaints and confide our miseries to it.

The women of the Third Estate are almost all born without fortune; their education is very neglected or very defective. . . . If nature has refused them beauty, they get married without dowry to unfortunate artisans, lead aimless, difficult lives stuck away in the provinces, and give birth to children they are incapable of raising. If, on the contrary, they are born pretty, without culture, without principles, without any idea of morals, they become the prey of the first seducer, commit a first sin, come to Paris to bury their shame, end by losing it altogether, and die victims of licentious ways. . . . Also, several, solely because they are born girls, are disdained by their parents, who refuse to set them up, preferring to concentrate their fortune on the head of a son whom they designate to carry on their name in the capital; for it is good that Your Majesty understands that we also have names to keep up. Or, if old age finds them spinsters, they spend it in tears and see themselves the object of the scorn of their nearest relatives. . . .

We ask to be enlightened, to have work, not in order to usurp men's authority, but in order to be better esteemed by them, so that we might have the means of living out of the way of misfortune and so that poverty does not force the weakest among us . . . to join the crowd of unfortunate beings who overpopulate the streets and whose debauched audacity is a disgrace to our sex and to the men who keep them company. . . .

We implore you, Sire, to set up free schools where we could learn our language on the basis of principles and religion and ethics. . . .

We ask to come out of the state of ignorance, to be able to give our children a sound and reasonable education so as to make of them subjects worthy of serving you. We will teach them to cherish the beautiful name of Frenchmen [and] we will transmit to them the love we have for Your Majesty.

COMPARE AND CONTRAST:

- Compare the demands made by the Abbé Sieyès on behalf of the Third Estate with the requests made by the women of the Third Estate to the king. Why did the women petition the king separately?

The Tennis Court Oath (June 20, 1789)

From the outset, the Estates-General was hampered by organizational disputes. After several weeks of frustration, the Third Estate invited the clergy and nobility to join them in organizing a new legislative body. Only a few of the lower clergy accepted, but the National Assembly was thus formed on June 17, 1789. Three days later they were accidentally locked out of their usual meeting place, and they marched to a nearby tennis court, where they took an oath to draft a new constitution for France. This is one of the most important documents of the revolution. The oath was taken orally and individually with but one vote in dissension. The president of the National Assembly was barely able to save the dissenter from bodily harm.

The National Assembly, considering that it has been summoned to establish the constitution of the kingdom, to effect the regeneration of public order, and to maintain the true principles of monarchy; that nothing can prevent it from continuing its deliberations in whatever place it may be forced to establish itself; and, finally, that wheresoever its members are assembled, there is the National Assembly.

Decrees that all members of this Assembly shall immediately take a solemn oath not to separate, and to reassemble wherever circumstances require, until the constitution of the kingdom is established and consolidated upon firm foundations; and that, the said oath taken, all members and each one of them individually shall ratify this steadfast resolution by signature.

Consider This:

- Read the Tennis Court Oath carefully. Does it call for radical action? Why is it considered to be one of the most important documents of the French Revolution?

FIGURE 5.1 *The Oath of the Tennis Court* by Jacques-Louis David. Having pledged their cooperation in the establishment of the National Assembly, members from the different estates took the famous oath to write a new constitution for France. (*Giraudon/Art Resource, NY*)

The Fall of the Bastille (July 14, 1789)

The Bastille was a fortress built to protect the eastern gates of Paris. It had also been used as a prison for political offenders of the old regime. Hence it served as a symbol of monarchical despotism. On July 14, 1789, a mob, irritated at the dismissal of a popular minister of the king, paraded through the streets of Paris, searching for arms and clashing with the military. They stormed the Bastille and slaughtered many of its small garrison. Although this act yielded few political prisoners of the king, the event would provide a catalyst to the revolution and is commemorated today in France with special reverence. Louis XVI, however, did not view it with such import. The entry in his diary for July 14, 1789, was *rien* ("nothing"), signifying that he failed to kill any game in his hunt that day. The following accounts of the fall of the Bastille are drawn from various witnesses and contemporaries of the event.

The Surrender

It was then that M. de Launay [commander of the forces of the Bastille] asked the garrison what course should be followed, that he saw no other than to blow himself up rather than to expose himself to having his throat cut by the people, from the fury of which they could not escape; that they must remount the towers, continue to fight, and blow themselves up rather than surrender.

The soldiers replied that it was impossible to fight any longer, that they would resign themselves to everything rather than destroy such a great number of citizens, that it was best to put the drummer on the towers to beat the recall, hoist a white flag, and capitulate. The governor, having no flag, gave them a white handkerchief. An officer wrote out the capitulation and passed it through the hole, saying that they desired to render themselves and lay down their arms, on condition of a promise not to massacre the troop; there was a cry of, "Lower your bridge; nothing will happen to you!"

The little drawbridge of the fort being first opened, Elie [one of the leaders of the attacking force] entered with his companions, all brave and honorable men, and fully determined to keep his word. On seeing him the governor went up to him, embraced him, and presented him with his sword, with the keys of the Bastille.

"I refused his sword," said Elie to me, "and took only the keys." His companions received the staff and the officers of the garrison with the same cordiality, swearing to serve them as guard and defense; but they swore in vain.

As soon as the great bridge was let down (and it is not known by what hand that was done) the people rushed into the court of the castle and, full of fury, seized on the troop of Invalides. Elie and the honest men who had entered with him exerted all their efforts to tear from the hands of the people the victims which they themselves had delivered to it. Ferocity held obstinately attached to its prey. Several of these soldiers, whose lives had been promised them, were assassinated; others were dragged like slaves through the streets of Paris. Twenty-two were brought to the Grève, and, after humiliations and inhuman treatment, they had the affliction of seeing two of their comrades hanged. When they were presented at the Hotel de Ville, a furious madman said to them: "You deserve to be hanged; and you shall be so presently." De Launay, torn

"The Fall of the Bastille" is from E. L. Higgins, ed., *The French Revolution as Told by Contemporaries* (Boston: Houghton Mifflin, 1966), pp. 98–100.

from the arms of those who wished to save him, had his head cut off under the walls of the Hotel de Ville. In the midst of his assassins, he defended his life with the courage of despair; but he fell under their number. De Losme-Salbray, his major, was murdered in the same manner. The adjutant, Mirai, had been so, near the Bastille. Pernon, an old lieutenant of the Invalides, was assassinated on the wharf Saint-Paul, as he was going to the hall. Another lieutenant, Caron, was covered with wounds. The head of the Marquis de Launay was carried about Paris by this same populace that he would have crushed had he not been moved to pity. Such were the exploits of those who have since been called the heroes and conquerors of the Bastille.

The King Informed of the Fall of the Bastille

When M. de Liancourt had made known to the king the total defection of his guards, the taking of the Bastille, the massacres that had taken place, the rising of two hundred thousand men, after a few moments' silence the king said, "It is then a revolt." "No, Sire," replied the duke. "It is a revolution."

CONSIDER THIS:

- Why was the fall of the Bastille such an important event? After reading the pertinent selections, discuss how important violence is in a revolution. Do most successful revolutions promote violence to some degree?

FIGURE 5.2 *The Storming of the Bastille* by Jean-Pierre Houel. When King Louis XVI was informed that the Bastille had been stormed by a Parisian crowd on July 14, 1789, he said, "It is then a revolt." "No, Sire," replied the duke. "It is a revolution." (*Corbis/Bettmann*)

Declaration of the Rights of Man (August 27, 1789)

The Declaration of the Rights of Man, issued by the National Assembly on August 27, 1789, served as a preamble to the French constitution, which was as yet unwritten. Its articles detail abuses of the old regime and were imitative of American bills of rights that had been attached to state constitutions. The declaration in turn influenced several European constitutions in the nineteenth century.

The representatives of the French people, organized as a National Assembly, believing that the ignorance, neglect, or contempt of the rights of man are the sole causes of public calamities and of the corruption of governments, have determined to set forth in a solemn declaration the natural, inalienable, and sacred rights of man, in order that this declaration, being constantly before all the members of the social body, shall remind them continually of their rights and duties; in order that the acts of the legislative power, as well as those of the executive power, may be compared at any moment with the objects and purposes of all political institutions and may thus be more respected; and, lastly, in order that the grievances of the citizens, based hereafter upon simple and incontestable principles, shall tend to the maintenance of the constitution and redound to the happiness of all. Therefore the National Assembly recognizes and proclaims, in the presence and under the auspices of the Supreme Being, the following rights of man and of the citizen:

Article 1: Men are born and remain free and equal in rights. Social distinctions may be founded only upon the general good.

Article 2: The aim of all political association is the preservation of the natural and imprescriptible rights of man. These rights are liberty, property, security, and resistance to oppression.

Article 3: The principle of all sovereignty resides essentially in the nation. No body nor individual may exercise any authority which does not proceed directly from the nation.

Article 4: Liberty consists in the freedom to do everything which injures no one else; hence the exercise of the natural rights of each man has no limits except those which assure to the other members of the society the enjoyment of the same rights. These limits can only be determined by law.

Article 5: Law can only prohibit such actions as are hurtful to society. Nothing may be prevented which is not forbidden by law, and no one may be forced to do anything not provided for by law.

Article 6: Law is the expression of the general will. Every citizen has a right to participate personally, or through his representative, in its formation. It must be the same for all, whether it protects or punishes. All citizens, being equal in the eyes of the law, are equally eligible to all dignities and to all public positions and occupations, according to their abilities, and without distinction except that of their virtues and talents.

"Declaration of the Rights of Man" is from James H. Robinson and Charles A. Beard, eds., *Readings in Modern European History*, vol. 1 (Boston: Ginn and Company, 1908), pp. 260–262.

Article 7: No person shall be accused, arrested, or imprisoned, except in the cases and according to the forms prescribed by law. Any one soliciting, transmitting, executing, or causing to be executed, any arbitrary order, shall be punished. But any citizen summoned or arrested in virtue of the law shall submit without delay, as resistance constitutes an offense.

Article 8: The law shall provide for such punishments only as are strictly and obviously necessary, and no one shall suffer punishment except it be legally inflicted in virtue of a law passed and promulgated before the commission of the offense.

Article 9: As all persons are held innocent until they shall have been declared guilty, if arrest shall be deemed indispensable, all harshness not essential to the securing of the prisoner's person shall be severely repressed by law.

Article 10: No one shall be disquieted on account of his opinions, including his religious views, provided their manifestation does not disturb the public order established by law.

Article 11: The free communication of ideas and opinions is one of the most precious of the rights of man. Every citizen may, accordingly, speak, write, and print with freedom, but shall be responsible for such abuses of this freedom as shall be defined by law.

Article 12: The security of the rights of man and of the citizen requires public military forces. These forces are, therefore, established for the good of all and not for the personal advantage of those to whom they shall be entrusted.

Article 13: A common contribution is essential for the maintenance of the public forces and for the cost of administration. This should be equitably distributed among all the citizens in proportion to their means.

Article 14: All the citizens have a right to decide, either personally or by their representatives, as to the necessity of the public contribution; to grant this freely; to know to what uses it is put; and to fix the proportion, the mode of assessment and of collection and the duration of the taxes.

Article 15: Society has the right to require of every public agent an account of his administration.

Article 16: A society in which the observance of the law is not assured, nor the separation of powers defined, has no constitution at all.

Article 17: Since property is an inviolable and sacred right, no one shall be deprived thereof except where public necessity, legally determined, shall clearly demand it, and then only on condition that the owner shall have been previously and equitably indemnified.

CONSIDER THIS:

- What are the most important ideas contained in the *Declaration of the Rights of Man*? Why was it essential to the French Revolution? What does it tell you about the old regime of Louis XVI and his predecessors?

- Do you believe (as did most of the philosophes) that so-called natural rights exist for all human beings and that a government should protect these rights? How is this natural rights argument reflected in the various documents of the revolution?

THEME: WOMEN IN HISTORY

AGAINST THE GRAIN

The Flip Side of Liberty

Declaration of the Rights of Woman (1791)

OLYMPE DE GOUGES

Olympe de Gouges was a butcher's daughter who became a dramatist, pamphleteer, and political activist for the cause of women's rights. She was disappointed that the *Declaration of the Rights of Man* did not address the political and social restrictions confronting women in the French state. Employing many of the natural rights arguments expounded by the philosophes, she painted revolutionary leaders as hypocrites and demanded a consistent application of Enlightenment freedoms to women so that they might become educated, politically aware, and active voters, able to administer a National Assembly of their own. Interestingly, she sought the help of Queen Marie Antoinette. De Gouges's loyalties transcended the political agenda of monarchists or republicans. She wanted respect and equality for women. Olympe de Gouges so irritated members of the Convention that they arrested her on charges of treason. After a perfunctory trial, her head was cut off by the guillotine on November 3, 1793.

KEEP IN MIND . . .

- Note Olympe de Gouges's condemnation of the hypocritical double standard imposed by "rational" male thinkers to justify their "greater" political equality.

To the Queen: Madame,

Little suited to the language one holds to with kings, I will not use the adulation of courtiers to pay you homage with this singular production. My purpose, Madame, is to speak frankly to you; I have not awaited the epoch of liberty to thus explain myself; I stirred myself as energetically in a time when the blindness of despots punished such noble audacity.

When the whole empire accused you and held you responsible for its calamities, I alone in a time of trouble and storm, I alone had the strength to take up your defense. I could never convince myself that a princess, raised in the midst of grandeur, had all the vices of baseness. . . .

Madame, may a nobler function characterize you, excite your ambition, and fix your attentions. Only one whom chance has elevated to an eminent position can assume the task of lending weight to the progress of the Rights of Woman and of hastening its success. . . . This is not the work of one day, unfortunately for the new regime. This revolution will happen only when all women are aware of their deplorable fate, and of the rights they have lost in society. Madame, support such a beautiful cause; defend this

"*Declaration of the Rights of Woman*" is from *Women in Revolutionary Paris 1789–1795. Selected Documents Translated with Notes and Commentary.* Translated with notes and commentary by Darline Gay Levy, Harriet Branson Applewhite, and Mary Durham Johnson (Urbana: University of Illinois Press, 1979), pp. 89–90; 90–93.

unfortunate sex, and soon you will have half the realm on your side, and at least one-third of the other half. . . .

There are my principles, Madame. . . . I am with the most profound respect, your most humble and most obedient servant,

DE GOUGES

> "Man, are you capable of being just? It is a woman who poses the question; you will not deprive her of that right at least. Tell me, what gives you sovereign empire to oppress my sex? Your strength? Your talents?"
>
> —OLYMPE DE GOUGES

The Rights of Women

Man, are you capable of being just? It is a woman who poses the question; you will not deprive her of that right at least. Tell me, what gives you sovereign empire to oppress my sex? Your strength? Your talents? Observe the Creator in his wisdom; survey in all her grandeur that nature with whom you seem to want to be in harmony, and give me, if you dare, an example of this tyrannical empire. Go back to animals, consult the elements, study plants, finally glance at all the modifications of organic mater, and surrender to the evidence when I offer you the means; search, probe, and distinguish, if you can, the sexes in the administration of nature. Everywhere you will find them mingled; everywhere they cooperate in harmonious togetherness in this immortal masterpiece.

Man alone has raised his exceptional circumstances to a principle. Bizarre, blind, bloated with science and degenerated—in a century of enlightenment and wisdom—into the crassest ignorance, he wants to command as a despot a sex which is in full possession of its intellectual faculties; he pretends to enjoy the Revolution and to claim his rights to equality in order to say nothing more about it.

Preamble

For the National Assembly to decree in its last sessions, or in those of the next legislature:

Mothers, daughters, sisters and representatives of the nation demand to be constituted into a national assembly. Believing that ignorance, omission, or scorn for the rights of woman are the only causes of public misfortunes and of the corruption of governments, [the women] have resolved to set forth in a solemn declaration the natural, inalienable, and sacred rights of woman in order that this declaration, constantly exposed before all the members of the society, will ceaselessly remind them of their rights and duties; in order that the authoritative acts of women and authoritative acts of men may be at any moment compared with and respectful of the purpose of all political institutions; and in order that citizens' demands, henceforth based on simple and incontestable principles, will always support the constitution, good morals, and the happiness of all.

Consequently, the sex that is as superior in beauty as it is in courage during the sufferings of maternity recognizes and declares in the presence and under the auspices of the Supreme Being, the following Rights of Woman and of Female Citizens:

Article 1: Woman is born free and lives equal to man in her rights. Social distinctions can be based only on the common utility.

Article 2: The purpose of any political association is the conservation of the natural and imprescriptible rights of woman and man; these rights are liberty, property, security, and especially resistance to oppression.

Article 4: Liberty and justice consist of restoring all that belongs to others; thus, the only limits on the exercise of the natural rights of woman are perpetual male tyranny; these limits are to be reformed by the laws of nature and reason.

Article 6: The law must be the expression of the general will; all female and male citizens must contribute either personally or through their representatives to its formation; it must be the same for all: male and female citizens, being equal in the eyes of the law, must be equally admitted to all honors, positions, and public employment according to their capacity and without other distinctions besides those of their virtues and talents.

Article 7: No woman is an exception; she is accused, arrested, and detained in cases determined by law. Women, like men obey this rigorous law.

Article 13: For the support of the public force and the expenses of administration, the contributions of woman and man are equal; she shares all the duties and all the painful tasks; therefore, she must have the same share in the distribution of position, employment, offices, honors, and jobs.

Article 16: No society has a constitution without the guarantee of rights and the separation of powers; the constitution is null if the majority of individuals comprising the nation have not cooperated in drafting it.

Article 17: Property belongs to both sexes whether united or separate; for each it is an inviolable and sacred right; no one can be deprived of it, since it is the true patrimony of nature, unless the legally determined public need obviously dictates it, and then only with a just and prior indemnity.

"Oh, women, women! When will you cease to be blind? What advantage have you received from the Revolution? A more pronounced scorn, a more marked disdain."

—OLYMPE DE GOUGES

Postscript

Woman, wake up; the tocsin of reason is being heard throughout the whole universe; discover your rights. The powerful empire of nature is no longer surrounded by prejudice, fanaticism, superstition, and lies. The flame of truth has dispersed all the clouds of folly and usurpation. Enslaved man has multiplied his strength and needs recourse to yours to break his chains. Having become free, he has become unjust to his companion. Oh, women, women! When will you cease to be blind? What advantage have you received from the Revolution? A more pronounced scorn, a more marked disdain. In the centuries of corruption you ruled only over the weakness of men. The reclamation of your patrimony, based on the wise decrees of nature—what have you to dread from such a fine undertaking? . . . Do you fear that our French legislators . . . long ensnared by political practices now out of date, will only say again to you: women, what is there in common between you and us? Everything, you will have to answer. If they persist in their weakness in putting this non sequitur in contradiction to their principles, courageously oppose the force of reason to the empty pretensions of superiority; unite yourselves beneath the standards of philosophy; deploy all the energy of your character, and you will soon see these haughty men, not groveling at your feet as servile adorers, but proud to share with you the treasures of the Supreme Being. Regardless of what barriers confront you, it is in your power to free yourselves; you have only to want to.

CONSIDER THIS:

- What are the thoughts of Olympe de Gouges on the topic of women's rights? Why did she, like the women of the Third Estate before her, address her plea to the monarch?

COMPARE AND CONTRAST:

- Compare the *Declaration of the Rights of Man* (1789) with Olympe de Gouges's "The Rights of Woman" (1791) point by point. What are the differences? Ultimately, why wasn't her vision of equality accepted?
- Olympe de Gouges spoke of reason as the alarm or bell signal ("the tocsin of reason") for revolution "being heard throughout the whole universe." What did she mean? She argued that men contradicted their support of the "principles of reason" in order to enjoy the "empty pretensions of superiority." Was she right? Was the *Declaration of the Rights of Man* an exposition of hypocrisy? Do you agree with William Wordsworth's quote at the beginning of the chapter that "a time of revolution is not the season of true liberty"?

THE BROADER PERSPECTIVE:

- De Gouges promoted a revolution in support of women's equality. She noted that "this revolution will happen only when all women are aware of their deplorable fate, and of the rights they have lost in society." What rights had women lost? Had they ever really possessed many rights? How modern is de Gouges's protest? Would her words have rung true during the women's movements for suffrage at the turn of the twentieth century and during the 1960s and 1970s?

Reflections on the Revolution (1790)

EDMUND BURKE

Edmund Burke (1729–1797) was a respected member of the English Parliament who gained extraordinary influence in public affairs through his writings. The following selection from his most famous work, *Reflections on the Revolution in France* (1790), gives evidence of his regret concerning the changes that had taken place during the first year of the revolution. Burke left a legacy of conservative thought that proved a solace to many whose status was jeopardized by revolutionary action. Burke's contributions to conservative political theory would provide a serious challenge to liberalism in the nineteenth century.

When I see the spirit of liberty in action, I see a strong principle at work; and this, for a while, is all I can possibly know of it. The wild gas, the fixed air is plainly broke loose: but we ought to suspend our judgment until the first effervescence is a little subsided, till the liquor is cleared, and until we see something deeper than the agitation of a troubled and frothy surface. I must be tolerably sure, before I venture publicly to congratulate men upon a blessing, that they have really received one. Flattery corrupts both the receiver and the giver; and adulation is not of more service to the people than to kings. I should therefore suspend my congratulations on the new liberty of France, until I was informed how it had been combined with government; with public

"Reflections on the Revolution" is from Edmund Burke, *Reflections on the Revolution in France*, in *The Works of the Right Honourable Edmund Burke*, vol. 2 (London: Henry G. Bohn, 1864), pp. 515–516.

force; with the discipline and obedience of armies; with the collection of an effective and well-distributed revenue; with morality and religion; with the solidity for property; with peace and order; with civil and social manners. All these (in their way) are good things too; and, without them, liberty is not a benefit while it lasts, and is not likely to continue long. The effect of liberty to individuals is, that they may do what they please: we ought to see what it will please them to do, before we risk congratulations, which may soon be turned into complaints. Prudence would dictate this in the case of separate insulated private men; but liberty, when men act in bodies, is power. Considerate people, before they declare themselves, will observe the use which is made of power; and particularly of so trying a thing as new power in new persons, of whose principles, tempers, and dispositions, they have little or no experience, and in situations where those who appear the most stirring in the scene may possibly not be the real movers. . . .

The age of chivalry is gone.—That of sophisters, economists, and calculators, has succeeded; and the glory of Europe is extinguished for ever. Never, never more, shall we behold that generous loyalty to rank and sex, that proud submission, that dignified obedience, that subordination of the heart, which kept alive, even in servitude itself, the spirit of an exalted freedom. The unbought grace of life, the cheap defense of nations, the nurse of manly sentiment and heroic enterprise is gone! It is gone, that sensibility of principle, that chastity of honour, which felt a stain like a wound, which inspired courage while it mitigated ferocity, which ennobled whatever it touched, and under which vice itself lost half its evil, by losing all its grossness. . . .

But now all is to be changed. All the pleasing illusions, which made power gentle, and obedience liberal, which harmonized the different shades of life, and which, by a bland assimilation, incorporated into politics the sentiments which beautify and soften private society, are to be dissolved by this new conquering empire of light and reason. All the decent drapery of life is to be rudely torn off. All the super-added ideas, furnished from the wardrobe of a moral imagination, which the heart owns, and the understanding ratifies, as necessary to cover the defects of our naked shivering nature, and to raise it to dignity in our own estimation, are to be exploded as a ridiculous, absurd, and antiquated fashion.

On this scheme of things, a king is but a man; a queen is but a woman; a woman is but an animal; and an animal not of the highest order. . . . On the scheme of this barbarous philosophy, which is the offspring of cold hearts and muddy understandings, and which is as void of solid wisdom, as it is destitute of all taste and elegance, laws are to be supported only by their own terrors, and by the concern, which each individual may find in them, from his own private speculations, or even spare to them from his own private interests. In the groves of their academy, at the end of every vista, you see nothing but the gallows. . . . When the old feudal and chivalrous spirit of Fealty, which, by freeing kings from fear, freed both kings and subjects from the precautions of tyranny, shall be extinct in the minds of men, plots and assassinations will be anticipated by preventive murder and preventive confiscation, and that long roll of grim and bloody maxims, which form the political code of all power, not standing on its own honour, and the honour of those who are to obey it. Kings will be tyrants from policy when subjects are rebels from principle. . . .

To make a government requires no great prudence. Settle the seat of power; teach obedience: and the work is done. To give Freedom is still more easy. It is not necessary to guide; it only requires to let go the rein. But to form a free government; that is, to temper together these opposite elements of liberty and restraint in one consistent work, requires much thought, deep reflection, a sagacious, powerful, and combining mind. This I do not find in those who take the lead in the National Assembly. Perhaps they are not so miserably deficient as they appear. I rather believe it. It would put them below the common level of human understanding. But when the leaders choose to make themselves bidders at an auction of popularity, their talents, in the construction of the state, will be of no service. They will become flatterers instead of legislators; the instruments, not the guides, of the people. If any of them should happen to propose a scheme of liberty, soberly limited, and defined with proper qualifications, he will be immediately outbid by his competitors, who will produce something more splendidly popular. Suspicions will be raised of his fidelity to his cause. Moderation will be stigmatized as the virtue of cowards; and compromise as the prudence of traitors; until, in hopes of preserving the credit which may enable him to temper, and moderate, on some occasions, the popular leader is obliged to become active in propagating doctrines, and establishing powers, that will afterwards defeat any sober purpose at which he ultimately might have aimed.

The improvements of the National Assembly are superficial, their errors fundamental.

Consider This:

- What were Edmund Burke's main criticisms of the revolution in France? Why did Burke anticipate plots, assassinations, and a "long roll of bloody maxims"? Was he right?

The Radicalization of the Revolution (1792–1794)

The Fall of Louis XVI (1792–1793)

On June 20, 1791, the royal family managed to get out of Paris. Traveling in disguise with false passports, they were detained and arrested in Varennes, about 150 miles from Paris. The king was disgraced and the monarchy suffered a humiliating blow. The months following the king's flight from Paris were tense and saw the eventual erosion of royalist support and the abolition of the monarchy in September 1792. Louis was indicted for treason on December 11, 1792. The king denied most of the charges and blamed the rest on others. Nevertheless, a small majority of votes in the Assembly sent him to the guillotine. The following excerpt is an eyewitness account of the execution by Henry Edgeworth de Firmont, the king's confessor, who accompanied Louis to the scaffold. Justification for regicide came two days later by way of a proclamation of the government to the French people. The last selection is from the memoirs of Mme Roland, a guiding spirit of the revolutionary Girondist faction who was eventually imprisoned and sent to the guillotine herself.

The Execution of Louis XVI (January 21, 1793)

HENRY EDGEWORTH DE FIRMONT

The carriage arrived . . . in the greatest silence, at the Place Louis XV, and came to a halt in the middle of a large empty space that had been left around the scaffold. This space was bordered with cannon; and beyond, as far as the eye could reach, was a multitude in arms. . . .

"The Execution of Louis XVI" is from E. L. Higgins, ed., *The French Revolution as Told by Contemporaries* (Boston: Houghton Mifflin, 1966), pp. 272–273.

As soon as the king descended from the carriage, three executioners surrounded him and wished to take off his coat. He repulsed them with dignity and took it off himself. The executioners, whom the proud bearing of the king had momentarily disconcerted, seemed then to resume their audacity and, surrounding him again, attempted to tie his hands. "What are you trying to do?" asked the king, withdrawing his hands abruptly.

"Tie you," replied one of the executioners.

"Tie me!" returned the king in an indignant tone. "No, I will never consent; do what you are ordered to do, but I will not be tied; renounce that idea." The executioners insisted, they lifted their voices, and seemed about to call for help in order to use force. . . .

"Sire," I said to him with tears, "in this new outrage I see only a final resemblance between Your Majesty and the Savior who is to reward you."

At these words he lifted his eyes to heaven with a sorrowing look that I cannot describe and turning to the executioners said: "Do what you wish; I will drain the cup to the dregs."

The steps that led to the scaffold were extremely steep in ascent. The king was obliged to hold to my arm, and by the pains he seemed to take, feared that his courage had begun to weaken; but what was my astonishment when, upon arriving at the last step, I saw him escape, so to speak, from my hands, cross the length of the scaffold with firm step to impose silence, by a single glance, upon ten or fifteen drummers who were in front of him, and with a voice so strong that it could be heard at the Pont-Tournant, distinctly pronounce these words forever memorable: "I die innocent of all the crimes imputed to me. I pardon the authors of my death, and pray God that the blood you are about to shed will never fall upon France."

FIGURE 5.3 "The executioners seized [Louis XVI's head] by the hair, and showed it to the multitude, whose cries of 'Long live the Republic!' resounded to the very bosom of the Convention."—Henry Edgeworth de Firmont. (*Corbis/Bettmann*)

The executioners seized him, the knife struck him, his head fell at fifteen minutes after ten. The executioners seized it by the hair, and showed it to the multitude, whose cries of "Long live the Republic!" resounded to the very bosom of the Convention, whose place of meeting was only a few steps from the place of execution.

Thus died, at the age of thirty-eight years, four months, and twenty-eight days, Louis, sixteenth of his name, whose ancestors had reigned in France for more than eight hundred years. . . .

Immediately after the execution, the body of Louis was transported to the cemetery of the ancient Church of the Madeleine. It was placed in a pit six feet square, close to the wall of the Rue d'Anjou, and dissolved instantly by a great quantity of quicklime with which they took the precaution to cover it.

Proclamation of the Convention to the French People (January 23, 1793)

Citizens, the tyrant is no more. For a long time the cries of the victims, whom war and domestic dissensions have spread over France and Europe, loudly protested his existence. He has paid his penalty, and only acclamations for the Republic and for liberty have been heard from the people.

We have had to combat inveterate prejudices, and the superstition of centuries concerning monarchy. Involuntary uncertainties and inevitable disturbances always accompany great changes and revolutions as profound as ours. This political crisis has suddenly surrounded us with contradictions and tumults.

But the cause has ceased, and the motives have disappeared; respect for liberty of opinion must cause these tumultuous scenes to be forgotten; only the good which they have produced through the death of the tyrant and of tyranny now remains, and this judgment belongs in its entirety to each of us, just as it belongs to the entire nation. The National Convention and the French people are now to have only one mind, only one sentiment, that of liberty and civic fraternity.

Now, above all, we need peace in the interior of the Republic, and the most active surveillance of the domestic enemies of liberty. Never did circumstances more urgently require of all citizens the sacrifice of their passions and their personal opinions concerning the act of national justice which has just been effected. Today the French people can have no other passion than that for liberty.

CONSIDER THIS:

- According to this document, the Convention blamed Louis for all the "contradictions and tumults" that accompanied the political crisis of the monarchy. They called for "liberty and civic fraternity," but in the next paragraph reveal that this required "the most active surveillance of the domestic enemies of liberty." What had happened to the definition of liberty in the resolution of political crisis?

THE BROADER PERSPECTIVE:

- Can you compare the attack on personal freedom that accompanied the execution of King Louis XVI with the restrictions placed on civil liberties in the United States as a result of the terrorist attacks of September 11, 2001? How did the Bush administration recalibrate democracy in the United States by sacrificing some personal liberties to the interests of national security? What does this tell you about political freedom even in the most stable of democracies?

"Proclamation of the Convention to the French People" is from E. L. Higgins, ed., *The French Revolution* as Told by Contemporaries (Boston: Houghton Mifflin, 1966), p. 392.

Reflections on Louis XVI

MME ROLAND

Louis XVI was not exactly the man they were interested in painting in order to discredit him. He was neither the stupid imbecile that they presented for the disdain of the people, nor the fine, judicious, virtuous man that his friends described. Nature had made him an ordinary man, who would have done well in some obscure station. He was ruined in being educated for the throne, and lost through mediocrity in a difficult period when he could have been saved only through genius and strength. An ordinary mind, brought up near the throne and taught from infancy to dissemble, acquires many advantages for dealing with people; the art of letting each see only what is suitable for him to see is for it only a habit to which practice gives an appearance of cleverness: one would have to be an idiot to appear stupid in such a situation. Louis XVI had moreover, a good memory and much activity; he never remained idle, and read a great deal. He knew well the various treaties made by France with the neighboring powers, and he was the best geographer in his kingdom. The knowledge of names, the exact application to the faces of the court personages to whom they belonged, of anecdotes personal to them, had been extended by him to all the individuals who appeared in some manner in the Revolution. But Louis XVI, without elevation of soul, without boldness of mind, without strength of character, still had his ideas narrowed and his sentiments perverted, so to say, by religious prejudices and Jesuitical principles. . . . If he had been born two centuries earlier, and if he had had a reasonable wife, he would have made no more noise in the world than many other princes of his race who have passed across the stage without having done much good or much harm.

CONSIDER THIS:

- According to Mme Roland, was Louis XVI a bad king? Note that in her opinion his fate might have been different had he a "reasonable wife." In 1791, Olympe de Gouges had appealed unsuccessfully to Marie Antoinette's sense of reason and nobility of character in promoting the political and social equality of women. Did women expect too much of Marie Antoinette? Did the French likewise expect too much of Louis?

THEME: WOMEN IN HISTORY

THE REFLECTION IN THE MIRROR

A Revolutionary Reality Check

An Update on the Political Rights of Women (1793)

In the midst of the revolution, with the recent execution of the king and the various political groups scrambling to consolidate their power, the official government (called the Convention) was presented with a complaint regarding the impending dissolution of the Society of Revolutionary Republican Women. An investigation was ordered, and the Committee of General Security presented the following recommendations to the Convention. The Convention subsequently voted to outlaw "women's societies and popular clubs."

Keep in Mind . . .

- What were the committee's specific reasons for rejecting the Society of Revolutionary Republican Women?

The Committee thought it should carry its investigation further. It raised the following questions: (1) Can women exercise political rights and take an active part in affairs of government? (2) Can they deliberate together in political associations or popular societies? With respect to these two questions, the Committee decided in the negative. . . .

We are going to put forward a few ideas which may shed light on [these questions]. In your wisdom you will know how to submit them to a thorough examination.

1. Should women exercise political rights and meddle in affairs of government? To govern is to rule the commonwealth by laws, the preparation of which demands extensive knowledge, unlimited attention and devotion, a strict immovability, and self-abnegation; again, to govern is to direct and ceaselessly to correct the action of constituted authorities. Are women capable of these cares and of the qualities they call for? In general, we can answer, no. Very few examples would contradict this evaluation.

The citizen's political rights are to debate and to have resolutions drawn up, by means of comparative deliberations, that relate to the interest of the state, and to resist oppression. Do women have the moral and physical strength which the exercise of one and the other of these rights calls for? Universal opinion rejects this idea.

2. Should women meet in political associations? The goal of popular associations is this: to unveil the maneuvers of the enemies of the commonwealth; to exercise surveillance both over citizens as individuals and over public functionaries—even over the legislative body; to excite the zeal of one and the other by the example of republican virtues; to shed light by public and in-depth discussion concerning the lack or reform of political laws. Can women devote themselves to these useful and difficult functions? No, because they would be obliged to sacrifice the more important cares to which nature calls them. The private functions for which women are destined by their very nature are related to the general order of society; this social order results from the differences between man and woman. Man is strong, robust, born with great energy, audacity, and courage; he braves perils [and] the intemperance of seasons because of his constitution; he resists all the elements; he is fit for the arts, difficult labors; and as he is almost exclusively destined for agriculture, commerce, navigation, voyages, war—everything that calls for force, intelligence, capability, so in the same way, he alone seems to be equipped for profound and serious thinking which calls for great intellectual effort and long studies which it is not granted to women to pursue.

"In general, women are ill suited for elevated thoughts and serious meditations. . . . We believe, therefore, that a woman should not leave her family to meddle in affairs of government."

What character is suitable for woman? Morals and even nature have assigned her functions to her. To begin educating men, to prepare children's minds and hearts for public virtues, to direct them early in life towards the good, to elevate their souls, to educate them in the political cult of liberty; such are their functions, after household cares. . . . When they have fulfilled all these obligations, they will have deserved well of the Fatherland. . . .

We must say that this question is related essentially to morals, and without morals, no republic. Does the honesty of woman allow her to display herself in public and to struggle against men? To argue in full view of a public about questions on which the salvation of the republic depends? In general, women are ill suited for elevated thoughts and serious meditations, and if, among ancient peoples, their natural timidity and modesty did not allow them to appear outside their families, then in the French Republic do you want them to be seen coming into the gallery to political assemblies as men do? abandoning both reserve—source of all the virtues of their sex—and the care of their family?

We believe, therefore, that a woman should not leave her family to meddle in affairs of government.

CONSIDER THIS:

- Assess the progress made by women to achieve political equality as noted in this document. Do you find it hypocritical that in a period where the "rights of man" are hotly contested, they don't apply to women? Women played an essential role in the success of the French Revolution but derived no benefit. Is this shocking to you? Assess the comments of Olympe de Gouges in this regard.

The Reign of Terror (1793–1794)

One of the most dramatic personalities of the French Revolution was Maximilien Robespierre (1758–1794), who dominated the principal policy-making body in the state, the Committee of Public Safety. An ardent democrat, Robespierre believed in a republic of virtue that demanded selfless adherence to republican ideals. Those who supported the monarchy or were more moderate in their republican zeal became threats to the success of the revolution and had to be eliminated. Terror, according to Robespierre, was "swift, inflexible justice" and therefore virtuous. The Reign of Terror, which lasted from 1793 to 1794, saw the execution by the guillotine of more than 25,000 people, from both the political left and right, many without proper trials.

Perhaps the most amiable of the radical political leaders was Camille Desmoulins. Although he was one of the first to preach and write about republican ideals, he harbored none of the fanaticism or cruelty that so energized and blinded his friend Robespierre. In the following selection, Desmoulins pleads for clemency and an end to the Terror. Ultimately, his voice threatened the authority of Robespierre, who sent Desmoulins, Danton, and other former adherents to the guillotine three months later.

"You Would Exterminate All Your Enemies by the Guillotine!" (December 20, 1793)

CAMILLE DESMOULINS

Is this liberty that we desire a mere empty name? Is it only an opera actress carried about with a red cap on, or even that statue, forty-six feet high, which David proposes to make? If by liberty you do not understand, as I do, great principles, but only a bit of stone, there never

"'You Would Exterminate All Your Enemies by the Guillotine!'" is from James H. Robinson and Charles A. Beard, eds., *Readings in Modern European History*, vol. 1 (Boston: Ginn and Company, 1908), pp. 307–308.

was idolatry more stupid and expensive than ours. . . . No, heaven-born liberty is no nymph of the opera, nor a red liberty cap, nor a dirty shirt and rags. Liberty is happiness, reason, equality, justice, the Declaration of Rights, your sublime constitution.

Would you have me recognize this liberty, have me fall at her feet, and shed all my blood for her? Then open the prison doors to the two hundred thousand citizens whom you call suspects, for in the Declaration of Rights no prisons for suspicion are provided for, only places of detention. Suspicion has no prison, but only the public accuser; there are no suspects, but only those accused of offenses established by law.

Do not think that such a measure would be fatal to the republic. It would, on the contrary, be the most revolutionary that you have adopted. You would exterminate all your enemies by the guillotine! But was there ever greater madness? Can you possibly destroy one enemy on the scaffold without making ten others among his family and friends? Do you believe that those whom you have imprisoned—these women and old men, these stragglers of the Revolution—are really dangerous? Only those among your enemies have remained among you who are cowardly or sick. The strong and courageous have emigrated. They have perished at Lyons or in the Vendee. The remnant which still lingers does not deserve your anger. . . .

Moreover, it has not been love of the republic, but curiosity, which has every day attracted multitudes to the Place de la Revolution [site of the executions]; it was the new drama which was to be enacted but once. . . .

I am of a very different opinion from those who claim that it is necessary to leave Terror as the order of the day. I am confident . . . that liberty will be assured and Europe conquered as soon as you have a Committee of Clemency. This committee will complete the Revolution, for clemency is itself a Revolutionary measure, the most efficient of all when it is wisely dealt out.

The Broader Perspective:

- Why was Desmoulins executed? How did he define liberty? Why did the French Revolution become increasingly radicalized, finally "devouring its own"?

THEME: THE VARIETIES OF TRUTH

The Artistic Vision

Jacques-Louis David and the Neoclassical Ideal

In the middle of the eighteenth century, artists turned to classicism once again in reaction to the frivolities of the highly ornamental Rococo style that did not offer much depth of expression or seriousness of purpose. The development of European art seemed to require a classical interlude with some regularity to balance great changes in artistic style. This return to classicism, however, was truly reflective of the intellectual undercurrent that found its most eloquent expression in the thinkers of the Enlightenment during the first decades of the eighteenth century.

The rationality and idealism of Enlightenment thought that established a seedbed for active revolution in late eighteenth-century France also proved attractive to artists. That Neoclassicism emerged as a coherent, artistic movement in France during this time must be attributed primarily to the influence of Jacques-Louis David.

David's lifespan from 1748 to 1823 encompasses one of the most dramatic periods in French history. He accepted commissions from King Louis XVI and witnessed the fall of the Bourbon dynasty, playing an active role during the revolution, even voting for the king's death in 1793. He was a member of the new revolutionary government called the Convention, a leader of the radical Jacobin faction, and an intimate of Robespierre. But after Robespierre's execution in 1794, David shifted to the camp of the ascending star, Napoleon Bonaparte, and through his stirring portraits he molded Napoleon's image and granted him visual glory to match his battlefield dramatics.

The attitude that glory was the preserve of those who risked all certainly appealed to David, who became involved in the radical political clubs that drew men of determination and resolve. Among them was Jean-Paul Marat. One of the intellectual leaders of the Jacobins, Marat suffered from a skin disease that required hours in the bath each day to give him relief from the irritation. On July 13, 1793, Charlotte Corday, a royalist sympathizer, arrived from Caen and proceeded to Marat's apartment. To gain entry, she presented a letter to his servant

FIGURE 5.4 *Napoleon Crossing the Alps* by Jacques Louis-David. (*Corbis/Bettmann*)

that read, "I have some secrets to tell you that are vital to the interests of the Republic. I am being persecuted for the sake of Liberty; I am wretched—that alone gives me a right to your protection." Entering the room, she pulled a knife and stabbed Marat as he sat in the bath. Corday was apprehended quickly and guillotined four days later. But things were just beginning for the apotheosis of Marat. At the meeting of the Convention the next day, Marat was eulogized as a guardian for liberty "whose only crime was that he constantly sacrificed himself for the sake of freedom." The Convention called on David to immortalize Marat with a painting and he responded, "I shall do it." This type of sober resolve energized David's paintings with a gravity and sense of purpose.

But there is something else going on here. The very directness of the painting belies its purpose as political propaganda and moral allegory. Some might have considered Marat a simple demagogue, but in David's skilled hands he becomes "the martyr of the Revolution," cut down in the midst of his labors for

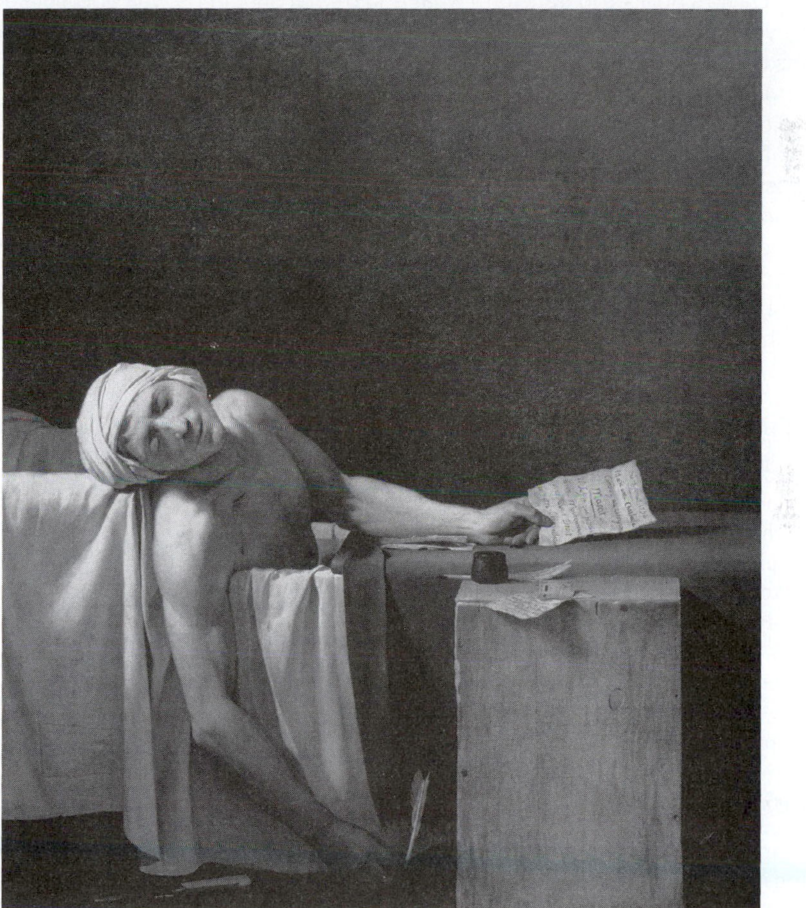

FIGURE 5.5 *The Death of Marat* by Jacques-Louis David. (*Corbis/Bettmann*)

freedom, at peace now, residing in the quiet eternity of memory. The light enters softly, blending into the stark background, a Christlike Marat almost as pietà, sacrificed by Judas the betrayer in the form of Charlotte Corday. Her note of entry is balanced on the simple woodblock and in his hand Marat holds a letter that reads, "You are to give this money to the mother of five whose husband died for his country." David likely made up the message to reinforce the betrayal of Charlotte Corday—Marat, the generous man whose life was snuffed out even in the act of charity. This was a grisly murder, but there is a measured, balanced, classical approach to the act. The blood trickles from the wound near Marat's collarbone, leading down to the murder weapon on the floor. There is a metamorphosis taking place, and the emphasis is not on the act of violence but on the afterglow, as if death has kissed Marat lovingly on the lips and taken his breath away. This is the truth that David wanted to believe, a truth of passionate faith in the ideal of revolution and its sanctification of any crime or deceit necessary for the people's freedom. Through this painting, he firmly enshrined Marat in the French pantheon of heroes.

David's abilities to transform what is into what should be was appreciated by the young general Napoleon Bonaparte, who first visited David's studio when he was twenty-eight years old. After the fall of Robespierre in 1794 and the end of the Terror, Napoleon offered David political cover by hiding him in his Italian camp to avoid the scrutiny of those reactionaries then seeking revenge for the excesses of the Terror. Their relationship was fruitful and symbiotic. David glorified the first consul of the state, not as a passive martyr à la Marat, but as neoclassical hero, the new Caesar, the imperial Charlemagne. Fiction and reality are merged in *Napoleon Crossing the Alps* (1801). David poses Napoleon atop his white steed, directing his armies over the Alps, much as did the Carthaginian general Hannibal. In fact, Napoleon made the journey on a donkey, but that wouldn't play for the mythical dimensions required. Image is all.

CONSIDER THIS:

- Jacques-Louis David was a great artist with expansive powers of observation, a refined and envied technique, a brilliance of conception, and a sophisticated understanding of the moment. Yet his vision was not only artistic but political. Possessed of an almost intuitive instinct for survival and prosperity, it is fair to ask whether David had the soul of an artist or the heart of a politician. Was he pure artist or expedient propagandist?

THE BROADER PERSPECTIVE:

- How are art and literature often employed as expressions of political ideals and goals? The vital question: To what extent are these paintings examples of great art or great propaganda? Can art and literature serve two masters (the creator and the patron) and still maintain their integrity as art forms?

- And when the patron is the political head of state, is the metamorphosis from art to propaganda inevitable? As an artist or poet, when the state calls as did Napoleon for David, as did Augustus for Livy, Virgil, and Horace, do you answer the call? Do you accept the challenge or the commission? Is there a price to pay? Can an artist be true to his or her personal vision without starving, or worse?

"Virtue and Terror": Speech to the Convention (February 5, 1794)

MAXIMILIEN ROBESPIERRE

As heads continued to roll during the first six months of 1794, radical leaders justified the executions through an evolving and distorted conception of liberty. The following speech by Robespierre justifies the use of terror and links it to virtue. The next document is a law that transferred the administration of the Terror from the Convention to the Committee of Public Safety. This enactment provided a general definition of an "enemy of the Republic" and increased the number of victims sacrificed to the purity of the revolution. Historians generally agree that this law not only damaged the ideals of the French Revolution but also was the ultimate cause of Robespierre's downfall. He fell victim to colleagues who feared his menacing power, and he himself was executed a month and a half after the law was ratified. With Robespierre's death, the Terror came to an end. The revolution continued but without the bloodshed that had devoured its own children.

What is the aim we want to achieve? The peaceful enjoyment of liberty and equality, the reign of that eternal justice whose laws have been engraved, not in stone and marble, but in the hearts of all men, even in the heart of the slave who forgets them or of the tyrant who denies them.

We want a state of affairs where all despicable and cruel passions are unknown and all kind and generous passions are aroused by the laws; where ambition is the desire to deserve glory and to serve the fatherland; where distinctions arise only from equality itself; where the citizen submits to the magistrate, the magistrate to the people and the people to justice; where the fatherland guarantees the well-being of each individual, and where each individual enjoys with pride the prosperity and the glory of the fatherland; where all souls elevate themselves through constant communication of republican sentiments and through the need to deserve the esteem of a great people; where the arts are the decorations of liberty that ennobles them, where commerce is the source of public wealth and not only of the monstrous opulence of a few houses.

In our country we want to substitute morality for egoism, honesty for honor, principles for customs, duties for decorum, the rule of reason for the tyranny of custom, the contempt of vice for the contempt of misfortune, pride for insolence, magnanimity for vanity, love of glory for love of money, good people for well-bred people, merit for intrigue, genius for wit, truth for pompous action, warmth of happiness for boredom of sensuality, greatness of man for pettiness of the great; a magnanimous, powerful, happy people for a polite, frivolous, despicable people—that is to say, all the virtues and all the miracles of the Republic for all the vices and all the absurdities of the monarchy.

In one word, we want to fulfill the wishes of nature, accomplish the destiny of humanity, keep the promises of philosophy, absolve Providence from the long reign of crime and tyranny.

What kind of government can realize these marvels? Only a democratic or republican government.

But what is the fundamental principle of the democratic or popular government, that is

"'Virtue and Terror'" is from Richard W. Lyman and Lewis W. Spitz, eds., *Major Crises in Western Civilization*, vol. 2 (New York: Harcourt, Brace & World, 1965), pp. 71–72.

to say, the essential strength that sustains it and makes it move? It is virtue: I am speaking of the public virtue which brought about so many marvels in Greece and Rome and which must bring about much more astonishing ones yet in republican France; of that virtue which is nothing more than love of the fatherland and of its laws.

If the strength of popular government in peacetime is virtue, the strength of popular government in revolution is both virtue and terror; terror without virtue is disastrous, virtue without terror is powerless. Terror is nothing but prompt, severe, and inflexible justice; it is thus an emanation of virtue; it is less a particular principle than a consequence of the general principle of democracy applied to the most urgent needs of the fatherland. It is said that terror is the strength of despotic government. Does ours then resemble despotism? Yes, as the sword that shines in the hands of the heroes of liberty resemble the one with which the satellites of tyranny are armed. Let the despot govern his brutalized subjects through terror; he is right as a despot. Subdue the enemies of liberty through terror and you will be right as founders of the Republic. The government of revolution is the despotism of liberty against tyranny.

CONSIDER THIS:

- Analyze this speech by Robespierre. How did he justify the use of terror in the promotion of revolution? Note, in particular, the juxtaposition of virtue and terror. In an ethical sense, can virtue ever be promoted by terror?

The Administration of Terror (June 10, 1794)

1. In the Revolutionary Tribunal there shall be a president and four vice-presidents, one public prosecutor, four substitutes for the public prosecutor, and twelve judges.
2. The jurors shall be fifty in number.
3. The Revolutionary Tribunal is instituted to punish the enemies of the people.
4. The enemies of the people are those who seek to destroy public liberty, either by force or by cunning.
5. The following are deemed enemies of the people: those who have instigated the re-establishment of monarchy, or have sought to disparage or dissolve the National Convention and the revolutionary and republican government of which it is the center;

   Those who have betrayed the Republic in the command of places and armies, or in any other military function, carried on correspondence with the enemies of the Republic, labored to disrupt the provisioning or the service of the armies;

   Those who have supported the designs of the enemies of France, either by countenancing the sheltering and the impunity of conspirators and aristocracy, by persecuting and calumniating patriotism, by corrupting the mandataries of the people, or by abusing the principles of the Revolution or the laws or measures of the government by false and perfidious applications;

   Those who have deceived the people or the representatives of the people, in order to lead them into undertakings contrary to the interests of liberty;

"The Administration of Terror" is from *A Documentary Survey of the French Revolution*, edited by John Hall Stewart, pp. 528–529.

Those who have sought to inspire discouragement, in order to favor the enterprises of the tyrants leagued against the Republic;

Those who have disseminated false news in order to divide or disturb the people;

Those who have sought to mislead opinion and to prevent the instruction of the people, to deprave morals and to corrupt the public conscience, to impair the energy and the purity of revolutionary and republican principles, or to impede the progress thereof, either by counter-revolutionary or insidious writings, or by any other machination; . . .

Finally, all who are designated in previous laws relative to the punishment of conspirators and counter-revolutionaries, and who, by whatever means or by whatever appearances they assume, have made an attempt against the liberty, unity, and security of the Republic, or labored to prevent the strengthening thereof.

7. The penalty provided for all offences under the jurisdiction of the Revolutionary Tribunal is death.
8. The proof necessary to convict enemies of the people comprises every kind of evidence, whether material or moral, oral or written, which can naturally secure the approval of every just and reasonable mind; the rule of judgments is the conscience of the jurors, enlightened by love of the Patrie; their aim, the triumph of the Republic and the ruin of its enemies; the procedure, the simple means which good sense dictates in order to arrive at a knowledge of the truth, in the forms determined by law.
9. Every citizen has the right to seize conspirators and counter-revolutionaries, and to arraign them before the magistrates. He is required to denounce them as soon as he knows of them.

Consider This:

- Because of this law, how easy was it to accuse and execute "conspirators and counterrevolutionaries?" Is "counterrevolutionary" simply another term for personal enemy? Did this law open the doors to those seeking to settle personal vendettas in the name of patriotism? What does this tell you about the process of revolution?

The Execution of Robespierre (July 28, 1794)

DURAND DE MAILLANE

Robespierre's turn had come at last. By fawning upon the people he had become their idol, and this will happen to any man who declaims against the rich, causing the people to hope for a division of the spoils. Through the populace, he ruled the Jacobin Club; through the Jacobin Club, the Convention and through the Convention, France. He dictated decrees and directed the administration. Nothing was done except by his orders or with his approval. His caprices were flattered, and his very manias were praised. The tribunal beheaded those he designated without investigation. His power seemed too terrible to his accomplices as it did to his victims. A number had been sacrificed already and others feared the same fate. They banded together to pull down the idol they themselves had set up.

[The committee of general security] ordered that he [Robespierre] be taken to the

"The Execution of Robespierre" is from E. L. Higgins, ed., *The French Revolution as Told by Contemporaries* (Boston: Houghton Mifflin, 1966), pp. 346, 361.

prison of the Conciergerie. His trial was short. On the following day he was guillotined, together with Saint-Just, Couthon, and his other accomplices. It was quite a distance from the Palais de Justice to the scaffold, and the immensity of the long Rue Saint-Honore had to be traversed. Along the whole course, the people pursued Robespierre with hoots and maledictions. He had been given a conspicuous place in the tumbril, his face half covered by a dirty, bloodstained cloth which enveloped his jaw. It may be said that this man, who had brought so much anguish to others, suffered during these twenty-four hours all the pain and agony that a mortal can experience.

THE BROADER PERSPECTIVE:

- With the execution of Robespierre, the Terror ended and the revolution entered another phase called Thermidor, where political radicals were purged and moderation became the watchword. In this last section, we have seen the great ironies and contradictions attending the process of political change with "enemies of the Revolution" (Desmoulins) juxtaposed with "martyrs of the Revolution (Marat), and "heroes of the Revolution"(Robespierre) pronounced enemies of the state and executed. Given this, compare these two quotes from former Supreme Court justice Louis Brandeis and former Senator Barry Goldwater:

> The greatest dangers to liberty lurk in insidious encroachment by men of zeal—well-meaning, but without understanding.
>
> —JUSTICE LOUIS D. BRANDEIS

> Extremism in the defense of liberty is no vice. And . . . moderation in the pursuit of justice is no virtue.
>
> —BARRY GOLDWATER (1964)

How are these perspectives relevant to a discussion of the French Revolution? Do you find these opinions to be valid? Why or why not?

NATIONALISM AND ROMANTICISM: "THE SPIRIT OF THE PEOPLE"

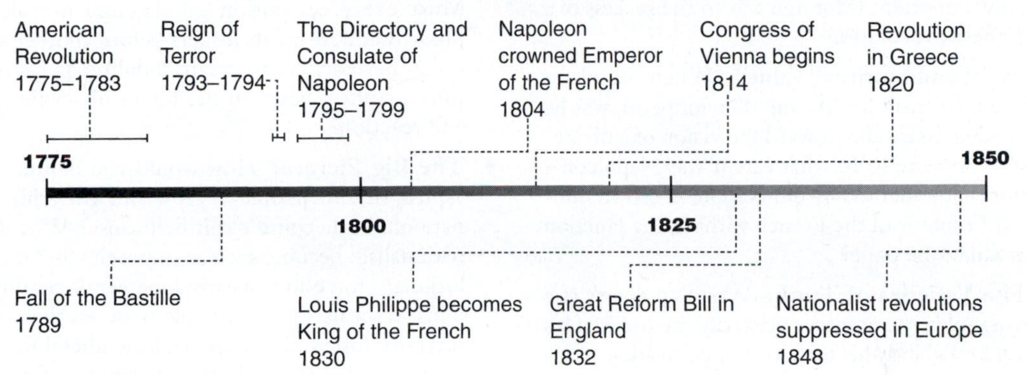

Do you know what astounds me most about the world? It is the impotence of force to establish anything. In the end, the sword is always conquered by the mind.

—NAPOLEON BONAPARTE (1808)

Nationhood is a baptismal rite which endows a people with its own character and rank in the brotherhood of nations.

—GIUSEPPE MAZZINI

Those nations in which no mixture of races has occurred are imperfect; and those in which its effects have disappeared are decrepit. A State which is incompetent to satisfy different races condemns itself; a State which labors to neutralize, to absorb, or to expel them, destroys its own vitality; a State which does not include them is destitute of the chief basis of self-government. The theory of nationality, therefore, is a retrograde step in history.

—LORD ACTON

CHAPTER THEMES

- **The Power Structure:** Did the French Revolution result in a democratic system of government for France or in the tyranny of Napoleon? How easily can the process of democracy degenerate into extremism? Is freedom, most importantly, just a state of mind?
- **Revolution and Historical Transition:** How contagious is the "revolutionary spirit"? Why were the ideals of the French Revolution so attractive to liberals and so threatening to conservatives of early nineteenth-century Europe? How was this "revolutionary moment" sustained

for the next fifty years, and what role did nationalism play in the promotion of revolution? Was Napoleon a conduit of progressive change or a threat to national stability?

- **Imperialism:** Many eighteenth-century French statesmen believed it was important to export the ideals of the French Revolution through war and imperialism. Is this a valid goal? Can one impose the ideals of democracy on other people? How important is foreign war to the success of a domestic revolution?
- **Social and Spiritual Values:** When Napoleon became consul for life and then emperor, was he moving inexorably toward the vision of a divine-right monarch? To what extent was Napoleon a spiritual leader? Why did Napoleon crown himself Emperor of the French without the sanction or aid of the pope?
- **The Varieties of Truth:** Was Napoleon's rise from soldier to emperor primarily the result of his military ability, his luck, or the cultivation of his image? Does one gain power through military or political ability and maintain power through creation of belief? Did the painter Jacques-Louis David actually create the image of Napoleon for posterity? Was it real?
- **The Individual and the Institution:** How important is the "hero" in history? Did Robespierre and Napoleon "create" and control the French Revolution? Or did they merely "ride the wave" of social and economic forces? Must every revolution go through a violent phase that devours its leaders before another so-called hero arrives to create stability? Is history thus a contest between the forces of revolution and reaction?
- **The Big Picture:** How would you define the "spirit of the people"? How did the idea of nationhood become a spiritual cause? Why did nationalism become such an important and revolutionary force in the early nineteenth century? This was a period of struggle between the conservative forces of stability and the liberal forces of change. Is change always a progressive force?

In October 1793, the artist Jacques-Louis David gazed through the crowd at a cart being drawn slowly toward the Place de la Revolution. Several guillotines had been set around the circle as vehicles for the "swift, inflexible justice" that was pouring from the revolutionary tribunals established during the previous summer to identify and hunt down any and all "enemies of the revolution." David understood the importance of the moment as he strained to draw quickly the sullen figure in the cart. When the blade severed the head of Queen Marie Antoinette, she became among the first victims of what was to be one of the bloodiest periods of French history. The Reign of Terror (1793–1794) claimed over 25,000 lives—first members of the royal family and nobility, then political opponents of the radical ruling Jacobin faction, then friends and associates who threatened the process, then the revolutionaries themselves. The thirst for blood transformed the noble ideals of the French Revolution into extremist rage born of fear and distrust, guided by lust for power.

Revolutions generally go through conservative and radical phases, and differences among revolutionaries often result in violence. The path toward freedom or despotism is then littered with bodies and bloodshed. In the power vacuum created by such chaos, the door is frequently left open for a transfer of power. During the French Revolution, an individual seized the initiative, filled the power vacuum, and altered its course. His name was Napoleon Bonaparte.

The mere name of Napoleon (1769–1821) evokes a wide array of emotions. As is the case with most influential individuals, he inspires controversy. Some historians have described him as a force for good, a lawgiver and reformer who spread revolutionary ideals throughout Europe. Others have viewed him as an egomaniac whose lust for conquest

FIGURE 6.1 *Marie Antoinette Taken to Her Execution.* Drawing by Jacques-Louis David. Having executed King Louis XVI in January, 1793, the revolutionary tribunals sent Queen Marie Antoinette to the guillotine in October. (*Art Resource, NY*)

overshadowed any other secondary achievements. Whatever final judgment one may make, it is clear that Napoleon Bonaparte had a brilliant mind, equally at home in the context of law and military strategy.

Napoleon was born in 1769 to a poor family of lesser nobility on the island of Corsica. The "Little Corporal," as he was called, went to French schools and obtained a commission as a French artillery officer. He was enthusiastic about the revolution of 1789 and was rewarded for his military service against the British with a promotion to brigadier general. After the fall of Robespierre in 1794, Napoleon's radical political associations threatened his career, but he was able to convince the new government of his loyalty. This government was called the Directory, and it was composed of people who had benefitted from the recent revolution and whose major goal was to perpetuate their own rule. Their chief opposition came from royalists, who supported a monarch as head of France and who had won a majority of the seats in the legislature in 1797. With the aid of Napoleon, the Directory succeeded in overthrowing the elected officials and placed their own supporters in the legislature. Napoleon then received a command against the Austrians and Sardinians that resulted in a swift victory for the French and eventual annexation of Italy. Napoleon was hailed as a hero. He decided to sail to Egypt to fight the British fleet and, it was hoped, cut off British contact and trade with its colonies in the East. However, the invasion of Egypt (1798) was a failure for the French; Napoleon abandoned his troops and returned to Paris, where he overthrew the Directory that he had once championed (November 10, 1799). Establishing a new government called the Consulate, he then issued the Constitution for the Year VIII (December 1799), which promoted liberal ideas such as universal manhood suffrage and a system of governmental checks and balances but in reality granted Napoleon virtual dictatorial power as first consul. His position was confirmed by a plebiscite that approved the new constitution by a vote of 3,011,077 to 1,567. Both the middle and lower classes seemed satisfied to accept the security that Napoleon offered.

Napoleon then quickly consolidated his rule by achieving peace with Austria and Britain and by restoring order at home. In 1801, he concluded a concordat with the Catholic church, which in fact resulted in the subordination of the church to the state; there would be no controversy between secular and religious authority in Napoleonic France. So satisfied were French citizens that in 1802 they voted Napoleon consul for life. In 1804, there was simply no one with enough authority to grant him the final accolade, so Napoleon crowned himself Napoleon I, Emperor of the French. The pope sat nearby watching the ceremony. Napoleon had achieved the ultimate authority, which had escaped even Charlemagne.

In his decade as emperor, Napoleon conquered most of Europe, spreading France's revolutionary ideals. It was at this time, too, that he paid great attention to domestic concerns and soon instituted reforms and programs, including a codification of laws known as the Napoleonic Code. His glory came to an end in 1814 when he was finally defeated by a coalition of European powers. Napoleon's brief return from exile was unsuccessful and resulted in his defeat by Lord Wellington at Waterloo. The victors agreed at the Congress of Vienna in 1815 that no single state should dominate Europe: Power must be balanced. Another Napoleon would not be tolerated. The great general was ingloriously exiled to St. Helena, an isolated and inaccessible rock in the Atlantic. He died there in 1821 of stomach cancer or, as some modern researchers advocate, the victim of gradual poisoning. Even in death, Napoleon remains a controversial figure.

In this chapter, we look at Napoleon's rise to power and especially his attempts to consolidate his position. Napoleon was certainly a military leader of genius, but his achievements often inspire philosophical rather than military analysis. His career raises questions about the nature of power and the ability of the individual to change the course of history. Is history motivated by social and economic forces over which individuals have no control? Or does the hero actually change history by force of personality and ability? Did Napoleon make France a great nation through his reforms and conquests? If so, does progress come about because of the imposition of reforms on a people? Was Napoleon, who overthrew the legitimate elected government of France and installed a dictatorship, necessary for the progress of a revolution dedicated to liberty and equality?

In this chapter, we also analyze the artistic and literary movement called Romanticism that existed contemporaneously with these political events. This was a revolutionary period in art, poetry, music, and literature as great creative figures such as Johann von Goethe, Ludwig van Beethoven, William Wordsworth, and Eugene Delacroix broke through the boundaries of established forms and created new standards of artistic expression. This was a movement inspired by the beauty and power of nature, by confidence in personal intuition and in the validity of the senses, and finally by the passion of nationalism, a watchword for the century.

The Napoleonic Era (1796–1815)

What is the throne?—a bit of wood gilded and covered with velvet. I am the state—I alone am the representative of the people. . . . France has more need of me than I of France.

—NAPOLEON BONAPARTE (1814)

Men of genius are meteors destined to be consumed in lighting up their century.

—NAPOLEON BONAPARTE (1791)

The Will to Power (1796–1802)

After the Reign of Terror (1793–1794), the French Revolution entered a moderate period that retreated from the violent radicalism of Robespierre. A new government called the Directory was formed, and it governed the French Republic rather ineffectively until 1799. In that year, Napoleon Bonaparte, who had supported the Directory and had earned fame as the military protector of the Republic, returned to Paris from his Egyptian campaign and promptly overthrew the government. In its place, he established the Consulate. Napoleon, as first consul, was given significant power over his other two colleagues. On December 15, 1799, the Consulate proclaimed the end of the French Revolution. The ideals that founded the Republic ostensibly had not changed, but the leadership certainly had. The following excerpt is from a conversation Napoleon had with one of his confidants in 1796, three years before coming into power. It reveals much about Napoleon's ambition.

On the Realities of Power (1796)

NAPOLEON BONAPARTE

What I have done so far is nothing. I am but at the opening of the career I am to run. Do you suppose that I have gained my victories in Italy in order to advance the lawyers of the Directory? Do you think, either, that my object is to establish a Republic? What a notion! A republic of thirty million people, with our morals and vices! How could that ever be? It is a chimera with which the French are infatuated but which will pass away in time like all others. What they want is glory and the gratification of their vanity; as for liberty, of that they have no conception. Look at the army! The victories which we have just gained have given the French soldier his true character. I am everything to him. Let the Directory attempt to deprive me of my command and they will see who is master. The nation must have a head, a head rendered illustrious by glory and not by theories of government, fine phrases, or the talk of idealists, of which the French understand not a whit. Let them have their toys and they will be satisfied. They will amuse themselves and allow themselves to be led, provided the goal is cleverly disguised.

CONSIDER THIS:

- What does the excerpt on Napoleon's political goals reveal about his commitment to the democratic ideals of the French Revolution? Compare Napoleon's political vision carefully with Machiavelli's ideas from *The Prince*. Was Machiavelli correct? Must any ideal in the political world remain of secondary importance to the necessity of gaining and maintaining power?
- Was Napoleon correct? Must the goals of power always be "cleverly disguised"? How important is deceit in gaining and maintaining power?

THE BROADER PERSPECTIVE:

- Has the nature of political power changed in our contemporary world or has technology simplified the "creation of belief" and thus made personal freedom even more difficult to maintain?

"On the Realities of Power" is from *Memoirs of Miot de Melito*, in James H. Robinson, ed.,*Translations and Reprints from the Original Sources of European History*, rev. ed., vol. 2, pt. 2 (Philadelphia: University of Pennsylvania Press, 1900), pp. 2–3.

The First Consul: "A Citizen Devoted to the Republic" (November 10, 1799)

NAPOLEON BONAPARTE

The next document is a proclamation to the French people that explains Napoleon's role in the overthrow of the Directory and the establishment of the Consulate. It is a fine example of effective propaganda.

On my return to Paris [from Egypt] I found division among all authorities, and agreement upon only one point, namely, that the Constitution was half destroyed and was unable to save liberty.

All parties came to me, confided to me their designs, disclosed their secrets, and requested my support; I refused to be the man of a party.

The Council of Elders summoned me; I answered its appeal. A plan of general restoration had been devised by men whom the nation has been accustomed to regard as the defenders of liberty, equality, and property; this plan required an examination, calm, free, exempt from all influence and all fear. Accordingly, the Council of Elders resolved upon the removal of the Legislative Body to Saint-Cloud; it gave me the responsibility of disposing the force necessary for its independence. I believe it my duty to my fellow citizens, to the soldiers perishing in our armies, to the national glory acquired at the cost of their blood, to accept the command.

The Councils assembled at Saint-Cloud; republican troops guaranteed their security from without, but assassins created terror within. Several deputies of the Council of Five Hundred, armed with stilettos and firearms, circulated threats of death around them.

The plans which ought to have been developed were withheld, the majority disorganized, the boldest orators disconcerted, and the futility of every wise proposition was evident.

I took my indignation and grief to the Council of Elders. I besought it to assure the execution of its generous designs; I directed its attention to the evils of the *Patrie* [Fatherland] . . . ; it concurred with me by new evidence of its steadfast will.

I presented myself at the Council of Five Hundred, alone, unarmed, my head uncovered, just as the Elders had received and applauded me; I came to remind the majority of its wishes, and to assure it of its power.

The stilettos which menaced the deputies were instantly raised against their liberator; twenty assassins threw themselves upon me and aimed at my breast. The grenadiers of the Legislative Body whom I had left at the door of the hall ran forward, placed themselves between the assassins and myself. One of these brave grenadiers had his clothes pierced by a stiletto. They bore me out.

At the same moment cries of "Outlaw" were raised against the defender of the law. It was the fierce cry of assassins against the power destined to repress them.

They crowded around the president, uttering threats, arms in their hands; they commanded him to outlaw me; I was informed of this: I ordered him to be rescued from their fury, and six grenadiers of the Legislative Body secured him. Immediately afterwards some grenadiers of the Legislative Body charged into the hall and cleared it.

The factions, intimidated, dispersed and fled. The majority, freed from their attacks, returned freely and peaceably into the meeting hall, listened to the proposals on behalf of public safety, deliberated, and prepared the salutary resolution which is to become the new and provisional law of the Republic.

Frenchmen, you will doubtless recognize in this conduct the zeal of a soldier of liberty, a citizen devoted to the Republic. Conservative, tutelary, and liberal ideas have been restored to their rights through the dispersal of the rebels who oppressed the Councils.

CONSIDER THIS:

- How did Napoleon come to power in 1799? Carefully read the statement he made on becoming consul. Pay particular attention to the vocabulary. How did Napoleon justify his overthrow of the Directory?
- Balance this public statement with the attitude found in the excerpt "On the Realities of Power." How did Napoleon use the rhetoric of the revolution to fashion his own dictatorship?

THE BROADER PERSPECTIVE:

- At the end of the eighteenth century, did France need less ideal and more practical inspiration and leadership to progress as a nation? Was Napoleon a hypocrite who saved France from chaos? If so, do you condemn him for his hypocrisy?

Suppression of the Newspapers (1800)

To consolidate the new regime, Napoleon sought to control the flow of information in the state. In the next document, note the reasons given for suppression of the newspapers.

The consuls of the Republic, considering that a part of the newspapers which are printed in the department of the Seine are instruments in the hands of the enemies of the Republic; that the government is particularly charged by the French people to look after their security, orders as follows:

1. The minister of police shall permit to be printed, published, and circulated during the whole course of the war only the following newspapers: . . . [Here follows the names of thirteen newspapers], and newspapers devoted exclusively to science, arts, literature, commerce, announcements and notices.

2. The minister of the general police shall immediately make a report upon all the newspapers that are printed in the other departments.

3. The minister of the general police shall see that no new newspaper be printed in the department of the Seine, as well as in all the other departments of the Republic.

4. The proprietors and editors of the newspapers preserved by the present order shall present themselves to the minister of the police in order to attest their character as French citizens, their residences and signatures, and they shall promise fidelity to the constitution.

5. All newspapers which shall insert articles opposed to the respect that is due to the social compact, to the sovereignty of the people and the glory of the armies, or which shall publish invectives against the governments and nations who are the friends or allies of the Republic, even when these articles may be extracts from foreign periodicals, shall be immediately suppressed.

6. The minister of the general police is charged with the execution of the present order, which shall be inserted in the Bulletin of the Laws.

"Suppression of the Newspapers" is from Frank M. Anderson, ed., *The Constitutions and Other Illustrative Documents of the History of France*, 2nd ed., revised (New York: Russell and Russell, 1908), p. 282.

Articles for the Catholic Church (1802)

Between July 1801 and April 1802, Napoleon sought to reorganize the religious institutions of France. The following selection is a legislative act of state that was promulgated without the pope's consent but enforced nevertheless. There were other similar pronouncements for Protestants (1802) and Jews (1808).

1. No bull, brief, rescript, decree, injunction, provision, signature serving as a provision, nor other documents from the court of Rome, even concerning individuals only, can be received, published, printed, or otherwise put into effect, without the authorization of the government.
4. No national or metropolitan council, no diocesan synod, no deliberative assembly, shall take place without the express permission of the government.
6. There shall be recourse to the Council of State in every case of abuse on the part of the Superiors and other ecclesiastical persons.

   The cases of abuse are usurpation or excess of power, contravention of the laws and regulations of the Republic, infraction of the rules sanctioned by the canons received in France, attack upon the liberties, privileges and customs of the Gallican church, and every undertaking or any proceeding which in the exercise of worship can compromise the honor of the citizens, disturb arbitrarily their consciences, or degenerate into oppression or injury against them or into public scandal.

CONSIDER THIS:

- On becoming first consul, Napoleon consolidated his position by suppressing the newspapers and reorganizing the state's religious institutions. Do you think these measures were consistent with democratic government? From Napoleon's perspective, why were these actions essential to the stability of the state?

The Imperial Mantle (1804–1806)

Five years after Napoleon became head of the French government as First Consul, then as Consul for Life, he moved to expand his power. On May 18, 1804, the Senate decreed that he should be made Emperor of the French. The people of France overwhelmingly approved of this measure through a plebiscite. Napoleon now had complete control of France's government and fate.

In the first excerpt, given before the legislative body of December 31, 1804, Napoleon recounts the reasons for establishing the government of the Empire in place of the Consulate. Note the importance of having the pope "officiate" at the coronation. In fact, Napoleon crowned himself emperor because he did not recognize the pope's authority as superior to his own. But why did the French people willingly submit to the despotism of Napoleon? In the second selection, the Comtesse de Rémusat (1780–1821), lady-in-waiting to Napoleon's wife, Josephine, and the author of some lively memoirs, gives her assessment. Appropriately, Napoleon found divine sanction for his power. The third offering recounts a catechism written during the reign of Louis XIV and modified to meet Napoleon's particular needs. Its questions and answers address the duties of French citizens toward their emperor.

"Articles for the Catholic Church" is from Frank M. Anderson, ed.,*The Constitutions and Other Illustrative Documents of the History of France*, 2nd ed., revised (New York: Russell and Russell, 1908), p. 299.

"The Only Salvation Lies in Hereditary Power" (December 1804)

NAPOLEON BONAPARTE

The internal situation of France is today as calm as it has ever been in the most peaceful periods. There is no agitation to disturb the public tranquility, no suggestion of those crimes which recall the Revolution. Everywhere useful enterprises are in progress, and the general improvements, both public and private, attest the universal confidence and sense of security. . . .

A plot conceived by an implacable government was about to replunge France into the abyss of civil war and anarchy. The discovery of this horrible crime stirred all France profoundly, and anxieties that had scarcely been calmed again awoke. Experience has taught that a divided power in the state is impotent and at odds with itself. It was generally felt that if power was delegated for short periods only, it was so uncertain as to discourage any prolonged undertakings or wide-reaching plans. If vested in an individual for life, it would lapse with him, and after him would prove a source of anarchy and discord. It was clearly seen that for a great nation the only salvation lies in hereditary power, which can alone assure a continuous political life which may endure for generations, even for centuries.

The Senate, as was proper, served as the organ through which this general apprehension found expression. The necessity of hereditary power in a state as vast as France had long been perceived by the First Consul. He had endeavored in vain to avoid this conclusion; but the public solicitude and the hopes of our enemies emphasized the importance of his task, and he realized that his death might ruin his whole work. Under such circumstances, and with such a pressure of public opinion, there was no alternative left to the First Consul. He resolved, therefore, to accept for himself, and two of his brothers after him, the burden imposed by the exigencies of the situation.

After prolonged consideration, repeated conferences with the members of the Senate, discussion in the councils, and the suggestions of the most prudent advisers, a series of provisions was drawn up which regulate the succession to the imperial throne. These provisions were decreed by a *senatus consultus* of the 28th Floreal last. The French people, by a free and independent expression, then manifested its desire that the imperial dignity should pass down in a direct line through the legitimate or adopted descendants of Napoleon Bonaparte, or through the legitimate descendants of Joseph Bonaparte, or of Louis Bonaparte.

From this moment Napoleon was, by the most unquestioned of titles, emperor of the French. No other act was necessary to sanction his right and consecrate his authority. But he wished to restore in France the ancient forms and recall those institutions which divinity itself seems to have inspired. He wished to impress the seal of religion itself upon the opening of his reign. The head of the Church, in order to give the French a striking proof of his paternal affection, consented to officiate at this August ceremony. What deep and enduring impressions did this leave on the mind of Napoleon and in the memory of the nation! What thoughts for future races! What a subject of wonder for all Europe!

In the midst of this pomp, and under the eye of the Eternal, Napoleon pronounced the inviolable oath which assures the integrity of the empire, the security of property, the perpetuity of institutions, the respect for Law,

"'The Only Salvation Lies in Hereditary Power'" is from James H. Robinson and Charles A. Beard, eds., *Readings in Modern European History*, vol. 1 (Boston: Ginn and Company, 1908), pp. 334–336.

and the happiness of the nation. The oath of Napoleon shall be forever the terror of the enemies of France. If our borders are attacked, it will be repeated at the head of our armies, and our frontiers shall never more fear foreign invasion.

Why the French Submitted to Napoleon's Rule (1804)

COMTESSE DE RÉMUSAT

I can understand how it was that men worn out by the turmoil of the Revolution, and afraid of that liberty which had long been associated with death, looked for repose under the dominion of an able ruler on who Fortune was seemingly resolved to smile. I can conceive that they regarded his elevation as a decree of destiny and fondly believed that in the irrevocable they should find peace. I may confidently assert that those persons believed quite sincerely that Bonaparte, whether as Consul or Emperor, would exert his authority to oppose the intrigues of faction and would save us from the perils of anarchy.

None dared to utter the word "republic," so deeply had the Terror stained that name; and the government of the Directory had perished in the contempt with which its chiefs were regarded. The return of the Bourbons could only be brought about by the aid of a revolution; and the slightest disturbance terrified the French people, in whom enthusiasm of every kind seemed dead. Besides, the men in whom they had trusted had one after the other deceived them; and as, this time, they were yielding to force, they were at least certain they were not deceiving themselves.

The belief, or rather the error, that only despotism could at that epoch maintain order in France was very widespread. It became the mainstay of Bonaparte; and it is due to him to say that he also believed it. The factions played into his hands by imprudent attempts which he turned to his own advantage. He had some grounds for his belief that he was necessary; France believed it, too; and he even succeeded in persuading foreign sovereigns that he constituted a barrier against republican influences, which, but for him, might spread widely. At the moment when Bonaparte placed the imperial crown upon his head there was not a king in Europe who did not believe that he wore his own crown more securely because of that event. Had the new emperor granted a liberal constitution, the peace of nations and of kings might really have been forever secured.

COMPARE AND CONTRAST:

- In 1804, Napoleon became Emperor of the French by decree of the senate. How does this position differ from that of First Consul for Life? Compare the reasons that Napoleon gives for assuming this position with those given when he became First Consul. Is there any pattern of justification?

THE BROADER PERSPECTIVE:

- Note that the people of France approved of Napoleon's rise to power and his assumption of titles by supporting him with plebiscites. Were they in fact limiting their own freedom? Is freedom, most importantly, just a state of mind? Does progress often depend on a restriction of freedom in the interests of stability and security?

"Why the French Submitted to Napoleon's Rule" is from James H. Robinson and Charles A. Beard, eds., *Readings in Modern European History*, vol. 1 (Boston: Ginn and Company, 1908), pp. 333–334.

The Imperial Catechism (April 1806)

Question: What are the duties of Christians toward those who govern them, and what in particular are our duties towards Napoleon I, our emperor?

Answer: Christians owe to the princes who govern them, and we in particular owe to Napoleon I, our emperor, love, respect, obedience, fidelity, military service, and the taxes levied for the preservation and defense of the empire and of his throne. We also owe him fervent prayers for his safety and for the spiritual and temporal prosperity of the state.

Question: Why are we subject to all these duties toward our emperor?

Answer: First, because God, who has created empires and distributes them according to his will, has, by loading our emperor with gifts both in peace and in war, established him as our sovereign and made him the agent of his power and his image on earth. To honor and serve our emperor is therefore to honor and serve God himself. Secondly, because our Lord Jesus Christ himself, both by his teaching and his example, has taught us what we owe to our sovereign. Even at his very birth he obeyed the edict of Caesar Augustus; he paid the established tax; and while he commanded us to render to God those things which belong to God, he also commanded us to render unto Caesar those things which are Caesar's.

Question: Are there not special motives which should attach us more closely to Napoleon I, our emperor?

Answer: Yes, for it is he whom God has raised up in trying times to reestablish the public worship of the holy religion of our fathers and to be its protector; he has reestablished and preserved public order by his profound and active wisdom; he defends the state by his mighty arm; he has become the anointed of the Lord by the consecration which he has received from the sovereign pontiff, head of the Church universal.

Question: What must we think of those who are neglecting their duties toward our emperor?

Answer: According to the apostle Paul, they are resisting the order established by God himself, and render themselves worthy of eternal damnation.

CONSIDER THIS:

- What comments can you make regarding Napoleon and religion? What role did religion play in the establishment of Napoleon's political power? Why is it essential in time of revolution for the state to control religious organization?

THE BROADER PERSPECTIVE:

- Should we characterize the protestant reformer John Calvin as a spiritual leader and Napoleon as a political leader? Or do the demands of controlling a spiritual or political movement blur the boundaries of such designations? To obtain effective control over people, must spiritual leaders grant themselves political power and must political leaders claim spiritual authority?

- Was Napoleon an absolute monarch in the tradition of Louis XIV? Was he a democrat or the first of the so-called modern dictators in the fascist mold of Mussolini and Hitler? Does the distinction between a democrat and a dictator blur when one is trying to achieve and consolidate power?

"The Imperial Catechism" is from James H. Robinson and Charles A. Beard, eds., *Readings in Modern European History*, vol. 1 (Boston: Ginn and Company, 1908), pp. 351–352.

The Military Genius

Beginning in 1792 and continuing throughout much of the revolution, France was at war against various coalitions of European nations. Revolutionary ideology was exportable and threatened the very foundation of enlightened despotism. As the French revolutionaries attacked the church, monarchy, and aristocracy, most of Europe, including Great Britain, reacted by repressing liberal reform movements. These wars at once threatened the revolution and also granted it purpose and unity. Napoleon, a military commander of genius and overreaching ambition, capitalized on this French spirit of the times and sought first to link himself with the revolutionary forces within the state and then, as consul and emperor, to dominate Europe both militarily and culturally from 1803 to his final defeat at Waterloo in 1815. In the process, he inspired France and certainly changed the course of history. Napoleon believed his actions were directed toward a destiny that he was compelled to achieve by fate. The next selection is a good example of this belief. It is an address to Dutch representatives on the annexation of Holland to the French empire in 1810.

"An End to the Woes of Anarchy" (1810)

NAPOLEON BONAPARTE

When Providence elevated me to the first throne in the world it became my duty, while establishing forever the destinies of France, to determine the fate of all those people who formed a part of the empire, to insure for all the benefits of stability and order, and to put an end everywhere to the woes of anarchy. I have done away with the uncertainty in Italy by placing upon my head the crown of iron. . . .

I gave you a prince of my own blood to govern you. . . . I have opened the continent to your industry, and the day will come when you shall bear my eagles upon the seas which your ancestors have rendered illustrious. You will then show yourself worthy of them and of me. . . .

CONSIDER THIS:

- What was Napoleon's view of his own destiny? Was he a progressive or destructive force in French history?

The Invasion of Russia (1812)

NAPOLEON BONAPARTE

The image of Napoleon and his glorious reputation as a military genius was cultivated through the paintings of Jacques-Louis David and the memoirs of Napoleon's commanders. Without doubt, Napoleon demonstrated organizational ability and strategic brilliance. This, coupled with a nearly limitless supply of well-trained French soldiers, allowed him to dominate and expand his control over the European continent.

"'An End to the Woes of Anarchy'" is from James H. Robinson and Charles A. Beard, eds., *Readings in Modern European History*, vol. 1 (Boston: Ginn and Company, 1908), pp. 355–356.

"The Invasion of Russia" is from James H. Robinson and Charles A. Beard, eds., *Readings in Modern European History*, vol. 1 (Boston: Ginn and Company, 1908), pp. 356–357.

Napoleon's grand ambitions, however, proved his undoing during his famous invasion of Russia through Poland in June 1812. The first selection is Napoleon's proclamation to his Grand Army at the outset of the Russian campaign. His boastful words turned to disaster as Napoleon was unable to engage the Russian army on favorable terms and left a burning Moscow to be dogged by constant surprise attacks, the ravages of hunger, and the devastation of the harsh Russian winter. The section ends with an account of the disaster from the memoirs of one of Napoleon's commanders, Wairy Louis Constant.

Soldiers, the second war of Poland has commenced. The first was brought to a close at Friedland and Tilsit. At Tilsit, Russia swore eternal alliance with France and war with England. She now violates her oaths, she refuses to give any explanation of her strange conduct, except on condition that the eagles of France shall repass the Rhine, leaving, by such a movement, our allies at her mercy. Russia is dragged along by a fate. Her destinies must be accomplished. Shall she then consider us degenerate? Are we no longer to be looked upon as the soldiers of Austerlitz [a Napoleonic victory]? She offers us the alternative of dishonor or war. The choice does not admit of hesitation. Let us march forward. Let us pass the Nieman [River]. Let us carry war into her territory. The second war of Poland will be as glorious to the French arms as was the first; but the peace which we shall conclude will be its own guaranty and will put an end to the proud and haughty influence which Russia has for fifty years exercised in the affairs of Europe.

At Our Headquarters at Wilkowiski
June 22,1815

"Everything Had Failed Us"

WAIRY LOUIS CONSTANT

The emperor awaited daylight in a poor hut, and in the morning said to Prince Berthier, "Well, Berthier, how can we get out of this?" He was seated in his room, great tears flowing down his cheeks, which were paler than usual; and the prince was seated near him. They exchanged few words, and the emperor appeared overcome by his grief. I leave to the imagination what was passing in his soul. . . .

On the 29th the emperor quitted the banks of the Beresina and we slept at Kamen, where his Majesty occupied a poor wooden building which the icy air penetrated from all sides through the windows, for nearly all the glass was broken. We closed the openings as well as we could with bundles of hay. A short distance from us, in a large lot, were penned up the wretched Russian prisoners whom the army drove before it. I had much difficulty in comprehending the delusion of victory which our poor soldiers still kept up by dragging after them this wretched luxury of prisoners, who could only be an added burden, as they required constant surveillance. When the conquerors are dying of famine, what becomes of the conquered? These poor Russians, exhausted by marches and hunger, nearly all perished that night. . . .

On the 3rd of December we arrived at Malodeczno. During the whole day the emperor appeared thoughtful and anxious. . . . At two leagues from Smorghoni, the duke of Vicenza summoned me and told me to go on

"'Everything Had Failed Us'" is from James H. Robinson and Charles A. Beard, eds., *Readings in Modern European History*, vol. 1 (Boston: Ginn and Company, 1908), pp. 357–360.

in front and give orders to have the six best horses harnessed to my carriage, which was the lightest of all, and keep them in constant readiness. I reached Smorghoni before the emperor, who did not arrive until the following night. . . . After supper the emperor ordered Prince Eugene to read the twenty-ninth bulletin and spoke freely of his plans, saying that his departure was essential in order to send help to the army. . . .

The emperor left in the night. By daybreak the army had learned the news, and the impression it made cannot be depicted. Discouragement was at its height, and many soldiers cursed the emperor and reproached him for abandoning them.

This night, the 6th, the cold increased greatly. Its severity may be imagined, as birds were found on the ground frozen stiff. Soldiers seated themselves with their heads in their hands and bodies bent forward in order thus to feel less the emptiness of their stomachs. . . . Everything had failed us. Long before reaching Vilna, the horses being dead, we received orders to burn our carriages and all their contents.

CONSIDER THIS:

- Napoleon has been called a military genius, and indeed his conquest of a large part of Europe would support that judgment. But after reading the accounts of his invasion and retreat from Russia, what perspective can you give on his character and qualities of leadership? Did he sacrifice the lives of soldiers to satiate his ego, or was his vision of a French empire worth dying for? Why did the soldiers of France support him even during his darkest days?

Exile and Death: The Hero in History

After the victory of the Duke of Wellington over the French forces at Waterloo in 1815, Napoleon was sentenced to permanent exile on the South Atlantic island of Saint Helena. The next selection from his diary gives indication of his dominant personality and spirit. However, he remained on this isolated rock until his death in 1821.

Napoleon in Exile: "We Stand as Martyrs to an Immortal Cause!"

NAPOLEON BONAPARTE

What infamous treatment they have held in store for us! This is the agony of death! To injustice, to violence, they add insult and slow torture! If I was so dangerous, why didn't they get rid of me? A few bullets in my heart or in my head would have settled it; there would have been some courage at least in such a crime! How can the Sovereigns of Europe permit the sacred nature of sovereignty to be attainted in me? Can't they see that they are killing themselves at St. Helena? I have entered their capitals as a conqueror; had I been moved by such motives, what would have become of them? They all called me their brother, and I had become so by the will of the people, the sanction of victory, the character of religion, the alliances of policy and of family. . . . Apart from that, who has there been in history with more partisans, more friends? Who has been more popular, more beloved? Who ever left behind more ardent regrets? Look at France: might not

"Napoleon in Exile" is from R. M. Johnston, ed., *The Corsican: A Diary of Napoleon's Life in His Own Words* (Boston: Houghton Mifflin, 1910), pp. 468–469.

one say that from this rock of mine I still reign over her? . . .

Our situation may even have good points! The Universe watches us! We stand as martyrs to an immortal cause! Millions of men weep with us, our country sighs, and glory has put on mourning! We struggle here against the tyranny of the gods, and the hopes of humanity are with us! Misfortune itself knows heroism, and glory! Only adversity was wanting to complete my career! Had I died on the throne, in the clouds of my almightiness, I would have remained a problem for many; as it is, thanks to my misfortunes, I can be judged naked.

The Role of Great Men in History

G. W. F. HEGEL

The career of Napoleon challenges us with a fundamental question: What is the role of the "great man" or "hero" in history? Can the course of history be changed by a dynamic individual of ability and resolve? Or does history progress by uncontrollable economic and social "forces"? The following selection is by G. W. F. Hegel, a German philosopher who believed that "heroes" such as Caesar, Alexander, and Napoleon were unconscious instruments of a "world spirit" (*Zeitgeist*) that lay behind the development of human history. The chosen passage reveals Hegel's thoughts about how heroes could change the course of history. Hegel is representative of the romantic belief, current in the early nineteenth century, that human history was connected with much larger spiritual forces.

Such are all great historical men—whose own particular aims involve those large issues which are the will of the World-Spirit. They may be called Heroes, inasmuch as they have derived their purposes and their vocation, not from the calm, regular course of things, sanctioned by the existing order: but from a concealed fount—one which has not attained to phenomenal, present existence—from that inner Spirit, still hidden beneath the surface, which, impinging on the outer world as on a shell, bursts it in pieces, because it is another kernel than that which belonged to the shell in question. They are men, therefore, who appear to draw the impulse of their life from themselves; and whose deeds have produced a condition of things and a complex of historical relations which appear to be only their interest, and their work.

Such individuals had no consciousness of the general idea they were unfolding, while prosecuting those aims of theirs; on the contrary, they were practical, political men. But at the same time they were thinking men, who had an insight into the requirements of the time—what was ripe for development. This was the very Truth for their age, for their world: the species next in order, so to speak, and which was already formed in the womb of time. It was theirs to know this nascent principle; the necessary, directly sequent step in progress, which their world was to take; to make this their aim, and to expend their energy in promoting it. World-historical men—the Heroes of an epoch—must, therefore, be recognized as its clear-sighted ones: their deed, their words are the best of that time.

"The Role of Great Men in History" is from G. W. F. Hegel, *The Philosophy of History*, trans. J. Sibree (New York: Dover, 1956), pp. 30–31. Reprinted by permission of the publisher.

THE BROADER PERSPECTIVE:

- How did Napoleon embody Hegel's conception of the term *hero*? Was the philosophy of Jean-Jacques Rousseau on the Social Contract every bit as much a force for the promotion of historical change as were the actions of Napoleon Bonaparte?

The Romantic Movement (1780–1830)

The dramatic events from the French Revolution in 1789 to the fall of Napoleon in 1815 transformed European social and political realities, and they also found expression in the art and literature of the day. The term *Romanticism* refers to an intellectual and cultural movement that was current from about 1780 to 1830 and beyond. It was in many ways a reaction to the structured rationalism of the Enlightenment and focused instead on passionate individualism and on the world of nature. The philosophes of the Enlightenment had sought to understand the natural world and were confident that phenomena could be explained through theory and experimentation. But the Romantic viewed the world differently. Natural beauty was to be engaged, not explained, and knowledge was more a matter of sense experience than of intellectual fortitude. Intuition, in fact, was more essential to understanding a world in flux than was an established method of inquiry. Romantic writers, artists, and musicians sought to break through established norms in search of new possibilities. In so many ways, the Romantic movement in the arts and literature paralleled the new political opportunities that were unfolding.

To understand Romanticism, one must be willing to suspend logic, trust intuition, and enter a world of natural beauty and foreboding terror, of idealistic passion fueled by the conviction that there is more to the world than can be explained.

Ode to the West Wind (1820)

PERCY BYSSHE SHELLEY

The fascination with and evocation of the power and beauty of nature was an important theme during the Romantic period. One of the founders of the English Romantic movement, William Wordsworth (1770–1850), once defined poetry as the "spontaneous overflow of powerful feelings." In the following selection, another leading English poet, Percy Bysshe Shelley (1792–1822), captures the Romantic vision of nature in his *Ode to the West Wind.* One feels the "wild spirit" of the West Wind—it is the only way to understand and truly know it.

O, wild West Wind, thou breath of Autumn's being,
Thou, from whose unseen presence the leaves dead
Are driven, like ghosts from an enchanter fleeing,

Yellow, and black, and pale, and hectic red,
Pestilence-stricken multitudes: O thou,
Who chariotest to their dark wintry bed

The wingèd seeds, where they lie cold and low,

"*Ode to the West Wind*" is from George Edward Woodberry, ed., *Complete Poetical Works of Percy Bysshe Shelley*, 8 vols. (Boston: Houghton Mifflin, 1892).

Each like a corpse within its grave, until
Thine azure sister of the Spring shall blow

Her clarion o'er the dreaming earth, and fill
(Driving sweet buds like flocks to feed in air)
With living hues and odors plain and hill:

Wild Spirit, which art moving every where;
Destroyer and preserver; hear, O, hear! . . .

Make me thy lyre, even as the forest is:
What if my leaves are falling like its own!
The tumult of thy mighty harmonies

Will take from both a deep autumnal tone,
Sweet though in sadness. Be thou, Spirit fierce,
My spirit! Be thou me, impetuous one!

Drive my dead thoughts over the universe
Like withered leaves to quicken a new birth!

And, by the incantation of this verse,
Scatter, as from an unextinguished hearth
Ashes and sparks, my words among mankind!
Be through my lips to unawakened earth

The trumpet of a prophecy! O, Wind,
If Winter comes, can Spring be far behind?

Consider This:

- How would you define the concept of "Romanticism"? What were the primary characteristics of the Romantic movement? Was it a revolution of sorts in the arts?
- How does the poem by Percy Bysshe Shelley capture the essence of the Romantic vision? What are the specific images that he evokes? How would you interpret the last line: "O, Wind / If Winter comes, can Spring be far behind?"

Terror and the Macabre: Frankenstein (1818)

MARY WOLLSTONECRAFT SHELLEY

The Romantic fascination with the natural world was accompanied by an expansive and creative vision of the potential of nature and the forces that existed beyond the limits of the human realm. This was an emotional response, a desire to participate in the fantastic, the forbidden, and the macabre forces that danced in the dreams and preyed on the fears of humankind.

Mary Shelley (1797–1851) was the daughter of the political philosopher William Godwin and the women's rights advocate Mary Wollstonecraft. She married the poet Percy Bysshe Shelley in 1814 and was introduced to his circle of literary friends. The idea of *Frankenstein* came to her during a vacation in Switzerland with her husband and the poet Lord Byron. Byron suggested that they write ghost stories. Her astonishing tale of an ambitious young scientist, Victor Frankenstein, and the monster he unleashes questions the very principles of life and the mysteries of nature. It forces us to consider ethical and religious issues, but more importantly we are introduced to the terror of the soul, the limits of the human mind, and the pathos of creation and destruction. Enter the laboratory of Dr. Frankenstein as he encounters his unnatural creation for the first time. . . .:

It was on a dreary night of November that I beheld the accomplishment of my toils. With an anxiety that almost amounted to agony, I collected the instruments of life around me, that I might infuse a spark of being into the lifeless thing that lay at my feet. It was already one in the morning: the rain pattered dismally against the panes, and my candle was nearly burnt out, when, by the glimmer of the half-extinguished light, I saw the dull yellow eye of the creature open; it breathed hard, and a convulsive motion agitated its limbs.

"*Frankenstein*" is from Mary Shelley, *Frankenstein, Or the Modern Prometheus* (London, 1818).

How can I describe my emotions at this catastrophe, or how delineate the wretch whom with such infinite pains and care I had endeavoured to form? His limbs were in proportion, and I had selected his features as beautiful. Beautiful! Great God! His yellow skin scarcely covered the work of muscles and arteries beneath; his hair was of a lustrous black, and flowing; his teeth of pearly whiteness; but these luxuriances only formed a more horrid contrast with his watery eyes, that seemed almost of the same colour as the dun-white sockets in which they were set, his shrivelled complexion and straight black lips.

The different accidents of life are not so changeable as the feelings of human nature. I had worked hard for nearly two years, for the sole purpose of infusing life into an inanimate body. For this I had deprived myself of rest and health. I had desired it with an ardour that far exceeded moderation; but now that I had finished, the beauty of the dream vanished, and breathless horror and disgust filled my heart. Unable to endure the aspect of the being I had created, I rushed out of the room and continued a long time traversing my bedchamber, unable to compose my mind to sleep. At length lassitude succeeded to the tumult I had before endured, and I threw myself on the bed in my clothes, endeavouring to seek a few moments of forgetfulness. But it was in vain; I slept, indeed, but I was disturbed by the wildest dreams. . . .

I thought that I held the corpse of my dead mother in my arms; a shroud enveloped her form, and I saw the grave-worms crawling in the folds of the flannel. I started from my sleep with horror; a cold dew covered my forehead, my teeth chattered, and every limb became convulsed; when by the dim and yellow light of the moon, as it forced its way through the window shutters, I beheld the wretch–the miserable monster whom I had created. He held up the curtain of the bed; and its eyes, if eyes they may be called, were fixed on me. His jaws opened and he muttered some inarticulate sounds, while a grin wrinkled his cheeks. He might have spoken, but I did not hear; one hand was stretched out, seemingly to detain me, but I escaped and rushed downstairs. I took refuge in the courtyard belonging to the house which I inhabited, where I remained during the rest of the night, walking up and down in the greatest agitation, listening attentively, catching and fearing each sound as if it were to announce the approach of the demoniacal corpse to which I had so miserably give life.

CONSIDER THIS:

- How does the excerpt from Mary Shelley's *Frankenstein* create the sense of dread and terror? What larger human themes does she propose? How has the concept of the reanimation of so-called dead tissue progressed from a Romantic idea to a reality in contemporary society? Can scientists now truly defy nature, create life, and redefine death as did the fictional Dr. Frankenstein?

THEME: SOCIAL AND SPIRITUAL VALUES

THE ARTISTIC VISION

Haunting the Soul: The Demonic Nightmare

The eighteenth century was an era in conflict between two dominant forces of the mind: reason and imagination. The Scientific Revolution and Enlightenment sought to explain the world in rational terms devoid of the obligations of faith. The human mind was empowered to challenge church and state, to provide new political and social opportunities. This was a structured intellectual process that seemed too confining, too sterile for many. Life, after all, was an emotional adventure of love and fear, beauty and sorrow—expressions of the spirit, of intuition and imagination.

Nowhere is this conflict more easily witnessed than in the daily transition between sleep and wakefulness. When awake, we are usually obligated to live in that world of reason, adhering to laws and social norms. But during sleep, our minds are freed and given full rein; we are often visited by dreams that offer insight to our unconscious fears and desires. One of the most important individuals to explore this dimension of Romanticism was the Swiss artist Johann Heinrich Füssli (1741–1825), better known in his adopted England as Henry Fuseli. He ranged far beyond the confines of Neoclassicism in exploring the murky areas of the unconscious.

Fuseli was originally trained as a priest, and although he took holy orders in 1761, he never ministered to a parish. After studying in Italy from 1770 to 1778, he settled in England where he exhibited some highly imaginative paintings that were generally well received. His most famous was *The Nightmare* (1781). In this

FIGURE 6.2 *The Nightmare* by Henry Fuseli. (*Art Resource, NY*)

painting, Fuseli portrays a woman in the midst of an erotic dream, hanging languorously off the edge of the bed. Surrounded by demons, she has entered that realm of the psyche where sex mingles with fear, where there is no rational limit imposed by the mores of society or religion. The rational world of wakefulness has evaporated and her nature as a sexual being, uncontrolled, unrepressed, defines the moment.

Perhaps the greatest artist of the eighteenth century, Francisco Goya (1728–1779) was initially an exponent of Neoclassical theory and composition. He became most influential as a portrait artist renown for his ability to unmask the interior truth deep within his subjects. But it is difficult to characterize him because he metamorphosed several times over a sixty-year working career. Fiercely independent, Goya seemed to work from a personal center of genius that enabled him to experiment with innovative techniques and venture into new realms of political and artistic expression.

Goya himself was particularly linked to images of evil beyond human constraint. His painting *Prometheus* is a dark psychological portrait that foreshadows an even darker period later in his life when he was sick and alone, prey to the irrational fears of death and more aware of the abyss of evil that threatened humankind. Among the most frightening paintings of this "dark period" after 1820 was *The Witches' Sabbath* (1821–1823). This is a graphic depiction of demonized souls gathered together at the very witching hour of night to answer Satan's call. Goya conjures him as a He-Goat leading the Black Mass, assisted by a witch in a white hood as seen from the rear.

The subject of the Black Mass was also visited by the great French writer, Victor Hugo (1802–1885). Hugo was best known for his elevated social conscience. His essays, plays, and novels exposed the miserable conditions among the French poor. But he also evinced a Romantic vision as early as 1826 when he brought out a new edition of his *Odes* to which he added fifteen *Ballades* centered around pictorial fantasies, dreams, and superstitions. Number 14 in the series, entitled "The Witches' Sabbath," starts with the description of a Gothic church at midnight as the Black Mass begins. In this excerpt, the souls of the damned have gathered from their tombs—witches, ghouls, vampires, and others in Satan's thrall—to dance amid flashing lights, flames, and boiling holy water.

"The Witches' Sabbath"

And their steps shake the arches colossal and high,
Disturbing the dead in their tombs close by.

From his tomb with sad moans
Each false monk to his stall
Glides, concealed in his pall,
That robe fatal to all,
Which burns into his bones.

Now a black priest draws nigh,
With a flame he doth fly
On the altar on high
He the cursed fire enthrones.

The dawn whitens the arches colossal and gray.
And drives all the devilish revellers away,
The dead monks retire to their graves 'neath the halls,
And veil their cold faces behind their dark palls.

—Victor Hugo

The Nationalist Vision

Volksgeist: "The Spirit of the People"

As Napoleon stormed through Europe, his armies not only spread fear and destruction but also ironically the Enlightenment idea of self-determination that had provided a foundation for the French Revolution. Napoleon was certainly no republican, but he helped channel the spirited rallying cries of the revolution into the vision of an expansive French state—bold and confident in the security of its military dominance and cultural superiority. France became the preeminent example of the possibilities of national zeal and focused commitment.

It was this zeal, combined with passionate leadership, that struck fear among the governments of Britain, Prussia, Austria, and Russia, finally victorious in coalition against Napoleon. The Congress of Vienna in 1815, led by Prince Klemens von Metternich of Austria and Viscount Castlereagh of Britain, settled borders, defined reparations, and envisioned a new Europe devoid of passion, committed to the principle of political stability. During the next decade from 1815 to 1825, conservative political forces dominated Europe with the establishment of the Congress System. Diplomatic representatives of the great powers planned to meet from time to time in a Congress to develop and enhance their relationships by molding a unified front, a bastion of security called the Concert of Europe. The primary purpose of the Concert was to maintain the balance of power among its members and to prevent one nation from taking action in international affairs without the consent of the others. In this way, the Concert could protect the principle of monarchical rule by maintaining domestic stability and international peace. The greatest threats to the Concert came from "upstart revolutionaries," infected with liberal ideas and nationalist conceit, who advocated redrawing the political boundaries of Europe along ethnic lines.

Nationalism became the most important and influential political ideology of the nineteenth and early twentieth centuries. Historians and philosophers as early as the late eighteenth century had promoted the concept of nationhood, a political organization composed of people linked by a common language, cultural tradition, and history. They argued that these common bonds should be administered by a responsive government and that the political borders of the nation should also be directly linked to ethnic boundaries. This idea was especially repugnant to the Austrian empire whose Germanic leaders ruled from Vienna over territory that included a vast majority of Slavic peoples.

During the nineteenth century, nationalists provided an ongoing challenge for the Concert and threatened the status quo throughout Europe as Irish nationalists sought independence from the control of Britain, as did Poles from Russia, Czechs, Slovenes, and Magyars from Austria, Serbs, Greeks, Albanians, Romanians, and Bulgarians from the Turkish Ottoman Empire. German nationalists argued political unity for all German-speaking peoples, a challenge that eventually pitted Austria against Prussia.

These nationalist movements, often divided in their diversity and conflicting visions of the future, were harnessed successfully with only a few exceptions by the paranoid efficiency of the dominant European powers. But nationalist dissidence was only one of the irritants faced by the conservative order. The other primary threat came from a liberal movement that derived its political vision from Enlightenment thought. This was a complex movement almost defying broad definition because they were rarely united politically or in agreement about specific demands. Liberals, however, were generally committed to the ideals of legal equality, religious tolerance, and political freedom. They were often academics or professionals like doctors, lawyers, and businessmen who believed in careers open to talent, unrestricted by the arbitrary power of government. Liberals feared the interference of a capricious king or ministers who operated for their own benefit beyond the confines of law. As such, liberals supported written constitutions providing for elected representative assemblies that required government ministers and monarchs to be responsible and responsive to their authority. These nineteenth-century liberals should not be confused with any modern definition of the word. They sought to guarantee their own political and economic freedoms and most often did not regard "the people" as anything but a theoretical proposition. Liberals often had little but scorn for the "unwashed masses," which proved limiting to their success. Indeed, liberalism and nationalism were not necessarily linked, and their interests were even directly antithetical at times. But they were certainly compatible in their drive for greater self-determination and opportunity for personal and ethnic freedom.

The following selection comes from the memoirs of Prince Klemens von Metternich (1773–1859), the chief minister of the Austrian Hapsburg Empire and the primary architect of the Treaty of Vienna in 1815. Metternich provided the guiding hand for the Congress System and fashioned the Concert of Europe with an almost spiritual commitment to the sanctity of the conservative order.

The Conservative Confession of Faith

PRINCE KLEMENS VON METTERNICH

"Europe," a celebrated writer has recently said, "inspires pity in a man of spirit and horror in a man of virtue."

It would be difficult to comprise in a few words a more exact picture of the situation at the time we are writing these lines!

Kings have to calculate the changes to their very existence in the immediate future; passions are let loose, and league together to overthrow everything which society respects as the basis of its existence; religion, public morality, laws, customs, rights, and duties—all are attacked, confounded, overthrown, or called into question. The great mass of the people are tranquil spectators of these attacks and revolutions, and of the absolute want of all means of defense. A few are carried off by the torrent, but the wishes of the immense majority are to maintain a repose which exists no longer, and of which even the first elements seem to be lost.

What is the cause of all these evils? By what methods has this evil established itself, and how is it that it penetrates into every vein of the social body? Do remedies still exist to arrest the progress of this evil, and what are they?

These are doubtless questions worthy of the consideration of every good man who is a true friend to order and public peace—two

"The Conservative Confession of Faith" is from Pierre Richard Metternich, ed., *Memoirs of Prince Metternich* (New York: Charles Scribner's Sons, 1881), pp. 454–475.

elements inseparable in principle, and which are at once the first needs and the first blessings of humanity. . . .

The Source of the Evil

Having now thrown a rapid glance over the present state of society, it is necessary to point out in a more particular manner the evil which threatens to deprive it, at one blow, of the real blessings, the fruits of genuine civilization, and to disturb it in the midst of its enjoyments. This evil may be described in one word—presumption; the natural effect of the rapid progression of the human mind towards the perfecting of so many things. This it is which at the present day leads so many individuals astray, for it has become an almost universal sentiment.

Religion, morality, legislation, economy, politics, administration, all have become common and accessible to everyone. Knowledge seems to come by inspiration; experience has no value for the presumptuous man; faith is nothing to him; he substitutes for it a pretended individual conviction, and to arrive at this conviction dispenses with all inquiry and with all study; for these means appear too trivial to a mind which believes itself strong enough to embrace at one glance all questions and all facts. Laws have no value for him, because he has not contributed to make them, and it would be beneath a man of his parts to recognize the limits traced by rude and ignorant generations. Power resides in himself; why should he submit himself to that which was only useful for the man deprived of light and knowledge? That which, according to him, was required in an age of reason and vigor, amounting to universal perfection, which the German innovators designate by the idea, absurd in itself, of the Emancipation of the People! Morality itself he does not attack openly, for without it he could not be sure for a single instant of his own existence; but he interprets its essence after his own fashion, and allows every other person to do so likewise, provided that other person neither kills nor robs him. . . .

Presumption makes every man the guide of his own belief, the arbiter of laws according to which he is pleased to govern himself, or to allow some one else to govern him and his neighbors; it makes him, in short, the sole judge of his own faith, his own actions, and the principles according to which he guides them. . . .

The Course Which the Evil Has Followed and Still Follows

France had the misfortune to produce the greatest number of these men. It is in her midst that religion and all that she holds sacred, that morality and authority, and all connected with them, have been attacked with a steady and systematic animosity, and it is there that the weapon of ridicule has been used with the most ease and success.

Drag through the mud the name of God and the powers instituted by His divine decrees, and the revolution will be prepared! Speak of a social contract, and the revolution is accomplished! The revolution was already completed in the palaces of Kings, in the drawing-rooms and boudoirs of certain cities, while among the great mass of the people it was still only in a state of preparation. . . .

In this memoir we have not yet touched on one of the most active and at the same time most dangerous instruments used by the revolutionists of all societies, a real power, all the more dangerous as it works in the dark, under a moral gangrene which is not slow to develop and increase. This plague is one of the worst which those Governments who are lovers of peace and of their people have to watch and fight against.

Do Remedies for This Evil Exist, and What Are They?

We look upon it as a fundamental truth, that for every disease there is a remedy, and that the knowledge of the real nature of the one should lead to the discovery of the other. Few men, however, stop thoroughly to examine a disease which they intend to combat. . . .

It is principally the middle classes of society which this moral gangrene has affected, and it is only among them that the real heads of the party are found.

For the great mass of the people it has no attraction and can have none. The labors to which this class—the real people—are obliged to devote themselves, are too continuous and too positive to allow them to throw themselves into vague abstractions and ambitions. The people know what is the happiest thing for them: namely, to be able to count on the morrow, for it is the morrow which will repay them for the cares and sorrows of today. The laws which afford a just protection to individual, to families, and to property, are quite simple in their essence. The people dread any movement which injures industry and brings new burdens in its train.

Men in the higher classes of society who join the revolution are either falsely ambitious men or, in the widest definition of the word, lost spirits. . . .

Europe thus presents itself to the impartial observer under an aspect at the same time deplorable and peculiar. We find everywhere the people praying for the maintenance of peace and tranquility, faithful to God and their Princes, remaining proof against the efforts and seductions of the factious who call themselves friends of the people and wish to lead them to an agitation which the people themselves do not desire!

We are convinced that society can no longer be saved without strong and vigorous resolutions on the part of the Government still free in their opinions and actions. We are also convinced that this may yet be, if the Governments face the truth, if they free themselves from all illusion, if they join their ranks and take their stand on a line of correct, unambiguous and frankly announced principles.

By this course the monarchs will fulfill the duties imposed upon them by Him who, by entrusting them with power, has charged them to watch over the maintenance of justice, and the rights of all, to avoid the paths of error, and tread firmly in the way of truth. . . .

Let the monarchs vigorously adopt this principle; let all their resolutions bear the impression of it. Let their actions, their measures, and even their words announce and prove to the world this determination—they will find allies everywhere. The government, in establishing the principle of stability, will in no way exclude the development of what is good, for stability is not immobility. But it is for those who are burdened with the heavy task of government to augment the well-being of their people!

Respect for all that is; liberty for every Government to watch over the well-being of its own people; a league between all Governments against factions in all States; contempt for the meaningless words which have become the rallying cry of the factious; respect for the progressive development of institutions in lawful ways; refusal on the part of every monarch to aid partisans under any mask whatever—such are happily the ideas of the great monarchs; the world will be saved if they bring them into action—it is lost if they do not.

Union between the monarchs is the basis of the policy which must now be followed to save society from total ruin. . . .

CONSIDER THIS:

- According to Metternich, "presumption" was the "evil" that threatened to deprive humanity of the blessings of civilization. What did he mean by this? Why were presumptuous men dangerous to society?
- Metternich spoke of the revolutionary threat to society as a disease, a "moral gangrene" that must be combated. What, in Metternich's opinion, did the people really want? What role did monarchs and governments have to play to crush these "seducers" of the people and establish the principle of stability? What was Metternich's solution to the threats against the conservative order?

Stirrings: The People and the Fatherland

JOHANN GOTTLIEB FICHTE

At the outset of the nineteenth century, both Italy and Germany were geographical regions that contained dozens of autonomous states within their general borders. Italy and Germany had remained a conglomeration of locally ruled duchies, kingdoms, and republics largely untouched by the process of political centralization that had enveloped England, France, and Spain during the fourteenth and fifteenth centuries. And although railways and tariff unions linked the economies of these regions, political unification for Italy and Germany was a slow and certainly contentious process in Europe until its resolution in 1871.

The vision of nationhood was largely defined by a small group of historians and literary scholars who collected popular stories and myths to serve as cultural beacons. The Brothers Grimm, for example, were ardent nationalists who traveled throughout Germany collecting and compiling their famous fairy tales that served as a common point of cultural reference.

The following selection is from the philosopher and fervent nationalist Johann Gottlieb Fichte (1762–1814), who glorified the common heritage of all Germans. In his addresses in 1807 and 1808, Fichte disclosed his frustrations with German disunity and provided the inspiration that fomented intellectual discussion and stirred the emotional yearnings of nationhood. It was just this type of so-called meddling that Metternich and the conservative order feared and wanted to suppress.

Our oldest common ancestors, the original people of the new culture, the Teutons, called Germans by the Romans, set themselves bravely in opposition to the overwhelming worldwide rule of the Romans. Did they not see with their own eyes the finest blossom of the Roman provinces beside them, the finer enjoyment in the same, together with laws, courts of justice, lictors' staves and axes in superabundance? Were not the Romans ready and generous enough to let them share in all these benefits? Did they not see proof of the famous Roman clemency in the case of several of their own princes, who allowed themselves to think that war against such benefactors of the human race was rebellion? For the compliant were decorated with the title of king and rewarded with posts of importance as leaders in the Roman army, with Roman sacrificial wreaths; and when they were expelled by their countrymen, the Romans furnished them with a refuge and support in their colonies. Had they no appreciation of the advantages of Roman culture, for better organization of their armies, for example, in which even Arminius himself did not refuse to learn the art of war? It cannot be charged against them that in any one of these respects they were ignorant. Their descendants have appropriated that culture, as soon as they could do so without loss of their own freedom, and as far as it was possible without loss of their distinctive character. Wherefore, then, have they fought for so many generations in bloody wars which have been repeatedly renewed with undiminished fury? A Roman writer represents their leaders as asking if anything else remained for them but to maintain their freedom or to die before they became slaves. Freedom was their possession, that they might

"Stirrings: The People and the Fatherland" is from Guy Carelton Lee, ed., *The World's Orators*, vol. 2 (New York: G. P. Putnam's Sons, 1900), pp. 190–193.

remain Germans, that they might continue to settle their own affairs independently and originally and in their own way, and at the same time to advance their culture and to plant the same independence in the hearts of their posterity. Slavery was what they called all the benefits which the Romans offered them, because through them they would become other than Germans, they would have to become semi-Romans. It was perfectly clear, they assumed, that every man, rather than become this, would die, and that a true German could wish to live only to be and to remain a German, and to have his sons the same.

They have not all died; they have not seen slavery; they have bequeathed freedom to their children. To their constant resistance the whole new world owes that it is as it is. Had the Romans succeeded in subjugating them also, and, as the Romans everywhere did, destroying them as a nation, the entire development of the human race would have taken a different direction, and it cannot be thought a better one. We who are the nearest heirs of their land, their language, and their sentiments, owe to them that we are still Germans, that the stream of original and independent life still bears us on; to them we owe that we have since then become a nation; to them, if now perhaps it is not at an end with us and the last drops of blood inherited from them are not dried in our veins, we owe all that which we have become. To them, even the other tribes, who have become to us aliens but through them our brethren, owe their existence; when they conquered eternal Rome, there were no others of all those peoples present; at that time was won for them the possibility of their future origin. . . .

These orations have attempted, by the only means remaining after others have been tried in vain, to prevent this annihilation of every noble action that may in the future arise among us, and this degradation of our entire nation. They have attempted to implant in your minds the deep and immovable foundations of the true and almighty love of the fatherland, in the conception of our nation as eternal and the people as citizens of our own eternity through the education of all hearts and minds.

CONSIDER THIS:

- How specifically did Johann Gottlieb Fichte glorify the Germanic tribes in their struggle against Rome? How did he define the German "people," and what was his purpose in this address?

The Duties of Man

GIUSEPPE MAZZINI

Before Italy finally became a single independent state under the pragmatic leadership of Count Camillo Cavour, unification was an ideal kept alive through the liberal beliefs of advocates such as Giuseppe Mazzini (1805–1872). Mazzini was called the "Soul of Italy" and advocated a passionate dedication to the nationalist cause. Active in the 1830s and 1840s, Mazzini led insurrections and linked the concept of nationality to God's humanizing mission on earth. Mazzini believed that nationality was a "baptismal rite which endows a people with its own character and rank in the brotherhood of nations." Through his writings, Mazzini helped define a basis for unification that proved influential in establishing a liberal constitutional monarchy in Italy by 1870. The following selection is from his address to Italian workers.

"The Duties of Man" is from Emilie Ashurst Venturi, *Joseph Mazzini: A Memoir* (London: Alexander and Shepherd, 1875), pp. 312–315.

Your first duties—first as regards importance—are, as I have already told you, towards Humanity. You are men before you are either citizens or fathers. Embrace the whole human family in your affection. Bear witness to your belief in the Unity of that family, consequent upon the Unity of God, and in that fraternity among the peoples which is destined to reduce that unity of action. . . .

But what can each of you, singly, do for the moral improvement and progress of Humanity? You can from time to time give sterile utterance to your belief; you may, on some rare occasions, perform some act of charity towards a brother man not belonging to your own land;—no more. But charity is not the watchword of the Faith of the Future. The watchword of the faith of the future is Association, and fraternal co-operation of all towards a common aim; and this is as far superior to all charity, as the edifice which all of you should unite to raise would be superior to the humble hut each one of you might build alone, or with the mere assistance of lending, and borrowing stone, mortar, and tools.

But, you tell me, you cannot attempt united action, distinct and divided as you are in language, customs, tendencies, and capacity. The individual is too insignificant, and Humanity too vast. . . .

This means was provided for you by God when he gave you a country; when, even as a wise overseer of labour distributes the various branches of employment according to the different capacities of the workmen, he divided Humanity into distinct groups or nuclei upon the face of the earth, thus creating the germ of Nationalities. Evil governments have disfigured the divine design. Nevertheless you may still trace it, distinctly marked out. . . . They have disfigured it by their conquests, their greed, and their jealousy even of the righteous power of others; disfigured it so far that if we except England and France—there is not perhaps a single country whose present boundaries correspond to that design.

These governments did not, and do not, recognize any country save their own families or dynasty, the egotism of caste. But the Divine design will infallibly be realized. Natural divisions, and the spontaneous, innate tendencies of the peoples, will take the place of the arbitrary divisions sanctioned by evil governments. The map of Europe will be re-drawn. The countries of the Peoples, defined by the vote of free men, will arise upon the ruins of the countries of kings and privileged castes, and between these countries harmony and fraternity will exist. And the common work of Humanity, of general amelioration and the gradual discovery and application of its Law of life, being distributed according to local development and advance. Then may each one of you, fortified by the power and the affection of many millions, all speaking the same language, gifted with the same tendencies, and educated by the same historical tradition, hope, even by your own single effort, to be able to benefit all Humanity.

O my brothers, love your Country! Our country is our Home, the house that God has given us, placing therein a numerous family that loves us, and whom we love; a family with whom we sympathize more readily, and whom we understand more quickly than we do others; and which, from its being centered round a given spot, and from the homogeneous nature of its elements, is adapted to a special branch of activity. Our country is our common workshop, whence the products of our activity are sent forth for the benefit of the whole world; wherein the tools and implements of labor we can most usefully employ are gathered together: nor may we reject them without disobeying the plan of the Almighty, and diminishing our own strength.

CONSIDER THIS:

- What are the main ideas contained in Mazzini's address to Italian workers? How did it appeal to them specifically? Why was Mazzini called the "Soul of Italy" by his adherents?

THEME: REVOLUTION AND HISTORICAL TRANSITION

THE REFLECTION IN THE MIRROR

The Greek Revolution of 1820

"To Avenge Ourselves Against a Frightful Tyranny"

The Concert of Europe faced its first challenges in the year 1820 as liberal revolts in support of written constitutions broke out in Spain and Naples. As Austria, Prussia, and Russia contemplated intervention to suppress the dissent, a third revolt erupted in Greece in 1822, which sought independence from the Ottoman Empire.

The Ottomans had long controlled the Balkan region that granted access through the Dardanelles to the Black Sea and the lucrative Eastern trade beyond. France and Britain hungered for commercial access; Russia and Austria coveted Balkan territory and access to the shrines of the Holy Land. Although liberals, Romantics, and nationalists all supported the Greek revolution unequivocally, the conservative Concert had to balance the geopolitical and economic benefits of supporting the revolution against the frightening prospect of appearing to support a nationalist revolt against established authority. Finally in 1827, Britain, France, and Russia signed the Treaty of London that demanded Turkish recognition of Greek independence, and they even sent troops and a joint fleet to support the Greeks. The following proclamation of independence from the Greek parliament provides justification for the revolution.

KEEP IN MIND . . .

- According to this proclamation, how did the Greeks justify their rebellion against Ottoman rule?

> "We find it no longer possible to suffer without cowardice and self-contempt the cruel yoke of the Ottoman power which has weighed upon us for more than four centuries."
> —THE GREEK PARLIAMENT

We descendants of the wise and noble peoples of Hellas, we who are the contemporaries of the enlightened and civilized nations of Europe, we who behold the advantages which they enjoy under the protection of the impenetrable aegis of the law, find it no longer possible to suffer without cowardice and self-contempt the cruel yoke of the Ottoman power which has weighed upon us for more than four centuries—a power that does not listen to reason and knows no other law than its own will, which orders and disposes everything despotically and according to its caprice. After this prolonged slavery we have determined to take arms to avenge ourselves and our country against a frightful tyranny, iniquitous in its very essence—an unexampled despotism to which no other rule can be compared.

The war which we are carrying on against the Turk is not that of a faction or the result of sedition. It is not aimed at the advantage of any single part of the Greek people; it is a national war, a holy war, a war the object of

"'To Avenge Ourselves Against a Frightful Tyranny'" is from *British and Foreign State Papers* (London: J. Harrison and Sons, 1829), Volume 9, pp. 629–630.

which is to reconquer the rights of individual liberty, of property and honor—rights which the civilized people of Europe, our neighbors, enjoy today; rights of which the cruel and unheard of tyranny of the Ottomans would deprive us—us alone—and the very memory of which they would stifle in our hearts.

Are we, then, less reasonable than other peoples, that we remain deprived of these rights? Are we of a nature so degraded and abject that we should be viewed as unworthy to enjoy the, condemned to remain crushed under a perpetual slavery and subjected, like beasts of burden or mere automatons, to the absurd caprice of a cruel tyrant who, like an infamous brigand, has come from distant regions to invade our borders? Nature has deeply engraved these rights in the hearts of all men; laws in harmony with nature have so completely consecrated them that neither three nor four centuries—nor thousand nor millions of centuries—can destroy them. . . .

Building upon the foundation of our natural rights, and desiring to assimilate ourselves to the rest of the Christians of Europe, our brethren, we have begun a war against the Turks, or rather, uniting all our isolated strength, we have formed ourselves into a single armed body, firmly resolved to attain our end, to govern ourselves by wise laws, or to be altogether annihilated, believing it to be unworthy of us, as descendants of the glorious peoples of Hellas, to live henceforth in a state of slavery fitted rather for unreasoning animals than for rational beings.

CONSIDER THIS:

- How influential were Enlightenment ideals and the example of the French Revolution in the Greek parliament's justification for independence?

COMPARE AND CONTRAST:

- Note the references in the Greek declaration of independence to the "descendants of the glorious peoples of Hellas." Compare this to Fichte's appeal to the "last drop of blood" inherited from Germanic ancestors on page 177. How important was past glory and honor to contemporary ethnic identity and pride?

Greece on the Ruins of Missolonghi (1826)

EUGÉNE DELACROIX

The Greek revolution of 1822 against Turkish control fired the senses and drew the support and participation of artists and literary figures. Its success became a marquee event for both the nationalists and liberals and inspired the poetry of Lord Byron and the paintings of Eugène Delacroix (1798–1863). Delacroix was perhaps the leading representative of Romantic painting. His imagination had been haunted by Goethe's *Faust* since he first saw it in London, and he produced several lithographs connected to the text. Delacroix also focused on classical subjects (*The Barque of Dante,* 1822) and on exotic material (*Algerian Women in Their Harem,* 1834). But his most inspirational work revealed a disposition for liberal political causes that were threatened by the conservative forces of reaction.

By 1825, the Ottoman Turks were unable to make any headway in suppressing the Greek rebellion so they sought help from the Egyptian commander Ibraghim-Pasha, who besieged the small but strategically important city of Missolonghi. The siege lasted for nearly a year before Missolonghi succumbed in April 1826. All surviving defenders were executed. In this painting, Delacroix presents us with the symbolic image of Greece in supplication amid the ruins of Missolonghi.

FIGURE 6.3 *Greece Expiring on the Ruins of Missolonghi* by Eugene Delacroix. (*Art Resource, NY*)

CONSIDER THIS:

- How does this painting ennoble the Greek cause for independence against the Ottoman Turks? Why is the female figure of Greece such a powerful symbolic image of strength and resolve even in supplication to Turkish barbarism?
- How does this painting reflect the image of the Turks as described in the Greek Declaration of Independence?

THE BROADER PERSPECTIVE:

- Why is it significant that Eugène Delacroix chose a female figure as the symbolic depiction of the nation of Greece in his painting *Greece on the Ruins of Missolonghi*? Why are allegorical figures often female?

1848: "A Great Outburst of Elemental Forces Had Begun"

CARL SCHURTZ

The demands of liberal and nationalist political factions that threatened the stability of the conservative order after the Congress of Vienna in 1815 had been defused with general success by the Concert of Europe. Although the Greek revolution of 1820 and the French rejection of the Bourbon monarchy in 1830 had presented challenges to the Congress System, the forces of change had largely been stifled by the monarchs of Europe. Everything seemed to change early in February 1848 as the corrupt regime of Louis Philippe was forced from power after rioting broke out among hungry and disgruntled Parisian workers. A Second French Republic was soon declared (1848–1852) and a new national assembly elected, but political instability reigned during the chaotic "June Days" when over 3,400 people were killed on the barricades and in street fighting against government troops.

The blaze of revolution that was first struck in Paris spread quickly throughout Europe to Austria, Italy, and Germany. And although these uncoordinated revolutions ultimately failed, they struck a chord of fear among the reactionary monarchs, so that by 1870, most had embraced liberal and nationalist agendas while still maintaining political control.

We can get a real sense of the chaos and exuberance that accompanied the outbreak of revolution from the account of Carl Schurtz, a nineteen-year-old university student in Bonn.

One morning, toward the end of February, 1848, I sat quietly in my attic-chamber, working hard at my tragedy of "Ulrich von Hutten," when suddenly a friend rushed breathlessly into the room, exclaiming: "What, you sitting here! Do you not know what has happened?"

"No, what?"

"The French have driven away Louis Philippe and proclaimed the republic."

I threw down my pen—and that was the end of "Ulrich von Hutten. I never touched the manuscript again. We tore down the stairs into the street, to the market-square, the accustomed meeting-place for all the student societies after their midday dinner. Although it was still forenoon, the market was already crowded with young men talking excitedly. There was no shouting, no noise, only agitated conversation. What did we want there? This probably no one knew. But since the French had driven away Louis Philippe and proclaimed the republic, something of course must happen here, too. Some of the students had brought their rapiers along, as if it were necessary at once to make an attack or to defend ourselves. We were dominated by a vague feeling as if a great outbreak of elemental forces had begun, as if an earthquake was impending of which we had felt the first shock, and we instinctively crowded together. . . .

[We discussed] what had happened and what was to come. In these conversations, excited as they were, certain ideas and catchwords worked themselves to the surface, which expressed more or less the feelings of the people. Now had arrived in Germany the day for the establishment of "German Unity,"

"1848: 'A Great Outburst of Elemental Forces Had Begun'" is from Carl Schurtz, *The Reminiscences of Carl Schurtz* (New York: Doubleday, Page & Co., 1908), Vol. I, pp. 107–112.

and the founding of a great, powerful national German Empire. In the first line, the convocation of a national parliament. Then the demands for civil rights and liberties, free speech, free press, the right of free assembly, equality before the law, a freely elected representation of the people with legislative power, responsibility of ministers, self-government of the communes, the right of the people to carry arms, the formation of a civic guard with elective officers, and so on—in short, that which was called a "constitutional form of government on a broad democratic basis." Republican ideas were at first only sparingly expressed. But the word democracy was soon on all tongues, and many, too, thought it a matter of course that if the princes should try to withhold from the people the rights and liberties demanded, force would take the place of mere petition. Of course, the regeneration of the fatherland must, if possible, be accomplished by peaceable means. . . . Like many of my friends, I was dominated by the feeling that at last the great opportunity had arrived for giving to the German people the liberty which was their birthright and to the German fatherland its unity and greatness, and that it was now the first duty of every German to do and to sacrifice everything for this sacred object. We were profoundly, solemnly in earnest. . . .

Great news came from Vienna. There the students of the university were the first to assail the Emperor of Austria with the cry for liberty and citizens' rights. Blood flowed in the streets, and the downfall of Prince Metternich was the result. The students organized themselves as the armed guard of liberty. In the great cities of Prussia there was a mighty commotion. . . . In the Prussian capital the masses surged upon the streets, and everybody looked for events of great import.

While such tidings rushed in upon us from all sides like a roaring hurricane, we in the little university town of Bonn were also busy preparing addresses to the sovereign, to circulate them for signature and to send them to Berlin. On the 18th of March, we too had our mass demonstration. A great multitude gathered for a solemn procession through the streets of the town. The most respectable citizens, not a few professors and a great number of students and people of all grades marched in close ranks. At the head of the procession, Professor Kinkel bore the tricolor black, red, and gold, which so long had been prohibited as the revolutionary flag. Arrived on the market-square he mounted the steps of the city hall and spoke to the assembled throng. He spoke with wonderful eloquence, his voice ringing out in its most powerful tones as he depicted a resurrection of German unity and greatness and of the liberties and rights of the German people, which now must be conceded by the princes or won by force by the people. And when at last he waved the black, red, and gold banner, and predicted to a free German nation a magnificent future, enthusiasm without bounds broke forth. People clapped their hands, they shouted, they embraced one another, they shed tears. . . .

While on that 18th of March we were parading through the streets, suddenly sinister rumors flew from mouth to mouth. It had been reported that the king of Prussia, after long hesitation, had finally concluded, like the other German princes, to concede the demands that were pouring upon him from all sides. But now a whispered report flew around that the soldiery had suddenly fired upon the people and that a bloody struggle was raging in the streets of Berlin.

CONSIDER THIS:

- What changes did the intellectual community of students and professors expect would occur in areas of Germany after the 1848 revolution in Paris and the establishment of the Second French Republic? What was the liberal agenda?

- Carl Schurz spoke of the "unity and greatness" of the German fatherland as well as the need for a "constitutional form of government on a broad democratic basis." He therefore linked liberal and nationalist ideals in his conception of "a free German nation." Why then didn't the German students reach out to the common people (who were driving the revolution in Paris) as allies in this vision? Why were the reactionary forces of the government able to suppress this German revolution? Does a revolution need mass participation from different social classes to be successful?

7

"A World to Win!": The Industrial Revolution

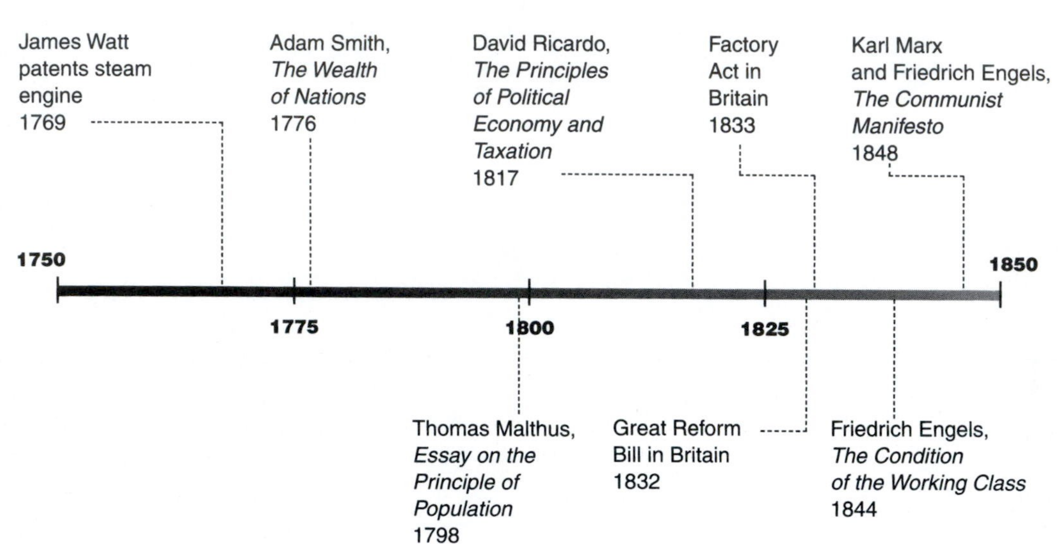

Two nations between whom there is no intercourse and no sympathy; who are as ignorant of each other's habits, thoughts and feelings as if they were . . . inhabitants of different planets; who are formed by a different breeding, are fed by a different food, are ordered by different manners, and are not governed by the same laws—the rich and the poor.

—Benjamin Disraeli

The inherent vice of capitalism is the unequal sharing of blessings; the inherent virtue of socialism is the equal sharing of miseries.

—Winston Churchill

The worth of a State, in the long run, is the worth of the individuals composing it.

—John Stuart Mill

Man is born free and everywhere he is in chains.

—Jean-Jacques Rousseau

CHAPTER THEMES

- **Revolution and Historical Transition:** What defines an economic or social revolution as opposed to a political revolution? Does one generally cause the other, or do all revolutions depend on a complex relationship among various elements? Can we define the Industrial Revolution as primarily technological?
- **Women in History:** How did the Industrial Revolution change the social relationships within the family and alter the nature of the workforce? Was this a progressive period for women?
- **The Individual and the Institution:** What role did the Catholic church play in addressing the struggle between capitalists and workers in the state? Does the church's social involvement represent a revitalization of the church and strike a new relationship between church and state in the modern world?
- **Social and Spiritual Values:** How would you define Marxism? Why did it become a popular social and economic policy in the nineteenth century? Although Marx repudiated religion, he became a spiritual leader for thousands of people. Can you explain this phenomenon?
- **The Big Picture:** How did the Industrial Revolution forever change the history of humankind? What were its social and economic consequences, and how are they still felt today? Have the transistor and microchip created a second Industrial Revolution with similar social and economic impacts? For civilization to progress, to move forward technologically, must there always be a price to pay in human suffering and abuse? Is it worth it?

The word *revolution* implies drastic change, most often political, which results in a new form of government. But there are other types of revolution as well. From the late eighteenth century to the late nineteenth century, Europe underwent a social and economic revolution that was the result of technological progress inspired by inventive minds. No longer would humans be harnessed to the land, completely dependent on the vicissitudes of nature for their livelihood; a new world was dawning, based in the city and filled with the prospect of employment and new lives. But this was not a move toward economic independence, for humans would soon be harnessed to an even more exacting master than the land: the machine.

Historically, the process of industrialization was a gradual one. The first stage of the Industrial Revolution began slowly, about 1760, and was made possible by several factors. First, Europe had reaped the benefits of an age of discovery during the sixteenth and seventeenth centuries. This fostered a commercial revolution that resulted in substantial economic growth. Indeed, the economic benefits of exploration were evident as nations sought to organize and compete on a grand scale. In addition, the English and French political revolutions of the seventeenth and eighteenth centuries began the ascendency of the middle class, which furnished the investment capital and expansive leadership necessary for the inception of the Industrial Revolution. At the same time, the population of Europe was growing dramatically, so much so that a rural-based economy simply could not support the growing tax requirements of governments and employ all who sought jobs.

These conditions were especially evident in England, where rural unemployment had been exacerbated by a conscious decision on the part of the wealthy landowners and the government itself to "enclose" farmland, release the tenantry from the security of farm labor, and use the land as pasture for sheep. Great profits were to be made in the textile trade, but the resulting displacement of the yeoman farmer added to the rural dilemma.

Yet England in the mid-eighteenth century was generally prosperous because it had developed a solid colonial foundation that provided ready markets for its goods. These markets were served by a maritime commercial and military fleet without peer and were supported by growing domestic production. This increase in the productive capacity of domestic industry resulted in large part from English ingenuity. The development of the flying shuttle, spinning jenny, and power loom in the mid-eighteenth century bespoke English technical superiority and advancement. The English had other natural advantages as well. Blessed with the existence of large quantities of coal and iron in close proximity, the English developed techniques for reducing the impurities in iron, thereby stimulating production; this eventually led to the development of the railroad in the mid-nineteenth century.

These new technologies were harnessed and organized in the factory. Men, women, and children were employed to keep the machines running, and the factory system was established to provide the greatest efficiency of material and labor, at the least expensive cost.

To many, industrialization became synonymous with progress. Increased production of goods meant greater potential for export, and this in turn created greater profit for the individual and government alike. The cultivation of new markets inspired competition among nations, exploration of new lands, and efficient management of time and labor. Yet industrialization, for all its glorification of the genius of the human mind, was never without its critics. It solved certain problems but created others. What, for instance, was to be done with those people who moved to the city in search of factory employment and found themselves among the technologically unemployed, as it were, looking for jobs that simply did not exist? And what of those who were fortunate enough to find work in the mills or the mines? The dull monotony and danger of their occupations, not to mention their subsistence living conditions, made life depressing. Factory workers dreaded unemployment, yet they could do little to change their condition. As long as competition, efficiency, and profit were the primary catalysts of the Industrial Revolution, the laborer would have to be sacrificed.

The conflicts raised by industrialization were all the more bewildering because they were unprecedented. How, for example, was government to respond to the complex problems created by industrial progress? This question was of primary importance for Britain, the first industrial area and the subject of this chapter. British industrialization was stimulated in the nineteenth century by the needs of national defense in view of the threat imposed by Napoleon. Criticism by reformers was not tolerated by the government, which viewed such acts as unpatriotic and incendiary. By the 1820s, however, tentative reforms were made that led to a rather prolonged debate resulting in the Reform Bill of 1832. This ensured that most middle-class British subjects would receive parliamentary representation and opened the franchise to some of the new industrial towns whose populations had never before been represented. In the following years, further reforms were legislated, such as the Factory Act of 1833, which limited the working hours of women and children in the textile mills and provided government inspection of the workplace. Still, reform was not won without struggle. In the 1830s and 1840s, writers and literary figures such as Charles Dickens and historian Thomas Carlyle and political organizations such as the Chartists advocated constitutional and social change. Liberalism was born as a political philosophy, and intellectuals such as John Stuart Mill (1806–1873) advocated workers' cooperatives, unions, and even women's suffrage.

Change was advocated from other directions as well. It was during this time that Karl Marx and Friedrich Engels observed the conditions of the working class in England and composed one of the most influential documents of the modern world—*The Communist Manifesto* (1848). According to Marx, the true revolutionary force in society was the workers (proletarians) who were dominated and abused by capitalists interested in profit at the workers' expense. As Marx wrote, "Let the ruling classes tremble at a Communist revolution. The proletarians have nothing to lose but their chains. They have a world to win." Other socialists less radical than Marx preached the need and inevitability of change to a more balanced society, based less on privilege and more on equality of opportunity.

The Industrial Revolution can thus be viewed in two ways: as a force for progress, an example of human ability to mold the environment, and as a demonstration of humans' abuse of each other, for the Industrial Revolution intensified class animosities and provided the catalyst for social change. The questions that emerge from this chapter are thus philosophical in nature yet practical in application. For civilization to progress, to move forward technologically, must there always be a price to pay in human suffering or abuse? And if that is the case, is it worth it? What indeed constitutes so-called progress? The twentieth century has experienced some of the greatest technological change, from the invention of the automobile to the exploration of space. Have we too paid a price?

Rural and Urban Transformations

During the eighteenth century, England was at the center of both agricultural and industrial revolutions. This was a time of great change and social upheaval as the introduction of new fertilizers and the process of crop rotation allowed farmers to produce crops more efficiently and in greater abundance. Landed aristocrats began to "engross," or add, to their holdings and to enclose this property for more efficient pasturage. As a result, the rural peasantry was often turned off the land and wandered the countryside with little hope of gainful employment. Increasing numbers of these "dependant poor" required charitable assistance and often drifted to the cities in search of new lives.

But in the urban factories, a parallel process occurred as the development of new machinery produced goods more economically and in greater quantity than ever before. Many artisans could not compete and were displaced from skilled positions. Workers protested these changes in the patterns of labor by demonstrating and even by destroying the new machinery they found so threatening to their livelihood.

The first selection is an analysis of the plight of the agricultural laborers. The second is a petition from the Leeds Woollen Workers, who demanded that machines not be used to prepare wool for spinning. The fear and frustration of trying to provide for a family in the face of such technological change fueled an ongoing debate on the nature of public assistance and the price to be paid for progress.

The Dependent Poor (1795)

DAVID DAVIES

III. *The practice of enlarging and engrossing of farms, and especially that of depriving the peasantry of all landed property, have contributed greatly to increase the number of dependent poor.*

"The Dependent Poor" is from David Davies, *The Case of Labourers in Husbandry Stated and Considered* (London, 1795), pp. 55–56.

The Land-owner, to render his income adequate to the increased expense of living, unites several small farms into one, raises the rent to the utmost, and avoids the expense of repairs. The rich farmer also engrosses as many farms as he is able to stock; lives in more credit and comfort than he could otherwise do; and out of the profits of *several farms*, makes an ample provision for *one family*. Thus thousands of families, which formerly gained an independent livelihood on those separate farms, have been gradually reduced to the class of day-laborers. But day-laborers are sometimes in want of work, and are sometimes unable to work; and in either case their sole resource is the parish. It is a fact, that thousands of parishes have not now half the number of farmers which they had formerly. And in proportion as the number of poor families has increased.

Thus depriving the peasantry of all landed property has beggared multitudes. It is plainly agreeable to sound policy, that as many individuals as possible in a state should possess an interest in the soil; because this attaches them strongly to the country and its constitution, and makes them zealous and resolute in defending them. But the gentry of this kingdom seem to have lost sight of this wise and salutary policy. Instead of giving to laboring people a valuable stake in the soil, the opposite measure has so long prevailed, that but few cottages, comparatively, have now *any* land about them. Formerly many of the lower sort of people occupied tenements of their own, with parcels of land about them, or they rented such of others. On these they raised for themselves a considerable part of their subsistence, without being obliged, as now, to buy all they want at shops. And this kept numbers from coming to the parish. But since those small parcels of ground have been swallowed up in the contiguous farms and inclosures, and the cottages themselves have been pulled down; the families which used to occupy them are crowded together in decayed farm-houses, with hardly ground enough about them for a cabbage garden: and being thus reduced to be *mere* hirelings, they are of course very liable to come to want. And not only the *men* occupying those tenements, but *their wives and children* too, could formerly, when they wanted work abroad, employ themselves profitably at home; whereas now, few of *these* are constantly employed, except in harvest; so that almost the whole burden of providing for their families rests upon the *men*. Add to this, that the former occupiers of small farms and tenements, though poor themselves, gave away something in alms to their poorer neighbors; a resource which is now much diminished.

Thus an amazing number of people have been reduced from a comfortable state of partial independence to the precarious condition of hirelings, who, when out of work, must immediately come to their parish. And the great plenty of working hands always to be had when wanted, having kept down the price of labor below its proper level, the consequence is universally felt in the increased number of dependent poor.

"How Are Men to Provide for Their Families?": A Workers' Petition (1786)

To the Merchants, Clothiers and all such as wish well to the Staple Manufactory of this Nation:

The Humble ADDRESS and PETITION of Thousands, who labour in the Cloth Manufactory SHEWETH that the

"'How Are Men to Provide for Their Families?'" is from J. F. C. Harrison, *Society and Politics in England, 1780–1960* (New York: Harper & Row, 1965), pp. 70–72.

Scribbling-Machines have thrown thousands of your petitioners out of employ, whereby they are brought into great distress, and are not able to procure a maintenance for their families, and deprived them of the opportunity of bringing up their children to labour: We have therefore to request, that prejudice and self-interest may be laid aside, and that you may pay that attention to the following facts, which the nature of the case requires.

The number of Scribbling-Machines extending about seventeen miles south-west of Leeds, exceed all belief, being no less than *one hundred and seventy*! And as each machine will do as much work in twelve hours, as ten men can in that time do by hand, (speaking within bounds) and they working night and day, one machine will do as much work in one day as would otherwise employ twenty men.

As we do not mean to assert anything but what we can prove to be true, we allow four men to be employed at each machine twelve hours, working night and day, will take eight men in twenty- four hours; so that, upon a moderate computation twelve men are thrown out of employ for every single machine used in scribbling; and as it may be supposed the number of machines in all the other quarters together, nearly equal those in the South-West, full four thousand men are left to shift for a living how they can, and must of course fall to the Parish, if not timely relieved. Allowing one boy to be bound apprentice from each family out of work, eight thousand hands are deprived of the opportunity of getting a livelihood.

We therefore hope, that the feelings of humanity will lead those who have it in their power to prevent the use of those machines, to give every discouragement they can to what has a tendency so prejudicial to their fellow-creatures.

This is not all; the injury to the Cloth is great, in so much that in Frizing, instead of leaving a nap upon the cloth, the wool is drawn out, and the Cloth is left thread-bare.

Many more evils we could enumerate, but we would hope, that the sensible part of mankind, who are not biased by interest, must see the dreadful tendency of their continuance; a depopulation must be the consequence; trade being then lost, the landed interest will have no other satisfaction but that of being *last devoured*. . . .

How are those men, thus thrown out of employ to provide for their families;–and what are they to put their children apprentice to, that the rising generation may have something to keep them at work, in order that they may not be like vagabonds strolling about in idleness? Some say, Begin and learn some other business.–Suppose we do; who will maintain our families, while we undertake the arduous task; and when we have learned it, how we have served our second apprenticeship, another machine may arise, which may take away that business also; so that our families, being half pined while we are learning how to provide them with bread, will be wholly so during the period of our third apprenticeship.

But what are our children to do; are they to be brought up in idleness? Indeed as things are, it is no wonder to hear of so many executions; for our parts, though we may be thought illiterate men, our conceptions are, that bringing children up to industry, and keeping them employed, is the way to keep them from falling into those crimes, which an idle habit naturally leads to.

These things impartially considered will we hope, be strong advocates in our favor; and we conceive that men of sense, religion and humanity, will be satisfied of the reasonableness, as well as necessity of this address, and that their own feelings will urge them to espouse the cause of us and our families.

Signed, on behalf of THOUSANDS, by
Joseph Hepworth Thomas Lobley
Robert Wood Thomas Blackburn

CONSIDER THIS:

- Discuss the plight of agricultural laborers as noted in the selection "The Dependent Poor." How did displacement from the land affect the security of the family? What are the arguments of the Leeds Woollen Workers? Do you find them compelling? If you were a Leeds woollen merchant, how would you counter the workers' claims?

The Urban Landscape

The Factory System

Sybil (1845)

BENJAMIN DISRAELI

One of the most ardent reformers who criticized working conditions was Benjamin Disraeli. A novelist and politician, he served as prime minister of Britain from 1867 to 1868 and from 1874 to 1880. His most famous novel, *Sybil, or the Two Nations,* vividly describes working and living conditions in factory towns. Disraeli hoped to gain working-class support for a group of reforming aristocrats in his Tory party. The following selection from this novel demonstrates the power of his prose.

They come forth: the mine delivers its gang and the pit its bondsmen, the forge is silent and the engine is still. The plain is covered with the swarming multitude: bands of stalwart men, broad-chested and muscular, wet with the toil, and black as the children of the tropics; troops of youth, alas! of both sexes, though neither their raiment nor their language indicates the difference; all are clad in male attire; and oaths that men might shudder at issue from lips born to breathe words of sweetness. Yet these are to be, some are, the mothers of England! But can we wonder at the hideous coarseness of their language, when we remember the savage rudeness of their lives? Naked to the waist, an iron chain fastened to a belt of leather runs between their legs clad in canvas trousers, while on hands and feet an English girl, for twelve, sometimes for sixteen hours a day, hauls and hurries tubs of coals up subterranean roads, dark, precipitous, and plashy; circumstances that seem to have escaped the notice of the Society for the Abolition of Negro Slavery. Those worthy gentlemen, too, appear to have been singularly unconscious of the sufferings of the little trappers, which was remarkable, as many of them were in their own employ.

See, too, these emerge from the bowels of the earth! Infants of four and five years of age, many of them girls, pretty and still soft and timid; entrusted with the fulfillment of responsible duties, the very nature of which entails on them the necessity of being the earliest to enter the mine and the latest to leave it. Their labour indeed is not severe, for that would be impossible, but it is passed in darkness and in solitude. They endure that

"*Sybil*" is from Benjamin Disraeli, *Sybil, or the Two Nations* (New York: M. Walter Dunne, 1904), pp. 199–200.

punishment which philosophical philanthropy has invented for the direst criminals, and which those criminals deem more terrible than the death for which it is substituted. Hour after hour elapses, and all that reminds the infant trappers of the world they have quitted, and that which they have joined, is the passage of the coal-wagons for which they open the air-doors of the galleries, and on keeping which doors constantly closed, except at this moment of passage, the safety of the mine and the lives of the persons employed in it entirely depend.

CONSIDER THIS:

- This passage from *Sybil* is both evocative and disturbing. Is it also a realistic vision or a rhetorical device? Do you detect an agenda? Does this lessen or increase its value as a reform document?

Testimony: "Not Many as Deformed as I Am" (1832)

In 1831 and 1832, the British government was under popular pressure to regulate factories and protect men, women, and children from abusive working conditions. The Sadler Committee was established and heard testimony from both workers and factory owners. The following selection clearly describes working conditions in a flax mill.

What age are you?—Twenty-three.

Where do you live?—At Leeds.

What time did you begin to work at a factory?—When I was six years old.

At whose factory did you work?—At Mr. Busk's.

What kind of mill is it?—Flax-mill.

What was your business in that mill?—I was a little doffer.

What were your hours of labour in that mill?—From 5 in the morning till 9 at night, when they were thronged.

For how long a time together have you worked that excessive length of time?—For about half a year.

What were your usual hours of labour when you were not so thronged?—From 6 in the morning till 7 at night.

What time was allowed for your meals?—Forty minutes at noon.

Had you any time to get your breakfast or drinking?—No, we got it as we could.

And when your work was bad, you hardly had anytime to eat at all?—No; we were obliged to leave it or take it home, and when we did not take it, the overlooker took it, and gave it to his pigs.

Do you consider doffing a laborious employment?—Yes.

Explain what it is you had to do?—When the frames are full, they have to stop the frames, and take the flyers off, and take the full bobbins off, and carry them to the roller; and then put empty ones on, and set the frame going again.

Does that keep you constantly on your feet?—Yes, there are so many frames, and they run so quick.

Your labour is very excessive?—Yes; you have not time for anything.

Suppose you flagged a little, or were too late, what would they do?—Strap us.

Are they in the habit of strapping those who are last in doffing?—Yes.

Constantly?—Yes.

"Testimony" is from *Parliamentary Papers, Reports from Committees, XV, "Labour of Children in Factories 1831–1832"* (London, 1832).

Have you ever been strapped?—Yes.

Severely?—Yes.

Is the strap used so as to hurt you excessively?—Yes, it is.

Were you strapped if you were too much fatigued to keep up with the machinery?—Yes; the overlooker I was under was a very severe man, and when we have been fatigued and worn out, and had not baskets to put the bobbins in, we used to put them in the window bottoms, and that broke the panes sometimes, and I broke one one time, and the overlooker strapped me on the arm, and it rose a blister, and I ran home to my mother.

How long did you work at Mr. Busk's?—Three or four years.

Where did you go to then?—Benyon's factory.

That was when you were about 10 years?—Yes.

What were you then?—A weigher in the card-room.

How long did you work there?—From half-past 5 till 8 at night.

Was that the ordinary time?—Till 9 when they were thronged.

What time was allowed for meals at that mill?—Forty minutes at noon.

Any time at breakfast or drinking?—Yes, for the card-rooms, but not for the spinning-rooms, a quarter of an hour to get their breakfast.

And the same for their drinking?—Yes.

So that the spinners in that room worked from half-past 5 till 9 at night?—Yes.

Having only forty minutes' rest?—Yes.

The carding-room is more oppressive than the spinning department?—Yes, it is so dusty they cannot see each other for dust.

It is on that account they are allowed a relaxation of those few minutes?—Yes; the cards get so soon filled up with waste and dirt, they are obliged to stop them, or they would take fire.

There is a convenience in that stoppage?—Yes, it is as much for their benefit as for the working people.

When it was not necessary no such indulgence was allowed?—No.

Never?—No.

Were the children beat up to their labour there?—Yes.

With what?—A strap; I have seen the overlooker go to the top end of the room, where the little girls hug the can to the back-minders; he has taken a strap, and a whistle in his mouth, and sometimes he has got a chain and chained them, and strapped them all down the room.

All the children?—No, only those hugging the cans.

What was his reason for that?—He was angry.

Had the children committed any fault?—They were too slow.

Were the children excessively fatigued at that time?—Yes, it was in the afternoon.

Were the girls so struck as to leave marks upon their skin?—Yes, they have had black marks many times, and their parents dare not come to him about it, they were afraid of losing their work.

If the parents were to complain of this excessive ill-usage, the probable consequence would be the loss of the situation of the child?—Yes.

In what part of the mill did you work?—In the card-room.

It was exceedingly dusty?—Yes.

Did it affect your health?—Yes; it was so dusty, the dust got upon my lungs, and the work was so hard; I was middling strong when I went there, but the work was so bad; I got so bad in health, that when I pulled the baskets down, I pulled my bones out of their places.

You dragged the baskets?—Yes; down the rooms to where they are worked.

And as you had been weakened by excessive labour, you could not stand that labour?—No.

It has had the effect of pulling your shoulders out?—Yes; it was a great basket that stood higher than this table a good deal.

How heavy was it?—I cannot say; it was a very large one, that was full of weights upheaped, and pulling the basket pulled my shoulders out of its place, and my ribs have grown over it.

You continued at that work?—Yes.

You think that work is too much for children?—Yes.

It is woman's work, not fit for children?—Yes.

Is that work generally done by women?—Yes.

How came you to do it?—There was no spinning for me.

Did they give you women's wages?—They gave me 5s. and the women had 6s. 6d.

What wages did you get as a spinner?—Six shillings.

Did you perceive that many other girls were made ill by that long labour?—Yes, a good many of them.

So that you were constantly receiving fresh hands to supply the places of those that could no longer bear their work?—Yes, there were fresh hands every week; they could not keep their hands.

Did they all go away on account of illness?—They were sick and ill with the dust.

Do you know whether any of them died in consequence of it?—No, I cannot speak to that.

You do not know what became of them?—No, we did not know that.

If a person was to take an account of a mill, and the hands in it that were ill, they would know very little of those who had suffered from their labour; they would be elsewhere?—Yes.

But you are sure of this, that they were constantly leaving on account of the excessive labour they had to endure?—Yes.

And the unhealthy nature of their employment?—Yes.

Did you take any means to obviate the bad effects of this dust?—No.

Did it make you very thirsty?—Yes, we drank a deal of water in the room.

Were you heated with your employment at the same time?—No, it was not so very hot as in the summer time; in the winter time they were obliged to have the windows open, it made no matter what the weather was, and sometimes we got very severe colds in frost and snow.

You were constantly exposed to colds, and were made ill by that cause also?—Yes.

You are considerably deformed in your person in consequence of this labour?—Yes, I am.

At what time did it come on?—I was about 13 years old when it began coming, and it has got worse since. . . .

Do you know of any body that has been similarly injured in their health?—Yes, in their health, but not many deformed as I am.

You are deformed in the shoulders?—Yes.

It is very common to have weak ankles and crooked knees?—Yes, very common indeed.

That is brought on by stopping the spindle?—Yes.

Do you know anything of wet-spinning?—Yes, it is very uncomfortable; I have stood before the frame till I have been wet through to my skin; and in winter time, when we have gone home, our clothes have been frozen, and we have nearly caught our death of cold.

Consider This:

- What was the "factory system"? How and why did it originate? What was it intended to do?
- According to the testimony for the Sadler Committee, what was it like to work in a factory? What passage lingers in your mind as the most disturbing or impressive example of the price of technological progress?

Child Labor

Children were an integral part of the factory system. Mine owners depended on small boys to enter and work in restrictive areas that could not accommodate adults. The mills were common sources of employment for children who were good with

"Child Labor" is from John Saville, ed., *Working Conditions in the Victorian Age* (Westmead, England: Gregg International Publishers Limited, 1973), pp. 130–132, 378–380. Reprinted by permission of the publisher.

their hands. Many parents condoned this and often forced their children to work because they depended on their children's wages to live at subsistence level. The following accounts were excerpted from various liberal journals such as the *Edinburgh Review,* the *Westminster Review*, and *Fraser's Magazine*; they reveal the social conscience of Victorian England.

With regard to the hours of work, the commissioners state, that when the work-people are in full employment, the regular hours of work for children and young persons are rarely less than eleven; more often they are twelve; in some districts they are thirteen; and in one district they are generally fourteen and upwards. Certainly, unless upon the ample testimony produced by the Commission, it would not be credible that there is one district in the centre of England in which children are regularly required to pursue the labours of the mine for fourteen and sixteen hours daily; but in Derbyshire, south of Chesterfield, from thirteen to sixteen hours are considered a day's work; from eleven to twelve hours are reckoned three quarters of a day's work; and eight hours make half a day's work.

"John Hawkins, eight years of age:—'Has worked in Sissons Pit, a year and a half; lives a mile from the pit; goes down from five to nine;' that is, this child, eight years old, is employed in the pit at work from five o'clock in the morning to nine at night, a period of 16 hours.—John Houghton, nine years old:—'Goes down from six to eight—it has been ten:' that is, this child is regularly employed at work in the pits 14 hours, and occasionally 16 hours.—Ephraim Riley, eleven years old:—'Had three miles to walk to the pit; left home at five o'clock, winter and summer, and did not get home again until nine o'clock at night (16 hours); his legs and thighs hurt him so with working so much that he remains in bed on Sunday mornings.'—John Chambers, thirteen years old:—'Has worked in pits since he was seven; works from six to nine or ten (from 15 to 16 hours). When first he worked in a pit he felt so tired, and his legs, arms, and back ached so much, that his brother has had to help him home many times. He could not go to school on a Sunday morning, he has been so stiff; he felt these pains until about a year since; he now feels tired, but his limbs do not ache as they did.'—James Creswell, fourteen years old:—'Has worked in pits four or five years; goes down at half-past six to nine, has this winter been after ten; half-days half-past six to three or four.'

"Of the fatigue of such labour, so protracted and carried on in such places of work, the following evidence exhibits a striking picture, and it will be observed that the witnesses of every class, children, young persons, colliers, underground stewards, agents, parents, teachers, and ministers of religion, all concur in making similar statements.

"John Bostock, aged seventeen, Babbington:—'Has often been made to work until he was so tired as to lie down on his road

FIGURE 7.1 Conditions in the mines were dismal and dangerous. Children were often used to "hurry coal" through low shafts, as shown in this drawing of 1842. (*Library of Congress*)

home until 12 o'clock, when his mother has come and led him home; he has done so many times when he first went to the pits; he has sometimes been so fatigued that he could not eat his dinner, but has been beaten and made to work until night; he never thought to play, was always too anxious to get to bed; is sure this is all true.'—John Leadbeater, aged eighteen, Babbington:—'Has two miles to go to the pit, and must be there before six, and works until eight; he has often worked all night, and been made by the butties to work as usual the next day; has often been so tired that he has lain in bed all Sunday. He knows no work so bad as that of a pit lad.'—Samuel Radford, aged nineteen, New Birchwood:—'Has been a week together and never seen daylight but on a Sunday, and not much then, he was so sleepy.'"

An imperfect abstract from the registration of deaths for the year 1838, gives a total, in England alone, of 349 deaths by violence in coal mines, and shows the most common causes of them:—

Cause of death	Under 13 years of age	13 and not exceeding 18 years of age	Over 18 years of age
Fell down the shafts	13	12	31
Fell down the shaft from the rope breaking	1	—	2
Fell out when ascending	—	—	3
Drawn over the pulley	3	—	3
Fall of stone out of a skip down the shaft	1	—	3
Drowned in the mines	3	4	15
Fall of stones, coal, and rubbish in the mines	14	14	69
Injuries in coal-pits, the nature of which is not specified	6	3	32
Crushed in coal-pits	—	1	1
Explosion of gas	13	18	49
Suffocation of choke-damp	—	2	6
Explosion of gunpowder	—	1	3
By tram-wagons	4	5	12
Total	58	60	229

We proceed now to notice the great Metal Manufactures and their influence upon the health and well being of the children and youths employed in them. . . . In the blast-furnaces, mills, and forges, great numbers of children and youths are employed in night sets, between 6 P.M. and 6 A.M.; and in the miscellaneous trades overtime is very common, a great number of children working as long as the men, viz. from 6 A.M. to 11 P.M. Little girls are employed in bellows-blowing (very hard work for children) for fourteen hours a-day, standing on platforms to enable them to reach the handle of the bellows. Night work, overtime, and the very nature of the employment, cannot but have a very disastrous influence on their health. The foundry-boys, it is admitted by the masters themselves, commence work at much too early an age, and are taxed far beyond their strength; and the children who work at home, in the various domestic manufactures, are so injured by premature labour, often commencing from the age of seven, that, as a rule, they are stunted, dwarfed, or deformed. An instance is given of a father having worked his three young boys from four in the morning until twelve at night for weeks together, until the other men 'cried shame upon him.' . . . Two girls, nine and ten years of age, were working as 'strikers' and a little girl of eight, occasionally relieved by a still younger one of six, was working the bellows. The gross earnings of this man amounted to two guineas per week. It may be doubted whether the world could not produce a more revolting instance of parental oppression than the spectacle of these two young girls, whose little hands would have been appropriately employed in hemming a kerchief or working a sampler, begrimed with the smoke, stifled with the heat and stunned with the din morning till night. A single instance of oppression has often had a greater effect in rousing indignation than the most powerful denunciation of a general wrong. The picture of these little Staffordshire girls thus unsexed by an imperious taskmaster, and that taskmaster their parent, is well adapted to expose for universal reprobation a system under which such an enormity could be possible, and to prove the necessity of immediate legislative interference.

A Defense of the Factory System (1835)

ANDREW URE

The factory system was not without its advocates. One of the most influential was Andrew Ure, a professor of applied science at the University of Glasgow. He was supportive of the efficiency and productive capabilities of mechanized manufacturing. Note how the major criticisms of the reformers (child labor, degrading and unhealthy work conditions, etc.) are methodically countered. Ure argued that the owners of the mills and mines were not devils but were actually abused themselves by the demands of the workers.

Proud of the power of malefaction, many of the cotton-spinners, though better paid, as we have shown, than any similar set of artisans in the world, organized the machinery of strikes through all the gradations of their people, terrifying or cajoling the timid or the passive among them to join their vindictive union. They boasted of possessing a dark tribunal, by the mandates of which they could paralyze every mill whose master did not comply with their wishes, and so bring ruin on the man who had given them profitable employment for many a year. By flattery or intimidation, they levied contributions from their associates in the privileged mills, which they suffered to proceed, in order to furnish spare funds for the maintenance of the idle during the decreed suspension of labour. In this extraordinary state of things, when the inventive head and the sustaining heart of trade were held in bondage by the unruly lower members, a destructive spirit began to display itself among

"A Defense of the Factory System" is from Andrew Ure, *The Philosophy of Manufactures* (London: Charles Knight, 1835), pp. 282–284, 290, 300–301, 309–311, 398–399.

some partisans of the union. Acts of singular atrocity were committed, sometimes with weapons fit only for demons to wield, such as the corrosive oil of vitriol, dashed in the faces of most meritorious individuals, with the effect of disfiguring their persons, and burning their eyes out of the sockets with dreadful agony.

The true spirit of turn-outs [strikes] among the spinners is well described in the following statement made on oath to the Factory Commission, by Mr. George Royle Chappel, a manufacturer of Manchester, who employs 274 hands, and two steam-engines of sixty-four horse power.

"I have had several turn-outs, and have heard of many more, but never heard of a turn-out for short time. I will relate the circumstances of the last turn-out, which took place on the 16th October, 1830, and continued till the 17th January, 1831. The whole of our spinners, whose average (weekly) wages were 2£. 13s. 5d., turned out at the instigation, as they told us at the time, of the delegates of the union. They said they had no fault to find with their wages, their work, or their masters, but the union obliged them to turn out. The same week three delegates from the spinners' union waited upon us at our mill, and dictated certain advances in wages, and other regulations, to which, if we would not adhere, they said neither our own spinners not any other should work for us again! Of course we declined, believing our wages to be ample, and our regulations such as were necessary for the proper conducting of the establishment. The consequences were, they set watches on every avenue to the mill, night and day, to prevent any fresh hands coming into the mill, an object which they effectually attained, by intimidating some, and promising support to others (whom I got into the mill in a caravan), if they would leave their work. Under these circumstances, I could not work the mill, and advertised it for sale, without any applications, and I also tried in vain to let it. At the end of twenty-three weeks the hands requested to be taken to the mill again on the terms that they had left it, declaring, as they had done at first, that the union alone had forced them to turn out. . . ."

FIGURE 7.2 "[The children] seemed to be always cheerful and alert, taking pleasure in the light play of their muscles, enjoying the mobility natural to their age."—Andrew Ure, *The Philosophy of Manufactures* (1835). (*Corbis/Bettmann*)

Nothing shows in a clearer point of view the credulity of mankind in general, and of the people of these islands in particular, than the ready faith which was given to the tales of cruelty exercised by proprietors of cotton-mills towards young children. The systems of calumny somewhat resembles that brought by the Pagans against the primitive Christians, of enticing children into their meetings in order to murder and devour them. . . .

No master would wish to have any wayward children to work within the walls of his factory, who do not mind their business without beating, and he therefore usually fines or turns away any spinners who are known to maltreat their assistants. Hence, ill-usage of any kind is a very rare occurrence. I have visited many factories, both in Manchester and in the surrounding districts, during a period of several months, entering the spinning rooms, unexpectedly, and often alone, at different times of the day, and I never saw a single instance of corporal chastisement inflicted on a child, nor indeed did I ever see children in ill-humour. They seemed to be always cheerful and alert, taking pleasure in the light play of their muscles, enjoying the mobility natural to their age. The scene of industry, so far from exciting sad emotions in my mind, was always exhilarating. It was delightful to observe the nimbleness with which they pieced the broken ends, as the mule-carriage began to recede from the fixed roller-beam, and to see them at leisure, after a few seconds' exercise of their tiny fingers, to amuse themselves in any attitude they chose, till the stretch and winding-on were once more completed. The work of these lively elves seemed to resemble a sport, in which habit gave them a pleasing dexterity. Conscious of their skill, they were delighted to show it off to any stranger. As to exhaustion by the day's work, they evinced no trace of it on emerging from the mill in the evening; for they immediately began to skip about any neighbouring playground, and to commence their little amusements with the same alacrity as boys issuing from a school. It is moreover my firm conviction, that if children are not ill-used by bad parents or guardians, but receive in food and raiment the full benefit of what they earn, they would thrive better when employed in our modern factories, than if left at home in apartments too often ill-aired, damp, and cold. . . .

Of all the common prejudices that exist with regard to factory labour, there is none more unfounded than that which ascribes to it excessive tedium and irksomeness above other occupations, owing to its being carried on in conjunction with the "unceasing motion of the steam-engine." In an establishment for spinning or weaving cotton, all the hard work is performed by the steam-engine, which leaves for the attendant no hard labour at all, and literally nothing to do in general; but at intervals to perform some delicate operation, such as joining the threads that break, taking the cops off the spindle, &c. And it is so far from being true that the work in a factory is incessant, because the motion of the steam-engine is incessant, that the fact is, that the labour is not incessant on that very count, because it is performed in conjunction with the steam-engine. Of all manufacturing employments, those are by far the most irksome and incessant in which steam-engines are not employed, as in lace-running and stocking-weaving; and the way to prevent an employment from being incessant, is to introduce a steam-engine into it. These remarks certainly apply more especially to the labour of children in factories. Three-fourths of the children so employed are engaged in piecing at the mules. "When the carriages of these have receded a foot and a half or two feet from the rollers," says Mr. Tufnell, "nothing is to be done, not even attention is required from either spinner or piecer." Both of them stand idle for a time, and in fine spinning particularly, for three-quarters of a minute, or more. Consequently, if a child remains at this business twelve hours daily, he has nine hours of inaction. And though he attends two mules, he has still six hours of non-exertion. Spinners sometimes dedicate these intervals to the perusal of books. The scavengers, who, in Mr. Sadler's report, have been described as being "constantly in a state of grief, always in terror, and every moment they have to spare stretched all their length upon the floor in a state of perspiration," may be observed in cotton factories idle for four minutes at a time, or moving about in a sportive mood, utterly unconscious of the tragical scenes in which they were dramatized. . . .

Mr. Hutton, who has been in practice as a surgeon at Stayley Bridge upwards of thirty-one years, and, of course, remembers the commencement, and has had occasion to trace the progress and effect, of the factory system, says that the health of the population has much improved since its introduction, and that they are much superior in point of comfort to what they were formerly. He also says that fever has become less common since the erection of factories, and that the persons employed in them were less attacked by the influenza in 1833, than other classes of work-people. Mr. Bott, a surgeon, who is employed by the operatives in Messrs. Lichfield's mills to attend them in all cases of sickness or accident, at the rate of one halfpenny a week (a sum which indicates pretty distinctly their small chances of ailment), says that the factory workmen are not so liable to epidemics as other persons; and that though he has had many cases of typhus fever in the surrounding district, nearly all the mill-hands have escaped, and not one was attacked by the cholera during its prevalence in the neighbourhood.

Compare and Contrast:

- How does Andrew Ure defend the factory system? What specific points does he address?
- Compare Ure's vision of the treatment of children and the benefits of child labor with the other accounts in this section.
- Do the descriptions of child labor and the testimony about degrading working conditions constitute a realistic and accurate portrayal of urban life during the Industrial Revolution, Or is this portrait an exaggeration? Are Andrew Ure's arguments persuasive? Why or why not?

Living Conditions

The living conditions of workers in urban industrial settings were a popular subject for reformers. One of the most important reformers, Friedrich Engels (1820–1895), was born to a family of German textile manufacturers. Engels was a keen observer of society and a talented urbane writer. His close friendship and collaboration with Karl Marx were instrumental in the dissemination and success of communist ideology. In the first selection, Engels describes the condition of the working class in Manchester, the primary manufacturing town in England. In the second, he exposes the threat to women and the family engendered by the factory system.

The Condition of the Working Class in England (1844)

FRIEDRICH ENGELS

Above Ducie Bridge, the left bank grows more flat and the right bank steeper, but the condition of the dwellings on both banks grows worse rather than better. He who turns to the left here from the main street, Long Millgate, is lost; he wanders from one court to another, turns countless corners, passes nothing but narrow, filthy nooks and alleys, until after a few minutes he has lost all clue, and knows not whither to turn. Everywhere half or wholly ruined buildings, some of them actually uninhabited, which means a great deal here; rarely a wooden or

"The Condition of the Working Class in England" is from Friedrich Engels, *The Condition of the Working Class in England in 1844* (London: Sonenschein & Co., 1892), pp. 51–53.

stone floor to be seen in the houses, almost uniformly broken, ill-fitting windows and doors, and a state of filth! Everywhere heaps of debris, refuse, and offal; standing pools for gutters, and a stench which alone would make it impossible for a human being in any degree civilised to live in such a district. The newly-built extension of the Leeds railway, which crosses the Irk here, has swept away some of these courts and lanes, laying others completely open to view. Immediately under the railway bridge there stands a court, the filth and horrors of which surpass all the others by far, just because it was hitherto so shut off, so secluded that the way to it could not be found without a good deal of trouble. I should never have discovered it myself, without the breaks made by the railway, though I thought I knew this whole region thoroughly. Passing along a rough bank, among stakes and washing-lines, one penetrates into this chaos of small one-storied, one-roomed huts, in most of which there is no artificial floor; kitchen, living and sleeping-room all in one. In such a hole, scarcely five feet long by six broad, I found two beds—and such bedsteads and beds!—which, with a staircase and chimney-place, exactly filled the room. In several others I found absolutely nothing, while the door stood open, and the inhabitants leaned against it. Everywhere before the doors refuse and offal; that any sort of pavement lay underneath could not be seen but only felt, here and there with the feet. This whole collection of cattle-sheds for human beings was surrounded on two sides by houses and a factory, and on the third by the river, and besides the narrow stair up the bank, a narrow doorway alone led out into another almost equally ill-built, ill-kept labyrinth of dwellings. . . .

Such is the Old Town of Manchester, and on re-reading my description, I am forced to

FIGURE 7.3 This 1872 engraving of Gustave Doré's *Over London by Rail* shows the crowded, polluted, urban living conditions that had developed during the Industrial Revolution. Friedrich Engels noted: "Everywhere heaps of debris, refuse and offal; standing pools for gutters, and a stench which alone would make it impossible for a human being . . . to live in such a district." (*Bridgeman Art Library International*)

admit that instead of being exaggerated, it is far from black enough to convey a true impression of the filth, ruin, and uninhabitableness, the defiance of all considerations of cleanliness, ventilation, and health which characterize the construction of this single district, containing at least twenty to thirty thousand inhabitants. And such a district exists in the heart of the second city of England, the first manufacturing city of the world. If any one wishes to see in how little space a human being can move, how little air—and such air!—he can breathe, how little civilisation he may share and yet live, it is only necessary to travel hither. True, this is the Old Town, and the people of Manchester emphasise the fact whenever any one mentions to them the frightful condition of this Hell upon Earth; but what does that prove? Everything which here arouses horror and indignation is of recent origin, belongs to the industrial epoch.

The Impact of the Factory System on Women and the Family

FRIEDRICH ENGELS

The employment of women at once breaks up the family; for when the wife spends twelve or thirteen hours every day in the mill, and the husband works the same length of time there or elsewhere, what becomes of the children? They grow up like wild weeds; they are put out to nurse for a shilling or eighteen pence a week, and how they are treated may be imagined.... That the general mortality among young children must be increased by the employment of the mothers is self-evident, and is placed beyond all doubt by notorious facts.

Women often return to the mill three or four days after confinement [for childbirth], leaving the baby, of course; in the dinner hour they must hurry home to feed the child and eat something, and what sort of suckling that can be is also evident.

Lord Ashley repeats the testimony of several workwomen:

"M. H., twenty years old, has two children, the youngest a baby, that is tended by the other, a little older. The mother goes to the mill shortly after five o'clock in the morning, and comes home at eight at night; all day the milk pours from her breasts so that her clothing drips with it."

"H. W. has three children, goes away Monday morning at five o'clock, and comes back Saturday evening; has so much to do for the children then that she cannot get to bed before three o'clock in the morning; often wet through to the skin, and obliged to work in that state. She said: 'My breasts have given me the most frightful pain, and I have been dripping wet with milk. '"

The use of narcotics to keep the children still is fostered by this infamous system, and has reached a great extent in the factory districts. Dr. Johns, Registrar in Chief for Manchester, is of opinion that this custom is the chief source of the many deaths from convulsions. The employment of the wife dissolves the family utterly and of necessity, and this dissolution, in our present society, which is based upon the family, brings the most demoralizing consequences for parents, as well as children....

Yet the working man cannot escape from the family, must live in the family, and the

"The Impact of the Factory System on Women and the Family" is from Friedrich Engels, *The Condition of the Working Class in England in 1844* (London: Sonnenschein & Co., 1892).

consequence is a perpetual succession of family troubles, domestic quarrels, most demoralizing for parents and children alike. Neglect of all domestic duties, neglect of the children, especially, is only too common among English working people, and only too vigorously fostered by the existing institutions of society. And children growing up in this savage way, amidst these demoralizing influences, are expected to turn out goody-goody and moral in the end! Verily the requirements are naive which the self-satisfied bourgeois makes upon the working man!

CONSIDER THIS:

- How does Engels's description of the impact of the factory system on women and the family seem to reflect some of the concerns of our contemporary society?

Reaction and Reform

Law and Liberty: The Liberal Truth

The Principle of Population (1798)

THOMAS MALTHUS

The Industrial Revolution began to develop in England while the economic practice of mercantilism was still widespread. Proponents of mercantilism argued that colonies existed for the benefit of the mother country, and indeed all economic activity should be regulated by the state for the good of the state. This concept was not in harmony with the rise of industrial capitalism. Adam Smith, in his important treatise *The Wealth of Nations* (1776), advocated the economic doctrine of laissez-faire. He contended that every human being is motivated primarily by self-interest and that the marketplace is regulated by its own competitive laws of supply and demand, profit and loss. Therefore, the market must be left alone (hence the name laissez-faire) and free from government controls and monopolies. Adam Smith soon became the "Patron Saint of Free Enterprise," and capitalism as a theory was born.

Two of the most important classical economists who subscribed to Smith's ideas were Thomas Malthus (1766–1834) and David Ricardo (1772–1823). Malthus employed statistics to develop the Malthusian doctrine: The world's population, unless checked by war, disease, famine, late marriage, or moral restraint, grows at a higher rate than the means of subsistence, resulting in a doubling of the population every twenty-five years. His prediction for world famine was pessimistic indeed.

I have read some of the speculations on the perfectibility of man and of society with great pleasure. . . . I ardently wish for such happy improvements. But I see great, and, to my understanding, unconquerable difficulties in the way of them. . . .

I think I may fairly make two postulates: First, that food is necessary to the existence

"The Principle of Population" is from Thomas Malthus, *An Essay on the Principle of Population As It Affects the Future Improvement of Society* (London, 1798).

of man. Secondly, that the passion between the sexes is necessary, and will remain nearly in its present state. These two laws, ever since we have had any knowledge of mankind, appear to have been fixed laws of our nature. . . .

Assuming, then, my postulates as granted, I say that the power of population is indefinitely greater than the power of the earth to produce subsistence for man.

Population, when unchecked, increases in a geometrical ratio. Subsistence only increases in an arithmetical ratio. A slight acquaintance with numbers will show the immensity of the first power in comparison with the second.

By that law of our nature which makes food necessary to the life of man, the effects of these two unequal powers must be kept equal.

This implies a strong and constantly operating check on population from the difficulty of subsistence. This difficulty must fall somewhere; and must necessarily be severely felt by a large portion of mankind. . . .

Of the Only Effectual Mode of Improving the Condition of the Poor

He who performs his duty faithfully . . . [will] not bring beings into the world for whom he cannot find the means of support. . . . If he cannot support his children they must starve; and if he marry in the face of a fair probability that he shall not be able to support his children, he is guilty of all the evils which he thus brings upon himself, his wife, and his offspring. It is clearly in his interest, and will tend greatly to promote his happiness, to defer marrying till by industry and economy he is in a capacity to support the children that he may reasonably expect from his marriage; and as he cannot in the meantime gratify his passions without violating an express command of God, and running a great risk of injuring himself, or some of his fellow-creatures, considerations of his own interest and happiness will dictate to him the strong obligation to a moral conduct while he remains unmarried.

Of the Consequences of Pursuing the Opposite Mode

Among the lower classes of society . . . the poor-laws afford a direct . . . encouragement to marriage, by removing from each individual that heavy responsibility, which he would incur by the laws of nature, for bringing beings into the world which he could not support. Our private benevolence has the same direction as the poor-laws, and almost invariably tends to encourage marriage, and to equalize as much as possible the circumstances of married and single men. . . .

[Until] the poor are undeceived with respect to the principal cause of their poverty, and taught to know that their happiness or misery must depend chiefly upon themselves, it cannot be said that, with regard to the great question of marriage, we leave every man to his free and fair choice.

Consider This:

- According to Malthus, why are private benevolence and government relief programs (poor laws) detrimental to improving the condition of the poor? How do they encourage marriage, and, as a result, greater poverty? Who ultimately bears responsibility for the condition of the poor?
- What was Malthus's solution to the problem of population and poverty? How important was moral responsibility to his solution? How can such a subjective factor as Christian morality influence a mathematical ratio between food supply, population, and poverty?

The Broader Perspective:

- How is the problem of poverty, welfare, and morality still a part of the political landscape? Was Malthus correct in his mathematical postulates? Or does such a human problem as poverty defy such "calculations"?

The Iron Law of Wages (1817)

DAVID RICARDO

David Ricardo, who had made a fortune on the London Stock Exchange, developed a theory, based to some extent on Malthus's analysis, that later came to be called the Iron Law of Wages. Ricardo believed that the wages of laborers must necessarily remain at a subsistence level because of the working class's unchecked rate of reproduction, which would continuously keep the supply of labor excessive. Ricardo advocated a restriction of so-called poor laws that were enacted by Parliament in the early nineteenth century to relieve the poor through governmental assistance. Ricardo thus became a champion of the rising industrial capitalists. A selection from his treatise *The Principles of Political Economy and Taxation* (1817) follows.

The friends of humanity cannot but wish that in all countries the laboring classes should have a taste for comforts and enjoyments, and that they should be stimulated by all legal means in their exertions to procure them. There cannot be a better security against a superabundant population. In those countries where the laboring classes have the fewest wants, and are contented with the cheapest food, the people are exposed to the greatest vicissitudes and miseries. They have no place or refuge from calamity; they cannot seek safety in a lower station; they are already so low that they can fall no lower. On any deficiency of the chief article of their subsistence there are few substitutes of which they can avail themselves and dearth to them is attended with almost all the evils of famine.

In the natural advance of society, the wages of labor will have a tendency to fall, as far as they are regulated by supply and demand; for the supply of laborers will continue to increase at the same rate, while the demand for them will increase at a slower rate. .   say that, under these circumstances, wages would fall if they were regulated only by the supply and demand of laborers; but we must not forget that wages are also regulated by the prices of the commodities on which they are expended.

As population increases, these necessaries will be constantly rising in price, because more labor will be necessary to produce them. If, then, the money wages of labor should fall, while every commodity on which the wages of labor were expended rose, the laborer would be doubly affected, and would be soon totally deprived of subsistence. . . . These, then, are the laws by which wages are regulated, and by which the happiness of far the greatest part of every community is governed. Like all other contracts, wages should be left to the fair and free competition of the market, and should never be controlled by the interference of the legislature.

The clear and direct tendency of the poor laws is in direct opposition to those obvious principles: it is not, as the legislature benevolently intended, to amend the condition of the poor, but to deteriorate the condition of both poor and rich; instead of making the poor rich, they are calculated to make the rich poor; and while the present laws are in force, it is quite in the natural order of things that the fund for the maintenance of the poor should progressively increase till it has absorbed all the net revenue of the country, or at least so much of it as the state shall leave to us, after satisfying its own never-failing demands for the public expenditure.

"The Iron Law of Wages" is from David Ricardo, *The Principles of Political Economy and Taxation* (London: J. M. Dent & Sons, Ltd., 1911), pp. 57, 61–63.

This pernicious tendency of these laws is no longer a mystery, since it has been fully developed by the able hand of Mr. Malthus; and every friend to the poor must ardently wish for their abolition. Unfortunately, however, they have been so long established, and the habits of the poor have been so formed upon their operation, that to eradicate them with safety from our political system requires the most cautious and skillful management. It is agreed by all who are most friendly to a repeal of these laws that, if it be desirable to prevent the most overwhelming distress to those for whose benefit they were erroneously enacted, their abolition should be effected by the most gradual steps.

It is a truth which admits not a doubt that the comforts and well-being of the poor cannot be permanently secured without some regard on their part, or some effort on the part of the legislature, to regulate the increase of their numbers, and to render less frequent among them early and improvident marriages. The operation of the system of poor laws has been directly contrary to this. They have rendered restraint superfluous, and have invited imprudence, by offering it a portion of the wages of prudence and industry.

The nature of the evil points out the remedy. By gradually contracting the sphere of the poor laws; by impressing on the poor the value of independence, by teaching them that they must look not to systematic or casual charity, but to their own exertions for support, that prudence and forethought are neither unnecessary nor unprofitable virtues, we shall by degrees approach a sounder and more healthful state.

No scheme for the amendment of the poor laws merits the least attention which has not their abolition for its ultimate object; and he is the best friend of the poor, and to the cause of humanity, who can point out how this end can be attained with the most security, and at the same time with the least violence. It is not by raising in any manner different from the present the fund from which the poor are supported that the evil can be mitigated. It would not only be no improvement, but it would be an aggravation of the distress which we wish to see removed, if the fund were increased in amount or were levied according to some late proposals, as a general fund from the country at large. . . . If by law every human being wanting support could be sure to obtain it, and obtain it in such a degree as to make life tolerably comfortable, theory would lead us to expect that all other taxes together would be light compared with the single one of poor rates. The principle of gravitation is not more certain than the tendency of such laws to change wealth and power into misery and weakness; . . . to confound all intellectual distinction; to busy the mind continually in supplying the body's wants; until at last all classes should be infected with the plague of universal poverty. Happily these laws have been in operation during a period of progressive prosperity, when the funds for the maintenance of labor have regularly increased, and when an increase of population would be naturally called for. But if our progress should become more slow; if we should attain the stationary state, from which I trust we are yet far distant, then will the pernicious nature of these laws become more manifest and alarming; and then, too, will their removal be obstructed by many additional difficulties.

Consider This:

- Discuss David Ricardo's ideas on the wages of laborers. Why were the poor laws to be regarded as destructive to the basic economic health of the state? Do you find his argument logical and compelling? Can you apply it to our contemporary society?

The Chartist Demands (1838)

Although the Factory Act of 1833 resulted in an improvement in factory working conditions and in restrictions on child labor, many critics favored more radical reform. The Chartist movement in Great Britain, which was popular in the 1840s, sought political participation and especially universal manhood suffrage as a means of improving the living conditions of the working poor. The following is an excerpt from the People's Petition of 1838, which articulated Chartist demands to the British House of Commons.

We, your petitioners, dwell in a land whose merchants are noted for enterprise, whose manufacturers are very skillful, and whose workmen are proverbial for their industry.

The land itself is goodly, the soil rich, and the temperature wholesome; it is abundantly furnished with the materials of commerce and trade; it has numerous and convenient harbours; in facility of internal communication it exceeds all others. For three-and-twenty years we have enjoyed a profound peace.

Yet, with all these elements of national prosperity, and with every disposition and capacity to take advantage of them, we find ourselves overwhelmed with public and private suffering.

We are bowed down under a load of taxes; which, notwithstanding, fall greatly short of the wants of our rulers; our traders are trembling on the verge of bankruptcy; our workmen are starving; capital brings no profit, and labour no remuneration; the home of the artificer is desolate, and the warehouse of the pawnbroker is full; the workhouse is crowded, and the manufactory is deserted. . . .

It was the found expectation of the people that a remedy for the greater part, if not for the whole, of their grievances, would be found in the Reform Act of 1832.

They were taught to regard that Act as a wise means to a worthy end; as the machinery of an improved legislation, when the will of the masses would be at length potential.

They have been bitterly and basely deceived.

The fruit which looked so fair to the eye has turned to dust and ashes when gathered.

The Reform Act has effected a transfer of power from one domineering faction to another, and left the people as helpless as before. . . .

Required as we are, universally, to support and obey the laws, nature and reason entitle us to demand, that in the making of the laws, the universal voice shall be implicitly listened to.

We perform the duties of freemen; we must have the privileges of freemen.

WE DEMAND UNIVERSAL SUFFRAGE

The suffrage to be exempt from the corruption of the wealthy, and the violence of the powerful, must be secret. . . .

WE DEMAND THE BALLOT

The connection between the representatives and the people, to be beneficial must be intimate. . . . To public safety as well as public confidence, frequent elections are essential.

WE DEMAND ANNUAL PARLIAMENTS

With power to choose, and freedom in choosing, the range of our choice must be unrestricted.

We are compelled, by the existing laws, to take for our representatives, men who are incapable of appreciating our difficulties, or who have little sympathy with them; merchants who have retired from trade, and no longer feel its harassings; proprietors of land who are alike ignorant of its evils and their cure; lawyers, by whom the honours of the

"The Chartist Demands" is from *The Life and Struggles of William Lovett* (New York: Knopf, 1920), pp. 478–481.

senate are sought after only as means of obtaining notice in the courts. . . .

We demand that in the future election of members of you Honourable House, the approbation of the constituency shall be the sole qualification; and that to every representative so chosen shall be assigned, out of the public taxes, a fair and adequate remuneration for the time which he is called upon to devote to the public service.

Finally, we would most earnestly impress on your Honourable House, that this petition has not been dictated by an idle love of change; that it springs out of no inconsiderate attachment to fanciful theories; but that it is the result of much and long deliberation, and of convictions, which the events of each succeeding year tend more and more to strengthen.

CONSIDER THIS:

- Who were the Chartists, and what were their demands for reform? Was this a political or social reform program?

A Middle-Class Perspective (1859)

SAMUEL SMILES

The classical economists such as Adam Smith and David Ricardo stressed the need for free enterprise in the marketplace and defied regulation by government. Other theoreticians accepted these principles of self-interest and self-determination and yet applied them more specifically to the social and political world. Jeremy Bentham (1748–1832) advocated a principle called *utilitarianism*, whereby all things could be judged on twin concepts of utility and happiness. The best government, for example, was one that ensured the greatest happiness for the greatest number of people. These utilitarians were also referred to as "philosophical radicals" because they lacked all reverence for tradition and believed that political, social, and economic problems could be addressed rationally, without reference to privilege or special interests. They were popularly characterized as unemotional intellectuals without a practical understanding of humanity.

For many members of the middle class, the Victorian Age was not characterized by the slums of Glasgow or the dirt of industry. To their thinking, perseverance and hard work resulted in a better life and were always rewarded. In his book *Self-Help* (1859), Samuel Smiles emphasized this principle through a series of biographies of men who had risen to fame and fortune. The guiding idea was that "the most important results in daily life are to be obtained, not through the exercise of extraordinary powers, such as genius and intellect, but through the energetic use of simple means and ordinary qualities with which nearly all human individuals have more or less been endowed." One was responsible for one's own fate; it was up to the individual to change a bad situation if so desired.

The object of the book briefly is, to re-inculcate these old-fashioned but wholesome lessons—which perhaps cannot be too often urged,—that youth must work in order to enjoy,—that nothing creditable can be accomplished without application and diligence,—that the student must not be daunted by difficulties, but conquer them by patience and

"A Middle-Class Perspective" is from Samuel Smiles, *Self-Help* (London: John Murray, 1882), pp. v, 1, 4.

perseverance,—and that, above all, he must seek elevation of character, without which capacity is worthless and worldly success is naught. If the author has not succeeded in illustrating these lessons, he can only say that he has failed in his object.

"Heaven helps those who help themselves" is a well-tried maxim, embodying in a small compass the results of vast human experience. The spirit of self-help is the root of all genuine growth in the individual; and, exhibited in the lives of many, it constitutes the true source of national vigor and strength. Help from without is often enfeebling in its effects, but help from within invariably invigorates. Whatever is done for men or classes, to a certain extent takes away the stimulus and necessity of doing for themselves; and where men are subjected to over-guidance and over-government, the inevitable tendency is to render them comparatively helpless.

Even the best institutions can give a man no active help. Perhaps the most they can do is, to leave him free to develop himself and improve his individual condition. But in all times men have been prone to believe that their happiness and well-being were to be secured by means of institutions rather than by their own conduct. Hence the value of legislation as an agent in human advancement has usually been much over-estimated. To constitute the millionth part of a Legislature, by voting for one or two men once in three or five years, however conscientiously this duty may be performed, can exercise but little active influence upon any man's life and character. Moreover, it is every day becoming more clearly understood, that the function of Government is negative and restrictive, rather than positive and active; being resolvable principally into protection—protection of life, liberty, and property. Laws, wisely administered, will secure men in the enjoyment of the fruits of their labour, whether of mind or body, at a comparatively small personal sacrifice; but no laws, however, stringent, can make the idle industrious, the thriftless provident, or the drunken sober. Reforms can only be effected by means of individual action, economy, and self-denial; better habits, rather than by greater rights. . . .

Daily experience shows that it is energetic individualism which produces the most powerful effects upon the life and action of others, and really constitutes the best practical education. Schools, academies, and colleges, give but the merest beginnings of culture in comparison with it. Far more influential is the life-education daily given in our homes, in the streets, behind counters, in workshops, at the loom and the plough, in counting-houses and manufactories, and in the busy haunts of men. This is that finishing instruction as members of society, which Schiller designated "the education of the human race," consisting in action, conduct, self-culture, self-control,—all that tends to discipline a man truly, and fit him for the proper performance of the duties and business of life,—a kind of education not to be learnt from books, or acquired by any amount of mere literary training. With his usual weight of words Bacon observes, that "Studies teach not their own use; but that is a wisdom without them, and above them, won by observation"; a remark that holds true of actual life, as well as of the cultivation of the intellect itself. For all experience serves to illustrate and enforce the lesson, that a man perfects himself by work more than by reading,—that it is life rather than literature, action rather than study, and character rather than biography, which tend perpetually to renovate mankind.

CONSIDER THIS:

- What was the attitude of Samuel Smiles toward the plight of the working class? Why would this opinion be considered "middle class"? What do you think of the principle of "self-help"?

Visions of a New World: The Socialist Truth

Utopian Socialism (1816)

ROBERT OWEN

One of the great personal success stories of the nineteenth century was Robert Owen. Born the son of a saddle maker, Owen left school at age nine and went to work in a draper's shop. At eighteen, he borrowed money and set up a small cotton mill in Manchester. Within ten years he was very wealthy and joint owner of the New Lanark mills, the largest textile operation in Scotland. But Owen was possessed with a desire to improve the lot of humanity. He provided higher wages and better working conditions for his employees and established free schools for their children. The New Lanark mills also returned a handsome profit. Owen sought government intervention and regulation to change conditions in industry. He could not understand why all factories could not be run on his utopian model. He is generally accepted in England as the founder of British socialism. The following address was delivered in 1816 on the opening of an "Institution for the Formation of Character" at New Lanark. Note the emphasis on morality as an essential ingredient of change.

Every society which exists at present, as well as every society which history records, has been formed and governed on a belief in the following notions, assumed as *first principles*:

First,—That it is in the power of every individual to form his own character.

Hence the various systems called by the name of religion, codes of law, and punishments. Hence also the angry passions entertained by individuals and nations towards each other.

Second,—That the affections are at the command of the individual. Hence insincerity and degradation of character.

Hence the miseries of domestic life, and more than one-half of all the crimes of mankind.

Third,—That it is necessary that a large portion of mankind should exist in ignorance and poverty, in order to secure to the remaining part such a degree of happiness as they now enjoy.

Hence a system of counteraction in the pursuits of men, a general opposition among individuals to the interests of each other, and the necessary effects of such a system,—ignorance, poverty, and vice.

Facts prove, however—

First,—That character is universally formed *for*, and not *by*, the individual.

Second,—That *any* habits and sentiments may be given to mankind.

Third,—That the affections are not under the control of the individual.

Fourth,—That every individual may be trained to produce far more than he can consume, while there is a sufficiency of soil left for him to cultivate.

Fifth,—That nature has provided means by which population may be at all times maintained in the proper state to give the greatest happiness to every individual, without one check of vice or misery.

Sixth,—That any community may be arranged, on a due combination of the foregoing principles, in such a manner, as not only to withdraw vice, poverty, and, in a great degree, misery, from the world, but also to place *every* individual under circumstances in which he shall enjoy more permanent happiness than

"Utopian Socialism" is from Robert Owen, *Address to the Workers of New Lanark* (1816).

FIGURE 7.4 The factory school at New Lanark mills. Robert Owen, a successful businessman and utopian socialist, believed that a humane working environment need not be sacrificed in order to maintain a fine profit. His industrial community included free schooling for the children of his workers. (*Picture Desk, Inc./Kobal Collection*)

can be given to *any* individual under the principles which have hitherto regulated society.

Seventh,—That all the assumed fundamental principles on which society has hitherto been founded are erroneous, and may be demonstrated to be contrary to fact. And—

Eighth,—That the change which would follow the abandonment of those erroneous maxims which bring misery into the world, and the adoption of principles of truth, unfolding a system which shall remove and for ever exclude that misery, may be effected without the slightest injury to any human being.

Here is the groundwork,—these are the data, on which society shall ere long be rearranged; and for this simple reason, that it will be rendered evident that it will be for the immediate and future interest of every one to lend his most active assistance gradually to reform society on this basis. I say gradually, for in that word the most important considerations are involved. Any sudden and coercive attempt which may be made to remove even misery from men will prove injurious rather than beneficial. Their minds must be gradually prepared by an essential alteration of the circumstances which surround them, for any great and important change and amelioration in their condition. They must be first convinced of their blindness: this cannot be effected, even among the least unreasonable, or those termed the best part of mankind, in their present state, without creating some degree of irritation. This irritation, must then be tranquillized before another step ought to be attempted; and a general conviction must be established of the truth of the principles on which the projected change is to be founded. Their introduction into practice will then become easy,—difficulties will vanish as we approach them,—and, afterwards, the desire to see the whole system carried immediately into effect will exceed the means of putting it into execution.

The principles on which this practical system is founded are not new; separately, or partially united, they have been often recommended by the sages of antiquity, and by modern writers. But it is not known to me that they have ever been thus combined. Yet it can be demonstrated that it is only by their being *all brought into practice together* that they are to be rendered beneficial to mankind; and sure I am that this is the earliest period in the history of man when they could be successfully introduced into practice.

Consider This:

- Robert Owen noted that "all the assumed fundamental principles on which society has hitherto been founded are erroneous." This is a bold statement. Which principles was he referring to? What did Owen propose as new principles for the best arrangement of society?
- What role does morality play in Owen's construction of a fair and equal society? Is character everything? Would Samuel Smiles have agreed?

The Communist Manifesto (1848)

KARL MARX AND FRIEDRICH ENGELS

The Communist Manifesto, written by Karl Marx (1818–1883) and Friedrich Engels in 1848, is the fundamental declaration of communist ideology. Marx was concerned with the process of change in history (dialectic). A keen observer of the industrial world around him, Marx saw the oppression of the worker (proletarian) by those who owned the means of production (bourgeoisie). Marx advocated a society that was devoid of capitalistic oppression, a society in which workers actually controlled the factories and regulated their own working conditions and environment. His call to revolution had little influence on the protests of 1848, but his ideas would serve as the foundation for the Russian Revolution in 1917 and are of great importance today.

Bourgeoisie and Proletariat

The history of all hitherto existing society is the history of class struggles.

Freeman and slave, patrician and plebeian, lord and serf, guildmaster and journeyman, in a word, oppressor and oppressed, stood in constant opposition to one another, carried on an uninterrupted, now hidden, now open fight, a fight that each time ended, either in a revolutionary reconstitution of society at large, or in the common ruin of the contending classes.

In the earlier epochs of history, we find almost everywhere a complicated arrangement of society into various orders, a manifold graduation of social rank. In ancient Rome we have patricians, knights, plebeian, slaves; in the Middle Ages, feudal lords, vassals, guildmasters, journeymen, apprentices, serfs; in almost all of these classes, again, subordinate gradations.

The modern bourgeois society that has sprouted from the ruins of feudal society, has not done away with class antagonisms. It has but established new classes, new conditions of oppression, new forms of struggle in place of the old ones.

Our epoch, the epoch of the bourgeoisie, possesses, however, this distinctive feature: it

"*The Communist Manifesto*" is from Karl Marx and Friedrich Engels, *The Communist Manifesto*, trans. Samuel Moore (New York: Socialist Labor Party, 1888).

has simplified the class antagonisms. Society as a whole is more and more splitting up into two great hostile camps, into two great classes directly facing each other: Bourgeoisie and Proletariat. . . .

Each step in the development of the bourgeoisie was accompanied by a corresponding political advance of the class. An oppressed class under the sway of the feudal nobility, an armed and self-governing association in the medieval commune, here independent urban republic (as in Italy and Germany), there taxable "third estate" of the monarchy (as in France), afterwards, in the period of manufacture proper, serving either the semifeudal or the absolute monarchy as a counterpoise against the nobility, and in fact, corner stone of the great monarchies in general, the bourgeoisie has at last, since the establishment of Modern Industry and of the world-market, conquered for itself, in the modern representative State, exclusive political sway. The executive of the modern State is but a committee for managing the common affairs of the whole bourgeoisie. . . .

The need of a constantly expanding market for its products chases the bourgeoisie over the whole surface of the globe. It must nestle everywhere, establish connections everywhere. . . .

The bourgeoisie, during its rule of scarce one hundred years, has created more massive and more colossal productive forces than have all preceding generations together. Subjection of Nature's forces to man, machinery, application of chemistry to industry and agriculture, steam-navigation, railways, electric telegraphs, clearing of whole continents for cultivation, canalization of rivers, whole populations conjured out of the ground—what earlier century had even a presentiment that such productive forces slumbered in the lap of social labor? . . .

In proportion as the bourgeoisie, i.e., capital, is developed, in the same proportion is the proletariat, the modern working-class, developed, a class of laborers, who live only so long as they find work, and who find work only so long as their labor increases capital. These laborers, who must sell themselves piecemeal, are a commodity, like every other article of commerce, and are consequently exposed to all the vicissitudes of competition, to all the fluctuations of the market.

Owing to the extensive use of machinery and to division of labor, the work of the proletarians has lost all individual character, and, consequently, all charm for the workman. He becomes an appendage of the machine, and it is only the most simple, most monotonous, and most easily acquired knack that is required of him. Hence, the cost of production of a workman is restricted, almost entirely, to the means of subsistence that he requires for his maintenance, and for the propagation of his race. But the price of commodity, and also of labor, is equal to its cost of production. In proportion, therefore, as the repulsiveness of the work increases, the wage decreases. Nay more, in proportion as the use of the machinery and division of labor increases, in the same proportion the burden of toil also increases, whether by prolongation of the working hours, by increase of the work enacted in a given time, or by increased speed of the machinery, etc.

Modern industry has converted the little workshop of the patriarchal master into the great factory of the industrial capitalist. Masses of laborers, crowded into the factory, are organized like soldiers. As privates of the industrial army they are placed under the command of a perfect hierarchy of officers and sergeants. Not only are they the slaves of the bourgeois class, and of the bourgeois State, they are daily and hourly enslaved by the machine, by the over-looker, and, above all, by the individual bourgeois manufacturer himself. The more openly despotism proclaims gain to be its end and aim, the more petty, the more hateful and the more embittering it is.

FIGURE 7.5 The grave memorial of Karl Marx at Highgate Cemetery in London: "The proletarians have nothing to lose but their chains. They have a world to win. Workers of the world, unite!" (*Perry M. Rogers*)

The less the skill and exertion or strength implied in manual labor, in other words, the more modern industry becomes developed, the more is the labor of men superseded by that of women. Differences of age and sex have no longer any distinctive social validity for the working class. All are instruments of labor, more or less expensive to use, according to their age and sex.

No sooner is the exploitation of the laborer by the manufacturer, so far at an end, that he receives his wages in cash, than he is set upon by the other portions of the bourgeoisie, the landlord, the shopkeeper, the pawnbroker, etc. . . .

But with the development of industry the proletariat not only increases in number, it becomes concentrated in greater masses, its strength grows, and it feels that strength more. The various interests and conditions of life within the ranks of the proletariat are more and more equalized, in proportion as machinery obliterates all distinctions of labor, and nearly everywhere reduces wages to the same low level. The growing competition among the bourgeois, and the resulting commercial crises, make the wages of the workers ever more fluctuating. The unceasing improvement of machinery, ever more rapidly developing, makes their livelihood more and more precarious; the collisions between individual workmen and individual bourgeois take more and more the character of collisions between two classes. Thereupon the workers begin to form combinations (Trades' Unions) against the bourgeois; they club together in order to keep up the rate of wages; they found permanent associations in order to make provision beforehand for these occasional revolts. Here and there the contest breaks out into riots.

Now and then the workers are victorious, but only for a time. The real fruit of their battle lies, not in the immediate result, but in the ever expanding union of the workers. This union is helped on by the improved means of communications that are created by modern industry, and that places the workers of different localities in contact with one another. It was just this contact that was needed to centralize the numerous local struggles, all of the same character, into one national struggle between classes. But every class struggle is a political struggle. . . .

This organization of the proletarians into a class, and consequently into a political party, is continually being upset again by the competition between the workers themselves. But it ever rises up again, stronger, firmer, mightier. It compels legislative recognition of particular interests of the workers, by taking advantage of the divisions among the bourgeoisie itself. Thus the ten-hour bill in England was carried. . . .

The essential condition for the existence, and for the sway of the bourgeois class, is the formation and augmentation of capital; the condition for capital is wage-labor. Wage-labor rests exclusively on competition between the laborers. The advance of industry, whose involuntary promoter is the bourgeoisie, replaces the isolation of the laborers, due to competition, by their revolutionary combination, due to association. The development of Modern Industry, therefore, cuts from under its feet the very foundation on which the bourgeoisie produces and appropriates products. What the bourgeoisie therefore produces, above all, are its own gravediggers. Its fall and the victory of the proletariat are equally inevitable.

Proletarians and Communists

In what relation do the Communists stand to the proletarians as a whole?

The Communists do not form a separate party opposed to other working class parties.

They have no interests separate and apart from those of the proletariat as a whole.

They do not set up any sectarian principles of their own, by which to shape and mould the proletarian movement.

The Communists are distinguished from the other working class parties by this only: 1. In the national struggles of the proletarians of the different countries, they point out and bring to the front the common interests of the entire proletariat independently of all nationality. 2. In the various stages of development which the struggle of the working class against the bourgeoisie has to pass through, they always and everywhere represent the interests of the movement as a whole.

The Communists, therefore, are on the one hand, practically, the most advanced and resolute section of the working class parties of every country, that section which pushes forward all other; on the other hand, theoretically, they have over the great mass of the proletariat the advantage of clearly understanding the line of march, the conditions, and the ultimate general results of the proletarian movement.

The immediate aim of the Communists is the same as that of all the other proletarian parties: formation of the proletariat into a class, overthrow of the bourgeois supremacy, conquest of political power by the proletariat.

The theoretical conclusions of the Communists are in no way based on ideas or principles that have been invented, or discovered, by this or that would-be universal reformer.

They merely express, in general terms, actual relations springing from an existing class struggle, from a historical movement going on under our very eyes. The abolition of existing property relations is not at all a distinctive feature of Communism.

All property relations in the past have continually been subject to historical change consequent upon the change in historical conditions.

The French Revolution, for example, abolished feudal property in favor of bourgeois property.

The distinguishing feature of Communism is not the abolition of property generally, but the abolition of bourgeois property. But modern bourgeois private property is the final and most complete expression of the system of producing and appropriating products, that is based on class antagonism, on the exploitation of the many by the few.

In this sense, the theory of the Communists may be summed up in the single sentence: Abolition of private property. . . .

The Communist revolution is the most radical rupture with traditional property-relations; no wonder that its development involves the most radical rupture with traditional ideas.

But let us have done with the bourgeois objections to Communism.

We have seen above, that the first step in the revolution by the working class, is to raise the proletariat to the position of ruling class, to win the battle of democracy.

The proletariat will use its political supremacy, to wrest, by degrees, all capital from the bourgeoisie, to centralize all instruments of production in the hands of the State, i.e., of the proletariat organized as the ruling class; and to increase the total of productive forces as rapidly as possible.

Of course, in the beginning, this cannot be effected except by means of despotic inroads on the rights of property, and on the conditions of bourgeois production; by means of measures, therefore, which appear economically insufficient and untenable, but which, in the course of the movement, outstrip themselves, necessitate further inroads upon the old social order, and are unavoidable as a means of entirely revolutionizing the mode of production.

These measures will of course be different in different countries.

Nevertheless in the most advanced countries the following will be pretty generally applicable:

1. Abolition of property in land and application of all rents of land to public purposes.
2. A heavy progressive or graduated income tax.
3. Abolition of all rights of inheritance.
4. Confiscation of the property of all emigrants and rebels.
5. Centralization of credit in the hands of the state, by means of a national bank with State capital and an exclusive monopoly.
6. Centralization of the means of communication and transport in the hands of the State.
7. Extension of factories and instruments of production owned by the State; the bringing into cultivation of waste lands, and the improvement of the soil generally in accordance with a common plan.
8. Equal liability of all to labor. Establishment of industrial armies, especially for agriculture.
9. Combination of agriculture with manufacturing industries; gradual abolition of the distinction between town and country, by a more equable distribution of population over the country.
10. Free education for all children in public schools. Abolition of children's factory labor in its present form. Combination of education with industrial production, etc., etc.

When, in the course of development, class distinctions have disappeared, and all production has been concentrated in the hands of a vast association of the whole nation, the public power will lose its political character. Political power, properly so called, is merely the organized power of one class for oppressing another. If the proletariat during its contest with the bourgeoisie is compelled, by the force of circumstances, to organize itself as a class, if, by means of a revolution, it makes itself the ruling class, and, as such, sweeps away by force the old conditions of production, then it will, along with these conditions, have swept away the conditions for the existence of class antagonisms, and of class generally, and will thereby have abolished its own supremacy as a class.

In place of the old bourgeois society, with its classes and class antagonisms, we shall have an association, in which the free development of each is the condition for the free development of all. . . .

In short, the Communists everywhere support every revolutionary movement against the existing social and political order of things.

In all these movements they bring to the front, as the leading question in each, the property question, no matter what its degree of development at the time.

Finally, they labor everywhere for the union and agreement of the democratic parties of all countries.

The Communists disdain to conceal their views and aims. They openly declare that their ends can be attained only by the forcible overthrow of all existing social conditions. Let the ruling classes tremble at a Communistic revolution. The proletarians have nothing to lose but their chains. They have a world to win. Workers of the world, unite!

CONSIDER THIS:

- What do you consider to be the most important ideas or statements that can be found in the excerpt on *The Communist Manifesto*? Why is this considered one of the most influential documents in Western civilization?

THEME: THE INSTITUTION AND THE INDIVIDUAL

THE REFLECTION IN THE MIRROR

A Papal Perspective: Rerum Novarum

One of the more influential associations against the abuses of industrialism was the Christian Socialist movement. It began in England about 1848 and stressed that one could overcome the evils of industrialism by following Christian principles: Brotherly love was preferable to ruthless competition and exploitation. Quite apart from this movement, but adhering to the same basic principles, was the Catholic church. Pope Leo XIII was an active commentator on political power and human liberty. In 1891, he issued the encyclical *Rerum Novarum*, which addressed the continuing struggle between capitalists and workers. This official opinion of the pope demonstrates the church's continuing interest in the affairs of the secular world.

"*Rerum Novarum*" is from Claudia Carlen Ihm, ed., *The Papal Encyclicals, 1878–1903*, vol. 2 (New York: McGrath Publishing Company, 1981), pp. 241–242, 244–246, 248, 255–256.

"A Yoke Little Better Than That of Slavery Itself"

POPE LEO XIII

Rights and Duties of Capital Labor

That the spirit of revolutionary change, which has long been disturbing the nations of the world, should have passed beyond the sphere of politics and made its influence felt in the cognate sphere of practical economics is not surprising. The elements of the conflict now raging are unmistakable, in the vast expansion of industrial pursuits and the marvelous discoveries of science; in the changed relations between masters and workmen; in the enormous fortunes of some few individuals, and the utter poverty of the masses; in the increased self-reliance and closer mutual combination of the working classes; as also, finally, in the prevailing moral degeneracy. The momentous gravity of the state of things now obtaining fills every mind with painful apprehension; wise men are discussing it; practical men are proposing schemes; popular meetings, legislatures, and rulers of nations are all busied with it—actually there is no question which has taken a deeper hold on the public mind.

Therefore, We thought it expedient now to speak on the condition of the working classes. It is a subject on which We have already touched more than once, incidentally. But in the present letter, the responsibility of the apostolic office urges Us to treat the question of set purpose and in detail, in order that no misapprehension may exist as to the principles which truth and justice dictate for its settlement. The discussion is not easy, nor is it void of danger. It is no easy matter to define the relative rights and mutual duties of the rich and of the poor, of capital and of labor. And the danger lies in this, that crafty agitators are intent on making use of these differences of opinion to pervert men's judgments and to stir up the people to revolt.

In any case we clearly see, and on this there is general agreement, that some opportune remedy must be found quickly for the misery and wretchedness pressing so unjustly on the majority of the working class: for the ancient working-men's guilds were abolished in the last century, and no other protective organization took their place. . . . Hence, by degrees it has come to pass that working men have been surrendered, isolated and helpless, to the hardheartedness of employers and the greed of unchecked competition. The mischief has been increased by rapacious usury, which, although more than once condemned by the Church, is nevertheless, under a different guise, but with like injustice, still practiced by covetous and grasping men. To this must be added that the hiring of labor and the conduct of trade are concentrated in the hands of comparatively few; so that a small number of very rich men have been able to lay upon the teeming masses of the laboring poor a yoke little better than that of slavery itself.

To remedy these wrongs the socialists, working on the poor man's envy of the rich, are striving to do away with private property, and contend that individual possessions should become the common property of all, to be administered by the State or by municipal bodies. They hold that by thus transferring property from private individuals to the community, the present mischievous state of things will be set to rights, inasmuch as each citizen will then get his fair share of whatever there is to enjoy. But their contentions are so clearly powerless to end the controversy that were they carried into effect the working man himself would be among the first to suffer. They are, moreover, emphatically unjust, for they would rob the lawful possessor, distort the functions of the State, and create utter confusion in the community. . . .

What is of far greater moment, however, is the fact that the remedy they propose is manifestly against justice. For, every man has by nature the right to possess property as his own. This is one of the chief points of distinction between man and the animal creation, for the brute has no power of self-direction, but is governed by two main instincts, which keep his powers on the alert, impel him to develop them in a fitting manner, and stimulate and determine him to action without any power of choice. One of these instincts is self-preservation, the other the propagation of the species. Both can attain their purpose by means of things which lie within range; beyond their verge the brute creation cannot go, for they are moved to action by their senses only, and in the special direction which these suggest. But with man it is wholly different. He possesses, on the one hand, the full perfection of the animal being, and hence enjoys at least as much as the rest of the animal kind, the fruition of things material. But animal nature, however perfect, is far from representing the human being in its completeness, and is in truth but humanity's humble handmaid, made to serve and to obey. It is the mind, or reason, which is the predominate element in us who are human creatures; it is this which renders a human being human, and distinguishes him essentially from the brute. And on this very account—that man alone among the animal creation is endowed with reason—it must be within his right to possess things not merely for temporary and momentary use, as other living things do, but to have and to hold them in stable and permanent possession. . . .

> "The great mistake . . . is to take up with the notion that class is naturally hostile to class."
>
> —POPE LEO XIII

The contention, then, that the civil government should at its option intrude into and exercise intimate control over the family and the household is a great and pernicious error. True, if a family finds itself in exceeding distress, utterly deprived of the counsel of friends, and without any prospect of extricating itself, it is right that extreme necessity be met by public aid, since each family is a part of the commonwealth. In like manner, if within the precincts of the household there occur grave disturbance of mutual rights, public authority should intervene to force each party to yield to the other its proper due; for this is not to deprive citizens of their rights, but justly and properly to safeguard and strengthen them. But rulers of the commonwealth must go no further; here, nature bids them stop. Paternal authority can be neither abolished nor absorbed by the State; for it has the same source as human life itself. . . . The socialists, therefore, in setting aside the parent and setting up a State supervision, act against natural justice, and destroy the structure of the home. . . .

The great mistake in regard to the matter now under consideration is to take up with the notion that class is naturally hostile to class, and that the wealthy and the working men are intended by nature to live in mutual conflict. So irrational and so false is this view that the direct contrary is the truth. Just as the symmetry of the human frame is the result of the suitable arrangement of the different parts of the body, so in a State is it ordained by nature that these two classes should dwell in harmony and agreement, so as to maintain the balance of the body politic. Each needs the other: capital cannot do without labor, nor labor without capital. Mutual agreement results in the beauty of good order, while perpetual conflict necessarily produces confusion and savage barbarity. Now, in preventing such strife as this, and in uprooting it, the efficacy of Christian institutions is marvelous and manifold. First of all, there is no intermediary more powerful than religion (whereof the Church is the interpreter and guardian) in drawing the rich and the working class together, by reminding each of its duties to the other, and especially of the obligations of justice.

> "To defraud any one of wages that are his due is a great crime which cries to the avenging anger of Heaven."
>
> —POPE LEO XIII

Of these duties, the following bind the proletarian and the worker: fully and faithfully to perform the work which has been freely and equitably agreed upon; never to injure the property, nor to outrage the person, of an employer; never to resort to violence in defending their own cause, nor to engage in riot or disorder; and to have nothing to do with men of evil principles, who work upon the people with artful promises of great results, and excite foolish hopes which usually end in useless regrets and grievous loss. The following duties bind the wealthy owner and the employer: not to look upon their work people as their bondsmen, but to respect in every man his dignity as a person ennobled by Christian character. They are reminded that, according to natural reason and Christian philosophy, working for gain is creditable, not shameful, to a man, since it enables him to earn an honorable livelihood; but to misuse men as though they were things in the pursuit of gain, or to value them solely for their physical powers—that is truly shameful and inhuman. Again justice demands that, in dealing with the working man, religion and the good of his soul must be kept in mind. Hence, the employer is bound to see that the worker has time for his religious duties; that he be not exposed to corrupting influences and dangerous occasions; and that he be not led away to neglect his home and family, or to squander his earnings. Furthermore, the employer must never tax his work people beyond their strength, or employ them in work unsuited to their sex and age. His great and principal duty is to give every one what is just. Doubtless, before deciding whether wages are fair, many things have to be considered; but wealthy owners and all masters of labor should be mindful of this—that to exercise pressure upon the indigent and the destitute for the sake of gain, and to gather one's profit out of the need of another, is condemned by all laws, human and divine. To defraud any one of wages that are his due is a great crime which cries to the avenging anger of Heaven. . . .

To sum up, then, We may lay it down as a general and lasting law that working men's associations should be so organized and governed as to furnish the best and most suitable means for attaining what is aimed at, that is to say, for helping each individual member to better his condition to the utmost in body, soul, and property. It is clear that they must pay special and chief attention to the duties of religion and morality, and that social betterment should have this chiefly in view; otherwise they would lose wholly their special character, and end by becoming little better than those societies which take no account whatever of religion. What advantage can it be to a working man to obtain by means of a society material well-being, if he endangers his soul for lack of spiritual food? "What doth it profit a man, if he gains the whole world and suffer the loss of his soul?" This, as our Lord teaches, is the mark of character that distinguishes the Christian from the heathen. . . . Let the working man be urged and led to the worship of God, to the earnest practice of religion. . . . Let him learn to reverence and love holy Church, the common Mother of us all; and hence to obey the precepts of the Church, . . . since they are the means ordained by God for obtaining forgiveness of sin and for leading a holy life. . . .

CONSIDER THIS:

- What was Pope Leo XIII's basic argument concerning the relationship between capital and labor? What specific measures does he advocate? How do his ideals compare with those of Karl Marx or Robert Owen?
- Note especially Pope Leo XIII's statement that "The great mistake . . . is to take up with the notion that class is naturally hostile to class, and that the wealthy and the working men are intended by nature to live in mutual conflict." Is this a naïve statement, or does the pope give a strong supporting argument?

THE BROADER PERSPECTIVE:

- How do you view the Industrial Revolution? Was it a progressive time that demonstrated human creativity, or was it born of human greed and exploitation of others who were less fortunate or less conscientious and, therefore, less determined to succeed?
- Is there always a price to pay in human suffering for a civilization to progress? How can you apply your ideas to our contemporary age?

"Mark Them with Your Dead!": The Scramble for Global Empire

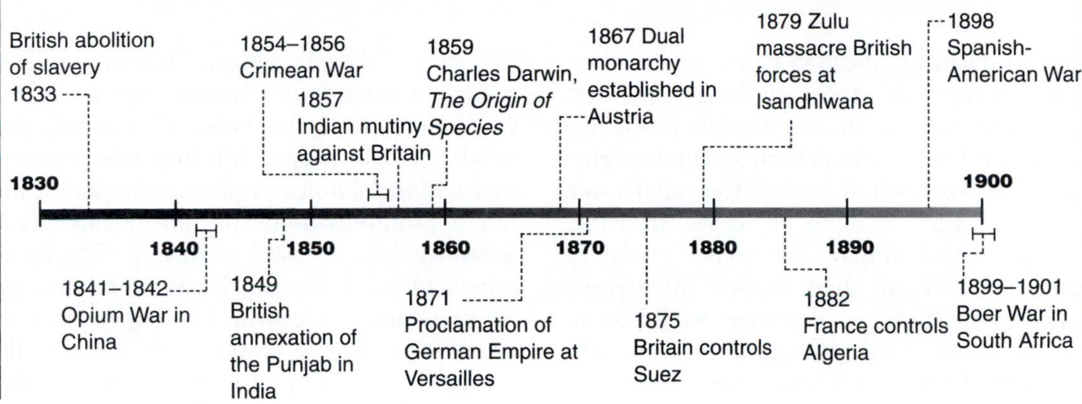

Just send in your Chief an' surrender–it's worse if you fights or you runs: You can go where you please, you can skid up the trees, but you can't get away from the guns!

—Rudyard Kipling

For how can man die better, Than facing fearful odds, For the ashes of his fathers, And the temples of his gods.

—Thomas Macaulay

I labored hard to avoid trouble and bloodshed. We gave up some country to the white man, thinking that then we could have peace. We were mistaken. The white men would not leave us alone.

—Chief Joseph

CHAPTER THEMES

- **Imperialism:** How did the new imperialism of the late nineteenth century differ from the colonialism of the fifteenth through eighteenth centuries? What political conditions had changed that compelled European nations to establish their control abroad?
- **The Institution and the Individual:** How did religious organizations encourage and support the various imperial efforts of European nations? What were the religious motives for controlling foreign populations? Was this blatantly hypocritical?
- **The Varieties of Truth:** How was propaganda used to create an image of peoples in Africa, India, and Asia that allowed European and U.S. governments to justify their imperialistic control? How

was science in particular distorted to create a new ethical perspective that made such expansion not just tolerable but socially responsible?

- **Revolution and Historical Transition:** Is imperialism such a part of human nature and social organization that it will always play a developmental role in world civilization?
- **The Big Picture:** Has world history always been dominated by a contentious and polarizing relationship between those who have and those who have not? To what extent is exploitation the watchword for economic and political progress? Or is justice the dominant force in the progress of world civilization?

The head of Charles "Chinese" Gordon, perhaps the most dashing and best regarded general in the British army, lay fixed on a tree in Omdurman, Sudan. Its sightless eyes were searching for the relief force that was not destined to arrive in time. Abdullah Muhammad, the Islamic visionary called the Mahdi, had warned the British garrison at Khartoum that there would be no escape from death for those who sought to control the Sudan and wage war against Allah. In February 1885, he made good his promise.

This act of resistance, at once brutal and defensible, underscores the contradictions that were inherent in the process of the so-called civilizing of the natives of Africa, America, and Asia during the nineteenth century. The poet Rudyard Kipling spoke to "the legions of the lost ones, to the cohort of the damned," those British soldiers who sacrificed their lives for the progress of civilization, for England—it was the "white man's burden." Of course, the British were not alone in their mission and sacrifice. The road to glory and pathway to higher civilization was littered with the dead of many villages, many nations, everyone innocent and fully justified in some way.

Nationalism and *imperialism* were two of the most important factors that shaped the nineteenth century. These terms, however, are difficult to define and have been used so loosely as nearly to be deprived of meaning. *Nationalism* involves devotion, a patriotism that implies unity and constructive action in the service of one's country. *Imperialism* is a policy of extending a nation's authority by establishing political or economic control over another area or people. It is important to note that nationalism need not cause imperialism, but it promotes domestic unity, which is a necessity for successful expansion. The term *expansion* is basically benign, connoting progress and dedication, but imperialism is often pejorative in connotation and recalls economic exploitation, racial prejudice, and even war. This chapter seeks to define more clearly the origins and parameters of European and American imperialism in the nineteenth century.

Imperialism and nationalism were certainly not introduced in the nineteenth century. During the Renaissance and Reformation eras in the fifteenth and sixteenth centuries, countries such as Spain, France, and England, which had previously been decentralized feudal areas, were united under the leadership of strong monarchs. Although this unity was often achieved initially by the sword, the benefits of centralized rule soon became apparent. Unity fostered pride and cooperation among compatriots and soon provided the energy and direction that made possible an age of exploration and discovery.

In essence, the establishment of colonial empires was profitable and patriotic. But by the nineteenth century, the age of colonial empire building was at an end. Spain, Portugal, and France had lost much of their old empires, Great Britain had lost her American colonies, and Germany was too divided internally to attempt to acquire new territory. Of the continental powers, only France under Napoleon was somewhat successful in establishing overseas colonies but realized only small gains. From 1800 to 1870, Britain acquired India, New Zealand, central Canada, and western Australia, but these territories generally were contiguous to areas Britain already held. There was a great deal of missionary activity from Christian organizations but little overt governmental support of that activity.

This period of relative disinterest did not last long. Suddenly, between 1870 and 1900, there was a general outburst of imperialistic activity among the nations of Europe and Japan. France, Belgium, Britain, and Portugal made extensive gains, especially in Africa. By 1871, both Italy and Germany had been born as nations under the aggressive political and military leadership of Camillo Cavour (1810–1861) and Giuseppe Garibaldi (1807–1882), in the case of Italy, and Otto von Bismarck (1815–1898), the first chancellor of the German Empire. Appealing to abstractions such as "fate" and "duty," politicians immediately sought new territories that would keep them economically and politically competitive with the other nations of Europe. It has been estimated that in this thirty-year period from 1870 to 1900, Europeans expanded their colonial empires by over 10 million square miles and nearly 150 million people. These intense economic rivalries were often expressed as well in political alliances. In 1882, the Triple Alliance was formed among Germany, Austria-Hungary, and Italy, and in 1907, the Triple Entente among Great Britain, France, and Russia. Such organized competition resulted in a polarization of European nations that contributed to the outbreak of World War I in 1914.

This drive for colonial acquisition was not limited to European powers, however. In 1854, Japan awoke from its centuries-long isolation from the world and quickly became a competitive force as the "Rising Sun" defeated Russian forces in the Russo-Japanese War of 1904–1905. The United States had come of age in the mid-nineteenth century by expanding to its "natural boundaries" of Mexico and the Pacific. Impelled by the dictates of a policy called "manifest destiny," U.S. settlers moved west in quest of new lives as farmers or in pursuit of gold in California. They were supported militarily by the U.S. government and ideologically by Christian missionaries who saw westward expansion as the fulfillment of the destiny of the United States, so ordained by God. Thus were Native Americans dehumanized and sent to reservations, and thus was Texas taken from Mexico in 1845. This expansion, however, was essentially domestic. The United States did not become involved in foreign adventures until 1898 when the Spanish-American War resulted in the cession of the Philippines, Cuba, Puerto Rico, and some smaller islands. The same arguments used by Europeans to legitimate their rule were now employed by the United States.

The imperialism of the late nineteenth century differed somewhat from the colonialism of the fifteenth to the eighteenth centuries. Earlier, nations had seized land with the intention of settling it with colonists or using it as a base from which to exploit the area economically. The new imperialism, as it was called, retained some of these goals but also introduced new ones. European nations now invested capital in what they termed a "backward region" and set about building productive enterprises while also improving the area with hygienic and transportation facilities. In so doing, the colonial powers employed native labor and made cooperative arrangements with local rulers (through either enrichment or intimidation). Their main purpose was to control the region, and if such arrangements proved inadequate, the colonial power had other options, which frequently resulted in full annexation.

The twentieth century also saw its share of imperialism. Determined to secure Germany's "place in the sun," Kaiser Wilhelm II led Germany to war in 1914. Adolf Hitler resurrected a moribund German people, reminded them of their national heritage, gave them self-respect, and promised them more living space through expansion to "natural boundaries." Hitler's territorial demands could not be satisfied and became one of the primary causes of World War II. After Hitler's defeat in 1945, the Soviet Union and the United States moved from their roles as allies to become rivals in the scramble for territory and influence in the remains of war-ravaged Europe. In a more contemporary setting, the United States fought a war in Vietnam to maintain "principles of democracy" in a country 7,500 miles from home. In 1979, the Soviet Union invaded Afghanistan and offered as justification the explanation that it was "asked in" by the Afghan people. In 1982, the Israelis invaded southern Lebanon in an attempt to eliminate dangerous Palestinian bases in the area; they ended up controlling Beirut itself. The United States in 1983 not only rescued American students from the perils of a coup d'état on the Caribbean island of Grenada but also stayed to ensure the establishment of a democratic regime. More recently, Panama was liberated from its dictator, Manuel Noriega, by U.S. forces in 1989, as was Kuwait from Saddam Hussein's Iraq in 1991, Afghanistan from the Taliban in 2001, and Iraq from Saddam in 2003. In the East, the communist Chinese government has controlled Tibet since 1951, and China remains committed to its unification with the "renegade province" of Taiwan. The questions abound: What are the responsibilities of great powers? Impelled by their concept of rightness and geopolitical advantage, do "superpowers" constitute forces for civilization or obstructions to the principle of self-determination? Are they vanguards of freedom or proponents of narrowly defined self-interest? It is important to gain the perspective that history offers.

"Send Forth the Best Ye Breed!": The Foundations of Imperialism

It is not to be doubted that this country [England] has been invested with wealth and power, with arts and knowledge, with the sway of distant lands, and the mastery of the restless waters, for some great and important purpose in the government of the world. Can we suppose otherwise than that it is our office to carry civilization and humanity, peace and good government, and, above all, the knowledge of the true God, to the uttermost ends of the earth?

—REVEREND JOHN WHEWELL

I am convinced that in the next century, people will slaughter each other by the millions because of the difference of a degree or two in the cephalic index [skull measurements]. It is by this sign . . . that men will be identified . . . and the last sentimentalist will be able to witness the most massive extermination of peoples.

—VACHER DE LAPOUGE (1887)

Lust for dominion inflames the heart more than any other passion.

—TACITUS

Racism and the Corruption of Science

The Descent of Man (1871)

CHARLES DARWIN

Charles Darwin altered the main currents of human thought when he published *The Origin of Species* in 1859. Before Darwin, the public believed that species of plants and animals had been created separately by God when he created the universe. Each species came into existence at once and had not changed since its creation. But Darwin's research led him to conclude that species of plants and animals had evolved by gradual and continuous changes that allowed them to adapt to their changing environments. Those species that were able to adapt were selected for survival, and those that failed simply perished. This thesis of "natural selection" gave rise to a host of popular slogans: "survival of the fittest" and "struggle of life." For some, evolution spelled inevitable progress. "There is warrant for the belief," wrote the influential philosopher Herbert Spencer, "that Evolution can end only in the establishment of the greatest perfection and the most complete happiness." But Darwin's work aroused bitter controversy because it contradicted the story of Genesis in the Bible and led to a continuing dispute between the competing demands of science and faith, which are still at issue today. Already in his *Origin of Species,* Darwin insisted on including humans in his theory. But it was not until 1871 that he published *The Descent of Man,* which bumped humankind from its preeminent position as God's most miraculous creation and connected it more intimately with chimpanzees and evolution. The following excerpt presents Darwin's ideas regarding natural selection and its scientific application to the world at large. These ideas would soon be distorted and misapplied by social Darwinists who sought to confirm racial superiority and to justify imperialism.

The main conclusion arrived at in this work, namely that man is descended from some lowly organized form, will, I regret to think be highly distasteful to many. But there can hardly be a doubt that we are descended from barbarians. The astonishment which I felt on first seeing a party of Fuegians on a wild and broken shore will never be forgotten by me, for the reflection at once rushed into my mind—such were our ancestors. These men were absolutely naked and bedaubed with paint, their long hair was tangled, their mouths frothed with excitement, and their expression was wild, startled, and distrustful. They possessed hardly any arts, and like wild animals lived on what they could catch; they had no government, and were merciless to every one not of their own small tribe. He who has seen a savage in his native land will not feel much shame, if forced to acknowledge that the blood of some more humble creature flows in his veins. For my own part I would as soon be descended from that heroic little monkey, who braved his dreaded enemy in order to save the life of his keeper, or from that old baboon, who descending from the mountains, carried away in triumph his young comrade from a crowd of astonished dogs—as from a savage who delights to torture his enemies, offers up bloody sacrifices, practices infanticide without remorse, treats his wives like slaves,

"*The Descent of Man*" is from Charles Darwin, *The Descent of Man*, vol. 2 (New York: P. F. Collier and Son, 1874), pp. 796–797.

knows no decency, and is haunted by the grossest superstitions.

Man may be excused for feeling some pride at having risen, though not through his own exertions, to the very summit of the organic scale; and the fact of his having thus risen, instead of having been aboriginally placed there, may give him hope for a still higher destiny in the distant future. But we are not here concerned with hopes or fears, only with the truth as far as our reason permits us to discover it; and I have given the evidence to the best of my ability. We must, however, acknowledge, as it seems to me, that man with all his noble qualities, with sympathy which feels for the most debased, with benevolence which extends not only to other men but to the humblest living creature, with his god-like intellect which has penetrated into the movements and constitution of the solar system—with all these exalted powers—Man still bears in his bodily frame the indelible stamp of his lowly origin.

CONSIDER THIS:

- Explain the ideas of Charles Darwin regarding "natural selection" and evolution. How do his theories as contained in *The Origin of Species* and *The Descent of Man* demonstrate a scientific approach to the development of nature? How would you explain the term *survival of the fittest*? What is his approach to human development as noted in his work? Why are Darwinist theories considered by some to be dangerous and irreligious?

The Standpoint of Science (1900)

KARL PEARSON

In general, imperialistic nations have felt compelled to justify their actions by explaining why they have taken control of territory or populations. One of the most popular justifications has been the policy of social Darwinism, a vulgarization of the scientific theory of Charles Darwin contained in *The Origin of Species* (1859). Social Darwinists held that only the fittest peoples would survive and that "lesser breeds" would of necessity perish or be taken over. Indeed, some argued that an empire was a living organism that must either grow or die. Racism, therefore, provided a potent thrust to imperial expansion. The next excerpt is from a lecture delivered in 1900 by the German scientist Karl Pearson, who presents racism as consistent with the directives of nature.

How many centuries, how many thousand of years, have the Kaffir or the Negro held large districts in Africa undisturbed by the white man? Yet their intertribal struggles have not yet produced a civilization in the least comparable with the Aryan. Educate and nurture them as you will, I do not believe that you will succeed in modifying the stock. History shows me one way, and one way only, in which a high state of civilization has been produced, namely, the struggle of race with race, and the survival of the physically and mentally fitter race. If you want to know whether the lower races of man can evolve a higher type, I fear the only course is to leave them to fight it out among themselves, and even then the struggle for existence between individual and individual, between tribe and tribe, may not be supported by that physical selection due to a particular

"The Standpoint of Science" is from Karl Pearson, *National Life from the Standpoint of Science*, 2nd ed. (Cambridge: Cambridge University Press, 1907), pp. 21–25.

climate on which probably so much of the Aryan's success depended.

If you bring the white man into contact with the black, you too often suspend the very process of natural selection on which the evolution of a higher type depends. You get superior and inferior races living on the same soil, and that coexistence is demoralizing for both. They naturally sink into the position of master and servant, if not admittedly or covertly into that of slave-owner and slave. Frequently they intercross, and if the bad stock be raised the good is lowered. Even in the case of Eurasians, of whom I have met mentally and physically fine specimens, I have felt how much better they would have been had they been pure Asiatics or pure Europeans. Thus it comes about that when the struggle for existence between races is suspended, the solution of great problems may be unnaturally postponed; instead of the slow, stern processes of evolution, cataclysmal solutions are prepared for the future. Such problems in suspense, it appears to me, are to be found in the Negro population of the Southern States of America, in the large admixture of Indian blood in some of the South American races, but, above all, in the Kaffir factor in South Africa.

You may possibly think that I am straying from my subject, but I want to justify natural selection to you. I want you to see selection as something which renders the inexorable law of heredity a source of progress which produces the good through suffering, an infinitely greater good which far outbalances the very obvious pain and evil. Let us suppose the alternative were possible. Let us suppose we could prevent the white man, if we liked, from going to lands of which the agricultural and mineral resources are not worked to the full; then I should say a thousand times better for him that he should not go than that he should settle down and live alongside the inferior race. The only healthy alternative is that he should go and completely drive out the inferior race. That is practically what the white man has done in North America. . . . The civilization of the white man is a civilization dependent upon free white labour, and when that element of stability is removed it will collapse like those of Greece and Rome. I venture to assert, then, that the struggle for existence between white and red man, painful and even terrible as it was in its details, has given us a good for outbalancing its immediate evil. In place of the red man, contributing practically nothing to the work and thought of the world, we have a great nation, mistress of many arts, and able, with its youthful imagination and fresh, untrammeled impulses, to contribute much to the common stock of civilized man. Against that we have only to put the romantic sympathy for the Red Indian generated by the novels of Cooper and the poems of Longfellow, and then—see how little it weighs in the balance! . . .

You will see that my view—and I think it may be called the scientific view of a nation—is that of an organized whole, kept up to a high pitch of internal efficiency by insuring that its numbers are substantially recruited from the better stocks, and kept up to a high pitch of external efficiency by contest, chiefly by way of war with inferior races, and with equal races by the struggle for trade-routes and for the sources of raw material and of food supply. This is the natural history view of mankind, and I do not think you can in its main features subvert it. Some of you may refuse to acknowledge it, but you cannot really study history and refuse to see its force. Some of you may realize it, and then despair of life; you may decline to admit any glory in a world where the superior race must either eject the inferior, or, mixing with it, or even living alongside it, degenerate itself. What beauty can there be when the battle is to the stronger, and the weaker must suffer in the struggle of nations and in the struggle of individual men? You may say: Let us cease to struggle; let us leave the lands of the world to the races that cannot profit by them to the full; let us cease to compete in the markets of the world. Well, we could do it, if we were a small nation living off the produce of our own soil, and a soil so worthless that no other race envied it and sought to appropriate it. We should cease to advance; but then we should naturally give up progress as a good which comes through suffering. I say it is impossible for a small rural community to stand apart from the world-contest and to stagnate, if no more powerful nation wants its possessions.

CONSIDER THIS:

- Explain social Darwinism and give several specific examples from the reading selections that demonstrate its practice and its use as justification for imperial expansion. What phrases and ideas are consistently used?

- What are some of the arguments of Karl Pearson? Are they compelling? Do you agree or disagree with the arguments of Charles Morris on war as a factor of civilization? Why?

THE BROADER PERSPECTIVE:

- To what extent is social Darwinism a corruption of Darwinist theories? Or is it simply a logical extension and application of the theories?

For God and Country

The Mandate System: Britain's Duty in Egypt (1890)

JOSEPH CHAMBERLAIN

The British in the late nineteenth century often justified their imperialism on the premise of duty. As a civilized power, it was imperative that they spread God's word and the fruits of civilization to those peoples who were not sufficiently advanced to develop them on their own. In essence, Britain held a nation "in trust" until the backward peoples could be educated and made ready to assume the responsibilities of self-government. The "mandate system," as it came to be called, is described in the following excerpt by the liberal statesman Joseph Chamberlain (1836–1914). The motive for British expansion in Egypt was not completely altruistic, however. Britain also wanted to protect the strategic Suez Canal, which controlled access to the riches of Britain's empire in India and the Far East. In 1882, Britain occupied Cairo and set about reorganizing the country. Chamberlain's address to Parliament must also be viewed in this light.

I want to say a word or two to you about the future. I am going to make a confession. I admit I was one of those—I think my views were shared by the whole Cabinet of Mr. Gladstone—who regretted the necessity for the occupation of Egypt. I thought that England had so much to do, such enormous obligations and responsibilities, that we might well escape, if we could, this addition to them; and, when the occupation was forced upon us, I looked forward with anxiety to an early, it might be even, to an immediate evacuation. The confession I have to make is that having seen what are the results of this occupation, having seen what is the nature of the task we have undertaken, and what progress we have already made towards its accomplishment, I have changed my mind. (*Cheers*) I say it would

"The Mandate System: Britain's Duty in Egypt" is from Joseph Chamberlain, *Foreign and Colonial Speeches* (London: George Routledge and Sons, 1897), pp. 41–44.

be unworthy of this great nation if we did not rise to the full height of our duty, and complete our work before we left the country. (*Cheers*) We have no right to abandon the duty which has been cast upon us, and the work which already shows so much promise for the advantage of the people with whose destinies we have become involved. This great alteration is due to the influence of a mere handful of your fellow-countrymen. . . .

They, by their persevering devotion, and their single-minded honesty, have wrought out this great work, and have brought Egypt from a condition which may fairly be described as one of ruin, to the promise of once more being restored to its ancient prosperity. I hear sometimes of pessimists who think the work of England is accomplished, who will tell you that we have lost the force and the capacity to govern. No; that is not true; and as long as we can spare from our abundance men like these, who, after all, are only ordinary Englishmen—men like these, who are able and willing to carry their zeal and their intelligence wherever it may conduce to the service of humanity, and to the honour of their native land—so long as we can do that we need not despair of the future of the United Kingdom. (*Cheers*) But we owe it to them, we owe it to ourselves, that their work shall not be in vain. You cannot revolutionise a country like Egypt—you cannot reform all that is wrong in her system, all that is poor and weak in the character of the people—in a few minutes, or a few years. Egypt has been submitted for centuries to arbitrary despotism. I believe there is hardly any time in her history, even if you go back to almost prehistoric ages, when she has not been in the grasp of some foreign ruler; and, under these circumstances, you cannot expect to find ready to your hands a self-governing people. They are not able—they cannot be able—to stand alone; and they do not wish to stand alone. They ask for your support and assistance, and without it, it is absolutely impossible that their welfare can be secured. If you were to abandon your responsibility, your retirement would be followed by an attempt once more to restore the old arbitrary methods and the old abuses, which in turn would no doubt be followed by anarchy and disorder; and then in time there would be again a foreign intervention, this time the intervention of some other European country. I have too much confidence in the public spirit of the country to believe that it will ever neglect a national duty. (Hear, hear.) A nation is like an individual; it has duties which it must fulfill, or else it cannot live honoured and respected as a nation. (*Loud cheers*)

CONSIDER THIS:

- Discuss the mandate system. What was it, and how is it evident in the speech by Joseph Chamberlain regarding Britain's duty in Egypt? Cite specific phrases in this regard.

"France Must Be a Great Country!" (1883)

JULES FERRY

The next selections comment on another motive for imperialism. The desire for power can be justified through the pride that one has in one's nation. Nationalism and imperialism seem to be intimately connected. And the European accumulation of empire in India and Africa during the nineteenth century certainly inspired the competitive juices. If Britannia "ruled the waves" and Germany deserved its "place

"'France Must Be a Great Country'" is from Ralph Austen, ed., *Modern Imperialism* (Lexington, Mass: D.C. Heath, 1969), pp. 70–73.

in the sun," then the process of global confrontation was necessary and an opportunity to demonstrate national superiority. So thought the French prime minister, Jules Ferry, in his 1883 speech to the assembly in Paris, and so too the German Kaiser Wilhelm II, who was certainly anxious to seize the opportunity for glory, as noted in the militaristic speech that follows.

Jules Ferry: Gentlemen, it embarrasses me to make such a prolonged demand upon the gracious attention of the Chamber, but I believe that the duty I am fulfilling upon this platform is not a useless one: it is as strenuous for me as for you, but I believe that there is some benefit in summarizing and condensing, in the form of arguments, the principles, the motives, and the various interests by which a policy of colonial expansion may be justified. . . .

In the area of economics, I will allow myself to place before you, with the support of some figures, the considerations which justify a policy of colonial expansion from the point of view of that need, felt more and more strongly by the industrial populations of Europe and particularly those of our won rich and hard working country: the need for export markets. . . .

Gentlemen, there is a second point, a second order of ideas to which I have to give equal attention, but as quickly as possible, believe me; it is the humanitarian and civilizing side of the question. On this point the honorable Camille Pelletan [a conservative politician] has jeered in his own refined and clever manner; he jeers, he condemns, and he says "What is this civilization which you impose with cannon-ball? What is it but another form of barbarism? Don't these populations, these inferior races, have the same rights as you? Aren't they masters of their own houses? Have they called upon you? You come to them against their will, you offer them violence, but not civilization." There, gentlemen is the thesis. . . . But, I must speak from a higher and more truthful plane. It must be stated openly that, in effect, superior races have rights over inferior races.

Jules Maigne: Oh! You dare to say this in the country which has proclaimed the rights of man!

M. De Gulloutet: This is a justification of slavery and the slave trade!

Jules Ferry: If M. Maigne is right, if the declaration of the rights of man was written for the black of equatorial Africa, then by what right do you impose regular commerce upon them? They have not called upon you.

Raoul Duval: We do not want to impose anything upon them. It is you who wish to do so!

Jules Maigne: To propose and to impose are two different things!

Georges Perin: In any case, you cannot bring about commerce by force.

Jules Ferry: I repeat that superior races have a right, because they have a duty. They have the duty to civilize inferior races. . . . Gentlemen, in Europe as it is today, in this competition of so many rivals which we see growing around us, some by perfecting their military or maritime forces, others by the prodigious development of an ever growing population; in a Europe, or rather in a universe of this sort, a policy of peaceful seclusion or abstention is simply the highway to decadence! Nations are great in our times only by means of the activities which they develop; it is not simply "by the peaceful shining froth of institutions" that they are great at this hour. . . .

[The Republican Party] has shown that it is quite aware that one cannot impose upon France a political ideal conforming to that of nations like independent Belgium and the Swiss Republic; that something else is needed for France; that she cannot be merely a free country, that she must also be a great country, exercising all of her rightful influence over the destiny of Europe, that she ought to propagate this influence throughout the world and carry everywhere that she can her language, her customs, her flag, her arms, and her genius.

CONSIDER THIS:

- According to the French prime minister Jules Ferry, why was it important for France to be a "great" country in 1883? What actions needed to be taken to make this a reality? Did Ferry answer his critics effectively?

Germany's Place in the Sun (1901)

KAISER WILHELM II

In spite of the fact that we have no such fleet as we should have, we have conquered for ourselves a place in the sun. It will now be my task to see to it that this place in the sun shall remain our undisputed possession, in order that the sun's rays may fall fruitfully upon our activity and trade in foreign parts, that our industry and agriculture may develop within the state and our sailing sports upon the water, for our future lies upon the water. The more Germans go out upon the waters . . . whether it be in journeys across the ocean, or in the service of the battleflag, so much the better will it be for us. For when the German has once learned to direct his glance upon what is distant and great, the pettiness which surrounds him in daily life on all sides will disappear.

As head of the empire I therefore rejoice over every citizen, whether from Hamburg, Bremen, or Lubeck, who goes forth with this large outlook and seeks new points where we can drive in the nail on which to hang our armor.

COMPARE AND CONTRAST:

- Compare Jules Ferry's vision of "greatness" with that of the German kaiser Wilhelm II. What is your reaction to the kaiser's proposal that Germany must seek "new points where we can drive in the nail on which to hang our armor"?

"The White Man's Burden" (1899)

RUDYARD KIPLING

In commemoration of successful U.S. imperialism in the Philippines, the great British poet Rudyard Kipling wrote "The White Man's Burden" in 1899. It reflects a devotion to the demands of empire and the duty of civilized nations. In Kipling's eyes, imperialism was a nationalistic venture, a heroic necessity.

"'Germany's Place in the Sun'" is from Christian Gauss, excerpted from *The German Emperor*, pp. 181–183. Copyright © 1915 Charles Scribner's Sons.

"'The White Man's Burden'" is from Rudyard Kipling, *Collected Verse* (New York: Doubleday and Page, 1911), pp. 215–217.

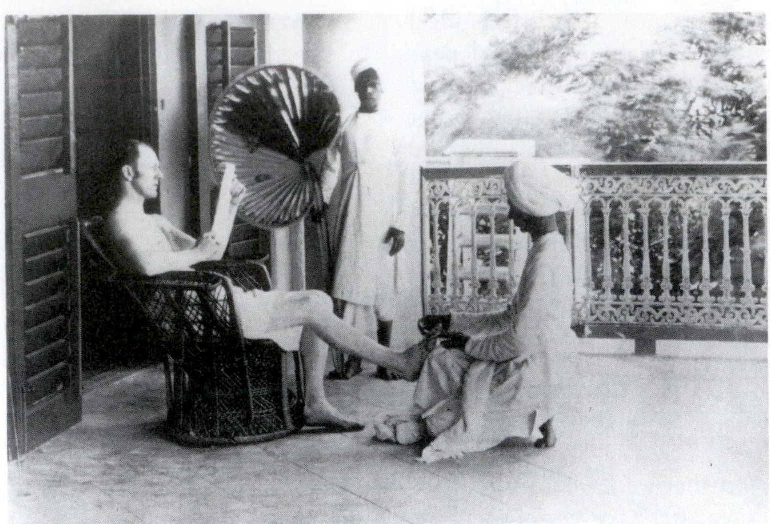

FIGURE 8.1 A British officer in India, ca. 1870: "Take up the White Man's burden / And reap his old reward: / The blame of those ye better, / The hate of those ye guard."—Rudyard Kipling. (*Getty Images, Inc.*)

Take up the White Man's burden—
Send forth the best ye breed—
Go bind your sons to exile
To serve your captive's need;
To wait in heavy harness,
On fluttered folk and wild—
Your new-caught, sullen peoples,
Half-devil and half-child.

Take up the White Man's burden—
In patience to abide,
To veil the threat of terror
And check the show of pride;
By open speech and simple,
An hundred times made plain
To seek another's profit,
And work another's gain

Take up the White Man's burden—
The savage wars of peace—
Fill full the mouth of Famine
And bid the sickness cease;
And when you goal is nearest
The end for others sought,
Watch sloth and heathen Folly
Bring all your hopes to nought.

Take up the White Man's burden—
No tawdry rule of kings,
But toil of serf and sweeper—
The tale of common things.
The ports ye shall not enter,
The roads ye shall not tread,
Go make them with your living,
And mark them with your dead.

Take up the White Man's burden—
And reap his old reward:
The blame of those ye better,
The hate of those ye guard—
The cry of hosts ye humour
(Ah, slowly!) toward the light:—
'Why brought he us from bondage,
Our loved Egyptian night?'

Take up the White Man's burden—
Ye dare not stoop to less—
Nor call too loud on Freedom
To cloke your weariness;
By all ye cry or whisper,
By all ye leave or do,

The silent, sullen peoples
Shall weigh your gods and you.

Take up the White Man's burden—
Have done with childish days—
The lightly proferred laurel,
The easy, ungrudged praise.
Comes now, to search your manhood
Through all the thankless years,
Cold, edged with dear-bought wisdom,
The judgment of your peers!

Compare and Contrast:

- Kipling's poem "The White Man's Burden" is the quintessential expression of the responsibility of race and the burdens of empire imposed on great nations for the benefit of lesser peoples. The mandate for superiors to govern inferiors was a heavy duty to be embraced of necessity and borne with dignity as befitted the altruistic agents of civilization. How do this source and other sources in this chapter define imperialism as an agent of "progress and civilization"?

THEME: IMPERIALISM

Against the Grain

The Zionist Movement

The Middle East has always been an important region in world history. It lies at the crossroads of Africa, Asia, and Europe, a location that has facilitated the exchange of ideas and commercial goods for thousands of years. Its strategic geopolitical position has also invited conflict over control of land and water rights, over access to sacred religious shrines, and, perhaps most importantly, over the very survival of the many peoples who claim title to a part of the region as a homeland.

The struggle to establish Jewish and Arab states in the area of Palestine bedeviled Middle Eastern politics and international diplomacy for most of the twentieth century and remains one of the most intransigent conflicts filtering into the twenty-first. This is truly an enduring struggle as both Jews and Palestinian Arabs claim the region as a homeland through ancient descent. According to the Bible, God led the Hebrew tribes out of bondage in Egypt to safety in Palestine, which was called "the land of Israel." The Palestinians claim descent through the Canaanites, Philistines, and other tribes who were the ancient inhabitants of this land known in Arabic as *Filastin*. For centuries, Jews and Palestinians had lived together on the land, controlled variously by Persians, Macedonians, Romans, Christians, and, after the Arab conquest in 637 C.E., Muslims.

The contest for statehood in Palestine began in earnest in the late nineteenth century as Jews and Arabs were caught in the tide of nationalism sweeping Europe at the time. Arabs sought independence from the degenerating control of the Ottoman Turkish Empire. And many Jews, who over the centuries had generally been displaced from the region in a series of dispersions (or diaspora), longed to return to Zion, a biblical name for Jerusalem, and found a state of their own.

Theodor Herzl (1860–1904), a Jewish journalist living in Austria, founded the Zionist movement in response to the virulent anti-Semitism in Europe. Zionism as a doctrine and movement advocated and justified the creation of a Jewish state in Palestine. In a short pamphlet entitled, *The Jewish State* (1896), Herzl posed the question whether Jews should continue to work for assimilation into European society or emigrate to Zion and a new state in "the promised land." The first excerpt details his plan. Many Jews who had suffered from persecution, especially in Russia during the 1880s, greeted Herzl's ideas with enthusiasm. But Jewish philanthropists and religious leaders were more hesitant. Undeterred, Herzl founded a Zionist newspaper (*Die Welt*) and transformed his ideas into an international political movement. The "Basel Program" of 1897 gave direction and continuity to the Zionist cause.

The Jewish State (1896)

THEODOR HERZL

The entire plan is in its essence perfectly simple, as it must be if it is to become comprehensible to all.

"Let sovereignty be granted us over a portion of the earth's surface that is sufficient for our rightful national requirements; we shall take care of everything else ourselves."
—THEODOR HERZL

Let sovereignty be granted us over a portion of the earth's surface that is sufficient for our rightful national requirements; we shall take care of everything else ourselves.

The creation of a new sovereign state is neither ludicrous nor impossible. After all, we have seen it happen in our own day—among nations which are not largely middle-class, as we are, but poorer, uneducated, and therefore weaker than ourselves. The governments of the countries scourged by anti-Semitism will be keenly interested in securing a sovereign status for us. . . .

As has already been stated, the departure of the Jews must not be imagined as a sudden one. It will be gradual, taking decades. The poorest will go first and make the land arable. In accordance with a predetermined plan, they will build roads, bridges, and railways, set up telegraphy installations; regulate rivers and provide themselves with homesteads. Their labor will bring trade, trade will create markets and markets will attract new settlers—for everyone will come voluntarily, at his own expense and his own risk. The labor that we put into the soil will enhance the value of the land. The Jews will soon realize that a new and permanent field has opened up for their spirit of enterprise which has heretofore been met with hatred and contempt. . . .

The emigrants standing lowest in the economic scale will gradually be followed by those of the next grade. Those who are now in desperate straits will go first. They will be led by the average intellects whom we overproduce and who are persecuted everywhere. . . . Let anyone who does not want to go along stay behind. The opposition of individuals is immaterial. Let all those who wish to join us line up behind our banner and fight for it with word, pen, and deed. . . .

[We] will negotiate with the present authorities of the country—under the protectorate of the European Powers, if the matter makes sense to them. We shall be able to offer the present authorities enormous advantages—assume part of their national debt, build new thoroughfares (which we should require ourselves), and do many other things. But the very creation of the Jewish State will be beneficial to the neighboring countries, because the cultivation of an area enhances the value of its surroundings, on a large as on a small scale. . . .

"*The Jewish State*" is from Theodor Herzl, *The Jewish State: An Attempt at a Modern Solution of the Jewish Question (Der Judenstaat)*, trans. by Jacob de Haas (New York: Federation of American Zionists, 1917). Translation modernized by the editor.

Palestine is our unforgettable historic homeland. The very name would be a powerfully moving rallying cry for our people. If His Majesty the Sultan were to give us Palestine, we could in return pledge ourselves to regulate the entire finances of Turkey. For Europe we could constitute part of the wall of defense against Asia; we would serve as an outpost of civilization against barbarism. As a neutral state we would remain in contact with all Europe, which would have to guarantee our existence. Some form of extraterritoriality under international law could be found for the Holy Places of Christendom. We would form a guard of honor around the Holy Places, answering for the fulfilment of this duty with our existence. This guard of honor would be the symbol of the solution of the Jewish Question after what were for us eighteen centuries of affliction.

The Basel Program (1897)

The aim of Zionism is to create for the Jewish people a home in Palestine secured by public law. The Congress contemplates the following means to the attainment of this end:

1. The promotion, on suitable lines, of the colonization of Palestine by Jewish agricultural and industrial workers.
2. The organization and binding together of the whole of Jewry by means of appropriate institutions, local and international, in accordance with the laws of each country.
3. The strengthening and fostering of Jewish national sentiment and consciousness.
4. Preparatory steps towards obtaining government consent, where necessary, to the attainment of the aim of Zionism.

Consider This:

- How would you define Zionism, and what are its goals? How specifically would Jewish settlement in Palestine take place?
- According to Herzl, how would the creation of a Jewish state benefit the European powers? Why was Herzl concerned with pleasing them?

The Broader Perspective:

- Herzl expected that the new Jewish state would be neutral and Europe would have to "guarantee our existence." In return, the Jews would "form a guard of honor around the Holy Places" of Christendom. What about the holy places of Islam? Is the absence of any mention of Arab peoples at this early juncture significant?

"The Basel Program" is from *The Jewish Chronicle* (September 3, 1897), p. 13.

"To Seek Another's Profit and Work Another's Gain"

It is the habit of every aggressor nation to claim that it is acting on the defensive.

—JAWAHARLAL NEHRU

The Englishman does everything on principle. He fights you on patriotic principles; he robs you on business principles; he enslaves you on imperial principles. . . . His watchword is always Duty; and he never forgets that the nation which lets its duty get on the side opposite to its interest is lost.

—NAPOLEON BONAPARTE

The right of conquest has no foundation other than the right of the strongest.

—JEAN-JACQUES ROUSSEAU

"Your New-Caught Sullen Peoples"

The eyes of both Eastern and Western powers had long been attracted to the trade and wealth of India. In the eighteenth century, the British took the lead in promoting agents of the East India Company, who advised and made treaty arrangements with local governors that excluded French and Dutch interests and gave Britain an unofficial dominion over the area. The British instituted a new office of governor-general in 1774 to oversee trade relations, to resolve conflicts among natives, and to control more effectively the region through local Indian princes. Parliament reviewed the actions of the governor-general and eventually regularized a policy of deposing these local Indian rulers and annexing the land as part of a growing world empire.

In April 1857, a widespread but unsuccessful rebellion against British rule in India broke out among Indian troops (called *sepoys*) fighting in the service of the East India Company. This revolt began in the Bengal army with the introduction of the new Enfield rifle; to load it the sepoys had to bite off the ends of cartridges lubricated in a mixture of pigs' and cows' lard. This oral contact with religiously forbidden substances was an insult to both Muslim and Hindu troops. When the sepoys refused the cartridges, they were shackled and put in jail. On May 10, their comrades shot several British officers and marched on Delhi. The rebellion spread quickly throughout northern India with massacres that provoked equally vicious British reprisals. After many desperate struggles, the British were able to suppress the revolt by July 1858.

To regard this mutiny as a bloody incident with a simple origin is to belie the social and economic complexities of the British presence in India. By 1820, it was evident that traditional Hindu society was being affected by the introduction of Western ideas and religious beliefs. The British governor-general, Lord Dalhousie, had introduced legislation to emancipate women and remove legal obstacles to the remarriage of Hindu widows. Christian converts were given property rights in the distribution of family estates, and it was even rumored that the British intended to end the Indian caste structure. The introduction of Western methods and educational curricula was a direct challenge to Hindu and Muslim orthodoxy. These actions threatened the traditional ruling Indian aristocracy by depriving it of its social position and administrative revenues.

The immediate result of the Indian mutiny of 1857 was a general restructuring of British administration. Great Britain abolished the East India Company in favor of direct rule by the government and rearranged the finances of India. The Indian army was also reorganized, and the British instituted a policy of consultation with Indian representatives that ended insensitive British-mandated social measures. But the failure of the mutiny confirmed British supremacy in India and opened the door to a gradual but inevitable breakdown of traditional Indian society. In return for political and economic control, the British brought educational and public works programs, roads, railways, telegraphs, and hygienic facilities. The annexation of India in 1858 and the establishment of the British Raj, or official administration, represented a tradeoff in technological and cultural influence. When British control ended with Indian independence in 1949, the culture and political traditions of the region had been dramatically altered.

The following selection is from the pen of Thomas Babington Macaulay, a literary figure and political liberal who argued that British rule in India was one of the highest achievements of English civilization. His vision of a proper education demonstrates the cultural insensitivity that contributed to the Indian mutiny of 1857.

Education in India: "The Intrinsic Superiority of Western Literature" (1835)

THOMAS BABINGTON MACAULAY

We now come to the gist of the matter. We have a fund to be employed as Government shall direct for the intellectual improvement of the people of this country. The simple question is, what is the most useful way of employing it?

All parties seem to be agreed on one point, that the dialects commonly spoken among the natives of this part of India contain neither literary nor scientific information, and are moreover so poor and rude that, until they are enriched from some other quarter, it will not be easy to translate any valuable work into them. It seems to be admitted on all sides, that the intellectual improvement of those classes of the people who have the means of pursuing higher studies can at present be effected only by means of some language not vernacular amongst them.

What then shall that language be? One-half of the committee maintain that it should be the English. The other half strongly recommend the Arabic and Sanscrit. The whole question seems to me to be–which language is the best worth knowing?

I have no knowledge of either Sanscrit or Arabic. But I have done what I could to form a correct estimate of their value. I have read translations of the most celebrated Arabic and Sanscrit works. I have conversed, both here and at home, with men distinguished by their proficiency in the Eastern tongues. I am quite ready to take the oriental leaning at the valuation of the orientalists themselves. I have never found one among them who could deny that a single shelf of a good European library was worth the whole native literature of India and Arabia. The intrinsic superiority of the Western literature is indeed fully admitted by those members of the committee who support the oriental plan of education.

It will hardly be disputed, I suppose, that the department of literature in which the Eastern writers stand highest is poetry. And I certainly never met with any orientalist who ventured to maintain that the Arabic and Sanscrit poetry could be compared to that of the great European nations. But when we pass from works of imagination to works in which facts are recorded and

"Education in India" is from H. Sharp, ed., *Selections from the Educational Records of the Government of India, Part I, 1781–1839* (Calcutta, 1920), pp. 110–112; 116.

general principles investigated, the superiority of the Europeans becomes absolutely immeasurable. It is, I believe, no exaggeration to say that all the historical information which has been collected from all the books written in the Sanscrit language is less valuable than what may be found in the most paltry abridgments used at preparatory schools in England. In every branch of physical or moral philosophy, the relative position of the two nations is nearly the same . . .

Nor is this all. In India, English is the language spoken by the ruling class. It is spoken by the higher class of natives at the seats of Government. It is likely to become the language of commerce throughout the seas of the East. It is the language of two great European communities which are rising, the one in the south of Africa, the other in Australia–communities which are every year becoming more important and more closely connected with our Indian empire. Whether we look at the intrinsic value of our literature, or at the particular situation of this country, we shall see the strongest reason to think that, of all foreign tongues, the English tongue is that which would be the most useful to our native subjects. . . .

To sum up what I have said. I think it clear . . . that we are free to employ our funds as we choose, that we ought to employ them in teaching what is best worth knowing, that English is better worth knowing than Sanscrit or Arabic, that . . . it is possible to make natives of this country thoroughly good English scholars, and that to this end our efforts ought to be directed.

In one point I fully agree with the gentlemen to whose general views I am opposed. I feel with them that it is impossible for us, with our limited means, to attempt to educate the body of the people. We must at present do our best to form a class who may be interpreters between us and the millions whom we govern–a class of persons Indian in blood and color, but English in tastes, in opinions, in morals, and in intellect.

CONSIDER THIS:

- Thomas Babington Macaulay did not mince words in his assessment of education in India. He believed in teaching the Indian population "what is best worth knowing." For Macaulay, what was worth knowing? Why was Arabic and Sanskrit poetry considered inferior to Western literature?

Foreign Children

ROBERT LOUIS STEVENSON

The Scottish writer Robert Louis Stevenson (1850–1894) is remembered primarily for his adventure novels, *Treasure Island* and *Kidnaped*. But he was also a poet and compiled a book of children's poetry toward the end of his life. The following selection reveals the vision of superiority that justified the argument for European control of "lesser peoples." The civilizing mandate was deeply inculcated in the education of the ruling classes.

Little Indian, Sioux or Crow,
Little frosty Eskimo,
Little Turk or Japanee,
O! don't you wish that you were me?

You have seen the scarlet trees
And the lions over seas;
You have eaten ostrich eggs,
And turned the turtles off their legs.

Such a life is very fine,
But it's not so nice as mine:
You must often, as you trod,
Have wearied *not* to be abroad.

You have curious things to eat,
I am fed on proper meat;
You must dwell beyond the foam,
But I am safe and live at home.

"*Foreign Children*" is from Robert Louis Stevenson, *Complete Poems: A Child's Garden of Verses* (New York: Scribner, 1912), p. 25.

Little Indian, Sioux or Crow,
Little frosty Eskimo,
Little Turk or Japanee,
O! don't you wish that you were me?

CONSIDER THIS:

- In his poem "Foreign Children," what point was Robert Louis Stevenson trying to make? Would you call this an arrogant poem? Why was Stevenson so confident in his perspective?

"The Great African Hunt"

CHARLES SEIGNOBOS

After the political unification of Germany and Italy by 1871, a stabilized Europe embarked on the "Great Hunt," the "scramble for empire" in Africa that provided the economic resources for industry and the image of authority so important in the vigorous competition for national prestige. Colonial enthusiasm had waned during the 1840s and 1850s when many politicians had denounced colonies as unprofitable and burdensome. But Europe's population was growing rapidly at a rate second only to the United States while the populations of Asia and Africa were essentially static. New colonies acted as a safety valve for a domestic population often burdened and unemployed by the great push toward industrialization, which actually created the need for new markets and resources to keep the factories producing at full capacity. Added to this were the exhortations of explorers and missionaries, who fed the imperial impulse with romantic visions of adventure and the will of God.

The following selection is from a general history of the period written by Charles Seignobos, a prominent French scholar at the time. Note his disdain for the importance of African history. The quest for power and its symbols among great nations were all that mattered. European imperialism became a state of mind that subverted the relevance of indigenous peoples and denied them a past.

By about 1880, the political geography of Europe was fixed; the attempt of any country to acquire territory at the expense of a neighbor would have precipitated an instantaneous armed conflict. Moreover, Europe had recovered from the fatigues which had accompanied the wars for the unification of the great nations, and regained its spirit of action; but its desire for expansion could now be satisfied only outside of Europe. All the continents, however, were occupied, except Africa, until then despised. The powers threw themselves upon that continent, so long scorned, and fairly dashed into the work of partition. The rivalry and the haste of the competitors was so great that one might well speak of "the great African hunt." Within twenty years almost everything was appropriated in Africa, and when the rivals wished to extend their borders further, they could only do so at the expense of the weaker among themselves.

The annals of Africa for twenty years (1880–1900) are practically limited to the story of the partition of the continent to its very heart. Its improvement and civilization have hardly begun; it has not yet passed out of the most rudimentary industrial state; and its development, of which there can be no question, will serve as a subject for the investigation of future historians. In itself the history of native Africa offers, with some few exceptions, no events of general interest. One may say,

"'The Great African Hunt'" is from James Harvey Robinson and Charles A. Beard, *Readings in Modern European History*, vol. II (Boston: Gin & Company, 1909), p. 448.

however, that the numberless African races have been happy because they have had no history. Some of them have had a little, but it is so confused that it cannot be told. Torrents of blood, which still flow in Africa, have been caused by the exploits of slave hunters, and by internecine pillage resulting from the general anarchy prevailing on a large scale; but the details of these horrors are so microscopic that they must be passed by with this general mention. The real object of our study should be the partition of Africa among the civilized nations.

CONSIDER THIS:

- Why was Africa so attractive to competing European powers in the late nineteenth century? Note Seignobos's assertion that "the history of Africa offers, with some few exceptions, no events of general interest." In fact, Africans "have been happy because they have had no history." How do African tribes record and preserve their histories? What do Seignobos's statements tell you about the justifications for European imperialism?

"A Natural Inclination to Submit to a Higher Authority" (1893)

SIR FREDERICK DEALTRY LUGARD

In spite of the organized resistance of African tribes, especially the Zulus, British tenacity and power prevailed. In his analysis of the "Scramble for Africa," Sir Frederick Lugard, British soldier and administrator of some of Britain's colonial possessions in the late nineteenth century, focused on the necessity of British action and the benefits that would naturally ensue. In 1893, fourteen years after the Zulu destruction of British forces at Isandhlwana in 1879, Lugard confidently proclaimed that Africans possessed "a natural inclination to submit to a higher authority."

The Chambers of Commerce of the United Kingdom have unanimously urged the retention of East Africa on the grounds of commercial advantage. The Presidents of the London and Liverpool chambers attended a deputation to her Majesty's Minister for Foreign Affairs to urge "the absolute necessity, for the prosperity of this country, that new avenues for commerce such as that in East Equatorial Africa should be opened up, in view of the hostile tariffs with which British manufacturers are being everywhere confronted." Manchester followed with a similar declaration; Glasgow, Birmingham, Edinburgh, and other commercial centers gave it as their opinion that "there is practically no middle course for this country, between a reversal of the free trade policy to which it is pledged, on the one hand, and a prudent but continuous territorial extension for the creation of new markets, on the other hand. . . .

The "Scramble for Africa" by the nations of Europe—an incident without parallel in the history of the world—was due to the growing commercial rivalry, which brought home to civilised nations the vital necessity of securing the only remaining fields for industrial enterprise and expansion. It is well, then, to realise that it is for our advantage—and not alone at the dictates of duty—that we have undertaken responsibilities in East Africa. It is in order to foster the growth of the trade of this country,

"'A Natural Inclination to Submit to a Higher Authority'" is from Sir Frederick Dealtry Lugard, *The Rise of Our East African Empire*, vol. 1 (London: William Blackwood and Sons, 1893), pp. 379–382.

and to find an outlet for our manufactures and our surplus energy, that our far-seeing statesmen and our commercial men advocate colonial expansion. . . .

There are some who say we have no right in Africa at all, that "it belongs to the natives." I hold that our right is the necessity that is upon us to provide for our ever-growing population—either by opening new fields for emigration, or by providing work and employment which the development of over-sea extension entails—and to stimulate trade by finding new markets, since we know what misery trade depression brings at home.

While thus serving our own interests as a nation, we may, by selecting men of the right stamp for the control of new territories, bring at the same time many advantages to Africa. Nor do we deprive the natives of their birthright of freedom, to place them under a foreign yoke. It has ever been the key-note of British colonial method to rule through and by the natives, and it is this method, in contrast to the arbitrary and uncompromising rule of Germany, France, Portugal, and Spain, which has been the secret of our success as a colonising nation, and has made us welcomed by tribes and peoples in Africa, who ever rose in revolt against the other nations named. In Africa, moreover, there is among the people a natural inclination to submit to a higher authority. That intense detestation of control which animates our Teutonic races does not exist among the tribes of Africa, and if there is any authority that we replace, it is the authority of the Slavers and Arabs, or the intolerable tyranny of the "dominant tribe."

CONSIDER THIS:

- How did Sir Frederick Lugard connect nationalism with the economic argument for imperialism? How did he respond to the arguments presented by critics of imperialism? How did he justify his support of imperial expansion?

THEME: IMPERIALISM

THE REFLECTION IN THE MIRROR

"The Judgement of Your Peers"

It would be inaccurate to characterize European imperialism in Africa and India as fully sanctioned by governments and supported by the popular will. Just as the voices of abolition were crucial in the destruction of slave economies, so too were critics who decried the arrogance and atrocities that were a part of the exploitation of these regions. The first selection is by the historian Frederick Starr, who experienced firsthand the fear and distrust that Asian and African peoples often felt for the "white man's face." His criticism is followed by that of Mark Twain, whose scathing wit and anguish at U.S. imperialism are evident in his reinterpretation of "The Battle Hymn of the Republic" (1900).

KEEP IN MIND . . .

- According to Frederick Starr, why did the white man's face inspire terror throughout the world?

The "White Man's Face": Terror in the Congo

FREDERICK STARR

Why should we pick out the Congo Free State for our assault? Atrocities occur wherever the white man with his thirst for gold comes into contact with "a lower people." He is ever there to exploit; he believes that they were created for exploitation. If we want to find cruelty, atrocities, all kinds of frightful maltreatment, we may find them in almost every part of Negro Africa. They exist in the French Congo, in German Africa, in Nigeria, even in Uganda. If we insist on finding them, we may find cruelty, dispossession, destruction of life and property, in all these areas. . . . Wherever British trade finds native custom standing in its way, we shall find cruelty. . . .

To me the real wonder is that there are any of the Congo peoples left. Think of the constant drain due to the foreign slave trade, continued from an early date until after the middle of the nineteenth century. Think of the continuous losses due to the barbarism of native chiefs and demands of native customs–to wars, cannibalism, execution, and ordeal. Think of the multitudes who have died from the diseases of the country and from pestilence introduced by the newcomers. . . .

Returned from the Congo country and a year and more of contact with the dark natives, I find that a curious and most disagreeable sensation has taken possession of me. I had read often and heard that other peoples find the faces of white men terrifying and cruel. The Chinese, the Japanese, and other peoples of Asia tell the same story. The white man's face is fierce and terrible. His great and prominent nose suggests the beak of some bird of prey. His fierce face causes babes to cry, children to run in terror, grown folk to tremble. I had been always inclined to think that this feeling was individual and trifling; that it was solely due to strangeness and lack of contact. Today I know better. Contrasted with the other faces of the world, the face of the fair white is terrible, fierce, and cruel. No doubt our intensity of purpose, or firmness and dislike of interference, our manner in walk and action and in speech all add to the effect. However that may be, both in Europe and our own land, after my visit to the blacks I see the cruelty and fierceness of the white man's face as I never would have believed was possible. For the first time I can appreciate fully the feelings of the natives. The white man's face is a dreadful prediction; where the white man goes, he devastates, destroys, depopulates. Witness America, Australia, and Africa.

The Battle Hymn of the Republic (Brought Down to Date)

MARK TWAIN

Mine eyes have seen the orgy of the
launching of the Sword;
He is searching out the hoardings where the
stranger's wealth is stored;
He hath loosed his fateful lightnings, and
with woe and death has scored;
HIS LUST IS MARCHING ON.

I have seen him in the watch-fires of a
hundred circling camps,
They have builded him an altar in the
Eastern dews and damps;
I have read his doomful mission by the dim
and flaring lamps—
HIS NIGHT IS MARCHING ON.

"The 'White Man's Face'" is from Frederick Starr, *The Truth About the Congo* (Chicago: Forbes & Co., 1907), pp. 105–106.

"The Battle Hymn of the Republic" is from Mark Twain, *The Complete Works of Mark Twain*, vol. 20 (New York: Harper Brothers, 1917), p. 465.

I have read his bandit gospel writ in
burnished rows of steel:
"As ye deal with my pretensions, so with
you my wrath shall deal;
Let the faithless son of Freedom crush the
patriot with his heel;
LO, GREED IS MARCHING ON!"

In a sordid slime harmonious, Greed was
born in yonder ditch,
With a longing in his bosom—and for
others' goods an itch—
As Christ died to make men holy, let men
die to make us rich—
OUR GOD IS MARCHING ON!

COMPARE AND CONTRAST:

- What do you think of Mark Twain's version of "The Battle Hymn of the Republic"? What point was he trying to make? Compare Twain's poem with Rudyard Kipling's "The White Man's Burden." Are they both honest and truthful?

9

FIN DE SIÈCLE: THE BIRTH OF THE MODERN ERA

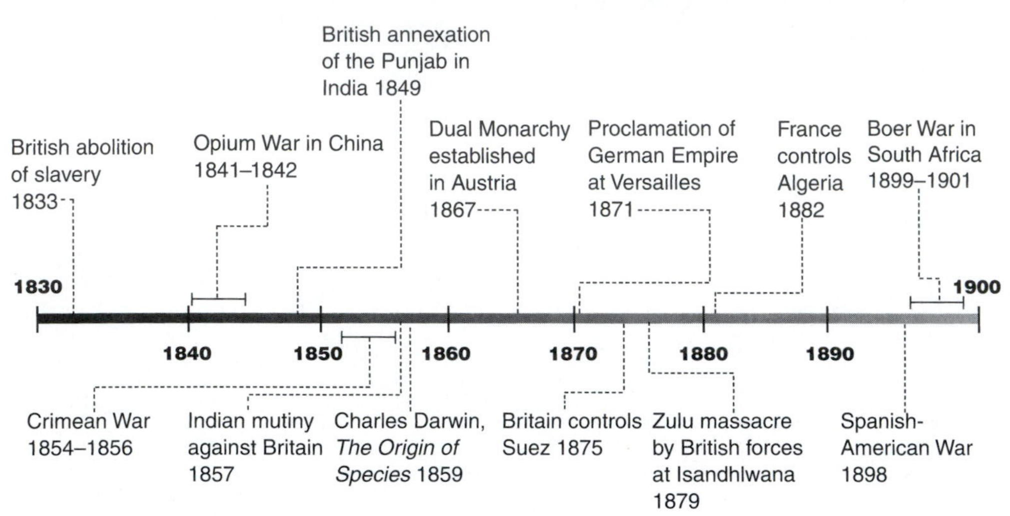

CHAPTER THEMES

- **The Individual and the Institution:** In the late nineteenth century, the optimistic Enlightenment ideals of reason and progress were replaced by lingering self-doubt and disconsolate isolation. Why did many intellectuals reject the institutions of church and state in an assertion of personal freedom? How was this challenge to the moral and political foundations of society reflected in the art and literature of the period?
- **Social and Spiritual Values:** How did nationalism and the fervent belief in the sanctity of one's nation and ethnic origins both contribute to a unified Europe and lead to the degeneration of personal freedom at home and abroad? How did nationalism become a spiritual factor in the political development of Europe?
- **The Varieties of Truth:** How did nationalist leaders lend credibility to the posturing and arrogant swagger of military glory that permeated the period and celebrated war as an instrument of national policy? Did this attitude pave the way for the destruction of the Great War in 1914?
- **Women in History:** The turn of the twentieth century proved to be a seminal time for the political organization of women as they fought stereotypes imposed on them by society. What were the expectations of women in society, and how did they begin to break the mold?
- **The Big Picture:** The end of the nineteenth century was an age of exploitation, innovation, and tremendous creative energy in the arts. How were these seemingly contradictory factors integrated into the political, economic, and social landscape of the time? How could a celebration of technology and war exist contemporaneously with a rejection of institutional values and reason?

The Political Unification of Italy and Germany

No other factor in history, not even religion, has produced so many wars as has the clash of national egotisms sanctified by the name of patriotism.

—PRESERVED SMITH

When any group sees itself as the bearer of civilization, this very belief will betray it into behaving barbarously at the first opportunity.

—SIMONE WEIL

During the first half of the nineteenth century, commitment to the goal of political unification that resided deep in the hearts of nationalists throughout Europe had resulted in several uprisings that challenged the supremacy of the conservative order. The greatest threat to the Concert of Europe had come in the year 1848–1849 with uncoordinated revolutions led variously by liberals and Romantic nationalists in Germany, Italy, France, and Austria that demanded written constitutions, self-determination, and political unification. In this crusade, they were wholly unsuccessful and left Germany and Italy in particular as regions on the map still without a national identity. During the next twenty-five years, however, many liberal goals were achieved, ironically through the efforts of the same conservative forces that had stifled all talk of political and social change. In Russia, the serfs were emancipated in 1861 by the decree of Tsar Alexander II, and in 1867 the Austrian emperor Franz Joseph compromised with Magyar demands by creating a separate Hungarian state and linking the new Austro-Hungarian Empire through a Dual Monarchy over which he reigned as titular head.

The issue of unification for Germany was coopted from the liberals through the conservative leadership of Otto von Bismarck (1815–1898). As prime minister of Prussia during the 1860s, Bismarck fought a series of strategic wars against Denmark, Austria, and France to incorporate territories into the North German Confederation. Bismarck was a master of deception and realpolitik who sought defensible borders by achieving limited goals. The unification of Germany and the creation of the German Empire, which was proclaimed after the defeat of Napoleon III in the Franco-Prussian war of 1870–1871, was the single most important political development of the nineteenth century and would have repercussions for Europe well into the next century under the leadership of Kaiser Wilhelm II and Adolf Hitler.

The tide of nationalism not only engulfed Germany but Italy as well. Fired by the romantic visions of an Italian republic under the leadership of Giuseppe Mazzini (1805–1872) and Giuseppe Garibaldi (1807–1882), respectively called the "Soul" and the "Sword" of Italy, the insurrections of 1848–1849 resulted in the ill-fated Roman Republic that was soon crushed by Austrian troops. Yet between 1852 and 1860, Italy was transformed into a constitutional monarchy, not by romantic nationalists but by the cool hand of Count Camillo Cavour (1810–1861), the prime minister of the north Italian kingdom of Piedmont. Through secret diplomacy, patience, and deceptive nuance, Cavour was able to provide a moderate political proposition attractive enough to both republicans and absolutists. Through his commitment to a constitutional monarchy led by the king of Piedmont, Victor Emmanuel II, he forged a political bond between the several Italian states. But Cavour often had to work uphill against the dynamism of Romantic republicanism, and after his death in 1861, Italy still needed to restrain and yet to integrate these important nationalist forces to achieve a lasting political unification.

Proclamation for the Liberation of Sicily (1860)

GIUSEPPE GARIBALDI

One of Mazzini's most devoted disciples was Giuseppe Garibaldi (1807–1882). A man of action, he was also an adventurer of ability who succeeded in gaining military support for the king of Piedmont, Victor Emmanuel II. In 1860, he organized a volunteer force to invade Sicily and offered the following appeal to the people. Note the emphasis on goals that transcend the individual boundaries and responsibilities of the small regions that previously composed Italy. Garibaldi successfully gained control of both Sicily and Naples.

Italians!—The Sicilians are fighting against the enemies of Italy, and for Italy. It is the duty of every Italian to succour them with words, money, and arms, and, above all, in person.

The misfortunes of Italy arise from the indifference of one province to the fate of the others.

The redemption of Italy began from the moment that men of the same land ran to help their distressed brothers.

Left to themselves, the brave Sicilians will have to fight, not only the mercenaries of the Bourbon, but also those of Austria and the Priest of Rome.

Let the inhabitants of the free provinces lift their voices in behalf of their struggling brethren, and impel their brave youth to the conflict.

Let the Marches, Umbria, Sabina, Rome, the Neapolitan, rise to divide the forces of our enemies.

Where the cities suffice not for the insurrection, let them send bands of their bravest into the country.

The brave man finds an arm everywhere. Listen not to the voice of cowards, but arm, and let us fight for our brethren, who will fight for us tomorrow.

A band of those who fought with me the country's battles marches with me to the fight. Good and generous, they will fight for their country to the last drop of their blood, nor ask for other reward than a clear conscience.

"Italy and Victor Emmanuel!" they cried, on passing the Ticino. "Italy and Victor Emmanuel!" shall re-echo in the blazing caves of Mongibello.

At this cry, thundering from the great rock of Italy to the Tarpeian, the rotten Throne of tyranny shall crumble, and, as one man, the brave descendants of Vespro shall rise.

To Arms! Let me put an end, once and for all, to the miseries of so many centuries. Prove to the world that it is no lie that Roman generations inhabited this land.

CONSIDER THIS:

- What was Garibaldi's purpose and goal in this proclamation? How did Garibaldi inspire his forces through an appeal to their patriotic loyalties? How did he use nationalism to effect policy?

"Proclamation for the Liberation of Sicily" is from *Public Documents, The Annual Register, 1860* (London: 1861), pp. 281–282.

Address to the Italian Parliament (1871)

KING VICTOR EMMANUEL II

Through years of idealistic and impassioned speeches by people like Giuseppe Mazzini, diplomatic maneuvering by Camillo Cavour, and the exercise of military might by Giuseppe Garibaldi, Italy became a unified, independent state in 1870 under the leadership of Victor Emmanuel II (1820–1878), former king of Piedmont. This excerpt from his address to the Italian Parliament in 1871 discusses some of the challenges that a new nation must face.

Senators and Deputies, gentlemen!

The work to which we consecrated our life is accomplished. After long trials of expiation Italy is restored to herself and to Rome. Here, where our people, after centuries of separation, find themselves for the first time solemnly reunited in the person of their representatives: here where we recognize the fatherland of our dreams, everything speaks to us of greatness; but at the same time it all reminds us of our duties. The joy that we experience must not let us forget them. . . .

We have proclaimed the separation of Church and State. Having recognized the absolute independence of the spiritual authority, we are convinced that Rome, the capital of Italy, will continue to be the peaceful and respected seat of the Pontificate. . . .

Economic and financial affairs, moreover, claim our most careful attention. Now that Italy is established, it is necessary to make it prosperous by putting in order its finances; we shall succeed in this only by persevering in the virtues which have been the source of our national regeneration. Good finances will be the means of re-enforcing our military organization. Our most ardent desire is for peace, and nothing can make us believe that it can be troubled. But the organization of the army and the navy, the supply of arms, the works for the defense of the national territory, demand long and profound study. . . .

Senators and deputies, a vast range of activity opens before you; the national unity which is today attained will have, I hope, the effect of rendering less bitter the struggles of parties, the rivalry of which will have henceforth no other end than the development of the productive forces of the nation.

I rejoice to see that our population already gives unequivocal proofs of its love of work. The economic awakening is closely associated with the political awakening. The banks multiply, as do the commercial institutions, the expositions of the products of art and industry, and the congresses of the learned. We ought, you and I, to favor this productive movement while giving to professional and scientific education more attention and efficiency, and opening to commerce new avenues of communication and new outlets. . . .

A brilliant future opens before us. It remains for us to respond to the blessings of Providence by showing ourselves worthy of bearing among the nations the glorious names of Italy and Rome.

Compare and Contrast:

- King Victor Emanuel in his address to Parliament appealed for political unity by "showing ourselves worthy of bearing among the nations the glorious

"Address to the Italian Parliament" is from Christine Walsh, ed., *Prologue: A Documentary History of Europe: 1846–1960.* Originally published by Cassell Australia Ltd. (1968), pp. 103–104. Reprinted by permission of Macmillan Publishing Company.

names of Italy and Rome." Compare this to Garibaldi's plea for Italians to "prove to the world that it is no lie that Roman generations inhabited this land." Both statements appeal to the legacy of the past, to Italians as inheritors of Roman greatness. How is past glory, therefore, linked to future success? Do modern Italians posses a genetic predisposition to political authority and cultural leadership by virtue of the achievements of the Roman Empire or the Florentine Renaissance? What makes a "great people"?

THE BROADER PERSPECTIVE:

- In the 1920s and 1930s, both Benito Mussolini and Adolf Hitler linked contemporary Italians and Germans with their national heritage. In fact, they characterized their authoritarian regimes as the "regenerators" of past glory. Has "extreme nationalism," not simply a love of country but a repudiation of other nations and peoples, been the cause of many conflicts?
- Can citizens of a democratic nation be patriotic and at the same time critical of the actions of political leaders? In this sense, how do you react to the Vietnam-era slogan "America—Love It or Leave It"? Are there other alternatives?
- Does a national crisis, such as the terrorist bombings of September 11, 2001, in New York City, virtually end open political debate as citizens and their elected representatives suppress political differences in exchange for a united response to the crisis? Is any criticism of presidential leadership therefore viewed as "unpatriotic"? Does the democracy then become vulnerable to a kind of despotism?
- Where is the line between patriotism and freedom? Can one ever become "too patriotic"—or is love of country the essence of our freedom and political stability?

"We Germans Fear God, and Nothing Else in the World": Speech to the Reichstag (1888)

OTTO VON BISMARCK

In 1862, Otto von Bismarck was appointed prime minister of Prussia. At that time he declared that German unity would be realized "not by speeches and majorities . . . but by blood and iron." By 1871, after several wars, Bismarck had formed the unified fatherland of which Fichte had dreamed: The nation of Germany existed under the leadership of Kaiser Wilhelm I. The following excerpt is from Bismarck's speech to the Reichstag (parliament) in 1888. Unity demands great goals.

Great complications and all kinds of coalitions, which no one can foresee, are constantly possible, and we must be prepared for them. We must be so strong, irrespective of momentary conditions, that we can face any coalition with the assurance of a great nation which is strong enough under circumstances to take her fate into her own hands. We must be able to face our fate placidly with that self-reliance and confidence in God which are ours when we are strong and our cause is just. And the government will see to it that the German cause will be just always.

We must, to put it briefly, be as strong in these times as we possibly can be, and we can be stronger than any other nation of equal numbers in the world. I shall revert to this later—but it would be criminal if we were not to make

"Speech to the Reichstag" is from Kuno Francke, ed., *The German Classics of the Nineteenth and Twentieth Centuries*, Volume 10 (1914), pp. 136–152. Translated by Edmund Von Mach.

use of our opportunity. If we do not need our full armed strength, we need not summon it. The only problem is the not very weighty one of money—not very weighty I say in passing, because I have no wish to enter upon a discussion of the financial and military figures, and of the fact that France has spent three milliards for the improvement of her armaments these last years, while we have spent scarcely one and one half milliards, including what we are asking of you at this time. But I leave the elucidation of this to the minister of war and the representatives of the treasury department.

When I say that it is our duty to endeavor to be ready at all times and for all emergencies, I imply that we must make greater exertions than other people for the same purpose, because of our geographical position. We are situated in the heart of Europe, and have at least three fronts open to an attack. France has only her eastern, and Russia only her western frontier where they may be attacked. We are also more exposed to the dangers of a coalition than any other nation, as is proved by the whole development of history, by our geographical position, and the lesser degree of cohesiveness, which until now has characterized the German nation in comparison with others. God has placed us where we are prevented, thanks to our neighbors, from growing lazy and dull. He has placed by our side the most warlike and restless of all nations, the French, and He has permitted warlike inclinations to grow strong in Russia, where formerly they existed to a lesser degree. Thus we are given the spur, so to speak, from both sides, and are compelled to exertions which we should perhaps not be making otherwise. The pikes in the European carp-pond are keeping us from being carps by making us feel their teeth on both sides. They also are forcing us to an exertion which without them we might not make, and to a union among us Germans, which is abhorrent to us at heart. By nature we are rather tending away, the one from the other. But the Franco-Russian press within which we are squeezed compels us to hold together, and by pressure our cohesive force is greatly increased. This will bring us to that state of being inseparable which all other nations possess, while we do not yet enjoy it. But we must respond to the intentions of Providence by making ourselves so strong that the pikes can do nothing but encourage us. . . .

If we Germans wish to wage a war with the full effect of our national strength, it must be a war which satisfies all who take part in it, all who sacrifice anything for it, in short the whole nation. It must be a national war, a war carried on with the enthusiasm of 1870, when we were foully attacked. I still remember the earsplitting, joyful shouts in the station at Köln. It was the same all the way from Berlin to Köln, in Berlin itself. The waves of popular approval bore us into the war, whether or not we wished it. That is the way it must be, if a popular force like ours is to show what it can do. . . . A war into which we are not borne by the will of the

FIGURE 9.1 Otto von Bismarck was a ruthless genius whose policy of German unification by "blood and iron" proved to have tremendous implications for the future. As Bismarck warned: "Attack the German nation anywhere, and you will find it armed to a man, and every man with the firm belief in his heart: God will be with us." (*National Archives and Records Administration*)

people will be waged, to be sure, if it has been declared by the constituted authorities who deemed it necessary; it will even be waged aggressively, and possibly victoriously, after we have once smelled fire and tasted blood, but it will lack from the beginning the nerve and enthusiasm of a war in which we are attacked. In such a one the whole of Germany from Memel to the Alpine Lakes will flare up like a powder mine; it will be bristling with guns, and no enemy will dare to engage this *furor teutonicus* which develops when we are attacked. We cannot afford to lose this factor of preeminence even if many military men—not only ours but others as well—believe that today we are superior to our future opponents. Our own officers believe this to a man, naturally. Every soldier believes this. He would almost cease to be a useful soldier if he did not wish for war, and did not believe that we would be victorious in it. If our opponents by any chance are thinking that we are pacific because we are afraid of how the war may end, they are mightily mistaken. We believe as firmly in our victory in a just cause as any foreign lieutenant in his garrison, after his third glass of champagne, can believe in his, and we probably do so with greater certainty. It is not fear, therefore, which makes us pacific, but the consciousness of our strength. We are strong enough to protect ourselves, even if we should be attacked at a less favorable moment, and we are in a position to let divine providence determine whether a war in the meanwhile may not become unnecessary after all.

I am, therefore, not in favor of any kind of an aggressive war, and if war could result only from our attack—somebody must kindle a fire, we shall not kindle it. Neither the consciousness of our strength, which I have described, nor our confidence in our treaties, will prevent us from continuing our former endeavors to preserve peace. In this we do not permit ourselves to be influenced by annoyances or dislikes. The threats and insults, and the challenges, which have been made have, no doubt, excited also with us a feeling of irritation, which does not easily happen with Germans, for they are less prone to national hatred than any other nation. We are, however, trying to calm our countrymen, and we shall work for peace with our neighbors, especially with Russia, in the future as in the past. . . .

We are easily influenced—perhaps too easily—by love and kindness, but quite surely never by threats! We Germans fear God, and nothing else in the world! It is this fear of God which makes us love and cherish peace. If in spite of this anybody breaks the peace, he will discover that ardent patriotism . . . has today become the common property of the whole German nation. Attack the German nation anywhere, and you will find it armed to a man, and every man with the firm belief in his heart: God will be with us.

CONSIDER THIS:

- According to Bismarck, why must Germany be armed? Does Bismarck advocate imperialism? How does he use God in his arguments? How does this relate to nationalism? How is religion (specifically Christianity) used in other sources as justification for imperial expansion?

THEME: SOCIAL AND SPIRITUAL VALUES

The Architectural Foundation

The Eiffel Tower

Great exhibitions during the nineteenth century served as testing grounds for mechanical innovations and new architectural ideas. The first was held within the glass enclosure of the Crystal Palace in 1851, and it was only two years later that New York City built its own crystal palace. Several cities throughout the world held successive exhibitions, but 1889 was the centenary year of the French Revolution and Paris wanted to host the world once again with a spectacular display. It clearly surpassed all earlier exhibitions in novelty and scale. The Machine Hall was a masterpiece of engineering and constructed almost exclusively from steel and glass. The public was clearly impressed and critics raved, but the hall was ultimately demolished, as befitting a temporary showcase.

The talk of the exhibition, however, was a tower that soared over 1,000 feet above the city. Gustave Eiffel, an engineer who was admired for his bridge over the Douro River in Portugal, was commissioned in 1887 to build, as he described it, "a bridge into the sky." Whereas the Machine Hall was admired by most, the Eiffel Tower seemed to be condemned by all. Constructed in just 17 months, Eiffel could boast that he had made a structure that would stand forever against all the elements. It indeed was a masterpiece of conception and precise execution. But it was considered to be an affront to the architecture of Paris and a wrought-iron eyesore without aesthetic value. It was, after all, built by an engineer "without any artistic sensibility." Based on construction diagrams and models

FIGURE 9.2 The Eiffel Tower (*Perry M. Rogers*)

alone, a petition was circulated and delivered to the exhibition authorities: "We, the writers, painters, sculptors, and architects come in the name of French good taste . . . to express our deep indignation that there should stand in the heart of our capital this . . . monstrous Eiffel Tower." Called by critics a "menace to French history," the tower serves today the very symbol of modern Paris.

But it is also important to view the Eiffel Tower in the context of political events outside the boundaries of aesthetic or artistic taste. In fact, the tower had its supporters in the French Third Republic. The period from 1870 to 1914 was a nightmare of political division and accusation between liberals in the press and the ruling conservative majority. Anti-Semitism was rife in Parisian society, and the conservatives, supported by the army and the Catholic church, quickly accused and convicted army captain Alfred Dreyfus on charges of treason in 1894. This conflict set Paris on fire for over a decade, drawing challenge lines in the sand and daring moderate voices to try to settle the issue. The charges against Dreyfus, who had been convicted on trumped-up evidence, were finally set aside in 1906, and he was released from his prison cell on Devil's Island just off the coast of French Guyana. The conservative coalition that had supported this injustice was shamed, and the Third Republic degenerated into a long period of ineffective chaos, where blame and defensive reaction aborted positive opportunities. Architectural controversies soon

FIGURE 9.3 The Basilica of the Sacred Heart (*Dorling Kindersley*)

spilled into this polluted well as conservatives decried the Eiffel Tower and instead championed the Basilica of the Sacred Heart (*Sacré Coeur*) under construction from 1873 to 1914. The French Roman Catholic church, the conservative arbiter of society, oversaw its construction high atop Montmartre as the symbol of national penance for sins committed during the Franco-Prussian war of 1870. Today, when viewing the gargoyles near the top of the cathedral of Notre Dame, you can easily see the Eiffel Tower and Sacré Coeur in polarized juxtaposition—two symbols of the political, spiritual, and architectural divisions in France at the turn of the century.

CONSIDER THIS:

- Why was the Eiffel Tower considered to be such a controversial addition to the urban landscape of Paris? Why was it so disturbing and criticized by architects and artists alike, those very individuals we might expect to be more open to the variety of creative expression? Was the Eiffel Tower the work of an architect or an engineer? Does this matter? Is there a difference between the two in the intent or approach?

COMPARE AND CONTRAST:

- Architecture often serves a specific purpose in society by expressing political or spiritual values. Does that mean, therefore, that to have credibility, must architecture be "politicized" or charged with a task?

- In this regard, what was the purpose of the Eiffel Tower? Compare the role played by the Basilica of the Sacred Heart. If they were not constructed for a political purpose, then why did the contending forces of conservatism and liberalism rally around them during the Third French Republic about the turn of the century?

The Woman Question and Anti-Feminism

I think it is unnecessary to take into consideration a system of education for girls; they can get no better teaching than that of their mothers. A public education does not suit them, for the reason that they are not called on to live in public; for them habit is everything, and marriage is the goal.

—NAPOLEON BONAPARTE (1806)

I myself have never been able to find out precisely what feminism is: I only know that people call me a feminist whenever I express sentiments that differentiate me from a doormat.

—REBECCA WEST (1913)

The desire of the man is for the woman, but the desire of the woman is for the desire of the man.

—MADAME DE STAËL

Europe at mid-century was a hotbed of intellectual and political activity. As the revolutions of 1848 spread throughout the great capitals of Europe, challenging conservative assumptions and promoting nationalist change, scientists were challenging the intellectual foundations of society. Charles Darwin's theory of evolution by natural selection, introduced in *The Origin of Species* (1859), and applied to human beings in *The Descent of Man* (1871), remained controversial even within the scientific community until the 1920s. In fact, during the last decade of the nineteenth century and the first decade of the twentieth century, philosophers, scientists, psychologists, and artists rejected many of the assumptions that governed the physical universe and the norms of bourgeois morality. The discovery of radium by Marie Curie (1869–1934), the development of quantum theory by Max Planck (1858–1947), and the relativity proposition of Albert Einstein (1879–1955) forced a reassessment of the nature of physical reality.

But the reassessment taking place in the scientific world in the latter part of the nineteenth century did not necessarily promote change in social relationships. The controversy surrounding new ideas in biology, evolution, and reproduction led many intellectuals to emphasize the role of women as a constant, stabilizing force in society. The mothering instinct was elemental to the woman, and many writers portrayed women as one dimensional. Their minds and bodies were simply not equipped for the stress and strain of active political life. They were creatures shackled to their emotions, susceptible to the illogic of feelings and instincts. Their role was clearly in the smaller world of the home, not in the university, or the professions, or the voting booth.

In reaction to such misogynistic attitudes, there arose in the mid-nineteenth century a feminist movement that concentrated first on achieving the vote for women. But in the process, female activists raised other questions regarding the role of women in society, in marriage, in the law courts, and in their general relationship with men.

The following selections attest to this struggle for recognition and equality. Many of the issues important at the end of the nineteenth century would be revisited in the decades after World War II as women made further strides toward political, economic, legal, and social equality in Western civilization.

Against Woman Suffrage (1884)

FRANCIS PARKMAN

At the heart of the women's movement during the nineteenth and early twentieth centuries was the demand for equal voting rights, or women's suffrage. The goal in America had been clearly detailed in a declaration of equal rights established at the Seneca Falls Convention in 1848. By 1852, the movement to secure the vote had picked up momentum. The reaction to such agitation was intense and polarizing. Advocates of the complete equality of women included the English philosopher John Stuart Mill, who together with his wife, Harriet, became a crusader for the cause. His fundamental tracts, *On Liberty* (1859) and *The Subjection of Women* (1869), were especially persuasive in advocating voting rights for women. Opposition forces, however, could also claim their intellectual champions.

The following selection comes from the pen of the great American historian Francis Parkman. A writer of unusual depth and narrative skill, Parkman was universally

"*Against Woman Suffrage*" is from Francis Parkman, *Some of the Reasons Against Woman Suffrage* (Printed at the Request of an Association of Women, 1884), pp. 1–7, 10–16.

acknowledged for his ability to characterize the figures of colonial American history. His account of the westward movement, *The Oregon Trail,* became one of the most popular personal narratives of the nineteenth century. He wrote this pamphlet against women's suffrage "at the request of an association of women." It reveals the attitudes and fears of conservatives in the face of an established threat to the status quo.

It has been said that the question of the rights and employment of women should be treated without regard to sex. It should rather be said that those who consider it regardless of sex do not consider it at all. . . . Whatever liberty the best civilization may accord to women, they must always be subject to restrictions unknown to the other sex, and they can never dispense with the protecting influences which society throws about them. A man, in lonely places, has nothing to lose but life and property; and he has nerve and muscles to defend them. He is free to go whither he pleases, and run what risks he pleases. Without a radical change in human nature, of which the world has never given the faintest sign, women cannot be equally emancipated. . . . Everybody knows that the physical and mental constitution of woman is more delicate than in the other sex; and, we may add, the relations between mind and body are more intimate and subtle. . . . It is these and other inherent conditions, joined to the engrossing nature of a woman's special functions, that have determined through all time her relative position. . . . Men did not make [these limitations], and they cannot unmake them. Through them, God and Nature have ordained that those subject to them shall not be forced to join in the harsh conflicts of the world militant. It is folly to ignore them, or try to counteract them by political and social quackery. . . .

The frequent low state of health among American women is a fact as undeniable as it is deplorable. In this condition of things, what do certain women demand for the good of their sex? To add to the excitements that are wasting them, other and greater excitements, and to cares too much for their strength, other and greater cares. Because they cannot do their own work, to require them to add to it the work of men, and launch them into the turmoil where the most robust sometimes fail. It is much as if a man in a state of nervous exhaustion were told by his physician to enter at once a foot-race or a boxing match.

Woman suffrage must have one of two effects. If, as many of its advocates complain, women are subservient to men, and do nothing but what they desire, then woman suffrage will have no other result than to increase the power of the other sex; if, on the other hand, women vote as they see fit, without regarding their husbands, then unhappy marriages will be multiplied and divorces redoubled. We cannot afford to add to the elements of domestic unhappiness.

One of the chief dangers of popular government is that of inconsiderate and rash legislation. . . . This danger would be increased immeasurably if the most impulsive and excitable half of humanity had an equal voice in the making of laws, and in the administration of them. . . . If the better class of women flatter themselves that they can control the others, they are doomed to disappointment. The female vote . . . is often more numerous, always more impulsive and less subject to reason, and almost devoid of the sense of responsibility. Here the bad politician would find his richest resources. He could not reach the better class of female voters, but the rest would be ready to his hand. Three fourths of them, when not urged by some pressing need or contagious passion, would be moved, not by principles, but by personal predilections.

Again, one of the chief arguments of the agitators is that government without the consent of the governed is opposed to inalienable right. But most women, including those of the best capacity and worth, fully consent that their fathers, husbands, brothers, or friends shall be their political representatives. . . . We venture to remind those who demand woman suffrage as a right that, even if it were so, the great majority of intelligent women could judge for themselves whether to exercise it better than the few who assume to teach them their duty. The agitators know well that, in spite of their persistent importunity, the majority of their sex are averse to the suffrage. . . .

On women of the intelligent and instructed classes depends the future of the nation. If they are sound in body and mind, impart this soundness to a numerous offspring, and rear them to a sense of responsibility and duty, there are no national evils that we cannot overcome. If they fail to do this their part, then the masses of the coarse and unintelligent, always of rapid increase, will overwhelm us and our institutions. When these indispensable duties are fully discharged, then the suffrage agitators may ask with better grace, if not with more reason, that they may share the political functions of men. . . .

Many women of sense and intelligence are influenced by the fact that the woman-suffrage movement boasts itself a movement of progress, and by a wish to be on the liberal or progressive side. But the boast is unfounded. Progress, to be genuine, must be in accord with natural law. If it is not, it ends in failure and in retrogression. To give women a thorough and wholesome training both of body and mind . . . [is] in the way of normal and healthy development: but to plunge them into politics, where they are not needed and for which they are unfit, would be scarcely more a movement of progress than to force them to bear arms and fight. . . .

Suppose, again, a foreign war in which the sympathies of our women were enlisted on one side or the other. Suppose them to vote against the judgment of the men that we should take part in it; or, in other words, that their male fellow citizens should fight whether they like it or not. Would the men be likely to obey?

There is another reason why the giving of the suffrage to women would tend to civil discord. . . . Most of us have had occasion to observe how strong the social rivalries and animosities of women are. They far exceed those of men. . . . The wives and daughters of the poor would bring into the contest a wrathful jealousy and hate against the wives and daughters of the rich, far more vehement than the corresponding passions in their husbands and brothers. . . .

The suffragists' idea of government is not practical, but utterly unpractical. It is not American, but French. It is that government of abstractions and generalities which found its realization in the French Revolution, and its apostle in the depraved and half-crazy man of genius, Jean Jacques Rousseau. The French had an excuse for their frenzy in the crushing oppression they had just flung off and in their inexperience of freedom. We have no excuse. Since the nation began we have been free and our liberty is in danger from nothing but its own excesses. . . .

Neither Congress, nor the States, nor the united voice of the whole people could permanently change the essential relations of the sexes. Universal female suffrage, even if decreed, would undo itself in time; but the attempt to establish it would work deplorable mischief. The question is, whether the persistency of a few agitators shall plunge us blindfold into the most reckless of all experiments; whether we shall adopt this supreme device for developing the defects of women, and demolish their real power to build an ugly mockery instead. For the sake of womanhood, let us hope not.

Consider This:

- Carefully note Francis Parkman's arguments against women's suffrage. Which ones could be applied to any political, social, religious, or ethnic group that strives for equal status with an incumbent authority? Which of his arguments do you find most specious? Which seem the most well founded and persuasive? Do you agree with his statement that "progress, to be genuine, must be in accord with natural law"?

"The Brain Weight of Women Is Five Ounces Less Than That of Men" (1887)

GEORGE ROMANES

Parkman's arguments against suffrage included the inability of women to participate effectively in the political arena, a world ill suited to their excitable and passionate nature. Women's physical anatomy and psychological composition underwent even closer scientific scrutiny during the late nineteenth century. This study flowed from the resounding confidence of the age in the discipline of science to solve the dilemmas and mysteries of past decades. Human relationships were left open to scientific inquiry, often with misleading and damaging results. Thus were Charles Darwin's theories on natural selection applied quite loosely to the human realm, with the excesses of social Darwinism the result. It is therefore not surprising that several fallacious scientific treatises like the following often confirmed in people's minds the inherent genetic inferiority of women. Such attitudes retarded progress toward social equality and proved influential even late into the twentieth century in justifying negative perceptions of women's ability to compete with men on an equal footing.

I will now briefly enumerate what appear to me the leading features of this distinction in the case of mankind, adopting the ordinary classification of mental faculties as those of intellect, emotion, and will.

Seeing that the average brain-weight of women is about five ounces less than that of men, on merely anatomical grounds we should be prepared to expect a marked inferiority of intellectual power in the former. Moreover, as the general physique of women is less robust than that of men—and therefore less able to sustain the fatigue of serious or prolonged brain action—we should also on physiological grounds be prepared to entertain a similar anticipation. In actual fact, we find that the inferiority displays itself most conspicuously in a comparative absence of originality, and this more especially in the higher levels of intellectual work. In her powers of acquisition [of knowledge] the woman certainly stands nearer to the man than she does in her powers of creative thought, although even as regards the former there is a marked difference. The difference, however, is one which does not assert itself till the period of adolescence. . . . But as soon as the brain, and with it the organism as a whole, reaches the stage of full development, it becomes apparent that there is a greater power of amassing knowledge on the

"'The Brain Weight of Women'" is from George J. Romanes, "Mental Differences Between Men and Women," *Nineteenth Century* 26 (1887), pp. 654–672.

part of the male. Whether we look to the general average or to the intellectual giants of both sexes, we are similarly met with the general fact that a woman's information is less wide and deep and thorough than that of a man. What we regard as a highly cultured woman is usually one who has read largely but superficially; and even in the few instances that can be quoted of extraordinary female industry—which on account of their rarity stand out as exceptions to prove the rule—we find a long distance between them and the much more numerous instances of profound erudition among men. . . .

But it is in original work . . . that the disparity is most conspicuous. . . . In no one department of creative thought can women be said to have at all approached men, save in fiction. Yet in poetry, music, and painting, if not also in history, philosophy, and science, the field has always been open to both. For . . . the disabilities under which women have laboured with regard to education, social opinion, and so forth, have certainly not been sufficient to explain this general dearth among them of the products of creative genius.

Lastly, with regard to judgment, I think there can be no real question that the female mind stands considerably below the male. It is much more apt to take superficial views of circumstances calling for decision, and also to be guided by less impartiality. Undue influence is more frequently exercised from the side of the emotions. . . . As a general rule, that the judgment of women is inferior to that of men has been a matter of universal recognition from the earliest times. The man has always been regarded as the rightful lord of the woman, to whom she is by nature subject, as both mentally and physically the weaker vessel.

But if woman has been a loser in the intellectual race as regards acquisition, origination, and judgment, she has gained, even on the intellectual side, certain very conspicuous advantages. First among these we must place refinement of the senses, or higher evolution of sense-organs. Next we must place rapidity of perception, which no doubt in part arises from this higher evolution of the sense-organs. . . .

Turning now to the emotions, we find that in woman, as contrasted with man, these are almost always less under control of the will—more apt to break away, as it were, from the restraint of reason, and to overwhelm the mental chariot in disaster. Whether this tendency displays itself in the overmastering form of hysteria, or in the more ordinary form of comparative childishness, ready annoyance, and a generally unreasonable temper, . . . we recognize it as more of a feminine than a masculine characteristic. . . .

Of course the greatest type of manhood, or the type wherein our ideal of manliness reaches its highest expression, is where the virtues of strength are purged from its vices. To be strong and yet tender, brave and yet kind, to combine in the same breast the temper of a hero with the sympathy of a maiden—this is to transform the ape and the tiger into what we know ought to constitute the man. And if in actual life we find that such an ideal is but seldom realised, this should make us more lenient in judging the frailties of the opposite sex. . . . This truth is, that the highest type of manhood can only then be reached when the heart and mind have been so far purified from the refuse of a brutal ancestry as genuinely to appreciate, to admire, and to reverence the greatness, the beauty, and the strength which have been made perfect in the weakness of womanhood.

CONSIDER THIS:

- What is the scientific evidence for arguing the general inferiority of women as presented by George Romanes in his article about the mental differences between men and women? How does Romanes damn women with "faint praise"?

"This Is the Logic of Demons!"

JOSEPHINE BUTLER

Between 1864 and 1886, English prostitutes were subject to the strict provisions of the Contagious Disease Acts. These acts required that any woman suspected of prostitution undergo detention (often for months) in a women's hospital, specifically established to provide internal medical examinations and treatments for venereal disease. The object of the acts was to protect soldiers and sailors in English cities. The women had no legal recourse for this detention, and the law took no action against the men who solicited their services and often themselves spread venereal disease. The Contagious Disease Acts angered middle-class women who saw them as promoting a double standard. These activists argued that poor women became victims of prostitution because inferior wages and inadequate working conditions often forced many into an immoral and destructive life.

One of the most vocal opponents of this treatment of poor women was Josephine Butler (1828–1906). She led the Ladies National Association for the Repeal of the Contagious Disease Acts; by 1883, she had achieved their suspension and, by 1886, their repeal. In the following selection from her book, *Personal Reminiscences of a Great Crusade* (1886), Butler explains her position.

Yes, prostitution kills the soul, even when it does not kill the body. This is the dialectic of evil, which follows its own inexorable course.

The partisans of this system say to us, however: "Society has a right to defend itself against physical evils which destroy it; it has a right to resort to any means when it has to deal not only with debauchery, but with debauchery which is a commerce; and these regulations, after all, only apply to the infamous creatures who sell themselves, and have put themselves beyond the pale of the law and of society: they are but the dirt of the street." Now I do not under-rate the abomination of paid debauchery. Yes, the vice which sells itself is abominable; what, then, shall we say of those who buy it? But there are distinctions to be made among those who sell. Let us look a little closer at the situation of the woman whom Governments have submitted to a regulation which is a complete and abject slavery. She deserves nothing but contempt you tell us! She is invariably as morally perverse as you tell us she is! I ask, how many of these girls are thrust upon the streets by abandonment after seduction, or dragged down by want into the infamy from which they cannot escape? What is you part in the matter? You engulf them further; you thrust them down lower; you throw on them the last shovelful of earth to hurl them to the abyss; you roll upon them the stone which cannot be removed except by a supernatural effort. "Ah! You have fallen, unfortunate creature," you say; "well, we will complete the work, we consummate your degradation: that which is already soiled shall be made still more vile." This is logic; but it is the logic of demons! . . .

I do not hide from myself the horror and the peril of the prostitution which exists where there are not these laws–the horror and danger of prostitution under every aspect, independently of the moral guilt of governments which guarantee it. We must enter upon a grand crusade, not only against legal prostitution, but against profligacy itself; we must form an

"'This Is the Logic of Demons!'" is from Josephine E. Butler, *Personal Reminiscences of a Great Crusade* (London: Horace Marshall & Son, 1911), pp. 119, 121.

indomitable league. . . . We must pursue vice up to its source; we must follow it in all its forms and in all its hiding-places; we must attack the unholy literature, the impure art, and the debased drama which are connected with it. Above all, we must combat the disastrous delusion, so fixed in many minds, that vice is an inevitable fatality; we must hold up before our youth the ideal of purity and of domestic worth.

CONSIDER THIS:

- What were the Contagious Disease Acts, and why was Josephine Butler opposed to the practice of prostitution? What was her ideal for women?

"I Incite This Meeting to Rebellion!" (1912)

EMMELINE PANKHURST

Emmeline Pankhurst (1858–1928) founded the Women's Social and Political Union in 1903 and was the leader of the militant suffragists until the beginning of World War I in 1914. She and her daughter Christabel disrupted political meetings, organized riots, and endured hunger strikes in prison to call attention to women's demands for the vote. Her tactics were not approved or shared by all women's reform organizations, but her methods became influential among more radical American suffragists. Pankhurst gave this speech just after having been released from prison for leading a violent demonstration in which the windows of several elegant London shops had been smashed by women wielding hammers.

It always seems to me when the anti-suffrage members of the [British] Government criticize militancy in women that it is very like beasts of prey reproaching the gentler animals who turn in desperate resistance when at the point of death. . . . Ladies and gentlemen, the only recklessness the militant suffragists have shown about human life has been about their own lives and not about the lives of others, and I say here and now that it never has been and never will be the policy of the Women's Social and Political Union recklessly to endanger human life. We leave that to the enemy. We leave that to the men in their warfare. It is not the method of women. . . . There is something that governments care far more for than human life, and that is the security of property, and so it is through property that we shall strike the enemy. From henceforward the women who agree with me will say, "We disregard your laws, gentlemen, we set the liberty and the dignity and the welfare of women above all such considerations, and we shall continue this war as we have done in the past; and what sacrifice of property, or what injury to property accrues will not be our fault. It will be the fault of that Government who admits the justice of our demands, but refuses to concede them. . . .

Be militant each in your own way. Those of you who can express your militancy by going to the House of Commons and refusing to leave without satisfaction, as we did in the early days—do so. . . . Those of you who can break windows—break them. Those of you who can still further attack the secret idol of property, so as to make the Government realize that property is as greatly endangered by women's suffrage as it was by the Chartists of old—do so.

And my last word to the Government: I incite this meeting to rebellion! . . . Take me,

"'I Incite This Meeting to Rebellion!'" is from Emmeline Pankhurst, *My Own Story* (New York: Hearst's International Library Co., 1914).

if you dare, but if you dare I tell you this: you will not keep me in prison.

CONSIDER THIS:

- Why was Emmeline Pankhurst so important to the women's movement? What tactics for achieving change did she advocate and practice? Why was property the focus of her campaign? Do you agree with her argument?

The Revolt Against Reason

I know my fate. One day my name will be associated with the memory of something tremendous—a crisis without equal on earth, the most profound collision of conscience, a decision that was conjured up against everything that had been believed, demanded, hallowed so far. I am no man—I am dynamite.

—FRIEDRICH NIETZSCHE

I welcome all signs that a more manly, a warlike age is now starting, an age which above all will honor valor again. . . . For, believe me, the secret which enables us to harvest in life the greatest fruitfulness and the greatest enjoyment is: to live dangerously! Build your cities under Vesuvius! Send your ships into uncharted seas! Live at war with your peers and yourselves!

—FRIEDRICH NIETZSCHE

Intellectual history, or the study of ideas, is an exciting, sometimes frustrating discipline. Ideas are abstract and intangible but often provide the foundation and justification for political and social change and thus are an important component of historical inquiry.

Europeans, at the turn of the century, could lay claim to a long intellectual heritage. The Enlightenment of the eighteenth century had emphasized rationalism and toleration, as well as an appreciation of the methods of scientific inquiry. The Romantic movement of the early nineteenth century valued feelings, intuition, the imagination, and artistic freedom as vital components in the exploration of human dimension. But by the mid-nineteenth century, science had once again attained prestige in the intellectual world as theories were advanced to explain, through rational scientific method, the development of human thought, social and economic interrelationships, and the evolution of plants and animals by natural selection. The emphasis on scientific method produced an intellectual skepticism toward anything that could not be proved by tangible evidence. Scholars sought to free themselves from the constraints of religion and Christian morality in particular. In his book *The Life of Jesus* (1835), David Friedrich Strauss questioned whether any genuine historical evidence could confirm the very existence of the preeminent religious figure in Western civilization.

During the second half of the nineteenth century, philosophy even confronted the rational processes of scientific inquiry. Perhaps human beings had to go further, beyond the attack on organized religion, beyond rational experimentation and postulation, to question the very source of our human values within the deep recesses of the mind. Sigmund Freud (1856–1939), with his theses on human motivation, the efficacy of dreams, and the complexities that lay beneath the calm human surface, gave birth to a new science of the mind: psychoanalysis.

More fervent even than understanding the complexities of the mind was the desire to tap the essence of the heart—the inner spirit of the soul wherein the truth of life was stored, a vision of pure God, unadulterated by the mask of the Catholic church or any other religious organization that sought to reveal the intent of God.

Fyodor Dostoevsky (1821–1881) was one of Russia's greatest novelists. He finished his most influential novel, *The Brothers Karamozov,* in 1880, near the end of his life. In it he created a vast panorama of humankind's eternal quest for spiritual insight. In the following selection from that novel, Dostoevsky envisions the Spanish Inquisition of the sixteenth century with the Grand Inquisitor confronting God himself. The Grand Inquisitor rejects the truth of God by substituting God's will with his own interpretation of morality on earth. Dostoevsky believed that knowledge of God must stem from the exploration of one's own soul without the optical illusion of Christianity. The rejection of Christianity was not a rejection of God but the rejection of any method of inquiry or institution that restricted the power of the human spirit to explore the beautiful, but hazardous, uncharted regions of the soul.

The Grand Inquisitor (1880)

FYODOR DOSTOEVSKY

[*Guards have detained God in a Seville prison to await judgment by the Grand Inquisitor, a cardinal of the Church. During the night the cardinal enters the cell and confronts God*]:

"Is it You? You? . . . Don't answer, be silent. What can You say, indeed? I know too well what You would say. And You have no right to add anything to what You have said of old. Why, then, have You come to hinder us? For You have come to hinder us, You know that. But do You know what will be tomorrow? I know not who You are and care not to know whether it is You or only a semblance of Him, but tomorrow I shall condemn You and burn You at the stake as the worst of heretics. And the very people who have today kissed Your feet, tomorrow at the faintest sign from me will rush to heap up the embers of Your fire. . . ."

"Why have You come now to hinder us? And why do You look silently and searchingly at me with Your mild eyes? Be angry. I don't want your love, for I do not love You. And what use is it for me to hide anything from You? Don't I know to Whom I am speaking? All that I say is known to You already. And is it for me to conceal from You our mystery? Perhaps it is Your will to hear it from my lips. Listen, then . . . ."

"Mankind as a whole has always striven to organise a universal state. There have been many great nations with great histories, but the more highly they were developed the more unhappy they were, for they felt more acutely than other people the craving for world-wide union. The great conquerors, Timors [Tammerlane] and Ghenghis-Khans, whirled like hurricanes over the face of the earth striving to subdue its people, and they too were but the unconscious expression of the same craving for universal unity. Had You taken the world and Caesar's purple, You would have founded the universal state and have given universal

"The Grand Inquisitor" is from Fyodor Dostoevsky, *The Brothers Karamozov* (New York: Modern Library, n.d.), pp. 310; 315–319. Translation has been modernized by the editor.

peace. For who can rule men if not he who holds their conscience and their bread in his hands. We have taken the sword of Caesar, and in taking it, of course, have rejected You and followed *him*. Oh, ages are yet to come of the confusion of free thought, of their science and cannibalism. For having begun to build their tower of Babel without us, they will end, of course, with cannibalism. But then the beast will crawl to us and lick our feet and spatter them with tears of blood. And we shall sit upon the beast and raise the cup, and on it will be written, 'Mystery.' But then, and only then, the reign of peace and happiness will come for men. You are proud of Your elect, but You have only the elect while we give rest to all. And besides, how many of those elect, those mighty ones who could become elect, have grown weary waiting for You, and have transferred and will transfer the powers of their spirit and the warmth of their heart to the other camp, and end by raising their *free* banner against You? You have lifted up that banner Yourself. But with us all will be happy and will no more rebel nor destroy one another as under Your freedom. Oh, we shall persuade them that they will only become free when they renounce their freedom to us and submit to us. And shall we be right or shall we be lying? They will be convinced that we are right, for they will remember the horrors of slavery and confusion to which Your freedom brought them. Freedom, free thought and science, will lead them into such straits and will bring them face to face with such marvels and insoluble mysteries, that some of them, the fierce and rebellious, will destroy themselves, others, rebellious but weak, will destroy one another, while the rest, weak and unhappy, will crawl fawning to our feet and whine to us: 'Yes, you were right, you alone possess His mystery, and we come back to you, save us from ourselves!'" . . .

"Too, too well they know the value of complete submission! And until men know that, they will be unhappy. Who is most to blame for their not knowing it, speak? Who scattered the flock will come together again and will submit once more, and then it will be once for all. Then we shall give them the quiet humble happiness of weak creatures such as they are by nature. Oh, we shall persuade them at last not to be proud. We shall show them that they are weak, that they are only pitiful children, but that childlike happiness is the sweetest of all. They will become timid and will look to us and huddle close to us in fear, as chicks to the hen. They will marvel at us and will be awe-stricken before us, and will be proud at our being so powerful and clever, that we have been able to subdue such a turbulent flock of thousands of millions. They will tremble impotently before our wrath, their minds will grow fearful, they will be quick to shed tears like women and children, but they will be just as ready at a sign from us to pass to laughter and rejoicing, to happy mirth and childish song. Yes, we shall set them to work, but in their leisure hours we shall make their life like a child's game, with children's songs and innocent dances. Oh, we shall allow them even sin, they are weak and helpless, and they will love us like children because we allow them to sin. We shall tell them that every sin will be expiated, if it is done with our permission, that we allow them to sin because we love them, and the punishment for these sins we take upon ourselves. And we shall take it upon ourselves, and they will adore us as their saviours who have taken on themselves their sins before god. And they will have no secrets from us. We shall allow or forbid them to live with their wives and mistresses, to have or not to have children–according to whether they have been obedient or disobedient–and they will submit to us gladly and cheerfully. The most painful secrets of their conscience, all, all they will bring to us, and we shall have an answer for all. And they will be glad to believe our answer, for it will save them from the great anxiety and terrible agony they endure at present in making a free decision for themselves. And all will be happy, all the millions of creatures except the hundred thousand who rule over them. For only we, we who guard the mystery, shall be unhappy. There will be thousands of millions of happy babes, and a hundred thousand sufferers who have taken upon themselves the curse of the knowledge of good and evil. Peacefully they will die, peacefully they will expire in Your name, and beyond the grave they will find nothing but death. But we shall keep the secret, and for their happiness we shall allure them with the reward of heaven and eternity. Though if there were anything in the other world, it certainly would not be for such as they. It is prophesied that You will come again in victory, You will come with Your chosen, the proud and strong, but we will say that they have only saved themselves, but we have saved all. We are told that the harlot who sits upon the beast, and holds in her hands the *mystery*, shall be put to shame, that the weak will rise up again, and will rend her royal purple and will strip naked her loathsome body [Rev. 17]. But then I will stand up and point out to Thee the thousand millions of happy children who have known no sin. And we who have taken their sins upon us for their happiness will stand up before You and say: 'Judge us if You can and dare.' Know that I do not fear You. Know that I too have been in the wilderness, I too have lived on roots and locusts, I too prized the freedom with which You the strong and powerful, thirsting 'to make up the number.' But I awakened and would not serve madness. I turned back and joined the ranks of those who have corrected Your work. I left the proud and went back to the humble, for the happiness of the humble. What I say to You will come to pass, and our dominion will be built up. I repeat, tomorrow You shall see that obedient flock who at a sign from me will hasten to heap up the hot cinders about the pile on which I shall burn You for coming to hinder us. For if any one has ever deserved our fires, it is You. Tomorrow I shall burn You. I have spoken."

CONSIDER THIS:

- In "The Grand Inquisitor," what is Fyodor Dostoevsky's message regarding Christianity? What is the role of the church in human society? Are you disturbed by this excerpt? What is the fate of God at the end of the confrontation?

Faith, Love, and Hope: "Enough! Enough!" (1887)

FRIEDRICH NIETZSCHE

Perhaps the most radical and powerful detractor of the positive value of reason was the German philosopher Friedrich Nietzsche (1844–1900). He was raised as a child prodigy and became a professor of classical philology at Basel University at the astonishing age of twenty-five. His first book, *The Birth of Tragedy* (1872), shocked the world of classical studies and was roundly condemned for its radical interpretations. Nietzsche was completely at odds with the values of his age. At various times in his career, he attacked democracy, Christianity, nationalism, rational analysis, and the so-called progressive nature of science. Nietzsche defined the political arena in terms of the "will to power." For Nietzsche, democratic political values and the concept of equal rights actively masked a "lust for power" that was at the heart of human nature. He introduced the concept of the *Übermensch,* or "Overman," who through his mental and physical authority would rise to dominate the weak. Christian morality, with its emphasis on peace and brotherly love, created a servile mentality. In the following selections from

"Faith, Love, and Hope" is from Friedrich Nietzsche, *The Genealogy of Morals* in *The Philosophy of Nietzsche* (New York: Modern Library, 1922), pp. 647–654.

his *Genealogy of Morals* (1887) and *The Gay Science* (1882), Nietzsche presents some of his most forceful ideas regarding the relationship between the "morality of slaves" and the "morality of aristocrats." Nietzsche emphasizes his desire to strip away the masks of society by declaring that "God is dead!" Human beings who so willed could create a new moral order that would reject the rational philosophy of the weak and replace it with a glorification of pride, assertiveness, and pure strength.

The profound, icy mistrust which the German provokes, as soon as he arrives at power–even at the present time–is always still an aftermath of that inextinguishable horror with which for whole centuries Europe has regarded the wrath of the blond Teuton beast. . . . Granted the truth of the theory now believed to be true, that the very *essence of all civilization* is to *train* out of man, the beast of prey, a tame and civilized animal, a domesticated animal, it follows indubitably that we must regard as the real *tools of civilization* all those instincts of reaction and resentment, by the help of which the aristocratic races, together with their ideals, were finally degraded and overpowered; though that has not yet come to be synonymous with saying that the bearers of those tools also *represented* the civilization. It is rather the contrary that is not only probable–nay, it is *palpable* today; these bearers of vindictive instincts that have to be bottled up, these descendants of all European and non-European slavery, especially of the pre-Aryan population–these people, I say, represent the *decline* of humanity! These "tools of civilization" are a disgrace to humanity, and constitute in reality more of an argument against civilization, more of a reason why civilization should be suspected. One may be perfectly justified in being always afraid of the blond beast that lies at the core of all aristocratic races, and in being on one's guard: but who would not a hundred times prefer to be afraid, when one at the same time admires, than to be immune from fear, at the cost of being perpetually obsessed with the loathsome spectacle of the distorted, the dwarfed, the stunted, the envenomed? And is that not our fate? What produces today our repulsion towards "man"?–for we *suffer* from "man," there is no doubt about it. It is not fear, it is rather that we have nothing more to fear from men; it is that the worm "man" is in the foreground and pullulates; it is that the "tame man," the wretched mediocre and unedifying creature, has learned to consider himself a goal and a pinnacle, an inner meaning, an historic principle, a "higher man"; yes, it is that he has a certain right so to consider himself, in so far as he feels that in contrast to that excess of deformity, disease, exhaustion, and effeteness whose odor is beginning to pollute present-day Europe, he at any rate has achieved a relative success, he at any rate still says "yes" to life. . . .

The Slave Morality

Will any one look a little into—right into–the mystery of how *ideals* are *manufactured* in this world? Who has the courage to do it? Come! . . . Now speak! What is happening below down yonder? Speak out! Tell what you see, many of the most dangerous curiosity–for now I am the listener.

"I see nothing, I hear the more. It is a cautious, spiteful, gentle whispering and muttering together in all the corners and crannies. It seems to me that they are lying; sugary softness adheres to every sound. Weakness is turned to *merit*, there is no doubt about it–it is just as you say."

Further!

"And the impotence which requites not, is turned to 'goodness,' craven baseness to meekness, submission to those whom one hates, to obedience (namely obedience to one of whom they say that he ordered this submission–they call him God). The inoffensive character of the weak, the very cowardice in which he is rich, his standing at the door, his forced necessity of waiting, gain here fine names, such as 'patience,' which is also called 'virtue'; not being able to avenge one's self, is called not wishing to avenge one's self, perhaps even forgiveness (for *they* know not what they do–we alone know what they do). They also talk of the 'love of their enemies' and swear thereby.

Further!

"They are miserable, there is no doubt about it, all these whisperers and counterfeiters in the corners. . . . But enough! Enough! I can endure it no longer. Bad air! Bad air! These workshops *where ideals are manufactured*–verily they reek with the crassest lies." . . .

Now do I hear for the first time that which they have said so often: 'We good, *we are the righteous*'–what they demand they call not revenge but 'the triumph of *righteousness*'; what they hate is not their enemy, no, they hate 'unrighteousness,' 'godlessness'; what they believe in and hope is not the hope of revenge, the intoxication of sweet revenge, . . . but the victory of God, of the *righteous God* over the 'godless'; what is left for them to love in this world is not their brothers in hate, but their 'brothers in love,' as they say, all the good and righteous on the earth."

And how do they name that which serves them as a solace against all the troubles of life–their phantasmagoria of their anticipated future blessedness?

"How? Do I hear right? They call it 'the last judgment' the advent of their kingdom, the kingdom of God'–but in the *meanwhile* they live 'in faith,' 'in love,' 'in hope.'"

Enough! Enough!

FIGURE 9.4 Portrait of Friedrich Nietzsche: "I am no man—I am dynamite!" *(Library of Congress)*

"God Is Dead!"

FRIEDRICH NIETZSCHE

Have you not heard of that mad man who on a bright morning lit a lantern, ran to the market place, and shouted incessantly, "I seek God! I seek God!" Among the many of those who do not believe in god and who were standing around there, he provoked much laughter. Shy, did god get lost? asked one. Did he lose his way like a child? asked another. Or is he hiding? Is he afraid of us? Has he left on a boat? Has he emigrated? Thus they shouted and laughed. The man jumped into their midst and pierced them with his glances.

"Whither is God?" he shouted. "I shall tell you. We have killed him—you and I. We all are his murderers. But how have we done it? How were we able to drink up the ocean? Who gave us the sponge to wipe out the whole horizon? What did we do when we unchained this earth from its sun? Whither is it moving now? Whither are we moving? Away from all suns? Are we not falling continually? Falling backward, sideward, forward, in all directions? Is there any up or down left? Are we not straying as through infinite nothingness? Do we not feel the breath of empty space? Has it not become colder? Is not night and more night coming on all the time? Must not lanterns be lit in the morning? Do we not yet hear the noise of the gravediggers who are burying God? Do we not begin to smell god's putrefaction? Gods, to, putrefy. God is dead. God will remain dead. And we have killed him. How shall we, the murderers of all murderers comfort ourselves? The holiest and mightiest of all that the world has ever owned has bled to death under our knives: who will wipe this blood off us? With what water can we clean ourselves? . . . Is not the greatness of this deed too great for us? Must not we ourselves become gods in order to seem worthy of it? There has never been a greater deed: whoever will be born after us, will be on account of this deed part of a higher history than all prior history."

Here the mad man became silent and glanced at his listeners; they too had become silent and stared at him with a strange feeling. Finally, he threw his lantern on the ground so that it broke into pieces and was extinguished. Then he said: "I have come too soon, my time has not come yet. This tremendous event is still on its way, it has not yet reached the ears of man. Lightning and thunder require time, the light of the stars requires time, deeds require time even after they are done, to be seen and heard. This deed is still more distant from them than the most distant stars–and yet they themselves have done it."

On the same day, we are told, the mad man entered a number of churches and there sang his *requiem aeternam deo*. Led out and questioned, he, according to the report, gave always the same reply, "What are these churches now if they are not the tombs and sepulchers of God?"

Consider This:

- What general ideas seem to flow through the selections of Friedrich Nietzsche? What are his thoughts concerning power, God, and Christianity? What does Nietzsche value? What does he mean by the declaration "Build your cities under Vesuvius! Send your ships into uncharted seas!"? How does Nietzsche embody the "revolt against reason" that was current at the end of the nineteenth century?

"'God Is Dead!'" is from Oscar Levy, ed., *The Complete Works of Friedrich Nietzsche*, trans. by Anthony M. Ludovici (London, 1911).

Part III

The Twentieth Century and Beyond

10

THE GREAT WAR (1914–1918)

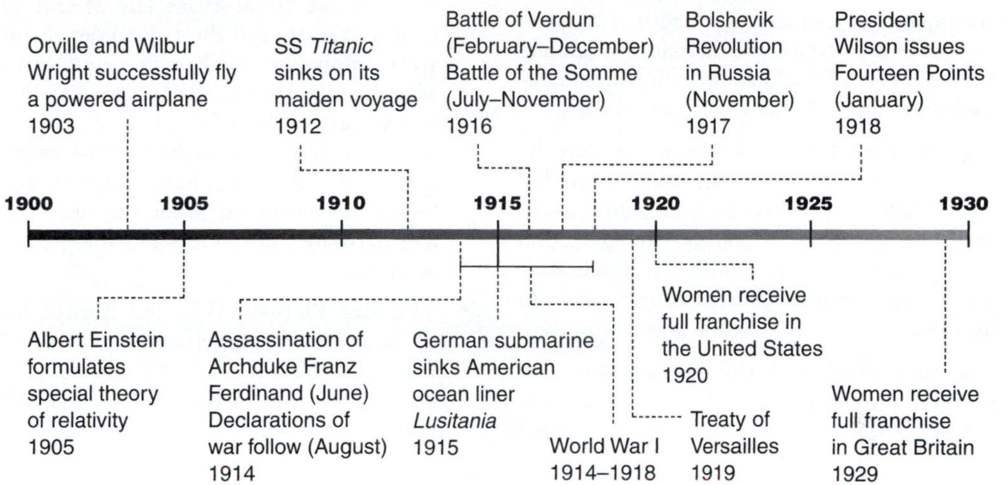

The next dreadful thing to a battle lost is a battle won.

—ARTHUR WELLESLEY, DUKE OF WELLINGTON

Only a general who was a barbarian would send his men to certain death against the concentrated power of my new gun.

—HIRAM MAXIM (INVENTOR OF THE MACHINE GUN)

The rain drives on, the stinking mud becomes evilly yellow, the shell holes fill up with green-white water, the roads and tracks are covered in inches of slime, the black, dying trees ooze and sweat and the shells never cease. They alone plunge overhead tearing away the rotting tree stumps. . . . It is unspeakable, Godless, hopeless.

—PAUL WALSH

What's the use of worrying, it never was worthwhile/So, pack up your troubles in your old kit bag and smile, smile, smile. . . .

—WORLD WAR I SONG

CHAPTER THEMES

- **The Power Structure:** The period beginning about 1870 witnessed a great competition for imperial expansion as both Germany and Italy had unified, and France, Austria, and Great Britain invested their monarchs with the guardianship of national pride. By 1918, however, the emperors of Austria and France, and the kaiser of Germany had all been deposed.

What happened and how had the structure of political power shifted?

- **Imperialism:** How did the intense economic and political rivalries between European governments lead to war? Was this the kind of war that European leaders expected to fight?
- **The Varieties of Truth:** What propaganda techniques and themes were used by European governments to establish a martial spirit among their soldiers? Did soldiers and diplomats actually believe this was "the war to end all wars"?
- **Women in History:** It has been said that the real victims of war are not the soldiers who kill and are killed but the women who support broken families, wander as homeless refugees, and sacrifice their sons and husbands to forces outside of their control. What is your reaction to this idea?
- **The Individual and the Institution:** The twentieth century has been described as a "century of holocaust" wherein the state dominated the individual and produced an ethical vacuum. Some have asserted that technology has created an impersonal world devoid of spiritual commitment. Do you agree? Is God dead?
- **Revolution and Historical Transition:** What impact did new military technology such as the machine gun, tank, airplane, and poisonous gas have on the Great War? Did World War I, World War II, and the Cold War encompass a transitional period between an "old world" where personal valor and courage were esteemed and a "new world" of impersonal, abstract war where the stakes were higher and the destruction of humanity a distinct possibility? Do technological advancements make war more destructive or more antiseptic—and therefore more acceptable?
- **The Big Picture:** Why did Europe lose an entire generation of men during the Great War? What did they die for? Did the peace settlements at the end of World War I make World War II inevitable?

After the defeat of Napoleon at the Battle of Waterloo in 1815, the victors at the Congress of Vienna decided that Europe had to be governed by a policy of deterrence that resisted dominance by any one country. Nations required comparable strength to maintain the balance of power and thus preserve the peace. Great Britain led the way and applied this policy successfully throughout the nineteenth century. During this time, however, Europe was changing. The Industrial Revolution had increased the demand for trade, and various countries sought markets in Africa and the East, establishing hegemony over a region by military force. Imperialism and competition abroad affected the sense of security and the balance of power that were crucial to the preservation of peace at home. In addition, new factors were being introduced that further threatened to disrupt the balance.

The first serious threat to the Pax Britannica of the nineteenth century came from the expansion of industry and the accompanying scientific progress. In the first decade of the twentieth century, new weapons were being developed, as were more rapid forms of communication and transportation, including the telegraph, the automobile, the railway, and the steamship. These technological advancements presented new possibilities for highly mobilized warfare that could be better coordinated and managed.

The second serious threat to the balance of European power in the late-nineteenth century was Germany. By 1870, the Prussians had unified north and west Germany through a policy of "blood and iron." The various regions of Germany had always been disunited, defying such masters as the Romans, Charlemagne, the Holy Roman Emperors, and Napoleon. But Kaiser Wilhelm I of Prussia (1797–1888), together with his master statesman Otto von Bismarck (1815–1898) and his general Count Helmut von Moltke, made highly effective use of the military capabilities of a thoroughly disciplined and well-supported army. To achieve unification, Prussia had beaten and humiliated the French in 1870 and succeeded in forging a unified German Reich. The balance of power had been upset and the lesson was clear: No nation in Europe could feel secure without training all of its young men for war, establishing a system of reserves, and creating a general staff that would prepare plans for potential wars and oversee a scheme for mobilization.

The concept of mobilization is very important in understanding why Europe and the world went to war. By 1914, every continental power had a complex plan and timetable for mobilizing against the most likely opponent or combination of enemies. When a country mobilized for war, its reserve troops were called to active duty, placed in the field, and supported with necessary rations, equipment, and armament. Timing was essential. Full mobilization took weeks, and it was important to get the process started before your enemy was ready to commit to such a policy. Hence the beginning of hostilities came when the various chiefs of state were convinced that military "necessity" required a mobilization order and that further delay would spell defeat by allowing the opponent to gain a military advantage that could not be overcome. Because mobilization involved a

FIGURE 10.1 This landscape of devastation in Belgium gives testimony to the mindless destruction that was such a part of the Great War. (*Reproduced by permission of the Trustees of the Imperial War Museum, London*)

radical shift of the economy to maximum production and troop movements could be detected by other nations within hours, the mobilization order could not be rescinded without the prospect of diplomatic and economic disaster. William H. McNeill, in *The Rise of the West*, notes that "the first weeks of World War I presented the amazing spectacle of vast human machines operating in a truly inhuman fashion and moving at least approximately according to predetermined and irreversible plans. The millions of persons composing the rival machines behaved almost as though they had lost individual will and intelligence." The "predetermined and irreversible" plans were centered on a military theory by Karl von Clausewitz that was accepted by all the general staffs of Europe: A swift and decisive battle that led to the initial destruction of the enemy's forces would achieve ultimate success. None planned for a long war—three or four months at most.

Thus the nations of Europe were powder kegs waiting to go off when in June 1914 the heir to the Austro-Hungarian Empire, the archduke Franz Ferdinand, was assassinated at Sarajevo. The diplomats talked and then the armies mobilized one by one. The "guns of August" soon enveloped Europe in a war that was to last not four months but four years. Over 8.5 million people were killed, with a total casualty count of more than 37.5 million.

This chapter gives an overall picture of World War I, or what has been more accurately called the Great War. This was war on a world scale, involving hostilities in Africa and the Balkans as well as an American presence. And it was war on some of the cruelest terms. Rules were changing. There were no longer strict orders to exempt the civilian population from harm. Nor were there moral constraints on the use of submarines, machine guns, and poisonous gas; all became permanent fixtures of conflict. The Great War stands unequaled in terms of blood sacrificed for miserable accomplishment. To die for a so-called "victory" of 100 yards of land needed justification, which was rarely forthcoming. The questions are disturbing and perhaps unanswerable: Why did commanders send their men repeatedly "over the top" of the trenches, across "no man's land," and into the bloody rain of machine gun fire? Why was this slaughter of human life condoned by the diplomats and even by the soldiers themselves? Why did Europe lose an entire generation of men?

As we look back on the twentieth century, our perspective is clearly focused at the midpoint, when the threat of fascism and all the attendant horrors of World War II seemed to be the defining moments of an age of anxiety. And yet, many historians believe that our modern world was fashioned at the outset of the century in the trenches of Europe, at the confluence of nineteenth-century arrogance and twentieth-century technology. Europe in 1914 was on the brink of "becoming." In a sense, the transition had been foreshadowed in one of the great cultural moments of the period. In 1913, the young Russian composer Igor Stravinsky premiered his new ballet to elite society in Paris. The *Rite of Spring* was a story of primal ritual, of sacrifice to the earth and the ceremonial renewal of life. The irregular rhythms, dissonant harmonies, and blatant sexuality shocked the crowd, which rioted in response.

The ritual of primal sacrifice would be played out during the next four years as the earth claimed so many human lives. When the war ended in 1918, the world of the nineteenth century had been forever altered. The thin veneer of civilization had been shattered and the nations of Europe had difficulty defining what had happened and why. Europe would be led out of this abyss of disillusionment and despair by those promising order and respect: Benito Mussolini and Adolf Hitler.

The Road to War (1900–1914)

Though the object of being a Great Power is to be able to fight a Great War, the only way of remaining a Great Power is not to fight one.

—A. J. P. Taylor

Diplomats are just as essential to starting a war as soldiers are for finishing it. . . . You take diplomacy out of war and the whole thing would fall flat in a week.

—Will Rogers

You may not be interested in war. But war is interested in you.

—Leo Tolstoy

The Celebration of War

Military glory! The image of victorious armies engaged in limited campaigns designed to further the righteous expansion of domain or to win security or to establish a national identity—this vision had fired the imagination of European leaders in the nineteenth century. War was an opportunity to parade all the trappings of authority: neatly pressed uniforms with braid and insignia, plumed helmets, polished swords that sparkled in the sun—all of this reflected the pomp and display that fed the egos and confirmed the superiority of class. War was a celebration of image. But this image was shallow, indeed, because just below the surface of the glitter lay the agony of pain and destruction.

The Crimean War (1854–1856) was the first campaign to be photographed. Through the senseless cavalry charges in the face of cannon, the degradation of cholera, and the lack of decisive victory, France, Britain, Russia, and Turkey denied the reality of the photographs and failed to register despair about this short and inconclusive war. The vision of victory with troops returning home covered in glory sustained in the imagination until the first battles of the Great War in 1914. The European accumulation of empire in India and Africa had inspired the competitive juices. If Britannia "ruled the waves" and Germany deserved its "place in the sun," then the process of conflict would not take long—and it would be glorious.

This attitude was a feature of the writings of the German historian Heinrich von Treitschke (1834–1896). From 1874 on, he held the chair of modern history at the University of Berlin. His ideal of power and heroism reflected the confidence in German military superiority, and it infected students and statesmen alike with the belief in Germany's right to rule. In the first selection from a lecture published posthumously, Germany's mission is clear: War was a necessity to be embraced.

"Without War, No State Could Exist"

HEINRICH VON TREITSCHKE

The essential function of the State is the conduct of war. The long oblivion into which this principle had fallen is a proof of how effeminate the science of government had become in civilian hands. . . .

Without war no State could exist. All those we know of arose through war, and the protection of their members by armed force remains their primary and essential task. War, therefore, will endure to the end of history, as long as there is multiplicity of States. The laws of human thought and of human nature forbid any alternative, neither is one to be wished for. The blind worshiper of an eternal peace falls into the error of isolating the State, or dreams of one which is universal, which we have already seen to be at variance with reason.

Even as it is impossible to conceive of a tribunal above the State, which we have recognized as sovereign in its very essence, so it is likewise impossible to banish the idea of war from the world. . . . The great strides which civilization makes against barbarism and unreason are only made actual by the sword. Between civilized nations also war is the form of litigation by which States make their claims valid. The argument brought forward in these terrible law suits of the nations compel as no argument in civil suits can ever do. . . .

Moreover war is a uniting as well as a dividing element among nations; it does not draw them together in enmity only, for through its means they learn to know and to respect each other's peculiar qualities.

It is important not to look upon war always as a judgment from God. Its consequences are impermanent; but the life of a nation is reckoned by centuries, and the final verdict can only be pronounced after the survey of whole epochs. . . .

The grandeur of war lies in the utter annihilation of puny man in the great conception of the State, and it brings out the full magnificence of the sacrifice of fellow-countrymen for one another. In the war the chaff is winnowed from the wheat. . . .

It is war which fosters the political idealism which the materialist rejects. What a disaster for civilization it would be if mankind blotted its heroes from memory. The heroes of a nation are the figures which rejoice and inspire the spirit of its youth, and the writers whose words ring like trumpet blasts become the idols of our boyhood and our early manhood. He who feels no answering thrill is unworthy to bear arms for his country. To appeal from this judgement to Christianity would be sheer perversity, for does not the Bible distinctly say that the ruler shall rule by the sword, and again that greater love hath no man than to lay down his life for his friend? To Aryan races, who are before all things courageous, the foolish preaching of everlasting peace has always been vain. They have always been men enough to maintain with the sword what they have attained through the spirit. . . .

But it is not worth while to speak further of these matters, for the God above us will see to it that war shall return again, a terrible medicine for mankind diseased.

Despite all this it is not denied that the progress of culture must make wars both shorter and rarer. They must become shorter and rarer owing to man's natural horror of bloodshed, as well as to the size and quality of modern armies, for it is impossible to see

"'Without War, No State Could Exist'" is from Heinrich von Treitschke, *Politics*, trans. by Blanche Dugdale (London: Constable, 1916).

FIGURE 10.2 The fears and aggression that permeated Europe at the outset of World War I are expressed in this painting by Rudolf Henneberg. Note the emphasis on the Kaiser's insatiable lust for world conquest and dominion. Was this the primary reason that the world went to war in 1914? (*The American Legion*)

how the burdens of a great war could long be borne under the present conditions. But it would be false to conclude that wars can ever cease. They neither can nor should, so long as the state is sovereign and stands among its peers. . . .

CONSIDER THIS:

- What are the arguments of Heinrich von Treitschke? Are you persuaded by his idea that "without war no state could exist"? Why do nations often celebrate war? Could this itself be a cause of war?

Establishing "Laws of War": The Hague Convention (1907)

There were those, however, who did not fall prey to the celebration of war. The Hague Convention of 1907 sought to promote peaceful coexistence by establishing "laws of war" that were intended to control or limit the destruction that always accompanies conflict; the convention was to meet next in 1915 but, ironically, was canceled because of the Great War.

SECTION II: HOSTILITIES

Chapter 1—Means of Injuring the Enemy, Sieges, and Bombardments

Article 22. The right of belligerents to adopt means of injuring the enemy is not unlimited.

Article 23. In addition to the prohibitions provided by special Conventions, it is especially forbidden—

(a) To employ poison or poisoned weapons;
(b) To kill or wound treacherously individuals belonging to the hostile nation or army;
(c) To kill or wound an enemy who, having laid down his arms, or having no longer the means of defence, has surrendered at discretion;

Article 25. The attack or bombardment, by whatever means, of towns, villages, dwellings, or buildings which are undefended is prohibited.

Article 26. The officer in command of an attacking force must, before commencing a bombardment, except in cases of assault, do all in his power to warn the authorities.

Article 27. In sieges and bombardments all necessary steps must be taken to spare, as far as possible, buildings dedicated to religion, art, science, or charitable purposes, historic monuments, hospitals, and places where the sick and wounded are collected, provided they are not being used at the time for military purposes. It is the duty of the besieged to indicate the presence of such buildings or places by distinctive and visible signs, which shall be notified to the enemy beforehand.

Article 28. The pillage of a town or place, even when taken by assault, is prohibited.

THE BROADER PERSPECTIVE:

- In 1864, the English prelate John Henry Cardinal Newman said, "There is such a thing as legitimate warfare: war has its laws; there are things which may fairly be done, and things which may not be done." Do you agree or disagree? Analyze the articles of the Hague Convention of 1907. Are "laws of war" so unrealistic? Which of the articles do you respect the most?

"Establishing 'Laws of War'" is from Carnegie Endowment for International Peace, *The Hague Conventions and Declarations of 1899 and 1907* (New York: Oxford University Press, 1915), pp. 116–118.

"Blind Obedience to Primitive Instincts" (1910)

NORMAN ANGELL

In 1910, historian Norman Angell challenged the whole doctrine that war had justification in the evolutionary law of survival of the fittest.

What are the fundamental motives that explain the present rivalry of armaments in Europe, notably the Anglo-German? Each nation pleads the need for defence; but this implies that someone is likely to attack, and has therefore a presumed interest in so doing. What are the motives which each State thus fears its neighbors may obey?

They are based on the universal assumption that a nation, in order to find outlets for expanding population and increasing industry, or simply to ensure the best conditions possible for its people, is necessarily pushed to territorial expansion and the exercise of political force against others. . . . It is assumed that a nation's relative prosperity is broadly determined by its political power; that nations being competing units, advantage in the last resort goes to the possessor of preponderant military force, the weaker goes to the wall, as in the other forms of the struggle for life. The author challenges this whole doctrine. . . .

War has no longer the justification that it makes for the survival of the fittest; it involves the survival of the less fit. The idea that the struggle between nations is a part of the evolutionary law of man's advance involves a profound misreading of the biological analogy.

The warlike nations do not inherit the earth; they represent the decaying human element. . . .

Are we, in blind obedience to primitive instincts and old prejudices, enslaved by the old catchwords and that curious indolence which makes the revision of old ideas unpleasant, to duplicate indefinitely on the political and economic side a condition from which we have liberated ourselves on the religious side? Are we to continue to struggle, as so many good men struggled in the first dozen centuries of Christendom—spilling oceans of blood, wasting mountains of treasure—to achieve what is at bottom a logical absurdity, to accomplish something which, when accomplished, can avail us nothing, and which, if it could avail us anything, would condemn the nations of the world to never-ending bloodshed and the constant defeat of all those aims which men, in their sober hours, know to be alone worthy of sustained endeavor?

Compare and Contrast:

- In 1910, Norman Angell declared that "warlike nations do not inherit the earth; they represent the decaying human element." Compare this to Heinrich von Treitschke's vision of war as a civilizing agent through which humankind makes strides against "barbarism and unreason." How can there be such a wide chasm between perspectives?
- Angell warns against "old prejudices enslaved by the old catchwords." Can you find some of these catch phrases that justify war in the writing of von Treitschke?

"'Blind Obedience to Primitive Instincts'" is from Norman Angell, *The Great Illusion* (New York: G. P. Putnam's Sons, 1913), pp. ix–xiii, 381–382.

THEME: THE INDIVIDUAL AND THE INSTITUTION

THE ARTISTIC VISION

Kandinsky and the Visual Language of War

Improvisation 30 (Cannons) (1913)

VASILY KANDINSKY

In 1912, the great ocean liner *Titanic* set sail from Britain to America. It was described as the quintessential expression of human technology—"unsinkable" said its creators. In 1985, the Titanic was finally discovered on the bottom of the Atlantic, the victim of a natural disaster on its maiden voyage when the impact from a collision with an iceberg split the ship in two. More than this, its sinking symbolized an ordered world on the path to destruction. Two years after the *Titanic* vanished, the world went to war, a war unparalleled in its ferocity and barbarism.

During this period of political tension from about 1900 to 1914, there was an explosion of intense artistic experimentation that gave rise to several movements including Cubism, the Fauves, Die Brücke, Der Blaue Reiter, Dadism, Futurism, and Constructionism. Many of the first avant-garde movements can be loosely grouped under the heading Expressionism because they generally rejected the Impressionist view of the world as superficial. The Expressionists dove to greater depths in their work. The world was rapidly changing. New scientific discoveries such as radium and elaborate mathematical postulates such as quantum theory or relativity revealed a more complex world that challenged Newton's physical laws as inadequate in unlocking the mysteries of the universe.

The potential for worldwide conflict was very real, and confidence invested in diplomacy or in human creations like the *Titanic* seemed misplaced. Fear permeated the European world. "Never has there been a time so disturbed by desperation, by the horrors of death," wrote the critic Hermann Bahr. "Never was man smaller. Never has he been more troubled. Never has joy been more absent and freedom more dead. Here is the cry of desperation; man cries out for his soul, a lone cry of anguish rises out of our time. Art also cries out in the dark, calling for help, appealing to the spirit: this is Expressionism."

Edvard Munch had an enormous influence on the German Expressionist school; French painters like Henri Matisse ushered in their own rejection of Impressionism and the academic system under the banner of Fauvism. Between the years 1910 and the opening of the Great War in 1914, the artistic community swam in a swirling pool of change where new ideas assumed a vibrancy in opposition to the staid and uncreative political and diplomatic worlds. European society had fashioned a "proud tower," as the historian Barbara Tuchman noted, in which the Belle Époque, or Golden Age, had meaning for only "a thin crust of the privileged class." The individual and the institution had reached a point of disconnect. Artists no longer were regularly employed to portray the glories of the state much beyond military recruitment posters. Instead, there was greater purpose in rebellion, in the energy of the self and the creation from within—this was the road to abstraction.

FIGURE 10.3 *Improvisation 30 (Cannons)* (1913) by Vasily Kandinsky (*The Art Institute of Chicago*)

One of the most important pioneers experimenting with abstraction was the Russian painter Vasily Kandinsky (1866–1934). After an academic career, Kandinsky made the leap to a life in art, "a luxury," he said "forbidden to a Russian." Kandinsky's artistic vision moved beyond the colors, lines, and shapes that depicted objects—they were distracting. He wanted to create a "visual language" that was capable of expressing his emotional center and the depth of his intellect. Kandinsky claimed that there was an "inner necessity" to art that revealed the soul in spontaneous expression. Between 1910 and 1917, Kandinsky painted a series of improvisations, allowing his unconscious spirit to evoke his inner profile in random assortment.

Improvisation No. 30 (Cannons) was influenced by the very intensity of the moment. "The presence of cannons in the picture," Kandinsky revealed, "could probably be explained by the constant war talk that has been going on throughout the year." What Kandinsky felt, what bubbled from his unconscious and was echoed by Stravinsky's dissonant harmonies and disjointed rhythms, would soon erupt on the battlefields of Europe in a sacrifice of innocents—the ultimate realization of Edvard Munch's greatest fears.

CONSIDER THIS:

- How does this painting by Kandinsky reflect the chaos of a European world bent on destruction? How was the sinking of the *Titanic* symbolic of the failure of industrial confidence and the "proud tower" of elite European civilization?
- *Cannons* flows from the unconscious emotions of the artist. Kandinsky's move toward abstraction was therefore an evolutionary process. Which elements in this painting are abstract and which are more distinct? What was Kandinsky trying to express?

The Lamps Go Out over Europe

The lamps are going out all over Europe; we shall not see them lit again in our lifetime.
—SIR EDWARD GREY, BRITISH FOREIGN MINISTER (AUGUST 3, 1914)

You will be home before the leaves have fallen from the trees.
—GERMAN KAISER WILHELM II TO HIS DEPARTING TROOPS (AUGUST 1914)

For decades the Balkan areas of Bosnia and Serbia had been in turmoil, causing the neighboring Austro-Hungarian Empire great anxiety. The Serbs had their own language and customs and had always been wary of Austrian attempts to unify the region politically, religiously, and culturally. Several extremist organizations, inspired by patriotic idealism, sought to eliminate the Austro-Hungarian presence through terror and violence. Among these organizations was the pan-Serbian nationalist group "Union or Death," also known as The Black Hand. Statutes of this representative group are included in the first selection.

The second selection recounts the famous assassination of the heir to the Austro-Hungarian throne, Archduke Franz Ferdinand. The murderer, a nineteen-year-old Serb student named Gavrilo Princip, was a member of a patriotic society similar to The Black Hand, called Narodna Odbrana. One of the leaders of this organization who was arrested along with Princip gave this firsthand account of the assassination, an event that propelled the world to war.

Statutes of "The Black Hand"

Article 1. This organization has been created with the object of realising the national ideal: The union of all the Serbs. All Serbs without distinction of sex, religion, place of birth, and all who are sincerely devoted to this cause, may become members.

Article 2. This organization prefers terrorist action to intellectual propaganda and for this reason must be kept absolutely secret from persons who do not belong to it.

Article 3. This organization bears the name "Union or Death."

Article 4. To accomplish its task, the organization:

"Statutes of 'The Black Hand'" is from W. Henry Cooke and Edith P. Stickney, *Readings in European International Relations* (Harper & Row, 1931), p. 309.

1. Brings influence to bear on Government circles, on the various social classes and on the whole social life of the Kingdom of Serbia, regarded as Piedmont.
2. Organizes revolutionary action in all territories inhabited by Serbs.
3. Outside the frontiers of Serbia uses every means available to fight the adversaries of this idea.
4. Maintains amicable relations with all states, peoples, organizations, and individuals who entertain feelings of friendship towards Serbia and the Serbian element.
5. Lends help and support in every way possible to all people and all organizations struggling for their national liberation and for their union.

Article 5. A central Committee having its headquarters at Belgrade is at the head of this organization and exercises executive authority. . . .

Article 25. Members of the organization are not known to each other personally. It is only the members of the Central Committee who are known to one another.

Article 26. In the organization itself the members are known by numbers. Only the Central Committee at Belgrade is to know their names. . . .

Article 31. Anyone who once enters the organization may never withdraw from it. . . .

Article 33. When the Central Committee at Belgrade has pronounced penalty of death [on one of the members] the only matter of importance is that the execution take place without fail. . . .

Assassination at Sarajevo: The Plot and Murder (June 28, 1914)

A tiny clipping from a newspaper, mailed without comment from a secret band of terrorists in Zagreb, capital of Croatia, to their comrades in Belgrade, was the torch which set the world afire with war in 1914. That bit of paper wrecked old, proud empires. It gave birth to new, free nations.

I was one of the members of the terrorist band in Belgrade which received it.

The little clipping declared that the Austrian Archduke Francis Ferdinand would visit Sarajevo, the capital of Bosnia, June 28, to direct army maneuvers in the neighboring mountains.

It reached our meeting place, the café called Zeatna Moruna, one night the latter part of April, 1914. To understand how great a sensation that little piece of paper caused among us when it was passed from hand to hand almost in silence, and how greatly it inflamed our hearts, it is necessary to explain just why the Narodna Odbrana existed, the kind of men that were in it, and the significance of that date, June 28, on which the Archduke dared to enter Sarajevo.

As every one knows, the old Austro-Hungarian Empire was built by conquest and intrigues, by sales and treacheries, which held in subjugation many peoples who were neither Austrian nor Hungarian. It taxed them heavily; it diverted the products of their toil to serve the wealth of the master state. It interfered in their old freedom by a multiplicity of laws administered with arrogance.

Several years before the war, a little group of us, thirty-five in all, living in several Bosnian and Herzegovinian cities and villages, formed the Narodna Odbrana, the secret society, the

"The Polt and Murder" is from *New York World,* June 28, 1924, the North American Newspaper Alliance.

aim of which was to work for freedom from Austria and a union with Serbia. So strict was the police vigilance in Bosnia and Herzegovina that we set up our headquarters in Belgrade, the capital of our mother country.

The men who were terrorists in 1914 embraced all classes. Most of them were students. Youth is the time for the philosophy of action. There were also teachers, tradesmen and peasants, artisans and even men of the upper classes were ardent patriots. They were dissimilar in everything except hatred of the oppressor.

Such were the men into whose hands the tiny bit of newsprint was sent by friends in Bosnia that April night in Belgrade. At a small table in a very humble café, beneath a flickering gas jet we sat and read it. There was no advice nor admonition sent with it. Only four letters and two numerals were sufficient to make us unanimous, without discussion, as to what we should do about it. They were contained in the fateful date, June 28.

How dared Francis Ferdinand, not only the representative of the oppressor but in his own person an arrogant tyrant, enter Sarajevo on that day? Such an entry was a studied insult.

June 28 is a date engraved deep in the heart of every Serb, so that the day has a name of its own. It is called the *vidovnan* [Saint Vitus Day]. It is the day on which the old Serbian kingdom was conquered by the Turks at the battle of Amselfelde in 1389. It is also the day on which in the second Balkan War the Serbian armies took glorious revenge on the Turk for his old victory and for the years of enslavement. . . .

As we read that clipping in Belgrade we knew what we would do to Francis Ferdinand. We would kill him to show Austria there yet lived within its borders defiance of its rule. We would kill him to bring once more to the boiling point the fighting spirit of the revolutionaries and pave the way for revolt.

Our decision was taken almost immediately. Death to the tyrant!

Then came the matter of arranging it. To make his death certain twenty-two members of the organization were selected to carry out the sentence. At first we thought we would choose the men by lot. But here Gavrilo Princip intervened. . . . From the moment Ferdinand's death was decided upon, he took an active leadership in its planning. Upon his advice we left the deed to members of our band, who were in and around Sarajevo, under his direction and that of Gabrinovic, a linotype operator on a Serbian newspaper. Both were regarded as capable of anything in the cause. . . .

The fateful morning dawned. Two hours before Francis Ferdinand arrived in Sarajevo all the twenty-two conspirators were in their allotted positions, armed and ready. They were distributed five hundred yards apart over the whole route along which the Archduke must travel from the railroad station to the town hall.

When Francis Ferdinand and his retinue drove from the station they were allowed to pass the first two conspirators. The motor cars were driving too fast to make an attempt feasible and in the crowd were many Serbians; throwing a grenade would have killed many innocent people.

When the car passed Gabrinovic, the compositor, he threw his grenade. It hit the side of the car, but Francis Ferdinand with presence of mind threw himself back and was uninjured. Several officers riding in his attendance were injured.

The cars sped to the Town Hall and the rest of the conspirators did not interfere with them. After the reception in the Town Hall General Potiorek, the Austrian Commander, pleaded with Francis Ferdinand to leave the city, as it was seething with rebellion. The Archduke was persuaded to drive the shortest way out of the city and to go quickly.

The road to the maneuvers was shaped like the letter V, making a sharp turn at the bridge over the River Nilgacka. Francis Ferdinand's car could go fast enough until it reached this spot but here it was forced to slow down for the turn. Here Princip had taken his stand.

As the car came abreast he stepped forward from the curb, drew his automatic pistol from his coat and fired two shots. The first struck the wife of the Archduke, the Archduchess Sofia, in the abdomen. She was an expectant mother. She died instantly.

The second bullet struck the Archduke close to the heart.

He uttered only one word, "Sofia"—a call to his stricken wife. Then his head fell back and he collapsed. He died almost instantly.

The officers seized Princip. They beat him over the head with the flat of their swords. They knocked him down, they kicked him, scraped the skin from his neck with the edges of their swords, tortured him, all but killed him.

The next day they put chains on Princip's feet, which he wore till his death. . . .

I was placed in the cell next to Princip's, and when Princip was taken out to walk in the prison yard I was taken along as his companion.

By Oct. 12, the date of Princip's trial, his prison sufferings had worn him to a skeleton. His sentence was twenty years imprisonment at hard labor, the death sentence being inapplicable because he was a minor.

Awakened in the middle of the night and told that he was to be carried off to another prison, Princip made an appeal to the prison governor:

"There is no need to carry me to another prison. My life here is already ebbing away. I suggest that you nail me to a cross and burn me alive. My flaming body will be a torch to light my people on their path to freedom."

Consider This:

- What role did secret organizations like the Black Hand play in the crisis of 1914 that led Europe into war?
- What inspired the political fanaticism that led to Gavrilo Princip's assassination of the Archduke?

The Broader Perspective:

- What is the role of fanatics in achieving political or nationalist freedom? Are religious fanatics any more or less justified in their violent acts than political fanatics?
- Note the impact of suicide bombers in promoting terror throughout the world. Has anything really changed in this regard since 1914? How effective is terror in changing policy?

"The Sword Is Drawn!" (August 18, 1914)

KAISER WILHELM II

For several years Europe had been diplomatically divided into two rival camps. The Triple Alliance was formed in 1882 among Germany, Italy, and Austria-Hungary. In 1907, the Triple Entente was established among Great Britain, France, and Russia. Both organizations were pledged by treaty to support their respective allies militarily should their mutual interests or existence be threatened. Thus the European world was shocked by the assassination of Archduke Franz Ferdinand. Poised on the brink

"'The Sword Is Drawn!'" is from Louis L. Snyder, ed., *Historic Documents of World War I* (Princeton, N. J.: Van Nostrand, 1958), pp. 80–81. Reprinted by permission of Louis Snyder.

of crisis, each nation took stock of its diplomatic commitments, its military arsenal, and its long-range goals. Such a slap in the face of the powerful Austro-Hungarian Empire by Serbian terrorists had wide-ranging implications. Response had to be quick to preserve the honor and integrity of the throne and to assure that such action would not invite further insolence, which could lead to outright revolt. There were other factors to consider as well. How would Russia react to a severe stand against the Serbs? Russia, after all, was a Slavic nation and promoting a policy that advocated the independence and cultural integrity of Balkan Slavs.

The Austrians sought German support in their plans to punish Serbia for the assassination of the Austrian heir. Germany would be an important ally in countering the potential hostility of Russia. On July 6, 1914, the German kaiser, Wilhelm II, sent a "blank check" telegram that guaranteed German support for whatever punishment Austria decided to inflict on Serbia. Austria thereupon declared war and started mobilizing its military forces. One by one, the European powers declared war on each other, constrained by the dictates of their alliance systems and by the necessity to obtain an advantage in mobilizing their military forces as quickly as possible.

The light of reason gave way to military timetables, national pride, and the celebration of war. Certain of their military superiority, the Germans expected a short conflict and looked forward to being home "before the leaves fall." As Kaiser Wilhelm drew his sword, European confidence, even arrogance, was about to meet the full fury of modern mechanized warfare. A door had closed, and the modern era was born amid the tragedy of the Great War.

Former generations as well as those who stand here today have often seen the soldiers of the First Guard Regiment and My Guards at this place. We were brought together then by an oath of allegiance which we swore before God. Today all have gathered to pray for the triumph of our weapons, for now that oath must be proved to the last drop of blood. The sword, which I have left in its scabbard for decades, shall decide.

I expect My First Guard Regiment on Foot and My Guards to add a new page of fame to their glorious history. The celebration today finds us confident in God in the Highest and remembering the glorious days of Leuthen, Chlum, and St. Privat. Our ancient fame is an appeal to the German people and their sword. And the entire German nation to the last man has grasped the sword. And so I draw the sword which with the help of God I have kept in its scabbard for decades. 'At this point the Kaiser drew his sword from its scabbard and held it high above his head.'

The sword is drawn, and I cannot sheathe it again without victory and honor. All of you shall and will see to it that only in honor is it returned to the scabbard. You are my guarantee that I can dictate peace to my enemies. Up and at the enemy! Down with the enemies of Brandenburg!

Three cheers for our army!

CONSIDER THIS:

- In any conflict there are underlying tensions within countries or between countries that depend on a precipitating action to upset the status quo. What was the spark that ignited the Great War, and what were the underlying causes for the conflict?

THE BROADER PERSPECTIVE:

- The war has sometimes been viewed as the logical outcome of the intense nationalism and imperialism of the late nineteenth century. Do you agree with this view? What evidence exists in this chapter that indicates nationalism and imperialism played a role in the Great War?

FIGURE 10.4 "Our ancient fame is an appeal to the German people and their sword. And the entire German nation to the last man has grasped the sword. . . . Three cheers for our army!"—Kaiser Wilhelm II. (*Corbis/Bettmann*)

"They Shall Not Pass": The Great War (1914–1918)

The Horror of Battle

The German strategy in August 1914 had been planned long in advance by Count Alfred von Schlieffen, German chief of staff until 1905. The essence of the strategy was to sweep through Belgium and overwhelm French defenses in one swift onslaught; about 90 percent of the German army would be used for that purpose while the remaining fraction, together with the Austrians, would hold off Russia. Once France was defeated, Germany and Austria-Hungary could concentrate their forces against the Russian army. Quite unexpectedly, however, the Belgians put up a gallant resistance, and the German attack was stalled long enough to upset the timetable. The British were able to land troops in Europe, and the war degenerated into a struggle for position that was characterized by trench warfare. New weapons such as the machine gun, the tank, and barbed wire eliminated thousands of men as attacks failed and comrades were left to die in the region between the trenches called "no man's land."

The following accounts of soldiers testify to the horrors of ceaseless shelling and destruction. The Battle of Verdun in 1916 raged for ten months, resulting in a combined total of about 1 million casualties. The Battle of the Somme lasted five months, with well over 1 million killed or wounded. Very little ground or tactical advantage was gained. Battle cries such as the French "They shall not pass" were indicative of the stalemated defensive war. In such a situation, propaganda leaflets dropped into enemy trenches by balloons attempted to gain advantage in what was as much psychological as physical combat.

The Battle of Verdun (February–December 1916)

During three days (February 26–29th) after their initial advance over devastated and useless ground, they assaulted with the greatest dash and determination the main French positions. But the defenders were now in strength; and the French guns at length took matters in hand. The German assaulting waves dashed themselves in vain against the Talou heights, the Pepper ridge, and the Vaux position. They were ripped open with cannon, broken by the French bayonets, and driven back with fearful slaughter, time and again. Finally the mauled and battered German columns collapsed, and they were withdrawn from the fray; the casualties of the assailants for the first full week of uninterrupted fighting being estimated, on the lowest computation, at 60,000.

For such heavy sacrifice the enemy technically had won nothing, although, as usual, he indulged in much boasting and he magnified tremendously the barren results he had obtained from the action—an insignificant and useless gain of ground, a few prisoners, and some disabled guns; this was really all he could show as the outcome of his plan which was meant to open to him the gates of Verdun and to place him in possession of the Heights of the Meuse. The French, who had lost 20,000 men, continued to hold Verdun and the main positions surrounding it. . . .

Thousands of projectiles are flying in all directions, some whistling, others howling, others moaning low, and all uniting in one infernal roar. From time to time an aerial torpedo passes, making a noise like a gigantic motor car. With a tremendous thud a giant shell bursts quite close to our observation post, breaking the telephone wire and interrupting all communication with our batteries.

A man gets out at once for repairs, crawling along on his stomach through all this place of busting mines and shells. It seems quite impossible that he should escape in the rain of shell, which exceeds anything imaginable; there has never been such a bombardment in war. Our man seems to be enveloped in explosions, and shelters himself from time to time in the shell craters which honeycomb the ground; finally he reaches a less stormy spot, mends his wires, and then, as it would be madness to try to return, settles down in a big crater and waits for the storm to pass.

Beyond, in the valley, dark-masses are moving over the snow-covered ground. It is German infantry advancing in packed formation along the valley to the attack. They look like a big gray carpet being unrolled over the country. We telephone through to the batteries and the ball begins.

"The Battle of Verdun" is from Charles F. Horne, ed., *Source Record of the Great War*, vol. 4 (Indianapolis, Ind.: The American Legion, 1931), pp. 45, 54–57. Reprinted by Permission of The American Legion.

FIGURE 10.5 The French soldier defending the stronghold of Verdun, where the German high command tried "to bleed the French army white" during ten months of fighting: "Despite the horror of it, despite the ceaseless flow of blood, one wants to see. One's soul wants to feed on the sight of the brute Boches falling." (*Reproduced by permission of the Trustees of the Imperial War Museum, London*)

The sight is hellish. In the distance, in the valley and upon the slopes, regiments spread out, and as they deploy fresh troops come pouring in.

There is a whistle over our heads. It is our first shell. It falls right in the middle of the enemy infantry. We telephone through, telling our batteries of their hit, and a deluge of heavy shells is poured on the enemy. Their position becomes critical. Through glasses we can see men maddened, men covered with earth and blood, falling one upon the other. When the first wave of the assault is decimated, the ground is dotted with heaps of corpses, but the second wave is already pressing on. Once more our shells carve awful gaps in their ranks. Nevertheless, like an army of rats the Boches [Germans] continue to advance in spite of our "marmites." Then our heavy artillery bursts forth in fury. The whole valley is turned into a volcano, and its exit is stopped by the barrier of the slain.

Despite the horror of it, despite the ceaseless flow of blood, one wants to see. One's soul wants to feed on the sight of the brute Boches falling. I stopped on the ground for hours, and when I closed my eyes I saw the whole picture again. The guns are firing at 200 and 300 yards, and shrapnel is exploding with a crash, scything them down. Our men hold their ground; our machine guns keep to their work, and yet they advance.

The Boches are returning again massed to the assault, and they are being killed in bulk. It makes one think that in declaring war the Kaiser had sworn the destruction of his race, and he would have shown good taste in doing so. Their gunfire is slackening now, and ours redoubles. The fort has gone, and if under its ruins there are left a few guns and gunners the bulk of the guns are firing from outside. The machine guns are coming up and getting in position, and our men are moving on in numerous waves.

I find a rifle belonging to a comrade who has fallen and join the Chasseurs with the fifty cartridges that I have left. What a fight it is, and what troops! From time to time a man falls, rises, shoots, runs, shoots again, keeps on firing, fights with his bayonet, and then, worn out, falls, to be trampled on without raising a cry. The storm of fire continues. Everything is on fire—the wood nearby, the village of Douaumont, Verdun, the front of Bezonvaux, and the back of Thiaumont. There is fire everywhere. The acid smell of carbonic acid and blood catches at our throats, but the battle goes on.

They are brave, but one of our men is worth two of theirs, especially in hand-to-hand fighting. . . . Our reinforcements continue to arrive. We are the masters.

CONSIDER THIS:

- In this account of the Battle of Verdun, truly one of the most devastating battles in military history, the narrating soldier says, "Despite the horror of it, despite the ceaseless flow of blood, one wants to see. One's soul wants to feed on the sight of the brute Boches falling." Why? Why this fascination in the midst of the carnage? Why does "one's soul" want to see?

The Battle of the Somme (July–November 1916)

The German Command was not thinking much about the human suffering of its troops. It was thinking, necessarily, of the next defensive line upon which they would have to fall back if the pressure of the British offensive could be maintained. . . . It was getting nervous. Owing to the enormous efforts made in the Verdun offensive the supplies of

"The Battle of the Somme" is from Charles F. Horne, ed., *Source Records of the Great War*, vol. 4 (Indianapolis, Ind.: The American Legion, 1931), pp. 248–251. Reprinted by permission of The American Legion.

ammunition were not adequate to the enormous demand.

The German gunners were trying to compete with the British in continuity of bombardments and the shells were running short. Guns were wearing out under this incessant strain, and it was difficult to replace them. General von Gallwitz received reports of "an alarmingly large number of bursts in the bore, particularly in the field guns."

In all the letters written during those weeks of fighting and captured by us from dead or living men there is one great cry of agony and horror.

"I stood on the brink of the most terrible days of my life," wrote one of them. "They were those of the battle of the Somme. It began with a night attack on August 13th–14th. The attack lasted till the evening of the 18th, when the English wrote on our bodies in letters of blood: 'It is all over with you.' A handful of the half-mad, wretched creatures, worn out in body and mind, were all that was left of a whole battalion. We were that handful."

In many letters this phrase was used. The Somme was called the "Bath of Blood" by the German troops who waded across its shell-craters, and in the ditches which were heaped with their dead. But what I have described is only the beginning of the battle, and the bath was to be filled deeper in the months that followed.

It was in no cheerful mood that men went away to the Somme battlefields. Those battalions of gray-clad men entrained without any of the old enthusiasm with which they had gone to earlier battles. Their gloom was noticed by the officers.

"Sing, you sheep's heads, sing!" they shouted.

They were compelled to sing, by order.

"In the afternoon," wrote a man of the 18th Reserve Division, "we had to go out again: we were to learn to sing. The greater part did not join in, and the song went feebly. Then we had to march round in a circle, and sing, and that went no better."

"After that we had an hour off, and on the way back to billets we were to sing '*Deutschland über Alles*,' but this broke down completely. One never hears songs of the Fatherland any more."

They were silent, grave-eyed men who marched through the streets of French and Belgian towns to be entrained for the Somme front, for they had forebodings of the fate before them. Yet none of their forebodings were equal in intensity of fear to the frightful reality into which they were flung.

THEME: WOMEN IN HISTORY

The Reflection in the Mirror

"World Without End": Women in War

War presents special burdens for women because sexual stereotypes are often reinforced by the impact of crisis. Although victory or defeat is usually calculated in numbers of men lost, position achieved, or territory gained in proportion to blood spilled, women endure the real dimension of tragedy. They maintain the home front, send their husbands and sons off to battle, struggle as refugees, and bear the sacrifice of war most intimately. Women have traditionally embodied the civilizing element in society as guardians of the hearth, who give life and cultivate the future by providing stability and continuity. For some, the Great War ripped this future apart and left only memories to assuage the grief. But many women also answered the call to arms as factory workers, nurses, and even as soldiers.

This selection is by Helen Thomas (1877–1967), a mother of three whose husband Edward, a distinguished poet, volunteered for combat. After Edward was killed by a shell at the front in 1917, Helen decided to write about their years together as a form of therapy. Her memoir *World Without End* reveals a personal intimacy in their relationship that profoundly contrasts with the impersonal brutality of the war. This scene took place on the night before Edward returned to the front for the last time.

"There Had Never Been Untruth Between Us"

HELEN THOMAS

I stir and stare stupidly at his luggage by the wall, and his roll of bedding, kit-bag, and suitcase. He takes out his prismatic compass and explains it to me, but I cannot see, and when a tear drops onto it, he just shuts it up and puts it away. Then he says, as he takes a book out of his pocket, "You see, your Shakespeare's Sonnets is already where it will always be. Shall I read you some?" He reads one or two to me. His face is grey and his mouth trembles, but his voice is quiet and steady. And soon I slip to the floor and sit between his knees, and while he reads, his hand falls over my shoulder and I hold it with mine.

"Shall I undress you by this lovely fire and carry you upstairs in my khaki greatcoat?" So he undoes my things, and I slip out of them; then he takes the pins out of my hair, and we laugh at ourselves for behaving as we so often do, like young lovers. . . .

> "I cannot stop crying. My body is torn with terrible sobs. I am engulfed in this despair like a drowning man by the sea. My mind is incapable of thought. . . ."
> —HELEN THOMAS

"I'll read to you till the fire burns low, and then we'll go to bed." Holding the book in one hand, and bending over me to get the light of the fire on the book, he puts his other hand over my breast, and I cover his hand with mine, and he reads from Antony and Cleopatra. He cannot see my face, nor I his, but his low, tender voice trembles as he speaks the words so full for us of poignant meaning. That tremor is my undoing. "Don't read any more. I can't bear it." All my strength gives way. I hide my face on his knee, and all my tears so long kept back come convulsively. He raises my head and wipes my eyes and kisses them, and wrapping his greatcoat round me carries me to our bed in the great, bare ice-cold room. Soon he is with me, and we lie speechless and trembling in each other's arms. I cannot stop crying. My body is torn with terrible sobs. I am engulfed in this despair like a drowning man by the sea. My mind is incapable of thought. . . . Edward did not speak except now and then to say some tender word or name, and hold me tight to him. "I've always been able to warm you haven't I?" "Yes" [he replied], "your lovely body never feels as cold as mine does. How is it that I am so cold when my heart is so full of passion? . . . But you must not make my heart cold with sadness, but keep it warm, for no one else but you has ever found my heart, and for you it was a poor thing after all." "No, no, no, your heart's love is all my life. I was nothing before you came and would be nothing without your love."

So we lay, all night, sometimes talking of our love and all that had been, and of the children, and what had been amiss and what right. We knew the best was that there had never been untruth between us. We knew all of each other, and it was right. So talking and crying and loving in each other's arms we fell asleep as the cold reflected light of the snow crept through the frost-covered windows.

CONSIDER THIS:

- What were the many roles that women played in the Great War? What makes the excerpt from Helen Thomas's memoir so powerful? Do women suffer a greater burden in war than men do?
- After World War I, women gained the vote in the United States and most European countries. Was this a reward for their war efforts in the factories and in combat?

THE BROADER PERSPECTIVE:

- Although some nations like Israel require military service of all men and women and do not restrict females from combat positions, many other Western countries have been slow to move in this direction. Why? How long will it be before women assume combat roles in the infantry? Why is it more difficult for society to see women as defenders of the state, as killers on the front lines?

No Man's Land

J. KNIGHT-ADKIN

No Man's Land is an eerie sight
At early dawn in the pale gray light.
Never a house and never a hedge
In No Man's Land from edge to edge,
And never a living soul walks there
To taste the fresh of the morning air.
Only some lumps of rotting clay,
That were friends or foemen yesterday.

What are the bounds of No Man's Land?
You can see them clearly on either hand,
A mound of rag-bags gray in the sun,
Or a furrow of brown where the earth
    works run
From the eastern hills to the western sea,
Through field or forest o'er river and lea;
No man may pass them, but aim you well
And Death rides across on the bullet or shell.

But No Man's Land is a goblin sight
When patrols crawl over at dead o' night;
Boche or British, Belgian or French,
You dice with death when you cross the trench.
When the "rapid," like fireflies in the dark,
Flits down the parapet spark by spark,
And you drop for cover to keep your head
With your face on the breast of the four
    months' dead.

The man who ranges in No Man's Land
Is dogged by the shadows on either hand
When the star-shell's flares, as it bursts
    o'erhead,
Scares the great gray rats that feed on the dead,

"*No Man's Land*" is from W. Reginald Wheeler, ed., *A Book of Verse of the Great War* (New Haven: Yale University Press, 1917), pp. 90–91.

FIGURE 10.6 Canadian soldiers go "over the top" in an effort to storm German fortifications at the battle of the Somme: "Only a general who was a Barbarian would send his men to certain death against the concentrated power of my new gun."—*Hiram Maxim* (inventor of the machine gun) (*National Archives and Records Administration)*

And the bursting bomb or the bayonet-snatch
May answer the click of your safety-catch.
For the lone patrol, with his life in his
hand,
Is hunting for blood in No Man's Land.

CONSIDER THIS:

- What are your most vivid impressions from the personal accounts of combat under the section "The Horror of Battle"? Granted that all wars are horrible, what made this war unique?

"What Are You Fighting For, Michel?"

They tell you that you are fighting to secure victory for your Fatherland. But have you ever thought about what you are fighting for?

You are fighting for the glory of, and for the enrichment of the Krupps. You are fighting to save the Kaiser, the Junkers and the War

"What Are You Fighting For, Michel?" is from George G. Bruntz, *Allied Propaganda and the Collapse of the German Empire in 1918*, Hoover War Library Publication No. 13 (Stanford, Calif: Stanford University Press, 1938), p. 99. Reprinted by permission of the publisher.

Lords who caused the war from the anger of the people.

The Junkers [German nobility] are sitting at home with their bejewelled wives and mistresses. Their bank accounts are constantly growing, accounts to which you and your comrades pay with your lives. For your wives and brides there are no growing bank accounts. They are at home working and starving, sacrifices like yourselves to the greed of the ruling class to whose pipes you have to dance.

What a dance! The dance of death. But yesterday you marched over the corpses of your comrades against the English cannon. Tomorrow another German soldier will march over your corpse.

You have been promised victory and peace. You poor fool! Your comrades were also promised these things more than three years ago. Peace indeed they have found—deep in the grave. But victory did not come.

Your Kaiser has adorned the glorious Hindenburg with the Iron Cross with golden beams. What has the Kaiser awarded to you? Ruin, suffering, poverty, hunger for your wives and children, misery, disease, and tomorrow the grave.

It is for the Fatherland, you say, that you go out as a brave patriot to death for the Fatherland.

But of what does your Fatherland consists? Is it the Kaiser with his fine speeches? Is it the Crown Prince with his jolly companions, who sacrificed 600,000 men at Verdun? Is it [Field Marshall] Hindenburg, who sits with [General] Ludendorf, both covered with medals many kilometers behind you and who plans how he can furnish the English with still more cannon fodder. Is it Frau Bertha Krupp for whom through year after year of war you pile up millions upon millions of marks? Is it the Prussian Junkers who cry out over your dead bodies for annexation?

No, the Fatherland is not any of these. You are the Fatherland, Michel! You and your sisters and your wives and your parents and your children. You, the common people are the Fatherland. And yet it is you and your comrades who are driven like slaves into the hell of English cannon-fire, driven by the command of the feelingless slave-drivers.

When your comrades at home were striking, they were shot at with machine guns. If you, after the war, strike a blow for your rights, the machine guns will be turned upon you, for you are fighting only to increase the power of your lords.

Do you perhaps believe your rulers who love war as you hate it? Of course not. They love war for it brings them advancement, honor, power, profit. The longer the war lasts, the longer they will postpone the revolution.

They promise you that you can compel the English to beg for peace. Do you really believe that? You have advanced a few kilometers but for every Englishman whom you have shot down, six Germans have fallen. And all America is still to come.

Your commanders report to you wonderful stories of English losses. But did they tell you that Germany in the first five days of battle lost 315,000 men? Arrayed against Germany in battle today stands the entire world because it knows that German rulers caused the war to serve their own greedy ambition. The entire power of the Western World stands behind England and France and America. Soon it will go forth to battle. Have you thought of that, Michel?

The Broader Perspective:

- What makes this propaganda leaflet an effective weapon?

- Must all soldiers be insulated from reality through propaganda to motivate them to risk death and kill the enemy?

THEME: THE INSTITUTION AND THE INDIVIDUAL

AGAINST THE GRAIN

Glory in the Skies: The Red Baron

"An Englishman for Breakfast"

BARON MANFRED VON RICHTHOFEN

While the infantryman was exposed to the frustration and chaos of land combat, there was another war that existed with less restriction. By 1916, airplanes had been developed for combat, and the sky became the haven for men who relished the opportunity to test individual skill in dogfights high above the earth. The romantic notion of the solitary warrior, with scarf flying high in the wind, was established by men who played by their own rules of honor and death in the air. Baron Manfred von Richthofen, a member of the Prussian aristocracy, became the ace of the war, shooting down eighty planes within two years before he himself was felled. In spite of his romantic aura, Richthofen was a methodical killer, a hunter with a morbid curiosity for death, who flew with his brains and not with the innocent courage of other pilots. The Red Baron discriminated between a sportsman and a butcher: "The latter shoots for fun. When I have shot down an Englishman, my hunting passion is satisfied for a quarter of an hour. If one of them comes down, I have a feeling of complete satisfaction. Only much, much later I have overcome my instinct and have become a butcher." The first excerpt is from his autobiography, *The Red Battle Flyer*; the second selection is an assessment of the Red Baron by one of his fellow pilots.

KEEP IN MIND . . .

- According to the Red Baron, what is the difference between the French and English fighting spirit? What does this say about the Red Baron himself?

My First English Victim (September 17, 1915)

We were all at the butts trying our machine guns. On the previous day we had received our new aeroplanes and the next morning Boelcke was to fly with us. We were all beginners. None of us had a success so far. Consequently everything that Boelcke told us was to us gospel truth. Every day, during the last few days, he had, as he said, shot one or two Englishmen for breakfast.

Slowly we approached the hostile squadron. It could not escape us. We had intercepted it, for we were between the Front and our opponents. If they wished to go back they had to pass us. We counted the hostile machines. They were seven in number. We were only five. All the Englishmen flew large bomb-carrying two-seaters. In a few seconds the dance would begin.

Boelcke had come very near the first English machine but he did not yet shoot. I followed. Close to me were my comrades. The Englishman nearest to me was traveling in a large boat painted with dark colors. I did not reflect very long but took my aim and shot.

Apparently he was no beginner, for he knew exactly that his last hour had arrived at

"An Englishman for Breakfast" is from Manfred von Richthofen, *The Red Battle Flyer* (New York: McBride Co., 1918), pp. 131–133.

the moment when I got at the back of him. At that time I had not yet the conviction "He must fall!" which I have now on such occasions, but on the contrary, I was curious to see whether he would fall. There is a great difference between the two feelings. When one has shot down one's first, second or third opponent, then one begins to find out how the trick is done.

In a fraction of a second I was at his back with my excellent machine. I gave a short series of shots with my machine gun. I had gone so close that I was afraid I might dash into the Englishman. Suddenly, I nearly yelled with joy for the propeller of the enemy machine had stopped turning. I had shot his engine to pieces; the enemy was compelled to land, for it was impossible for him to reach his own lines.

The Englishman landed close to the flying ground of one of our squadrons. I was so excited that I landed also and my eagerness was so great that I nearly smashed up my machine. The English flying machine and my own stood close together. I rushed to the English machine and saw that a lot of soldiers were running towards my enemy. When I arrived I discovered that my assumption had been correct. I had shot the engine to pieces and both the pilot and observer were severely wounded. The observer died at once and the pilot while being transported to the nearest dressing station. I honored the fallen enemy by placing a stone on his beautiful grave.

English and French Flying (February 1917)

The great thing in air fighting is that the decisive factor does not lie in trick flying but solely in the personal ability and energy of the aviator. A flying man may be able to loop and do all the stunts imaginable and yet he may not succeed in shooting down a single enemy. In my opinion the aggressive spirit is everything and that spirit is very strong in us Germans. Hence we shall always retain the domination of the air.

The French have a different character. They like to put traps and to attack their opponents unawares. That cannot easily be done in the air. Only a beginner can be caught and one cannot set traps because an aeroplane cannot hide itself. The invisible aeroplane has not yet been discovered. Sometimes, however, the Gaelic blood asserts itself. The Frenchmen will then attack. But the French attacking spirit is like bottled lemonade. It lacks tenacity.

The Englishmen, on the other hand, one notices that they are of Germanic blood. Sportsmen easily take to flying, and Englishmen see in flying nothing but a sport. They take a perfect delight in looping the loop, flying on their back, and indulging in other stunts for the benefit of our soldiers in the trenches. All these tricks may impress people who attend a Sports Meeting, but the public at the battle-front is not as appreciative of these things. It demands higher qualifications than trick flying. Therefore, the blood of English pilots will have to flow in streams.

> "The blood of English pilots will have to flow in streams."
> —MANFRED VON RICHTHOFEN

"On the Other Side of the Boundary"

ERNST UDET

What a man he was! The others, admittedly, were doing their share, but they had wives at home, children, a mother or a profession. And only on rare occasions could they forget it. But Richthofen always lived on the other side of the boundary which we

"'On the Other Side of the Boundary'" is from Ernst Udet, *Ace of the Black Cross*, trans. Kenneth Kirkness (London: Newnes, 1937), p. 72.

FIGURE 10.7 The aerial dogfight. "In my opinion the aggressive spirit is everything and that spirit is very strong in us Germans. . . . Therefore, the blood of English pilots will have to flow in streams."—Baron Manfred von Richthofen (*Corbis/Bettmann*)

crossed only in our great moments. When he fought, his private life was thrust ruthlessly behind him. Eating, drinking and sleeping were all he granted life, and then only the minimum that was necessary to keep flesh and blood in working order. He was the simplest man I ever met. He was a Prussian through and through. A great soldier.

CONSIDER THIS:

- Apart from the physical differences, how was war in the air different from war on land? Is killing more palatable when it is romanticized? Do you find the Red Baron to be an exciting or intriguing personality? A great soldier? Or simply a deranged butcher?

It Is Sweet and Proper to Die for One's Country

One of the oldest puzzles of politics is who is to regulate the regulators. But an equally baffling problem, which has never received the attention it deserves, is who is to make wise those who are required to have wisdom.

—JOHN KENNETH GALBRAITH

Wilfred Owen, a poet and soldier who was killed a week before the war ended, wrote that the "Lie" of the conflict lay in the belief that it was honorable and proper to give your life for the benefit of your country (*Dulce et decorum est pro patria mori*). Indeed, the war seemed to people an absurd and tragic event. Why were they fighting? Why did old men send young men off to die "for their country"? How could poisonous gas, which burned out the lungs and led to a painfully slow death, be justified—or submarines, which destroyed under cover, thus eliminating a "fair fight"? The rules of war had changed. Disillusionment was evident in mutinies and in the poetry written in the trenches and in the letters sent home. It was not enough to be complimented by your general for victory in battle.

Five Souls

W. N. EWER

FIRST SOUL—
I was a peasant of the Polish plain;
I left my plow because the message ran:
Russia, in danger, needed every man
To save her from the Teuton; and was slain.
I gave my life for freedom—this I know;
For those who bade me fight had told me so.

SECOND SOUL—
I was a Tyrolese, a mountaineer;
I gladly left my mountain home to fight
Against the brutal, treacherous Muscovite;
And died in Poland on a Cossack spear.
I gave my life for freedom—this I know;
For those who bade me fight had told me so.

THIRD SOUL—
I worked in Lyons at my weaver's loom,
When suddenly the Prussian despot hurled
His felon blow at France and at the world;
Then I went forth to Belgium and my doom.
I gave my life for freedom—this I know;
For those who bade me fight had told me so.

FOURTH SOUL—
I owned a vineyard by the wooded Main,
Until the Fatherland, begirt by foes
Lusting her downfall, called me, and I rose
Swift to the call—and died in fair Lorraine.
I gave my life for freedom—this I know;
For those who bade me fight had told me so.

FIFTH SOUL—
I worked in a great shipyard by the Clyde,
There came a sudden word of wars declared,
Of Belgium, peaceful, helpless, unprepared,
Asking our aid; I joined the ranks, and died.
I gave my life for freedom—this I know;
For those who bade me fight had told me so.

"*Five Souls*" is from W. Reginald Wheeler, ed., *A Book of Verse of the Great War* (New Haven, Conn: Yale University Press, 1917), pp. 46–47.

FIGURE 10.8 "This is the way the world ends/Not with a bang but a whimper."—T. S. Eliot. (*Library of Congress*)

A German War Letter: "One Blood-Soaked, Corpse-Strewn Field"

RICHARD SCHMIEDER, Student of Philosophy, Leipzig
Born January 24th, 1888.
Killed July 14th, 1916, near Bethenville.

In the Trenches near Vaudesincourt, March 13th, 1915.

Anybody who, like myself, has been through the awful days near Penthy since the 6th of February, will agree with me that a more appalling struggle could not be imagined. It has been a case of soldier against soldier, equally matched and both mad with hate and anger, fighting for days on end over a single square of ground, till the whole tract of country is one blood-soaked, corpse-strewn field. . . . On February 27th, tired out and utterly exhausted in body and mind, we were suddenly called up to reinforce the VIIIth Reserve Corps, had to reoccupy our old position at Ripont, and were immediately attacked by the French with extraordinary strength and violence. It was a gigantic murder, by means of bullets, shells, axes, and bombs, and there was such a thundering, crashing, bellowing and screaming as might have heralded the Day of Judgment.

In three days, on a front of about 200 yards, we lost 909 men, and the enemy casualties must

"A German War Letter" is from *German Students' War Letters*, translated and arranged from the original edition of Dr. Philipp Witkop by A. F. Wedd (New York: E. P. Dutton, 1929), pp. 208–209. Reprinted by permission of Methuen and Company.

have amounted to thousands. The blue French cloth mingled with the German grey upon the ground, and in some places the bodies were piled so high that one could take cover from shell-fire behind them. The noise was so terrific that orders had to be shouted by each man into the ear of the next. And whenever there was a momentary lull in the tumult of battle and the groans of the wounded, one heard, high up in the blue sky, the joyful song of birds! Birds singing just as they do at home in spring-time! It was enough to tear the heart out of one's body!

Don't ask about the fate of the wounded! Anybody who was incapable of walking to the doctor had to die a miserable death; some lingered in agony for hours, some for days, and even for a week. And the combatants stormed regardlessly to and fro over them: 'I can't give you a hand,—You're for the Promised Land,—My Comrade good and true.' A dog, dying in the poorest hovel at home, is enviable in comparison.

There are moments when even the bravest soldier is so utterly sick of the whole thing that he could cry like a child. When I heard the birds singing at Ripont, I could have crushed the whole world to death in my wrath and fury. If only those gentlemen—Grey, Asquith, and Poincaré—could be transported to this spot, instead of the war lasting ten years, there would be peace tomorrow!

CONSIDER THIS:

- Evaluate the statement "It is sweet and proper to die for one's country." Is it an "old Lie" as Wilfred Owen said? Was this war a game started by the old, fought by the young, and suffered by the innocent? What about patriotism and honor? Were they hollow concepts in this war? How about in World War II or in Vietnam, or, more recently, in the Persian Gulf War, or the Iraq War, or the war against terrorism?

Aftermath: The Light That Failed

"This Is the Way the World Ends"

On November 9, 1918, the German kaiser abdicated his throne and fled the country. The armistice, which ended the war, was signed on November 11. The European world of 1914 had been shattered, people were changed, and the foremost question was how to begin again.

The Great War was a turning point in the history of Western civilization. The bluster of European achievement, the creation of armed states with myopic and rigid alliance systems, mobilization timetables, and uncreative leadership led the world to the greatest mass destruction yet experienced by human beings. Political arrogance had been supported in this endeavor by the perversions of science, which had produced the mechanized destruction of machine guns and the unimaginable pain of poisonous gas. Many worried that the West was an empty shell, a carcass on the desert, guilty of hubris and worthy of decline. Over the next twenty years, Europeans battled homelessness and despair, unemployment and economic dislocation. This was the so-called "lost generation," searching for an explanation, appalled by the reflection in the mirror, and looking for new inspiration. The following selections reveal this weariness and search for meaning. The first is from the diary of Anna Eisenmenger, an Austrian whose son returned home after the armistice a changed man.

A German Soldier Returns Home: "A Complete Stranger"

ANNA EISENMENGER

Karl looked very ill. He had no underlinen or socks. His uniform was dirty and in rags. "Mother, I am famished!" he said, and walking straight into the kitchen without waiting for me to bring him something he began to devour our rations of bread and jam. "Forgive me, Mother, but we have got into the habit of taking what we can find." He only greeted us very casually and did not notice until much later that Erni, who had come in to welcome him on Liesbeth's arm, was wounded. "Hullo! So it's caught you too!" and then, still hurriedly chewing and swallowing: "Well, just wait! We'll pay them out yet, the war profiteers and parasites. We've grown wiser out there in the trenches, far wiser than we were. Everything must be changed, utterly changed."

I got ready the bath and clean underlinen. After his bath Karl went straight to bed, but he was too excited to sleep, although it was almost 11 o'clock at night. He telephoned to Edith, and then he made us all come to his bedside, for he wanted to tell us about himself. He told us that. . . the Italians had gone on attacking in spite of the Armistice. For another whole day they had fired on our retreating columns in the Fellathal and had captured several divisions. That, however, was the only victory they had won. It was contemptible, but war made every one base and contemptible. He had become so too. . . . After the proclamation of the Armistice all military discipline went to pieces. Everyone was intent only on getting home and made for home by the way that seemed to him quickest and surest. The men trampled down whatever stood in their way, even if the obstacle were their own officers. Woe to the officers who were unpopular with their men. . . . In the next war there would be no one foolish enough to risk his life, they would see to that. . . . Karl was evidently in a nervous, overexcited state, but he went on talking, and only after I had entreated him several times did he consent to try to get to sleep.

"We are all tired, Karl, and it is already past midnight. . . ."

"Do you know, Mother, how I feel here? In a clean bed, washed and fed? As if I were in heaven. . . . Oh no, there is no heaven so beautiful. . . . As if I were in a beautiful dream . . . and in that dream I shall try to find sleep."

We left Karl's room in order to go to bed ourselves. As I was helping Erni undress, he said: "Mother, Karl seems to me like a complete stranger."

Although I was nervously and physically exhausted, sleep refused to close my eyelids. For a long, long time I lay awake, agitated by the horrors of the War. I found myself marvelling that civilised human beings could live through all the brutalities which war entailed for themselves and others without going utterly to pieces. . . .

Treaty Concerning Submarines and Poisonous Gases in Warfare (1922)

This treaty of 1922 was an attempt to civilize war and to protect the lives of noncombatants by regulating submarine warfare and by banning the use of poisonous gas. Both weapons were considered to have been immorally used during the war and remained a subject of controversy.

The United States of America, the British Empire, France, Italy and Japan, hereinafter referred to as the Signatory Powers, desiring to make more effective the rules adopted by civilized nations for the protection of the lives of neutrals and noncombatants at sea in time of

"A German Soldier Returns Home" is from Anna Eisenmenger, *Blockade: The Diary of an Austrian Middle-Class Woman, 1914–1924* (London: Constable Publishers, 1932), pp. 39–42. Reprinted by permission of the publisher.

"Treaty Concerning Submarines and Poisonous Gases" is from *Department of State Bulletin* (February 6, 1922).

war, and to prevent the use in war of noxious gases and chemicals, have determined to conclude a Treaty to this effect:

Article I

The Signatory Powers declare that among the rules adopted by civilized nations for the protection of the lives of neutrals and noncombatants at sea in time of war, the following are to be deemed an established part of international law:

(1) A merchant vessel must be ordered to submit to visit and search to determine its character before it can be seized.

A merchant vessel must not be attacked unless it refuse to submit to visit and search after warning, or to proceed as directed after seizure.

A merchant must not be destroyed unless the crew and passengers have been first placed in safety.

(2) Belligerent submarines are not under any circumstances exempt from universal rules above stated; and if a submarine can not capture a merchant vessel in conformity with these rules the existing law of nations requires it to desist from attack and from seizure and to permit the merchant vessel to proceed unmolested.

Article IV

The Signatory Powers recognize the practical impossibility of using submarines as commerce destroyers without violating, as they were violated in the recent war of 1914–1918, the requirements universally accepted by civilized nations for the protection of the lives of neutrals and noncombatants, and to the end that the prohibition of the use of submarines as commerce destroyers shall be universally accepted as a part of the law of nations, they now accept that prohibition as henceforth binding as between themselves and they invite all other nations to adhere thereto.

Article V

The use in war of asphyxiating, poisonous or other gases, and all analogous liquids, materials or devices, having been justly condemned by the general opinion of the civilized world and a prohibition of such use having been declared in treaties to which a majority of the civilized Powers are parties.

The Signatory Powers, to the end that this prohibition shall be universally accepted as a part of international law binding alike the prohibitions, agree to be bound thereby as between themselves and invite all other civilized nations to adhere thereto.

The Broader Perspective:

- Note the treaty of 1922 concerning submarines and poisonous gas. Why were these weapons considered immoral at the time? By mutual consent, poisonous gas was not used in World War II—yet this was a "total war." Does total war preclude "laws of humanity"?

- In the same sense, consider the Persian Gulf War of 1990–1991 or the war against terrorism beginning in 2001. Because modern technology now provides laser-controlled missiles to destroy specific targets, do such so-called "surgical strikes" allow us to fight antiseptic campaigns where civilian casualties are considerably reduced and war is thus made more palatable and civilized?

"If You Want to Endure Life—Prepare for Death"

SIGMUND FREUD

Among the most controversial figures of the twentieth century was the Austrian physician and psychoanalyst Sigmund Freud (1856–1939). Freud sought to apply the critical methods of science to the understanding of the human unconscious. His research centered on sexuality and the interpretation of dreams in his explanation of human motivation. He portrayed the mind as an area in which the irrational amoral instincts (id) struggle with the restrictive demands of society (superego). The ego seeks to reconcile these conflicting forces to maintain a stable existence. Freud's work stripped humanity of the privacy of its inner nature and led to a revolution in human understanding that has only recently been challenged. In this selection Freud comments on the great impact the war had on the modern attitude toward death.

[A primary factor] to which I attribute our present sense of estrangement in this once lovely and congenial world is the disturbance that has taken place in the attitude which we have hitherto adopted towards death.

That attitude was far from straightforward. To anyone who listened to us we were of course prepared to maintain that death was the necessary outcome of life, that everyone owes nature a death and must expect to pay the debt–in short, that death was natural, undeniable and unavoidable. In reality, however, we were accustomed to behave as if it were otherwise. We showed an unmistakable tendency to put death on one side, to eliminate it from life. We tried to hush it up; indeed we even have a saying [in German]: "To think of something as though it were death." That is, as though it were our own death, of course. It is indeed impossible to imagine our own death; and whenever we attempt to do so we can perceive that we are in fact still present as spectators. Hence the psycho- analytic school could venture on the assertion that at bottom no one believes in his own death, or, to put the same thing in another way, that in the unconscious every one of us is convinced of his own immortality. . . .

It is evident that war is bound to sweep away this conventional treatment of death. Death will no longer be denied; we are forced to believe in it. People really die; and no longer one by one, but many, often tens of thousands, in a single day. And death is no longer a chance event. To be sure, it still seems a matter of chance whether a bullet hits this man or that; but a second bullet may well hit the survivor; and the accumulation of deaths puts an end to the impression of chance. Life has, indeed, become interesting again; it has recovered its full content. . . .

To sum up: our unconscious is just as inaccessible to the idea of our own death, just as murderously inclined towards strangers, just as divided (that is, ambivalent) towards those we love, as was primaeval man. But how far we have moved from this primal state in our conventional and cultural attitude towards death!

It is easy to see how war impinges on this dichotomy. It strips us of the later accretions of civilization, and lays bare the primal man in each of us. It compels us once more to be heroes who cannot believe in their own death; it stamps strangers as enemies, whose death is to be brought about or desired; it tells us to

"'If You Want to Endure Life—Prepare for Death'" is from James Strachey, trans. and ed., *Standard Edition of the Complete Works of Sigmund Freud*, vol. 14 (London: Hogarth Press Ltd., 1957), pp. 280–281.

disregard the death of those we love. But war cannot be abolished; so long as the conditions of existence among nations are so different and their mutual repulsion so violent, there are bound to be wars. The question then arises: Is it not we who should give in, who should adapt ourselves to war? Should we not confess that in our civilized attitude towards death we are once again living psychologically beyond our means, and should we not rather turn back and recognize the truth? Would it not be better to give death the place in reality and in our thoughts which is its due, and to give a little more prominence to the unconscious attitude towards death which we have hitherto so carefully suppressed? This hardly seems as advanced to higher achievement, but rather in some respects a backward step–a regression; but it has the advantage of taking the truth more into account, and of making life more tolerable for us once again. To tolerate life remains, after all, the first duty of all living beings. Illusion becomes valueless if it makes this harder for us.

We recall the old saying: *Si vis pacem, para bellum.* If you want to preserve peace, arm for war.

It would be in keeping with the times to alter it: *Si vis vitam, para mortem.* If you want to endure life, prepare yourself for death.

CONSIDER THIS:

- What did Freud mean by this statement: "If you want to endure life, prepare yourself for death"? Was this the problem? With all the bluster for war and the benefits that would ensue from victory, did the European governments fail to prepare their countrymen for death?

- Do you agree with Freud that "war cannot be abolished" and that it is "we who should adapt ourselves to war"? Why should human beings try to prevent war? Why not reconcile ourselves to it as Freud suggested?

11

The Russian Revolution and the Development of the Soviet State (1917–1939)

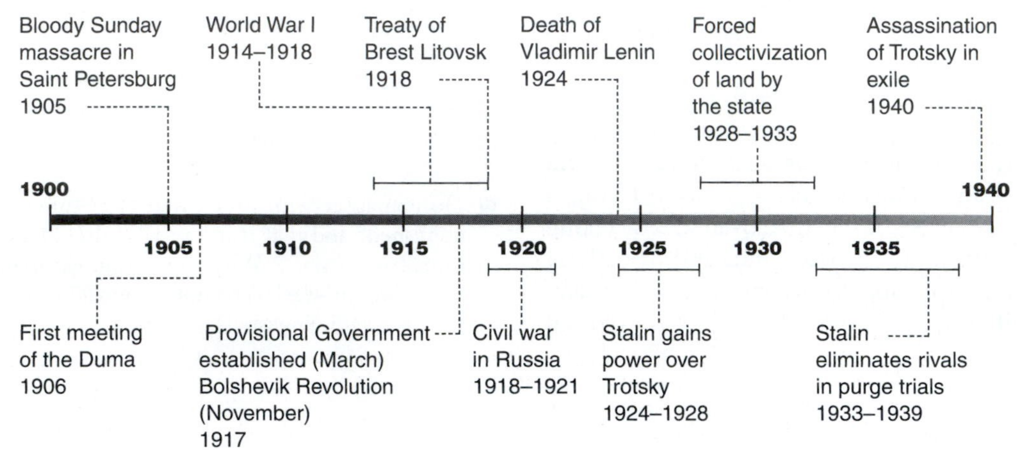

CHAPTER THEMES

- **Revolution and Historical Transition:** Against great odds, why were the Bolsheviks able to overthrow the Provisional Government and come to power in Russia in 1917? How would you compare the Russian Revolution to the French Revolution or the Nazi revolution in Germany?
- **The Power Structure:** What are the components of totalitarian government? How does it differ from fascism? How did the character of Stalin's government differ from that of Lenin or Hitler?
- **Women in History:** How did Lenin's vision of women's roles and responsibilities differ from that of Hitler in Nazi Germany? Did women have greater equality of opportunity under the Soviet system than they did in other Western societies?
- **The Individual and the Institution:** Karl Marx argued that the individual had minimal influence on the social and economic forces that propelled historical events. How then does one explain the crucial role of Lenin in the Russian Revolution? Marx also predicted that the state under communism would eventually "wither away" rather than grow more pervasive, as happened under Stalin. What happened?
- **The Big Picture:** Is a government based on fear and oppression doomed to fail? Or is totalitarian rule workable and even preferable in some ways to democracy? Is freedom really the natural condition of human beings?

The events of the year 1917 remain among the most significant in the history of the twentieth century. The world was in the midst of a war that could no longer be viewed as glorious and patriotic but had degenerated in people's minds to what war really is—suffering, destruction, and death. In such a crisis, it is important for governments to justify their actions, inspire soldiers, and assuage the populace. Statesmen require domestic stability to focus attention on the war effort. However, Russia was not afforded this tranquility, and the monarchy of Tsar Nicholas II fell in March 1917, a prelude to a power struggle that by November of that year would see the imposition of a new regime, born of Marxist revolutionary philosophy and led by Vladimir Ulyanov, better known as Lenin (1870–1924). This was a complex revolution, and any simplification distorts the intricacy of events and political philosophies. Yet, for our purposes, it can be divided into three separate but related phases: the revolution of 1905, the March revolution of 1917, and the Bolshevik revolution of November 1917. This chapter seeks to unravel the conditions and pressures that led to the overthrow of the Romanov dynasty and the eventual Bolshevik seizure of power.

As in the French and American revolutions, social and economic conditions, as well as ideology, played an important role in providing the underlying causes and inspiration for revolution. TsarNicholas II was heir to a long tradition of autocracy that regarded change as dangerous to the stability of the dynasty. In the nineteenth century alone, TsarAlexander I (1801–1825) continued the long-standing policy of absolutism, and his successor, Nicholas I (1825–1855), became Europe's most reactionary monarch with the slogan "Autocracy, Orthodoxy, and National Unity." Under Nicholas's leadership, Russia became a closed society. Nicholas employed a secret police and a network of paid informers that successfully exiled over 150,000 people to the frigid wastes of Siberia. And yet there existed reform movements. Alexander Herzen (1812–1870), called the "father of Russian liberalism," advocated moderate socialist policies. But other dissidents were not so polite. Mikhail Bakunin (1814–1876) founded the anarchist movement and advocated the use of terror to effect change. Tsar Alexander II (1855–1881) instituted a series of liberal measures, including the emancipation of Russian serfs (1861), and reforms of the judiciary, army, and local and municipal governments. Yet his actions, although revolutionary for the absolutist government of Russia, were incomplete, and his failure to provide a constitution led to growing opposition and a populist movement (Narodnik) that preached revolution to the peasant masses and was suppressed by the tsar. On March 13, 1881, Alexander II was assassinated by the terrorist group People's Will—ironically on the very day he had signed a decree that was to lead to constitutional reform. His son, Alexander III (1881– 1894), refused to conform to the decree and set about reimplementing a policy of reactionary oppression. Thus when Nicholas II came to the throne in 1894, a long tradition of violent repression and terrorist response already existed.

One of the most influential philosophies that gave inspiration to the Russian Revolution was Marxism. Karl Marx and Friedrich Engels published the *Communist Manifesto* in 1848. In it they advocated a classless society that would come about through struggle between the exploiting bourgeoisie or middle-class capitalists and the working class, or proletariat. Marx intoned, "Workers of the world unite! You have nothing to lose but your chains!" Marx's ideas became popular among the Russian revolutionary intelligentsia, and converts met in secret societies throughout Europe and Russia to discuss and plan action. One of his most dedicated disciples was Lenin. By 1905, Tsar Nicholas II's political opposition was more firmly organized. The Social Democratic Party had been formed among industrial workers and was truly Marxist in philosophy. Yet party members differed among themselves; the Menshevik faction was more moderate and wanted to concentrate on improving the lot of the industrial worker, instead of concentrating on the world revolution that Marx predicted would become a reality. The other faction of the Social Democrats, the Bolsheviks, were led by Lenin and were more extreme in their insistence on a core of "professional revolutionaries," dedicated to the immediate overthrow of capitalist society. Other political groups existed in 1905 as well, including the Constitutional Democratic Party (Cadets) and the Social Revolutionary Party, which sought agricultural land reform.

Although Russian tsars had long resisted demands for basic civil rights, equality before the law, and representative government, Nicholas II especially seemed to live in a vacuum—his own world of yachts and tennis, crystal and caviar. He remained unaware of the plight of the Russian peasantry, half starved and oppressed by landlords who often confiscated their land, or of the urban worker who was burdened by low wages and long hours. Following the massacre of Russian workers during a peaceful demonstration in January 1905 (called "Bloody Sunday"), the popular outcry forced the tsar to establish an Imperial Duma, or representative assembly, and to provide a new constitution, guaranteeing civil rights for the people. The first phase of the Russian Revolution had taken place. Still, the Duma had no real authority over the tsar, and its liberal recommendations were stifled. From 1906 to 1907, Nicholas merely dismissed Dumas that sought to encroach on his power. From 1907 to 1916, the Dumas were controlled by the tsar through voting restrictions and altered election laws.

In the summer of 1914, Europe gravitated toward disaster. When Germany declared war on Russia (August 1, 1914), France supported its Russian ally. On August 4, Great Britain also joined in the struggle against Germany and Austria. The Great War had begun. Conditions among the Russian people deteriorated as thousands died in battle or as victims of disease or famine. The refugee problem was acute, and people wandered homeless throughout Russia. The government was simply not able to cope with the economic and logistic demands of military mobilization and war. In March 1917, the tsar was persuaded to abdicate, hoping that such action would assure Russia's continued participation in the war. This action came as a surprise to almost everyone. Even the most vitriolic detractors of the tsarist regime, notably Lenin in Switzerland, were caught off guard. The second phase of the revolution had just begun.

With the fall of the tsar, a power vacuum existed, and the competition to fill it was intense. A Provisional Government was chosen from members of the sitting Imperial Duma. The Provisional Government generally was made up of liberals and moderate socialists who promised an elected Constituent Assembly that was representative of the Russian people; they also pledged to draw up a new constitution that guaranteed civil liberties. However, the Provisional Government also supported Russia's continuation of the war. The other competitor for power was the Petrograd Soviet of Workers and Soldiers' Deputies. A *soviet* was simply a council of elected representatives that advocated reforms for the working classes. The soviets were generally composed of Social Revolutionaries, Mensheviks, and initially only a minority of Bolsheviks. They regarded the war as a struggle between capitalists at the expense of the working classes (proletariat) and therefore wanted Russia to cease hostilities immediately. However, the Petrograd Soviet did not advocate armed rebellion against the Provisional Government. On the contrary, some members of the Soviet even believed that they held a kind of dual power with it. No one proposed a government of national unity, and this lack of cooperation was to prove fatal to political stability.

Perhaps too much was expected of the Provisional Government. Soldiers wanted an end to the war, peasants needed more land, the workers in the cities demanded better living conditions, the national and religious minorities

FIGURE 11.1 This dramatic portrait of Lenin as the heroic leader of the Russian Revolution created a sense of urgency and compelling energy that was so vital in establishing the destined communist utopia of Karl Marx. Images like this also created distrust among Western governments, which feared the Soviet rhetoric of "world revolution." (*Alexander Gerasimov, "Lenin at the Tribune," 1930. Tretyakov Gallery, Moscow, Russia. Scala/Art Resource, NY*)

of Russia wanted official recognition, as well as political and cultural autonomy, and the Allies wanted Russia's continued support in the war. For a temporary government composed of people who lacked experience and an organized plan of action, the burden was too great.

Lenin arrived in Petrograd in April and started organizing the opposition. As leader of the more radical Bolshevik faction of the Social Democratic Party, he denounced the Provisional Government and worked independently of the other socialist groups in an effort to seize control. Lenin proclaimed "all power to the soviets" and in July led a premature uprising that failed. Several Bolsheviks were arrested (including Lenin's brilliant associate Leon Trotsky), but Lenin escaped to Finland. Bolshevik fortunes changed when the leader of the Provisional Government, Alexander Kerensky (1881–1970), was confronted with a military rebellion—a right-wing revolt led by General Lavr Kornilov that was quelled only with the assistance of the Petrograd Soviet. In November 1917, Lenin, against the judgment of some of his colleagues, made another attempt to topple the Provisional Government. This time he was successful and his Bolshevik faction of radical socialists was able to maintain its power. This third phase of the Russian Revolution established a regime of a very different order.

The Provisional Government failed for many reasons. The members had little experience in government and administration and could not counter the effective propaganda of Lenin, which offered "Peace, Bread, and Land." Kerensky believed that he had an obligation to act in a legal democratic fashion, to demonstrate that his leadership was progressive and superior to that of the tsar. Lenin played by his own rules and would not share power. His organization and insistence on the rightness of his ideas, coupled with a measure of luck, produced a revolution that indeed shook the world.

Lenin's Bolshevik government survived a counterrevolutionary threat from supporters of the tsar as the civil war came to an end in 1921. Lenin had started the transition toward Marx's concept of a communist society, but he fell ill in 1922 and died two years later. His position as leader of the revolution would eventually be assumed by Joseph Stalin (1879–1953). Under Stalin's brutal direction, and the leadership of his successors, the Soviet Union emerged as a formidable political, military, and ideological adversary to the United States in the late twentieth century.

From 1945 to 1989, the two countries lived under a cloud of mutual suspicion, fostered by intense propaganda, massive nuclear arsenals, and geopolitical competition. Only in the 1990s, with the collapse of the Soviet Union and the subsequent Russian preoccupation with domestic affairs, did the rhetoric cool, the Cold War end, and the future seem to present more opportunities for cooperation. Viewed from this perspective, the Russian Revolution of 1917 and Stalin's institution of totalitarian rule remain among the most significant political events of the modern world.

The Provisional Government (March–November 1917)

Just think what's going on around us! And that you and I should be living at such a time. Such a thing happens only once in an eternity. Just think of it, the whole of Russia has had its roof torn off, and you and I and everyone else are out in the open! And there's nobody to spy on us. Freedom! Real freedom, not just talk about it, freedom dropped out of the sky, freedom beyond our expectations.

——BORIS PASTERNAK (*DOCTOR ZHIVAGO*)

"Shall the Romanov Dynasty Remain?" (March 15, 1917)

IZVESTIA

World War I proved especially disastrous for Russia. The army suffered tremendous losses against a German onslaught of superior force and preparation. Misery, famine, and disease descended on the Russian people, and thousands were dislocated and wandered aimlessly as refugees. Tsar Nicholas II feared a general uprising and finally decided to abdicate his throne in favor of his brother, the Grand Duke Michael. But the tide had turned, and the question was posed by the newspaper *Izvestia*: "Shall the Romanov Dynasty Remain?"

The revolutionary people should carry through to the end the revolution and the democratization of its political and social organization. To return to the old is unthinkable. The revolutionary people should organize the State in the way that will best satisfy its interests, strength and great zeal, and will make impossible a new attempt on its rights and liberty. This can be done by handing the power over to the people, that is to say, by forming a democratic republic, in which the officers of government are elected by universal equal, secret, and direct suffrage. All the revolutionary elements in Russia, who have made tremendous sacrifices in the fight and the forging of freedom, should strive for such a government.

If the power were entrusted to a monarch, one, with his responsible ministry, the latter might make an attempt on the liberty of the people and bind it with chains of slavery. Then again, in a constitutional monarchy there is the right of succession which again creates the possibility of rulers of the type of Nicholas, the Last.

In a constitutional monarchy, the army serves not the people, but the monarch, giving him great power, which he could use to harm the people.

The Romanov dynasty is now overthrown. . . . There must be no going back to it. The revolutionary people will find enough strength to form a new republican government, which will guarantee its rights and freedom.

"A New, Free Russia Is Born": First Declaration of the Provisional Government (March 19, 1917)

After the abdication of the tsar in March 1917, a temporary body called the Provisional Government was installed to maintain stability in the country until a representative Constituent Assembly could be elected by the Russian people. The Petrograd Soviet, an elected council of workers and soldiers, immediately threatened the authority of the Provisional Government. Lenin, who had just arrived from Switzerland, reasserted leadership of the Bolshevik Party and set forth his demands as noted in the last selection, the famous *April Theses*.

"Shall the Romanov Dynasty Remain?" is from Frank A. Golder, ed., *Documents of Russian History (1914–1917)*, trans. Emanuel Aronsberg (New York: The Century Company, 1927), pp. 296–297.

"First Declaration of the Provisional Government" is from Frank A. Golder, ed., *Documents of Russian History (1914–1917)*, trans. Emanuel Aronsberg (New York: The Century Company, 1927), pp. 311–313.

Citizens of Russia:

A great event has taken place. By the mighty assault of the Russian people, the old order has been overthrown. A new, free Russia is born. The great revolution crowns long years of struggle. By the act of October 17, [30] 1905, under the pressure of the awakened popular forces, Russia was promised constitutional liberties. Those promises, however, were not kept. The First State Duma, interpreter of the nation's hopes, was dissolved. The Second Duma suffered the same fate, and the Government, powerless to crush the national will, decided, by the act of June 3, [16] 1907, to deprive the people of a part of those rights of participation in legislative work which had been granted.

In the course of nine long years, there were taken from the people, step by step, all the rights that they had won. Once more the country was plunged into an abyss of arbitrariness and despotism. All attempts to bring the Government to its senses proved futile, and the titanic world struggle, into which the country was dragged by the enemy, found the Government in a state of moral decay, alienated from the people, indifferent to the fate of our native land, and steeped in the infamy of corruption. Neither the heroic efforts of the army, staggering under the crushing burdens of internal chaos, nor the appeals of the popular representatives who had united in the face of the national peril, were able to lead the former Emperor and his Government into the path of unity with the people. And when Russia, owing to the illegal and fatal actions of her rulers, was confronted with gravest disasters, the nation was obliged to take the power into its own hands.

The unanimous revolutionary enthusiasm of the people, fully conscious of the gravity of the moment, and the determination of the State Duma, have created the Provisional Government, which considers it to be its sacred and responsible duty to fulfill the hopes of the nation, and lead the country out onto the bright path of free civic organization.

The Government trusts that the spirit of lofty patriotism, manifested during the struggle of the people against the old regime, will also inspire our valiant soldiers on the field of battle. For its own part, the Government will make every effort to provide our army with everything necessary to bring the war to a victorious end.

The Government will sacredly observe the alliances which bind us to other powers, and will unswervingly carry out the agreements entered into by the Allies. While taking measures to defend the country against the foreign enemy, the Government will, at the same time, consider it to be its primary duty to make possible the expression of the popular will as regards the form of government, and will convoke the Constituent Assembly within the shortest time possible, on the basis of universal, direct, equal, and secret suffrage, also guaranteeing participation in the elections to the gallant defenders of our native land, who are now shedding their blood on the fields of battle.

The Constituent Assembly will issue the fundamental laws, guaranteeing to the country the inalienable rights of justice, equality, and liberty. Conscious of the heavy burden which the country suffers because of the lack of civic rights, which lack stands in the way of its free, creative power at this time of violent national commotion, the Provisional Government deems it necessary, at once, before the convocation of the Constituent Assembly, to provide the country with laws for the safeguard of civic liberty and equality, in order to enable all citizens freely to apply their spiritual forces to creative work for the benefit of the country. The Government will also undertake the enactment of legal provisions to assure to all citizens, on the basis of universal suffrage, an equal share in the election of local governments.

At this moment of national liberation, the whole country remembers with reverent gratitude those who, in the struggle for their political and religious convictions, fell victims to the vindictive old regime, and the Provisional Government will regard it as its joyful duty to bring back from their exile, with full honors, all those who have suffered for the good of the country.

In fulfilling these tasks, the Provisional Government is animated by the belief that it will thus execute the will of the people, and that the whole nation will support it in its honest efforts to insure the happiness of Russia. This belief inspires it with courage. Only in the common effort of the entire nation and the Provisional Government can it see a pledge of triumph of the new order.

March 19, 1917

"Proletarians Unite!": Policy of the Petrograd Soviet (March 27, 1917)

Comrade-proletarians, and toilers of all countries:

We, Russian workers and soldiers, united in the Petrograd Soviet of Workers' and Soldiers' Deputies, send you warmest greetings and announce the great event. The Russian democracy has shattered in the dust the age-long despotism of the Tsar and enters your family [of nations] as an equal, and as a mighty force in the struggle for our common liberation. Our victory is a great victory for the freedom and democracy of the world. The chief pillar of reaction in the world, the "Gendarme of Europe" is no more. May the earth turn to heavy granite on his grave! Long live freedom! Long live the international solidarity of the proletariat, and its struggle for final victory!

Our work is not yet finished: the shades of the old order have not yet been dispersed, and not a few enemies are gathering their forces against the Russian revolution. Nevertheless our achievement so far is tremendous. The people of Russia will express their will in the Constituent Assembly, which will be called as soon as possible on the basis of universal, equal, direct, and secret suffrage. And it may already be said without a doubt that a democratic republic will triumph in Russia. The Russian people now possess full political liberty. They can now assert their mighty power in the internal government of the country and in its foreign policy. And, appealing to all people who are being destroyed and ruined in the monstrous war, we announce that the time has come to start a decisive struggle against the grasping ambitions of the governments of all countries; the time has come for the people to take into their own hands the decision of the question of war and peace.

Conscious of its revolutionary power, the Russian democracy announces that it will, by every means, resist the policy of conquest of its ruling classes, and it calls upon the peoples of Europe for concerted, decisive action in favor of peace.

We are appealing to our brother-proletarians of the Austro-German coalition, and, first of all, to the German proletariat. From the first days of the war, you were assured that by raising arms against autocratic Russia, you were defending the culture of Europe from Asiatic despotism. Many of you saw in this a justification of that support which you were giving to the war. Now even this justification is gone: democratic Russia cannot be a threat to liberty and civilization.

We will firmly defend our own liberty from all reactionary attempts from within, as well as from without. The Russian revolution will not retreat before the bayonets of conquerors, and will not allow itself to be crushed by foreign military force. But we are calling to you: Throw off the yoke of your semi-autocratic rule, as the

"Policy of the Petrograd Soviet" is from Frank A. Golder, ed., *Documents of Russian History (1914–1917)*, trans. Emanuel Aronsberg (New York: The Century Company, 1927), pp. 325–326.

Russian people have shaken off the Tsar's autocracy; refuse to serve as an instrument of conquest and violence in the hands of kings, landowners, and bankers—and then by our united efforts, we will stop the horrible butchery, which is disgracing humanity and is beclouding the great days of the birth of Russian freedom.

Toilers of all countries: We hold out to you the hand of brotherhood across the mountains of our brothers' corpses, across rivers of innocent blood and tears, over the smoking ruins of cities and villages, over the wreckage of the treasures of civilization;—we appeal to you for the reestablishment and strengthening of international unity. In it is the pledge of future victories and the complete liberation of humanity.

Proletarians of all countries, Unite!
PETROGRAD SOVIET OF WORKERS' AND SOLDIERS' DEPUTIES

CONSIDER THIS:

- Analyze the demands of the Provisional Government and the Petrograd Soviet just after the abdication of the tsar. How are they similar and what are their differences?

The April Theses (April 20, 1917)

V. I. LENIN

The class conscious proletariat can consent to a revolutionary war, which would really justify revolutionary defencism, only on condition: (a) that the power of government pass to the proletariat and the poor sections of the peasantry bordering on the proletariat; (b) that all annexations be renounced in deed as well as in words; (c) that a complete and real break be made with all capitalist interests.

In view of the undoubted honesty of the mass of the rank-and-file believers in revolutionary defencism, who accept the war as a necessity only and not as a means of conquest; in view of the fact that they are being deceived by the bourgeoisie, it is necessary thoroughly, persistently and patiently to explain their error to them, to explain the indissoluble connection between capital and the imperialist war, and to prove that *it is impossible* to end the war by a truly democratic, non-coercive peace without overthrow of capital.

The widespread propaganda of this view among the army on active service must be organised.

Fraternisation

(2) The specific feature of the present situation in Russia is that it represents a transition from the first stage of the revolution—which owing to the insufficient class consciousness and organisation of the proletariat, led to the assumption of power by the bourgeoisie—*to the second stage*, which must place power in the hands of the proletariat and the poor strata of the peasantry.

This transition is characterised, on the one hand, by a maximum of freedom (Russia is *now* the freest of all the belligerent countries in the world); on the other, by the absence of violence in relation to the masses, and, finally, by the naive confidence of the masses in the government of capitalists, the worst enemies of peace and socialism.

This specific situation demands on our part an ability to adapt ourselves to the specific requirements of Party work among unprecedently large masses of proletarians who have just awakened to political life.

"*The April Theses*" is from Martin McCauley, ed., *The Russian Revolution and the Soviet State* (New York: Barnes & Noble, 1975), pp. 52–54. Reprinted by permission of Palgrave Macmillan.

(3) No support must be given to the Provisional Government, the utter falsity of all its promises must be exposed, particularly of those relating to the renunciation of annexations. Exposure, and not the unpardonable illusion-breeding 'demand' that this government, a government of capitalists, should cease to be an imperialist government.

(4) The fact must be recognised that in most of the Soviets of Workers' Deputies our Party is in a minority, and so far in a small minority, as against *a bloc of all* the petty-bourgeois opportunist elements, who have yielded to the influence of the bourgeoisie and are the conveyors of its influence to the proletariat. . . .

It must be explained to the masses that the Soviet of Workers' Deputies is the *only possible* form of revolutionary government and that therefore our task is, as long as *this* government submits to the influence of the bourgeoisie, to present a patient, systematic, and persistent *explanation* of its errors and tactics, an explanation especially adapted to the practical needs of the masses.

As long as we are in the minority we carry on the work of criticising and exposing errors and at the same time advocate the necessity of transferring the entire power of state to the Soviets of Workers' Deputies, so that the masses may by experience overcome their mistakes.

(5) Not a parliamentary republic—to return to a parliamentary republic from the Soviets of Workers' Deputies would be a retrograde step—but a republic of Soviets of Workers,' Agricultural Labourers' and Peasants' Deputies throughout the country, from top to bottom. Abolition of the police, the army and the bureaucracy.

(6) The agrarian programme must be centered around the Soviets of Agricultural Labourers' Deputies.

Confiscation of All Landed Estates

Nationalisation of *all* lands in the country, the disposal of such *lands* to be in the charge of the local Soviets of Agricultural Labourers' and Peasants' Deputies. The organisation of separate soviets of Deputies of the Poor Peasants. The creation of model farms on each of the large estates. . . .

(7) The immediate amalgamation of all banks in the country into a single national bank, control over which shall be exercised by the Soviet of Workers' Deputies.

(8) Our *immediate* task shall be not the 'introduction of socialism,' but to bring social production and distribution of products at once under the control of the Soviet of Workers' Deputies.

(9) Party tasks:

(a) Immediate summoning of a Party congress.

(b) Alteration of the Party programme, mainly:

1. On the question of imperialism and the imperialist war;
2. On the question of our attitude towards the state and our demand for a 'commune state.'
3. Amendment of our antiquated minimum programme;

(c) A new name for the Party.

(10) A new International.

Consider This:

- What did Lenin advocate in his *April Theses*? What was the purpose of this document?
- Lenin characterized the overthrow of the tsar and the creation of the Provisional Government as the first stage of the revolution. What was the second stage that he hoped to accomplish? Was this in keeping with the theory of revolution that was expounded in Marx's *Communist Manifesto*?

The Bolshevik Revolution (November–December 1917)

The essence of Bolshevism, the essence of Soviet power, lies in exposing the fraud and hypocrisy of bourgeois democracy, in abolishing the private ownership of the land, the factories, and in concentrating all political power in the hands of the toilers and the exploited masses.

—V. I. LENIN

Even if for every hundred correct things we did, we committed ten thousand mistakes, our revolution would still be—and it will be in the judgment of history—great and invincible; for this is the first time that the working people are themselves building a new life.

—V. I. LENIN

The Overthrow of the Provisional Government: "A New Page in the History of Russia"

V. I. LENIN

The Bolshevik faction, led by Lenin and his very competent colleague Leon Trotsky, had suffered reversals during an abortive uprising in July 1917. Trotsky was imprisoned and Lenin fled to Finland. Finally in November 1917, Lenin persuaded his faction that the time was ripe for a coup. The first selection is Lenin's speech after his successful storming of the Winter Palace in Petrograd. Note the critical editorial from the newspaper *Izvestia* on November 8. It was the last before the Bolsheviks censored the press. Lenin's seizure of power also included the establishment of a secret police (Cheka), an institution that had been used (in another form) by the autocratic tsar to eliminate opposition.

Comrades, the workmen's and peasant's revolution, the need of which the Bolsheviks have emphasized many times, has come to pass.

What is the significance of this revolution? Its significance is, in the first place, that we shall have a soviet government, without the participation of bourgeoisie of any kind. The oppressed masses will of themselves form a government. The old state machinery will be smashed into bits and in its place will be created a new machinery of government by the soviet organizations. From now on there is a new page in the history of Russia, and the present, third Russian revolution shall in its final result lead to the victory of Socialism.

One of our immediate tasks is to put an end to the war at once. But in order to end the war, which is closely bound up with the present capitalistic system, it is necessary to overthrow capitalism itself. In this work we shall have the aid of the world labor movement, which has already begun to develop in Italy, England, and Germany.

A just and immediate offer of peace by us to the international democracy will find everywhere a warm response among the international proletariat masses. In order

"The Overthrow of the Provisional Government" is from Frank A. Golder, ed., *Documents of Russian History (1914–1917)*, trans. Emanuel Aronsberg (New York: The Century Company, 1927), pp. 618–619.

to secure the confidence of the proletariat, it is necessary to publish at once all secret treaties.

In the interior of Russia a very large part of the peasantry has said: Enough playing with the capitalists; we will go with the workers. We shall secure the confidence of the peasants by one decree, which will wipe out the private property of the landowners. The peasants will understand that their only salvation is in union with the workers.

We will establish a real labor control on production.

We have now learned to work together in a friendly manner, as is evident from this revolution. We have the force of mass organization which has conquered all and which will lead the proletariat to world revolution.

We should now occupy ourselves in Russia in building up a proletarian socialist state.

Long live the world-wide socialistic revolution!

"Little Good Is to Be Expected" (November 8, 1917)

IZVESTIA

Yesterday we said that the Bolshevik uprising is a made adventure and today, when their attempt is crowned with success, we are of the same mind. We repeat: that which is before us is not a transfer of power to the Soviets, but a seizure of power by one party—the Bolsheviks. Yesterday we said that a successful attempt meant the breaking up of the greatest of the revolution—the Constituent Assembly. Today we add that it means, also, the breaking up of the Congress of Soviets, and perhaps the whole soviet organization. They can call themselves what they please; the fact remains that the Bolsheviks alone took part in the uprising. All the other socialistic and democratic parties protest against it.

How the situation may develop we do not know, but little good is to be expected. We are quite confident that the Bolsheviks cannot organize a state government. As yesterday, so today, we repeat that what is happening will react worst of all on the question of peace.

Censorship of the Press (November 9, 1917)

V. I. LENIN

In the trying critical period of the revolution and the days that immediately followed it the Provisional Revolutionary Committee was compelled to take a number of measures against the counter-revolutionary press of different shades.

Immediately outcries were heard from all sides that the new, socialist power had violated a fundamental principle of its programme by encroaching upon the freedom of the press.

The Workers' and Peasants' Government calls the attention of the population to the fact that what this liberal facade actually conceals is freedom for the propertied classes, having taken hold of the lion's share of the entire press, to poison, unhindered, the minds and obscure the consciousness of the masses.

Everyone knows that the bourgeois press is one of the most powerful weapons of the bourgeoisie. Especially at the crucial moment

"'Little Good Is to Be Expected'" is from Frank A. Golder, ed., *Documents of Russian History (1914–1917)*, trans. Emanuel Aronsberg (New York: The Century Company, 1927), p. 619.

"Censorship of the Press" is from Martin McCauley, ed., *The Russian Revolution and the Soviet State* (New York: Barnes & Noble, 1975), pp. 190–191. Reprinted by permission of Palgrave Macmillan.

when the new power, the power of workers and peasants, is only affirming itself, it was impossible to leave this weapon wholly in the hands of the enemy, for in such moments it is no less dangerous than bombs and machine-guns. That is why temporary extraordinary measures were taken to stem the torrent of filth and slander in which the yellow and green press would be only too glad to drown the recent victory of the people.

As soon as the new order becomes consolidated, all administrative pressure on the press will be terminated and it will be granted complete freedom within the bounds of legal responsibility, in keeping with a law that will be broadest and most progressive in this respect.

However, being aware that a restriction of the press, even at critical moments, is permissible only within the limits of what is absolutely necessary, the Council of People's Commissars resolves:

General Provisions on the Press

1. Only those publications can be suppressed which (1) call for open resistance or insubordination to the Workers' and Peasants' Government; (2) sow sedition through demonstrably slanderous distortion of facts; (3) instigate actions of an obviously criminal, i.e. criminally punishable, nature.
2. Publications can be proscribed, temporarily or permanently, only by decision of the Council of People's Commissars.
3. The present ordinance is of a temporary nature and will be repealed by a special decree as soon as normal conditions of social life set in.

Chairman of the Council of People's Commissars

VLADIMIR ULYANOV (LENIN)

CONSIDER THIS:

- What measures did Lenin take to protect the position of the Bolsheviks once they had achieved power? How did Lenin justify censorship of the press? Do fallacies or inconsistencies exist in his argument? Note especially the vocabulary. For example, how is the phrase "workmen's and peasants' revolution" used?
- How was the *Izvestia* newspaper editorial dangerous to the Bolshevik Revolution?

Establishment of the Secret Police (December 20, 1917)

V. I. LENIN

The Commission is to be called the All-Russian Extraordinary Commission for the Struggle with Counter-Revolution and Sabotage and is to be attached to the Council of People's Commissars.

The duties of the Commission are to be as follows:

1. To investigate and nullify all acts of counter-revolution and sabotage throughout Russia, irrespective of origin.
2. To bring before the Revolutionary Tribunal all counter-revolutionaries and saboteurs and to work out measures to combat them.
3. The Commission is to conduct the preliminary investigation only, sufficient to suppress (the counter-revolutionary act). The Commission is to be divided into sections: (1) the information (section) (2) the organization section (in charge of organizing the struggle with counter-revolution

"Establishment of the Secret Police" is from Martin McCauley, ed., *The Russian Revolution and the Soviet State* (New York: Barnes & Noble, 1975), pp. 181–182. Reprinted by permission of Palgrave Macmillan.

throughout Russia) with branches, and (3) the fighting section.

The Commission shall be set up finally tomorrow. Then the fighting section of the All-Russian Commission shall start its activities. The Commission shall keep an eye on the press, saboteurs, right Socialist Revolutionaries and strikers. Measures to be taken are confiscation, imprisonment, confiscation of cards, publication of the names of the enemies of the people, etc.

Chairman of the Council of People's Commissars

V. Ulyanov (Lenin)

Consider This:

- What were the duties of the secret police? What elements of society was this organization directed against?

The Broader Perspective:

- The tsar also had an active secret police that protected against "enemies of the monarchy." What is the difference between "enemies of the monarchy" and "enemies of the people"? Is a secret police, therefore, a necessary instrument for maintaining power, regardless of political philosophy?

Dissolution of the Constituent Assembly (December 1917)

V. I. LENIN

A major responsibility of the Provisional Government had been to organize an election and establish a Constituent Assembly that was truly representative of the Russian people. Lenin, after achieving power through political manipulation and force of arms, decided to hold the election anyway. The results were not encouraging because the Bolsheviks were soundly defeated. Lenin, however, would not concede defeat and chose to dissolve the Constituent Assembly instead. Note Lenin's reasons for his actions.

At its very inception, the Russian revolution produced the Soviets of Workers,' Soldiers' and Peasants' Deputies as the only mass organization of all the working and exploited classes capable of giving leadership to the struggle of these classes for their complete political and economic emancipation.

Throughout the initial period of the Russian revolution the Soviets grew in number, size and strength, their own experience disabusing them of the illusions regarding compromise with the bourgeoisie, opening their eyes to the fraudulence of the forms of bourgeois-democratic parliamentarism, and leading them to the conclusion that the emancipation of the oppressed classes was unthinkable unless they broke with these forms and with every kind of compromise. Such a break came with the October [November] Revolution, with the transfer of power to the Soviets.

The Constituent Assembly, elected on the basis of lists drawn up before the October Revolution, was expressive of the old correlation of political forces, when the conciliators and Constitutional-Democrats were in power.

The working classes learned through experience that old bourgeois parliamentarism had outlived its day, that it was utterly incompatible with the tasks of Socialism, and that only class institutions (such as the Soviets) and not national ones were capable of

"Dissolution of the Constituent Assembly" is from Martin McCauley, ed., *The Russian Revolution and the Soviet State* (New York: Barnes & Noble, 1975), pp. 184–186. Reprinted by permission of Palgrave Macmillan.

overcoming the resistance of the propertied classes and laying the foundations of socialist society.

Any renunciation of the sovereign power of the Soviets, of the Soviet Republic won by the people, in favour of bourgeois parliamentarism and the Constituent Assembly would now be a step backwards and would cause a collapse of the entire October Workers' and Peasants' Revolution.

By virtue of generally known circumstances the Constituent Assembly, opening on January 18, gave the majority to the party of Right-Wing Socialist-Revolutionaries, the party of Kerensky, Avksentev and Chernov. Naturally, this party refused to recognize the programme of Soviet power, to recognize the Declaration of Rights of the Working and Exploited People, to recognize the October Revolution and Soviet power. . . .

Obviously, under such circumstances the Constituent Assembly can only serve as a cover for the struggle of the bourgeois counter-revolution to overthrow the power of the Soviets.

In view of this, the Central Executive Committee resolves:

The Constituent Assembly is hereby dissolved.

CONSIDER THIS:

- What arguments did the Bolsheviks give to justify the dissolution of the Constituent Assembly? What gave them the authority to invalidate an assembly that was chosen by vote of the Russian people? Why did the Bolsheviks allow the election to occur in the first place?

A Self-Portrait (March 7, 1921)

V. I. LENIN

This is a questionnaire that all delegates to the Tenth All Russian Congress of the Russian Communist Party had to fill out. This was Lenin's view of himself in 1921.

Name: Ulyanov (Lenin), Vladimir Ilyich

Party organization: Central Committee, Russian Communist Party

Number of delegate mandate (voting/advisory): No. 21 advisory

By whom elected: Central Committee

No. of Party members represented at meeting at which elected: Central Committee—19 members

Which All-Russian party Congresses have you attended: All except July (August?) 1917

Date of birth—age: 1870—51 years

State of health: Good

Family—no. of members of dependents: Wife and sister

Nationality: Russian

Native tongue: Russian

Knowledge of other languages: English, German, French—poor, Italian—very poor

What parts of Russia do you know well, and how long have you lived there: Know Volga country where I was born best; lived there until age 17

Have you been abroad (when, where, how long): In a number of West European countries—1895, 1900–1905, 1908–1917

Military training: None

Education: Graduate (passed examination as extern) Petrograd University Law Faculty, 1891

Basic occupation before 1917: Writer

Special training: None

"A Self-Portrait" is from Warren B. Walsh, ed., *Readings in Russian History*, 3rd ed. (Syracuse, N.Y.: Syracuse University Press, 1959), pp. 622–623. Reprinted by permission of the publisher.

FIGURE 11.2 Portrait of V. I. Lenin (October 1918). Could the Russian Revolution have succeeded without Lenin's firm direction? (*Library of Congress*)

Occupation since 1917 besides Party, Soviet, trade union, and similar work: Besides those enumerated, only writing

What trade union do you belong to: Union of Journalists

Positions held since 1917: October 1917 to March 1921; Moscow; Council People's Commissars and Council of Labor and Defense; Chairman

Present position: Since October 1917; Moscow; Chairman, Council of People's Commissars and Council of Labor and Defense

How long have you been a member of the R.C.P. [Bolsheviks]: Since 1894

Have you ever belonged to any other parties: No

Participation in the revolutionary movement before 1917: Illegal Social-Democratic circles; member of the Russian Social-Democrats Workers' Party since its foundation. 1892–3, Samara; 1894–5, St. Petersburg; 1895–7, prison; 1898–1900, Siberia; 1900–05, abroad; 1905–07, St. Petersburg; 1908–1917, abroad

Penalties incurred for revolutionary activities: 1887 prison; 1895–7 prison; 1898–1900 Siberia; 1900 prison

How long in prison: Several days and 14 months

How long at hard labor: None

How long in exile: Three years

How long a political refugee: 9–10 years

Party functions since 1917: October 1917 to March 1921, Moscow, Member of the Central Committee

Present Party function: As above

Have you ever been tried by the courts of the RSFSR or of the Party: No

Date: March, 1921

Signature of delegate: V. Ulyanov (Lenin)

CONSIDER THIS:

- What social or economic conditions contributed to the outbreak of the Russian Revolution? Although the Russian Revolution involved such strong personalities as Kerensky, Trotsky, and Stalin, it was Lenin who was the guiding spirit. Analyze his self-portrait. What kind of a man emerges?

THE BROADER PERSPECTIVE:

- In Marxist theory, the individual is of little or no importance in contributing to the social and economic forces that result in the eventual destruction of capitalism and capitalist society. If so, how then does one explain Lenin? What was his role in the revolution? Without his presence, would the Russian Revolution have succeeded? To what extent can the individual change the course of history?

The Aftermath of Revolution

A proletarian revolution is never proletarian.

—WILL DURANT

Everyone has the right to sacrifice himself for a cause he deems deserving. No one has the right to sacrifice others or to incite others to sacrifice themselves for an ideal.

—KARL POPPER

Those who hold the power also write the history.

—PLATO

State and Revolution: The Transition from Capitalism to Communism (August 1917)

V. I. LENIN

The Bolsheviks were thrust into a difficult situation on achieving power. Lenin was true to his slogan "Peace, Bread, and Land" and took Russia out of the war, negotiating a peace with Germany (Brest-Litovsk) that conceded much Russian territory. Lenin then applied his energies to quelling a civil war that pitted his Red Army (led by Trotsky) against the White forces, which consisted of supporters of the tsar or of other anti-Bolshevik elements. The tsar's execution in 1918 removed a possible impediment to the progress of the revolution. The civil war ended in 1921, and Lenin spent the next three years until his death consolidating his gains and preparing for Russia's transition from a capitalist to a communist state. In this, Lenin endeavored to apply Marxist theory to the realities of the situation. The first selection is from a pamphlet entitled *State and Revolution* written in August 1917, two months before the Bolshevik seizure of power. In it Lenin discusses this crucial period of transition. Events were to move in logical progression: from bourgeois capitalism to the dictatorship of the proletariat, to the "withering away" of the state, and finally to the justice and equality of the purely communist society. But things did not quite go as planned. The chaos of the civil war and a great drought rendered the socialization of the economic system an unrealistic proposition. Lenin thus allowed a "partial return to capitalism" by permitting the revival of private industry and authorizing the peasantry to produce and trade for profit as part of his New Economic Plan (NEP). Although Russia would still move toward Marx's dream of a truly communist existence, the journey would take longer than Lenin expected.

Earlier the question was put thus: to attain its emancipation, the proletariat must overthrow the Bourgeoisie, conquer political power and establish its own revolutionary dictatorship.

Now the question is put somewhat differently: the transition from capitalist society, developing towards Communism, towards a Communist society, is impossible without a

"*State and Revolution*" is from V. I. Lenin, *State and Revolution* (New York: International Publishers, 1971), pp. 71–74.

"political transition period," and the state in this period can only be the revolutionary dictatorship of the proletariat.

What, then, is the relation of this dictatorship to democracy?

We have seen that the *Communist Manifesto* simply places side by side the two ideas: the "transformation of the proletariat into the ruling class" and the "establishment of democracy." On the basis of all that has been said above, one can define more exactly how democracy changes in the transition from capitalism to Communism.

In capitalist society, under the conditions most favourable to its development, we have more or less complete democracy in the democratic republic. But this democracy is always bound by the narrow framework of capitalist exploitation, and consequently always remains, in reality, a democracy for the minority, only for the possessing classes, only for the rich. . . .

Democracy for an insignificant minority, democracy for the rich—that is the democracy of capitalist society. If we look more closely into the mechanism of capitalist democracy, everywhere, both in the . . . details of suffrage (residential qualification, exclusion of women, etc.), and in the technique of the representative institutions . . . on all sides we see restriction after restriction upon democracy. These restrictions, exceptions, exclusions, obstacles for the poor, seem slight, especially in the eyes of one who has himself never known want and has never been in close contact with the oppressed classes in their mass life (and nine-tenths, if not ninety-nine hundredths, of the bourgeois publicists and politicians are of this class), but in their sum total these restrictions exclude and squeeze out the poor from politics and from an active share in democracy.

Marx splendidly grasped this *essence* of capitalist democracy, when . . . he said that the oppressed were allowed once every few years, to decide which particular representatives of the oppressing class should be in parliament to represent and repress them!

But from this capitalist democracy—inevitably narrow, subtly rejecting the poor, and therefore hypocritical and false to the core—progress does not march onward, simply, smoothly and directly, to "greater and greater democracy," as the liberal professors and petty-bourgeois opportunists would have us believe. No, progress marches onward, i.e., towards Communism, through the dictatorship of the proletariat; it cannot do otherwise, for there is no one else and no other way to *break the resistance* of the capitalist exploiters.

But the dictatorship of the proletariat—i.e., the organisation of the vanguard of the oppressed as the ruling class for the purpose of crushing the oppressors—cannot produce merely an expansion of democracy. *Together* with an immense expansion of democracy which *for the first time* becomes democracy for the poor, democracy for the people, and not democracy for the rich folk, the dictatorship of the proletariat produces a series of restrictions of liberty [by itself oppressing] the exploiters, the capitalists. We must crush them in order to free humanity from wage-slavery; their resistance must be broken by force; it is clear that where there is suppression there is also violence, there is no liberty, no democracy.

Engels expressed this splendidly . . . when he said . . . that "as long as the proletariat still needs the state, it needs it not in the interests of freedom, but for the purpose of crushing its antagonists; and as soon as it becomes possible to speak of freedom, then the state, as such, ceases to exist."

Democracy for the vast majority of the people, and suppression by force, i.e., exclusion from democracy, of the exploiters and oppressors of the people—this is the modification of democracy during the *transition* from capitalism to Communism.

Only in Communist society, when the resistance of the capitalists has been completely broken, when the capitalists have disappeared, when there are no classes (i.e., there is no difference between the members of society in their relation to the social means of production), *only then* "the state ceases to exist," and "*it becomes possible to speak of freedom*." Only then a really full democracy, a democracy without any exceptions, will be possible and will be realised. And only then will democracy itself begin to *wither away* due to the simple fact that, free from capitalist slavery, from the untold horrors, savagery, absurdities and infamies of capitalist exploitation, people will gradually *become accustomed* to the observance of the elementary rules of social life that have been known for centuries and repeated for thousands of years in all school books; they will become accustomed to observing them without force, without compulsion, without subordination, without the *special apparatus* for compulsion which is called the state.

The expression "the state *withers away*," is very well chosen, for it indicates both the gradual and the elemental nature of the process. Only habit can, and undoubtedly will, have such an effect; for we see around us millions of times how readily people get accustomed to observe the necessary rules of life in common, if there is no exploitation, if there is nothing that causes indignation, that calls forth protest and revolt and has to be *suppressed*.

Thus, in capitalist society, we have a democracy that is curtailed, poor, false; a democracy only for the rich, for the minority. The dictatorship of the proletariat, the period of transition to Communism, will, for the first time, produce democracy for the people, for the majority, side by side with the necessary suppression of the minority—the exploiters. Communism alone is capable of giving a really complete democracy, and the more complete it is the more quickly will it become unnecessary and wither away of itself. . . .

Again, during the *transition* from capitalism to Communism, suppression is *still* necessary; but it is the suppression of the minority of exploiters by the majority of exploited. . . . Finally, only Communism renders the state absolutely unnecessary, for there is *no one* to be suppressed—"no one" in the sense of a *class*, in the sense of a systematic struggle with a definite section of the population.

CONSIDER THIS:

- Lenin maintained that a democratic republic "is always bound by the narrow framework of capitalist exploitation" and consequently always remains "a democracy for the minority, . . . only for the rich." How did Lenin propose to extend true democracy to the working poor, to the proletariat?

- How did Lenin define "the dictatorship of the proletariat"? Why could this dictatorship "free humanity from wage-slavery"? How can any dictatorship insure freedom?

THE BROADER PERSPECTIVE:

- In *State and Revolution*, Lenin emphasized the Marxist doctrine that the state will "wither away" and be replaced by the true freedom of a worker's paradise without exploitation—the complete equality of communism. This utopian vision of the future has inspired humanitarians and ignited the fires of revolution for over 150 years. It also provided the springboard for the twentieth-century totalitarian dictatorships of Joseph Stalin in the Soviet Union and Mao Zedong in China that resulted in the deaths of millions of people. In fact, the Marxist vision of equality has never been successfully implemented in a modern state. Why then does the ideal live on? Why didn't the state "wither away"? Why did it grow ever more dominant?

"Days of Grueling Work"

ALEXANDRA KOLLONTAI

Lenin envisioned an egalitarian future, one that included women as integral members of society, valued for their talents and abilities. His wife Krupsaya was an important intellectual force who played a seminal role as Lenin's ideological adviser in the struggle to achieve revolution. Alexandra Kollontai (1873–1952) was another powerful voice in the administration of the incipient Soviet state. She was a member of the Central Committee, the most important policy-making body of the Bolshevik Party, and became People's Commissar of Social Welfare. Kollontai was proud of her authority and accomplishments, as noted in the first selection from her autobiography. Lenin's thoughts on the role of women in the new state are included in the succeeding selection.

I was given my full freedom of movement one month before the decisive struggle, the November (Bolshevik) Revolution of 1917. Again my work piled up. Now the ground work was to be set for a systematic women-workers movement. The first conference of women workers was to be called. It also took place and it coincided with the overthrow of the Provisional Government and the establishment of the Soviet Republic.

At that time, I was a member of the highest Party body, the Central Committee, and I voted for the policy of armed uprising. . . . Then came the great days of the November Revolution. The sleepless nights, the permanent sessions. And, finally, the stirring declarations: "The Soviets take power!" "The Soviets address an appeal to the peoples of the world to put an end to the war." "The land is socialized and belongs to the peasants!"

The Soviet Government was formed. I was appointed People's Commissar (Minister) of Social Welfare. I was the only woman in the cabinet and the first woman in history who had ever been recognized as a member of a government. When one recalls the first months of the Workers' government, months which were so rich in magnificent illusions, plans, ardent initiatives to improve life, to organize the world anew, months of the real romanticism of the Revolution, one would in fact like to write about all else save about one's self. I occupied the post of Minister of Social Welfare from November of 1917 to April of 1918. It was not without opposition that I was received by the former officials of the Ministry. Most of them sabotaged us openly and simply did not show up for work. But precisely this office could not interrupt its work, come what may, since in itself, it was an extraordinarily complicated operation. It included the whole welfare program for the war-disabled, hence for hundreds of thousands of crippled soldiers and officers, the pension system in general, foundling homes, homes for the aged, orphanages, hospitals for the needy, the work-shops making artificial limbs, the administration of the educational system, clinical hospitals for women. In addition, a whole series of educational institutes for young girls were also under the direction of this ministry. One can easily imagine the enormous demands these tasks made upon a small group of people who, at the same time, were novices in State administration. In a clear awareness of these difficulties, I formed an auxiliary council in which experts such as physicians, jurists, and pedagogues were represented alongside the workers and the minor officials of the Ministry. The sacrifice, the energy with which the minor employees

"'Days of Grueling Work!'" is from Alexandra Kollontai, *The Autobiography of a Sexually Emancipated Communist Woman*, edited by Iring Fetscher and translated by Salvatore Attanasio (New York: Herder and Herder, 1971), pp. 34–37.

bore the burden of this difficult task was truly exemplary. It was not only a matter of keeping the work of the Ministry going, but also of initiating reforms and improvements. New, fresh forces replaced the sabotaging officers of the old regime. A new life stirred in the offices of the formerly highly conservative Ministry. Days of grueling work! And at night the sessions of the councils of the People's Commissar under Lenin's chairmanship. . . .

In my opinion, the most important accomplishment of the People's Commissariat, however, was the legal foundation of a Central Office for Maternity and Infant Welfare.

The Communist Emancipation of Women (1920)

V. I. LENIN

The thesis must clearly point out that real freedom for women is possible only through communism. The inseparable connection between the social and human position of the woman, and private property in the means of production, must be strongly brought out. . . . And it will also supply the basis for regarding the woman question as a part of the social question, of the workers' problem, and so bind it firmly to the proletarian class struggle and the revolution. The Communist women's movement must itself be a mass movement, a part of the general mass movement. Not only of the proletariat, but of all the exploited and oppressed, all the victims of capitalism or any other mastery. . . . We must win over to our side the millions of toiling women in the towns and villages. Win them for our struggles and in particular for the communist transformation of society. There can be no real mass movement without women. . . .

Could there be more damning proof of [female exploitation] than the callous acquiescence of men who see how women grow worn out in the petty, monotonous household work, their strength and time dissipated and wasted, their minds growing narrow and stale, their hearts beating slowly, their will weakened? Of course, I am not speaking of the ladies of the bourgeoisie who shove onto servants the responsibility of all household work, including the care of children. What I am saying applies to the overwhelming majority of women, to the wives of workers and to those who stand all day in a factory.

So few men—even among the proletariat—realize how much effort and trouble they could save women, even quite do away with, if they were to lend a hand in "woman's work." But no, that is contrary to the "right and dignity of a man." They want their peace and comfort. The home life of the woman is a daily sacrifice to a thousand unimportant trivialities. The old master right of the man still lives in secret. His slave takes her revenge, almost secretly. The backwardness of women, their lack of understanding for the revolutionary ideals of the man decrease his joy and determination in fighting. They are like little worms which, unseen slowly but surely rot and corrode. I know the life of the worker, and not only from books. Our Communist work among the women, our political work, embraces a great deal of educational work among men. We must root out the old "master" idea to its last and smallest root, in the party and among the masses. That is one of our political tasks, just as is the urgently necessary task of forming a staff of men and women

"The Communist Emancipation of Women" is from V. I. Lenin, *The Woman Question* (New York: International Publishers Co., 1951), pp. 89–90, 93–94.

comrades, well trained in theory and practice, to carry on party activity among working women.

The government of the proletarian dictatorship, together with the Communist Party and trade unions, is of course leaving no stone unturned in the effort to overcome the backward ideas of men and women, to destroy the old Communist psychology. In law there is naturally complete equality of rights for men and women. And everywhere there is evidence of a sincere wish to put this equality into practice. We are bringing the women into the social economy, into legislation and government. All educational institutions are open to them, so that they can increase their professional and social capacities. We are establishing communal kitchens and public eating-houses, laundries and repair shops, infant asylums, kindergartens, children's homes, educational institutes of all kinds. In short, we are seriously carrying out the demand in our program for the transference of the economic and educational functions of the separate household to society. That will mean freedom for the women from the old household drudgery and dependence on man. That enables her to exercise to the full her talents and her inclinations. . . . We have the most advanced protective laws for women workers in the world, and the officials of the organized workers carry them out. We are establishing maternity hospitals, homes for mothers and children, mothercraft clinics, organizing lecture courses on child care, exhibitions teaching mothers how to look after themselves and their children, and similar things. We are making the most serious efforts to maintain women who are unemployed and unprovided for.

We realize clearly that that is not very much, in comparison with the needs of the working women, that it is far from being all that is required for their real freedom. But still, it is tremendous progress, as against conditions in tsarist-capitalist Russia. It is even a great deal compared with conditions in countries where capitalism still has a free hand. It is a good beginning in the right direction, and we shall develop it further. With all our energy, you may believe that. For every day of the existence of the Soviet state proves more clearly that we cannot go forward without the women.

Consider This:

- What was Alexandra Kollontai's role in the Russian Revolution? What qualities of character did she display that were important for the administration of the Soviet state?
- What was Lenin's main message to the women of the new Soviet Union? How would supporting the Bolshevik Revolution benefit women?
- What are the "backward" capitalist ideas about men and women that the Proletarian Dictatorship and Communist Party sought to destroy? Did the communists eventually succeed in establishing an egalitarian society?

"Stalin Is Too Rude" (January 4, 1923)

V. I. LENIN

In 1922, Lenin suffered the first of a series of strokes that gradually incapacitated him until his death in 1924. His leadership of the revolution was thus interrupted at a crucial time. Lenin worried about a successor and expected Leon Trotsky to continue his policies. He doubted Joseph Stalin's character, as he revealed in a note written about a year before his death.

"'Stalin Is Too Rude'" is from Warren B. Walsh, ed., *Readings in Russian History*, 3rd ed. (Syracuse, N.Y.: Syracuse University Press, 1959), p. 626. Reprinted by permission of the publisher.

Stalin is too rude and this defect, which can be freely tolerated in our midst and in contacts among us Communists, can become an intolerable defect in one holding the position of the Secretary General. Because of this, I proposed that the comrades consider ways and means by which Stalin can be removed from this position and another man selected, a man who, above all, would differ from Com. Stalin in only one quality, namely, attitude toward his comrades, less capricious temper, etc. This circumstance could appear to be a meaningless trifle. I think, however, that from the viewpoint of preventing a split and from the viewpoint of what I have written above concerning the relationship between Stalin and Trotsky, this is not a trifle, or if it is one, then it is a trifle which can acquire a decisive significance.

THEME: THE VARIETIES OF TRUTH

AGAINST THE GRAIN

Red Terror: Stalin Versus Trotsky

Stalin's Falsification of History (1927)

LEON TROTSKY

In 1922, when Lenin's stroke removed him from active leadership of the Communist Party, a struggle broke out among Lenin's chief lieutenants for control. Leon Trotsky appeared to be the most logical choice, for he had been, together with Lenin, the primary ideological force behind the Russian Revolution and had proved his organizational ability during the civil war of 1918 by managing the Red Army. He was eventually outmaneuvered, however, by Joseph Stalin, who in his capacity as general secretary of the Communist Party was in a position to control the delegates to the party congress. Stalin's control over the administrative levers of the party allowed him to eliminate all rivals.

The next source reveals the infighting between communist factions before Stalin's consolidation of power. The Commission for the Study of Party History had been established by the Secretariat to censor works that might conflict with the official history of the communist revolution, which was being compiled in commemoration of the tenth anniversary in 1927. Stalin's ascendance was evident as the commission constructed its history in accordance with his personal vision. By reinterpreting and falsifying documents, Trotsky's persona as the ideological soul of the revolution was downgraded to the status of "traitor." Trotsky submitted the following defense of his contributions to the commission, but it was never published. He had lost the power struggle and was dismissed from the party, exiled to Siberia in 1928, and deported to Turkey a year later. Trotsky was eventually murdered in Mexico at the hands of Stalin's assassins in 1940.

"Stalin's Falsification of History" is from Leon Trotsky, *The Real Situation in Russia*, trans. by Max Eastman (New York: Harcourt Brace World, 1928), pp. 241–242.

Keep in Mind...

- In Trotsky's view, how did Stalin distort the historical record of the Russian Revolution?

It was said long ago: A truthful man has this advantage, that even with a bad memory, he never contradicts himself. A disloyal, unscrupulous, a dishonest man has always to remember what he said in the past, in order not to shame himself. Comrade Stalin . . . is trying to construct a new history of the [Bolshevik] revolution. . . .

> "Only a limited mind like Stalin's could imagine that these pitiful secretarial machinations will make men forget the gigantic events of modern history."
> ——Leon Trotsky

I will just say this: During the time when I stood in opposition to the Bolshevik party, during that period when my differences with Bolshevism reached their highest point, the distance separating me from the views of Lenin was never as great as the distance which separates the present position of Stalin-Bukharin from the very foundations of Marxism and Leninism. . . .

In all those—very few—questions upon which Stalin has attempted to occupy an independent position, or has merely given,

FIGURE 11.3 Leon Trotsky stands at the center of a ring of Russian soldiers as he raises his arm and passionately addresses the troops. "Comrade Stalin is trying to construct a new history of the Bolshevik revolution."—Leon Trotsky (*Corbis/Bettman*)

without the immediate direction of Lenin, his own answer upon big problems, he has always and invariably . . . occupied an opportunist position. . . .

You can juggle citations, hide the reports of your own speeches, forbid the propagation of the letters and articles of Lenin, fabricate yards of dishonestly selected quotations. You can suppress, conceal, and burn up historical documents. You can extend your censorship even to the photographic and moving-picture records of revolutionary events. All these things Stalin is doing. But the results will not justify his hopes. Only a limited mind like Stalin's could imagine that these pitiful secretarial machinations will make men forget the gigantic events of modern history.

CONSIDER THIS:

- Trotsky was direct in his criticism of Stalin's efforts to distort the past for future gain. Trotsky called his efforts "pitiful machinations" that would not succeed in making "men forget the gigantic events of modern history." And yet, Stalin's "limited mind" won the power struggle and Trotsky was murdered. What does that tell you about power and the importance of controlling "truth" in a revolution?

THE BROADER PERSPECTIVE:

- Truth has been called the "daughter of time." It is often a casualty of the moment, subject to distortion by sycophants and power brokers for political advantage and short-term gain. But in the larger perspective of history, will truth eventually prevail? Can Stalin now be viewed for what he really was? Or is truth fragile, vulnerable, and so susceptible to the continuing demands of political fortune that it is more often than not an accidental by-product of history?

The Development of the Totalitarian State

Now you see what they've brought Russia to! They'll make you equal to the peasants, deprive you of your privileges, and recall the old affronts into the bargain. Bad times are coming. . . . It depends on whose hands the government falls into, otherwise we shall be brought to utter disaster.

—MIKHAIL SHOLOKHOV (*AND QUIET FLOWS THE DON*)

The Russian dictatorship of the proletariat has made a farce of the whole Marxist vision: developing a powerful, privileged ruling class to prepare for a classless society, setting up the most despotic state in history so that the state may wither away, establishing by force a colonial empire to combat imperialism and unite the workers of the world.

—HERBERT J. MULLER

Judged in terms of its own aspirations, the Communist regime was a monumental failure; it succeeded in one thing only—staying in power. But since for Bolsheviks power was not an end in itself, but a means to an end, its mere retention does not qualify the experiment as a success.

—RICHARD PIPES

The Soviet Control of Society

After establishing his dictatorship over the Communist Party, Stalin moved to consolidate his control over all aspects of Soviet society. Stalin's practical mind was in direct contrast to the ideologue Trotsky. Stalin rejected Trotsky's emphasis on immediate world revolution and embarked on the rapid large-scale industrialization of the Soviet Union. He sought to create "socialism in one country" and understood that Lenin's revolution had taken place in at best an imperfectly industrialized country, one that would have difficulty competing with the productive capacity of Western capitalism. In the mid-1920s, Stalin decided to continue the New Economic Policy (NEP) that Lenin had developed to establish rudimentary capitalism and increase production among shop workers and peasants. But by 1928, he had taken steps to replace this with an economy planned and directed by the state. In 1928, the first Five-Year Plan was introduced for "expansion of the national economy." The plan prioritized heavy industry and the construction of steel mills, dams for the production of hydraulic electricity, and plants for the production of automobiles and chemicals.

The goals of this "command economy" were impressive: steel production was to go from 4.2 million tons to 10 million tons; coal from 35 million to 150 million tons, electric power from 5 million to 22 million kilowatt-hours. In the following speech, Stalin explains the importance of industrialization.

Industrialization: "Either Perish or Overtake Capitalistic Countries" (1931)

JOSEPH STALIN

Science, technical experience, knowledge, are all things that can be acquired. We may not have them today, but tomorrow we will. The main thing is to have the passionate Bolshevik desire to master technique, to master the science of production. Everything can be achieved, everything can be overcome, if there is a passionate desire to do so.

It is sometimes asked whether it is not possible to slow down the tempo somewhat, to put a check on the movement. No, comrades, it is not possible! The tempo must not be reduced! On the contrary, we must increase it as much as is within our powers and possibilities. This is dictated to us by our obligations to the workers and peasants of the USSR. This is dictated to us by our obligations to the working class of the whole world. . . . To slacken the tempo would mean falling behind. And those who fall behind get beaten. But we do not want to be beaten. No, we refuse to be beaten! . . .

In the past we had no fatherland, nor could we have one. But now that we have overthrown capitalism and power is in our hands, in the hands of the people, we have a fatherland, and we will defend its independence. Do you want our socialist fatherland to be beaten and to lose its independence? If you do not want this you must put an end to its backwardness in the shortest possible time and develop genuine Bolshevik tempo in building up its socialist system of economy. There is no

"Industrialization: 'Either Perish or Overtake Capitalistic Countries' " is from Joseph Stalin, *Problems of Leninism* (Moscow: Foreign Languages Publishing House, 1953), pp. 455–456.

other way. That is why Lenin said on the eve of the October Revolution: "Either perish, or overtake and outstrip the advanced capitalist countries." We are fifty or a hundred years behind the advanced countries. We must make good this distance in ten years. Either we do it, or we shall be crushed.

CONSIDER THIS:

- Stalin noted that "everything can be achieved, everything can be overcome, if there is a passionate desire to do so." If the transition to a communist society was inevitable in Marxist theory, why did this speech carry such an urgent, competitive message? Was the Soviet Union fighting for its life?

Collectivization and the Liquidation of the Kulaks (1929)

JOSEPH STALIN

Collectivized agriculture, in which all land was owned by the proletariat and worked in common for the benefit of the whole community, had always been considered an integral aspect of communism. Although Karl Marx had little to say about its organization, this was a preeminent problem for Lenin and later Stalin. Lenin had conceived of the peasantry as a rural proletariat of agricultural workers who also belonged to the "working class." All income after expenses and taxes from the collective farm were to be shared based on the total number of workdays performed by each member of the collective. The farmers were also permitted a "private plot" of not more than one acre for use as a garden, and a cow, pigs, and chickens. In the 1920s the government offered special subsidies and favorable tax treatments to join the collective farms, but by 1928 only one peasant in sixty had joined. The first Five-Year Plan called for 17.5 percent of the cultivated land to be organized as collective farms. But there was great resistance, especially from a class of prosperous middle-class farmers called Kulaks. They had prospered because of their efficiency and expected to reap the benefits of their dedicated labor. Stalin decided to force the issue and declared the Kulaks to be class enemies, as the following account confirms. Communist squads from the cities were sent into the countryside to seize the grain and livestock of the Kulaks. In response, the Kulaks often burned their property in defiance. They were executed by the thousands.

Can Soviet power and the work of socialist construction rest for any length of time on two different foundations: on the most large-scale and concentrated socialist industry, and the most scattered and backward, small-commodity peasant farming? No, they cannot. Sooner or later this would be bound to end in the complete collapse of the whole national economy.

What, then, is the solution? The solution lies in enlarging the agricultural units, in making agriculture capable of accumulation, of expanded reproduction, and in thus transforming the agricultural bases of our national economy. But how are the agricultural units to be enlarged?

There are two ways of doing this. There is the *capitalist* way, which is to enlarge the agricultural units by introducing capitalism in agriculture—a way which leads to the impoverishment of the peasantry and to the development of capitalist enterprises in agriculture. We reject this way as incompatible with the Soviet economic system.

"Collectivization and the Liquidation of the Kulaks" is from Joseph Stalin, *Problems of Leninism* (Moscow: Foreign Languages Publishing House, 1953), pp. 392–393, 409, 411–412.

There is a second way: the *socialist* way, which is to enlarge the agricultural units to introduce collective farms and state farms in agriculture, the way which leads to the amalgamation of the small-peasant farms into large collective farms, employing machinery and scientific methods of farming, and capable of developing further, for such agricultural enterprises can achieve expanded reproduction.

And so, the question stands as follows: either one way or the other, either *back*—to capitalism, or *forward*—to socialism. There is no third way, nor can there be. . . .

What does this mean? It means that we have passed from the policy of *restricting* the exploiting proclivities of the Kulaks to the policy of *eliminating* the Kulaks as a class. This means that we have made, and are still making, one of the decisive turns in our whole policy. . . .

Could we have undertaken such an offensive against the Kulaks five years or three years ago? Could we then have counted on success in such an offensive? No, we could not. That would have been the most dangerous adventurism. . . . Why? Because we still lacked a wide network of state and collective farms in the rural districts which could be used as strongholds in a determined offensive against the Kulaks. Because at that time we were not yet able to *substitute* for the capitalist production of the Kulaks the socialist production of the collective farms and state farms. . . .

Now we are able to carry on a determined offensive against the Kulaks, to break their resistance, to eliminate them as a class and substitute for their output the output of the collective farms and state farms. No, the Kulaks are being expropriated by the masses of poor and middle peasants themselves, by the masses who are putting solid collectivization into practice. Now, the expropriation of the Kulaks in the regions of solid collectivization is no longer just an administrative measure. Now, the expropriation of the Kulaks is an integral part of the formation and development of the collective farms. Consequently it is now ridiculous and foolish to discourse on the expropriation of the Kulaks. You do not lament the loss of the hair of one who has been beheaded.

There is another question which seems no less ridiculous: whether the Kulaks should be permitted to join the collective farms. Of course not, for they are sworn enemies of the collective-farm movement.

CONSIDER THIS:

- According to Stalin, why did the Kulaks need to be "eliminated as a class"? Why did some citizens have to be forced to take the communist road?

"For the Fatherland!" (1936)

PRAVDA

During the First Five-Year Plan, overall living standards in the Soviet Union diminished 35 percent, especially in the countryside. But by pouring nearly 35 percent of the gross national product into new production, the goals of the first plan were more or less accomplished. The Second and Third Five-Year Plans followed, but the Soviet people saw little benefit from their labor, and the standard of living remained

"'For the Fatherland'" is from *The Communist Conspiracy, Part I: Communism Outside the U.S.*, Section B: the USSR, U.S. House of Representatives Report No. 2241, 84th Congress, 2nd Session (Washington, D.C.: Government Printing Office, 1956), pp. 287–288.

essentially unchanged. Criticism of Stalin's programs increased, especially among his supporters. The result was to purge or eliminate any opposition in political circles, the military, and the artistic community. Lenin had established the Cheka, or "secret police," to combat "counterrevolution," but Stalin honed this organization into a formidable intelligence unit that specialized in foreign espionage and domestic surveillance. Stalin made his secret police the primary instrument of his ruthless purges. They conducted interrogations, tortures, and trials, and expedited the incarceration of dissidents in the Siberian labor camps known as the "Gulag."

The climax of the purge trials came in 1938 when several former revolutionaries who had planned the Russian Revolution with Lenin were condemned and executed. These included "Trotskyites" and "Bukharinites," whose opposition was especially troubling. Stalin's victims even included heads of the secret police, who simply vanished one day and were quickly replaced. Stalin thus used terror effectively and maintained his preeminent authority by making sure there were no entrenched or safe positions in the state. The estimated numbers of his purge victims including Kulaks range from 10 to 20 million. Even when compared with Adolf Hitler's imposition of the Holocaust, Stalin was perhaps history's greatest mass murderer.

The first selection is from the official organ of the Communist Party, *Pravda* (meaning "Truth"). The proclamation of patriotism served as justification for intensifying the penalties of treason. The following accounts of the purge trials and the Gulag give evidence of the nature of Stalin's dominance.

For our fatherland! This call fans the flame of heroism, the flame of creative initiative in pursuits and all fields of our rich life. For our fatherland! This call arouses millions of workers and alerts them in the defence of their great country.

The defence of the fatherland is the supreme law of life. And he who raises his hand against his country, he who betrays his country should be destroyed.

Today we publish the decree of the Central Executive Committee of the USSR regarding the supplementing of the statutes of the state criminal code with articles on treason. The Soviet country is very dear to the workers. . . . They have paid for it dearly in blood and suffering in their struggle with exploiters and interventionists and they will not allow anyone to betray their country and will not allow anyone to bargain with her interests.

For high treason, for acts detrimental to the country's military might, or state independence, or inviolability of her territories, for espionage, for divulging military or state secrets, for deserting to the enemy, or escaping across the border, the Soviet court will punish the guilty by shooting or by confiscating all his property. In the case of a civilian, some leniency will be shown according to circumstances, and for the death penalty will be substituted the confiscation of his property or imprisonment for ten years. For a person in military service, however, for treason there will be only one measure of punishment—execution by shooting with confiscation of all his property. Individual members of his family are also responsible for the acts of traitors. In the case of the escape or flight across the border of a person in military service, all mature members of his family, if they are implicated in aiding the criminal, or knew of his intentions and did not report them to the authorities, are punished by imprisonment for five to ten years with confiscation of all their property.

The other members of the family of the traitor and all his dependents at the time he committed treason are subject to disfranchisement and exile to some remote region in Siberia for five years.

Traitors should be punished unmercifully. On the other hand, if a person in military service was aware of a plot to betray the government or of an act of betrayal and did not report this to the authorities, he is subject to imprisonment for ten years. One cannot be a neutral observer where the interests of the country or the workers and peasants are concerned. This is a terrible crime; this is complicity in the crime.

This decree of the Central Executive Committee gives the workers of the great Soviet Union a new weapon in their hands in the struggle against the enemies of the proletariat dictatorship. The one hundred and seventy million working people who regard the Soviet land as their own mother who has nursed them to a happy and joyous life will deal with the traitors of their fatherland with all their force. For the fatherland, for its honor and glory, might and well-being!

The Purge Trials: "Traitors Must Be Shot Like Dirty Dogs!" (1938)

ANDREI VYSHINSKY

The Trotskyites and Bukharinites, . . . the leading lights of which are now in the prisoners' dock is not a political party, nor a political tendency, but a band of felonious criminals, and not simply felonious criminals, but of criminals who have sold themselves to enemy intelligence services, criminals whom even ordinary felons treat as the basest, the lowest, the most contemptible, the most depraved of the depraved. . . .

The investigation established, and I deem it necessary to remind you of this here in its full scope, Comrades Judges, that in 1918, immediately following the October Revolution, . . . Bukharin and his group of so-called "Left Communists," and Trotsky with his group . . . organized a conspiracy against Lenin as the head of the Soviet government.

Bukharin and the other conspirators, as can be seen from the materials of the investigation, aimed at . . . overthrowing the Soviet government, arresting and killing Lenin, Stalin, and Sverdlov [secretary of the Party from 1917 to 1919], and forming a new government made up of Bukharinites. . . .

It has been proved that this bloc consisted of agents of the intelligence services of several foreign states, it has been proved that the [Trotskyites] regularly engaged in espionage on behalf of these states and supplied their intelligence services with most important state secret material. . . .

It has been proved that the bloc had organized, but fortunately for us had not succeeded in effecting, a number of terrorist acts against the leaders of our Party and government. . . .

Our whole country, from young to old, is awaiting and demanding one thing: the traitors and spies who were selling our country to the enemy must be shot like dirty dogs! Our people are demanding one thing: crush the accursed reptile!

Time will pass. The graves of the hateful traitors will grow over with weeds and thistle, they will be covered with eternal contempt of honest Soviet citizens, of the entire Soviet

"The Purge Trials: 'Traitors Must Be Shot Like Dirty Dogs!'" is from *Report of Court Proceedings: The Case of the Anti-Soviet Bloc of Rights and Trotskyites* (Moscow: People's Commissariat of Justice of the USSR, 1938), English edition, pp. 696–697.

people. But over us, over our happy country, our sun will shine with its luminous rays as bright and as joyous as before. Over the road cleared of the last scum and filth of the past, we, our people, with our beloved leader and teacher, the great Stalin, at our head, will march as before onwards and onwards, towards communism!

The Gulag: "Stalin's Sadistic Nature Thirsted for Blood!" (1938)

Certain Trotskyites, including Vladimir Ivanov, Kossior, and Trotsky's son, Sergei Sedov, a modest and likeable youth, who had imprudently refused to follow his parents into exile in 1928, were taken in a special convoy to Moscow. We can only believe that Stalin was not satisfied simply to hurl them into the tundra; his sadistic nature thirsted not only for blood; he wished first to immeasurably humiliate them and torture them, coercing them into false self-accusations. Ivanov and Kossior disappeared without trace behind the walls of the Lubyanka prison. As for Sergei Sedov, after a "treatment" at the Lubyanka he was "tried" at Sverdlovsk, where he had worked as an engineer at the electric station; according to the newspaper stories, "he recalled having devoted himself to acts of sabotage" and other "crimes," for which he was condemned to be shot. . . .

The whole winter of 1937–38 some prisoners, encamped in barracks at the brickyard, starved and waited for a decision regarding their fate. Finally, in March, three NKVD [Secret Police] officers, with Kashketin at their head, arrived by plane at Vorkuta, coming from Moscow. They came to the brickyard to interrogate the prisoners. Thirty to forty were called each day, superficially questioned five to ten minutes each, rudely insulted, forced to listen to vile name-calling and obscenities. Some were greeted with punches in the face; Lt. Kashketin himself several times beat up one of them, the Old Bolshevik Virap Virapov, a former member of the Central Committee of Armenia. . . .

Two days later, there was a new call, this time of forty names. Once more there was a ration of bread. Some, out of exhaustion, could no longer move; they were promised a ride in a cart. Holding their breath, the prisoners remaining in the barracks heard the grating of the snow under the feet of the departing convoy. For a long time there was no sound; but all on the watch still listened. Nearly an hour passed in this way. Then, again, shots resounded in the tundra; this time, they came from much further away, in the direction of the narrow railway which passed three kilometers from the brickyard. The second "convoy" definitely convinced those remaining behind that they had been irremediably condemned.

The executions in the tundra lasted the whole month of April and part of May. Usually one day out of two, or one day out of three, thirty to forty prisoners were called. It is characteristic to note that each time, some common criminals, repeaters, were included. In order to terrorize the prisoners, the officials, from time to time, made publicly known by means of local radio, the list of those shot. Usually broadcasts began as follows: "For counter-revolutionary agitation, sabotage, brigandage in the camps, refusal to work, attempts to escape, the following have been shot . . ." followed by a list of names of some

"The Gulag: 'Stalin's Sadistic Nature Thirsted for Blood!' " is from "Trotskyites at Vorkuta: An Eyewitness Report," *International Socialist Review*, vol. 24, no. 3 (Summer 1963), p. 97.

political prisoners mixed with a group of common criminals.

At the beginning of May, a group of women were shot. . . . At the time of execution of a male prisoner, his imprisoned wife was automatically liable to capital punishment; and when it was a question of well-known members of the Opposition, this applied equally to any of his children over the age of twelve.

Consider This:

- Why did Stalin purge so many opponents? Were purges necessary to create the "workers' paradise" promised by Karl Marx? Or did the purges have anything to do with Marxism at all?
- The 1936 constitution of the Soviet Union guaranteed citizens freedom of speech, press, and assembly. In view of this, how do you account for Stalin's liquidation of the Kulaks, the purge trials, and the establishment of the Gulag?

The Broader Perspective:

- Must revolutions go through a radical phase of blood lust before they stabilize? Compare the French Revolution and the Russian Revolution in this regard. Did the elimination of "enemies of the people" have anything to do with the ideals of the French Revolution or the establishment of a Marxist egalitarian society? At the end of the day, are revolutions all about power and not ideals? Was Machiavelli right? Do the ends always justify the means?

THEME: THE POWER STRUCTURE

The Reflection in the Mirror

The Orwellian World of 1984

"Power Is in Tearing Human Minds to Pieces"

GEORGE ORWELL

Under the tenets of Stalinism the state became a dominant force and exercised complete control over all political, social, and economic affairs. Thus total control, or totalitarianism, was the most sophisticated expression of authoritarian government that had developed through the fascist societies of Hitler and Mussolini. Fascism and communism theoretically were diametrically opposed, the former advocating the subordination of all elements to the needs of the state, the latter seeking the withering away of the state. Yet Stalin's perversion of Marxist orthodoxy allowed the creation of a state even more encompassing than fascist Germany or Italy. The following selection is from George Orwell's famous novel *1984*, in which he discusses the real implications of totalitarian power.

"The real power, the power we have to fight for night and day, is not power over things, but over men." O'Brien paused, and for a moment assumed again his air of a schoolmaster questioning a promising pupil: "How does one man assert his power over another, Winston?"

Winston thought. "By making him suffer," he said.

"'Power Is in Tearing Human Minds to Pieces'" is from George Orwell, *Nineteen Eighty-Four* (New York: Harcourt, Brace and Company, 1949), pp. 269–271.

> "If you want a picture of the future, imagine a boot stamping on a human face—forever."
> —GEORGE ORWELL

"Exactly. By making him suffer. Obedience is not enough. Unless he is suffering, how can you be sure that he is obeying your will and not his own? Power is in inflicting pain and humiliation. Power is in tearing human minds to pieces and putting them together again in new shapes of your own choosing. Do you begin to see, then, what kind of world we are creating? It is the exact opposite of the stupid hedonistic Utopias that the old reformers imagined. A world of fear and treachery and torment, a world of trampling and being trampled upon, a world which will grow not less but more merciless as it refines itself. Progress in our world will be progress toward more pain. The old civilizations claimed that they were founded on love and justice. Ours is founded upon hatred. In our world there will be no emotions except fear, rage, triumph, and self-abasement. Everything else we shall destroy—everything. Already we are breaking down the habits of thought which have survived from before the Revolution. We have cut the links between child and parent, and between man and man, and between man and woman. No one dares trust a wife or a child or a friend any longer. But in the future there will be no wives and no friends. Children will be taken from their mothers at birth, as one takes eggs from a hen. The sex instinct will be eradicated. Procreation will be an annual formality like the renewal of a ration card. We shall abolish the orgasm. Our neurologists are at work upon it now. There will be no loyalty, except loyalty toward the Party. There will be no love, except the love of Big Brother. There will be no laughter, except the laugh of triumph over a defeated enemy. There will be no art, no literature, no science. When we are omnipotent we shall have no more need of science. There will be no distinction between beauty and ugliness. There will be no curiosity, no employment of the process of life. All competing pleasures will be destroyed. But always——do not forget this, Winston——always there will be the intoxication of power, constantly increasing and constantly growing subtler. Always, at every moment, there will be the thrill of victory, the sensation of trampling on an enemy who is helpless. If you want a picture of the future, imagine a boot stamping on a human face—forever."

COMPARE AND CONTRAST:

- The competing ideologies of the Cold War engendered fear and distrust between the United States and the Soviet Union. Compare the fear expressed in our need to learn "how to spot a communist" (p. 468) with the fear that Orwell describes in his vision of the future. Which one really frightens you?

THE BROADER PERSPECTIVE:

- After reading this excerpt from George Orwell's *1984*, what images remain in your mind? What is the essence of power? Could you foresee a modern state with that amount of control over society?

- As we become more advanced technologically, does the threat to personal freedom increase? How do humans remain free in mind and body?

The Soviet State Ideal

The Creation of "Stalinism" (1934)

JOSEPH STALIN

The nineteenth-century political thinker Karl Marx had established the philosophical tenets of communism in 1848 that had guided Lenin, Trotsky, and other revolutionaries toward the establishment of a communist society. Marx was specific about his vision of a community of workers, the proletariat, which would work in harmony after the state had "withered away." Marx was notoriously unspecific, however, regarding the details or time span of this process. Thus revolutionaries like Lenin were left on their own to make whatever practical accommodations were necessary to implement Marx's vision. Lenin was a devoted Marxist and tried to remain faithful to his general principles. But Stalin, while outwardly professing Marxism, reinterpreted the primary doctrines. In the following address at the Seventeenth Party Congress in 1934, Stalin enunciated his revised conception of Marxism. In fact, it was his rejection of the guiding influence of Marx and the imposition of his own philosophy that might best be termed "Stalinism." Note carefully Stalin's views of the maintenance of class warfare, rather than the "withering away" of the state's influence; the emphasis on inequality, rather than a community of equals; and the importance of individual effort to effect change, rather than the unyielding influence of impersonal social and economic forces.

It goes without saying that a classless society cannot come of itself, spontaneously, as it were. It has to be achieved and built by the efforts of all the working people, by strengthening the organs of the dictatorship of the proletariat, by intensifying the class struggle, by abolishing classes, by eliminating the remnants of the capitalist classes, and in battles with enemies both internal and external.

The point is clear, one would think. And yet, who does not know that the promulgation of his clear and elementary thesis of Leninism has given rise to not a little confusion and to unhealthy sentiments among a section of Party members? The thesis that we are advancing towards a classless society—which was put forward as a slogan—was interpreted by them to mean a spontaneous process. And they began to reason in this way: If it is a classless society, then we can relax the class struggle, we can relax the dictatorship of the proletariat, and get rid of the state altogether, since it is fated to wither away soon in any case. They dropped into a state of mooncalf ecstasy, in the expectation that soon there will be no classes, and therefore no class struggle, and therefore no cares and worries, and therefore we can lay down our arms and retire—to sleep and to wait for the advent of a classless society. . . .

It goes without saying that if this confusion of mind and these non-Bolshevik sentiments obtained a hold over the majority of our Party, the Party would find itself demobilized and disarmed. . . .

[Some] people evidently think that socialism calls for equalization, for levelling the requirements and the individual lives of the members of society. Needless to say, such an assumption has nothing in common with Marxism, with Leninism. By equality Marxism means, not equalization of individual

"The Creation of 'Stalinism'" is from Joseph Stalin, *Problems of Leninism* (Moscow: Foreign Languages Publishing House, 1953), pp. 631–632, 635.

requirements and individual life, but the abolition of classes, i.e., a) the equal emancipation of all working people from exploitation after the capitalists have been overthrown and expropriated; b) the equal abolition for all of private property in the means of production after they have been converted into the property of the whole of society; c) the equal duty of all to work according to their ability, and the equal right of all working people to receive remuneration according to the amount of work performed (socialist society); d) the equal duty of all to work according to their ability, and the equal right of all working people to receive remuneration according to their needs (communist society). Furthermore, Marxism proceeds from the assumption that people's tastes and requirements are not, and cannot be identical, equal, in regard to quality or quantity, either in the period of socialism or in the period of communism. That is the Marxian conception of equality. . . .

CONSIDER THIS:

- In 1924, Stalin, in true Marxist fashion, argued that the Communist Party was the instrument in the hands of the people for achieving the dictatorship of the proletariat. He noted that "when classes disappear and the dictatorship of the proletariat withers away, the Party will also wither away." How does this statement compare with his ideas ten years later in 1934 concerning the creation of "Stalinism"? What does this tell you about Stalin? Was he an orthodox Marxist, or was he merely adapting Marxism to fit the demands of the time—or the needs of his own authority?

COMPARE AND CONTRAST:

- Compare the vision of Stalin on capitalism versus communism, on the duty of citizens to the state and on the future of communism, with the remarks made by Mikhail Gorbachev and Vladimir Putin on pages 477–484. What happened to the "Soviet miracle"? Why did the Soviet Union fail?

Literature and the Soviet Ideal: "The Craftsmen of Culture" (1934)

MAXIM GORKY

With the launching of the First Five-Year Plan in 1928, Stalin decided that the creative arts (literature, dance, music, and the visual arts) had to be mobilized to support the state efforts to industrialize the economy and collectivize agriculture. All artistic endeavors had to be intelligible to the masses, so creativity and experimentation were condemned. Themes suggested to creative artists included industrial construction, the fight against external aggression and internal subversion, and the glory of life on collective farms. Socialist realism became the order of the day, and the state demanded that artists and writers depict Soviet society not as it was but as it was supposed to be. Music was to be melodic and firmly grounded in folk themes, art could not be abstract, and modern and jazz dance were barred. The result was an outpouring of poster art depicting scenes from the Russian Revolution or portraits of Marx and Lenin. Ballet was locked into a classical mode or focused on revolutionary themes.

"Literature and the Soviet Ideal" is from H. G. Scott, ed., *Problems of Soviet Literature* (Moscow: Cooperative Publishing Society of Foreign Workers in the USSR, 1935), pp. 53–54, 64–67.

The famous revolutionary writer Maxim Gorky became the leading advocate of Soviet realism. In the following selection, he discussed the new standards of Soviet literature at a writers' conference in 1935.

The Communist-Leninist Party, the workers' and peasants' government of the Union of Socialist Soviets, which have destroyed capitalism throughout the length and breadth of tsarist Russia, which have handed over political power to the workers and the peasants, and which are organizing a free classless society, have made it the object of their daring, sage, and indefatigable activity to free the working masses from the age-old yoke of an old and outworn history, of the capitalist development of culture, which today has glaringly exposed all its vices and its creative decrepitude. And it is from the height of this great aim that we honest writers of the Union of Soviets must examine, appraise and organize our work. . . .

As the principal hero of our books we should choose labor, i.e. a person, organized by the processes of labor, who in our country is armed with the full might of modern technique, a person who, in his turn, so organizes labor that it becomes easier and more productive, raising it to the level of an art. . . .

The party leadership of literature must be thoroughly purged of all philistine influences. Party members active in literature must not only be the teachers of ideas which will muster the energy of the proletariat in all countries for the last battle for its freedom; the party leadership must, in all its conduct, show a morally authoritative force. This force must imbue literary workers first and foremost with a consciousness of their collective responsibility for all that happens in their midst. Soviet literature, with all its diversity of talents, and the steadily growing number of new and gifted writers, should be organized as an integral collective body, as a potent instrument of socialist culture. . . . The idea, of course, is not to restrict individual creation, but to furnish it with the widest means of continued powerful development. . . .

The high standard demanded of literature, which is being rapidly remolded by life itself and by the cultural revolutionary work of Lenin's party, is due to the high estimation in which the party holds the importance of the literary art. There has never been a state in the world where science and literature enjoyed such comradely help, such care for the raising of professional proficiency among the workers of art and science.

The proletarian state must educate thousands of first-class "craftsmen of culture," "engineers of the soul." This is necessary in order to restore to the whole mass of the working people the right to develop their intelligence, talents and faculties—a right of which they have been deprived everywhere else in the world. This aim, which is a fully practicable one, imposes on us writers the need of strict responsibility for our work and our social behavior. This places us not only in the position, traditional to realist literature, of "judges of the world and men," "critics of life," but gives us the right to participate directly in the construction of a new life, in the process of "changing the world." The possession of this right should impress every writer with a sense of his duty and responsibility for all literature, for all the aspects in it which should not be there. . . .

Consider This:

- What are the main points that Maxim Gorky makes about Soviet literature? What was the purpose of the "craftsmen of culture" and the "engineers of the soul"?

Our Country:
"A Dream Come True" (1937)

A. STETSKY

In the late 1930s, as Stalin moved to consolidate his power by destroying any opposition through the purges, he also began a campaign to export propaganda for consumption abroad that would influence public opinion and confirm the "Soviet miracle" as an industrial and military power. The so-called Soviet "ideal" is nowhere better explained than in this utopian vision of Soviet progress.

The land of the Soviets differs from the capitalist world in that here the power belongs to the toilers themselves—to the workers and peasants. In our country there are no private owners of factories and banks, of land and manors. All the mills and factories, all the mines, railways and banks, and all the land, forests and mineral wealth . . . belong to the toilers themselves, organized in the Soviet socialist state.

There are no capitalists in our country, no stockbrokers, no landlords, no Kulaks, nor any of the classes which in bourgeois countries oppress and rob the workers and peasants. . . . The working class of our country, acting in alliance with the toiling peasantry, has created the social system of which the best representatives of the toiling people have dreamed for centuries. . . . The USSR is the first country in the world where socialism reigns victorious. . . .

Soviet industry has made giant strides during the period of the Second Five-Year Plan [1933–1937]. Wretched and beggarly does the industry of pre-war Russia now appear to us compared with the mighty and up-to-date industry of the USSR. . . . One of the aims of the policy of industrializing the USSR was to overtake and outstrip the foremost capitalist countries economically and technically. The rapid development of Soviet industry . . . advanced our country to first place in Europe with respect to output of tractors, and first place in the world with respect to output of harvester combines. . . .

If exploitation was to be ended completely, the whole system in the countryside had to be changed. The Communists set about explaining to the peasants that only large-scale, collective farming could put an end to their poverty and their enslavement to the Kulaks. The USSR had built up a powerful, up-to-date industry. Agriculture could not be allowed to lag behind industry. It was impermissible that, with a large-scale, highly developed socialist industry, agriculture should consist of a sea of small and dwarf farms.

The Communists explained to the peasants that the only way they could escape from their poverty was to abandon the ancient habit of each household working its separate farm. The Soviet government aided the peasants in every way—by loans, seed, and agricultural implements, and by curbing the Kulaks and placing restrictions on their exploiting proclivities. But at the same time, the Communist Party and the Soviet government made it clear to the peasants that the only sure way they could escape from poverty and exploitation altogether was to form collective farms. . . . That is why the Bolsheviks, in leading the struggle of the workers and peasants for the victory of socialism, insistently directed the peasants towards

"Our Country" is from A. Stetsky, ed., *Our Country* (Moscow: Cooperative Publishing Society of Foreign Workers in the USSR, 1937), pp. 7–8, 19–20, 23, 27–28, 43–45, 79.

FIGURE 11.4 This police mugshot of a young Stalin after an arrest contrasts with his subsequent position as General Secretary of the Communist Party. Stalin's "cult of personality" permeated social, political, and cultural life in the Soviet Union. The Marxist vision of a state that was supposed to "wither away" had been replaced with the totalitarian control of a dictator. (*Library of Congress*)

collectivization, towards large-scale collective, co-operative farming. . . .

The cultural level of our country is rising with the rise in the standard of living of the people. Ever since the dictatorship of the proletariat was set up, the Party and the Soviet government have been steadily working to completely abolish illiteracy, that accursed heritage of the tsarist regime. In 1920, two-thirds of the population were still illiterate, but by 1936 the proportion of illiterates had dropped to 10 per cent. . . .

Education in our country is open to everybody—juvenile or adult. The workers under the Soviet system, where exploitation is unknown, have the shortest working day in the world. They possess great opportunities for cultural development and rational recreation. Russian workers before the revolution on an average worked 10 or 11 hours a day. Under the Soviet system the working day has been fixed at 7 hours, and for some branches at 6 hours. . . .

The development of culture in the USSR has been accompanied by the development of science. Scientific institutions and research laboratories have sprung up all over the country. There is no branch of knowledge in which Soviet scientists are not active and to which they have not made important contributions. . . . Soviet science is working hand in hand with our industry and is serving the cause of socialist development and the emancipation of humanity from the blind forces of nature.

Soviet science strives to master nature, to make it the servant of man and to place upon its shoulders the burdensome forms of physical labor which are detrimental to the health and strength of man. . . .

The people of our Soviet country are stretching to their full height. They are justly proud of their great gains. And they have expressed their joy and warm gratitude to their beloved leader in their song:

"And we who have conquered, we sing it so
 proudly,
The Stalinist epoch we honor as one,
We sing of our new life so happy and
 splendid,
We sing of the joy of our victories won.
From border to border, o'er valley and
 mountain,
Where loudly the airplane's swift motor roars,
Of Stalin the wise, the dearly beloved,
The song of the peoples triumphantly soars."

CONSIDER THIS:

- Do you think the selection "Our Country: 'A Dream Come True'" is a valuable and convincing piece of propaganda? Why or why not? All of these works were created in the middle to late 1930s. What do you think of the juxtaposition of this expression of Soviet idealism with the purge trials that were taking place within the Soviet Union?

THEME: THE VARIETIES OF TRUTH

THE ARTISTIC VISION

Engineers of the Soul: The Soviet Creation of Belief

Industrial Worker and Collective Farm Girl (1937)

VERA MUKHINA

By the mid-1930s, most of the Russian avant-garde artists who had flourished in the 1920s were either dead or in exile. Those who stayed in the Soviet Union either embraced the dictates of Soviet Realism and became "engineers of the soul" or resisted state repression by conjuring up their personal vision masked by a dense, almost impenetrable imagery that was then criticized by government officials. The photographer Alexander Rodchenko, for example, was denounced for a series of photos he took of young Soviet "Pioneers": "Why does the Pioneer look upwards? It is not ideologically correct. Pioneers and the youth of the Communist Party must look ahead."

The International Exhibition of 1937 in Paris became a magnet for the expression of political ideology through art and architecture. The Soviet and German pavilions faced each other across a deep ideological divide. The German pavilion, designed by Hitler's architect Albert Speer, was topped with a Prussian eagle; the Soviet pavilion sported a massive sculpture by Vera Mukhina called *Industrial Worker and Collective Farm Girl.* Almost 80 feet tall, it served as the visual embodiment of the Marxist ideal—the cooperation of the industrial and agricultural sectors, the unity of the proletarians in the establishment of a worker's paradise. As Stalin's purges were reaching their bloody climax, Mukhina's worker, holding a hammer and the farm girl a sickle, stride forth in lock step toward a common vision of the future.

FIGURE 11.5 *Industrial Worker and Collective Farm Girl* (1936) by Vera Mukhina. (*Corbis/Bettmann*)

CONSIDER THIS:

- What was the purpose of this sculpture by Vera Mukhina? How effective was it as a reflection of Marxist ideology? Would you call it art? Why or why not?

- *Industrial Worker and Collective Farm Girl* is made of steel and stands over 80 feet high. Why is scale such an issue in disseminating a political message? Is it a utilitarian matter? The bigger the scale, the greater the impression for the greatest number of people? This sculpture represents a collective ideological vision. When this collective vision is made more personal through armbands, insignia, uniforms, flags, and the like, does it become more or less effective?

THE BROADER PERSPECTIVE:

- *Industrial Worker and Collective Farm Girl* has been called "a rare masterpiece of Soviet realism." Does this imply that it is art? Can propaganda ever be considered art?

- Shortly after the International Exhibition of 1937, Mukhina's sculpture was returned to Russia where it towered over the Moscow skyline. But after the fall of the Soviet Union in 1990, it was first threatened and then simply became irrelevant, suffering the indignity of graffiti and the decay of time. Before long, parking lots and apartments blocked its view and obscured its pointless message. In 2000, however, Russian authorities brought back the old Soviet national anthem and asked the poet who wrote the words in 1943 to compose a new set of verses that reflected the current vision of the state. This wave of nostalgia engulfed Mukhina's sculpture as well. In 2001, the Kremlin decided to restore *Industrial Worker and Collective Farm Girl* and construct a new pedestal containing a museum, thereby making the sculpture three times higher. We often think that propaganda has a lifespan and that great art is timeless. Do you think this is true? What new relevance and purpose has the sculpture assumed in the view of the Russian government? Has it now transcended the boundaries of propaganda and become art?

12

Europe Between the Wars: Fascism and the Nazi Rise to Power (1919–1939)

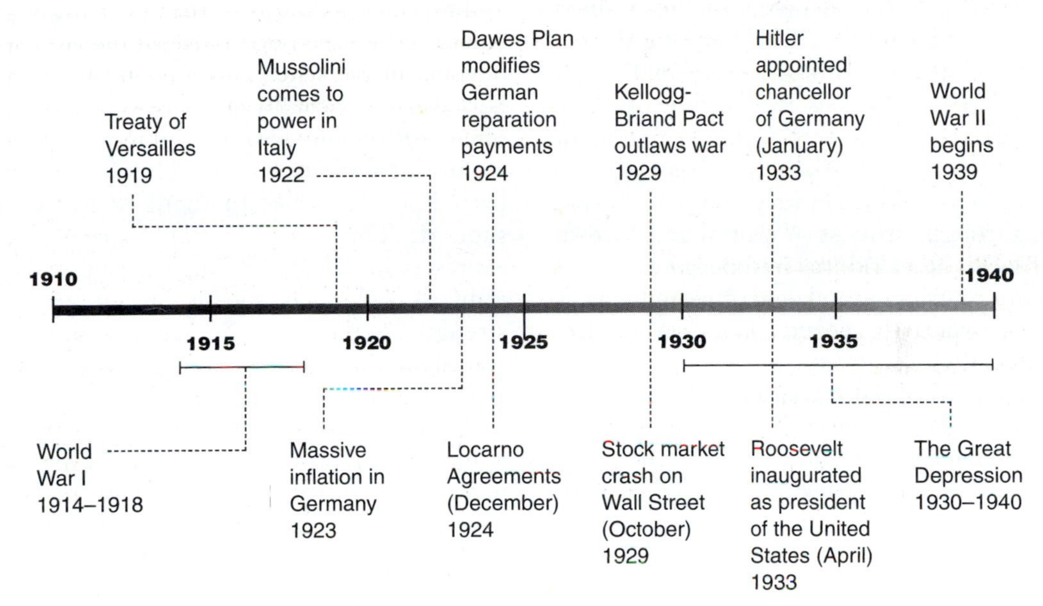

CHAPTER THEMES

- **The Power Structure:** What is fascism, and why was it so popular in the 1920s and 1930s? Why did democracy fail in Germany and Italy? What is totalitarianism, and how did Hitler's control over Germany differ from Stalin's control over the Soviet Union?
- **Revolution and Historical Transition:** Is it legitimate to speak of a fascist revolution in Italy and Germany? Mussolini and Hitler came to power legally. How did their revolutions differ from Napoleon's revolution in France or Lenin's revolution in Russia?
- **The Varieties of Truth:** How were the Nazis aided in their rise to power by creating belief in their cause? What elements of their propaganda appealed to most Germans?
- **Women in History:** What were the role and expectation of women and children in the Nazi state? How did the image differ from the reality?
- **The Individual and the Institution:** How important were Hitler and Mussolini in changing the course of European history? Were the political, social, and economic conditions right for historical change, or did these leaders create the conditions of their success?
- **The Big Picture:** Is fascism dead, or will it always exist? Does modern communication technology make it even more dangerous? Why does fascism

seem to strike a responsive chord in human nature? Is freedom most importantly a thing of the mind? If the institutions of government are controlled, yet appear to be free, and if you feel that you are free, are you free?

With the end of the war in 1918, Europe entered a new age of change and development. Democratic governments had won "the war to make the world safe for democracy," and the aggressive German monarchy had been abolished. Indeed, most other European nations adopted or maintained democratic institutions. The dominant theme, however, in the political history of Europe from 1919 to 1939 is the decline of these democratic governments. By the beginning of World War II in 1939, authoritarian regimes had been established in Italy, Germany, Spain, and throughout most of central and eastern Europe. The world was introduced to two of the most intriguing and destructive individuals of the twentieth century: Benito Mussolini and Adolf Hitler.

To understand the success of Hitler and the Nazis in particular, we must first look at the doctrine of fascism to which Hitler and many other twentieth-century dictators have subscribed. Fascism varies in its particular details of application, but in the simplest of terms, it is a doctrine that sanctifies the interests of the state and minimizes the rights of the individual. Fascism promotes as its great benefit the stability and security of the state.

Nearly all fascist governments have certain features in common. For example, fascism was born in direct opposition to liberal democracy, and as such regards personal freedom as dangerous to the stability of the state. Democracy, according to fascist doctrine, promotes individual expression and self-aggrandizement, which in turn results in disagreement and class conflict. Fascists also oppose socialism and communism because they promote the welfare of the masses over the good of the state. Communism, in fact, with its Leninist emphasis on the immediacy of world revolution, has dangerous potential for destabilization by its very insistence on class warfare. Fascism also depends on extreme nationalism. This goes far beyond the patriotic love of one's nation but is based on pride in the allegedly unique characteristics and achievements of a "special" people. Fascist national pride, therefore, is exclusive and implies a hostility toward other countries that are considered inferior in their outlook, governmental organization, or national heritage. This hostility is a unifying factor and often vented against particular minority groups within the state itself. Thus Hitler promoted hatred of the Jews as a rallying point for his support. This fascist national pride often expresses itself through imperialism because military and economic expansion actually strengthens the state. Because stability and security of the state are the watchwords of fascism, it is important to implement a strong, highly centralized, and efficient government that only dictatorial rule can provide. One man with total control over the affairs of state ensures coordination and consistency of rule. Such a dictatorship is achieved and maintained through control of the national army but most practically through paramilitary organizations like secret police, private armies, and bodyguards, which do not hesitate to use violence.

Fascism traditionally derives its support from the right-wing, or conservative, forces of society. The military represents, by its very nature, order and discipline. Big industrialists want to enjoy the lucrative profits that state stability affords; in a fascist society, general workers' strikes, which can often cripple an economy and interrupt production, are forbidden. Socially, fascism derives its mass support from the lower middle class. In general, these are people who have worked hard within the confines of society to attain some measure of self-respect. Sociologically, they are individuals of commitment and pride who harbor dreams of social mobility, have faith in traditional values, and love their country; they have much to lose from instability and chaos. The fascist totalitarian regime is intended to eliminate class conflict by concentrating the energy of all its members in the service of the state.

Fascism is often born of the frustration and discontent of people who have been in some way humiliated or robbed of their dignity either as individuals or collectively as a nation. According to the philosopher Eric Hoffer, in his book *The True Believer* (New York: Harper & Row, 1951), people who are most susceptible to mass movements are filled with the burden of their present existence and seek inspiration from those who have a vision of a proud and stable future.

Fascism first took hold in Italy during the 1920s when unemployment greeted returning war veterans and disruptive strikes crippled the economy. Liberal middle-class politicians lost control of the state, and four socialist governments fell in three years. In addition, Italy felt deprived of the fruits of victory from its involvement in World War I. It failed to obtain any of the German colonies in Africa and was frustrated in its attempt to acquire Albania as well. Amid this frustration and dislocation, Benito Mussolini rose to power with his Italian National Fascist Party ("Black Shirts"). Mussolini (1883–1945) promised stability and the vision of a "corporate state" in which each individual worked for the welfare of the entire nation. Mussolini guaranteed employment and satisfactory wages for labor but did not permit strikes. He favored industrialists by allowing them lucrative profits and gave respect to Italy by closely identifying his regime with the glorious heritage of the ancient Roman Empire. Mussolini succeeded in giving Italy direction and dignity, but he accomplished this through suppression of civil rights and individual liberties. He was, indeed, the quintessential fascist.

But perhaps the most important and influential of the authoritarian regimes in the subsequent history of Europe was established legally in Germany by Adolf Hitler and the National Socialist Party.

After the abolition of the aggressive German monarchy in 1918, the Weimar Republic was established amid lofty ideals. Yet it labored under the burden of antirepublican pressures from the army, judiciary, bureaucracy, and even monarchists who wanted to reinstate the kaiser. Germany had never had a strong democratic tradition and had been united under a central monarch for only about fifty years. The German republic was also weakened because it had been created during a time of national defeat and humiliation. Critics used the Weimar Republic as a scapegoat for Germany's ills and accused its democratic leaders of betraying the German armies by making an unacceptable peace. Faced with the threat of communist revolution in Germany and economic dislocation, which was prompted by incredible price inflation and devaluation of currency, the Weimar Republic struggled through the early 1920s. Even during a period of relative economic stability after 1924, the leaders of the republic were unable to foster a coherent program because of the conflicting demands of coalition government.

In the summer of 1929, Germany felt the first effects of the worldwide depression. By the winter of 1929–1930, 3 million Germans were unemployed, a figure that increased to 6 million by 1933. The deepening depression made it increasingly difficult for the various parties in the coalition government to work together. In the elections of 1930, the moderate and prorepublican parties suffered a significant defeat; the greatest gains were made by the National Socialist Party, headed by Adolf Hitler. The Nazis, as its members were called, had been a small violent group on the fringes of antirepublican politics during the early 1920s. But by 1930, their membership had increased greatly, and they were the most dynamic of the antidemocratic parties. Their success and popularity lay in providing, or at least promising, something for everyone.

The Nazis promised a renegotiation of peace treaties and reestablishment of German honor and power to those who saw Germany's greatness shattered by the defeat in 1918 and the Treaty of Versailles in 1919. They promised efficient authoritarianism to those who were frustrated by the inadequacy of republican politics. The Nazis promised a strong economy to those (especially in the middle class) whose savings were threatened by the depression. Hitler also promised protection to the industrialists whose profits and very existence were jeopardized by the communist movement.

The central doctrine, however, of the National Socialist party was anti-Semitism. In his autobiography, *Mein Kampf* (My Struggle), and in speeches and party announcements, Hitler blamed the Jews for the economic crises of the 1920s. The inflation and depression, he argued, had been caused by Jewish international financiers. The Nazis also believed that the Jews controlled the international communist movement. Jews had to be excluded from German life, they concluded. In the unstable and violent years after 1929, more and more Germans seemed willing to accept this explanation for their difficult times.

As Hitler's influence grew, his followers advocated a violent seizure of power. Although he sanctioned violent political disruption and intimidation, Hitler insisted on attaining power legally. On January 30, 1933, after much political maneuvering, Hitler was appointed chancellor of the Weimar Republic. By July 1934, Hitler had legally altered the Weimar constitution, changed the nature of the republic, removed all Jews and "politically unreliable" people from the bureaucracy, dissolved all opposition political parties, and purged the army. On August 2, 1934, President von Hindenburg died, and Hitler combined the offices of president and chancellor. The army formally supported these developments by swearing "unconditional obedience to the Führer of the German Reich and People, Adolf Hitler." Hitler then began fashioning his own dictatorship.

In this chapter, we look carefully at the political, social, and economic conditions that existed in Germany during the 1920s and early 1930s in an effort to understand why the Nazis were able to gain power. Themes that emerge from the material include the use of racism and propaganda in the pursuit of power, as well as the role of the individual in history. Could Hitler have risen to lead Germany had he not been presented with the devastating social and economic conditions of the time? To what extent did Hitler change the course of history? In essence, why did Germany follow the leadership of Adolf Hitler? The complicated political maneuverings are not at issue here. Rather, it is important to try to understand people in crisis.

The Legacy of World War I

Power is given only to him who dares to stoop and seize it. There is only one thing that matters, just one thing: you have to dare!

—FYODOR DOSTOEVSKY

Tyranny consists in the desire of universal power beyond its scope; it is the wish to have in one way what can only be had in another.

—BLAISE PASCAL

The Rise of Benito Mussolini

Before discussing the Nazi rise to power, one must understand the doctrine of fascism to which most of the right-wing dictatorships in the decades between the wars adhered. Benito Mussolini (1883–1945) was perhaps its most articulate spokesman. Mussolini was born the son of a blacksmith and worked as a schoolteacher and day laborer before becoming editor of a socialist newspaper prior to World War I. He supported Italy's entry into the war and was wounded in the conflict. In 1919, he was one of many small-time candidates trying to make a mark in Italian politics. An amazing orator and opportunist, Mussolini presented a message of order and action that won him the support of working- and middle-class Italians who had been hit hard by the inflation that plagued Europe after the war. Mussolini even organized terrorist squads to contribute to the very instability that drew him adherents.

By 1922, the fascists controlled local governments in many cities in northern Italy. Mussolini initiated a march on Rome that met with no resistance from King Victor Emmanuel III. Concerned with violence and his personal safety, the king asked Mussolini to become prime minister and form a government. Although Mussolini had achieved power legally, he did not enjoy even a near majority in the Chamber of Deputies. He immediately disrupted the parliamentary government with threats and physical acts of violence against its elected members. Mussolini was then given temporary dictatorial powers by the king to stabilize the political situation; he soon turned these into a permanent and personal dominance.

The first two excerpts come from Mussolini's autobiography and represent the official fascist interpretation of events leading to his assumption of power in Italy. Focus carefully on his reasons for taking action. The last selection is perhaps the quintessential defining statement of fascism. Mussolini believed that the twentieth century was a new historical epoch that required a different political premise based on popular loyalty to the state and supported by violent force.

"The State's Authority Was Ready for the Grave!" (1922)

BENITO MUSSOLINI

Milan, our greatest modern city, was in the power of political anarchy. Those same military forces who would have been able easily to take the situation in hand and dominate it were put at the mercy of the local authorities. They were even obliged to ask the authorities for the flour to make bread for the troops! The stations, situated at the boundaries of the district of Milan, had in store heaps on heaps of goods; or course these stores decayed or deteriorated and were at the mercy of ware-house and freight-car robbers. At length, after thirteen days, on the morning of June twenty-fourth [1922] and after a meeting on behalf of the striking railway employees during which there was a fusillade of firearms, with dead and wounded, the railway men, overpowered by the indignation which had spread through the whole body of citizens, were convinced that it was better to return to work. But the state's authority was dead; it was now ready for the grave. . . .

"The State's Authority Was Ready for the Grave!" is from Benito Mussolini, *My Autobiography* (New York: Charles Scribner's Sons, 1928), pp. 110–111, 119–120.

I called to Milan the responsible chiefs of the Fascist movement, the representatives of the Po Valley, of Upper Italy, of the towns and countrysides. Those present were not many, but they were men resolved to take any risk. I made them understand, as I had suddenly understood, that through newspaper propaganda, or by example, we would never attain any great successes. It was necessary to beat the violent adversary on the battlefield of violence.

As if a revelation had come to me, I realized that Italy would be saved by one historic agency—in an imperfect world, sometimes inevitable still—righteous force. Our democracy of yesterdays had died; its testament had been read; it had bequeathed us nothing but chaos.

The Fascist March on Rome (October 26, 1922)

BENITO MUSSOLINI

Suddenly, when I knew that everything was ready, I issued from Milan, through the . . . correspondents of all the Italian newspapers, my proclamation of revolution. . . . Here is the text of the memorable document:

> Fascisti! Italians!
>
> The time for determined battle has come! Four years ago at this season the national army loosed the final offensive which brought it to Victory. Today the army of the black shirts [Fascists] again takes possession of that Victory, which has been mutilated, and going directly to Rome, brings Victory again to the glory of that Capitol. . . . By order of the Duce all the military, political and administrative functions of the party management are taken over by a secret Quadrumvirate of Action with dictatorial powers.
>
> The army, the reserve and safeguard of the Nation, must not take part in this struggle. . . . Fascism, furthermore, does not march against the police, but against a political class both cowardly and imbecile, which in four long years has not been able to give a Government to the Nation. Those who form the productive class must know that Fascism wants to impose nothing more than order and discipline upon the Nation and to help to raise the strength which will renew progress and prosperity. The people who work in the fields and in the factories, those who work in the railroads or in offices, have nothing to fear from the Fascist Government. Their just rights will be protected. We will even be generous with unarmed adversaries.
>
> Fascism draws its sword to cut the multiple Gordian knots which tie and burden Italian life. We call God and the spirit of our five hundred thousand dead to witness that only one impulse sends us on, that only one passion burns within us—the impulse and the passion to contribute to the safety and greatness of our Country.
>
> Fascisti of all Italy!
>
> Stretch forth like Romans your spirits and your sinews! We must win. We will. Long live Italy! Long live Fascism!
>
> "The Quadrumvirate"

At night there reached me the first news of bloody clashes in Cremona, Alessandri and Bologna, and of the assaults on munitions factories and upon military barracks. . . . Fascism was under arms, it was dominating the centers of national life, it had a very well-defined aim, it had followed deliberately an extra-parliamentary path and it could not allow its victory to be mutilated or adulterated in such a manner. That was my exact answer to the mediators of the union

"The Fascist March on Rome" is from Benito Mussolini, *My Autobiography* (New York: Charles Scribner's Sons, 1928), pp. 176–177, 184, 205–207.

between the National right and Fascism. No compromise! . . .

On the afternoon of the 29th, I received a very urgent telephone call from Rome. General Cittadini, first aide-de-camp of His Majesty the King, asked me very kindly to go to Rome because the King, having examined the situation, wanted to charge me with forming a ministry. . . .

Italy needed what? An avenger! Her political and spiritual resurrection needed a worthy interpreter. It was necessary to cauterize the virulent wounds, to have strength, and to be able to go against the current. It was necessary to eliminate evils which threatened to become chronic. It was necessary to curb political dissolution. I had to bring to the blood stream of national life a new, serene and powerful lymph of the Italian people.

Voting was reduced to a childish game; it had already humiliated the nation for entire decades. It had created a perilous structure far below the heights of the duties of any new Italy. I faced numberless enemies. I had created new ones—I had few illusions about that! The struggle, in my opinion, had to have a final character: it had to be fought as a whole over the most diverse fields of action. . . .

From petty discords and quarrels of holiday and Sunday frequency, from many-colored political partisanships, from peasant strifes, from bloody struggles, from the insincerity and duplicity of the press; from parliamentary battles and maneuvers, from the vicissitudes of representative lobbies, from hateful and useless debates and snarling talk, we finally climbed up to the plane of a unified nation, to a powerful harmony—dominated, inspired and spiritualized by Fascism. That is not my judgment, but that of the world.

After my speech of November 16th, 1922, in the Chamber of Deputies, I obtained approval for my declaration by 306 votes against 116. I asked and without difficulty obtained full powers.

Consider This:

- According to the excerpts from Mussolini's autobiography, why was it necessary "to beat the violent adversary on the battlefield of violence"? What did Mussolini mean by this? Did Mussolini save Italy from the destructive weariness of chaos? Why did he call himself the "avenger" of Italy?

The Doctrine of Fascism: "This Will Be the Century of the State"

BENITO MUSSOLINI

Fascism was not the nursling of a doctrine worked out beforehand with detailed elaboration; it was born of the need for action and it was itself from the beginning practical rather than theoretical; it was not merely another political party but, even in the first two years, in opposition to all political parties as such. . . . If one were to re-read . . . the report of the meeting in which the *Fasci Italiani di Combáttimento* "Italian Bands of Combat" were constituted, one would there find no ordered expression of doctrine, but a series of aphorisms, anticipations, and aspirations which, when refined by time from the original ore, were destined after some years to develop into an ordered series of doctrinal concepts, forming the Fascists' political doctrine—different from all others either of the past or the present day. . . .

"The Doctrine of Fascism" is from Benito Mussolini, "The Political and Social Doctrine of Fascism," in *International Conciliation*, no. 306 (January 1935), pp. 5–17. Reprinted by permission of the Carnegie Endowment for International Peace.

We want to accustom the working-class to real and effectual leadership, and also to convince them that it is no easy thing to direct an industry or a commercial enterprise successfully. . . . We shall combat every retrograde idea, technical or spiritual. . . . When the succession to the seat of government is open, we must not be unwilling to fight for it. We must make haste; when the present regime breaks down, we must be ready at once to take its place. It is we who have the right to the succession, because it was we who forced the country into the War, and led her to victory. . . .

The years which preceded the March to Rome were years of great difficulty, during which the necessity for action did not permit research of any complete elaboration of doctrine. The battle had to be fought in the towns and villages. There was much discussion, but—what was more important and more sacred—men died. They knew how to die. Doctrine, beautifully defined and carefully elucidated, with headlines and paragraphs, might be lacking; but there was to take its place something more decisive—Faith. . . . But, since there was inevitably some lack of system, the adversaries of Fascism have disingenuously denied that it had any capacity to produce a doctrine of its own, though that doctrine was growing and taking shape under their very eyes . . . in the laws and institutions of the regime as enacted successively in the years 1926, 1927 and 1928. . . .

Above all, Fascism, the more it considers and observes the future and the development of humanity quite apart from political considerations of the moment, believes neither in the possibility nor the utility of perpetual peace. It thus repudiates the doctrine of Pacifism—born of a renunciation of the struggle and an act of cowardice in the face of sacrifice. War alone brings up to its highest tension all human energy and puts the stamp of nobility upon the peoples who have the courage to meet it. All other trials are substitutes, which never really put men into the position where they have to make the great decision—the alternative of life or death. Thus a doctrine which is founded upon this harmful postulate of peace is hostile to Fascism. . . . This anti-pacifist spirit is carried by Fascism even in the life of the individual. . . . The Fascist accepts life and loves it, knowing nothing of and despising suicide; he rather conceives of life as duty and struggle and conquest, life which would be high and full, lived for oneself, but above all for others—those who are at hand and those who are far distant contemporaries, and those who will come after. . . .

Such a conception of life makes Fascism the complete opposite of that doctrine, the base of the so-called scientific and Marxian Socialism, the materialist conception of history; according to which the history of human civilization can be explained simply through the conflict of interests among the various social groups and by the change and development in the means and instruments of production. That the changes in the economic field . . . have their importance no one can deny; but that these factors are sufficient to explain the history of humanity excluding all others is an absurd delusion. Fascism now and always, believes in holiness and in heroism; that is to say, in actions influenced by no economic motive, direct or indirect. . . . And above all Fascism denies that class war can be the preponderant force in the transformation of society. . . .

After Socialism, Fascism combats the whole complex system of democratic ideology; and repudiates it, whether in its theoretical premises or in its practical application. Fascism denies that the majority, by the simple fact that it is a majority, can direct human society; it denies that numbers alone can govern by means of a periodical consultation, and it affirms the immutable, beneficial, and fruitful inequality of mankind, which can never be permanently leveled through the mere operation of a mechanical process such as universal suffrage. The democratic regime may be defined as from time to time giving the people the illusion of sovereignty, while the real effective sovereignty lies in the hands of other concealed and irresponsible forces. Democracy is a regime nominally without a king, but it is ruled by many kings—more absolute, tyrannical, and ruinous than one sole king, even though a tyrant. . . .

Political doctrines pass, but humanity remains; and it may rather be expected that this will be a century of Fascism. For if the nineteenth century was the century of individualism (Liberalism always signifying individualism) it may be expected that this will be the century of collectivism, and hence the century of the State. . . .

The foundation of Fascism is the conception of the State. Fascism conceives of the State as an absolute, in comparison with which all individuals or groups are relative, only to be conceived of in their relation to the State. . . .

The Fascist State has drawn into itself even the economic activities of the nation, and through the corporative social and educational institutions created by it, its influence reaches every aspect of the national life and includes, framed in their respective organizations, all the political, economic and spiritual forces of the nation. A State which reposes upon the support of millions of individuals who recognize its authority, are continually conscious of its power and are ready at once to serve it, is not the old tyrannical State of the medieval lord nor has it anything in common with the absolute governments either before or after 1789. The individual in the Fascist State is not annulled but rather multiplied, just in the same way that a soldier in a regiment is not diminished but rather increased by the number of his comrades. The Fascist State organizes the nation, but leaves a sufficient margin of liberty to the individual; the latter is deprived of all useless and possibly harmful freedom, but retains what is essential. . . .

The Fascist State is an embodied will to power and government; the Roman tradition is here an ideal of force in action. According to Fascism, government is not so much a thing to be expressed in territorial or military terms as in terms of morality and the spirit. It must be thought of as an empire—that is to say, a nation which directly or indirectly rules other nations, without the need for conquering a single square yard of territory. For Fascism, the growth of empire, that is to say the expansion of the nation, is an essential manifestation of vitality, and its opposite a sign of decadence. Peoples which are rising, or rising again after a period of decadence, are always imperialist: any renunciation is a sign of decay and of death.

Fascism is the doctrine best adapted to represent the tendencies and the aspirations of a people, like the people of Italy, who are rising again after many centuries of abasement and foreign servitude. But empire demands discipline, the coordination of all forces and a deeply felt sense of duty and sacrifice; . . . for never before has the nation [Italy] stood more in need of authority, of direction, and of order. If every age has its own characteristic doctrine, there are a thousand signs which point to Fascism as the characteristic doctrine of our time. For if a doctrine must be a living thing, this is proved by the fact that Fascism has created a living faith; and that this faith is very powerful in the minds of men, is demonstrated by those who have suffered and died for it.

CONSIDER THIS:

- According to Benito Mussolini, what are the primary tenets of fascist doctrine? Why was he especially critical of socialism (Marxism) and democracy? Do you find his arguments compelling or flawed? Why is war such an important requirement for the fascist state?

COMPARE AND CONTRAST:

- What did Mussolini mean by "[the individual] is deprived of all useless and possibly harmful freedom, but retains what is essential"? What is "harmful freedom" as opposed to "essential freedom"? In what ways was Hitler's concept *offascism* (as expressed in the various documents) consistent or inconsistent with Mussolini's concept?

"Germany in Her Deepest Humiliation"

"I Resolved Now to Become a Politician"

ADOLF HITLER

On November 11, 1918, German representatives signed terms of surrender and the Great War came to an end. Although they were clearly beaten militarily, defeat came as a shock to the majority of Germans because they had been told, as late as September, that victory was certain. Adolf Hitler, a corporal at the time, was gassed during the night of October 13, 1918. While recuperating in a military hospital, he heard rumors of German surrender.

But then as the old gentleman tried to continue and began to tell us that now we had to end the long war, that even our fatherland would now be submitted to severe oppressions in the future, that now the War was lost and that we had to surrender to the mercy of the victors . . . that the armistice should be accepted with confidence in the generosity of our previous enemies . . . there I could stand it no more. It was impossible for me to stay any longer. While everything began to go black again before my eyes, stumbling, I groped my way back to the dormitory, threw myself on my cot and buried my burning head in the covers and pillows. . . .

Now all had been in vain. In vain all the sacrifices and deprivations, in vain the hunger and thirst of endless months, in vain the hours during which, gripped by the fear of death, we nevertheless did our duty, and in vain the death of two millions who died thereby. Would not the graves of all the hundred of thousands open up, the graves of those who once had marched out with faith in the fatherland, never to return? Would they not open up and send the silent heroes, covered with mud and blood, home as spirits of revenge, to the country that had so mockingly cheated them of the highest sacrifice which in this world man is able to bring to his people? Was it for this that they had died, the soldiers of August and September, 1914, was it for this that the regiments of volunteers followed the old comrades in the fall of the same year? Was it for this that boys of seventeen sank into Flanders Fields? Was that the meaning of the sacrifice which the German mother brought to the fatherland when in those days, with an aching heart, she let her most beloved boys go away, never to see them again? Was it all for this that now a handful of miserable criminals was allowed to lay hands on the fatherland? . . .

I resolved now to become a politician.

"Stabbed in the Back" (1919)

PAUL VON HINDENBURG

The following is a statement by the German field marshal Paul von Hindenburg (1847–1934) to the Committee of Enquiry in November 1919. The committee was established to investigate charges that Germany had provoked the war and committed war

"'I Resolved Now to Become a Politician'" is from *Mein Kampf*, by Adolf Hitler, trans. Ralph Manheim, pp. 266–269.

"'Stabbed in the Back'" is from John W. Wheeler-Bennet, *Wooden Titan: Hindenburg in Twenty Years of German History, 1914–34*, pp. 235–236.

crimes. Hindenburg was one of the most influential German commanders during World War I and later became president of the German Weimar Republic (1925–1934). His statement reveals the dissatisfaction and betrayal that many Germans felt upon surrender.

In spite of the superiority of the enemy in men and materials, we could have brought the struggle to a favorable conclusion if determined and unanimous cooperation had existed between the army and those at home. But while the enemy showed an ever greater will for victory, divergent party interests began to show themselves with us. These circumstances soon led to a breaking up of our will to conquer. . . . Our operations therefore failed, as they were bound to, and the collapse became inevitable; the Revolution was merely that last straw. As an English General has truly said, "The German Army was stabbed in the back." It is plain enough on whom the blame lies.

Consider This:

- After four devastating years of war, the kaiser abdicated his throne and Germany surrendered. Why? According to Hitler and von Hindenburg, who was to blame?

The Treaty of Versailles (1919)

The Treaty of Versailles, which was signed by Germany on June 28, 1919, was a dictated peace designed to affix blame and to punish. The reduction of the army to 100,000 men and the territorial clauses, which eliminated areas abundant in natural resources, were viewed with outrage. The Germans were particularly incensed by the reparation clauses and the statement of German responsibility for the war contained in Article 231.

Article 227: The Allied and Associated Powers publicly arraign William II of Hohenzollern, formerly German Emperor, for a supreme offence against international morality and the sanctity of treaties.

A special tribunal will be constituted to try the accused, thereby assuring him the guarantees essential to the right of defense. It will be composed of five judges, one appointed by each of the following Powers: namely, the United States of America, Great Britain, France, Italy and Japan.

In its decision the tribunal will be guided by the highest motives of international policy, with a view to vindicating the solemn obligations of international undertakings and the validity of international morality. It will be its duty to fix the punishment which it considers should be imposed.

Article 228: The German Government recognizes the right of the Allied and Associated Powers to bring before military tribunals persons accused of having committed acts of violation of the laws and customs of war. Such persons shall, if found guilty, be sentenced to punishments laid down by law.

Article 231: The Allied and Associated Governments affirm and Germany accepts the responsibility of Germany and her allies for causing all the loss and damage to which the Allied and Associated Governments and their nationals have been subjected as a consequence

"The Treaty of Versailles" is from *Great Britain, State Papers*, vol. 112 (1919), pp. 104 ff.

of the war imposed upon them by the aggression of Germany and her allies.

Article 232: The Allied and Associated Governments recognize that the resources of Germany are not adequate . . . to make complete reparation for all such loss and damage.

The Allied and Associated Governments, however, require, and Germany undertakes, that she will make compensation for all damage done to the civilian population of the Allied and Associated Powers . . . by such aggression by land, by sea, and from the air. . . .

Article 428: As a guarantee for the execution of the present Treaty by Germany, the German territory situated to the west of the Rhine together with the bridgeheads, will be occupied by Allied and Associated troops for a period of fifteen years from the coming into force of the present Treaty.

Article 430: In case either during the occupation or after the expiration of the fifteen years referred to above the Reparation Commission finds that Germany refuses to observe the whole or part of her obligations under the present Treaty with regard to reparation, the whole or part of the areas specified will be reoccupied immediately by the Allied and Associated forces.

Article 431: If before the expiration of the period of fifteen years Germany complies with all the undertakings resulting from the present Treaty, the occupying forces will be withdrawn immediately.

CONSIDER THIS:

- What did Germany lose as a result of these provisions of the Treaty of Versailles?
- Analyze especially Article 231. Why was this so difficult for Germany to bear? Can you justify this provision?

THE BROADER PERSPECTIVE:

- How did the provisions of the Treaty of Versailles leave an "open wound" in the fabric of the German Weimar Republic? Was it too much to argue in 1919 that World War II was inevitable?

The Weimar Republic

Order is the mother of civilization and liberty; chaos is the midwife of dictatorship.

—WILL DURANT

It is too difficult to think nobly when one only thinks to get a living.

—JEAN-JACQUES ROUSSEAU

Germany's Unstable Democracy: The Best and Worst of Times

The Weimar Republic, burdened by the specter of defeat and shame, was impotent to meet the economic and political problems of the 1920s. The portion of the constitution that follows reflects the liberal idealism of the Social Democratic, Catholic Center, and Democratic parties that shaped it. Although there was much opposition to these beliefs from the National Socialist (Nazi) Party, among others, many Germans were still loyal to the republic, as the second selection reveals.

The Weimar Constitution: Fundamental Rights and Duties of the Germans (1919)

Section I: The Individual

Article 109: All Germans are equal before the law. Men and women have the same fundamental civil rights and duties. Public legal privileges or disadvantages of birth or of rank are abolished. Titles of nobility . . . may be bestowed no longer. . . . Orders and decorations shall not be conferred by the state. No German shall accept titles or orders from a foreign government.

Article 110: Citizenship of the Reich and the states is acquired in accordance with the provisions of a Reich law. . . .

Article 111: All Germans shall enjoy liberty of travel and residence throughout the whole Reich. . . .

Article 112: Every German is permitted to emigrate to a foreign country. . . .

Article 114: Personal liberty is inviolable. Curtailment or deprivation of personal liberty by a public authority is permissible only by authority of law.

Persons who have been deprived of their liberty must be informed at the latest on the following day by whose authority and for what reasons they have been held. They shall receive the opportunity without delay of submitting objections to their deprivation of liberty.

Article 115: The house of every German is his sanctuary and is inviolable. Exceptions are permitted only by authority of law. . . .

Article 117: The secrecy of letters and all postal, telegraph, and telephone communications is inviolable. Exceptions are inadmissible by national law.

Article 118: Every German has the right, within the limits of the general laws, to express his opinion freely by word, in writing, in print, in picture form, or in any other way. . . . Censorship is forbidden. . . .

Section II. The General Welfare

Article 123: All Germans have the right to assemble peacefully and unarmed without giving notice and without special permission. . . .

Article 124: All Germans have the right to form associations and societies for purposes not contrary to the criminal law. . . .

Article 126: Every German has the right to petition. . . .

Section III. Religion and Religious Societies

Article 135: All inhabitants of the Reich enjoy full religious freedom and freedom of conscience. The free exercise of religion is guaranteed by the Constitution and is under public protection. . . .

Article 137: There is no state church. . . .

Section IV. Education and the Schools

Article 144: The entire school system is under the supervision of the state. . . .

Article 145: Attendance at school is compulsory. . . .

"The Weimar Constitution" is from Louis L. Snyder, ed., *Documents of German History*, pp. 390–392.

Section V: Economic Life

Article 151: The regulation of economic life must be compatible with the principles of justice, with the aim of attaining humane conditions of existence for all. Within these limits the economic liberty of the individual is assured. . . .

Article 152: Freedom of contract prevails . . . in accordance with the laws. . . .

Article 153: The right of private property is guaranteed by the Constitution. . . . Expropriation of property may take place . . . by due process of law. . . .

Article 159: Freedom of association for the preservation and promotion of labor and economic conditions is guaranteed to everyone and to all vocations. All agreements and measures attempting to restrict or restrain this freedom are unlawful. . . .

Article 161: The Reich shall organize a comprehensive system of [social] insurance. . . .

Article 165: Workers and employees are called upon to cooperate, on an equal footing, with employers in the regulation of wages and of the conditions of labor, as well as in the general development of the productive forces. . . .

CONSIDER THIS:

- After analyzing the Weimar constitution, do you regard it as a liberal, visionary framework for a strong democracy? Was it a workable constitution?

COMPARE AND CONTRAST:

- Compare the provisions of the Weimar constitution to those of the U.S. Constitution. Was the Weimar constitution the quintessential expression of eighteenth-century Enlightenment values?

Loyalty to the Weimar Republic

LILO LINKE

A procession was formed, headed by the military band with triangles and drums and clarinets and followed by the members of the movement, two abreast, holding their torches in their upraised hands. We marched through the town, our ghostly magnified shadows moving restlessly over the fronts of the houses.

Never before had I followed the flag of the Republic, which was now waving thirty yards in front of me, spreading its colours overhead, the black melting in one with the night, the red glowing in the light of the torches, and the gold overshining them like a dancing sun. It was not just a torchlight march for me, it was a political confession. I had decided to take part in the struggle for German democracy. I wanted to fight for it although I knew that this meant a challenge to my parents and my whole family, who all lived with their eyes turned towards the past and thought it disloyal and shameful to help the Socialists.

We marched out of the town to the cemetery, where the first President of the Republic, Fritz Ebert, has been buried. Silently we assembled round the grave. Wilhelm Wismar, national leader of the Young Democrats and youngest member of the Reichstag, stepped forward and spoke slowly the oath.

"We vow to stand for the Republic with all our abilities and strength."

"Loyalty to the Weimar Republic" is from *Restless Days: A German Girl's Autobiography*, by Lilo Linke, pp. 278–280.

"We vow to work for the fulfillment of the promises given to the German people in the Weimar Constitution."

"We vow to shield and defend democracy against all its enemies and attackers whoever they might be."

And out of the night in a rolling echo two thousand citizens of tomorrow answered, repeating solemnly word for word:

"We vow to stand for the Republic with all our abilities and strength."

"We vow to work for the fulfillment of the promises given to the German people in the Weimar Constitution."

"We vow to shield and defend democracy against all its enemies and attackers whoever they might be."

CONSIDER THIS:

- Why was Lilo Linke so excited about the possibilities of the new Weimar constitution?
- Because Germany had no democratic tradition and the Weimar constitution thus structured a new and very different political experience, do you think that older Germans were as idealistic and enthusiastic as Lilo Linke was?

Inflation: "The Boiling Kettle of a Wicked Witch"

LILO LINKE

Inflation, or the decline in the value of currency with an attendant rise in prices, engulfed Germany in the early 1920s, reaching a peak in 1923. The following accounts reflect some of the difficulties and frustrations felt by people of the time. The middle classes were especially affected, and their hard-earned savings became worthless. Both Lilo Linke and Konrad Heiden witnessed the hardship of these days. Heiden was particularly active against the Nazis in street confrontations as a student at the University of Munich in 1923.

The time for my first excursions into life was badly chosen. Rapidly Germany was precipitated into the inflation, thousands, millions, milliards of marks whirled about, making heads swim in confusion. War, revolution, and the wild years after had deprived everyone of old standards and the possibility of planning a normal life. Again and again fate hurled the helpless individual into the boiling kettle of a wicked witch. Now the inflation came and destroyed the last vestige of steadiness. Hurriedly one had to make use of the moment and could not consider the following day.

The whole population had suddenly turned into maniacs. Everyone was buying, selling, speculating, bargaining, and dollar, dollar, dollar was the magic word which dominated every conversation, every newspaper, every poster in Germany. Nobody understood what was happening. There seemed to be no sense, no rules in the mad game, but one had to take part in it if one did not want to be trampled underfoot at once. Only a few people were able to carry through to the end and gain by the inflation. The majority lost everything and broke down, impoverished and bewildered.

The middle class was hurt more than any other, the savings of a lifetime and their small fortunes melted into a few coppers. They had to sell their most precious belongings for ten milliard inflated marks to buy a bit of food or an absolutely necessary coat, and their pride and dignity were bleeding out of many wounds. Bitterness remained for ever in their hearts. Full of hatred, they accused the international financiers, the Jews and Socialists—their old enemies—of having exploited their distress. They never forgot and never forgave and were the first to lend a willing ear to Hitler's fervent preaching.

In the shop, notices announced that we should receive our salaries in weekly parts; after a while we queued up at the cashier's desk every evening, and before long we were paid twice daily and ran out during the lunch hour to buy a few things, because as soon as the new rate of exchange became known in the early afternoon our money had again lost half its value.

In the beginning I did not concern myself much with these happenings. They merely added to the excitement of my new life, which was all that mattered to me. Living in the east of Berlin and in hard times, I was long accustomed to seeing people around me in hunger, distress, and poverty. My mother was always lamenting that it was impossible for her to make both ends meet, my father—whenever he was at home—always asking what the deuce she had done with all the money he had given her yesterday. A few tears, a few outbreaks more did not make a difference great enough to impress me deeply.

Yet, in the long run, the evil influence of the inflation, financially as well as morally, penetrated even to me. Berlin had become the center of international profiteers and noisy new rich. For a few dollars they could buy the whole town, drinks and women, horses and houses, virtue and vice, and they made free use of these possibilities.

The Devaluation of Currency

KONRAD HEIDEN

They all stood in lines outside the pay-windows, staring impatiently at the electric wall clock, slowly advancing until at last they reached the window and received a bag full of paper notes. According to the figures inscribed on them, the paper notes amounted to seven hundred thousand or five hundred million, or three hundred and eighty billion, or eighteen trillion marks—the figures rose from month to month, then from week to week, finally from day to day. With their bags the people moved quickly to the doors, all in haste, the younger ones running. They dashed to the nearest food store, where a line had already formed. Again they moved slowly, oh how slowly, forward. When you reached the store, a pound of sugar might have been obtainable for two millions; but, by the time you came to the counter, all you could get for two millions was half a pound, and the saleswoman said the dollar had just gone up again. With the millions and billions you bought sardines, sausages, sugar, perhaps even a little butter, but as a rule the cheaper margarine—always things that would keep for a week, until next pay-day, until the next stage in the fall of the mark.

CONSIDER THIS:

- Why was inflation and the consequent devaluation of currency so devastating to German life?

"The Devaluation of Currency" is from *Der Fuehrer*, by Konrad Heiden, trans. Ralph Manheim, p. 126.

The Broader Perspective:

- Why was the National Socialist Party able to rise to power? What were the main political, social, and economic problems of the 1920s and early 1930s, and what were the solutions offered by the Nazis? Why was the Weimar Republic unable to cope with the major problems facing Germany? Was its destruction inevitable?

Hitler's Response to Germany's Problems

The National Socialist German Worker's Party was but one of several minor parties that existed during the chaos of the early 1920s. The clearly articulated Nazi program of 1920 formed the basis of Hitler's campaign against the Weimar Republic. The succeeding selections of speeches and rally announcements not only reveal Nazi ideology but also testify to the dynamism of Nazi propaganda.

The Nazi Program (1920)

The program is the political foundation of the NSDAP [Nazi Party] and accordingly the primary political law of the State. It has been made brief and clear intentionally.

All legal precepts must be applied in the spirit of the party program.

Since the taking over of control, the Fuehrer has succeeded in the realization of essential portions of the Party program from the fundamentals to the detail.

The Party Program of the NSDAP was proclaimed on the 24 February 1920 by Adolf Hitler at the first large Party gathering in Munich and since that day has remained unaltered. Within the national socialist philosophy is summarized in 25 points:

1. We demand the unification of all Germans in the Greater Germany on the basis of the right of self-determination of peoples.
2. We demand equality of rights for the German people in respect to the other nations; abrogation of the peace treaties of Versailles and St. Germain.
3. We demand land and territory [colonies] for the sustenance of our people, and colonization for our surplus population.
4. Only a member of the race can be a citizen. A member of the race can only be one who is of German blood, without consideration of creed. Consequently no Jew can be a member of the race.
5. Whoever has no citizenship is to be able to live in Germany only as a guest, and must be under the authority of legislation for foreigners.
6. The right to determine matters concerning administration and law belongs only to the citizen. Therefore we demand that every public office, of any sort whatsoever, whether in the Reich, the county or municipality, be filled only by citizens. . . .
7. We demand that the state be charged first with providing the opportunity for a livelihood and way of life for citizens. If it is impossible to sustain the total population of the State, then the members of foreign nations (non-citizens) are to be expelled from the Reich.

"The Nazi Program" is from "National Socialist Yearbook, 1941," Office of the U.S. Chief Counsel for Prosecution of Axis Criminality, *Nazi Conspiracy and Aggression* (Washington, D.C.: Government Printing Office, 1946), vol. 4, pp. 208–211.

8. Any further immigration of non-citizens is to be prevented. We demand that all non-Germans, who have immigrated to Germany since the 2 August 1914, be forced immediately to leave the Reich.
9. All citizens must have equal rights and obligations.
10. The first obligation of every citizen must be to work both spiritually and physically. . . .
13. We demand the nationalization of all [previous] associated industries [trusts].
14. We demand a division of profits of all heavy industries.
15. We demand an expansion on a large scale of old age welfare.
16. We demand the creation of a healthy middle class and its conservation. . . .
18. We demand struggle without consideration against those whose activity is injurious to the general interest. Common national criminals, usurers . . . and so forth are to be punished with death, without consideration of confession or race.
20. The state is to be responsible for a fundamental reconstruction of our whole national education program, to enable every capable and industrious German to obtain higher education and subsequently introduction into leading positions. . . .
21. The State is to care for the elevating of national health by protecting the mother and child, by outlawing child-labor, by the encouragement of physical fitness, by means of the legal establishment of a gymnastic and sport obligation, by the utmost support of all organizations concerned with the physical instruction of the young.
23. We demand legal opposition to known lies and their promulgation through the press. In order to enable the provision of a German press, we demand, that: (a) All writers and employees of the newspapers appearing in the German language be members of the race: (b) Non-German newspapers be required to have the express permission of the State to be published. They may not be printed in the German language: © Non-Germans are forbidden by law any financial interest in German publications, or any influence on them, and as punishment for violations the closing of such a publication as well as the immediate expulsion from the Reich of the non-German concerned. Publications which are counter to the general good are to be forbidden. We demand legal prosecution of artistic and literary forms which exert a destructive influence on our national life, and the closure of organizations opposing the above made demands.
24. We demand freedom of religion for all religious denominations within the state so long as they do not endanger its existence or oppose the moral senses of the Germanic race. The Party as such advocates the standpoint of a positive Christianity without binding itself confessionally to any one denomination. It combats the Jewish-materialistic spirit within and around us, and is convinced that a lasting recovery of our nation can only succeed from within on the framework: common utility precedes individual utility.
25. For the execution of all of this we demand the formation of a strong central power in the Reich. Unlimited authority of the central parliament over the whole Reich and its organizations in general. The forming of state and profession chambers for the execution of the laws made by the Reich within the various states of the confederation. The leaders of the Party promise, if necessary by sacrificing their own lives, to support the execution of the points set forth above without consideration.

COMPARE AND CONTRAST:

- Compare the constitution of the Weimar Republic with the Nazi program of 1920. How are they similar in outlook, and what are the main differences? Pay particular attention to the presentation of specific points and the vocabulary.

FIGURE 12.1 Drawing of Adolf Hitler in uniform: "I resolved now to become a politician." On January 30, 1933, the Nazis celebrated the appointment of Adolf Hitler as chancellor of the Weimar Republic. The dismantling of the Weimar Constitution began almost immediately. *(Library of Congress)*

"We Fashion Once More a Hammer—a German Sword!"

ADOLF HITLER

With the armistice begins the humiliation of Germany. If the Republic on the day of its foundation had appealed to the country: "Germans, stand together! Up and resist the foe! The Fatherland, the Republic expects of you that you fight to your last breath," then millions who

"'We Fashion Once More a Hammer—a German Sword!'" is from Norman H. Baynes, trans. and ed., *The Speeches of Adolf Hitler, April 1922–August 1939*, vol. 1 (London: Oxford University Press for the Royal Institute of International Affairs, 1942), pp. 59–60.

are now enemies of the Republic would be fanatical Republicans. Today they are the foes of the Republic not because it is a Republic but because this Republic was founded at the moment when Germany was humiliated, because it so discredited the new flag that men's eyes must turn regretfully towards the old flag.

So long as this Treaty stands there can be no resurrection of the German people; no social reform of any kind is possible! The Treaty was made in order to bring 20 million Germans to their deaths and to ruin the German nation. But those who made the Treaty cannot set it aside. As its foundation our Movement formulated three demands:

1. Setting aside of the Peace Treaty.
2. Unification of all Germans.
3. Land and soil [*Grund und Boden*] to feed our nation.

Our movement could formulate these demands, since it was not our Movement which caused the War, it has not made the Republic, it did not sign the Peace Treaty.

There is thus one thing which is the first task of this Movement: it desires to make the German once more National, that his Fatherland shall stand for him above everything else. It desires to teach our people to understand afresh the truth of the old saying: He who will not be a hammer must be an anvil. An anvil are we today, and that anvil will be beaten until out of the anvil we fashion once more a hammer, a German sword!

Nazi Political Rally Announcement (February 1921)

NATIONAL SOCIALIST GERMAN WORKERS' PARTY

Fellow Citizens!

A year ago we called you to the Zirkus Krone. For the first time we invited you to a giant protest against making Germany defenseless by disarmament. We declared that this making her defenseless would be the prelude for the loss of Upper Silesia.

For the second time we invite you to resist against the Paris Dictate. We called it the permanent enslavement of Germany. . . .

Poverty no longer begins to appear, it is here. And though one does not feel it in the armchairs of the parliaments and in the soft cushions of our people's leaders it is felt all the more by the millions who have been cheated, by the masses of the people who do not live by cheating, profiteering and usury, but by the sweat of their honest work. But we are not only a poor people, we are also a miserable people.

We have forgotten the millions of our fellow citizens who once, during a long four and a half years, bled for Germany's existence on innumerable battlefields, and of whom our fatherland has been robbed by a cruel fate.

We have forgotten the millions of those Germans who longingly await the day which brings them home to a country that even as the poorest would still present the happiness of being their fatherland. We have forgotten the Rhineland and Upper Silesia, forgotten German-Austria and the millions of our brothers in Czechoslovakia, forgotten Alsace-Lorraine and the Palatinate, and while our beloved Germany thus lies dismembered, powerless and torn, disgracefully robbed, a colony of the international world criminals, there—we dance.

We invite you to come Thursday, February 2, 1921, to a GIANT DEMONSTRATION for a coming GREATER GERMANY to the Zirkus Krone, Engineer Rudolf JUNG, Deputy of the Prague Parliament, and Party Member Adolf HITLER will speak about:

'GERMANY IN HER DEEPEST HUMILIATION'

Beginning 8 P.M., end 10 P.M.
Jews not admitted

To cover expenses of the hall and posters, admission M.I. War invalids free.

Fellow citizens, white collar and manual workers, Germans from all countries of our fatherland, come in masses!

[The meeting was attended by more than 7,000 persons.]

THE BROADER PERSPECTIVE:

- Did the victory of National Socialism in Germany depend on Adolf Hitler? How important was he to the Nazi movement? To what extent can the individual mold the events of history? What conditions in a state present the greatest opportunity for individual assertion of will and power?

Nazi Appeal and Victory

There is nothing more terrible than ignorance in action.

—JOHANN VON GOETHE

Remember this, take it to heart, live by it, die for it if necessary: true patriotism, the only rational patriotism, is loyalty to the Nation ALL the time, loyalty to the Government when it deserves it.

—MARK TWAIN

Nazi Propaganda

Although the 1920s proved to be a difficult decade for the Weimar Republic amid extreme inflation and political turbulence, several signs of progress lent hope for the future. German reparation payments to the victors of World War I were restructured under the more liberal terms of the Dawes Plan of 1924. In 1925, the German foreign minister Gustav Stresemann initiated a conference at Locarno where Germany and France met as equals to establish firm boundaries and "preserve their respective nations from the scourge of war" by providing for the peaceful settlement of any dispute that might eventually arise between them. This "Spirit of Locarno" was a positive influence in Europe until 1929 when the stock market crash in the United States and the succeeding economic depression also proved disastrous for European stability.

No European country was more fragile politically and economically than Germany. The Nazis were quick to exploit the moment with an array of propaganda. To rise to power, an organization or individual must promote ideas, gain converts, and feed on the mistakes of the opposition. Where no problems exist, they must be created, and where they are real, they must be exposed and used to advantage. Such is the nature and purpose of propaganda. The first selection is a pamphlet composed in 1930 by Dr. Joseph Goebbels, the future minister of propaganda for the Third Reich. It was important to focus on enemies, whether they were cowards, communists, or Jews, because fear and hatred can often unify a people more readily than positive ideas.

Unity must also be achieved through leadership. Above anything else, the Nazis promoted faith over rational thought. The National Socialist program could be reduced to two words: Adolf Hitler. His mythic presence is seen in the second selection, which appeared in the newspaper *Völkischer Beobachter* just before an election on March 13, 1932. As Hitler noted, "The most brilliant propaganda technique must concentrate on a few points and repeat them over and over." He understood that in troubled times, people want a simple explanation for their pain and insecurity—and then they want the pain to go away.

Nationalists, Socialists, and Jews (1930)

JOSEPH GOEBBELS

Why Are We Nationalists?

We are NATIONALISTS because we see in the NATION the only possibility for the protection and the furtherance of our existence.

The NATION is the organic bond of a people for the protection and defense of their lives. He is nationally minded who understands this IN WORD AND IN DEED.

Today, in GERMANY, NATIONALISM has degenerated into BOURGEOIS PATRIOTISM, and its power exhausts itself in tilting at windmills. . . .

Young nationalism has its unconditional demands. BELIEF IN THE NATION is a matter of all the people, not for individuals of rank, a class, or an industrial clique. The eternal must be separated from the contemporary. The maintenance of a rotten industrial system has nothing to do with nationalism. I can love Germany and hate capitalism; not only CAN I do it, I also MUST do it. The germ of the rebirth of our people LIES ONLY IN THE DESTRUCTION OF THE SYSTEM OF PLUNDERING THE HEALTHY POWER OF THE PEOPLE.

WE ARE NATIONALISTS BECAUSE WE, AS GERMANS, LOVE GERMANY. And because we love Germany, we demand the protection of its national spirit and we battle against its destroyers.

Why Are We Socialists?

We are SOCIALISTS because we see in SOCIALISM the only possibility for maintaining our racial existence and through it the reconquest of our political freedom and the rebirth of the German state. SOCIALISM has its peculiar form first of all through its comradeship in arms with the forward-driving energy of a newly awakened nationalism. Without nationalism it is nothing, a phantom, a theory, a vision of air, a book. With it, it is everything, THE FUTURE, FREEDOM, FATHERLAND!

It was a sin of the liberal bourgeoisie to overlook THE STATEBUILDING POWER OF SOCIALISM. It was the sin of MARXISM to degrade SOCIALISM to a system of MONEY AND STOMACH.

We are SOCIALISTS because for us THE SOCIAL QUESTION IS A MATTER OF NECESSITY AND JUSTICE, and even beyond that A MATTER FOR THE VERY EXISTENCE OF OUR PEOPLE.

DOWN WITH POLITICAL BOURGEOIS SENTIMENT: FOR REAL NATIONALISM!

DOWN WITH MARXISM: FOR TRUE SOCIALISM!

UP WITH THE STAMP OF THE FIRST GERMAN NATIONAL SOCIALIST STATE!

AT THE FRONT THE NATIONAL SOCIALIST GERMAN WORKERS PARTY! . . .

Why Do We Oppose the Jews?

We are ENEMIES OF THE JEWS, because we are fighters for the freedom of the German people. THE JEW IS THE CAUSE AND THE BENEFICIARY OF OUR MISERY. He has used the social difficulties of the broad masses of our people to deepen the unholy split between Right and Left among our people. He has made two halves of Germany. He is the real cause for our loss of the Great War.

The Jew has no interest in the solution of Germany's fateful problems. He CANNOT have any. FOR HE LIVES ON THE FACT THAT THERE HAS BEEN NO SOLUTION. If we could make the German people a unified community and give them freedom before the world, then the Jew can have no place among us. He has the best trumps in his hands when a people lives in inner and outer slavery. THE JEW IS RESPONSIBLE FOR OUR MISERY AND HE LIVES ON IT.

That is the reason why we, AS NATIONALISTS and AS SOCIALISTS, oppose the Jew. HE HAS CORRUPTED OUR RACE, FOULED OUR MORALS, UNDERMINED OUR CUSTOMS, AND BROKEN OUR POWER.

THE JEW IS THE PLASTIC DEMON OF THE DECLINE OF MANKIND.

THE JEW IS UNCREATIVE. He produces nothing. HE ONLY HANDLES PRODUCTS. As long as he struggles against the state, HE IS A REVOLUTIONARY; as soon as he has power, he preaches QUIET AND ORDER, so that he can consume his plunder at his convenience.

ANTI-SEMITISM IS UN-CHRISTIAN. That means, then, that he is a Christian who looks on while the Jew sews straps around our necks. TO BE A CHRISTIAN MEANS: LOVE THY NEIGHBOR AS THYSELF! MY NEIGHBOR IS ONE WHO IS TIED TO ME BY HIS BLOOD. IF I LOVE HIM, THEN I MUST HATE HIS ENEMIES. HE WHO THINKS GERMAN MUST DESPISE THE JEWS. The one thing makes the other necessary.

WE ARE ENEMIES OF THE JEWS BECAUSE WE BELONG TO THE GERMAN PEOPLE. THE JEW IS OUR GREATEST MISFORTUNE.

It is not true that we eat a Jew every morning at breakfast.

It is true, however, that he SLOWLY BUT SURELY ROBS US OF EVERYTHING WE OWN.

THAT WILL STOP, AS SURELY AS WE ARE GERMANS.

Free Germany! (1932)

The National Socialist movement has been assembled as a fighting squad around its leader. Today it calls on the entire German people to join its ranks, and to blaze a path that will bring Adolf Hitler to the head of the nation, and thus

"Free Germany" is from *Völkischer Beobatchter* (March 3, 1932), p. 1. See also, Office of the U.S. Chief Counsel for Prosecution of Axis Criminality, *Nazi Conspiracy and Aggression* (Washington, D.C.: Government Printing Office, 1946), vol. 5, p. 246 (PS-2511).

Lead Germany to Freedom

Hitler is the password for everyone who believes in Germany's resurrection.

Hitler is the last hope of those who were deprived of everything: of farm and home, of savings, employment, survival; and who have but one possession left: their faith in a just Germany which will once again grant to its citizens honor, freedom, and bread.

Hitler is the word of deliverance for millions who are in despair and see in this name alone, a pathway to new life and creativity.

Hitler was handed down the legacy of the two million dead German comrades of the Great War, who died not for the current government's systematic destruction of our nation, but for Germany's future.

Hitler is the man of the people who is hated by the enemy because he understands and fights for the German people.

Hitler is the furious will of Germany's youth, which is fighting amidst a tired generation, for new opportunities; German youth neither can nor will abandon its faith in a better future for Germany. Therefore, Hitler is the password and the fiery signal of all who wish for a German future.

On March 13, all of them will cry out to the failed leaders of the old system who promised them freedom and dignity, and delivered only stones and words instead: We have known enough of you. Now you are to know us!

Hitler Will Win Because the People Want His Victory!

Munich, March 3, 1932

CONSIDER THIS:

- Analyze the propaganda documents included in this chapter. In particular, what messages does Goebbels promote in "Nationalists, Socialists, and Jews"? Is he logical in the presentation of his arguments, or can you find inconsistencies? What emotions does the propaganda exploit?
- What is the message in "Free Germany!"? Would you call it effective propaganda?

THE BROADER PERSPECTIVE:

- Konrad Heiden, in his book *Der Führer*, stated that "Hitler was able to enslave his own people because he gave them something that even the traditional religions could no longer provide, the belief in a meaning to existence beyond the narrowest self-interest" (p. v). How do you see this statement reflected in the various sources?

Nazi Victory by the Numbers: Elections to the German Reichstag (1924–1932)

The statistical table here reveals the increasing popularity of the National Socialist Party from 1924, when the Nazis first appeared on a ballot, to 1932, the last free election before Hitler's accession to power. Note the direct relationship of Nazi popularity to the unemployment figures.

"Elections to the German Reichstag" is from *Statisches Jahrbuch* (1933), p. 19. See also, Office of the U.S. Chief Counsel for Prosecution of Axis Criminality, *Nazi Conspiracy and Aggression* (Washington, D.C.: Government Printing Office, 1946), vol. 5, p. 252 (PS-2514).

Elections to the German Reichstag (1924–1932)

	May 4, 1924	**December 7, 1924**	**May 20, 1928**	**September 14, 1930**	**July 31, 1932**	**November 6, 1932**
Number of eligible voters (in millions)	38.4	39.0	41.2	43.0	44.2	44.2
Votes cast (in millions)	29.7	30.7	31.2	35.2	37.2	35.7
National Socialist German Workers' Party (Nazi)	1,918,000 6.6%	908,000 3%	810,000 2.6%	6,407,000 18.3%	13,779,000 37.3%	11,737,000 33.1%
German Nationalist People's Party (Conservative)	5,696,000 19.5%	6,209,000 20.5%	4,382,000 14.2%	2,458,000 7%	2,187,000 5.9%	3,131,000 8.8%
Center Party (Catholic)	3,914,000 13.4%	4,121,000 13.6%	3,712,000 12.1%	4,127,000 11.8%	4,589,000 12.4%	4,230,000 11.9%
Democratic Party (The German State Party)	1,655,000 5.7%	1,921,000 6.3%	1,506,000 4.9%	1,322,000 3.8%	373,000 1%	339,000 1%
Social Democratic Party	6,009,000 20.5%	7,886,000 26%	9,153,000 29.8%	8,575,000 24.5%	7,960,000 21.6%	7,251,000 20.4%
Communist Party	3,693,000 12.6%	2,712,000 9%	3,265,000 10.6%	4,590,000 13.1%	5,370,000 14.3%	5,980,000 16.9%

Unemployment in Germany (1924–1932)*

1924	1928	1930	July 31, 1932	October 31, 1932
978,000	1,368,000	3,076,000	5,392,000	5,109,000

*The figures are those of annual average unemployment, except for 1932, where some precise end-of-the-month figures are available, and the two dates that coincide with the Reichstag elections are given.

CONSIDER THIS:

- Statistics often reveal much after close analysis. What statements about the comparative strength of political parties can you make based on these data? Which party lost the most support from 1924 to 1932? How successful was the Communist Party? What relationships do you see between political election and unemployment?

FIGURE 12.2 This photograph of Benito Mussolini and Adolf Hitler expresses the image of discipline and vision that was so much a part of fascist propaganda. They both rose to power amidst the political and economic dislocation of the 1920s and 1930s. "Order is the mother of civilization and liberty; chaos is the midwife of dictatorship."—Will Durant. (*Corbis/Bettmann*)

Chancellor to Dictator

By 1932, the Nazis had emerged as Germany's strongest single party. Hitler demanded the chancellorship of the Weimar Republic. The president, Paul von Hindenburg, disliked Hitler and resisted entrusting all governmental authority to a single party that "held to such a one-sided attitude toward people with convictions different from theirs." But on January 30, 1933, Hindenburg gave in to political pressure and popular demand and appointed Hitler chancellor. The Nazis were confirmed in power and immediately began to dismantle the Weimar constitution. On the night of February 27, 1933, the Reichstag building burned. The Nazis blamed the communists and issued the "Decree for the Protection of the People and State," an article of which is presented in the first selection.

The second selection is the famous Enabling Act, which allowed Hitler and his Reich Cabinet to issue laws that could deviate from the established constitution yet could not practically be challenged by representatives of the Reichstag. Its overwhelming passage (444 to 94) gave the destruction of parliamentary democracy an appearance of legality; from then on, the Reichstag became a rubber stamp of approval for Hitler's decrees. The succeeding documents show the conversion of Hitler's chancellorship to a dictatorship.

Decree for the Protection of the People and State (February 28, 1933)

In virtue of Section 48 (2) of the German Constitution, the following is decreed as a defensive measure against Communist acts of violence endangering the state:

Article 1

Sections 114, 115, 117, 118, 123, 124, and 153 of the Constitution of the German Reich are suspended until further notice. Thus, restrictions on personal liberty, on the right of free expression of opinion, including freedom of the press, on the right of assembly and the right of association, and violations of the privacy of postal, telegraphic, and telephone communications, and warrants for house-searches, orders for confiscations as well as restrictions on property, are also permissible beyond the legal limits otherwise prescribed.

The Enabling Act (March 24, 1933)

The Reichstag has passed the following law and, with the approval of the Reichsrat "upper house," will be promulgated after it first has been established that it satisfies the requirements for legislation altering the Constitution.

Article 1: In addition to the procedure for the passage of legislation outlined in the Constitution, the Reich Cabinet is also authorized to enact laws.

Article 2: The national laws enacted by the Reich Cabinet may deviate from the Constitution provided they do not affect the position of the Reichstag and the Reichsrat. The powers of the President are not affected.

Article 3: The national laws enacted by the Reich Cabinet shall be prepared by the Reich Chancellor and published in the official newspaper. They become effective, unless otherwise specified, on the day following their publication.

"Decree for the Protection of the People and State" is from Office of the U.S. Chief Counsel for Prosecution of Axis Criminality, *Nazi Conspiracy and Aggression* (Washington, D.C.: Government Printing Office, 1946), vol. 1, p. 126 (PS-1390).

"The Enabling Act" is from Johannes Hohlfeld, ed., *Documente der Deutschen Politik und Geschichte von 1848 bis zur Genenwart*, Volume 4: *Die Zeit der nationalsozialistischen Diktatur, 1933–1945* (Berlin, n.d.), p. 40.

Articles 68–77 of the Constitution [concerning the enactment of new legislation] do not apply to the laws enacted by the Reich Cabinet.

Article 4: Treaties of the Reich with foreign states which concern matters of domestic legislation do not require the consent of the assemblies participating in legislation. The Reich Cabinet has the authority to issue the necessary provisions for implementing these treaties.

Article 5: This law comes into effect on the day of its publication.

Law Against the New Formation of Parties (July 14, 1933)

The government has passed the following law, which is hereby proclaimed:

Article 1: The only political party existing in Germany is the National Socialist German Workers' Party.

Article 2: Whoever maintains the organization of another political party, or founds a new political party, shall be punished at hard labor for up to three years, or be sentenced to prison between six months and three years, unless other regulations provide for a harsher punishment.

The Chancellor
s. ADOLF HITLER

The Minister of the Interior
s. FRICK

The Minister of Justice
s. GURTNER

Law Concerning the Head of the German State (August 1, 1934)

The government has passed the following law, which is hereby proclaimed:

Article 1: The office of Reich President shall be combined with that of Reich Chancellor. Therefore, all the functions heretofore exercised by the Reich President are transferred to the Führer and Reich Chancellor, Adolf Hitler. He has the authority to appoint his deputy.

Article 2: This law goes into force upon the death of Reich President von Hindenburg.

CONSIDER THIS:

- Many have viewed the Nazi rise to power as a legitimate act, fully sanctioned by law. Others have called it a revolution in which Hitler seized power. After reading these documents, what do you think? To what extent was Hitler justified in stressing the legality of the Nazi assumption of power?

COMPARE AND CONTRAST:

- Compare Hitler's rise to power with that of Mussolini. In what ways were Mussolini's rhetoric and political techniques similar to Hitler's? How were their situations different?

"Law Against the New Formation of Parties" is from Johannes Hohlfeld, ed., *Documente der Deutschen Politik und Geschichte von 1848 bis zur Genenwart*, Volume 4: *Die Zeit der nationalsozialistischen Diktatur, 1933–1945* (Berlin, n.d.), p. 83.

"Law Concerning the Head of the German State" is from Johannes Hohlfeld, ed., *Documente der Deutschen Politik and Geschichte von 1848 bis zur Genenwart*, Volume 4: *Die Zeit der national sozialistischen Diktatur, 1933–1945* (Berlin, n.d.), pp. 83–84.

The Role of the Family in the Nazi State

Once Hitler and his National Socialist Party were firmly seated in power, he began to enact legislation designed to restrict Jews and other racial groups whose presence threatened his plans for a racially pure society. The German family became the cornerstone of the new social policy. The role of women in the state as wives and mothers was crucial to Hitler's sense of the future and the establishment of his "thousand-year" Reich. Two weeks after Hitler received 88 percent of the votes in a plebiscite and assumed the title "Reichführer," he delivered the following speech at Nuremberg and articulated his vision of the role of women in the Nazi state.

"Our Fanatical Fellow-Combatants" (September 8, 1934)

ADOLF HITLER

If one says that man's world is the State, his struggle, his readiness to devote his powers to the service of the community, one might be tempted to say that the world of woman is a smaller world. For her world is her husband, her family, her children, and her house. But where would the greater world be if there were no one to care for the small world? How could the greater world survive if there were none to make the cares of the smaller world the content of their lives? . . . Providence has entrusted to woman the cares of that world which is peculiarly her own, and only on the basis of this smaller world can the man's world be formed and built up. These two worlds are never in conflict. They are complementary to each other, they belong together as man and woman belong together. . . .

Every child that a woman brings into the world is a battle, a battle waged for the existence of her people. Man and woman must therefore mutually value and respect each other when they see that each performs the task which Nature and Providence have ordained. And from this separation of the functions of each there will necessarily result this mutual respect. It is not true, as Jewish intellectuals assert, that respect depends upon the overlapping of the spheres of activity of the sexes: this respect demands that neither sex should try to do that which belongs to the other's sphere. Respect lies in the last resort in this: that each knows that the other is doing everything which is necessary to maintain the whole community. . . .

We National Socialists have for many years protested against bringing woman into political life; that life in our eyes was unworthy of her. A woman said to me once: You must see to it that women go into Parliament; that is the only way to raise the standard of Parliamentary life. I do not believe, I answered, that man should try to raise the level of that which is bad in itself. And the woman who enters into this business of Parliament will not raise it, it will dishonor her. I would not leave to woman what I intend to take away from men. My opponents thought that in that case we would never gain women for our Movement, but in fact we gained more women than all the other parties together, and I know we should have won over the last German woman if she had only had the opportunity to study Parliament and the

"'Our Fanatical Fellow-Combatants'" is from Raoul de Roussy de Sales, ed., *My New Order* (New York: Reynal & Hitchcock, Inc., 1941), pp. 286–289. Reprinted by permission of Harcourt Brace Jovanovich.

dishonoring role which women have played there. . . .

So our Women's Movement is for us not something which inscribes on its banner as its program the fight against man, but something which sets on its program the common fight of woman together with man: For the new National Socialist community of the people was set on a firm basis precisely because we gained in millions of women our truest, our fanatical fellow-combatants, women who fought for the common life in the service of the common task of maintaining life, who in that combat did not set their gaze on rights which a Jewish intellectualism mirrored before their eyes, but rather on duties which nature imposes on all of us in common. . . .

The program of our National Socialist Women's Movement has in truth but one single point, and that point is The Child—that tiny creature which must be born and should grow strong, for in the child alone the whole life-struggle gains its meaning. . . . It is a glorious sight, this golden youth of ours: we know that it is the Germany of the future when we shall be no more. What we create and construct, that youth will maintain. For youth we work; it is that fact which gives its significance to all this effort of ours.

CONSIDER THIS:

- According to Hitler's speech of September 8, 1934, what was the intended role of women in the Nazi state? Why was the establishment of family stability with all roles clearly defined so important to the future of Nazi society?

"The Disenfranchisement of Women"

HANNA SCHMITT

Hitler's vision of German women as "fellow-combatants" in the struggle to achieve the ideal National Socialist community was not accepted by all, including Hanna Schmitt, as the following selection on the disenfranchisement of women attests.

In 1918 German women were given the active and passive franchise. From that time on, they were represented in the parliaments of the Reich, the states and the communities. The progressive and socialist parties in particular sent women representatives to these bodies. The only exception was the Nazi party and once the dictatorship was in power, it was this party that expelled women from parliaments and deprived them again of their public functions. Thousands of women who formerly had been active in state and communal positions experienced the hostile attitude of the new regime. In numerous cases they were turned out of hospitals and schools where they were employed as physicians, school principals and valuable teachers.

Mr. Goebbels tried to explain the measure in his own peculiar brand of dishonest pathos: "When we exclude women from public life, we give them back their honor." . . .

Women have disappeared from editorial offices and are deprived of professorships. There is no room for them in laboratories. If they are suspect for racial and ideological reasons, the regime persecutes them even more ruthlessly than men. For they are out of favor not only because of their convictions but also because of their sex, which, according to National Socialism, places them on a lower level than the male.

This is particularly evident in the economic and social life of women. An official

"The Disenfranchisement of Women" is from Eleanor S. Riemer and John C. Fout, eds., *European Women* (New York: Schocken Books, 1980), pp. 111–113.

decree issued on April 27, 1933, shortly after Hitler's seizure of power, said: "Management is to see to it that all married women employees ask for their discharge. If they do not comply voluntarily, the employer is free to dismiss them upon ascertaining that they are economically protected some other way." Thousands of employees lost their positions by this decree, married as well as single women, who were simply told that parents or other members of their families could take care of them. . . .

And what about the private life of women? The Nazis claim to honor housewives and mothers above all. But this honor is denied to a great number of mothers. It does not cover, for example, the mothers of illegitimate children. They bear the burden of care but are morally disqualified and do not get the benefit of the necessary legal protection.

Marriage is subject to the severest restrictions. Women who have been in a concentration camp must provide proof before marriage that they are in perfect physical and mental health, racially pure and not dependent on public relief. The threat of sterilization hangs over many women like the sword of Damocles. Every woman with a physical defect, be it ever so slight, must make it known to the authorities. The doors are wide open for denunciation and vindictive vengeance. . . .

The most tender and intimate relationship held sacred by all civilized peoples is that between mother and child. But with what brutality does National Socialism often tear asunder these bonds. If, for example, a mother is Jewish and the father Aryan, the child is taken away from the mother in case of divorce to avoid exposure to "Jewish influences." The fate of Jewish mothers is especially tragic in small towns. They must look on as their children grow up in isolation which has a devastating effect on the young minds. . . .

Women who are silent, women who serve, are not free women. For only free women can develop their characters to the fullest, be it in pursuit of studies or at work, as housewives and mothers. A nation that honors its women honors itself. However much it may boast of national virtues, a regime that oppresses the women shows contempt for the people and at the same time for those who are responsible for the future, the mothers of its children.

Compare and Contrast:

- According to Hanna Schmitt, in what ways were women restricted in Nazi society? Schmitt noted that "women who are silent, women who serve, are not free women." Compare this statement with the Nazi vision of women as "fanatical fellow combatants."
- Compare Hitler's conception of women and the family with that of V. I. Lenin in the preceding chapter on the Russian Revolution entitled "The Communist Emancipation of Women." (page 326). Why are the expressed roles of women in these two states so different?

Hitler Youth: "Tough as Leather, Hard as Krupp Steel"

ADOLF HITLER

Any political or religious movement that seeks stability and longevity must ultimately cultivate the loyalty of those who will inherit the future. Hitler established several

"Hitler Youth" is from Norman H. Baynes, trans. and ed., *The Speeches of Adolf Hitler, April 1922–1939*, vol. 1 (London: Oxford University Press for the Royal Institute of International Affairs, 1942), pp. 542–545.

youth organizations for boys and girls that sought to inculcate the values and ideals that would maintain his authority in the future. Ten-year-olds were taught to "serve the Führer" by stressing the virtues of duty, obedience, and strength. The following speech at a party rally in Nuremberg demonstrates how earnestly the Nazis looked to the future.

Each year at the gatherings of youth at the Parteitage (Nuremberg Party Day celebrations) I note the difference: in each year I see the same development which we can discern today in all the other spheres of German life. Our people grows continuously more disciplined, more taut, more sturdy, and youth begins to do the same. . . .

What we wish from our German youth is different from what past generations asked. In our eyes the German youth of the future must be slim and slender, swift as the greyhound, tough as leather, and hard as Krupp steel. We must educate a new type of manhood so that our people does not go to ruin amongst all the degeneracy of our day. We do not talk, we act. We have undertaken to educate this people in a new school, to give it an education which begins in youth and shall never come to an end. . . .

Everyone is bound to serve his people, everyone is bound to arm himself for that service, to steel his body, to prepare and fortify his mind. And the sooner these preparations begin, the better. . . .

Nothing is possible if there is not a single will which issues its commands and which the others must always obey, beginning from above and ending only at the lowest point. And that is alongside of the training and hardening of the body the second great task. We are a "following," and that means that it is our duty to "follow," to obey. We must educate our whole people so that wherever one is appointed to command the others recognize their duty to obey him, because perhaps an hour later they in their turn will be called upon to command and can only do so precisely as others render to them obedience. That is the expression of an authoritarian State, not of a weak chattering democracy; and in the authoritarian State everyone is proud to owe obedience because he knows: I shall in just the same way find obedience when I have to give a command. . . .

If the others fail to understand us, that need not trouble us. . . . We are no bullies. If the rest of the world misconceives us in our discipline, we cannot help it. From this discipline of ours there will come fewer brawls for the world than from the parliamentary democratic chaos of today. We go our own way: we do not wish to cross the way of another. Would that the others would let us pursue our way in peace! . . . But never do we wish to forget that only the strong deserves friendship, only the strong keeps friendship. And so our will is to make ourselves strong: that is our solution!

CONSIDER THIS:

- Hannah Schmitt in her criticism of the Nazi vision of the family noted: "The most tender and intimate relationship held sacred by all civilized peoples is that between mother and child. But with what brutality does National Socialism often tear asunder these bonds." How is this statement validated in the cultivation of Hitler Youth?

- How did the Nazi state shape the future by symbolically separating children from their parents and admitting them to the greater German family with Hitler as Leader—as "Father"? Through physical and mental indoctrination, how were children transformed into the "Iron Youth" of the Third Reich?

FIGURE 12.3 In this photograph of a 1938 Nazi party rally, members of the Hitler Youth demonstrate their discipline and loyalty to Adolf Hitler. The Iron Youth of the future, "swift as greyhounds, tough as leather, hard as Krupp steel." (*National Archives and Records Administration*)

Conversion and Resistance

The people of Germany were generally enthusiastic about Hitler, his image of a strong, successful fatherland, and his promises of prosperity. Membership in the National Socialist Party rose steadily. Some people found that joining the Nazis was even more than a political experience; for them it was almost a religious conversion. The following section presents the experience of two such converts, the first by Joseph Goebbels, who became Hitler's minister of propaganda.

"Now I Know Which Road to Take"

JOSEPH GOEBBELS

Someone was standing up and had begun to talk, hesitatingly and shyly at first. . . . Then suddenly the speech gathered momentum. I was caught, I was listening. . . . The crowd began to stir. The haggard grey faces were reflecting hope. . . . Two seats to my left, an old officer was crying like a child. I felt alternately hot and cold. . . . It was as though guns were thundering. . . . I was beside myself. I was shouting hurrah. Nobody seemed surprised. The man up there looked at me for a moment. His blue eyes met my glance like a flame. This was a command. At that moment I was reborn. . . . Now I know which road to take.

[Goebbels became member No. 8,762.]

"I Had Given Him My Heart"

KURT LUDECKE

Hitler's words were like a scourge. When he spoke of the disgrace of Germany, I felt ready to spring on any enemy . . . glancing around, I saw that his magnetism was holding these thousands as one. . . . I was a man of 32, weary of disgust and disillusionment, a wanderer seeking a cause . . . a yearner after the heroic without a hero. The intense will of the man, the passion of his sincerity, seemed to flow from him into me. I experienced a feeling that could be likened only to a religious conversion. . . . I felt sure that no-one who heard Hitler that night could doubt he was the man of destiny. . . . I had given him my heart.

THE BROADER PERSPECTIVE:

- Carefully read the conversion accounts of Joseph Goebbels and Kurt Ludecke. Why did they join the Nazi Party? In his book *The True Believer*, the philosopher Eric Hoffer described such converts as "permanent misfits." He noted

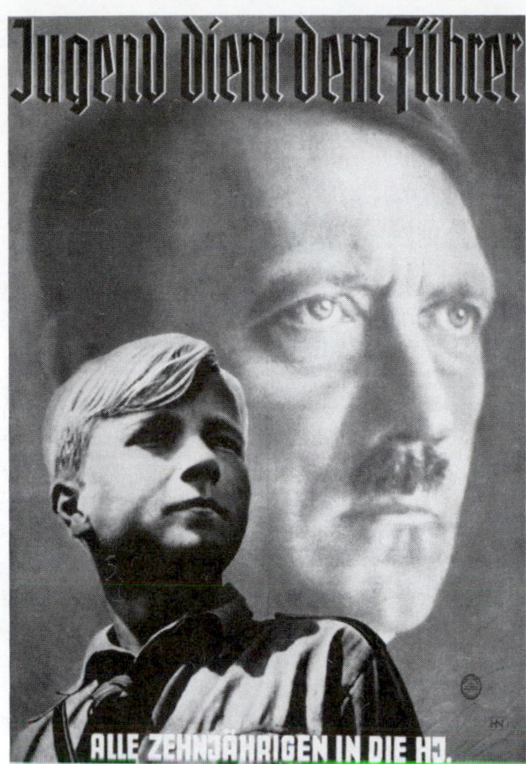

FIGURE 12.4 Nazi propaganda poster: "Youth Serve the Führer. All ten-year-olds in Hitler Youth." *(Library of Congress)*

that no achievement can give them a sense of fulfillment; they pursue goals passionately but never arrive: "The permanent misfits can find salvation only in a complete separation from the self; and they usually find it by losing themselves in the compact collectivity of a mass movement. By renouncing individual will, judgment, and ambition, and dedicating all their powers to the service of an eternal cause, they are at last lifted off the endless treadmill which can never lead them to fulfillment. A rising mass movement attracts and holds a following not by its doctrine or promises, but by the refuge it offers from the anxieties [and] barrenness of an individual existence." What do you think about this idea?

- Is this lack of meaning, the "barrenness of individual existence," the reason people often become fanatical devotees to a cause? Can a structured society prevent fanaticism by engaging those who are disaffected loners or those who reject the values of the mainstream? How could this be done because society most often represents mainstream values? Do religious or political interest groups therefore offer "refuge" to the rejected and the possibility for a new engagement with life?

THEME: THE INDIVIDUAL AND THE INSTITUTION

AGAINST THE GRAIN

Guilty! Guilty! Guilty!

Leaflets of "The White Rose" (1942)

HANS AND SOPHIE SCHOLL

It must be remembered that there were still many Germans who were alarmed at Hitler's actions. The degree to which the German people resisted the Nazi regime has been an ongoing and important topic of research among historians. Resistance was not simply confined to intellectuals, and many dissident Germans were incarcerated in concentration camps along with Jews, Gypsies, and homosexuals. One of the more courageous acts of defiance came from a group of university students and young professionals who called themselves "the White Rose."

In the summer of 1942, leaflets of the White Rose were nailed on poster boards, handed out to the public, and distributed through the mail. They contained attacks on the cultural and political policies of the National Socialist regime. In particular, members of the White Rose accused the Nazis of atrocities against the Jews. Their goal was to resist and obstruct the government through passive resistance. Hans and Sophie Scholl were leaders of the movement. Hans attended medical school and had served in the German army with the rank of sergeant. His sister Sophie first worked as a kindergarten teacher and then attended the University of Munich as a science and philosophy student. They were apprehended in February 1942, accused of treason, and executed that same month after a perfunctory trial. The following is an excerpt from the second leaflet they distributed.

KEEP IN MIND . . .

- According to the White Rose, who should be condemned for the success of Nazi ideology and brutality?

It is impossible to engage in intellectual discourse with National Socialism because it is not an intellectually defensible program. It is false to speak of a National Socialist philosophy, for if there were such an entity, one would have to try by means of analysis and discussion either to prove its validity or to combat it. In actuality, however, we face a totally different situation. At its very inception this movement depended on the deception and betrayal of one's fellow man; even at that time it was inwardly corrupt and could support itself only by constant lies. After all, Hitler states in an early edition of "his" book (a book written in the worst German I have ever read, in spite of the fact that it has been elevated to the position of the Bible in this nation of poets and thinkers): "It is unbelievable to what extent one must betray a people in order to rule it." If at the start this cancerous growth in the nation was not particularly noticeable, it was only because there were still enough forces at work that operated for the good, so that it was kept under control. As it grew larger, however, and finally in an ultimate spurt of growth attained ruling power, the tumor broke open, as it were, and infected the whole body. The greater part of its former opponents went into hiding. The German intellectuals fled to their cellars, there, like plants struggling in the dark, away from light and sun, gradually to choke to death. Now the end is at hand. Now it is our task to find one another again, to spread information from person to person, to keep a steady purpose, and to allow ourselves no rest until the last man is persuaded of the urgent need of his struggle against this system. When thus a wave of unrest goes through the land, when "it is in the air," when many join the cause, then in a great final effort this system can be shaken off. After all, an end in terror is preferable to terror without end. . . .

Since the conquest of Poland [1939], three hundred thousand Jews have been murdered in this country in the most bestial way. Here we see the most frightful crime against human dignity, a crime that is unparalleled in the whole of history. For Jews, too, are human beings—no matter what position we take with respect to the Jewish question—and a crime of this dimension has been perpetrated against human beings. Someone may say that the Jews deserved their fate. This assertion would be a monstrous impertinence. . . .

"For Jews, too, are human beings—no matter what position we take with respect to the Jewish question—and a crime of this dimension has been perpetrated against human beings."
—The White Rose

Why do the German people behave so apathetically in the face of all these abominable crimes, crimes so unworthy of the human race? Hardly anyone thinks about that. It is accepted as fact and put out of mind. The German people slumber on in their dull, stupid sleep and encourage these fascist criminals; they give them the opportunity to carry on their depredations; and of course they do so. Is this a sign that the Germans are brutalized in their simplest human feelings, that no chord within them cries out at the sight of such deeds, that they have sunk into a fatal consciencelessness from which they will never, never awake? It seems to be so, and will certainly be so, if the German does not at last start up out of his stupor, if he does not protest wherever and whenever he can against this clique of criminals, if he show no sympathy for these hundreds of thousands of victims. He must evidence not only sympathy; no, much more: a sense of complicity in guilt. For through his apathetic behavior he gives these evil men the opportunity to act as they do; he tolerates this "government" which has taken upon itself such an infinitely great burden of guilt; indeed, he himself is to blame for the fact that it came about at all! Each man wants to be exonerated of a guilt of this kind, each one continues on his way with the most placid, the calmest conscience. But he cannot be exonerated; he is guilty, guilty, guilty!

Up until the outbreak of the war the larger part of the German people was blinded; the Nazis did not show themselves in their true aspect. But now, now that we have recognized them for what they are, it must be the sole and first duty, the holiest duty of every German to destroy these beasts!

Consider This:

- In the leaflet distributed by the White Rose, Hans and Sophie Scholl ask the question "Why do the German people behave so apathetically in the face of all these abominable crimes? . . . Is this a sign that the Germans are brutalized in their simplest human feelings?" How would you answer these questions? Why didn't more Germans join in the resistance?

THE BROADER PERSPECTIVE:

- Some historians have recently proposed that the success of the Nazi regime was based fundamentally on the deep roots of anti-Semitism inherent in German society and on the willingness of the German population to support Nazi authoritarianism and its consequent abuse. What do you think of this proposition? Are homogeneous societies like Germany or Japan more vulnerable to "national shame" or "patriotic passion"?
- Let's expand on the implications of that idea: Was the victory of Adolf Hitler and the National Socialist Party consistent with the racism, militarism, and blind obedience to authority that mark German national character? Can you describe French, Italian, British, Russian, or American character? Is there even such a thing as "national character," and is it legitimate to explain historical events on the basis of such a representation?

FIGURE 12.5 In this photograph of the Nazi leadership, Adolf Hitler, Luftwaffe Commander Hermann Goering, and Propaganda Minister Joseph Goebbels demand the blind commitment to the "Thousand Year Reich" that the White Rose opposed: "It must be the sole and first duty, the holiest duty of every German to destroy these beasts!"—Sophie Scholl (*Library of Congress*)

13

"The Abyss Also Looks into You": War and Holocaust (1939–1945)

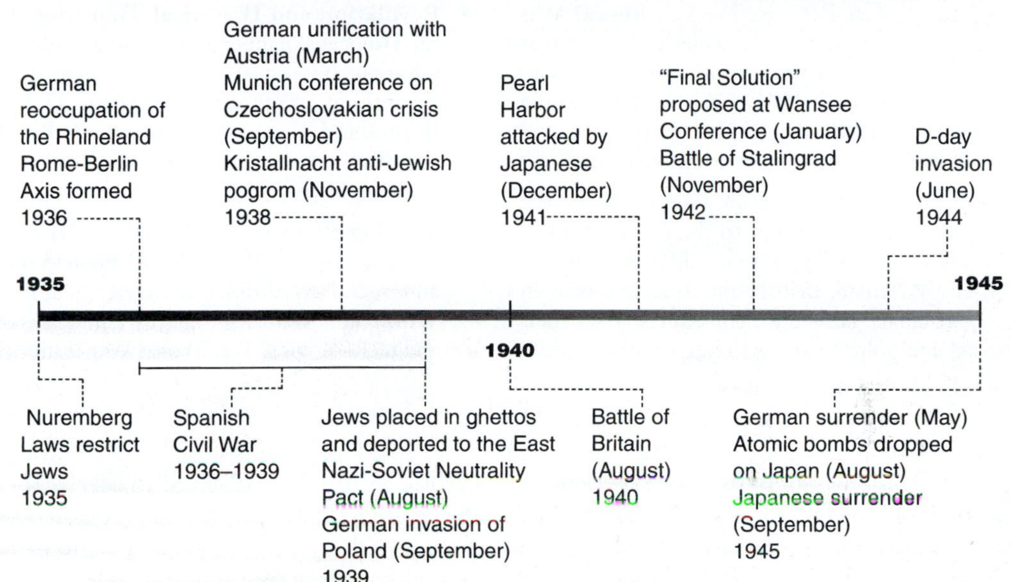

War will never be avoided until babies come into the world with larger cerebrums and smaller adrenal glands.

—H. L. Mencken

War is an ugly thing, but not the ugliest of things; the decayed and degraded state of moral and patriotic feeling which thinks nothing worth a war, is worse. . . . A war to protect other human beings against tyrannical injustice; a war to give victory to their own ideas of right and good, and which is their own war, carried on for an honest purpose by their own free choice—is often the means of their regeneration.

—John Stuart Mill

This is no war for domination or imperial aggrandizement or material gain. . . . It is a war . . . to establish on impregnable rocks, the rights of the individual and it is a war to establish and revive the stature of man.

—Winston Churchill

There was never a good war or a bad peace.

—Benjamin Franklin

The real trouble with war is that it gives no one a chance to kill the right people.

—Ezra Pound

CHAPTER THEMES

- **Imperialism:** Was the German and Japanese desire to expand and acquire more territory the primary cause of World War II? Was the same kind of imperialism the root cause of World War I?
- **The Varieties of Truth:** Why has World War II been termed the "Good War" in the United States and the "Great Patriotic War" in Russia? Was there a distinct clash of ideologies and values that provided the primary motivation for Allied victory? Why was World War II never billed as the "war to end all wars"? Had Europeans and Americans grown less naïve and more cynical?
- **Women in History:** How essential were the contributions of women to the prosecution of World War II? What were the different expectations of German, British, and American women in particular? How did their efforts affect their social and political status in the postwar years?
- **Social and Spiritual Values:** After the massive destruction of World War I, how were soldiers motivated a scant twenty years later to engage once again in war? Was there something spiritual, almost sacred, in the image of Mother Russia that motivated 12 million Russian soldiers to sacrifice their lives?
- **Revolution and Historical Transition:** Could the Holocaust happen again, and would contemporary technology make genocide a reality? Can the ethnic cleansing by Serbian soldiers in Bosnia and Kosovo be likened to the "Final Solution" of the Nazis? What is the value of studying history?
- **The Big Picture:** Was World War II merely a continuation of World War I? Or had political and social conditions changed so much that World War II was set apart by new ideologies and technologies? Was World War II inevitable?

At the conclusion of the Great War in November 1918, the peoples of Europe paused amid their ruined cities, twisted landscapes, and shattered lives to consider the remnants of Western civilization. They understood that an era had truly ended. They had passed from the structured formalism of polite Victorian society, from an era of effete monarchs, to a world of disillusioned reality. An entire generation of men had been sacrificed to aggressive monarchs, shortsighted politicians, incompetent generals, and the ruinous effects of modern military technology. Everywhere people sought to justify the many lives that had been lost—some might say wasted—on the battlefields of Europe. This had been "the war to make the world safe for democracy," "the war to end all wars." It was termed the "Great War" because no one could envision another of such magnitude and destructive capacity. And yet, as we now view the twentieth century, we refer to it as the First World War, to be followed twenty years later by another that was truly global in scope and far more destructive, consuming the lives and property of over 30 million people.

Some historians have viewed the First and Second World Wars as one conflict with an intervening period of "festering peace," as the Greek historian Thucydides might have termed it. There is no doubt that the origins of the Second World War certainly sprang in part from the harsh peace that had been imposed on the Germans in the Treaty of Versailles in 1919. Adolf Hitler had used the restrictions, reparations, and guilt imposed on the struggling German Weimar Republic in the 1920s to remind the German populace of a distant past of dignity and glorious culture that could once again be gained by following a regimen of discipline and devotion to the nation and to the Führer. After coming to power in 1933 and gaining success in solving some of the employment and monetary problems engendered by the Great Depression, Hitler obtained the confidence and mass support of a majority of Germans. He worked carefully to persuade through propaganda and punish through terror. By 1936, the Nazi state had consolidated its domestic situation and was eager to be recognized by the international community as an equal, no longer burdened by reparations or military and territorial restrictions. Feeling buoyed by his domestic success, Hitler invited the world to the 1936 Olympics in Berlin as a way of showcasing German discipline and talent.

But his vision was focused on a broader agenda to be gained, if possible, by subtlety and, if not, by intimidation and force. Hitler sought to incorporate territory into the German Reich to which Germany had historical or racial connections. This need for *Lebensraum*, or "living space," was essential, Hitler argued, for the development of the German nation. In 1936, Hitler reoccupied the Rhineland, a region between Germany and France, in defiance of the Treaty of Versailles. To his surprise, he encountered little reaction from Great Britain and France, which were charged with guaranteeing the provisions of Versailles. Hitler's next step in obtaining more territory for the Reich was the *Anschluss*, or unification with Austria, in March 1938. This was achieved when Germany invaded Austria the day before a plebiscite on unification was to be held because Hitler feared defiance and a defeat at the polls. His assertive policy of incorporation reached its apex in September 1938 as Hitler demanded the Sudentenland of Czechoslovakia, where ethnic Germans resided and were (as he claimed) abused. As a result of the Munich agreements, Hitler gained access to this territory.

At each step, Hitler was confronted and pacified by the figure of British prime minister Neville Chamberlain, who believed that Hitler could be satisfied and war averted by conceding territory and respect to Germany. This policy of appeasement, as it came to be called, depended on the assumption that Germany's demands were legitimate and limited. It is to Hitler's credit that he understood the domestic divisions within Britain and France and was able to take bold risks at crucial times. As the concessions mounted and Hitler realized his visions of greater "living space" for the German Volk and the consolidation of a greater German Reich that would last "a thousand years," he moved into areas that could no longer be viewed as having special significance to German history and culture. Hitler's desire to link the Reich with East Prussia by a corridor through Poland was the final straw in Chamberlain's appeasement concessions, and the line was drawn. War broke out on September 3, 1939, after Hitler had invaded Poland two days earlier.

World War II, however, is not simply the story of Hitler and Chamberlain. The world was enrolled as the Axis alliance joined together the other fascist powers of Italy and Japan. The influence and independence of Benito Mussolini soon faded amid the dominance and military power of Germany. Japan had pursued its own policy of imperialism in the Far East by grabbing valuable mineral-rich areas like Manchuria from China and by imposing its presence in Indochina and Malaya in pursuit of oil and tin. Japanese relations with the United States were tenuous at best. The fascist Japanese government under the leadership of General Hideki Tojo received sanction from Emperor Hirohito to cripple the U.S. fleet at Pearl Harbor to prevent any restriction of an aggressive Japanese policy. The "Rising Sun" of Japan would not be restrained.

The war itself gave new meaning to the definition of destruction. The world now fell to the unleashed might of mechanized warfare supported by the full commitment of national will. Societies were transformed as men went to war and women moved to the factories. Civilian populations felt the pain of war as never before. Cities were bombed and refugees were rarely spared—this was total war, war with no restriction and no innocents. Ultimately, the developing technologies of war blurred the boundaries of civilization as nuclear weapons were finally detonated over the Japanese cities of Hiroshima and Nagasaki.

World War II truly causes a pause in the consideration of civilization. For the Russians, this was the "Great Patriotic War." In the eyes of the Western powers it became "the Good War," the struggle against the evil of Hitler, Mussolini, and Tojo. There was purpose and justification for our destruction. And yet at the conclusion of hostilities in 1945, the world had not been "made safe for democracy." The Soviet Union had indeed made a "strange bedfellow" in the war against fascism, but the Cold War against Soviet authoritarianism would continue for an additional forty years. With the looming specter of the "Red Menace" and the subsequent undeclared wars in Korea and Vietnam, the claim was never made that the Good War was the "war to end all wars."

The Road to War (1938–1939)

There is no avoiding war; it can only be postponed to the advantage of others.

—NICCOLÒ MACHIAVELLI

All war represents a failure of diplomacy.

—TONY BENN

An appeaser is one who feeds a crocodile, hoping it will eat him last.

—SIR WINSTON CHURCHILL

To delight in war is a merit in the soldier, a dangerous quality in the captain, and a positive crime in the statesman.

—GEORGE SANTAYANA

What a country calls its vital economic interests are not the things which enable its citizens to live, but the things which enable it to make war. Petrol is more likely than wheat to be a cause of international conflict.

—SIMONE WEIL

The Czechoslovak Crisis (September 1938–March 1939)

One of the crucial turning points of German history occurred in March 1936 when Adolf Hitler remilitarized the region between Germany and France called the Rhineland. The security of this region was guaranteed by the Treaty of Versailles (1919) and the Locarno Agreements of 1925. In all respects, both Britain and France had a legal right to resist. But a rising tide of pacifism in Europe prevented British support of France and reinforced France's own commitment to a defensive rather than offensive posture. Hitler evaluated the situation and decided to test the strength and determination of the Allied powers. To his relief, neither country did anything except register a mild protest with the League of Nations. In retrospect, the Allies lost an important opportunity to stop Hitler, whose tiny German force in the Rhineland would have easily been overwhelmed by the French army. Such a failure may well have led to the political overthrow of Hitler's regime because the German military commanders had generally not supported the gamble to remilitarize the Rhineland.

The German union with Austria in 1938 was another clear violation of the Treaty of Versailles, but that arrangement was clearly dead by 1938, as neither Great Britain nor France was willing to enforce its provisions. The Allied response slowly crystallized into a policy of appeasement based on the assumption that Germany had legitimate grievances and Hitler's goals were limited and rational. With perfect hindsight, the remilitarization of the Rhineland and German union with Austria were but the beginning of a German power play that eventually resulted in war.

It was the Czechoslovak crisis, however, that defined the term *appeasement*. Behind British negotiations of this policy was the fear that another general war might break out, with all the concomitant horrors that had characterized World War I. Britain, led by its prime minister, Neville Chamberlain, hoped to negotiate and make reasonable concessions to Germany to avert the possibility of war.

With the addition of Austria to the Reich, Germany now surrounded Czechoslovakia on three sides. Czechoslovakia itself was an affront to Hitler. It had been created after World War I as a check on Germany and was democratic and allied to both France and the Soviet Union. It also had a German population of about 3.5 million, which was concentrated in an area near the German border called the Sudetenland. These Sudeten Germans had been agitating for greater privileges and even autonomy in the Czech state. Chamberlain was so concerned that Hitler might invade Czechoslovakia and thus threaten European peace that he proposed a conference at Hitler's mountain retreat on September 15, 1938. In the following speech delivered three days before his meeting with Chamberlain, Hitler recounts his version of the misery of Sudeten Germans.

"The Misery of the Sudeten Germans Is Indescribable" (September 12, 1938)

ADOLF HITLER

I am speaking of Czechoslovakia. . . . Amongst the majority of the nationalities which are suffering oppression in this State there are to be found three and a half million Germans, that is to say about as many people of our race as, for example, the whole population of Denmark. But these Germans—they too are God's creatures. The Almighty did not create them in order that by means of a State-construction designed at Versailles they should be given over

"'The Misery of the Sudeten Germans Is Indescribable'" is from Norman H. Baynes, trans. and ed., *The Speeches of Adolf Hitler, April 1922–1939*, vol. 1 (London: Oxford University Press for the Royal Institute of International Affairs, 1942), pp. 1489–1490, 1499. Reprinted by permission of the Royal Institute of International Affairs.

to a hated alien Power. And He did not create the seven million Czechs that they should watch over and take under their care—much less that they should outrage and torture—these three and a half millions.

The conditions in this State, as is generally known, are intolerable. Here in political life over seven and a half millions in the name of the right of self-determination of a certain Mr. Wilson [President Woodrow Wilson] are deprived of their right of self-determination. In economic life these seven and a half millions are being systematically ruined and thus devoted to a slow process of extermination. This misery of the Sudeten Germans is indescribable. It is sought to annihilate them. As human beings they are oppressed and scandalously treated in an intolerable fashion. When three and a half million members of a people which numbers nearly eighty millions may not sing a song they like simply because it does not please the Czechs, or when they are beaten until the blood flows solely because they wear stockings the sight of which offends the Czechs, or when they are terrorized and ill-treated because they use a form of greeting which the Czechs dislike, although they use it only in greeting each other and not in greeting Czechs, when they are hunted and harried like helpless wild-fowl for every expression of their national sentiment—this may perhaps cause the worthy representatives of our democracies no concern: they may possibly welcome it since in this case only some three and a half million Germans are in question; but I can only say to the representatives of these democracies that this does concern us, and that if these tortured creatures can of themselves find no justice and no help they will get both from us. The depriving of these people of their rights must come to an end. . . . All of us have the duty never again to bow the head beneath an alien will. Let that be our vow. So help us God!

CONSIDER THIS:

- Hitler referred to the Sudeten Germans as "tortured creatures." Why were they in misery?

FIGURE 13.1 In this photograph taken during the Munich conference in September 1938, Adolf Hitler and Benito Mussolini discuss the fate of Czechoslovakia with British Prime Minister Neville Chamberlain. Chamberlain's policy of appeasing Hitler failed, and the world went to war a year later (*National Archives and Records Administration*)

"Czechoslovakia Has Ceased to Exist" (March 15, 1939)

ADOLF HITLER

Returning home from his meeting with Hitler to criticism from the British Parliament and press, Chamberlain justified his actions to the House of Commons on September 28. The next day he met with Mussolini and Hitler at Munich, where Britain guaranteed Czechoslovak security in exchange for their concession of territory to Germany.

With the Munich agreement, Chamberlain believed that he had secured "peace with honor. I believe it is peace for our time." It was not. The Czech state was rapidly torn up as Poland and Hungary took territory and the Slovaks demanded a state of their own. Finally Hitler broke his agreement and occupied Prague on March 15, 1939. Czechoslovakia had ceased to exist, and appeasement had ended any illusions that Hitler's only goal was to restore Germans to the Reich. The following documents reveal the bitter reality of the moment.

Only a few months ago [September 1938] Germany was compelled to protect her fellow-countrymen living in well defined settlements against the unbearable Czecho-Slovakian terror regime; and during the last weeks the same thing has happened on an ever increasing scale. This is bound to create an intolerable state of affairs within an area inhabited by citizens of so many nationalities.

These national groups, to counteract the renewed attacks against their freedom and life, have now broken away from the Prague Government. Czecho-Slovakia has ceased to exist. Since Sunday at many places wild excesses have broken out, amongst the victims of which are again many Germans. Hourly the number of oppressed and persecuted people crying for help is increasing. From areas thickly populated by German-speaking inhabitants, which last autumn Czecho-Slovakia was allowed by German generosity to retain, refugees robbed of their personal belongings are streaming into the Reich.

Continuation of such a state of affairs would lead to the destruction of every vestige of order in an area in which Germany is vitally interested, particularly as for over a thousand years it formed a part of the German Reich.

In order definitely to remove this menace to peace and to create the conditions for a necessary new order in this living space, I have today resolved to allow German troops to march into Bohemia and Moravia. They will disarm the terror gangs and the Czech forces supporting them, and protect the lives of all who are menaced. Thus they will lay the foundations for introducing a fundamental reordering of affairs which will be in accordance with a thousand-year history and will satisfy the practical needs of the German and Czech peoples.

Berlin, 15 March 1939 (*Signed*)

ADOLF HITLER

CONSIDER THIS:

- Were Hitler's motives altruistic? Was he really the protector of German honor and the guarantor of justice? Why was British prime minister Neville Chamberlain willing to buy this argument?

"'Czechoslovakia Has Ceased to Exist'" is from the Office of the U.S. Chief Counsel for Prosecution of Axis Criminality, *Nazi Conspiracy and Aggression* (Washington, D.C.: Government Printing Office, 1946), vol. 8, pp. 402–403 (050-TC).

"I Bitterly Regret What Has Now Occurred" (March 15, 1939)

NEVILLE CHAMBERLAIN

A further point which I would make is this: Hitherto the German Government in extending the area of their military control have defended their action by the contention that they were only incorporating in the Reich neighboring masses of people of German race. Now for the first time they are effecting a military occupation of territory inhabited by people with whom they have no racial connection. These events cannot fail to be a cause of disturbance to the international situation. They are bound to administer a shock to confidence, all the more regrettable because confidence was beginning to revive and to offer a prospect of concrete measures which would be of general benefit.

In a speech which I made at Birmingham on 30th January last I pointed out that we ought to define our aims and attitude, namely, our determination to search for peace. I added that I felt it was time now that others should make their contribution to a result which would overflow in benefits to many besides those immediately concerned. It is natural, therefore, that I should bitterly regret what has now occurred. But do not let us on that account be deflected from our course. Let us remember that the desire of all the peoples of the world still remains concentrated on the hopes of peace and a return to the atmosphere of understanding and good will which has so often been disturbed. The aim of this Government is now, as it has always been, to promote that desire and to substitute the method of discussion for the method of force in the settlement of differences. Though we may have to suffer checks and disappointments, from time to time, the object that we have in mind is of too great significance to the happiness of mankind for us lightly to give it up or set it on one side.

The Invasion of Poland (September 1939)

The occupation of Prague by German troops in March 1939 was a tremendous blow to Chamberlain's foreign policy. Two weeks later, the British government responded to public opinion by joining with France to guarantee the independence of Poland. Hitler now wanted to incorporate the Polish port city of Danzig into the German Reich and demanded access to this eastern city through a "corridor" that would link Germany with East Prussia. Hitler apparently did not take the Franco-British guarantee seriously, as revealed by the following notes taken at a conference at Obersalzberg in which he considered his options.

"Our Enemies Are Little Worms" (August 22, 1939)

ADOLF HITLER

It was clear to me that a conflict with Poland had to come sooner or later. I had already made this decision in the spring, but I thought I would first turn against the West in a few years, and only afterwards against the East. But the sequence of events cannot be fixed. Also one must not close one's eyes to a threatening situation. I wanted first of all to establish

"'I Bitterly Regret What Has Now Occurred'" is from *Parliamentary Debates*, 5th series, vol. 345 (1939), col. 440.

"'Our Enemies Are Little Worms'" is from the Nuremberg Military Tribunals, *Trials of War Criminals* (Washington, D.C.: Government Printing Office, 1947–1949), vol. 26, pp. 338–344 (PS-798).

an acceptable relationship with Poland in order to fight first against the West. But this plan, which was agreeable to me, could not be executed since fundamentals have changed. It became clear to me that Poland would attack us in case of a conflict with the West. Poland wants access to the sea. . . . It became clear to me that under the circumstances conflict with Poland could arise at an inopportune moment. I enumerate as reasons for this reflection: my own personality and that of Mussolini.

Essentially it depends on me, my existence, because of my political ability. Furthermore, the fact that probably no one will ever again have the confidence of the whole German people as I do. There will probably never again be a man in the future with more authority than I have. My life is, therefore, a factor of great value. But I can be eliminated at any time by a criminal or an idiot.

The second personal factor is the Duce [Mussolini]. His life is also a decisive factor. If something happens to him, Italy's loyalty to the alliance will no longer be certain. The basic attitude of the Italian Court is against the Duce. Above all, the Court sees in the expansion of the empire a burden. The Duce is the man with the strongest nerves in Italy. . . .

On the other side, negative picture, as far as decisive personalities are concerned. There is no outstanding personality in England or France. For us it is easy to make decisions. We have nothing to lose; we can only gain. Our economic situation is such, because of our limitations, that we cannot hold out more than a few years. Goring can confirm this. We have no other choice; we must act. Our opponents risk much and can gain only a little. England's stake in a war is unimaginably great. Our enemies have leaders who are below the average. No personalities. No masters, no men of action. . . .

All these fortunate circumstances will no longer prevail in two or three years. No one knows how long I shall live. Therefore war is better now. . . .

Relations with Poland have become unbearable. My Polish policy hitherto was opposed to the ideas of the people. My proposals to Poland [regarding Danzig and the Corridor] were disturbed by England's intervention. Poland changed her tone towards us. A state of tension which lasts for any length of time is intolerable. The initiative cannot be allowed to pass to the others. This moment is more favorable than it will be in two to three years. An attempt on my life or Mussolini's could change the situation to our disadvantage. One cannot eternally stand opposite one another with cocked rifle. . . .

England and France are under an obligation, neither is in a position to fulfil it. There is no actual rearmament in England, just propaganda. . . . England's position in the world is very precarious. She will not take any risks. . . . France lacks men (decline of the birth-rate). Little has been done for rearmament. The artillery is obsolete. . . .

The enemy had another hope, that Russia would become our enemy after the conquest of Poland. The enemy did not count on my great power of determination. Our enemies are little worms. I saw them in Munich.

I was convinced that Stalin would never accept the English offer. Russia has no interest in maintaining Poland, and Stalin knows that it will be the end of his regime no matter whether his soldiers come out of a war victorious or beaten. . . . I brought about the change of attitude towards Russia gradually. In connection with the commercial treaty we got into political conversation. Proposal of a non-aggression pact. Then came a general proposal from Russia. Four days ago I took a special step, with the result that Russia answered yesterday that she was ready to sign. The personal relations with Stalin are established. The day after tomorrow [German foreign minister] von Ribbentrop will conclude the treaty. Now Poland is in the position in which I wanted her. . . .

Today's publication of the non-aggression pact with Russia acted as a bombshell. The consequences cannot be foreseen. Stalin has also said that this course will be of benefit to both countries. The effect on Poland will be tremendous.

CONSIDER THIS:

- What do these notes tell you about Hitler as a man and leader? What was he willing to risk? Had he characterized his political allies and enemies correctly?

"At Dawn We Crossed into Poland" (September 1, 1939)

LIEUTENANT BARON TASSLIO VON BOGENHARDT

The next day, August 23, 1939, Hitler formally revealed a neutrality pact that he had signed with the Soviet Union. Joseph Stalin had resented having been cut out of the Munich negotiations by the West and felt he would have to bear the brunt of any future war with Germany. The most bitter ideological rivals thus became allies. This pact shocked the Western powers and paved the way for Hitler's conquest of Poland by removing the threat of Soviet retaliation from the East in exchange for allowing Russia to occupy the Baltic states of Estonia, Latvia, and Lithuania. Neville Chamberlain made a last attempt to impress on the German government the seriousness of the situation. Britain would no longer appease Hitler's demands and was willing to support Polish independence by going to war. When Hitler invaded Poland on September 1, war was declared.

The German attack on Poland instituted a new form of warfare called *blitzkrieg*, or "lightning war." The emphasis was on speed and focused aggression through massed armored columns of tanks supported by airpower. The Germans quickly overwhelmed Polish defenses, as the first account by a German officer indicates. Chamberlain's radio address and speech in Parliament on September 3 reveal the abridgment of his hopes and the ultimate failure of his policy of appeasement.

The ordering of general mobilization came almost on top of Britain's and France's guarantee of Poland; reservists were called up, vehicles and troops mobilized and ammunition distributed. We loaded our tanks and trucks onto the train and travelled for three days to Paprad in Slovakia, where we waited about ten miles from the Polish border. Several of us went up to the frontier to reconnoitre, and after the third day we got orders to move up during the night. At dawn we crossed into Poland.

The whole thing was so like an occupation of a manoeuvre that we could hardly believe this was really war; it all seemed too well-ordered and familiar. There was virtually no resistance, and for days on end we advanced towards the Polish Ukraine. There were rumors of sharpshooters and partisans, but I never saw or heard anything of them, except for the occasional sound of a shot in the distance. There was a certain amount of sporadic fighting when we got to the river barriers, but the Luftwaffe [Air Force] had already cleared the way for us. Their Stuka dive-bombers were deadly accurate, and as there was no opposition they had it all their own way. The roads and fields were swarming with unhappy peasants who had fled in panic from their villages when the bombing began, and we passed hundreds and hundreds of Polish troops walking dejectedly towards Slovakia. The Poles seemed to be completely apathetic, and there were so many prisoners that nobody bothered to guard them or even tell them where to go.

"At Dawn We Crossed into Poland" is from Louis Hagen, *Follow My Leader* (London: Wingate, 1951), p. 24.

"Everything I Have Hoped for Has Crashed into Ruins" (September 3, 1939)

NEVILLE CHAMBERLAIN

Radio Address to the British People

I am speaking to you from the Cabinet Room at 10, Downing Street. This morning the British Ambassador in Berlin handed the German Government a final note stating that unless we heard from them by 11 o'clock that they were prepared at once to withdraw their troops from Poland a state of war would exist between us. I have to tell you now that no such undertaking has been received, and that consequently this country is at war with Germany.

You can imagine what a bitter blow it is to me that all my long struggle to win peace has failed. Yet I cannot believe that there is anything more or anything different that I could have done that would have been more successful.

Up to the very last it would have been quite possible to have arranged a peaceful and honorable settlement between Germany and Poland. But Hitler would not have it. He had evidently made up his mind to attack Poland whatever happened, and although he now says he put forward reasonable proposals which were rejected by the Poles, that is not a true statement.

The Proposals were never shown to the Poles, nor to us, and, though they were announced in a German broadcast on Thursday night, Hitler did not wait to hear comments on them, but ordered his troops to cross the Polish frontier. His action shows convincingly that there is no chance of expecting that this man will ever give up his practice of using force to gain his will. He can only be stopped by force.

We and France are today, in fulfillment of our obligations, going to the aid of Poland, who is so bravely resisting this wicked and unprovoked attack upon her people. We have a clear conscience. We have done all that any country could do to establish peace, but a situation in which no word given by Germany's ruler could be trusted and no people or country could feel themselves safe had become intolerable. And now that we have resolved to finish it, I know that you will all play your part with calmness and courage. . . .

Address to the House of Commons

This is a sad day for all of us, and to none is it sadder than to me. Everything that I have worked for, everything that I have hoped for, everything that I have believed in during my public life, has crashed into ruins. There is only one thing left for me to do; that is, to devote what strength and powers I have to forwarding the victory of the cause for which we have to sacrifice so much. I cannot tell what part I may be allowed to play myself. I trust I may live to see the day when Hitlerism has been destroyed and a liberated Europe has been reestablished.

CONSIDER THIS:

- Winston Churchill was the most outspoken opponent to Chamberlain's policy of appeasement and noted that "an appeaser is one who feeds a crocodile hoping he will eat him last." Although Churchill's assessment of Hitler's motives proved to be correct, can Chamberlain be blamed for trying to secure political stability and international peace through concession?

THE BROADER PERSPECTIVE:

- Do the roots of appeasement lie in the myopic diplomacy that produced the 1919 Treaty of Versailles at the conclusion of World War I? Do you agree with Benjamin Franklin that "There was never a good war or a bad peace"? Or are you in Niccolò Machiavelli's camp and believe that "There is no avoiding war; it can only be postponed to the advantage of others"?

"'Everything I Have Hoped for Has Crashed into Ruins'" is from *Parliamentary Debates*, 5th series, vol. 340 (1939).

FIGURE 13.2 "Europe on the Eve of World War II." Germany's secret neutrality pact with the Soviet Union allowed Hitler to invade Poland on September 1, 1939. Britain had guaranteed Poland's independence and declared war on Germany two days later. (From *The War in Maps: An Atlas of the New York Times Maps*, 4/e by Francis Brown and Lucas Manditch. Copyright © 1942, 1943, 1946, 1973 by Oxford University Press, Inc., renewed 1973 by Francis Brown. Reprinted by permission of the publisher.)

Total War (1939–1943)

The aims of battle and the fruits of conquest are never the same; the latter have their value and only the saint rejects them, but their hint of immortality vanishes as soon as they are held in the hand.

—E. M. Forster

It takes twenty years of peace or more to make a man; it takes only twenty seconds of war to destroy him.

—Baudouin I, King of Belgium

What war has always been is a puberty ceremony. It's a rough one, but you went away a boy and came back a man, maybe with an eye missing or whatever, but godammit you were a man and people had to call you a man thereafter.

—Kurt Vonnegut

The Battlefield and the Home Front

The German invasion of Poland was so successful that the Russians moved quickly to claim their division of Poland and the Baltic countries of Estonia, Latvia, and Lithuania. After this, events slowed dramatically into a *sitzkrieg*, or "phony war," as Germany consolidated its gains and prepared for the next phase of war. In April, Hitler invaded Denmark and Norway and followed this with attacks on Belgium and the Netherlands. France had relied for its defense on the renowned Maginot Line, a series of artillery fortifications built after World War I to repel an attack. But the new German mobilized warfare, together with the fact that the fortifications were never completed through Belgium to the sea, allowed the Germans to maneuver around and through the Maginot Line. The French army, poorly led by generals who could not fathom the changes in mechanized warfare since 1918, collapsed. Hitler defeated France in five weeks.

The fall of France in June 1940 left Britain alone to fight the Germans. Hitler expected the British to negotiate an arrangement that allowed Britain to retain its empire if Germany could rule the European continent. British opposition to such an accommodation was assured with the appointment of Winston Churchill as prime minister in May 1940.

Churchill had been a vocal critic of Neville Chamberlain's appeasement policies and inspired his nation through a series of speeches and an aura of dogged determination to resist the Nazi menace. Although the United States was officially neutral and dominated by isolationist sentiments, it still helped Britain survive by sending warships and military supplies through a mutually beneficial lend-lease arrangement.

The following speeches by Churchill in the British Parliament reveal his dynamic qualities of leadership. He was a great orator who understood how to inspire the British people to unify and resist regardless of the cost.

Alone: "Their Finest Hour" (June 18, 1940)

WINSTON CHURCHILL

The Battle of France is over. I expect that the Battle of Britain is about to begin. Upon this battle depends the survival of Christian civilization. Upon it depends our own British life, and the long continuity of our institutions and our Empire. The whole fury and might of the enemy must very soon be turned on us. Hitler knows that he will have to break us in this island or lose the war. If we can stand up to him, all Europe may be free and the life of the world may move forward into broad, sunlit uplands. But if we fail, then the whole world, including the United States, including all that we have known and cared for, will sink into the abyss of a new Dark Age made more sinister, and perhaps more protracted, by the lights of perverted science. Let us therefore brace ourselves to our duties and so bear ourselves that, if the British Empire and its Commonwealth last for a thousand years, men will still say, "This was their finest hour."

The Battle of Britain: "So Much Owed by So Many to So Few" (August 20, 1940)

WINSTON CHURCHILL

The gratitude of every home in our Island, in our Empire, and indeed throughout the world, except in the abodes of the guilty, goes out to the British airmen who, undaunted by odds, unwearied in their constant challenge and mortal danger, are turning the tide of the world war by their prowess and by their devotion. Never in the field of human conflict was so much owed by so many to so few. All hearts go out to the fighter pilots, whose brilliant actions we see with our own eyes day after day; but we must never forget that all the time, night after night, month after month, our bomber squadrons travel far into Germany, find their targets in the darkness by the highest navigational skill, aim their attacks, often under the heaviest fire, often with serious loss, with deliberate careful discrimination, and inflict shattering blows upon the whole of the technical and war-making structure of the Nazi power. On no part of the Royal Air Force does the weight of the war fall more heavily than on the daylight bombers who will play an invaluable part in the case of invasion and whose unflinching zeal it has been necessary in the meanwhile on numerous occasions to restrain.

London Aflame!

MRS. ROBERT HENREY

The Battle of Britain began in August 1940 with German attacks on the airfields of southeastern England. But in early September, seeking revenge for British bombing raids on German cities, the Nazis switched their attacks to London. For two months,

"Alone" is from *Parliamentary Debates*, 5th series, vol. 362 (1940), cols. 60–61.

"The Battle of Britain" is from *Parliamentary Debates*, 5th series, vol. 364 (1940), cols. 1166–1167.

"London Aflame!" is from Mrs. Robert Henrey, *London Under Fire, 1940–1945* (London: J. M. Dent & Sons, Ltd., 1969), pp. 36–37, 43–44.

life in London was transformed as the air raid siren and blackout curtains signaled the daily ritual of night bombings.

Much of the city was destroyed, and over 15,000 people were killed. British inhabitants went underground to the subways where life continued as babies were born, friendships formed, and the survivors were tallied. Mrs. Robert Henrey, a mother who lived in London's West End, recounts the activity.

As the battle for London continued, the face of the West End changed; but as far as possible its inhabitants attempted to carry on as usual. Crowds filed through the streets an hour before dusk carrying their mattresses on their way to the tube stations and public shelters. . . .

Bombs fell by day as well as by night. We became accustomed to the sudden drone of an airplane in the middle of the morning, the screech of a bomb, the dull crash of its explosion and the smell of cordite that filled the air a moment later. The sight of a burned-out bus unexpectedly in Berkeley Square, the ruins of a shop still half-hidden in a cloud of dust, streets that were impassable because of time bombs, enemy planes that burst in mid air sending down large chunks of fuselage, the pilots gliding down with their parachutes, became the normal things of life. . . . Almost every night some landmark near us would go up in dust, and yet our building continued to stand. . . .

From the very first night of the battle for London [1940], because of the fires in the east which lit up the dome, St. Paul's Cathedral had become a symbol of London's defiance. As long ago as the night of the 12th September a large delayed-action bomb hurtled down south of the granite posts and buried itself twenty-seven feet deep. Everybody knew that if it exploded there would be nothing left of St. Paul's. For three days men worked to dig it out. Then it was driven in state to Hackney Marches on a lorry under the command of Lt. Davies, a Canadian who became a national hero.

Even for a very ordinary housewife living with her baby in the West End, St. Paul's could never for long be out of her mind. Almost every evening from the flat roof of Carrington House we peered east and prayed that it might stand.

The Japanese Attack on Pearl Harbor

Although American support of the British through lend-lease arrangements might have justified a German declaration of war against the United States, Hitler knew that his chances for victory in Europe were greater without the involvement of the "sleeping giant." In fact, the United States may not have overcome its isolationist caution and entered the European conflict had not war been thrust on it in the Pacific.

Since the early 1930s, Japan had been forging a policy of conquest in Asia. Japan had conquered the mineral-rich Chinese region of Manchuria in 1931 and renamed it Manchukuo. After allying itself with Germany and Italy and signing a neutrality pact with the Soviet Union, Japan exploited the weakness of Britain and France abroad. In July 1941, the Japanese occupied Indochina. In response, the United States and Britain froze Japanese assets and cut off oil supplies. Without control over the Indonesian oil fields and the supplies of rubber and tin in Malaya, Japanese plans for expansion would fail. The solution, imposed by a war faction in the Japanese government led by General Hideki Tojo, was to end the constraint of the United States.

On Sunday morning, December 7, 1941, while Japanese representatives were still negotiating in Washington, Japan launched a surprise air attack on the U.S. naval base at Pearl Harbor, Hawaii. Its aim was to severely cripple America's ability to respond to Japanese aggression in the Pacific and allow Japan to consolidate its gains before the United States could rebuild its fleet. Eyewitness accounts of the disaster follow, and the section ends with President Roosevelt's famous request in Congress for a declaration of war against Japan.

"I Saw My Maker on Sunday"

PRIVATE NICHOLAS GAYNOS

December 9, 1941

Dear Folks,

Well, I'm okay and feeling fine. We sure had a hot time here for a while and I thought that my end had come—God, was it hell. I'll give you an eyewitness account of the Japanese air raid on Pearl Harbor and Hickam Field on Sunday, 7 December 1941. This ought to make a good news copy for the *Bridgeport Post*.

Well, Sunday as usual, all of the men were sleeping late because we had no work to do. I was sound asleep, having gone to bed at 4:30 A.M. after being relieved of duty. It was exactly 7:55 when I was almost tossed out of bed by a terrific roar and the ensuing concussion. Most of the fellows also got up and, on looking out the window, we could see flames about five hundred feet high and huge clouds of smoke coming from Pearl Harbor.

No one thought it was war until we looked out of our eastern windows and saw some of our hangars in flames. Somebody yelled, "They are Japanese planes," but nobody believed it. We all ran out of the barracks and looked skyward. It was plain to see them. They were only from fifty to one hundred feet off the ground, and the huge red circle under their wings proved their identity. Some of them had huge torpedoes under the fuselage almost as long as the ship itself.

The thunder of bombs and the staccato of machine guns made such a deafening roar you had to yell to be heard a few feet away. The splintering of wood as fifty-caliber bullets ripped through the wooden barracks was mixed with screams of men as they ran from one shelter to another. We soon collected our senses and the full realization that war was here.

Some men cried, some laughed, others were terrified, some just couldn't seem to understand what it was all about. I soon had my senses under control and jumped in a car headed for my post. With a hail of bullets and with the planes roaring right over our heads, we raced down the street. I arrived at my transmitters and dove into a hole caused by an exploded bomb. One young fellow was dead, and his legs stuck out of the hole. It reminded me of a book I once read back home. I stayed here until things had quieted down and then scurried for safety in my flimsy office. We all knew they would be back soon so we hurriedly made preparations for their return. It was at 10:20 when the second attack came.

I was busy removing a radio truck to safety. Three men and I kept working as they dived into the big barracks and dropped load after load of bombs. The very ground shook, and my ears were ringing. By this time they spotted my equipment and headed straight for my men and me. I was lying in a small hole

"I Saw My Maker on Sunday" is from Paul Joseph Travers, *Eyewitness to Infamy: An Oral History of Pearl Harbor* (New York: Madison Books, 1991), pp. 48–50.

about ten feet to the right of my trucks. As the planes dove down at us, I could peek out under the brim of my tin helmet and see them spitting fire at us. The ground in front of me was spraying up and I could see the bombs leave the planes and head straight down at us. One of them was a one-thousand-pound bomb and landed fifty feet on my right. Three kids with a machine gun were shooting at the plane and the bomb landed almost on them. It blew them sky-high—gun and all.

The dirt and stones fell all over us and I ached all over. I emptied my forty-five pistol time after time into the planes, but it was futile. I thumbed my nose as they roared right over my head. We all swore like hell.

The planes were still roaring around strafing us unmercifully as those of us that were alive got into cars and started to pick up the dead and wounded. One of the kids who was blown up with the machine gun was lying about fifty feet away. I tried to pick him up and he fell apart in my arms. He was covered with dirt and smiling. We rushed as many as we could to the hospital and gave first aid to those lying near us. Things were now getting quiet and then ambulances, nurses, and trucks came to pick up the men. Some of the things were so ghastly I cannot write of them. All I can say is that my baptism under fire sure was hell on earth and I saw my Maker on Sunday, December 7, 1941.

The USS Arizona: "Some Sort of Hellish Nightmare!"

SEAMAN JOHN RAMPLEY

On 7 December, a beautiful, clear, typical island day dawned. Being Sunday, the entire ship would be on "holiday routine." Sunrise over the harbor on Sunday was in itself a religious experience. With the stillness and quietness which surrounded the water, it was as if every Sunday was an Easter sunrise service. Certainly, this Sunday was to be no exception. . . .

Within moments, general quarters were sounded. "This is no drill. I repeat, this is no drill," echoed down the steel corridors of the ship. The words sent a cold, shuttering chill down my spine. At our battle stations on the fourteen-inch guns, there was little to do but pray. In the space of a few seconds, some men made up for twenty and more years of tardy prayers. Inside the turret, there was an eerie silence. Everyone seemed afraid to breathe, much less speak, as if that would somehow give away our position to the enemy or attract the attention of one of the bombs. We waited anxiously for some word from topside. Even though we were protected by the heavy plating of the turret, we felt helpless and defenseless, not being able to take any kind of action to defend ourselves and our fellow sailors. We could hear the thunder and feel the ship shudder as the bombs fell upon her. At one point in time, we felt a tremendous jolt, as if the ship had been lifted up in the air and slammed back down. Little did we realize that this was the fatal blow for the Arizona. Rivets popped from the steel walls and flew about the place. . . .

After what seemed like an eternity, the order came over the speakers, "All hands abandon ship." I looked around for some comfort, but all my shipmates seemed to have the same awareness as myself. Our life together aboard the old Arizona was over. I climbed down the ladder on the outside of the turret. Everywhere I touched or grabbed onto the

"The USS *Arizona*" is from Paul Joseph Travers, *Eyewitness to Infamy: An Oral History of Pearl Harbor* (New York: Madison Books, 1991), pp. 140–142.

FIGURE 13.3 "A date which will live in infamy." The Japanese attack on the American naval base at Pearl Harbor, Hawaii, on December 7, 1941, brought the United States into World War II. This picture shows the destruction of the battleships Arizona, Tennessee, and West Virginia. (*National Archives and Records Administration*)

ship, I felt the effects of the fires and explosions. The ship had become a piece of molten steel, a kind of giant tea kettle, where heat was being transferred to all metal and steel parts. . . . Finally being outside the turret, it looked as if the rest of the ship was a blazing inferno, encircled by a wall of fire which was quickly closing in. I remember looking around the deck and seeing my shipmates from the deck division with their bodies burned black or lying on the deck bleeding from open wounds. Some men were screaming and jumping over the side of the ship. Others were spread about the deck in various positions, crying and moaning in agony. Charred and mutilated bodies were scattered everywhere in the wreckage of the ship. They lay crumpled like broken dolls who had been picked up in the air by some giant hand and slammed against the structures of the ship. With all the smoke and fire on the decks, it seemed difficult to catch one's breath. . . . All around, the air was filled with the smell of burning oil and burning flesh. It was a smell which lingered in the air like a heavy fog, saturating one's clothes and body.

I walked, then crawled, very calmly and carefully to the side of the ship and looked down into the water. The water was partially covered with oil, most of which was burning. . . . From where I stood, all I could see forward was a crumbling mass of twisted metal that had only minutes before been the proud superstructure. The command to abandon ship was being repeated over and over again. Enemy planes were still strafing the ship when I made the decision to jump. The warm water was certainly a refresher. When I came to the surface, I was hoping that the whole thing was a bad dream, some sort of hellish nightmare. . . . I began swimming toward Ford Island. The swim wasn't far, but it was very exhausting swimming an obstacle course filled with oil, debris, and bodies. I reached the island in relatively good shape, considering the ordeal which I had been through. After a short rest and a couple of mouthfuls of water, I got my second wind and was ready to help wherever needed.

It wasn't until many hours later that I learned so many of my shipmates were dead. Of the fifteen from my boot platoon that I went aboard with, I was the only one who survived.

"A Date Which Will Live in Infamy"

PRESIDENT FRANKLIN DELANO ROOSEVELT

Yesterday, December 7, 1941—a date which will live in infamy—the United States of America was suddenly and deliberately attacked by naval and air forces of the Empire of Japan.

The United States was at peace with that nation and, at the solicitation of Japan, was still in conversation with its Government and its Emperor looking toward the maintenance of peace in the Pacific. . . .

It will be recorded that the distance of Hawaii from Japan makes it obvious that the attack was deliberately planned many days or even weeks ago. During the intervening time the Japanese Government has deliberately sought to deceive the United States by false statements and expressions of hope for continued peace.

The attack yesterday on the Hawaiian Islands has caused severe damage to American naval and military forces. Very many American lives have been lost. In addition American ships have been reported torpedoed on the high seas between San Francisco and Honolulu. . . .

As Commander-in-Chief of the Army and Navy I have directed that all measures be taken for our defense. Always will we remember the character of the onslaught against us. No matter how long it may take us to overcome this premeditated invasion, the American people in their righteous might will win through to absolute victory. . . .

With confidence in our armed forces—with the unbounded determination of our people—we will gain the inevitable triumph—so help us God.

I ask that the Congress declare that since the unprovoked and dastardly attack by Japan on Sunday, December seventh, a state of war has existed between the United States and the Japanese Empire.

CONSIDER THIS:

- After reading the documents and firsthand accounts of the Japanese attack on Pearl Harbor, what images stand out in your mind? Was the attack well planned? How did the Japanese miscalculate?

"'A Date Which Will Live in Infamy'" is from Department of State, *Bulletin*, December 13, 1941, p. 474.

Women in the Factories: "My Hands Are as Smooth as the Steel I Worked on" (August 1943)

ELIZABETH HAWES

Perhaps the most amazing feat of logistical supply in history occurred after the disaster at Pearl Harbor when American industry was transformed to produce the implements of war. Much more than the economy was altered, however. An entire society was transformed as men went to war and women went into the factories.

"Rosie the Riveter" became an endearing image of women who decided to leave their jobs as homemakers, teachers, and salesclerks to become crane operators and machinists. At proving grounds, women loaded and tested machine guns and antiaircraft weapons. Women became guards at plants, foundry workers, hydraulic press operators, and miners. In January 1942, 4,000 women were employed as war workers. Within a year the number had swollen to 43,000.

The standard workweek was forty-eight hours (six days of eight hours each) with only Sundays off, and many women routinely worked overtime. Many doubted that women could handle the long hours and grind of grueling, repetitious work. But most women truly felt that their contributions were essential to victory, and they proved to themselves and to the country that they could compete in traditional male occupations. The following account explains the demands and benefits of wartime factory work for women.

A few months ago, when everybody was talking about the production crisis—can women do it?—will women do it?—how are you going to make women do it?—I began to murmur that I guessed I'd go into a factory and find out how the wheels went round. . . .

Now that I've worked a few months in a plant—on the graveyard shift too—the only wonder to me is that all the women in the USA aren't storming the factory gates. I'm convinced that any healthy woman can work in a factory—and like it. My biggest regret is that I had to leave because I'd agreed to do some writing. My biggest ambition is to get back.

Sure, I caught a bad cold. My hands aren't soft any more but they're as smooth as the steel I worked on. . . . So what! All the other women had to do cleaning and laundry as well as cooking and shopping. I was spared that. . . .

The plant itself was exciting. It's one of the Wright aeronautical plants in northern New Jersey—I believe the biggest airplane engine plant in the country. You feel you're in a small town, only the streets are lined with machines. Electric trucks honk at you constantly and people on bicycles flip past as you wend your way from the locker room to your machine a mile or so distant. There are no windows. Air conditioning and thousands of long blue lights take the place of the breezes and the sun. . . .

It was a great pleasure to me that nobody gave a darn who anyone was or whether you'd ever had your picture in the paper or shaken hands with the Duchess of Windsor or Gertie Lawrence. . . . Of course there are little discords. The foremen and subforemen are honestly scared to death of us women. When first you arrive they look at you out of the corner of their eyes. . . . Every woman machinist has to endure sheer torture from her fellow male employees at one point in her career. You

"Women in the Factories" is from Elizabeth Hawes, "My Life on the Midnight Shift," *Woman's Home Companion* (August 1943), pp. 24, 47.

discover that you can't work without tools and that the company doesn't provide all of them. First you borrow from your lead man or somebody near by who owns a toolbox. Ultimately you buy your own toolbox and quite a few dollars' worth of wrenches, hammers, micrometers and such.

The men see that now you think you're a mechanic. Some honestly don't believe the Lord ever intended women to be mechanics. Others are infuriated by your presumption that you can do their work. . . .

Thank heaven, none of the women in the plant had ever been told by "authoritative sources," as I had, that the women of the USA are unpatriotic—that they're just working for money.

They are working for money—money to feed their kids, money to keep their homes together—so their sons and husbands can fight. They never speak of being useful because it might sound boastful. It might sound as if you were taking credit for losing sleep, for tending sick children at home, for not having time to shop carefully and for still turning up at work.

But mostly I want to go back to Wright's new plant because I think the women who work in war plants, and the men who first help them and then work with them are the luckiest people in the world. There's an equality developing there unlike any I've ever seen. Joe was an Italian—Nel, a Negro—Suzy, Irish—there were Germans, Poles, Hungarians, Gentiles, Jews. Slowly you could see there was no difference between any two of us. Gradually everybody was beginning to work as one unit. When you see something like that happening you feel you're not just doing a job to help win the war. You also have the profound pleasure of seeing the future peace being worked out before your eyes.

CONSIDER THIS:

- Elizabeth Dawes wondered why "all the women in the USA aren't storming the factory gates" and regretted the fact that she had to leave to do some writing: "My biggest ambition is to get back." Why was she so enthusiastic? What obstacles did she have to overcome, and what did she prove to herself and to others?

COMPARE AND CONTRAST:

- Compare the wartime experience of the American factory worker, Elizabeth Dawes, to that of Mrs. Robert Henrey, the young British mother who survived the blitz bombing of London in 1940 and after on pages 398–399. What were their roles during World War II? Reflect on the diversity of experience and the changing expectations of women during times of war.

The Jewish Holocaust (1923–1945)

I mean the clearing out of the Jews, the extermination of the Jewish race. . . . Most of you must know what it means when 100 corpses are lying side by side, or 500, or 1,000. To have stuck it out and at the same time. . . to have remained decent fellows, that is what has made us hard. This is a page of glory in our history which has never been written and is never to be written. . . .

—HEINRICH HIMMLER TO HIS S.S. OFFICERS

In spite of everything, I still believe that people are really good at heart.

—ANNE FRANK

Whoever fights monsters should see to it that in the process he does not become a monster; and when you look long into an abyss, the abyss also looks into you.

—FRIEDRICH NIETZSCHE

Despair is no solution. I know that. What is the solution? Hitler had one. And he tried it while a civilized world kept silent. I remember. And I am afraid.

—ELIE WIESEL

The name *Adolf Hitler* has become synonymous with evil. Much of this reputation has been derived from his attempt to commit genocide, to exterminate an entire race of people. One of the more distinctive differences between Italian fascism under Benito Mussolini (1883–1945) and the Nazi movement was Hitler's use of anti-Semitism. Hitler demanded that Germany be composed of racially pure Aryan stock. The blond, blue-eyed German, untainted by inferior blood, became Hitler's ideal and the image he tried to cultivate in his propaganda. Hitler saw the Jews as the source of all of Germany's trouble. According to Hitler, Jews were cowards who did not support the fatherland in the Great War. They had deep communist sympathies, controlled international finance, and dominated the most important offices in government. Jews also controlled the purse strings of the nation and thus prevented worthier and more talented individuals from holding jobs and contributing to German culture. Indeed, Hitler had once been a frustrated artist in Vienna who blamed his failure on such Jewish influence. Hitler understood that hatred often unifies a nation more readily than love. In troubled times, people want a simple explanation for their pain and insecurity. For Hitler, and consequently for Germany, that explanation was the Jew.

Anti-Semitism certainly did not originate with Hitler. Jews had been persecuted since the Middle Ages and even blamed for such things as outbreaks of bubonic plague. Still, never before was there such a systematic, methodical attempt to exterminate an entire ethnic group.

Although Hitler had exhibited his racism from the early 1920s in speeches and writings, and he had incorporated it into the philosophy of national socialism, nothing could be implemented until the Nazis came into power. By 1935, Jews were excluded from citizenship by law to preserve German blood and honor. Germany was saturated with propaganda that presented the Jew as an immoral pervert whose presence was a threat to the health and morality of the German community. Nazi policy slowly evolved toward deportation and then toward isolation of the Jews in city ghettos. The "Final Solution" to the Jewish problem actually began in June 1941. As Hitler's armies drove into Russia, special mobile killing units (*Einsatzgruppen*) were set up and followed just behind the front lines. For eighteen months, the *Einsatzgruppen* operated and killed over 1.3 million Jews. The Nazis also built several concentration camps generally designed to house workers and remove Jews from society. The treatment of prisoners was cruel, and hundreds of thousands died of exhaustion, starvation, and disease. The Nazi commitment to Jewish extermination even exceeded the bounds of practicality. Although there was a widespread shortage of labor throughout German-controlled Europe during the war, the Nazis continued to wipe out valuable workers. The camps, run by Hitler's private army called the S.S. (*Schutzstaffel*), often served as holding pens until the inmates were sent by train to six death camps located in Poland. Created solely for the task of killing, the camps at Auschwitz and Treblinka have become infamous—over 2.7 million Jews were eliminated, 1 million in Auschwitz alone. Thousands of other undesirable people such as Gypsies, Slavs, and even dissident Germans were also killed.

Many questions arise out of the Holocaust that make this a particularly important and relevant historical problem. How could such a violation against humanity have happened? Could it happen again? Can one view the Jewish Holocaust as a precedent that legitimized the dropping of the atomic bomb on Hiroshima and Nagasaki? Can one say "War is hell" and let it go at that? How deep and penetrating is the racial argument? Do we all have prejudices, that, if exploited properly, can lead to such results? The urgency of these questions is intensified when we consider other issues: the policy of "ethnic cleansing" by the Serbs in Bosnia or the influence of the Ku Klux Klan; the millions who were murdered by Stalin during Soviet collectivization, industrialization, and the Great Purges of the 1930s; the butchery in Rwanda; the ruthlessness of the Cambodian dictator Pol Pot; or the maniacal ranting of Muammar Gaddafi or Saddam Hussein.

Not forgetting is the responsibility of the living.

"The Jews Are the Cause of Our Misfortune!"

Anti-Semitism was one of the cornerstones of Nazi dogma. When Hitler became chancellor in 1933, he began the process of excluding Jews from life in the German Reich. Note the charges that are leveled against the Jews in one of Hitler's early speeches. Indeed, Jews felt compelled to defend themselves against accusations that they were in control of international finance and the German government or that they were cowards who forsook Germany in World War I. With the adoption of the Nuremberg Laws in 1935, Hitler excluded Jews from German citizenship and made provisions to restrict their social relations.

The Jewish Peril (April 1923)

ADOLF HITLER

The German people was once clear thinking and simple: why has it lost these characteristics? Any inner renewal is possible only if one realizes that this is a question of race: America forbids the yellow peoples to settle there, but this is a lesser peril than that which stretches out its hand over the entire world—the Jewish peril. Many hold that the Jews are not a race, but is there a second people anywhere in the wide world which is so determined to maintain its race?

As a matter of fact the Jew can never become a German however often he may affirm that he can. If he wished to become a German, he must surrender the Jew in him. And that is not possible: he cannot, however much he tries, become a German at heart, and that for several reasons: first because of his blood, second because of his character, thirdly because of his will, and fourthly because of his actions. His actions remain Jewish: he works for the "greater idea" of the Jewish people.

"The Jewish Peril" is from Norman H. Baynes, trans. and ed., *The Speeches of Adolf Hitler, April 1922–1939*, vol. 1 (London: Oxford University Press for the Royal Institute of International Affairs, 1942), pp. 59–60. Reprinted by permission of the Royal Institute of International Affairs.

Because that is so, because it cannot be otherwise, therefore the bare existence of the Jew as part of another State rests upon a monstrous lie. It is a lie when he pretends to the peoples to be a German, a Frenchman, etc.

What then are the specifically Jewish aims? To spread their invisible State as a supreme tyranny over all other States in the whole world. The Jew is therefore a disintegrator of peoples. To realize his rule over the peoples he must work in two directions: in economics he dominates peoples when he subjugates them politically and morally: in politics he dominates them through the propagation of the principles of democracy and the doctrines of Marxism—the creed which makes a Proletarian a Terrorist in the domestic sphere and a Pacifist in foreign policy. Ethically the Jew destroys the peoples both in religion and in morals. He who wishes to see that can see it, and him who refuses to see it no one can help. The Jew, whether consciously or unconsciously, whether he wishes it or not, undermines the platform on which alone a nation can stand.

We are now met by the questions: Do we wish to restore Germany to freedom and power? If "yes": then the first thing to do is to rescue it from him who is ruining our country. Admittedly it is a hard fight that must be fought here. We National Socialists on this point occupy an extreme position: but we know only one people: it is for that people we fight and that is our own people. . . . We want to stir up a storm. Men must not sleep: they ought to know that a thunder-storm is coming up. We want to prevent our Germany from suffering, as Another did, the death upon the Cross.

We may be inhumane, but if we rescue Germany we have achieved the greatest deed in the world! We may work injustice, but if we rescue Germany then we have removed the greatest injustice in the world. We may be immoral, but if our people is rescued we have once more opened up the way for morality!

"Not a Single Jew" (1932)

Jewish World Finance

Today, capital formation takes place in large industry. Its largest enterprises are almost entirely dominated by non-Jewish interests: Krupp, Vereinigte Stahlwerke, Klockner, Stinnes, Siemeins, Stumm, I. G. Farben, Hugenberg, Hapag, Nordlloyd.

International connections are concentrated most heavily in those industries in which Jews are without influence or altogether unrepresented: the German-French iron cartel, wooden matches trust, oil trust, potash industry, and shipping conventions are all "clean of Jews," and so are the international chemical cartel, nylon production and all the other raw material and key industries in which Jews have no influence either as owners or directors. . . .

Jewish Government

The anti-Semites assert that the German government is full of Jews. The 19 post-war cabinets consisted of 237 ministers of whom three (Preuss and twice Rathenau) were Jews and four (Landsberg, Gradnauer, and twice Hilferding) of Jewish descent. The last few governments have had no Jewish ministers.

In the German provinces, the situation is not different: none of the provincial cabinets contain a Jew. The administration is not full of

"'Not a Single Jew'" is from Raul Hilberg, ed., *Documents of Destruction* (Chicago: Quadrangle Books, 1971), pp. 8–11. Reprinted by permission of the author.

Jews, either. For example, in Prussia, among the twelve chief presidents, thirty-five government presidents and four hundred provincial counsellors, there is not a single Jew. . . .

The Jews in World War I

Of 538,000 Jews in Germany, more than 96,000 were under arms, including 10,000 volunteers; about 80,000 were on the front lines, 35,000 received decorations, 23,000 were promoted, including more than 2000 to officer rank (without medical corps). One hundred sixty-eight Jews who volunteered as flyers are known by name. At the top of the list is Lieutenant D. R. Frankl who received the *Pour le merite* [combat medal] and who like 29 other Jewish flyers was killed in battle.

Twelve thousand Jewish soldiers did not see their homeland again; they *died a hero's death for their German fatherland*. More than 10,000 of their names have now been recorded with personal information, unit, and number. The dead of Hamburg, Alsace-Lorraine and ceded Posen (with its relatively large Jewish population) have not yet been registered.

It is heartless to demand today that the widows and orphans, parents and brothers, brides and relatives of 12,000 fallen Jews be deprived of equality in Germany.

Consider This:

- What are the specific charges leveled against the Jews by Hitler in his speech, "The Jewish Peril"? Why can't Jews be Germans?
- How strong is the Jewish argument in defense against Hitler's attacks that Jews were cowards and controlled the Weimar government and world finance? Why did the German people believe Hitler?

"I Got You at Last, You Little German Girl!"

ERNST HIEMER

In 1936, Germany hosted the Olympic Games and Hitler ordered the temporary removal of anti-Jewish placards to appease foreign opinion. Still, anti-Semitic propaganda continued to flow, especially from *Der Stürmer*, a sensationalistic journal published by Julius Streicher. The following excerpt is from a book for older children called *Der Giftpilz* (The Poisonous Mushroom), which presented the Jew as an evil deviate who preyed on the innocence of children.

"It is almost noon," he said, "now we want to summarize what we have learned in this lesson. What did we discuss?"

All the children raise their hands. The teacher calls on Karl Scholz, a little boy on the first bench. "We talked about how to recognize a Jew."

"Good! Now tell us about it!"

Little Karl takes the pointer, goes to the blackboard and points to the sketches.

"One usually recognizes a Jew by his nose. The Jewish nose is crooked at the end. It looks like the figure 6. Therefore it is called the 'Jewish Six.' Many non-Jews have crooked noses, too. But their noses are bent, not at the end but further up. Such a nose is called a hook nose or eagle's beak. It has nothing to do with a Jewish nose."

"Right!" says the teacher. "But the Jew is recognized not only by his nose. . . ." The boy continues. "The Jew is also recognized by his lips. His lips are usually thick. Often the lower lip hangs down. This is called 'sloppy.' And the Jew is also recognized by his eyes. His eyelids

"'I Got You at Last'" is from the Office of the U.S. Chief of Counsel for the Prosecution of Axis Criminality, *Nazi Conspiracy and Aggression* (Washington, D.C.: Government Printing Office, 1947), vol. 4, pp. 358–359 (PS-1778).

are usually thicker and more fleshy than ours. The look of the Jew is lurking and sharp."

Then the teacher goes to the desk and turns over the blackboard, on its back is a verse. The children recite it in chorus:

From a Jew's countenance—the evil devil
talks to us,
The devil, who in every land—is known as
evil plague.
If we shall be free of the Jew—and again will
be happy and glad,
Then the youth must struggle with us—to
subdue the Jew devil.

Inge sits in the reception room of the Jew doctor. She has to wait a long time. She looks through the journals which are on the table. But she is almost too nervous to read even a few sentences. Again and again she remembers the talk with her mother. And again and again her mind reflects on the warnings of her leader of the BDM [League of German Girls]: "A German must not consult a Jew doctor! And particularly not a German girl! Many a girl that went to a Jew doctor to be cured, found disease and disgrace!"

When Inge had entered the waiting room, she experienced an extraordinary incident. From the doctor's consulting room she could hear the sound of crying. She heard the voice of a young girl: "Doctor, doctor leave me alone!"

Then she heard the scornful laughing of a man. And then all of a sudden it became absolutely silent. Inge had listened breathlessly.

"What may be the meaning of all this?" she asked herself and her heart was pounding. And again she thought of the warning of her leader in the BDM.

Inge was already waiting for an hour. Again she takes the journals in an endeavor to read. Then the door opens. Inge looks up. The Jew appears. She screams. In terror she drops the paper. Frightened she jumps up. Her eyes stare into the face of the Jewish doctor. And this face is the face of the devil. In the middle of this devil's face is a huge crooked nose. Behind the spectacles two criminal eyes. And the thick lips are grinning. A grinning that expresses: "Now I got you at last, you little German girl!"

And then the Jew approaches her. His fleshy fingers stretch out after her. But now Inge has her wits. Before the Jew can grab hold of her, she hits the fat face of the Jew doctor with her hand. Then one jump to the door. Breathlessly she escapes the Jew house.

CONSIDER THIS:

- How does this account distort the image of Jews? Why was this effective propaganda? Did people want to believe this? Did these stories merely "confirm" their suspicions?

The Radicalization of Anti-Semitism (1938–1941)

On November 9–10, 1938, the Nazis, in retaliation for the assassination of a German diplomat, set fire to Jewish synagogues and systematically destroyed 7,500 Jewish stores. The incident became known as *Kristallnacht* (Crystal Night) because of the broken glass that covered the street. A few days later, Reich Marshal Hermann Goering called a meeting of some of the Nazi hierarchy (Reinhard Heydrich and Joseph Goebbels) to place ultimate responsibility for the destruction on the Jews. It was decided that the Jews would have to pay for the damage they "provoked." In the first selection, note the mention of ideas (separate schools, badges, and ghettos) that were soon implemented. Hitler gave little doubt as to his intentions regarding the Jews in a speech given before the Reichstag in 1939. Joseph Goebbels, the minister of propaganda, capitalized on this official anti-Semitic stance of the German government in his tract, which blamed the war on the Jews.

"Jewish Ghettos Shall Have to Be Created" (November 12, 1938)

Goering: I should not want to leave any doubt, gentlemen, as to the aim of today's meeting. We have not come together merely to talk again, but to make decisions, and I implore the competent agencies to take all measures for the elimination of the Jew from German economy and to submit them to me, as far as it is necessary. . . .

Furthermore, I advocate that the Jews be eliminated from all positions in public life in which they may prove to be provocative. . . . Jews should not be allowed to sit around in German parks. I am thinking of the whispering campaign on the part of Jewish women in the public gardens at Fehrbelliner Platz. They go and sit with German mothers and their children and begin to gossip and incite. I see in this a particularly grave danger. I think it is imperative to give the Jews certain public parks, not the best ones—and tell them: "You may sit on these benches," these benches shall be marked, "For Jews only." Besides that they have no business in German parks. Furthermore, Jewish children are still allowed in German schools. That's impossible. It is out of the question that any boy should sit beside a Jewish boy in a German gymnasium and receive lessons in German history. Jews ought to be eliminated completely from German schools; they may take care of their own education in their own communities. . . .

Heydrich: As another means of getting the Jews out, measures for Emigration are to be taken in the rest of the Reich for the next 8 to 10 years.

The highest number of Jews we can possibly get out during one year is 8,000 to 10,000. Therefore, a great number of Jews will remain. Because of Aryanizing and other restrictions, Jewry will become unemployed. The remaining Jews gradually become proletarians. Therefore, I shall have to take steps; to isolate the Jew so he won't enter into the German normal routine of life. On the other hand, I shall have to restrict the Jew to a small circle of consumers, but I shall have to permit certain activities within professions; lawyers, doctors, barbers, etc. This question shall also have to be examined.

As for the isolation, I'd like to make a few proposals regarding police measures which are important also because of their psychological effect on public opinion. For example, whoever is Jewish according to the Nuremberg laws shall have to wear a certain insignia. That is a possibility which shall facilitate many other things. I don't see any danger of excuses, and it shall make our relationship with the foreign Jew easier.

Goering: A uniform?

Heydrich: An insignia. This way we could also put an end to it that the foreign Jews who don't look different from ours, are being molested.

Goering: But, my dear Heydrich, you won't be able to avoid the creation of ghettos on a very large scale, in all the cities. They shall have to be created.

"'Jewish Ghettos Shall Have to Be Created'" is from Office of the U.S. Chief of Counsel for the Prosecution of Axis Criminality, *Nazi Conspiracy and Aggression* (Washington, D.C.: Government Printing Office, 1947), vol. 4, pp. 426, 432–434 (PS-1816).

"The Annihilation of the Jewish Race in Europe!" (January 30, 1939)

ADOLF HITLER

One thing I should like to say on this day which may be memorable for others as well as for us Germans. In the course of my life I have very often been a prophet, and have usually been ridiculed for it. During the time of my struggle for power it was in the first instance only the Jewish race that received my prophecies with laughter when I said that I would one day take over the leadership of the State, and with it that of the whole nation, and that I would then among other things settle the Jewish problem. Their laughter was uproarious, but I think that for some time now they have been laughing on the other side of their face. Today I will once more be a prophet: if the international Jewish financiers in and outside Europe should succeed in plunging the nations once more into a world war, then the result will not be the Bolshevizing of the earth, and thus the victory of Jewry, but the annihilation of the Jewish race in Europe!

"The Jews Are to Blame!" (1941)

JOSEPH GOEBBELS

World Jewry's historic guilt for the outbreak and expansion of this war is so evident and proven that little more need be said. The Jews wanted their war and now they have it. But the Führer's prophecy that he explained in his Reichstag speech of January 30, 1939 is also coming true: if the Jews who control international finance succeed in dragging the nations of the world into another war, the outcome would not be the Bolshevization of the world and therefore the victory of the Jews, but rather the complete annihilation of the Jewish race in Europe.

We are now witnessing the real test of this prophecy. The Jews are experiencing a difficult, but well-deserved fate. Save your pity—for they aren't even worth your regret. By starting this war, the Jews have badly estimated the forces at their disposal and are suffering the same gradual destruction that they had planned for us. They would certainly not hesitate to destroy us if they had the power. It's in accordance with their own law—"An eye for an eye, a tooth for a tooth"—that they now face utter destruction. . . . So, although I've said it before, let me repeat once again:

1. The Jews are our destruction. They provoked and started this war. Through it, they plan to destroy the German state and nation. They must be denied.
2. There is no difference between Jews. Every Jew is a sworn enemy of the German people. If he doesn't seem hostile, it is because he is a sneak and a coward, not because his heart is free of hatred.

"'The Annihilation of the Jewish Race in Europe'" is from Norman H. Baynes, trans. and ed., *The Speeches of Adolf Hitler, April 1922–1939*, vol. 1 (London: Oxford University Press for the Royal Institute of International Affairs, 1942), pp. 740–741. Reprinted by permission of the Royal Institute of International Affairs.

"'The Jews Are to Blame'" is from Joseph Goebbels, "Die Juden Sind Schuld," *Das Reich* (November 16, 1941) contained in Hans Dieter Müller, *Facsimilie Querschnitt durch das Reich* (Munich, 1964), pp. 100–101.

3. Every German soldier who dies in this war is the responsibility of the Jews. They must pay for their guilt.
4. Anyone wearing a Jewish star is a marked enemy of the nation. Anyone who associates with the Jew socially is one of them and should be treated with contempt as a deserter to the Fatherland.
5. The Jews enjoy the protection of the enemy nations. No further proof is needed of their destructive role among our people.
8. If a Jew commits a sentimental act, he's just depending on your forgetfulness. Show him right away that you see right through him and punish him with contempt.
9. After his defeat, an honorable enemy deserves generosity. But the Jew is no honorable enemy—he only pretends to be one.
10. The Jews are to blame for this war. However we treat them can never do them any wrong—they have more than deserved it. . . .

The Final Solution (1942–1945)

By 1940, the Nazis had embarked on a policy that was designed to cleanse the German homeland of Jews by confining them to ghettos in cities, especially in Poland. There the Nazis could control them and, upon demand, export them to concentration camps where they would be put to work or die. But in July 1941, preparations were made for a secretive "Final Solution" to the Jewish problem. It was discussed in more detail at the Wansee Conference in January 1942, as the following excerpts indicate.

"A Complete Solution to the Jewish Question" (July 31, 1941)

HERMANN GOERING

To: The Chief of the Security Police and the Security Service; SS-Gruppenfuehrer Heydrich

Complementing the task that was assigned to you on 24 January 1939, which dealt with the carrying out of emigration and evacuation, a solution of the Jewish problem, as advantageous as possible, I hereby charge you with making all necessary preparations in regard to organizational and financial matters for bringing out a complete solution to the Jewish question in the German sphere of influence in Europe.

Wherever other governmental agencies are involved, these are to cooperate with you. I charge you furthermore to send me, before long, an overall plan concerning the organizational, factual and material measures necessary for the accomplishment of the desired solution to the Jewish question.

The Broader Perspective:

- This is a very cryptic decree. What was the "Jewish question"? What was the "desired solution to the Jewish question"?

"'A Complete Solution to the Jewish Question'" is from the Office of the U.S. Chief Counsel for Prosecution of Axis Criminality, *Nazi Conspiracy and Aggression* (Washington, D.C.: Government Printing Office, 1947), vol. 3, pp. 525–526 (PS-710).

The Wansee Conference (January 20, 1942)

II. At the beginning of the meeting the Chief of the Security Police and the SD, SS Lieutenant General Heydrich, reported his appointment by the Reich Marshal to service as Commissioner for the Preparation of the Final Solution of the European Jewish Problem, and pointed out that the officials had been invited to this conference in order to clear up the fundamental problems. The Reich Marshal's request to have a draft submitted to him on the organizational, factual, and material requirements with respect to the Final Solution of the European Jewish Problem, necessitated this previous general consultation by all the central offices directly concerned, in order that there should be coordination in the policy.

The primary responsibility for the administrative handling of the Final Solution of the Jewish Problem will rest centrally with the Reich Leader SS and the Chief of the German Police (Chief of the Security Police and the SD)—regardless of geographic boundaries.

The Chief of the Security Police and the SD thereafter gave a brief review of the battle conducted up to now against these enemies. The most important are—

(a) Forcing the Jews out of the various fields of the community life of the German people.
(b) Forcing the Jews out of the living space [*Lebensraum*] of the German people.

Meanwhile, in view of the dangers of emigration during the war and in view of the possibilities in the East, the Reich Leader SS and Chief of the German Police had forbidden the emigrating of the Jews.

III. The emigration program has now been replaced by the evacuation of the Jews to the East as a further solution possibility, in accordance with previous authorization by the Fuehrer.

These actions are of course to be regarded only as a temporary substitute; nonetheless, here already, the coming Final Solution of the Jewish Question is of great importance. In the course of this Final Solution of the European Jewish Problem, approximately 11 million Jews are involved.

Under proper direction the Jews should now in the course of the Final Solution be brought to the East in a suitable way for use as labor. In big labor gangs, with separation of the sexes, the Jews capable of work are brought to these areas and employed in road building, in which task undoubtedly a great part will fall out through natural diminution.

The remnant that finally is able to survive all this—since this is undoubtedly the part with the strongest resistance—must be treated accordingly since these people, representing a natural selection, are to be regarded as the germ cell of a new Jewish development. (See the experience of history.)

In the program of the practical execution of the Final Solution, Europe is combed through from the West to the East.

The evacuated Jews are brought first group by group into the so-called transit ghettos, in order to be transported from these farther to the East.

CONSIDER THIS:

- What solutions to the Jewish problem were presented at the Wansee Conference? On the basis of this evidence and on the directive of Hermann Goering, how would you define the "Final Solution"? What did it entail? Why was there no specific talk of extermination in these documents?

"The Wansee Conference" is from the Nuremberg Military Tribunals, *Trials of War Criminals* (Washington, D.C.: Government Printing Office, 1947–1949), vol. 13, pp. 211–213.

The Death Camps: "Work Makes You Free"

The "Final Solution" ordered the implementation of a policy of genocide. Hitler wanted to rid the world of a people whom he found responsible for most of humanity's ills. The following selections present the Nazi system of extermination. Much of the testimony in this section comes from the Nuremberg trial proceedings in 1946. Hermann Gräbe ("The Pit") was a German construction engineer working in Ukraine in 1942. Kurt Gerstein ("Gas") was the S.S. head of Disinfection Services in early 1942. The gassing of Jews did not take place at concentration or death camps alone, as noted by the selection "Mobile Killing." This is a top-secret dispatch concerning the *Einsatzgruppen* that often followed advancing troops. Nuremberg testimony regarding Nazi medical experiments and excerpts from the autobiography and testimony of Rudolf Hoess are also included. Hoess was commandant of the notorious Auschwitz death camp and was himself executed there in 1947 after being judged guilty of crimes against humanity.

Sites of Nazi Concentration Camps

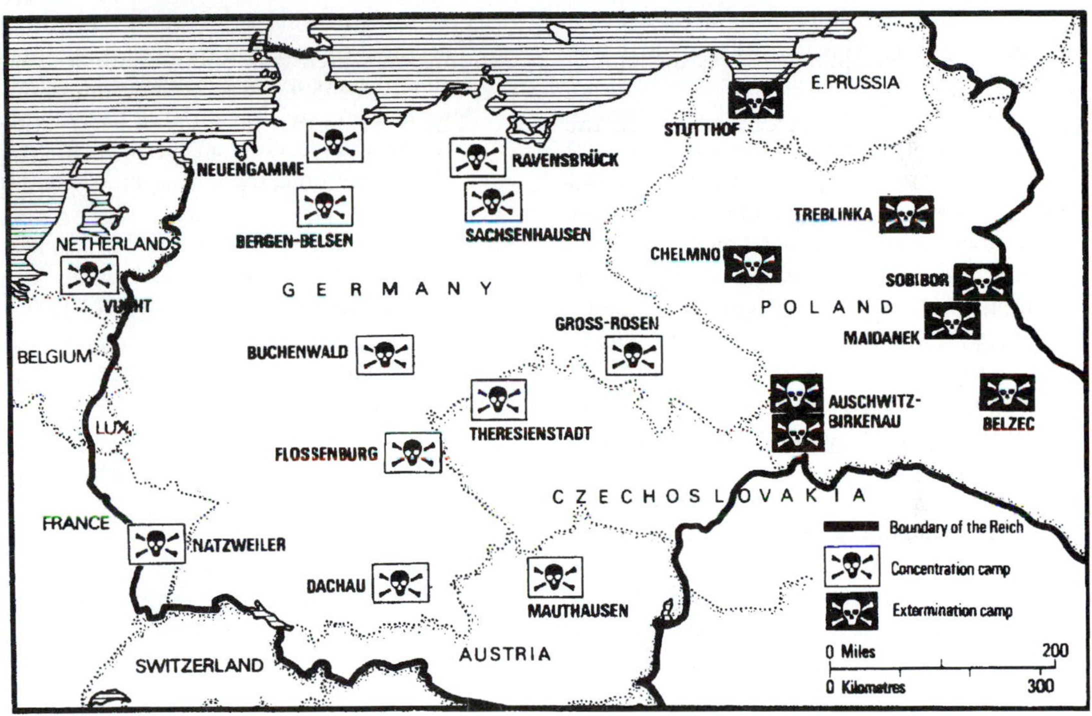

FIGURE 13.4 "Sites of Nazi Concentration Camps" is from Louis L. Snyder, *Encyclopedia of the Third Reich* (New York: McGraw-Hill Book Company, 1976), p. 57. Copyright © 1976 by McGraw-Hill, Inc. Appears by permission of the publisher, Marlowe & Company.

Genocide

RUDOLF HOESS

I, Rudolf Franz Ferdinand Hoess, being first duly sworn, depose and say as follows:

1. I am forty-six years old, and have been a member of the NSDAP since 1922; a member of the SS since 1934; a member of the Waffen-SS since 1939. I was a member from 1 December 1934 of the SS Guard Unit, the so-called Deaths-head Formation [*Totenkopf Verband*].
2. I have been constantly associated with the administration of concentration camps since 1934, serving at Dachau until 1938; then as Adjutant in Sachenhausen from 1938 to May 1, 1940, when I was appointed Commandant of Auschwitz. I commanded Auschwitz until 1 December 1943, and estimate that at least 2,500,000 victims were executed and exterminated there by gassing and burning, and at least another half million succumbed to starvation and disease making a total dead of about 3,000,000. This figure represents about 70% or 80% of all persons sent to Auschwitz as prisoners, the remainder having been selected and used for slave labor in the concentration camp industries. Included among the executed and burnt were approximately 20,000 Russian prisoners of war (previously screened out of Prisoner of War cages by the Gestapo) who were delivered at Auschwitz in Wehrmacht transports operated by regular Wehrmacht officers, 100,000 German Jews, and great numbers of citizens, mostly Jewish from Holland, France, Belgium, Poland, Hungary, Czechoslovakia, Greece, or other countries. We executed about 400,000 Hungarian Jews alone at Auschwitz in the summer of 1944. . . .
4. Mass executions by gassing commenced during the summer of 1941 and continued until fall 1944. I personally supervised executions at Auschwitz until the first of December 1943 and know by reason of my continued duties . . . that these mass executions continued as stated above. All mass executions by gassing took place under the direct orders, supervisions, and responsibility of RSHA [Reich Security Main Office]. I received all orders for carrying out these mass executions directly from RSHA. . . .
6. The "final solution" of the Jewish question meant the complete extermination of all Jews in Europe. I was ordered to establish extermination facilities at Auschwitz in June 1941. At that time, there were already in the general government three other extermination camps; Belzek, Treblinka, and Wolzek. These camps were under the Einsatzkommando of the Security Police and SD. I visited Treblinka to find out how they carried out their extermination. The Camp Commandant at Treblinka told me that he had liquidated 80,000 in the course of one-half year. He was principally concerned with liquidating all the Jews from the Warsaw ghetto. He used monoxide gas and I did not think that his methods were very efficient. So when I set up the extermination building at Auschwitz, I used Cyclon B, which was a crystallized prussic acid which we dropped into the death chamber from a small opening. It took from 3 to 15 minutes to kill the people in the death chamber depending upon climatic conditions. We

"Genocide" is from the Office of the U.S. Chief of Counsel for the Prosecution of Axis Criminality, *Nazi Conspiracy and Aggression* (Washington, D.C.: Government Printing Office, 1947), vol. 6, pp. 787–790 (PS-3868).

FIGURE 13.5 Entrance to Dachau, the concentration camp outside of Munich (*Perry M. Rogers*)

knew when the people were dead because their screaming stopped. We usually waited about one-half hour before we opened the doors and removed the bodies. After the bodies were removed our special commandos took off the rings and extracted the gold from the teeth of the corpses.

7. Another improvement we made over Treblinka was that we built our gas chambers to accommodate 2,000 people at one time, whereas at Treblinka their 10 gas chambers only accommodated 200 people each. The way we selected our victims was as follows: we had two SS doctors on duty at Auschwitz to examine the incoming transports of prisoners. The prisoners would be marched by one of the doctors who would make spot decisions as they walked by. Those who were fit for work were sent into the Camp. Others were sent immediately to the extermination plants. Children of tender years were invariably exterminated since by reason of their youth they were unable to work. Still another improvement we made over Treblinka was that at Treblinka the victims almost always knew that they were to be exterminated and at Auschwitz we endeavored to fool the victims into thinking that they were to go through a delousing process. Of course, frequently they realized our true intentions and we sometimes had riots and difficulties due to that fact. Very frequently women would hide their children under their clothes but of course when we found them we would send the children in to be exterminated. We were required to carry out these exterminations in secrecy but of course the foul and nauseating stench from the continuous burning of bodies permeated the entire area and all of the people living in the surrounding communities knew that exterminations were going on at Auschwitz.

8. We received from time to time special prisoners from the local Gestapo office. The SS doctors killed such prisoners by injections of benzine. Doctors had orders to write ordi-

FIGURE 13.6 One of the ovens in the crematoria at Dachau (*Perry M. Rogers*)

nary death certificates and could put down any reason at all for the cause of death.

9. From time to time we conducted medical experiments on women inmates, including sterilization and experiments relating to cancer. Most of the people who died under these experiments had been already condemned to death by the Gestapo. . . .

I understand English as it is written above. The above statements are true; this declaration is made by me voluntarily and without compulsion; after reading over the statements, I have signed and executed the same at Nuremberg, Germany, on the fifth day of April 1946.

Rudolf Franz Ferdinand Hoess
Subscribed and sworn to before me this
5th day of April 1946, at Nuremberg,
Germany Smith W. Brookhart Jr., Lt.
Colonel, IGD

The Pit

HERMANN GRÄBE

On October 5, 1942, when I visited the building office at Dubno, my foreman told me that in the vicinity of the site, Jews from Dubno had been shot in three large pits, each about 30 metres long and 3 metres deep. About 1,500 persons had been killed daily. All the 5,000 Jews who had still been living in Dubno before the pogrom were to be liquidated. As the shooting had taken place in his presence, he was still much upset.

Thereupon, I drove to the site accompanied by my foreman and saw near it great mounds of earth, about 30 metres long and 2 metres high. Several trucks stood in front of the mounds. Armed Ukrainian militia drove the people off the trucks under the supervision of an S.S. man. The militiamen acted as guards on the trucks and drove them to and from the pit. All these people had the regulation yellow patches on the front and back of their clothes, and thus could be recognized as Jews.

My foreman and I went directly to the pits. Nobody bothered us. Now I heard rifle shots in quick succession from behind one of the earth mounds. The people who had got off the trucks—men, women and children of all ages—had to undress upon the orders of an S.S. man, who carried a riding or dog whip. They had to put down their clothes in fixed places, sorted according to shoes, top clothing and underclothing. I saw a heap of shoes of about 800 to 1,000 pairs, great piles of underlinen and clothing.

Without screaming or weeping, these people undressed, stood around in family groups, kissed each other, said farewells, and waited for a sign from another S.S. man, who stood near the pit, also with a whip in his hand. During the fifteen minutes that I stood near I heard no complaint or plea for mercy. I watched a family of about eight persons, a man and a woman both about fifty with their children of about one, eight and ten, and two grown-up daughters of about twenty to twenty-nine. An old woman with snow-white hair was holding the one-year old child in her arms and singing to it and tickling it. The child was cooing with delight. The couple were looking on with tears in their eyes. The father was holding the hand of a boy about ten years old and speaking to him softly; the boy was fighting his tears. The father pointed to the sky, stroked his head, and seemed to explain something to him.

At that moment the S.S. man at the pit shouted something to his comrade. The

FIGURE 13.7 "I remember and I am afraid."—Elie Wiesel. (*Yad Vashem, Jerusalem*)

latter counted off about twenty persons and instructed them to go behind the earth mound. Among them was the family which I have mentioned. I well remember a girl, slim and with black hair, who, as she passed close to me pointed to herself and said "23." I walked around the mound and found myself confronted by a tremendous grave. People were closely wedged together and lying on top of each other so that only their heads were visible. Nearly all had blood running over their shoulders from their heads. Some of the people shot were still moving. Some were lifting their arms and turning their heads to show that they were still alive. The pit was already two-thirds full. I estimated that it already contained about 1,000 people.

Gas

KURT GERSTEIN

In January, 1942, I was named chief of the Waffen SS technical disinfection services, including a section for extremely toxic gases. . . . SS Gruppenfuhrer Globocnik was waiting for us at Lublin. He told us, "This is one of the most secret matters there are, even the most secret.

Anybody who talks about it will be shot immediately." He explained to us that there were three installations:

1. Belzec, on the Lublin-Lwow road. A maximum of 15,000 people per day.
2. Sobibor (I don't know exactly where it is), 20,000 people a day.
3. Treblinka, 120 kilometers NNE of Warsaw.
4. Maidanek, near Lublin (under construction).

Globocnik said: "You will have to disinfect large piles of clothing coming from Jews, Poles, Czechs, etc. Your other duty will be to improve the workings of our gas chambers, which operate on the exhaust from a Diesel engine. We need a more toxic and faster working gas, something like prussic acid. . . .

The following morning, a little before seven there was an announcement: "The first train will arrive in ten minutes!" A few minutes later a train arrived from Lemberg: 45 cars with more than 6,000 people. Two hundred Ukrainians assigned to this work flung open the doors and drove the Jews out of the cars with leather whips. A loud speaker gave instructions: "Strip, even artificial limbs and glasses. Hand all money and valuables in at the 'valuables window.' Women and young girls are to have their hair cut in the 'barber's hut.' "

Then the march began. Barbed wire on both sides, in the rear two dozen Ukrainians with rifles. They drew near. Wirth and I found ourselves in front of the death chambers. Stark naked men, women, children, and cripples passed by. A tall S.S. man in the corner called to the unfortunates in a loud minister's voice: "Nothing is going to hurt you! Just breathe deep and it will strengthen your lungs. It's a way to prevent contagious diseases. It's a good disinfectant!" They asked him what was going to happen and he answered: "The men will have to work, build houses and streets. The women won't have to do that, they will be busy with the housework and the kitchen." This was the last hope for some of these poor people, enough to make them march toward the death chambers without resistance. The majority knew everything; the smell betrayed it! They climbed a little wooden stairs and entered the death chambers, most of them silently, pushed by those behind them. A Jewess of about forty with eyes like fire cursed the murderers; she disappeared into the gas chambers after being struck several times by Captain Wirth's whip . . . . All were dead after thirty-two minutes! Jewish workers on the other side opened the wooden doors. They had been promised their lives in return for doing this horrible work, plus a small percentage of the money and valuables collected. The men still standing, like columns of stone, with no room to fall or lean. Even in death you could tell the families, all holding hands. It was difficult to separate them while emptying the rooms for the next batch. The bodies were tossed out, blue, wet with sweat and urine, the legs smeared with excrement and menstrual blood. Two dozen workers were busy checking mouths which they opened with iron hooks. "Gold to the left, no gold to the right." Others checked anus and genitals, looking for money, diamonds, gold, etc. Dentists knocked out gold teeth, bridges and crowns, with hammers. . . .

Then the bodies were thrown into big ditches near the gas chambers, about 100 by 20 by 12 meters. After a few days the bodies swelled and the whole mass rose up 2–3 yards because of the gas in the bodies. When the swelling went down several days later, the bodies matted down again. They told me later they poured Diesel oil over the bodies and burned them on railroad ties to make them disappear.

Mobile Killing

Kiev, 16 May 1942

Field Post Office
No 32704
B Nr 40/42

TOP SECRET

To: SS-Obersturmbannfuehrer Rauff
Berlin, Prinz-Albrecht-Str. 8

pers.
R/29/5 Pradel n.R
b/R

Sinkkel [?] b.R., p 16/6

The overhauling of vans by groups D and C is finished. . . .

I ordered the vans of group D to be camouflaged as house trailers by putting one set of window shutters on each side of the small van and two on each side of the larger vans, such as one often sees on farm-houses in the country. The vans became so well-known, that not only the authorities, but also the civilian population called the van "death van," as soon as one of these vehicles appeared. It is my opinion, the van cannot be kept secret for any length of time, not even camouflaged. . . .

I ordered that during application of gas all the men were to be kept as far away from the vans as possible, so they should not suffer damage to their health by the gas which eventually would escape. I should like to take this opportunity to bring the following to your attention: several commands have had the unloading after the application of gas done by their own men. I brought to the attention of the commanders of the Sonder-Kommando [special unit] concerning the immense psychological injuries and damages to their health which that work can have for those men, even if not immediately, at least later on. The men complained to me about headaches which appeared after each unloading. Nevertheless prisoners called for that work, could use an opportune moment to flee. To protect the men from these damages, I request orders be issued accordingly.

The application of gas usually is not undertaken correctly. In order to come to an end as fast as possible, the driver presses the accelerator to the fullest extent. By doing that the persons to be executed suffer death from suffocation and not death by dozing off as was planned. My directions now have proved that by correct adjustment of the levers death comes faster and the prisoners fall asleep peacefully. Distorted faces and excretions, such as could be seen before, are no longer noticed.

Today I shall continue my journey to group B, where I can be reached with further news.

Signed: D. Becker
SS Untersturmfuehrer

Nazi Medical Experiments

DR. FRANZ BLAHA

From the middle of 1941 to the end of 1942, some 500 operations were performed on healthy prisoners [at Dachau]. These were for the instruction of SS medical students and doctors and included operations on the stomach, gall bladder, and throat. They were

"Mobile Killing" is from the Office of the U.S. Chief Counsel for Prosecution of Axis Criminality, *Nazi Conspiracy and Aggression* (Washington, D.C.: Government Printing Office, 1946), vol. 3, pp. 418–419 (PS-501).

"Nazi Medical Experiments" is from the Office of the U.S. Chief of Counsel for the Prosecution of Axis Criminality, *Nazi Conspiracy and Aggression* (Washington, D.C.: Government Printing Office, 1947), vol. 5, pp. 949–955 (PS-3249).

performed by students and doctors with only two years training, although they were very dangerous and difficult. . . . Many prisoners died on the operating table and many others from later complications. I performed the autopsies. . . .

During my time at Dachau, I was familiar with many kinds of experiments carried on there. The victims never volunteered but were forced to submit to these operations. Dr. Klaus Schilling conducted malaria experiments on about 1200 people between 1941 and 1945. Himmler personally ordered him to conduct these experiments. The victims were either bitten by mosquitoes or given injections of malaria sporozoites; treatments included quinine, pyrifer, neosalvarsam, antipyrin, pyramidon, and a drug called 2516 Behring. I performed autopsies on those who died from these experiments. About 30–40 died from the malaria itself, and 300–400 from later diseases that were fatal because of the physical condition resulting from the malaria attack. There were also deaths from overdoses of neosalvarsam and pyramidon. . . .

In 1942 and 1943, experiments were conducted by Dr. Sigmund Rascher to determine the effects of changes in air pressure. As many as 25 persons at a time were put into a specially constructed van where pressure could be increased or decreased at will, in order to see the effects of high altitude and rapid descent by parachute. . . . Most of the victims in these experiments died from internal hemorrhaging of the lungs or brain. Survivors coughed blood when taken out of the van. It was my job to remove the bodies as soon as they were dead and send the internal organs to Munich for study. About 400–500 prisoners were experimented on. . . .

Dr. Rascher also conducted cold-water experiments to find ways of reviving airmen who fell in the ocean. The subject was placed in ice water and kept there until unconscious. Blood was taken from his neck and tested with each degree change in his body temperature. . . . The lowest body temperature obtained was 19% C., but most of the men died at 25% or 26%. When they were removed from the water, attempts were made to revive them by artificial sunlight, hot water, electro therapy, or animal warmth. For the latter, prostitutes were used, the body of the unconscious man being placed between two of the women. Himmler was present at one such experiment. . . . About 300 prisoners were used. The majority died. Of those who survived, many became mentally deranged. . . .

Liver-puncture experiments were performed on healthy people and on others who had diseases of the stomach and gall bladder. A needle was jabbed into the person's liver and a small piece extracted. No anaesthetic was used. The experiment was very painful and often had serious results when the stomach or a large blood vessel was punctured. Many persons died from these tests, involving Polish, Russian, Czech and German prisoners. . . .

It was a common practice to remove the skin from dead prisoners, which I was ordered to do on many occasions. Drs. Rascher and Wolter in particular asked for the skin from backs and chests. It was chemically treated, placed in the sun to dry, and then cut into various sizes for use as saddles, riding breeches, gloves, slippers, and ladies' handbags. Tattooed skin was especially valued by SS men. Russians, Poles, and other inmates were used in this way, but it was forbidden to cut the skin of a German prisoner. . . . Sometimes we did not have enough bodies with good skin and Rascher would say, "All right, you will get the bodies." The next day we would receive 20 or 30 bodies of young people, [who] had been shot in the neck or struck on the head so the skin would not be injured. . . .

Commandant of Auschwitz

RUDOLF HOESS

I must emphasise here that I have never personally hated the Jews. It is true that I looked upon them as the enemies of our people. But just because of this I saw no difference between them and the other prisoners, and I treated them all in the same way. I never drew any distinctions. In any event the emotion of hatred is foreign to my nature. But I know what hate is, and what it looks like. I have seen it and I have suffered it myself.

When the Reichsfuhrer SS modified his original Extermination Order of 1941, by which all Jews without exception were to be destroyed, and ordered instead that those capable of work were to be separated from the rest and employed in the armaments industry, Auschwitz became a Jewish camp. It was a collecting place for Jews, exceeding in scale anything previously known.

Whereas the Jews who had been imprisoned in former years were able to count on being released one day and were thus far less affected psychologically by the hardships of captivity, the Jews in Auschwitz no longer had any such hope. They knew, without exception, that they were condemned to death, that they would live only so long as they could work.

Nor did the majority have any hope of a change in their sad lot. They were fatalists. Patiently and apathetically, they submitted to all the misery and distress and terror. The hopelessness with which they accepted their impending fate made them psychologically quite indifferent to their surroundings. This mental collapse accelerated its physical equivalent. They no longer had the will to live, everything had become a matter of indifference to them, and they would succumb to the slightest physical shock. Sooner or later, death was inevitable. I firmly maintain from what I have seen that the high mortality among the Jews was due not only to the hard work, to which most of them were unaccustomed, and to the insufficient food, the overcrowded quarters and all the severities and abuses of camp life, but principally and decisively to their psychological state. . . .

What I have just written applies to the bulk, the mass of the Jewish prisoners. The more intelligent ones, psychologically stronger and with a keener desire for life, that is to say in most cases those from the western countries, reacted differently.

These people, especially if they were doctors, had no illusions concerning their fate. But they continued to hope, reckoning on a change of fortune that somehow or other would save their lives. They also reckoned on the collapse of Germany, for it was not difficult for them to listen to enemy propaganda.

For them the most important thing was to obtain a position which would lift them out of the mass and give them special privileges, a job that would protect them to a certain extent from accidental and mortal hazards, and improve the physical conditions in which they lived.

They employed all their ability and all their will to obtain what can truly be described as a "living" of this sort. The safer the position the more eagerly and fiercely it was fought for. No quarter was shown, for this was a struggle in which everything was at stake. They flinched from nothing, no matter how desperate, in their efforts to make such safe jobs fall vacant and then to acquire them for themselves. Victory usually went to the most unscrupulous man or woman. Time and again I heard of these struggles to oust a rival and win his job. . . .

So it can be seen that even in a small prison the governor is unable to prevent such behavior; how much more difficult was it in a concentration camp the size of Auschwitz! I was certainly severe and strict. Often perhaps, when I look at it now, too severe and too strict.

In my disgust at the errors and abuses that I discovered, I may have spoken many hard words that I should have kept to myself. But I was never cruel, and I have never maltreated anyone, even in a fit of temper. A great deal happened in Auschwitz which was done ostensibly in my name, under my authority and on my orders, which I neither knew about nor sanctioned. But all these things happened in Auschwitz and so I am responsible. For the camp regulations say: the camp commandant is fully responsible for everything that happens in his sphere.

Consider This:

- After reading through the accounts concerning the death camps, what are your feelings? What statements by Rudolf Hoess, the commandant of Auschwitz, in his autobiography stand out in your mind? Why? How does he free himself from guilt while still accepting it?

THEME: REVOLUTION AND HISTORICAL TRANSITION

Against the Grain

Jewish Resistance

As Rudolph Hoess noted in his autobiography, many Jews went to their deaths as lambs to slaughter without struggling against their apparent fate. Still, it is misleading to characterize the acts of the condemned under duress as devoid of courage. In fact, there was constant Jewish resistance to the Nazis in the camps and ghettos. A Jewish Fighting Organization was active in the Warsaw ghetto, and resistance continued from January to mid-May 1943, when the Jews were finally defeated. Joseph Goebbels was rather surprised at their tenacity, as the excerpt from his diary indicates. An account by the Nazi S.S. chief in Warsaw of the destruction of the ghetto follows. The last selection is a manifesto of a Jewish resistance organization in the Vilna ghetto dated a month after the revolt at the Treblinka death camp in August 1943.

Keep in Mind . . .

- Note the methodical process of human destruction in the Warsaw ghetto. How did the Jews resist their oppressors?

Nazi Problems in the Warsaw Ghetto (May 1, 1943)

JOSEPH GOEBBELS

Reports from the occupied areas contain no sensational news. The only noteworthy item is the exceedingly serious fights in Warsaw between the police and even a part of our Wehrmacht on the one hand and the rebellious Jews on the other. The Jews have actually succeeded in making a defensive position of the Ghetto. Heavy engagements are being

"Nazi Problems" is from *The Goebbels Diaries* by Louis P. Lochner, pp. 350–351.

fought there which led even to the Jewish Supreme Command's issuing daily communiques. Of course this fun won't last very long. But it shows what is to be expected of the Jews when they are in possession of arms. Unfortunately, some of their weapons are good German ones, especially machine guns. Heaven only knows how they got them.

The Destruction of the Warsaw Ghetto (May 1943)

JÜRGEN STROOP

On 23 April 1943 the Reichsführer SS issued through the higher SS and Police Führer East at Cracow his order to complete the combing out of the Warsaw Ghetto with the greatest severity and relentless tenacity. I therefore decided to destroy the entire Jewish residential area by setting every block on fire, including the blocks of residential buildings near the armament works. One concern after the other was systematically evacuated and later destroyed by fire. In almost every case, the Jews then emerged from their hiding places and dug-outs. Not infrequently, the Jews stayed in the burning buildings until, because of the heat and the fear of being burned alive, they preferred to jump down from the upper storeys after having thrown mattresses and other upholstered articles into the street from the burning buildings. With their bones broken, they still tried to crawl across the streets into blocks of buildings which had not yet been set on fire or were only partly in flames. Often Jews changed their hiding places during the night, by moving into the ruins of burnt-out buildings, taking refuge there until they were found by our patrols. Their stay in the sewers also ceased to be pleasant after the first week. From the street we could frequently hear loud voices coming through the sewer shafts. Then the men of the Waffen SS, the police or the Wehrmacht engineers courageously climbed down the shafts to bring out the Jews and not infrequently they then stumbled over Jews already dead, or were shot at. It was always necessary to use smoke candles to drive out the Jews. Thus, one day we opened 183 sewer entrance holes and at a fixed time lowered smoke candles into them, so that the bandits fled from what they believed to be gas to the center of the former Ghetto, where they could then be pulled out of the sewer holes. A great number of Jews, beyond counting, were exterminated by the blowing up of the sewers and dug-outs. . . .

> "I decided to destroy the entire Jewish residential area by setting every block on fire"
> —JÜRGEN STROOP

Only through the continuous and untiring work of all involved did we succeed in catching a total of 56,065 Jews, whose extermination can be proved. To this should be added the number of Jews who lost their lives in explosions or fires, whose numbers could not be ascertained.

During the large-scale operation the Aryan population was informed by posters that it was strictly forbidden to enter the former Jewish Ghetto and that anybody caught within the former Ghetto without a valid pass would be shot. At the same time these posters informed the Aryan population again that the death penalty would be imposed on

"The Destruction of the Warsaw Ghetto" is from Jeremy Noakes and Geoffrey Pridham, eds., *Documents on Nazism, 1919–1945*, pp. 491–492. Reprinted by permission of A. D. Peters & Co. Ltd.

anyone who intentionally gave refuge to a Jew, especially on anyone who lodged, supported or concealed a Jew outside the Jewish residential area. The large-scale action was terminated on 16 May 1943 with the blowing up of the Warsaw synagogue at 20.15 hours.

Manifesto of the Jewish Resistance in Vilna (September 1943)

Offer armed resistance! Jews, defend yourselves with arms!

The German and Lithuanian executioners are at the gates of the ghetto. They have come to murder us! Soon they will lead you forth in groups through the ghetto door.

Tens of thousands of us were despatched. But we shall not go! We will not offer our heads to the butcher like sheep.

Jews, defend yourselves with arms!

Do not believe the false promises of the assassins or believe the words of the traitors.

Anyone who passes through the ghetto gate will go to Ponar! [Death Camp]

And Ponar means death!

> "Jews, we have nothing to lose. . . . Active resistance alone can save our lives and our honor."

Jews, we have nothing to lose. Death will overtake us in any event. And who can still believe in survival when the murderer exterminates us with so much determination? The hand of the executioner will reach each man and woman. Flight and acts of cowardice will not save our lives. Active resistance alone can save our lives and our honor.

Brothers! It is better to die in battle in the ghetto than to be carried away to Ponar like sheep. And know this: within the walls of the ghetto there are organized Jewish forces who will resist with weapons.

Support the revolt!

Do not take refuge or hide in the bunkers, for then you will fall into the hands of the murderers like rats.

Jewish people, go out into the squares. Anyone who has no weapons should take an ax, and he who has no ax should take a crowbar or a bludgeon!

For our ancestors!

For our murdered children!

Avenge Ponar!

Attack the murderers!

In every street, in every courtyard, in every house within and without the ghetto, attack these dogs!

Jews, we have nothing to lose! We shall save our lives only if we exterminate our assassins.

Long live liberty! Long live armed resistance! Death to the assassins!

The Commander of the F.P.A.
Vilna, the Ghetto, September 1, 1943.

The Broader Perspective:

- Some have argued that the Jews were passive in their resistance to Nazi aggression. Do these sources bear this out? Is it legitimate to blame the Jews for being willing participants in their own extermination?

"Manifesto of the Jewish Resistance in Vilna" is from *An Anthology of Holocaust Literature*, eds. J. Glatstein, I. Knox, and S. Margoshes (Philadelphia: The Jewish Publication Society, 1969), pp. 332–333. Reprinted by permission of the publisher.

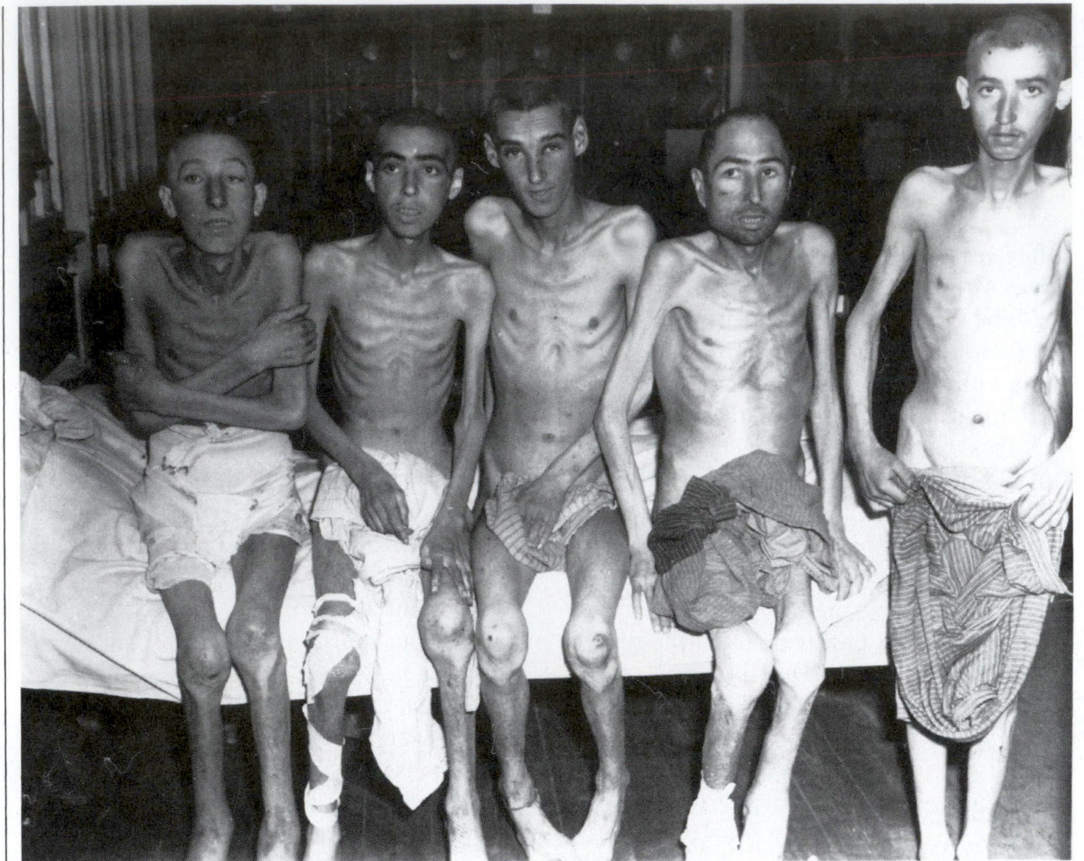

FIGURE 13.8 Emaciated prisoners at a recently liberated German concentration camp (*Library of Congress*)

Götterdämmerung: The Final Destruction (1944–1945)

War alone brings up to their highest tension all human energies and imposes the stamp of nobility upon the peoples who have the courage to make it.

—BENITO MUSSOLINI

When you lose a friend, you have an overpowering desire to go back home and yell in everybody's ear, 'This guy was killed fighting for you. Don't forget him—ever.' Keep him in your mind when you wake up in the morning and when you go to bed at night. Think of him as a guy who wanted to live every bit as much as you do.

—BILL MAULDIN

People came streaming out of burning Hiroshima looking like ghosts, silent from shock, eyes staring, terribly burned with their skin hanging in strips, arms outstretched as if pleading for help.

REVEREND KIYOSKI TANIMOTO

The D-Day Invasions (June 6, 1944)

By 1944, with Allied victories in North Africa, Italy, and Russia beginning to turn the tide of battle, the Allied High Command, led by General Dwight Eisenhower, had developed plans for the invasion of Europe. The Germans were aware that an invasion was imminent and had constructed formidable defenses along the French coast under the direction of Field Marshal Erwin Rommel. But the Germans could not defend the entire coast with equal troop strength and focused more of their attention on the area surrounding Calais, which marked the shortest invasion route across the English Channel. Because British intelligence had secretly broken German codes and could better estimate the strength of enemy defenses, the decision was made to invade along the Normandy beaches.

An amphibious assault is a delicate operation, and even the most meticulous plans are vulnerable to changes of wind and weather. The operation was a high-risk gamble that cost thousands of lives but resulted in the establishment of a "second front" against the Germans. The next drive was to Berlin itself.

The following personal accounts of "The Longest Day" capture the confusion and heroism displayed by soldiers in the greatest amphibious operation in history. The fiftieth anniversary commemorative speech by President Clinton on June 6, 1994, offers perspective on the cost and importance of this day.

The Paratrooper: "He Was Blown Away"

KEN RUSSELL

I was just a boy, seventeen—I should have been in high school rather than in a strange country. I should have been going to school. I think my class was graduating that night. Sainte-Mere-Eglise was the area that we had to take, and as we came in, there was a building on fire. The fire gave light for miles around, and we came in and when we saw the fire, we jumped. I knew we were in trouble, and it was so horrifying, because most of our stick were killed.

They didn't even hit the ground. They hit the telephone poles—Lieutenant Cadish, H. T. Bryant, and Laddie Tlapa landed on telephone poles down the street, and it was like they were crucified there. Coming down, one fellow had a Gammon grenade on his hip, and I looked to my right, and I saw the guy, and instantaneously, I looked around and there was just an empty parachute coming down. He was blown away.

I got hit in the hand—just a kind of a valley up through my hand. To be honest, I was trying to hide behind my reserve chute, because you could hear the shells hitting. We were all sitting ducks coming down. The

"The Paratrooper" is from Ronald J. Drez, *Voices of D-Day* (Baton Rouge: Louisiana State University Press, 1994), pp. 132–133.

heat drew the nylon chutes toward the fire, and the air to feed the fire was actually drawing us into it, and I saw one trooper land in the fire. I heard him scream one time before he was engulfed, and he didn't scream any more.

When I came down, I knew that we were going to hit in the town, but I didn't know exactly where. I finally hit the roof of the church first and a couple of my suspension lines went around the church steeple and I slid off the roof. I was hanging on the edge of the roof, and when Steele had come down, his chute covered the steeple.

While I was there, a buck sergeant who was in our unit who had jumped from our plane by the name of John Ray came down. I was on the right side of the church, and Steele was hung up on the steeple, and Sergeant Ray came down and missed the edge of the church, but he hit in front of it. A Nazi soldier, billeted on the next street behind the church, came around from behind the church. He was a red-haired German soldier, and he came to shoot Steele and myself, who were still hanging there. As he came around, he shot Ray in the stomach. Ray being a sergeant, had been armed with a .45 pistol, and while he was dying in agony, got his .45 out and when this German soldier started turning around to us, Ray shot him in the back of the head and killed him.

FIGURE 13.9 American troops land on Normandy beach during the D-day assault, June 6, 1944: "I waded through the waist-deep water, watching many of my buddies fall alongside of me. The water was being shot up all around, and many a bullet ricocheted off the water."—Harold Baumgarten (*Corbis/Bettmann*)

The Assault on Omaha Beach: "I'm Hit! I'm Hit!"

HAROLD BAUMGARTEN

At 7:00 A.M. I saw the beach with its huge seawall at the foot of a massive 150-foot bluff. We'd made it. And then an 88-millimeter shell landed right in the middle of the LCA [landing craft] on the side of us, and splinters of the boat, equipment, and bodies were thrown into the air. Lieutenant Donaldson cautioned us to get down. Bullets were passing through the thin wooden sides of our vessel. The ramp was lowered and the inner door was opened. In a British LCA, we could only get out one at a time, and a German machine gun trained on the opening took a heavy toll of lives. Many of my thirty buddies went down as they left the LCA.

I got a bullet through the top of my helmet first, and then as I waded through the deep water, a bullet aimed at my heart hit the receiver of my M-1 rifle as I carried it at port arms, embedding itself in my ammunition. I waded through the waist-deep water, watching many of my buddies fall alongside of me. The water was being shot up all around, and many a bullet ricocheted off the water. Clarius Riggs, who left the assault boat in front of me, went under, shot to death, and eight or ten feet to my right, just as we hit the beach, I heard a hollow thud and I saw Private Robert Ditmar hold his chest and yell, "I'm hit! I'm hit!" I hit the ground and watched him as he continued to go forward ten more yards and then trip over a tank obstacle. As he fell, his body made a complete turn and he lay sprawled on the damp sand with his head facing the German, his face looking skyward. He seemed to be suffering from shock, and was yelling, "Mother, Mom . . ." as he kept rolling around on the sand.

There were three or four others wounded and dying right near him. Sergeant Barnes got shot down right in front of me, and Lieutenant Donaldson, and another sergeant had a gaping wound in the upper right corner of his forehead. He was walking crazily in the water, without his helmet, and then he got down on his knees and started praying with his rosary beads, and at that moment the Germans cut him in half with their deadly cross fire. The fire came from a pillbox [machine gun emplacement] built into the mountain on the right flank of the beach. We had snipers firing at us from the vantage points in front of us and from dugouts and pillboxes. I saw the reflection from the helmet of one of the snipers, and took aim, and later on found out I got a bull's-eye. It was the only shot that rifle fired, because the rifle broke in half and I had to throw it away. The shot that had hit my rifle must have shattered the wood. . . .

Finally, I came to dry sand, and there was another hundred yards to go, and I started across the sand, crawling very fast. When I reached the stone wall without further injury, I looked back on the beach I had crossed and saw two of our battalion's twelve special tanks knocked out in the water, a dead man hanging out of the turret of one of them. The other one fired his 75-millimeter gun shells right into the pillbox on the right flank and could not knock them out.

At the wall, I met a fellow from Company B from my boat team named Dominick Surrow, a boy from Georgia about my age, a rugged fellow, who looked at my face and said, "Stay here, I'm going to run down the beach and get help." He got killed.

"The Assault on Omaha Beach" is from Ronald J. Drez, *Voices of D-Day* (Baton Rouge: Louisiana State University Press, 1994), pp. 215–217.

I watched him being washed around by the incoming water, and I saw the bodies of my buddies who had tried in vain to clear the beach. It looked like the beach was littered with the refuse of a wrecked ship that were the dead bodies of what once were the proud, tough, and the well-trained combat infantrymen of the 1st Battalion of the 116th Infantry.

I saw Sergeant Draper and Vargos and all of Company A dying in the water to my left. . . . There was no medical aid available at this time, and many had bled to death and many drowned. I ran down the wall to the left a hundred yards or so, giving a hand to many of the wounded who were trying to pull themselves against the wall. . . .

Lying in the sand in front of the Vierville draw was our boat's walkie-talkie radio man and my best buddy, PFC Robert Garbed of Newport News, Virginia. He was facedown with his back to the enemy, probably spun around by the force of a bullet. . . .

Sergeant Cecil Bredan dressed my face wound. I had received five individual wounds that day in Normandy.

THE BROADER PERSPECTIVE:

- How would you define heroism? Were the soldiers who landed on the Normandy beaches heroes? Or were they just doing their jobs, as were the Allied soldiers in Italy, North Africa, or the Philippines—as were German soldiers dying in Russia? Is victory the determinant of heroism? Because the victors write the history, what constitutes a heroic act?

THEME: THE INSTITUTION AND THE INDIVIDUAL

THE REFLECTION IN THE MIRROR

Fiftieth Anniversary of D-Day

The fiftieth anniversary commemorative speech by President Clinton on June 6, 1994, offered perspective on the cost and importance of D-day.

"When They Were Young, These Men Saved the World"

PRESIDENT BILL CLINTON

In these last days of ceremonies, we have heard wonderful words of tribute. Now we come to this hallowed place that speaks, more than anything else, in silence. Here on this quiet plateau, on this small piece of American soil, we honor those who gave their lives for us fifty crowded years ago.

Today, the beaches of Normandy are calm. If you walk these shores on a summer's day, all you might hear is the laughter of children playing on the sand, or the cry of seagulls overhead, or perhaps the ringing of a distant church bell—the simple sounds of freedom barely breaking the silence.

But June 6th, 1944 was the least ordinary day of the 20th century. On that chilled dawn, these beaches echoed with the sounds of staccato gunfire, the roar of aircraft, the thunder of bombardment. And through the wind and the waves came the soldiers, out of

"When They Were Young, These Young Men Saved the World" is from President Bill Clinton, speech delivered at the United States National Cemetery above Omaha Beach, Colleville-sur-Mer, France, on June 6, 1994. Contained in *Vital Speeches of the Day*, July 1, 1994, pp. 546–547.

their landing craft and into the water, away from their youth and toward a savage place many of them would sadly never leave.

They had come to free a continent—the Americans, the British, the Canadians, the Poles, the French Resistance, the Norwegians and the others—they had all come to stop one of the greatest forces of evil the world has ever known.

As news of the invasion broke back home in America, people held their breath. In Boston, commuters stood reading the news on the electric sign at South Station. In New York, the Statue of Liberty, its torch blacked out since Pearl Harbor, was lit at sunset for 15 minutes. . . .

During those first hours on bloody Omaha nothing seemed to go right. Landing craft were ripped apart by mines and shells. Tanks sent to protect them had sunk, drowning their crews. Enemy fire raked the invaders as they stepped into chest-high water and waded past the floating bodies of their comrades. And as the stunned survivors of the first wave huddled behind a seawall, it seemed the invasion might fail.

Hitler and his followers had bet on it. They were sure the Allied soldiers were soft, weakened by liberty and leisure, by the mingling of races and religion. They were sure their totalitarian youth had more discipline and zeal.

But then, something happened. Although many of the American troops found themselves without officers on unfamiliar ground, next to soldiers they didn't know, one by one, they got up. They inched forward and together in groups of threes and fives and tens, the sons of democracy improvised and mounted their own attacks. At that exact moment on these beaches, the forces of freedom turned the tide of the 20th century. . . .

Today, many of them are here among us. Oh, they may walk with a little less spring in their step and their ranks are growing thinner, but let us never forget—when they were young, these men saved the world. . . .

Millions of our GI's did return home from that war to build up our nations and enjoy life's sweet pleasures. But on this field, there are 9,386 who did not. . . . They were the fathers we never knew, the uncles we

FIGURE 13.10 The British cemetery near the D-Day beaches at Bayeux *(Perry M. Rogers)*

never met, the friends who never returned, the heroes we can never repay. They gave us our world. And those simple sounds of freedom we hear today are their voices speaking to us across the years. . . .

Fifty years ago, the first Allied soldiers to land here in Normandy came not from the sea, but from the sky. They were called Pathfinders, the first paratroopers to make the jump. Deep in the darkness they descended upon these fields to light beacons for the airborne assaults that would soon follow. Now, near the dawn of a new century, the job of lighting those beacons falls to our hands.

> "To you who brought us here, I promise, we will be the new pathfinders, for we are the children of your sacrifice."
> —PRESIDENT BILL CLINTON

To you who brought us here, I promise, we will be the new pathfinders, for we are the children of your sacrifice.

"Like Cherry Blossoms in the Spring": The Fall of Japan

In 1943, U.S. forces began a campaign of island hopping in hopes of capturing several strategic islands that would provide important bases for an eventual assault on Japan. By March 1945, the islands of Iwo Jima and Okinawa had fallen despite determined Japanese resistance. The Japanese High Command realized the gravity of the moment and focused their resistance with suicide attacks on U.S. ships and aircraft carriers by using Japanese planes filled with explosives. These planes, called *kamikazes*, were named after the "Divine Wind" that had saved Japan from Mongolian invasion in the thirteenth century. The following diary account is from a kamikaze pilot who was about to sacrifice his life with honor and dignity.

Kamikaze: "Death and I Are Waiting"

ENSIGN HEIICHI OKABE

22 February 1945

I am actually a member at last of the Kamikaze Special Attack Corps. My life will be rounded out in the next thirty days. My chance will come! Death and I are waiting. The training and practice have been rigorous, but it is worthwhile if we can die beautifully and for a cause.

I shall die watching the pathetic struggle of our nation. My life will gallop in the next few weeks as my youth and life draw to a close. . . .

The sortie has been scheduled for the next ten days. I am a human being and hope to be neither saint nor scoundrel, hero nor fool—just a human being. As one who has spent his life in wistful longing and searching, I die resignedly in the hope that my life will serve as a "human document."

"Kamikaze" is from Rikihei Inoguchi and Tadashi Nakajima, *The Divine Wind* (Annapolis, Md.: United States Naval Institute, 1958), pp. 207–208.

The world in which I lived was too full of discord. As a community of rational human beings it should be better composed. Lacking a single great conductor, everyone lets loose with his own sound, creating dissonance where there should be melody and harmony.

We shall serve the nation gladly in its present painful struggle. We shall plunge into enemy ships cherishing the conviction that Japan has been and will be a place where only lovely homes, brave women, and beautiful friendships are allowed to exist.

What is the duty today? It is to fight.

What is the duty tomorrow? It is to win.

What is the daily duty? It is to die.

We die in battle without complaint. I wonder if others, like scientists, who pursue the war effort on their own fronts, would die as we do without complaint. Only then will the unity of Japan be such that she can have any prospect of winning the war.

If, by some strange chance, Japan should suddenly win this war it would be a fatal misfortune for the future of the nation. It will be better for our nation and people if they are tempered through real ordeals which will serve to strengthen.

Like cherry blossoms
In the spring,
Let us fall
Clean and radiant.

Consider This:

- Why did the Japanese resort to suicide attacks on U.S. aircraft carriers during 1944 and 1945? What general impression do you receive from the letter written by the kamikaze pilot? Was the Japanese government asking a greater sacrifice from these suicide pilots than the British and American governments asked of their pilots and soldiers during the D-day invasions? How do you interpret the phrase of Ensign Heiiche Okabe that should Japan suddenly win the war "it would be a fatal misfortune for the future of the nation"? What did he mean? Was he a Japanese national hero?

The Destruction of Hiroshima (August 6, 1945)

HARRY S. TRUMAN

On August 6, 1945, the world entered the nuclear age with the detonation of the atomic bomb over the city of Hiroshima, Japan. Persuaded by the argument that such use would ultimately save Allied lives, President Truman ordered another bomb dropped on Nagasaki two days later. The first selection is Truman's announcement of the event and explanation of his decision. It is followed by the human toll of the destruction as seen through the eyes of a Japanese doctor and a woman whose husband never returned home.

The Japanese surrendered, and World War II finally came to an end. The United States responsibly attempted to control the destructive power it had unleashed, but the race was on to match America's technological achievement. The escalation of nuclear arms became a focal point for the Cold War competition between the United States and the Soviet Union for the next forty years.

Sixteen hours ago an American airplane dropped one bomb on Hiroshima, an important Japanese Army base. That bomb had more power than 20,000 tons of T.N.T. It had more than two thousand times the blast power of the British "Grand Slam" which is the

"The Destruction of Hiroshima" is from *Public Papers of the President*, Harry S Truman, 1947 (Washington, D.C.: Government Printing Office, 1963), pp. 197–200.

largest bomb ever yet used in the history of warfare.

The Japanese began the war from the air at Pearl Harbor. They have been repaid many fold. And the end is not yet in sight. With this bomb we have now added a new and revolutionary increase in destruction to supplement the growing power of our armed forces. In their present form these bombs are now in production and even more powerful forms are in development. It is an atomic bomb. It is a harnessing of the basic power of the universe. The force from which the sun draws its power has been loosed against those who brought war to the Far East.

Before 1939, it was the accepted belief of scientists that it was theoretically possible to release atomic energy. But no one knew any practical method of doing it. By 1942, however, we knew that the Germans were working feverishly to find a way to add atomic energy to the other engines of war with which they hoped to enslave the world. But they failed. We may be grateful to Providence that the

FIGURE 13.11 Explosion of the atomic bomb over Hiroshima, Japan (August 6, 1945). (*National Archives and Record Administration*)

Germans got the V-1's and V-2's late and in limited quantities and even more grateful that they did not get the atomic bomb at all. . . .

We are now prepared to obliterate more rapidly and completely every productive enterprise the Japanese have above ground in any city. We shall destroy their docks, their factories, and their communications. Let there be no mistake; we shall completely destroy Japan's power to make war. . . .

I shall recommend that the Congress of the United States consider promptly the establishment of an appropriate commission to control the production and use of atomic power within the United States. I shall give further consideration and make further recommendations to the Congress as to how atomic power can become a powerful and forceful influence towards the maintenance of world peace.

Consider This:

- Do you think that President Truman was justified in his use of the atomic bomb on Hiroshima and Nagasaki? Does "total war" have limits? Is there an acceptable versus unacceptable degree of destruction, and where is the line of demarcation?
- The first and only time nuclear weapons have been directed against human beings occurred in 1945. For those born after this date, can the terror of that long-ago event maintain our allegiance toward arms control, or must we have an example of an atomic explosion every generation or so to promote the seriousness of negotiation? Will people forget the horrors of Hiroshima the further they are removed by time from the experience?

"They Had No Faces"

DR. MICHIHIKO HACHIYA

Dr. Tabuchi, an old friend from Ushita, came in [to the hospital ward]. His face and hands had been burned, though not badly, and after an exchange of greetings, I asked if he knew what had happened.

"I was in the back yard pruning some trees when it exploded," he answered. "The first thing I knew, there was a blinding white flash of light, and a wave of intense heat struck my cheek. This was odd, I thought, when in the next instant there was a tremendous blast."

"The force of it knocked me clean over," he continued, "but fortunately, it didn't hurt me; and my wife wasn't hurt either. But you should have seen our house! It didn't topple over, it just inclined. I have never seen such a mess. Inside and out everything was simply ruined. Even so, we are happy to be alive. . . .

After a pause, Dr. Tabuchi made ready to go.

"Don't go," I said. "Please tell us more of what occurred yesterday."

"It was a horrible sight," said Dr. Tabuchi. "Hundreds of injured people who were trying to escape to the hills passed our house. The sight of them was almost unbearable. Their faces and hands were burnt and swollen; and great sheets of skin had peeled away from their tissues to hang down like rags on a scarecrow. They moved like a line of ants. All through the night, they went past our house, but this morning they had stopped. I found them lying on both sides of the road so thick that it was impossible to pass without stepping on them."

"'They Had No Faces'" is from Michihiko Hachiya, *Hiroshima Diary: The Journal of a Japanese Physician, August 6-September 30, 1945*, translated and edited by Warner Wells, M. D. (Chapel Hill: The University of North Carolina Press, 1955), pp. 14–15.

I lay with my eyes shut while Dr. Tabuchi was talking, picturing in my mind the horror he was describing. I neither saw nor heard Mr. Katsutani when he came in. It was not until I heard someone sobbing that my attention was attracted, and I recognized my old friend. I had known Mr. Katsutani for many years and knew him to be an emotional person, but even so, to see him break down made tears come to my eyes. . . .

Mr. Katsutani paused for a moment to catch his breath and went on: "I *really* walked along the railroad tracks to get here, but even they were littered with electric wires and broken railway cars, and the dead and wounded lay everywhere. When I reached the bridge, I saw a dreadful thing. It was unbelievable. There was a man, stone dead, sitting on his bicycle as it leaned against the bridge railing. It is hard to believe that such a thing could happen!"

He repeated himself two or three times as if to convince himself that what he said was true and then continued: "It seems that most of the dead people were either on the bridge or beneath it. You could tell that many had gone down to the river to get a drink of water, and had died where they lay. I saw a few live people still in the water, knocking against the dead as they floated down the river. There must have been hundreds and thousands who fled to the river to escape the fire and then drowned.

"The sight of the soldiers, though, was more dreadful than the dead people floating down the river. I came onto I don't know how many, burned from the hips up; and where the skin had peeled, their flesh was wet and mushy. They must have been wearing their military caps because the black hair on top of their heads was not burned. It made them look like they were wearing black lacquer bowls.

"And they had no faces! Their eyes, noses and mouths had been burned away, and it looked like their ears had melted off. It was hard to tell front from back. One soldier, whose features had been destroyed and was left with his white teeth sticking out, asked me for some water, but I didn't have any. I clasped my hands and prayed for him. He didn't say anything more. His plea for water must have been his last words. The way they were burned, I wonder if they didn't have their coats off when the bomb exploded."

The Aftermath of War

Nuremberg: The Crimes of the Nazi Regime

JUSTICE ROBERT H. JACKSON

In the spring of 1945, Allied troops fought their way into the heart of Nazi Germany. Infamous concentration camps such as Dachau and Buchenwald were liberated by soldiers; the German inhabitants of the area were forced to view the horrors perpetrated by their "neighbors." Judgment was demanded, and an international court was established in Nuremberg. Its responsibility was to pass sentence on the various Nazi leaders after first examining documentary evidence and

"Nuremberg: The Crimes of the Nazi Regime" is from Office of the U.S. Chief of Counsel for the Prosecution of Axis Criminality, *Nazi Conspiracy and Aggression* (Washington, D.C.: Government Printing Office, 1947), Supplement A, pp. 15–16, 44.

transcripts of oral testimony. No court has ever attained such universal recognition. Transcripts and documents of the proceedings fill forty-two large volumes. The following selection is from the summation of Justice Robert H. Jackson, the chief American prosecutor.

The Nazi movement will be an evil memory in history because of its persecution of the Jews, the most far-flung and terrible racial persecution of all time. Although the Nazi party neither invented nor monopolized anti-Semitism, its leaders from the very beginning embraced it, and exploited it. They used it as "the psychological spark that ignites the mob." After the seizure of power, it became an official state policy. The persecution began in a series of discriminatory laws eliminating the Jews from the civil service, the professions, and economic life. As it became more intense it included segregation of Jews in ghettos, and exile. Riots were organized by party leaders to loot Jewish business places and to burn synagogues. Jewish property was confiscated and a collective fine of a billion marks was imposed upon German Jewry. The program progressed in fury and irresponsibility to the "final solution." This consisted of sending all Jews who were fit to work to concentration camps as slave laborers, and all who were not fit, which included children under 12 and people over 50, as well as any others judged unfit by an SS doctor, to concentration camps for extermination. . . .

The chief instrumentality for persecution and extermination was the concentration camp, sired by defendant Goering and nurtured under the overall authority of defendants Frick and Kaltenbrunner.

The horrors of these iniquitous places have been vividly disclosed by documents and testified to by witnesses. The Tribunal must be satiated with ghastly verbal and pictorial portrayals. From your records it is clear that the concentration camps were the first and worst weapons of oppression used by the National Socialist State, and that they were the primary means utilized for the persecution of the Christian Church and the extermination of the Jewish race. This has been admitted to you by some of the defendants from the witness stand. In the words of defendant Frank: "A thousand years will pass and this guilt of Germany will still not be erased." . . .

It is against such a background that these defendants now ask this Tribunal to say that they are not guilty of planning, executing, or conspiring to commit this long list of crimes and wrongs. They stand before the record of this trial. . . . If you were to say of these men that they are not guilty, it would be as true to say there has been no war, there are no slain, there has been no crime.

CONSIDER THIS:

- In your opinion, was justice served and the dead avenged by the Nuremberg trials and execution of Nazi leaders?

THE BROADER PERSPECTIVE:

- In a way, was the Holocaust the inevitable outcome of the racist and Social Darwinist ideas discussed in Chapter 8, "The Scramble for Global Empire"? Was the Holocaust "conditioned" by the expendability of life that was so characteristic of battles during World War I? Was the Holocaust itself a precedent for the U.S. bombing of Hiroshima? As you look at the world today, give some examples of attitudes, specific organizations, or individuals that might threaten reoccurrence of genocide. What can be done?

- During the Nuremberg trials of Nazi war criminals in 1946, testimony regarding medical experiments and the atrocities of the death camps was presented (see pages 417–430) as "crimes against humanity." The court set itself up as arbiters of genocide and war crimes as defined against a standard of "inhumanity." Can such a court define what is humane or inhumane? Is there a "human sanction" against genocide? Many have criticized such an overwhelming authority to impose justice as defined by some abstract international standard regarding actions committed during time of war. What do you think? Do you agree with Nuremberg prosecutor Jackson that "if you were to say of these men that they are not guilty, it would be as true to say there has been no war, there are no slain, there has been no crime."

■ Do you think that the International War Crimes Tribunal in the Hague can render a legitimate judgment against the Serb leaders charged with "crimes against humanity" in Bosnia and Kosovo from 1992 to 1996? Are we as human beings subject to specific standards of human behavior? If we all have "natural rights" to life and liberty, is there an inherent approbation against inhumane acts that would deprive us of those natural rights?

The Existential Perspective (1956)

JEAN-PAUL SARTRE

At the close of World War II, humanity paused, much as it had at the end of the Great War in 1918, stunned by the prolonged destruction that shook the very foundations of world civilization. But in 1945, there was a clear winner and a clear loser. This time there was joy, a celebration that evil had been vanquished and the world made safe from the horrors of fascism. Still, Europe was in ruins, over 30 million people lay dead or wounded, and the new threat, the Soviet Union, with its totalitarian government and "creeping communism," was the next obstacle to freedom. The postwar world would again pick up the pieces of its destruction and rearrange its alliances to reflect the new realities. The century had begun with devastation, followed at midpoint by even greater annihilation—and the looming potential to destroy the human race. Such events demand reflection. The existentialist philosopher Jean-Paul Sartre comments on the carnage and lends perspective to the age of anxiety. The responsibility for war, life, and death, according to Sartre, was a burden that could not be shirked and was not easily borne. The alienation of the individual from society was an axiom for the intellectual crisis that followed World War II.

The essential consequence of our earlier remarks is that man, being condemned to be free, carries the weight of the whole world on his shoulders; he is responsible for the world and for himself as a way of being. . . . Thus there are no *accidents* in a life. . . . If I am mobilized in a war, this war is *my* war; it is in my image and I deserve it. I deserve it first because I could always get out of it by suicide or by desperation; these ultimate possibilities are those which must always be present for us when there is a question of envisaging a situation. For lack of getting out of it, I have *chosen* it. This can be due to inertia, to cowardice in the face of public opinion, or because I prefer certain other values to the value of the refusal to join in the war (the good opinion of my relatives, the honor of my family, etc.). Any way you look at it, it is a matter of a choice. This choice will be repeated later on again and again without a break until the end of the war. . . . Thus, totally free, undistinguishable from the period for which I have chosen to be the meaning, as profoundly responsible for the war as if I had myself declared it, unable to live without integrating it in my situation, engaging myself in it wholly and stamping it with my seal, *I must be without remorse or regrets as I am without excuse; for from*

"The Existential Perspective" is from Jean-Paul Sartre, *Existentialism and Human Emotions* (New York: Philosophical Library, 1957), pp. 52–54, 56–57.

the instant of my upsurge into being, I carry the weight of the world by myself alone without anything or any person being able to lighten it.

Consider This:

- According to Jean-Paul Sartre, why are there no "accidents" in life? Why has existentialism often been called a "depressing philosophy"?
- If being "free" is usually considered an advantageous human condition, why does the existentialist believe he is "condemned to be free"? Do you think Albert Einstein was correct in his assessment that "as long as there will be man, there will be wars"?

14

COLD WAR CONFRONTATION AND THE DYNAMICS OF CHANGE (1945–2006)

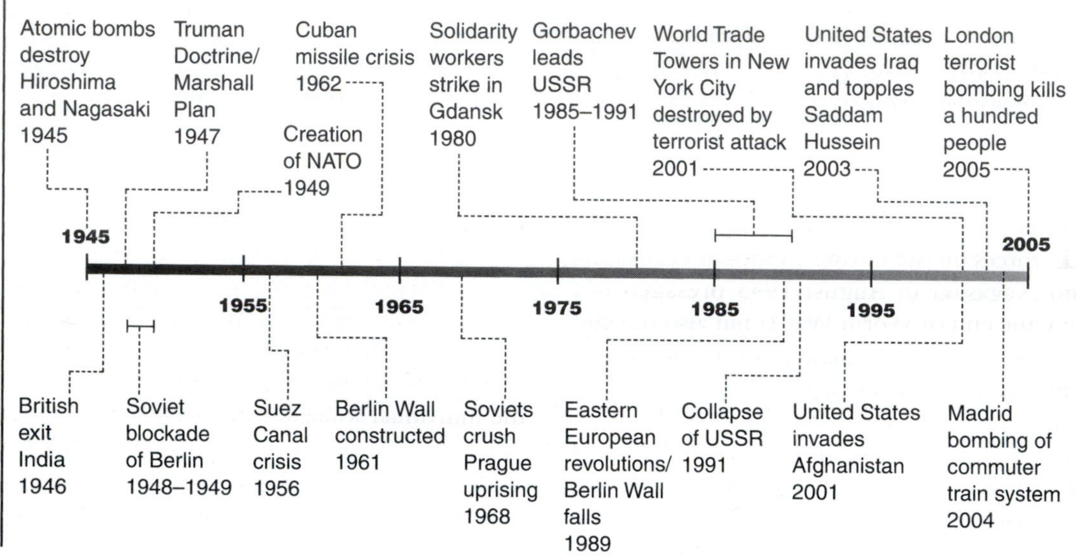

CHAPTER THEMES

- **The Power Structure:** Was the Cold War an ideological struggle between two different systems of government, or did it have very little to do with government at all? What was the root cause of the Cold War?
- **Imperialism:** Was the Cold War just another term for "ideological imperialism?" Was the Cold War really about the accumulation of territory or about the winning of "hearts and minds?" How did this differ from nineteenth-century imperialism?
- **The Varieties of Truth** Just how does one spot a communist? Were the fear and distrust during the Cold War real, or were they manufactured by governments seeking justification for authority?
- **Beliefs and Spirituality:** How did the Cold War transform the concepts of freedom and tyranny, of democracy and totalitarianism into a spiritual realm where abstractions obscured reality? Was nuclear destruction such a threat that each side deified its leaders and transformed its ideologies into pure Truth, to be supported without equivocation?
- **Women in History:** What political, social, and economic strides have women made in the last 150 years? Have women attained true equality with men in our contemporary society? How much influence has Madison Avenue advertising had on the definition of women's roles in society? Do movies and advertising create images or

reflect them? Has the women's movement run its course, or will there always be a need to redefine the relationship between the sexes?

- **Historical Change and Transition:** How did the technological revolution of the late twentieth century alter not only the way we live but also the way in which we perceive reality? Have the great advances in transistors, microchips, personal computers, faxes, cell phones, and e-mail allowed us unparalleled access to information and at the same time placed our personal privacy and security in jeopardy? Is technological progress always a two-edged sword? Has it empowered terrorist organizations and given revolutionaries new credibility as agents of change? Will the acceleration of change lead to the acceleration of decline?
- **The Big Picture:** How should we measure progress in civilization? Is it a quantifiable commodity linked to advances in technology? Or is the ethical development of humanity the only real determinant of whether a society has evolved and progressed? Is human nature basically good or evil? Is this the fundamental question that must be answered before political systems can be developed or social programs instituted? Where are we headed in the twenty-first century, and what is the value of studying history?

The use of atomic weapons by American forces on the Japanese cities of Hiroshima and Nagasaki in August 1945 presaged not only the end of World War II but also the end of an era. The world entered the nuclear age when modern science joined with military necessity to produce an astonishing desolation. The horrors of trench warfare, poisonous gas, dislocated refugees, and the deprivation and starvation that had plagued the victims of two world wars could not compare with the new possibilities: Human beings had finally discovered a way to destroy themselves and their world. The power unleashed by the splitting of the atom had created a completely new distribution of power. Those countries that had access to the necessary materials and technologies were in a position to dominate and impose their will on less developed regions. As the people of Europe struggled to find food and shelter, to repair their lives and mourn their dead, another game was being played with the ultimate risk at stake. This was a contest between good and evil, between freedom and domination—between the United States and the Soviet Union.

The uneasy relationship between the United States and the Soviet Union was not created at the end of World War II. Its roots were deep and primarily philosophical. The United States had been founded on the principles of the eighteenth-century Enlightenment. There existed "natural rights" that were the birthright of each individual: life, liberty, and property. The government was to exist in balance with its citizens, protecting the rights of the individual while seeing to the general welfare of its population. Capitalism, with its inherent emphasis on private enterprise and the reward of individual ability, hard work, and perseverance, blended nicely with the ideals of the democratic political system. As it was applied in the United States, capitalism was not always successful and not always fair. It was regulated by the federal government at various intervals to protect the general welfare of the citizenry. But the American commitment to personal liberty was never in question. The fear of communism as a threat to the so-called "American way" was inculcated in the public consciousness in the first decades of the twentieth century.

The Soviet Union was founded on a different philosophical premise. It was created in 1917 when the Bolshevik party seized power from the Provisional Government that had opposed the absolutism of the Russian tsar and was both democratic and capitalistic. The Bolsheviks were led by Vladimir Lenin, a disciple of the German philosopher Karl

Marx. Marx had developed the economic theory of communism, which decried the exploitation of workers by middle-class entrepreneurs who sought a profit at all costs. Marx's complex philosophy argued that the conflict engendered by competing capitalistic forces would eventually lead to a communist society where the state would "wither away" and all people would live in harmony, giving what labor they could to the community and taking just what they needed to live a life of mutual respect and tolerance. Communism theoretically looks to the best in human nature—that people are basically good and will share the necessities of life with others. Thus Marx expected "world revolution" that would free people from the class exploitation of capitalism: "The proletarians have nothing to lose but their chains. They have a world to win. Workers of the world unite!"

Note that communism is an economic theory not a political system. If anything, the state is supposed to remove itself from the life of its citizens. Marx believed that the world would naturally evolve toward communism, but he left no practical plans for the application of his ideas. Lenin based the Russian Revolution of 1917 on Marx's philosophy but found himself having to make adjustments in Marx's theory. Americans felt threatened by the coming "world revolution," which sought the overthrow of their cherished principles of individualism and capitalism. The United States even sent troops to Russia to fight against the communists in 1918 when Lenin had not yet consolidated control of the government.

Communism therefore became a great evil in the American mind. When Lenin died in 1924 and Joseph Stalin struggled for control of the new Soviet state, further modifications in Marx's philosophy confirmed American fears. Instead of the Soviet state withering away, Stalin increased its authority and actually redefined Marxism to justify his reorganization of agriculture and industry to protect the Soviet state from hostile Western democracies. From about 1928 to 1940, Stalin imprisoned and eliminated millions of Russians who resisted his authority. Secret police and a Siberian prison system known as the Gulag sought to maintain total control over the population. The term *totalitarian* was coined to describe this complete imprisonment of society to the dictatorship of the state.

It was therefore with great delicacy that the Western Allies in 1940 decided to sleep with the enemy, as it were, and join Stalin in the crusade against Hitler and Nazism during World War II. This was from the first an expedient relationship—Hitler, the "Great Evil," had to be vanquished, and Stalin became a tolerable, lesser evil.

But with the victory over Hitler assured in 1945, Europe became the battleground once again for a new war—the Cold War. As European governments licked their wounds and looked to the immediate needs of their citizens, they retreated from the empires that they had established and depended on for decades. Britain removed itself from controlling interests in Africa, India, and the Middle East; France loosened its control over countries in Africa and Southeast Asia. Into this power vacuum flowed the interests of the new emerging superpowers, each trying to compete for the hearts and minds as well as the territory of the remnants. Even though the Soviet Union had suffered the greatest losses (nearly 18 million military and civilian dead) of all combatants in World War II, the need to maintain and expand its position in the face of perceived Western encroachment became Stalin's obsession. By 1946, Winston Churchill spoke of an Iron Curtain that had descended over Eastern Europe, trapping Hungary, Czechoslovakia, Bulgaria, Romania, Poland, and East Germany in the communist sphere of influence. The United States sought to reinforce Western democracies by providing financial aid through the Marshall Plan in 1947. The United States also moved to halt Soviet expansionism in 1947 by proclaiming the Truman Doctrine, which justified intervention against communist movements. Containment of communist "world revolution" became the watchword of American foreign policy throughout the 1950s and 1960s.

The Cold War between the United States and the Soviet Union lasted from about 1945 to 1990. This was a bipolar arrangement in which the world in a sense was held hostage by two nations, philosophically opposed to one another, paranoid about losing face and territory to the unspeakable "evil" of the other. New alliance systems like NATO and the Warsaw Pact were developed to achieve a balance of power. Military competition was intense as both countries expended billions to develop new weapons systems and accumulate more tanks, more missiles, more bombers. The world became a dangerous place in the 1960s as the arms race was on, fueled by military theories that demanded "parity" with the enemy. Mutually Assured Destruction (MAD) was presented as a security measure—if each side could destroy the other many times over, then it would be too dangerous to start a war with a "first strike." The balance of power was thus maintained and peace assured by building ever more sophisticated weaponry, whose mere threat was enough to keep the peace.

This is not to say that there were not outbreaks of hot war. The Korean "police action" (1950–1953), the Cuban "missile crisis" (1962), and the Vietnam "conflict" (1960–1975) were euphemistic struggles in which the two superpowers "fought," often through surrogates without formally declaring war, to achieve geopolitical position and influence over strategic regions of the world.

There was a price to pay for the tension of the Cold War, even if the world was spared a nuclear holocaust. Weapon systems developed during the 1980s such as the B-1 bomber, the M-1 tank, stealth fighter aircraft, and the laser-based Strategic Defense Initiative (SDI, or "Star Wars") cost hundreds of billions of dollars and drove defense expenditures to nearly a quarter of the national budget.

In the Soviet Union, the expense of competing in the arms race proved fatal. The Soviets could put cosmonauts in space and sophisticated MIG fighters in the air, but they could not put bread on the table or refrigerators in the houses of Soviet citizens. The managed economy of a Soviet state that was supposed to have withered away proved disastrous as the workforce became apathetic and inefficient. The Soviets were never able to solve the many ethnic problems that plagued the unity of their political system, and, more importantly, the government was never able to cultivate the trust and commitment of its people that are essential to success and stability. By the time Mikhail Gorbachev came on the scene in 1985 with his policies of *glasnost* ("openness") and *perestroika* ("political restructuring"), social and economic problems were spinning out of control. The ossified political leadership that had survived Stalin by committing itself to his policies, methods, and priorities for so long could not prepare the Soviet Union for the future.

By 1991, the Soviet Union had collapsed, with its empire of dependent countries broken apart and left to fend for themselves. The United States had won the Cold War and rejoiced in its so-called "victory," the triumph of capitalism over communism, of right over wrong, of good over evil. But it is up to each of us to assess the damage wrought by fifty years of distrust and destructive competition.

The world in the year 2000 was very different from what it was in 1945 when the evil of Hitler could be defined and destroyed. After the Cold War from 1991 to 2001, when there was no longer an evil to be vanquished, the United States as the sole remaining superpower seemed adrift in foreign affairs. Which road to take? What did we stand for, and what were we willing to fight and die for? These questions were answered on September 11, 2001, when the twin towers of the World Trade Center in

FIGURE 14.1 The erection of the Berlin Wall in August 1961 separated East and West Berlin but also symbolized the Cold War rivalry that had developed between the United States and the Soviet Union. (*Perry M. Rogers*)

New York City collapsed after two hijacked commercial jetliners, turned into missiles by Islamic militants, slammed into them, thus destroying the lives of thousands, jeopardizing the nation's economy, and shaking the confidence and security of the American people. A same-day attack on the Pentagon and the subsequent anthrax contamination of the mail produced a defensive reaction as the United States prepared for a new war, a war on terrorism with the great evil redefined as Osama bin Laden, the wealthy Saudi exile and mastermind of the al-Qaeda terrorist network. As the United States provided leadership in this ongoing struggle, old enemies like Russia were themselves given new opportunities to refashion their images and redefine their loyalties. President John Kennedy was correct when he noted: "History teaches us that enmities between nations do not last forever. . . . The tide of time and events will often bring surprising changes in the relations between nations and neighbors." We are witnessing the transition to a new paradigm where nations that have enjoyed a dominant military or economic status must confront their vulnerabilities or perhaps lose their superpower designation. New threats to old power relationships, including international terrorism and militant Islam, create new expediencies, alliances, and opportunities for a greater alienation or integration of the world community. The twenty-first century unfolds.

Retrenchment (1945–1965)

The Reconstruction of Europe

It is logical that the United States should do whatever it is able to do to assist in the return of normal economic health in the world, without which there can be no political stability and no assured peace.

—George Marshall

At the end of World War II, Europe lay in ruins, crushed physically and psychologically by the incessant bombing and catastrophic death spiral of the Nazi regime. People wandered the landscape starving, homeless, and detached from even the barest essentials of life. For the second time in a generation, Europeans faced the world as vulnerable indigents, happy to be alive but desperate. The United States was determined to lay a foundation of stability that would relieve the population and contain Soviet influence in the region.

The first step was to follow through on Woodrow Wilson's failed vision of a League of Nations that he had personally promoted in the Treaty of Versailles. President Roosevelt fought for a newly structured international organization called the United Nations. In June 1945, a month after the German surrender was concluded, the Charter of the United Nations was signed. This organization was dedicated to the proposition that international cooperation was not only preferable to war but also possible to attain.

The new United Nations provided a necessary idealistic proposition for drawing countries together in support of diplomatic solutions to world crises. But it did little to solve the economic and social dislocation of Europe that opened the region to the influence of communism. The Marshall Plan, introduced in 1947 by U.S. secretary of state George Marshall (1880–1959), provided economic aid to European countries, thus allowing them to rebuild their infrastructure and stabilize their societies. The Marshall Plan eventually restored prosperity to Europe, thereby supporting democracies that in turn helped contain the Soviet Union.

The Marshall Plan (June 1947)

George C. Marshall

The truth of the matter is that Europe's requirements for the next three or four years of foreign food and other essential products—principally from America—are so much greater than her present ability to pay that she must have substantial additional help or face economic, social, and political deterioration of a very grave character.

The remedy lies in breaking the vicious circle and restoring the confidence of the European people in the economic future of their own countries and of Europe as a whole. The manufacturer and the farmer throughout wide areas must be able and willing to exchange their products for currencies the continuing value of which is not open to question.

"The Marshall Plan" is from *Department of State Bulletin* (June 15, 1947), pp. 1159–1160.

Aside from the demoralizing effect on the world at large and the possibilities of disturbances arising as a result of the desperation of the people concerned, the consequences to the economy of the United States should be apparent to all. It is logical that the United States should do whatever it is able to do to assist in the return of normal economic health in the world, without which there can be no political stability and no assured peace. Our policy is directed not against any country or doctrine but against hunger, poverty, desperation, and chaos. Its purpose should be the revival of a working economy in the world so as to permit the emergence of political and social conditions in which free institutions can exist. Such assistance, I am convinced, must not be on a piecemeal basis as various crises develop. Any assistance that this Government may render in the future should provide a cure rather than a mere palliative. Any government that is willing to assist in the task of recovery will find full cooperation, I am sure, on the part of the United States Government. Any government which maneuvers to block the recovery of other countries cannot expect help from us. Furthermore, governments, political parties, or groups which seek to perpetuate human misery in order to profit therefrom politically or otherwise will encounter the opposition of the United States.

It is already evident that, before the United States Government can proceed much further in its efforts to alleviate the situation and help start the European world on its way to recovery, there must be some agreement among the countries of Europe as to the requirements of the situation and the part those countries themselves will take in order to give proper effect to whatever action might be undertaken by this Government. It would be neither fitting nor efficacious for this Government to undertake to draw up unilaterally a program designed to place Europe on its feet economically. This is the business of the Europeans. The initiative, I think, must come from Europe. The role of this country should consist of friendly aid in the drafting of a European program and of later support of such a program so far as it may be practical for us to do so. The program should be a joint one, agreed to by a number, if not all, European nations.

An essential part of any successful action on the part of the United States is an understanding on the part of the people of America of the character of the problem and the remedies to be applied. Political passion and prejudice should have no part. With foresight, and a willingness on the part of our people to face up to the vast responsibility which history has clearly placed upon our country, the difficulties I have outlined can and will be overcome.

Program for the Welfare State: The Beveridge Report

Europeans were certainly not waiting for American aid to rescue them. Among the most active countries in seeking to provide relief to their citizens was Great Britain. In 1942, Parliament set up a commission headed by Sir William Beveridge to develop ideas for a system of social insurance. The Beveridge Report laid down a revolutionary socialist pathway for Britain that would task the government with responsibility for the health and welfare of its population. This was a "comprehensive policy of social progress" that with ongoing revision remains in effect today.

"Program for the Welfare State" is from *Social Insurance and Allied Services: Report by Sir William Beveridge* (Cmd. 6404). London: His Majesty's Stationary Office, 1942, pp. 5–9.

The first task of the committee has been to attempt for the first time a comprehensive survey of the whole field of social insurance and allied services, to show just what provision is now made and how it is made for many different forms of need. . . . In proceeding from this first comprehensive survey of social insurance to the next task—of making recommendations—three guiding principles may be laid down at the outset:

The first principle is that any proposals for the future, while they should use to the full the experience gathered in the past, should not be restricted by consideration of sectional interests established in the obtaining of that experience. Now, when the war is abolishing landmarks of every kind, is the opportunity for using experience in a clear field. A revolutionary moment in the world's history is a time for revolutions, not for patching.

The second principle is that organisation of social insurance should be treated as one part only of a comprehensive policy of social progress. Social insurance fully developed may provide income security; it is an attack upon Want. But Want is one only of five giants on the road of reconstruction and in some ways the easiest to attack. The others are Disease, Ignorance, Squalor, and Idleness.

The third principle is that social security must be achieved by cooperation between the State and the individual. The State should offer security for service and contribution. The State in organising security should not stifle incentive, opportunity, responsibility; in establishing a national minimum, it should leave room and encouragement for voluntary action by each individual to provide more than that minimum for himself and his family.

The plan for Social Security set out in this Report is built upon these principles. It uses experience but is not tied by experience. It is put forward as a limited contribution to a wider social policy, though as something that could be achieved now without waiting for the whole of that policy. It is, first and foremost, a plan of insurance—of giving in return for contributions benefits up to subsistence level, as of right and without means test, so that individuals may build freely upon it. . . .

The Plan for Social Security . . . starts from a diagnosis of want. . . . This is the main conclusion to be drawn: abolition of want requires a double-distribution of income, through social insurance and by family needs. Abolition of want requires, first, improvement of State insurance, that is to say provision against interruption and loss of earning power. . . .

Abolition of want requires, second, adjustment of incomes, in periods of earning as well as in interruption of earning, to family needs, that is to say in one form or another it requires allowances for children. . . .

By a double re-distribution of income through social insurance and children's allowances, want, as defined in the social surveys, could have been abolished in Britain before the present war. . . . The income available to the British people was ample for such a purpose. The Plan for Social Security set out in this Report takes abolition of want after this war as its aim. It includes as its main method compulsory social insurance, with national assistance and voluntary insurance as subsidiary methods. It assumes allowances for dependent children, as part of its background. The plan assumes also establishment of comprehensive health and rehabilitation services and maintenance of employment, that is to say avoidance of mass unemployment, as necessary conditions of success in social insurance.

The main feature of the Plan for Social Security is a scheme of social insurance against interruption and destruction of earning power and for special expenditure arising at birth, marriage or death. The scheme embodies six fundamental principles: flat rate of subsistence benefit; flat rate of contribution; unification of administrative responsibility; adequacy of benefit; comprehensiveness; and classification. . . . Based on them and in combination with national assistance and voluntary insurance as subsidiary methods, the aim of the Plan for Social Security is to make want under any circumstances unnecessary.

CONSIDER THIS:

- What was the Marshall Plan and why was it instituted? Did it achieve its aims?
- According to the Beveridge Report, what were the "five giants" blocking the road to reconstruction? How did the Report plan to "slay" these giants? What role was the government to play?
- The Beveridge Report argued that Britain faced an extraordinary moment that required revolutionary Action, not a "patch." How revolutionary was this new "welfare state"? Why was the government so confident in its ability to solve the problem of "want"?

THE BROADER PERSPECTIVE:

- In his book *Why War*? (Paris, 1933), the great physicist Albert Einstein wrote, "Mankind can only gain protection against the danger of unimaginable destruction and wanton annihilation if a supranational organization has alone the authority to produce or possess [nuclear] weapons. . . and the legal right and duty to solve all the conflicts which in the past have led to war." What is your reaction to this opinion? To what extent are organizations like the United Nations and Amnesty International useful and effective? Would it make a difference if they did not exist?

The Retreat from Empire

India is prepared to take risks and face dangers. We do not want the so-called protection of the British Army and Navy. We will shift for ourselves.

—JAWAHARLAL NEHRU (1944)

Long years ago we made a tryst with destiny, and now the time comes when we shall redeem our pledge, not wholly or in full measure, but very substantially. At the stroke of the midnight hour, while the world sleeps, India will awake.

—JAWAHARLAL NEHRU (1947)

We solemnly declare to the world that Vietnam has the right to be a free and independent country.

—HO CHI MINH

If the Arab people really want freedom and independence, we must depend on ourselves alone.

—GAMAL ABDUL NASSER

In the first two decades after World War II, Europe licked its wounds and struggled to implement new social agendas and to reestablish production and economic prosperity amid the political insecurity of the Cold War. The conflict and tension of the period was played out while another movement, in many ways even more dramatic and important, was changing the lives of people throughout the world.

During the nineteenth century and especially during the 1870s, European countries had launched out in an orgy of competitive expansion, establishing colonial outposts from where they could dominate native populations and siphon off the natural resources of the region for the aggrandizement of "king and country" and the glory of God. But the doctrine of the self-determination of nations that had been advocated in the Paris peace talks of 1919 energized native political leaders, many of whom, such as Mohandas K. Gandhi, Jawaharlal Nehru, and Ho Chi Minh, had been educated in Europe as liberals, socialists, or communists.

The process of decolonization, therefore, came both as a result of the inability of distracted European governments to sustain control over their colonial holdings and rising nationalist movements filled with deep-seated resentment for past injustices. The European retreat from empire was not a systematic process and did not come easily to Great Britain or France. It was a difficult and grudging realization that Britannia no longer ruled the waves and French glory would have to be obtained with less dramatic panache.

But it was hard to deny the energy and determination of leaders like Ho Chi Minh (1892–1969). A sophisticated and erudite patriot, Ho Chi Minh was educated in Paris where he became a committed communist. His Viet Minh nationalist movement against French rule in Indochina was inspired by Enlightenment values of self-determination and political equality. He had fought with the Allies against the Japanese, and upon their defeat in September 1945, Ho declared the independence of Vietnam under the direction of a coalition of nationalists and communists, as noted in the following selection. The road toward independence would be long and hard as first the French and then the United States viewed Vietnam as the front line of Cold War contention and struggled to control the region until 1975, when the last American troops and civilian personnel were evacuated.

Vietnam: "Determined to Fight to the Bitter End" (1945)

HO CHI MINH

"All men are created equal. They are endowed by their Creator with certain unalienable Rights; among these are Life, Liberty, and the pursuit of Happiness."

This immortal statement was made in the Declaration of Independence of the United States of America in 1776. In a broader sense, this means: All the peoples on the earth are equal from birth, all the peoples have a right to live, to be happy and free.

The Declaration of the French Revolution made in 1791 on the Rights of man and the Citizen also states: "All men are born free and with equal rights, and must always remain free and have equal rights."

Those are undeniable truths.

Nevertheless, for more than eighty years, the French imperialists, abusing the standard of Liberty, Equality, and Fraternity, have violated our Fatherland and oppressed our fellow citizens. They have acted contrary to the ideals of humanity and justice.

In the field of politics, they have deprived our people of every democratic liberty. They have enforced inhuman laws; . . . They have built more prisons than schools. They have mercilessly slain our patriots; they have drowned our uprisings in rivers of blood. . . . In the field of economics, they have fleeced us to the backbone, impoverished our people and devastated our land. They have robbed us of our rice fields, our mines, our forests, and our raw materials. They have monopolized the issuing of bank notes and the export trade. They have invented numerous unjustifiable taxes and reduced our people, especially our peasantry, to a state of extreme poverty. They have hampered the prospering of our national

"Vietnam" is from Ho Chi Minh, *Selected Works* (Hanoi: Foreign Languages Publishing House, 1977).

bourgeoisie; they have mercilessly exploited our workers.

In the autumn of 1940, when the Japanese fascists violated Indochina's territory to establish new bases in their fight against the Allies, the French imperialists went down on their bended knees and handed over our country to them. Thus, from that date, our people were subjected to the double yoke of the French and the Japanese. Their sufferings and miseries increased. . . .

From the autumn of 1940, our country had in fact ceased to be a French colony and had become a Japanese possession. After the Japanese had surrendered to the Allies, our whole people rose to regain our national sovereignty and to found the Democratic Republic of Vietnam. The truth is that we have wrested our independence from the Japanese and not from the French.

The French have fled, the Japanese have capitulated, Emperor Boa Dai has abdicated. Our people have broken the chains which for nearly a century have fettered them and have won independence for the Fatherland. Our people at the same time have overthrown the monarchic regime that has reigned supreme for dozens of centuries. In its place has been established the present Democratic Republic.

For these reasons, we, members of the Provisional Government, representing the whole Vietnamese people, declare that from now on we break off all relations of a colonial character with France; we repeal all the international obligation that France has so far subscribed to on behalf of Vietnam, and we abolish all the special rights the French have unlawfully acquired in our Fatherland.

The whole Vietnamese people, animated by a common purpose, are determined to fight to the bitter end against any attempt by the French colonialists to reconquer their country.

We are convinced that the Allied nations, which at Teheran and San Francisco have acknowledged the principles of self-determination and equality of nations, will not refuse to acknowledge the independence of Vietnam.

A people who have courageously opposed French domination for more than eighty years, a people who have fought side by side with the Allies against the fascists during these last years, such a people must be free and independent.

For these reasons, we solemnly declare to the world that Vietnam has the right to be a free and independent country—and in fact it is so already. The entire Vietnamese people are determined to mobilize all their physical and mental strength, to sacrifice their lives and property in order to safeguard their independence and liberty.

CONSIDER THIS:

- According to Ho Chi Minh, in what ways did the French abuse the Vietnamese people?
- How did Ho Chi Minh's declaration of Vietnamese independence in 1945 reflect the Enlightenment values on which the United States had declared the legitimacy of its own freedom in 1776? Why did the Untied States ultimately regard Vietnam's sovereign independence as illegitimate and fight a war to "save the Vietnamese from themselves?"

British Rule in India (1946)

JAWAHARLAL NEHRU

Perhaps the most successful political transition during the process of decolonization occurred on the Indian subcontinent as the "Jewel in the Crown" of Britain's empire achieved independence. The subject had been discussed repeatedly during the

"British Rule in India" is from Jawaharlal Nehru, *The Discovery of India* (New York: John Day Company, 1946), pp. 304–306. Reprinted by permission of Sonia Gandhi and the Jawaharlal Nehru Memorial Fund.

1920s and 1930s. During World War II, the Congress Party in India continued to demand progress in the negotiations over independence from Britain even as the Indian army fought with the British against the Japanese in Burma. The war drained Britain of the will and the economic resources to hold on to India, and negotiations began in earnest. In 1946, a compromise between Muslims and the Congress Party about the administration of regions in the new India seemed to have satisfied both parties, but it fell apart. The Muslim leader, Jinnah, was looking to a new Muslim state separate from India. Amid violent confrontations between Hindus and Muslims in the streets of Calcutta, in which six thousand were killed, Jinnah remarked, "We shall have India divided, or we shall have India destroyed." In the face of civil war, Jawaharlal Nehru conceded the creation of a homeland for Muslims to be called Pakistan. Only the seventy-seven-year-old Mohandas Gandhi clung to the dream of a united India. On August 15, 1947, Britain handed over power to two countries, India and Pakistan. Nehru became the first president of an independent India, and although disputes between India and Pakistan continued to dull the celebration, the British Raj had come to an end and a new era had begun. In the following selection, Nehru provides justification for India's independence.

Then there was the Indian Army, consisting of British and Indian troops, but officered entirely by Englishmen. This was reorganized repeatedly, especially after the Mutiny of 1857, and ultimately became organizationally linked up with the British Army. This was so arranged as to balance its different elements and keep the British troops in key positions. . . . The primary function of these forces was to serve as an army of occupation—"internal Security Troops" they were called, and a majority of these were British. The Frontier Province served as a training ground for the British Army at India's expense. The field army (chiefly Indian) was meant for service abroad and it took part in numerous British imperial wars and expeditions, India always bearing the cost. Steps were taken to segregate Indian troops from the rest of the population.

Thus India had to bear the cost of her own conquest, and then of her transfer (or sale) from the East India Company to the British crown and for the extension of the British empire to Burma and elsewhere, and expeditions to Africa, Persia, etc., and for her defense against Indians themselves. She was not only used as a base for imperial purposes, without any reimbursement for this, but she had further to pay for the training of part of the British Army in England—"capitation" charges these were called. Indeed, India was charged for all manner of other expenses incurred by Britain, such as the maintenance of British diplomatic and consular establishments in China and Persia, the entire cost of the telegraph line from England to India, part of the expenses of the British Mediterranean fleet, and even the receptions given to the sultan of Turkey in London.

The buildings of railways in India, undoubtedly desirable and necessary, was done in an enormously wasteful way. The government of India guaranteed five percent interest on all capital invested, and there was no need to check or estimate what was necessary. All purchases were made in England.

The civil establishment of government was also run on a lavish and extravagant scale, all the highly paid positions being reserved for Europeans. The process of Indianization of the administrative machine was very slow and only became noticeable in the twentieth century. This process, far from transferring any power to Indian hands, proved yet another method of strengthening British rule. The really key positions remained in British hands, and Indians in the administration could only function as the agents of British rule.

To all these methods must be added the deliberate policy, pursued throughout the period of British rule, of creating divisions among Indians, of encouraging one group at the cost of the other. This policy was openly admitted in the early days of their rule, and indeed it was a natural one for an imperial power. With the growth of the nationalist movement, that policy took subtler and more dangerous forms, and though denied, functioned more intensively than ever.

Nearly all our major problems today have grown up during British rule and as a direct result of British policy: the princes; the minority problem; various vested interests, foreign and Indian; the lack of industry and the neglect of agriculture; the extreme backwardness in the social services; and, above all, the tragic poverty of the people. This attitude to education has been significant in Kaye's *Life of Metcalfe*, it is stated that . . . "it was our policy . . . to keep the natives of India in the profoundest state of barbarism and darkness, and every attempt to diffuse the light of knowledge among the people, either of our own or of the independent states, was vehemently opposed and resented."

Imperialism must function in this way or else it ceases to be imperialism. The modern type of finance imperialism added new kinds of economic exploitation which were unknown in earlier ages. The record of British rule in India during the nineteenth century must necessarily depress and anger an Indian, and yet it illustrates the superiority of the British in many fields, not least in their capacity to profit by our disunity and weaknesses. A people who are weak and who are left behind in the march of time invite trouble and ultimately have only themselves to blame. If British imperialism with all its consequences was, in the circumstances, to be expected in the natural order of events, so also was the growth of opposition to it inevitable, and the final crisis between the two.

CONSIDER THIS:

- How did India contribute to the imperial success of the British Empire?
- How was India forced to pay for its own enslavement by the British?
- What specific modern problems did Nehru attribute to British policy in India? Why were the British able to rule India for so many years?

THE BROADER PERSPECTIVE:

- British prime minister Clement Attlee maintained in 1946 that "the British Commonwealth and Empire is not bound together by chains of external compulsion. It is an association of free peoples." If that was true, why was there such a struggle for independence in India?

The Arab Nationalist Movement and the Creation of Israel

Palestine is the cement that holds the Arab world together, or it is the explosive that blows it apart.

—YASSER ARAFAT

My generation swore on the Altar of God that whoever proclaims the intent of destroying the Jewish state or the Jewish people, seals his fate.

—MENACHEM BEGIN

We have always said that in our war with the Arabs, we had a secret weapon—no alternative.

—GOLDA MEIR

The tormenting dilemma of the Middle East is this: either we have one people too many, or one state too few.

—Afif Safieh

Arab nationalism as an ideology and as a primary factor in the politics of the Middle East is a comparatively recent development. It was only after World War I, in the mandated territories under British and French rule, that a comprehensive doctrine of Arab nationhood was formulated. But the roots of Arab nationalism go back to the nineteenth century, when Muslim states in North Africa and South Asia were subjugated militarily by European powers, and Islam as a system of belief and social organization was ridiculed and belittled in comparison with Western learning, philosophy, and technical expertise. A response to this attitude came from early Arab revolutionaries such as Jamal al-Din (1838–1897), commonly known as al-Afghani, who lived among Indian Muslims, was expelled from Egypt for dissident activities, and edited an underground newspaper in Paris, preaching Muslim unity and solidarity in the face of European encroachment.

After victory in World War I, Britain and France carved up the Arab portions of the defeated Ottoman Empire into zones of influence, or "mandates." Although the mandates for Syria and Iraq were designed to prepare those countries for independence, the mandate for Palestine was intended to bolster Britain's strategic presence in the region while accommodating Zionist goals. The Arabs were furious that Britain had reneged on its wartime support for Arab self-determination. As more Jews emigrated into the region in the 1930s to escape Nazi persecution, Arab nationalists broke into rebellion in 1936.

The following document is a manifesto from the First Arab Students' Congress held in Brussels in December 1938. It is an expression of frustration and an attempt to define and promote Arab unity in response to the effects of European diplomacy.

The Arab Homeland: "Compromise Is National Treason" (1938)

Our National Pact

I am an Arab, and I believe that the Arabs constitute one nation. The sacred right of this nation is to be sovereign in her own affairs. Her ardent nationalism drives her to liberate the Arab homeland, to unite all its parts, and to found political, economic, and social institutions more sound and more compatible than the existing ones. The aim of this nationalism is to raise up the standard of living and to increase the material and the spiritual good of the people; it also aspires to share in working for the good of the human collectivity; it strives to realize this by continuous work based on national organization.

I pledge myself to God, that I will strive in this path to my utmost, putting the national interest above any other consideration.

First Principles

The Arabs: All who are Arab in their language, culture, and loyalty, those are the Arabs. The Arab is the individual who belongs to the nation made up of those people.

"The Arab Homeland" is from Sylvia Haim, ed., *Arab Nationalism: An Anthology* (Berkeley: University of California Press, 1962), pp. 100–102.

The Arab Homeland: It is the land which has been or is, inhabited by an Arab majority, in the above sense, in Asia and Africa. As such it is a whole which cannot be divided or partitioned. It is a sacred heritage no inch of which may be trifled with. Any compromise in this respect is invalid and is national treason.

Arab Nationalism: It is the feeling for the necessity of independence and unity which the inhabitants of the Arab lands share. It is based on the unity of the homeland, of language, culture, history, and a sense of the common good.

The Arab Movement: It is the new Arab renaissance which pervades the Arab nation. Its motive force is her glorious past, her remarkable vitality and the awareness of her present and future interests. This movement strives continuously and in an organized manner toward well-defined aims. These aims are to liberate and unite the Arab homeland, to found political, economic, and social organizations more sound than the existing ones, and to attempt afterward to work for the good of the human collectivity and its progress. These aims are to be realized by definite means drawn from the preparedness of the Arabs and their particular situation, as well as from the experience of the West. They will be realized without subscribing to any particular creed of the modern Western ones such as Fascism, Communism, or Democracy.

Foreign Elements in the Arab Countries

We have said that the Arab countries belong to the Arabs and that benefits therefrom must accrue to them. By Arabs we mean those whom the political report has included under this appellation. As for those elements who are not Arabized and who do not intend to be Arabized, but are, rather, intent on putting obstacles in the way of the Arab nation, they are foreign to the Arab nation. The most prominent problem of this kind is that of the Jews in Palestine.

If we looked at the Jews in Palestine from an economic angle, we would find that their economy is totally incompatible with the Arab economy. The Jews are attempting to build up a Jewish state in Palestine and to bring into this state great numbers of their kind from all over the world. Palestine is a small country, and they will therefore have to industrialize it so that this large number of inhabitants can find subsistence. And in order to make their industry a success, they will have to find markets for their products. For this they depend on the Arab market; their products will therefore flood the Arab countries and compete with Arab industries. This is very harmful to the Arabs.

Moreover, Palestine, placed as it is between the Arab countries in Asia and Africa, occupies an important position in land, sea, and air communications. A foreign state in Palestine will impede these communications and have a harmful effect on commerce. And even if the Jews in Palestine presented no danger other than the economic, this would be enough for us to oppose them and to put an end to their intrigues, so that we may ensure for our country a happy and glorious future.

Among the dangerous alien elements in the Arab countries are the foreign colonies such as the Italians in Troplitania, the French, and the Frenchified Jews in Tunisia, Algeria, and Morocco. The danger of these elements is akin to that of the Jews in Palestine, even though less prominent and less critical.

CONSIDER THIS:

- How did the Arab Students' Congress define the Arab homeland, Arab nationalism, and the goals of the Arab Movement?
- Why were the Jews in Palestine a threat to the Arabs? Are you persuaded by the economic argument?
- If one of the goals of the Arab Movement was to work "for the good of the human collectivity and its progress," why must Arabs oppose a Jewish state?

Proclamation of the State of Israel (1948)

To forestall Arab hostility and maintain political stability in the Middle East during the anticipated war with Germany in 1939, the British indicated that they would end the mandate over Palestine within ten years if possible and restricted Jewish immigration to the region. At this point, the Jews felt betrayed and Britain wanted out of the quicksand altogether.

At the end of the war in 1945, Britain announced its intention to leave Palestine and transferred the problem to the newly created United Nations. The UN passed a resolution to partition Palestine into independent Jewish and Arab states with Jerusalem becoming an international zone administered by the UN in permanent trusteeship. The Arabs were bitter that the new Jewish state would be given more than half the territory of Palestine, although the Jews constituted only a third of the population. The Arabs rejected the plan, and fighting broke out. Israel declared itself a sovereign state on May 14, 1948, in the following proclamation. The next day, Arab armies from Syria, Egypt, Lebanon, Transjordan, and Iraq attacked Israel. With their backs to the wall, the Israelis took advantage of their united command, forcing the Arab armies back and extending their control to 78 percent of the territory, more than it would have received under the UN plan. By mid-1949, Israel had concluded armistices with the demoralized Arab nations. This was a tenuous peace because no Arab state conceded Israel's right to exist.

The land of Israel was the birthplace of the Jewish people. Here their spiritual, religious and national identity was formed. Here they achieved independence and created a culture of national and universal significance. Here they wrote and gave the Bible to the world.

Exiled from Palestine, the Jewish people remained faithful to it in all the countries of their dispersion, never ceasing to pray and hope for their return and the restoration of their national freedom.

Impelled by this historic association, Jews strove throughout the centuries to go back to the land of their fathers and regain their statehood. In recent decades they returned in masses. They reclaimed the wilderness, revived their language, built cities and villages, and established a vigorous and ever-growing community, with its own economic and cultural life. They sought peace yet were prepared to defend themselves. They brought the blessing of progress to all inhabitants of the country.

In the year 1897, the First Zionist Congress, inspired by Theodor Herzl's vision of the Jewish State, proclaimed the right of the Jewish people to national revival in their own country.

This right was acknowledged by the Balfour Declaration of November 2, 1917, and reaffirmed by the Mandate of the League of Nations, which gave explicit international recognition to the historic connection of the Jewish people with Palestine and their right to reconstitute their National Home.

The Nazi holocaust, which engulfed millions of Jews in Europe, proved anew the urgency of the reestablishment of the Jewish State, which would solve the problem of Jewish homelessness by opening the gates to all Jews and lifting the Jewish people to equality in the family of nations.

"Proclamation of the State of Israel" is from *Foreign Relations of the United States, 1948. Volume V: The Near East, South Asia and Africa, Part 2* (Washington D.C.: United States Government Printing Office, 1976), pp. 976–978.

The survivors of the European catastrophe, as well as Jews from other lands, proclaiming their right to a life of dignity, freedom and labor, and undeterred by hazards, hardships and obstacles, have tried unceasingly to enter Palestine.

In the Second World War, the Jewish people in Palestine made a full contribution in the struggle of the freedom-loving nations against the Nazi evil. The sacrifices of their soldiers and the efforts of their workers gained them title to rank with the peoples who founded the United Nations.

On November 29, 1947, the General Assembly of the United Nations adopted a Resolution for the establishment of an independent Jewish State in Palestine, and called upon the inhabitants of the country to take such steps as may be necessary on their part to put the plan into effect.

This recognition by the United Nations of the right of the Jewish people to establish their independent State may not be revoked. It is, moreover, the self-evident right of the Jewish people to be a nation, as all other nations, in its own sovereign State.

ACCORDINGLY, WE, the members of the National council, representing the Jewish people in Palestine and the Zionist movement of the world, . . . by virtue of the natural and historic right of the Jewish people and of the Resolution of the General Assembly of the United Nations, HEREBY PROCLAIM the establishment of the Jewish State in Palestine, to be called ISRAEL. . .

We offer peace and unity to all the neighboring states and their peoples, and invite them to cooperate with the independent Jewish nation for the common good of all.

Our call goes out to the Jewish people all over the world to rally to our side in the task of immigration and development and to stand by us in the great struggle for the fulfillment of the dream of generations—the redemption of Israel.

CONSIDER THIS:

- On what bases does this proclamation justify the creation of the state of Israel?
- This proclamation advocated the "reestablishment" of the Jewish state as if Jews had once had a political homeland and had lost it. What is this passage referring to?
- Is this proclamation the realization of Theodor Herzl's dream for the establishment of a Jewish state? Is Zionism a positive or negative movement?
- This proclamation argued that it was the "self-evident right of the Jewish people to be a nation." In what way is this right "self-evident?" Why didn't the Palestinians have a "self- evident" right?

The Arab Revolution (1958)

GAMAL ABDEL NASSER

The war from 1948 to 1949 that followed Israel's declaration of sovereignty resulted in major population shifts. About 133,000 Arabs remained in the new state of Israel and became citizens while an estimated 600,000 to 750,000 fled the area. Most of these entered the West Bank territory that was under the control of Jordan, and the rest went south to the Gaza Strip, occupied by Egypt in 1949, and to other Arab states, especially Syria and Lebanon. These Palestinians, with their political aspirations dashed, wandered the landscape as refugees, often trying to establish their

"The Arab Revolution" is from *President Gamal Abdel-Nasser's Speeches and Press-Interviews*, March 9, 1958 (Cairo: United Arab Republic Information Department, 1958), pp. 95–98.

lives in states that, although Arab, were not always receptive to a new population competing for jobs and economic relief. The Palestinian exodus was paralleled by an influx of 500,000 Jews into Israel from Arab states and war-torn Europe. Many Palestinians ended up in refugee camps run by the United Nations where, in their poverty and unemployment, they kept alive a sense of national identity that would later find expression in political associations like the Palestine Liberation Organization (PLO).

Perhaps the most demonstrative advocate of Arab nationalism was Gamal Abdel Nasser (1918–1970). The son of a postal clerk, Nasser was active in student demonstrations against British control of Egypt in 1935. He led the 1952 Egyptian revolution that ousted the corrupt King Farouk, and he became president of Egypt in 1954. But Nasser did not become a popular and charismatic leader in the international arena until the Suez crisis of 1956, when he defied Britain and France by nationalizing the Suez Canal and defending it against counterattack. This event was of seminal importance in the world's eyes because it revealed weaknesses in the exhausted European imperial powers and underscored the possibilities of Arab nationalism. In fact, Nasser saw himself as the international spokesman for Arab liberation and envisioned a united Arab state. But domestic difficulties and his aggressive confrontation with Israel in 1967 constrained his potential. The following speech on the Suez Canal incident and his vision of Arab unity testify to his dominant will and influence on Arab nationalism.

This, my dear brethren, was the great conspiracy carried out by imperialism at the outbreak of World War I. The forces of imperialism allied themselves then with the Arab people in order to have them stage a revolution, and when the Arab revolution broke out during the First World War, it called for the liberation of the Arab peoples and allied itself with imperialism and with Britain. But has Britain been true to the promises it made to the Arab peoples? Have the Arab people been able to achieve their liberty and independence? . . . Britain did not fulfill its promises. Furthermore, the whole region was divided between Britain and France. Britain failed its allies and carried out the Balfour Declaration by giving Palestine to the Zionists thus establishing the national home they craved. Having reached this stage in their experience with the imperialist powers, the Arab people became convinced, that if they really wanted freedom, they should depend only on themselves and their own strength and not on any alliance with imperialism or with Britain. . . . The fact is, imperialism does not want us to be strong or to be united. If we really want freedom and independence, we must depend on ourselves alone. We must learn our lessons from the past and know that any alliance with imperialism results in weakness, despotism, and occupation. . . .

The revolution in Egypt was launched in 1952, and we all proclaimed that it had a vital scope that included the whole Arab area. . . . This, my dear brethren, is the true Arab revolution which depends solely on the Arab peoples in every Arab country. This is the revolution which believed in you—you, the Arab peoples in every Arab country as well as elsewhere. This is the revolution which refused to join any foreign or imperialist alliances to achieve its freedom, for freedom stands in open contradiction to imperialism which can only imply slavery. This is the revolution which depended first on God and then on the Arab peoples everywhere. It rose to fight Zionism, to fight imperialism and its agents.

This is the revolution we can pride ourselves on and say that it grew up in our soil, from our blood and from our hearts, the revolution that expressed Arab feelings and aspirations. This is the revolution which has suffered no contamination because it firmly believed in God, and in the Arab people everywhere. These beliefs it considered were the power which could defeat the navies and land forces of the Big Powers. You remember, my brethren, how at Port-Said, when we were besieged by the Big Powers [Suez Canal crisis of 1956], you rose from Syria, Lebanon and practically every Arab country to support your brethren in Egypt. Our unity of heart succeeded in defeating their naval forces, in destroying the Big Powers, and causing them to slide down to rank among second-class powers. God willing, our unity will never suffer any weakness. No power in the world can drive us apart. They may succeed in raising artificial partitions or boundaries, they may succeed in winning over some agents in the area, but they cannot reach those hearts who firmly believed in their right to freedom and independence, those hearts that believed that their unity was the only way to strength. They may succeed in having agents in the Arab fatherland, but they will never succeed in suppressing the feelings of the Arab peoples.

CONSIDER THIS:

- According to Nasser, to be independent, what must the Arabs do?
- Nasser states that the Arab revolution rose "to fight Zionism, to fight imperialism and its agents." Is Zionism an imperialistic philosophy? Who are the "agents" Nasser mentions? Who are the "Big Powers"?

THE BROADER PERSPECTIVE:

- After Nasser's death in 1970, several politicians from the Middle East tried to assume leadership of a pan-Arab movement, among them Anwar Sadat of Egypt and Saddam Hussein of Iraq. Why is it so difficult to lay claim to Arab leadership? Was such political leadership a goal of Osama bin Laden's terrorist attacks against the United States in 2001? Or was his focus limited to the cultivation of Islamic religious unity?

The Cold War (1945–1990)

The "Superpower" Rivalry

Whether you like it or not, history is on our side. We will bury you.

—NIKITA KHRUSHCHEV

History teaches us that enmities between nations . . . do not last forever. However fixed our likes and dislikes, the tide of time and events will often bring surprising changes in the relations between nations and neighbors.

—JOHN F. KENNEDY

The term *Cold War* describes the era of uneasy relations between the Western Allies and the Soviet Union after World War II from 1945 to about 1990. Each was competing for influence in Europe through propaganda and troop placement. In the first excerpt, the Soviet leader Joseph Stalin offered a glimpse of the ideological combat that was to be waged in the future. A month later, Winston Churchill, who had largely directed the British war effort, warned the West of the deceptive Soviet Union in his famous Iron Curtain speech.

The Soviet Victory: Capitalism Versus Communism (February 1946)

JOSEPH STALIN

It would be wrong to believe that the Second World War broke out accidentally or as a result of the mistakes of some or other statesmen, though mistakes certainly were made. In reality, the war broke out as an inevitable result of the development of world economic and political forces on the basis of modern monopoly capitalism.

Marxists have stated more than once that the capitalist system of world economy conceals in itself the elements of general crisis and military clashes, that in view of this in our time the development of world capitalism takes place not as a smooth and even advance but through crises and war catastrophes.

The reason is that the unevenness of the development of capitalist countries usually results, as time passes, in an abrupt disruption of the equilibrium within the world system of capitalism, and that a group of capitalist countries which believes itself to be less supplied with raw materials and markets usually attempts to alter the situation and re-divide the "spheres of influence" in its own favor by means of armed force. . . . This results in the splitting of the capitalist world into two hostile camps and in war between them.

Perhaps the catastrophes of war could be avoided if there existed the possibility of re-distributing periodically raw materials and markets among the countries in accordance with their economic weight—by means of adopting coordinated and peaceful decisions. This, however, cannot be accomplished under present capitalist conditions of the development of world economy. . . .

As to our country, for her the war was the severest and hardest of all the wars our Motherland has ever experienced in her history. But the war was not only a curse. It was at the same time a great school in which all the forces of the people were tried and tested. The war laid bare all the facts and events in the rear and at the front, it mercilessly tore off all the veils and covers which had concealed the true faces of States, governments, and parties, and placed them on the stage without masks, without embellishments, with all their shortcomings and virtues.

And so, what are the results of the war?. . .

Our victory means, in the first place, that our Soviet social system has won, that the Soviet social system successfully withstood the trial in the flames of war and proved its perfect viability.

It is well known that the foreign press more than once asserted that the Soviet social system is a "risky experiment" doomed to failure, that the Soviet system is a "house of cards," without any roots in life, imposed upon the people by the organs of the "Cheka" [secret police], that a slight push from outside would be enough to blow this "house of cards" to smithereens.

Now we can say that the war swept away all these assertions of the foreign press as groundless. The war has shown that the Soviet social system is a truly popular system, which has grown from the people and enjoys its powerful support, that the Soviet social system is a perfectly viable and stable form of organization of society.

More than that, the point is now not whether the Soviet social system is viable or not, since after the objective lessons of the war no single skeptic now ventures to come out with doubts concerning the viability of the Soviet social system. The point now is that the

"The Soviet Victory" is from Embassy of the U.S.S.R., Speech Delivered by J. V. Stalin at a Meeting of Voters of the Stalin Electoral Area of Moscow (Washington, D.C.: Government Printing Office, 1946).

Soviet social system has proved more viable and stable than a non-Soviet social system, that the Soviet social system is a better form of organization of society than any non-Soviet social system.

CONSIDER THIS:

- According to Stalin, what did the Russian victory in World War II mean for the future of the Soviet system? What kind of "Soviet victory" was this?

"An Iron Curtain Has Descended Across the Continent" (March 1946)

SIR WINSTON CHURCHILL

I now come to the . . . danger which threatens the cottage home and ordinary people, namely tyranny. We cannot be blind to the fact that the liberties enjoyed by individual citizens throughout the United States and British Empire are not valid in a considerable number of countries, some of which are very powerful. In these states control is forced upon the common people by various kinds of all-embracing police governments, to a degree which is overwhelming and contrary to every principle of democracy. The power of the state is exercised without restraint, either by dictators or by compact oligarchies operating through a privileged party and a political police. It is not our duty at this time, when difficulties are so numerous, to interfere forcibly in the internal affairs of countries whom we have not conquered in war, but we must never cease to proclaim in fearless tones the great principles of freedom and the rights of man, which are the joint inheritance of the English-speaking world and which, through Magna Carta, the Bill of Rights, the habeas corpus, trial by jury, and the English common law find their famous expression in the Declaration of Independence. . . .

A shadow has fallen upon the scenes so lately lighted by the Allied victory. Nobody knows what Soviet Russia and its Communist international organization intends to do in the immediate future, or what are the limits, if any, to their expansive and proselytizing tendencies. . . . From Stettin in the Baltic to Trieste in the Adriatic, an iron curtain has descended across the continent. Behind that line lie all the capitals of the ancient states of central and eastern Europe. Warsaw, Berlin, Prague, Vienna, Budapest, Belgrade, Bucharest, and Sofia, all these famous cities and the populations around them lie in the Soviet sphere and all are subject, in one form or another, not only to Soviet influence but to a very high and increasing measure of control from Moscow. Athens alone, with its immortal glories, is free to decide its future at an election under British, American, and French observation.

In a great number of countries, far from the Russian frontiers and throughout the world, Communist fifth columns are established and work in complete unity and absolute obedience to the directions they receive from the Communist center. Except in the British Commonwealth, and in the United States, where communism is in its infancy, the Communist parties and fifth columns constitute a growing challenge and peril to Christian civilization. These are somber facts for anyone to have to recite on the morrow of a victory gained by so much splendid comradeship in arms and in the cause of freedom and democracy, and we

"'An Iron Curtain Has Descended Across the Continent'" is from *Congressional Record*, 79th Congress, 2nd session, pp. A1145–A1147.

should be most unwise not to face them squarely while time remains. . . .

On the other hand, I repulse the idea that a new war is inevitable, still more that it is imminent. It is because I am so sure that our fortunes are in our own hands and that we hold the power to save the future, that I feel the duty to speak out now that I have occasion to do so. I do not believe that Soviet Russia desires war. What they desire is the fruits of war and the indefinite expansion of their power and doctrines. But what we have to consider here today while time remains, is the permanent prevention of war and the establishment of conditions of freedom and democracy as rapidly as possible in all countries.

Our difficulties and dangers will not be removed by closing our eyes to them; they will not be removed by mere waiting to see what happens; nor will they be relieved by a policy of appeasement. What is needed is a settlement, and the longer this is delayed, the more difficult it will be and the greater our dangers will become. From what I have seen of our Russian friends and allies during the war, I am convinced that there is nothing they admire so much as strength, and there is nothing for which they have less respect than for military weakness. For that reason the old doctrine of a balance of power is unsound. We cannot afford, if we can help it, to work on narrow margins, offering temptations to a trial of strength. If the western democracies stand together in strict adherence to the principles of the United Nations Charter, their influence for furthering these principles will be immense and no one is likely to molest them. If, however, they become divided or falter in their duty, and if these all-important years are allowed to slip away, then indeed catastrophe may overwhelm us all.

Consider This:

- What policy was Churchill advocating in his Iron Curtain speech? Was he pessimistic or optimistic about the possibility of war?

The Truman Doctrine (March 1947)

HARRY S. TRUMAN

In the first months of 1946, President Truman received urgent requests from the Greek government for economic assistance, which, it was hoped, would put an end to the chaos and strife hindering its recovery from the war. Hoping to forestall communist dissidents who were threatening the stability of the government, Truman appealed to Congress to appropriate such financial assistance. He also asked for military as well as economic aid to Turkey. The controversial Truman Doctrine, as it came to be called, committed the United States to an active policy of promoting ideological divisions between it and the Soviet Union, and it further escalated Cold War tensions.

One of the primary objectives of the foreign policy of the United States is the creation of conditions in which we and other nations will be able to work out a way of life free from coercion. This was a fundamental issue in the war with Germany and Japan. Our victory was won over countries which sought to impose their will, and their way of life, upon other nations.

To ensure the peaceful development of nations, free from coercion, the United States

"The Truman Doctrine" is from *Public Papers of the President*, Harry S. Truman, 1947 (Washington, D.C.: Government Printing Office, 1963), pp. 177–180.

has taken a leading part in establishing the United Nations. The United Nations is designed to make possible lasting freedom and independence for all its members. We shall not realize our objectives, however, unless we are willing to help free peoples to maintain their free institutions and their national integrity against aggressive movements that seek to impose upon them totalitarian regimes. This is no more than a frank recognition that totalitarian regimes imposed upon free peoples, by direct or indirect aggression, undermine the foundations of international peace and hence the security of the United States.

The peoples of a number of countries of the world have recently had totalitarian regimes forced upon them against their will. The Government of the United States has made frequent protests against coercion and intimidation, in violation of the Yalta agreement, in Poland, Rumania, and Bulgaria. I must also state that in a number of other countries there have been similar developments.

At the present moment in world history nearly every nation must choose between alternative ways of life. The choice is too often not a free one.

One way of life is based upon the will of the majority, and is distinguished by free institutions, representative government, free elections, guarantees of individual liberty, freedom of speech and religion, and freedom from political oppression.

The second way of life is based upon the will of a minority forcibly imposed upon the majority. It relies upon terror and oppression, a controlled press and radio, fixed elections, and the suppression of personal freedoms.

I believe that it must be the policy of the United States to support free peoples who are resisting attempted subjugation by armed minorities or by outside pressures.

I believe that we must assist free peoples to work out their own destinies in their own way.

I believe that our help should be primarily through economic and financial aid which is essential to economic stability and orderly political processes.

The world is not static, and the status quo is not sacred. But we cannot allow changes in the status quo in violation of the Charter of the United Nations by such methods as coercion, or by such subterfuges as political infiltration. In helping free and independent nations to maintain their freedom, the United States will be giving effect to the principles of the Charter of the United Nations. . . .

The seeds of totalitarian regimes are nurtured by misery and want. They spread and grow in the evil soil of poverty and strife. They reach their full growth when the hope of a people for a better life has died.

We must keep that hope alive.

The free peoples of the world look to us for support in maintaining their freedoms.

If we falter in our leadership, we may endanger the peace of the world—and we shall surely endanger the welfare of this Nation.

Great responsibilities have been placed upon us by the swift movement of events.

I am confident that the Congress will face these responsibilities squarely.

CONSIDER THIS:

- Winston Churchill once said, "I do not believe that Soviet Russia desires war. What it desires is the fruits of war and the indefinite expansion of their power and doctrines." Do you think he was right?

- How would you define the Truman Doctrine? In a sense, was it an "ideological declaration of war" against a legitimate Soviet threat to the values and political security of the Western world?

THE BROADER PERSPECTIVE:

- The Truman Doctrine championed political freedom in response to the totalitarian threat posed by the Soviet Union. But hadn't the Untied States just defeated the fascist threat to freedom with the help of the Soviet Union? How did two allies in the war to vanquish the evil of despotism so quickly become enemies?

■ How difficult is it for a government to refashion the public perception of good and evil? Do we define our friends and enemies on the basis of short-term expediency or compatible ideology? If the United States stands for the values of freedom and independence described in the Truman Doctrine, why did we often support right-wing dictatorships in Latin America, Iran, Iraq, and the Philippines during the height of the Cold War? What does this say about ideology and the complexities and inconsistencies of foreign policy?

An Assessment of Communism (1953)

THEODORE WHITE

Distrust and tension between the United States and the Soviet Union continued to mount in 1948 as the Russians stopped all traffic, including food transports, through their zone of German occupation to the Western-occupied sector of Berlin. From June 1948 to May 1949, the United States airlifted supplies to the people of Allied-controlled Berlin and defied Soviet heavy-handedness. This tenacious policy in the face of Soviet aggression was termed *containment*. By 1950, it was natural to begin assessing the events that had transpired during the first half of the century and to speculate on developments for the future. In 1953, the Soviet leader Joseph Stalin died, and many wondered how this might change the face of communism and subsequently the nature of the Cold War. Theodore White, a journalist who had spent much of his early career in China and became famous for his political analysis of the presidency, offered this view of communism in 1953.

Americans are so frightened by the evil in communism that they fail to see that the greatest danger is not the evil but the attraction in it. Only Americans live in a society in which communism can seduce no healthy mind. Most of our senior Allies and the myriad-man countries who live outside our Alliance are made of people who stand transfixed by fear of communism and its sinister charm at the same time.

The magic appeal in the Communist faith is simple. It is the belief that pure logic applied to human affairs is enough to change the world and cure it of all its human miseries. It is buttressed by the belief that the processes of history are governed by certain "scientific" laws, which automatically guarantee the triumph of communism when the situation is ripe, if only its protestants have the courage to strike and act.

This simple credo carries an almost irresistible attraction to two kinds of people everywhere in the world: first, to small coteries of able and ambitious young men hungry for the ecstasy of leadership, and, secondly, to larger masses of ignorant people who have just begun to hope.

To both these schools of converts, the fatal flaw in the Communist faith is neither apparent nor important. This fatal flaw is embedded in the nature of human beings whenever they gather politically. Human beings tend to be illogical. The logic of which communism boasts is never certain, therefore, of success in any political operation unless simultaneously it imposes so rigid a discipline as to make ordinary people mere bodies in the sequence of their masters' planning. Logic cannot succeed if its premises are to be shaken over and over again by vagrant human emotions allowed freely to express themselves in all their passion and frailty. Any political organization which sets out to be totally logical thus calls for total discipline; total discipline inevitably requires police, and police bring terror.

"An Assessment of Communism" is from Theodore H. White, *Fire in the Ashes* (New York: William Sloane Associates Publishers, 1953), pp. 318–320.

But the weakness of communism lies less in the calculated immorality of terror than in the inevitable internal appetite of the discipline. The discipline feeds on itself; it shrinks the area of discussion and decision into ever narrower, ever tighter, ever more cramped circles. Fewer and fewer men have less and less access to the raw facts which are necessary for wise judgment. The discipline they control and impose inevitably sneaks back to weaken them, to blind or deafen them into stupidity and error.

To those who come to communism out of ambition or out of misguided intelligence, this flaw is not immediately apparent. Each of this type of convert cherishes the illusion until too late that the ever-shrinking circle of discipline will leave him safe at its center of creative leadership, rather than crushed and tortured as discipline contracts about his own soft human body. To the second category of converts, those who come to it out of hunger and ignorance, this flaw in communism (even if it could be explained to them) seems unimportant. They have always been excluded from decision and control over their own lives. Communism promises them simply "more"; they are ready to believe. The hungrier and more ignorant they are, the more difficult it is to explain to them that their own hopes and welfare are directly dependent on the freedom of creative minds, with which they are unfamiliar, to think independently of all discipline.

To the Western world, so challenged by communism, this flaw in the adversary presents a grotesque problem. Communism's prison-logical system of human organization grows in strength decade by decade even as its leadership becomes less and less capable of wise and sensible decision. For all its dynamism and strength, the Communist world falls into blunders with increasing frequency, blunders which are only rectified by great wrenchings of policy that shake the world with disaster. To deal with communism, one must recognize both its strength and its blunders clearly. . . .

Such an event as the death of Stalin, by shaking the superstructure of discipline, by admitting for a brief moment the clash of several opinions and the consequent opportunity for a slightly larger area of discussion at the summit, has given the Communist machinery of politics a momentary opportunity to review some of its errors. But, unless communism ceases to be communism, the process of discipline calls for a new tightening of control, a new struggle to apply the logic of a single man to a world of dark and uncertain phenomena.

CONSIDER THIS:

- According to Theodore White, what two kinds of people "everywhere in the world" are attracted to communism? Why?

- What is the "fatal flaw" inherent in the "Communist faith?" Is communism really governed by "scientific laws" or does it only promise "pure logic" to illogical human beings?

How to Spot a Communist (1955)

By the mid-1950s, the ideological and political polarization between capitalist and communist countries had become institutionalized. The world was an open battlefield in the contest for the hearts and minds of the masses. Complex concepts were simplified and distorted by government propaganda mills to create so-called "truth"

"How to Spot a Communist" was first issued by First Army Headquarters in a pamphlet entitled *How to Spot a Communist.* It was reprinted by *U.S.A., An American Magazine of Fact and Opinion*, in a special supplement on June 22, 1955. Copyright © 1955 by U.S.A. Contained in Anthony Bouscaren, ed., *A Guide to Anti-Communist Action* (Chicago: Henry Regnery Company, 1958), pp. 174–185.

and revise it to suit the needs of the moment. The gray area between the moral absolutes of good and evil, of freedom and tyranny that beckoned to rational thinkers was a dangerous no-man's-land of unappreciated dissent. Activists were often denounced as unpatriotic and suspect—blacklisted in McCarthyist purges or relegated to the Soviet prison system in Siberia known as the Gulag. Many in the United States and the Soviet Union grew disillusioned with the "self-evident" freedoms of democracy or the "pure Marxist vision" that had degenerated into Cold War paranoia.

The following article was issued by the U.S. First Army Headquarters for public dissemination and reveals this Cold War paranoia that was so much a part of the decade of the 1950s.

Events of recent years have made it obvious that there is no fool-proof way of detecting a Communist. The Communist individual is no longer a "type" exemplified by the bearded and coarse revolutionary with time bomb in briefcase. U.S. Communists come from all walks in life, profess all faiths, and exercise all trades and professions. In addition, the Communist Party, USA, has made concerted efforts to go underground for the purpose of infiltration.

If there is no fool-proof system in spotting a Communist, there are, fortunately, indications that may give him away. These indications are often subtle but always present, for the Communist, by reason of his "faith," must act and talk along certain lines.

While a certain heaviness of style and preference for long sentences is common to most Communist writing, a distinct vocabulary provides the . . . more easily recognized feature of the "Communist Language."

Even a superficial reading of an article written by a Communist or a conversation with one will probably reveal the use of some of the following expressions: integrative thinking, vanguard, comrade, hootenanny, chauvinism, book-burning, syncretistic faith, bourgeois-nationalism, jingoism, colonialism, hooliganism, ruling class, progressive, demagogy, dialectical, witch-hunt, reactionary, exploitation, oppressive, materialist.

This list, selected at random, could be extended almost indefinitely. While all of the above expressions are part of the English language, their use by Communists is infinitely more frequent than by the general public. . . .

The tell-tale signs of the "Communist Religion" are not easy to detect. There is, above all, a rigidity in views insofar as they pertain to the Communist doctrine. This is not to say that the Communist lacks persuasiveness or variety of expression. It does mean, however, that he will stubbornly cling to the "line" even when proven wrong in debate. The Communist has implicit faith in Marxist philosophy and in the truth of the "line" as transmitted from Moscow. Because of this faith, he cannot and will not give ground when challenged on basic Marxist issues or political pronouncements made by his leaders. The possibility of compromising on these issues is utterly beyond his comprehension. . . .

His "religion," then, can give away the Communist. His naive and unquestioning acceptance of the "line," his refusal to accept criticism are excellent indications. Last but not least, the Communist feels a strong compulsion to speak his "faith" and can frequently be spotted by his never-ceasing attempts at conversion of others.

The "Communist Logic". . . is diametrically opposed to our own. Thus, the Communist refers to the iron curtain police states as "democracies," and any defensive move on the part of the Western powers is condemned as "aggression." The Communist thus builds for himself a topsy-turvy world with a completely distorted set of values. For this reason, it is practically impossible to win an argument with a hard-core Communist. . . . The Communist mind cannot and will not engage in a detached examination of ideas. Talking to a Communist about his own ideas, then, is like listening to a phonograph record. His answers will invariably follow a definite pattern because he can never admit, even hypothetically, that the basis for his ideas may not be sound. This attitude is typical not only for the individual but also on a national scale. . . . The answer is final and no arguments are permitted so far as the Communists are concerned. The Communist, then, is not really "logical." The finality of his arguments and the completeness of his condemnation marks him clearly, whether as a speaker, a writer or a conversation partner.

In addition to these very general principles common to Communist tactics, a number of specific issues have been part of the Communist arsenal for a long period of time. These issues are raised not only by Communist appeals to the public, but also by the individual Party member or sympathizer who is a product of his Communist environment. They include: "McCarthyism," violation of civil rights, racial or religious discrimination, immigration laws, anti-subversive legislation, any legislation concerning labor unions, the military budget, "peace."

While showing standard opposition to certain standard issues, the U.S. Communist has traditionally identified himself with certain activities in the hope of furthering his ultimate purposes. Such hobbies as "folk dancing" and "folk music" have been traditionally allied with the Communist movement in the United States. . . . The reason for their choice [of hobbies] is not altogether an attempt to hide political activities. The Communist's fondness for everything that comes from "the people" is not an entirely theoretical preference and has found expression in his everyday life. Most Communists are likely to show preference for group activities rather than such bourgeois forms of recreation as ballroom dancing. . . .

A study such as this can lead to only one certain conclusion: There is no sure-fire way of spotting a Communist. . . . The principle difficulty involved is the distinction between the person who merely dissents in the good old American tradition and the one who condemns for the purpose of abolishing that tradition.

In attempting to find the answer to the question: "Is this man a Communist?" a check-list such as this can prove helpful, although in itself it cannot provide the answer:

- Does the individual use unusual language? ("Communist Language")
- Does he stubbornly cling to Marxist ideals without being willing to question them?
- Does he condemn our American institutions and praise those of Communist countries?
- Does he pick on any event, even the most insignificant occurrences in this country for his criticism?
- Is he secretive about certain of his contacts?
- Does he belong to groups exploiting controversial subjects?

Above all, the approach to the problem of discovering Communists must be detached and completely free from prejudice. Using some of the clues mentioned in this study in connection with a factual approach provides the best system at present of spotting a Communist.

CONSIDER THIS:

- After analyzing this selection, what do you consider to be its most and least effective arguments? Just how do you spot a communist? How do vocabulary, logic, and religion easily give away him away?

- Do you find any hypocrisy in this document? Is it a public service message or an example of "capitalist propaganda?"

"The Victory of Communism Is Inevitable": Speech to the 22nd Communist Party Congress (1962)

NIKITA KHRUSHCHEV

Although there may have been hope that the fears of the Cold War would be reduced, the decade from 1955 to 1966 was especially intense in its rhetoric and ideological conflict. As Khrushchev menacingly said of capitalist states in 1956, "Whether you like it or not, history is on our side. We will bury you!" This was the era of Senator Joseph McCarthy, who played on the fears of Americans with his deceitful rantings that communists had infiltrated the highest echelons of government. It was during this time (1961) that the Berlin Wall was built, sealing off the city into communist and democratic sectors—a symbolic as well as practical measure. And finally in 1962, the two superpowers nearly went to nuclear war as President Kennedy demanded the removal of Soviet missiles from Cuba. The following excerpt is from Khrushchev's speech to the 22nd Congress of the Communist Party. Note the argument carefully.

The most rabid imperialists, acting on the principle of "after us the deluge," openly voice their desire to undertake a new war venture. The ideologists of imperialism, intimidating the peoples, try to instill a kind of philosophy of hopelessness and desperation. Hysterically they cry: "Better death under capitalism than life under communism." They do not like free peoples to flourish, you see. They fear that the peoples in their countries too will take the path of socialism. Blinded by class hatred, our enemies are ready to doom all mankind to the catastrophe of war. The imperialists' opportunities to carry out their aggressive designs, however, are becoming smaller and smaller. They behave like a feeble and greedy old man whose powers have been exhausted, whose physical capacity has weakened, but whose avid desires remain. . . .

As long as the imperialist aggressors exist, we must be on guard, keep our powder dry, improve the defense of the socialist countries, their armed forces and the state security agencies. If, in the face of common sense, the imperialists dare attack the socialist countries and plunge mankind into the abyss of a world war of annihilation, this mad act of theirs would be their last, it would be the end of the whole system of capitalism. (*Applause.*)

Our party clearly understands its tasks, its responsibility, and will do everything in its power to see to it that the world socialist system continues to grow stronger, gathers fresh strength and develops. We believe that in the competition with capitalism socialism will win. (*Prolonged applause.*) We believe that this victory will be won in peaceful competition and not by way of unleashing a war. We have stood, we stand and we will stand by the positions of peaceful competition of states with different social systems; we will do everything to strengthen world peace. (*Prolonged applause.*)

The most important component of our party's foreign policy activities is *the struggle for general and complete disarmament*. The Soviet Union has been waging this struggle for many years now, and doing so firmly and perseveringly. We have always been resolutely opposed to the arms race, since rivalry in this

"Speech to the 22nd Communist Party Congress" is from *Current Soviet Policies*, IV (New York, 1962), pp. 44–45, 50, 77. Reprinted by permission of *The Current Digest*.

sphere in the past not only saddled the peoples with a terrible burden but inevitably led to world wars. We are even more resolutely opposed to the arms race now that there has been a colossal technical revolution in the art of war and the use of today's weapons would inevitably entail the deaths of hundreds of millions of people.

The stockpiling of these weapons, proceeding as it is in a setting of cold war and war hysteria, is fraught with disastrous consequences. All that has to happen is for the nerves of some fellow in uniform to crack while he is on duty at a "push-button" somewhere in the West, and things may happen that will bring more than a little misfortune upon the peoples of the whole world.

Naturally, when we put forward a program of general and complete disarmament, we are talking not about the unilateral disarmament of socialism in the face of imperialism or vice versa, but about universal renunciation of arms as a means of solving problems at issue among states. . . .

The example of the Soviet Union inspires all progressive mankind. Never has the great vital force of Marxist-Leninist teaching been so clearly evident as in our days, now that socialism has triumphed fully and finally in the Soviet Union, the cause of socialism is winning new victories in the countries of the world socialist commonwealth, and the international Communist and workers' movement and the national liberation struggle of peoples are growing and expanding tempestuously.

The revolution awakened the great energy of peoples, which is transforming the world on the principles of socialism and communism. Colossal changes are taking place and will take place throughout the world under the influence of the successes of communism.

The victory of communism is inevitable! (*Stormy applause.*)

The great army of Communists and of Marxist-Leninists acts as the vanguard of the peoples in the struggle for peace, for social progress and for communism, the bright future of mankind. New and ever newer millions of people will assemble and rally under the great banner of communism. The cause of progress, the cause of communism will triumph! (*Stormy applause.*)

Long live the great and heroic Soviet people, the builders of communism! (*Stormy applause.*)

Long live the indestructible unity and fraternal friendship of the peoples of the world socialist camp! (*Stormy applause.*)

Long live the heroic party of the Communists of the Soviet Union, created and tempered in struggle by the great Lenin! (*Stormy applause.*)

Long live the indestructible unity of the international Communist and workers' movement and the fraternal solidarity of the proletarians of all countries! (*Stormy applause.*)

Long live peace the world over! (*Stormy applause.*)

Under the all-conquering banner of Marxism-Leninism, under the leadership of the Communist Party, forward to the victory of communism! (*Stormy, prolonged applause, turning into an ovation. All rise.*)

CONSIDER THIS:

- What are the main points about capitalism and communism that Khrushchev stressed in his speech to the 22nd Communist Party Congress?

- Khrushchev characterized the Soviet Union as an unwilling participant in the arms race, a true advocate of "complete disarmament." And yet the USSR was willing to deploy nuclear missiles in Cuba. Why was he so confident that the "example of the Soviet Union inspires all progressive mankind" and that the "victory of communism is inevitable?" After analyzing this document, do you agree or disagree with Theodore White's assessment of communism on pages 467–468.

THEME: THE POWER STRUCTURE

Against the Grain

Dissent in the "Evil Empire"

Russia is doomed to be governed by fools; she knows no other way.

—Alexander Solzhenitsyn

The autopsy of history is that all great nations commit suicide.

—Arnold Toynbee

During the early 1970s, the Soviet Union and United States, under the leadership of Leonid Brezhnev and Richard Nixon, respectively, demonstrated cooperation through cultural exchanges and even negotiated a Strategic Arms Limitation Treaty (SALT) in 1972. This policy of détente, as it was called, was a hopeful sign that the world was becoming a safer place. But internally, the Soviet Union continued to stifle dissent in an effort to preserve the integrity of its image as a united and stable state, proof of the success and superiority of the communist philosophy.

The next selection is from the dissident writer Alexander Solzhenitsyn. A winner of the Nobel Prize for Literature in 1970, his fame was secured by his book *The Gulag Archipelago* (1973), which examined the brutal Soviet prison system in Siberia. Exiled in 1974, Solzhenitsyn commanded international recognition and focused concern on the inadequacies and repression of Soviet society.

Keep in Mind . . .

- What were the specific criticisms of Solzhenitsyn in his 1974 dissent against the policies of the Soviet Union?

"What Have You to Fear?" (1974)

ALEXANDER I. SOLZHENITSYN

But what about us? Us, with our unwieldiness and our inertia, with our flinching and inability to change even a single letter, a single syllable, of what Marx said in 1848 about industrial development? Economically and physically we are perfectly capable of saving ourselves. But there is a road block on the path to our salvation—the sole Progressive World View. If we renounce industrial development, what about the working class, socialism, Communism, unlimited increase in productivity and all the rest? Marx is not to be corrected, that's revisionism. . . .

But you are already being called "revisionists" anyway, whatever you may do in the future. So wouldn't it be better to do your duty soberly, responsibly and firmly, and give up the dead letter for the sake of a living people who

"'What Have You to Fear?'" is an excerpt from Alexander I. Solzhenitsyn, *Letter to the Soviet Leaders* (New York, 1974), pp. 25–26, 41–43, 56–58.

are utterly dependent on your power and your decisions? And you must do it without delay. Why dawdle if we shall have to snap out of it sometime anyway? Why repeat what others have done and loop the agonizing loop right to the end, when we are not too far into it to turn back? If the man at the head of the column cries, "I have lost my way," do we absolutely have to plow right on to the spot where he realized his mistake and only there turn back? Why not turn and start on the right course from wherever we happen to be?. . .

This Ideology [Marxism] that fell to us by inheritance is not only decrepit and hopelessly antiquated now; even during its best decades it was totally mistaken in its predictions and was never a science.

A primitive, superficial economic theory, it declared that only the worker creates value and failed to take into account the contribution of either organizers, engineers, transportation or marketing systems. It was mistaken when it forecast that the proletariat would be endlessly oppressed and would never achieve anything in a bourgeois democracy—if only we could shower people with as much food, clothing and leisure as they have gained under capitalism! It missed the point when it asserted that the prosperity of the European countries depended on their colonies—it was only after they had shaken the colonies off that they began to accomplish their "economic miracles." It was mistaken through and through in its prediction that socialists could never come to power except through an armed uprising. It miscalculated in thinking that the first uprisings would take place in the advanced industrial countries—quite the reverse. And the picture of how the whole world would rapidly be overtaken by revolutions and how states would soon wither away was sheer delusion, sheer ignorance of human nature. And as for wars being characteristic of capitalism alone and coming to an end when capitalism did—we have already witnessed the longest war of the twentieth century so far, and it was not capitalism that rejected negotiations and a truce for fifteen to twenty years; and God forbid that we should witness the bloodiest and most brutal of all mankind's wars—a war between two Communist superpowers. Then there was nationalism, which this theory also buried in 1848 as a "survival"—but find a stronger force in the world today! And it's the same with many other things too boring to list.

Marxism is not only not accurate, is not only not a science, has not only failed to predict *a single event* in terms of figures, quantities, time-scales or locations. . . —it absolutely astounds one by the economic and mechanistic crudity of its attempts to explain that most subtle of creatures, the human being, and that even more complex synthesis of millions of people, society. Only the cupidity of some, the blindness of others and a craving for *faith* on the part of others can serve to explain this grim jest of the twentieth century: how can such a discredited and bankrupt doctrine still have so many followers in the West! In *our* country are left the fewest of all! We who have had a taste of it are only pretending willy-nilly. . . .

"How can such a discredited and bankrupt doctrine still have so many followers in the West! In *our* country are left the fewest of all! We who have had a taste of it are only pretending willy-nilly. . . ."
— ALEXANDER I. SOLZHENITSYN

So that the country and people do not suffocate, and so that they all have the chance to develop and enrich us with ideas, allow competition on an equal and honorable basis—not for power, but for truth—between all ideological and moral currents, in particular between *all religions*. . . . Allow us a free art and literature, the free publication not just of political books—God preserve us!—and exhortations and election leaflets; allow us philosophical, ethical, economic and social studies, and you will see what a rich harvest it brings and how it bears fruit—for the good of Russia. . . .

What have you to fear? Is the idea really so terrible? Are you really so unsure of yourselves? You will still have absolute and impregnable power, a separate, strong and exclusive Party, the army, the police force, industry, transportation, communications, mineral wealth, a monopoly of foreign trade, an artificial rate of exchange for the ruble—but let the people breathe, let them think and develop! If you belong to the people heart and soul, there can be nothing to hold you back!

After all, does the human heart not still feel the need to atone for the past?

Your dearest wish is for our state structure and our ideological system never to change, to remain as they are for centuries. But history is not like that. Every system either finds a way to develop or else collapses.

THE BROADER PERSPECTIVE:

- In this source, Solzhenitsyn accuses Soviet authorities of being insecure in their authority and afraid to face the threat to their power that political restructuring and an open attitude would bring. Is ideology the culprit here? Must governments based on a strict ideology resist all change as a threat to truth?

- Solzhenitsyn argued that "every system either finds a way to develop or else collapses." Do you think this is true? Can you give any contemporary examples?

"A World Turned Upside Down!": The Gorbachev Era and Beyond

There is nothing more difficult to take in hand, more perilous to conduct, or more uncertain in its success than to take the lead in a new order of things.

—NICCOLÒ MACHIAVELLI

Much of what accumulated in the stifling and repressive atmosphere of Stalinism and stagnation, and is now surfacing, is far from pleasant and constructive. But this has to be tolerated. This is what a revolution is all about. Its primary function is always to give people freedom. And perestroika *with its democratization and* glasnost *has already fulfilled its primary task.*

—MIKHAIL GORBACHEV

Many people feel empty, a world that seemed so strong just collapsed. Forty years have been wasted on stupid strife for the sake of an unsuccessful experiment.

—GEORGE KONRAD

In the end we beat them with Levi 501 jeans. Seventy-two years of Communist indoctrination and propaganda was drowned out by a three-ounce Sony Walkman. A huge totalitarian system . . . has been brought to its knees because nobody wants to wear Bulgarian shoes. Now they're lunch, and we're number one on the planet.

—P. J. O'ROURKE

During the presidency of Jimmy Carter, the Soviet Union invaded the sovereign state of Afghanistan (December 1979), an act that drew international criticism and contributed to the Carter Doctrine of January 1980: Any threat upon American oil interests in the Persian Gulf would be considered provocative and tantamount to war. In 1981, Ronald Reagan was inaugurated as president, having won the election in part on a get-tough stance toward the USSR His verbal attacks characterized the Soviet Union as "the Evil Empire" and "the focus of evil in the world." Such rhetoric did little to encourage cooperation between the two nations.

A new era in international relations dawned on the death of the old-guard Soviet leader Constantine Chernenko in 1985. His government had been transitional, a geriatric accommodation to the demands of a new-style Soviet leadership waiting in the wings. Mikhail Gorbachev was forty-eight years old when he secured entry to the Politburo in 1979 and only fifty-four when he assumed the position of general secretary of the Communist Party in 1985. A career bureaucrat with primary assignments in agricultural administration, Gorbachev was nevertheless ready to embark on a radical departure from established Soviet policies. He sought to define and implement the new concepts of *perestroika* ("restructuring") and *glasnost* ("openness") through which he hoped to liberalize the political, economic, and cultural bases of Soviet society. Change was imminent, but no one could predict its full impact on travel restrictions and emigration, censorship, state control of artistic expression, and ultimately political organization itself through democratization and self-determination of ethnic nationalities.

Gorbachev's initial declarations in 1985 were met with international and domestic astonishment. Gorbachev was hailed in the West as the "man of the century," personally responsible for overcoming the legacy of Stalinism, for eliminating an authoritarian mind-set, for offering flexible positions on arms reduction in pursuit of a safer world. The "Evil Empire" was fast losing its threatening aura as each of the Eastern European satellite nations broke away from Soviet control in popular revolutions throughout 1989. This time there was no military attempt to maintain Soviet control as in Hungary (1956) and in Czechoslovakia (1968). The symbolic culmination of this process occurred on November 10, 1989, with the destruction of the Berlin Wall by the people of East and West Germany.

But Mikhail Gorbachev also faced severe opposition at home, both from the political right, which feared chaos and a loss of influence, and from the political left, led by Boris Yeltsin, who argued that *perestroika* was not being instituted fast enough or with a deep democratic conviction. Also in the late 1980s, the various ethnic minorities in the Soviet republics of Armenia, Azerbaijan, and Georgia began testing the limits of Gorbachev's commitment to democracy and self-determination of peoples. So too did the Baltic states of Estonia, Latvia, and Lithuania seek to break away from the Soviet "Union" and once again run their own affairs independently of Moscow.

Add to this turmoil a tense domestic background of deprivation as evidenced by food shortages and a heritage of consumer neglect, and Gorbachev was pressed at every turn. However, he was a maneuverer, a political tactician, an orchestrator of change. In an effort to maintain the union of the Soviet republics, Gorbachev tried to run a center position against the divergent agendas of the reformists and conservatives. He promised the former continued democratization and progress toward a market economy, and he reassured the latter that he was a loyal Communist Party man, who would respect them and protect their traditional interests. In late 1990, Gorbachev felt the need to conciliate the right wing of the party, which was increasingly concerned about demonstrations of independence in the republics. Gorbachev regarded this placation as necessary for the maintenance of his authority, but it drove away some of the most talented and avid reformers in the Gorbachev orbit. Eduard Shevardnadze resigned as foreign minister and warned of dictatorship.

On August 19, 1991, Shevardnadze's fears threatened to become reality as hard-line members of Gorbachev's advisory cabinet tried to institute a coup d'état. Gorbachev was confined in the Crimea for three days while an "emergency committee" of eight coup leaders explained that he was "ill" and needed a long rest. The incompetency of the conspirators, the refusal of the army and KGB security forces to fire on the Russian people, and, most important, the defiance of the Soviet citizenry and their commitment to the tenets of popular sovereignty resulted in the swift collapse of the coup. But the Soviet state emerged from this drama a changed entity. Boris Yeltsin, the popularly elected president of the Republic of Russia, now seemed to hold the keys to the future. By August 24, Gorbachev's cabinet had been reappointed with reformers scrutinized by Yeltsin; the Communist Party newspaper, *Pravda,* had been shut down; and Gorbachev had resigned from his position as general secretary of the Communist Party. Indeed, the Communist Party was in complete disarray after having ruled the country for nearly seventy-five years. Each of the Baltic states as well as the Ukraine and other Soviet republics had declared independence, a foreshadowing of the dissolution of the Soviet empire. Some scholars have hailed this as the "Second Russian Revolution." That revolution left Gorbachev behind. He had styled himself a reforming communist and a convinced socialist, an image essential to the initial phases of reform. Paradoxically, this close identification with the Communist Party afforded him the path to success, but it also sowed the seeds of failure. Gorbachev faced the great challenge of transition, of creating revolution and controlling it at the same time. As Lenin, Napoleon, Robespierre, and the Roman emperor Augustus understood in earlier ages, it is difficult to hold on to a world turned upside down.

The following selections recount the transitional dilemmas that faced the Russian people as they coped with political instability, social chaos, economic dislocation, and ethnic rebellion.

Perestroika *and the Socialist Renewal of Society (September 11, 1989)*

MIKHAIL GORBACHEV

Good evening, comrades, I am here to talk to you about our current affairs. The situation in the country is not simple. We all know and feel this. Everything has become entangled in a tight knot: scarcity on the consumer goods market, conflicts in ethnic relations, and difficult and sometimes painful processes in the public consciousness, resulting from the over-

"*Perestroika* and the Socialist Renewal of Society" is from Mikhail Gorbachev, speech delivered to the people of the U.S.S.R., September 11, 1989. Contained in *Vital Speeches of the Day*, October 15, 1989, pp. 5–7.

coming of distortions and from the renewal of socialism. People are trying to understand where we have found ourselves at the moment, evaluating the pluses and minuses of the path we have covered during the last four-plus years, the development of democracy and the pace of the economic and political reforms.

It is only natural that people want to know the real causes of our weaknesses and failures in carrying out specific programs for *perestroika* and in tackling urgent problems and to find out why the situation in some areas has deteriorated rather than improved.

In short, political life today is characterized by intense debate. But the main thing I want to emphasize is that the mass of people have become involved in this movement and they play an every growing role in discussing and accomplishing social, economic, and political tasks.

Comrades, this is a fact of fundamental importance because it gives *perestroika* the elements of constructive and businesslike effort and helps overcome people's alienation from power. Yet one cannot fail to see a different trend. Against the background of heated debate and a rapid succession of events, things are happening that must not be ignored or left unaccounted for. Efforts are being made to discredit *perestroika* from conservative, leftist and sometimes unmistakably anti-socialist positions. One can hear in this discordant choir voices predicting an imminent chaos and speculation about the threat of a coup and even civil war. It is a fact that some people would like to create an atmosphere of anxiety, despair and uncertainty in society. . . .

In effect, the conservative forces are trying to impose on us such evaluations of the situation that would provoke resistance to *perestroika* and mold in people's mind the view that the process of change begun in society should be halted or at least slowed down; these forces demand that the old command methods of government should be restored. Otherwise, they say, chaos will set in. Meanwhile, the leftist elements suggest tackling extremely difficult problems in one go, without taking into account our actual possibilities or the interests of society. Such demands are presented as concern for the people and its well-being.

Recommendations have also been made lately from which one can assume that our only "salvation" is renouncing the values of socialism and conducting *perestroika* in the capitalist manner. Such views do exist. Needless to say, such ideas go against the grain of *perestroika*, which implies socialist renewal of society. . . .

True, *perestroika* is meeting with many difficulties. But it is radical change, a revolution in the economy and in policy, in the ways of thinking and in people's consciousness, in the entire pattern of our life. Besides, we have not been able to avoid mistakes in our practical actions in the course of *perestroika*.

But *perestroika* has opened up realistic opportunities for society's renewal, for giving society a new quality and for creating truly humane and democratic socialism. It has returned to the great nation a sense of dignity and given the Soviet people a sense of freedom. It is a powerful source of social, spiritual, and, I should say, patriotic energy for decades to come.

That is why we must do everything to continue *perestroika* on the basis of the ideas and principles proclaimed by the party. And we must not stop. We must continue along the way of changes we have embarked upon. . . . The community is casting off its illusions. It no longer believes that there are simple solutions to be brought ready-made from above for all our problems. . . .

I think it very important that the community is coming to better understand the primary link between *perestroika* and labor—dedicated, creative, efficient work fully implementing every worker's knowledge and abilities. This is essential because until recently, we concentrated not so much on labor as on the distribution of benefits. One could think that redistribution of fictitious wealth was all *perestroika* was about. We have at last begun to shed this delusion. . . .

The Government of the U.S.S.R. is elaborating a program of extraordinary measures to improve the economy and, above all, to normalize the consumer market. The program is to be submitted to the Congress of People's Deputies. We believe that this program will give clear answers to the questions of how and when the most urgent social and economic problems will be solved. I think society will not accept it if the program does not determine clear and concrete measures, stages, and time limits as well as the responsibility of the republic and local bodies and labor collectives. I presume that this package may include unpopular, probably tough and even painful measures. This will be justified, however, only if they are prompted by the need to get out of the present situation.

Shortages, which arouse the sharpest criticisms and discontent of the people, are a special issue. The government is to give an explanation on this urgent social problem and come up with practical measures shortly. . . .

Of major political importance will be the laws on republic and regional cost-accounting and self-government. They are an important step toward realistically strengthening the sovereignty of the republics and expanding the rights of the local Soviets [councils].

The party, which is society's consolidating and vanguard force, has a unique role to play in this process. Those who strive to use the difficulties of the transition period for certain unseemly purposes and try to undermine the influence of the party should know that they will not succeed. We are sure that with all the critical sentiments concerning the activities of some or other party committee or communists, the working people realize perfectly well the importance of the party of Lenin for the fate of socialism, which today is inseparable from the success of *perestroika*. On the other hand, it is clear that the new tasks call for a deep renewal of the party.

By restructuring itself, getting rid of all that hinders its activities, overcoming dogmatism and conservatism, mastering a new style and new methods of work, renewing its personnel, and working side by side with the working people, the Communist Party of the Soviet Union will be able to fulfill its role of the political vanguard of society. The party will firmly pursue the policy of *perestroika*, heading the revolutionary transformation of society. We should realistically assess all processes and phenomena of the present-day situation, show restraint, see clearly where we are and not become confused. On this basis we should draw conclusions for our action at the given moment and in the future. We must act responsibly and prudently, without deviating from the course of *perestroika* in society. Dear comrades, I wish you success in work, determination and firm spirit.

Gorbachev's Resignation: "This Society Has Acquired Freedom" (December 25, 1991)

MIKHAIL GORBACHEV

Dear fellow countrymen, compatriots. Due to the situation which has evolved as a result of the formation of the Commonwealth of Independent States, I hereby discontinue my activities at the post of President of the Union of Soviet Socialist Republics.

I am making this decision on considerations of principle. I firmly came out in favor of the independence of nations and sovereignty for the republics. At the same time, I support the preservation of the union state and the integrity of this country. The developments took a differ-

"Gorbachev's Resignation" is from Mikhail Gorbachev, speech delivered over Russian television on December 25, 1991. Contained in *Vital Speeches of the Day*, January 15, 1992, pp. 194–195.

ent course. The policy prevailed of dismembering this country and disuniting the state, which is something I cannot subscribe to. . . .

This being my last opportunity to address you as President of the U.S.S.R., I find it necessary to inform you of what I think of the road that has been trodden by us since 1985. I find it important because there have been a lot of controversial, superficial, and biased judgments made on this score. Destiny so ruled that when I found myself at the helm of this state it already was clear that something was wrong in this country.

We had a lot of everything—land, oil and gas, other natural resources—and there was intellect and talent in abundance. However, we were living much worse than people in the industrialized countries were living and we were increasingly lagging behind them. The reason was obvious even then. This country was suffocating in the shackles of the bureaucratic command system. Doomed to cater to ideology, and suffer and carry the onerous burden of the arms race, it found itself at the breaking point.

All the half-hearted reforms—and there have been a lot of them—fell through, one after another. This country was going nowhere and we couldn't possibly live the way we did. We had to change everything radically. It is for this reason that I have never had any regrets—never had any regrets—that I did not use the capacity of General Secretary just to rein in this country for several years. I would have considered it an irresponsible and immoral decision. I was also aware that to embark on reform of this caliber and in a society like ours was an extremely difficult and even risky undertaking. But even now, I am convinced that the democratic reform that we launched in the spring of 1985 was historically correct.

The process of renovating this country and bringing about drastic change in the international community has proven to be much more complicated than anyone could imagine. However, let us give its due to what has been done so far. This society has acquired freedom. It has been freed politically and spiritually, and this is the most important achievement that we have yet fully come to grips with. And we haven't, because we haven't learned to use freedom yet. However, an effort of historical importance has been carried out. The totalitarian system has been eliminated, which prevented this country from becoming a prosperous and well-to-do country a long time ago. A breakthrough has been effected on the road of democratic change.

Free elections have become a reality. Free press, freedom of worship, representative legislatures and a multi-party system have all become reality. Human rights are being treated as the supreme principle and top priority. Movement has been started toward a multi-tier economy and the equality of all forms of ownership is being established. . . .

We're now living in a new world. An end has been put to the Cold War and to the arms race, as well as to the mad militarization of the country, which has crippled our economy, public attitudes and morals. The threat of nuclear war has been removed. Once again, I would like to stress that during this transitional period, I did everything that needed to be done to insure that there was reliable control of nuclear weapons. We opened up ourselves to the rest of the world, abandoned the practices of interfering in others' internal affairs and using troops outside this country, and we were reciprocated with trust, solidarity, and respect. . . .

All this change had taken a lot of strain, and took place in the context of fierce struggle against the background of increasing resistance by the reactionary forces, both the party and state structures, and the economic elite, as well as our habits, ideological bias, the sponging attitudes. The change ran up against our intolerance, a low level of political culture and fear of change. That is why we have wasted so much time. The old system fell apart even before the new system began to work. Crisis of society as a result aggravated even further.

FIGURE 14.2 "We have paid with all our history and tragic experience for these democratic achievements, and they are not to be abandoned, whatever the circumstances, and whatever the pretexts. Otherwise, all our hopes for the best will be buried."—Mikhail Gorbachev. (*American Publishing*)

I'm aware that there is popular resentment as a result of today's grave situation. I note that authority at all levels, and myself are being subject to harsh criticisms. I would like to stress once again, though, that the cardinal change in so vast a country, given its heritage, could not have been carried out without difficulties, shock and pain.

The August [1991] coup brought the overall crisis to the limit. The most dangerous thing about this crisis is the collapse of statehood. I am concerned about the fact that the people in this country are ceasing to become citizens of a great power and the consequences may be very difficult for all of us to deal with. I consider it vitally important to preserve the democratic achievements which have been attained in the last few years. We have paid with all our history and tragic experience for these democratic achievements, and they are not to be abandoned, whatever the circumstances, and whatever the pretexts. Otherwise, all our hopes for the best will be buried. I am telling you all this honestly and straightforwardly because this is my moral duty. . . .

I am very much concerned as I am leaving this post. However, I also have a feeling of hope and faith in you, your wisdom and force of spirit. We are heirs of a great civilization and it now depends on all and everyone whether or not this civilization will make a comeback to a new and decent living today. . . . Of course, there were mistakes made that could have been avoided, and many of the things that we did could not have been done better. But I am positive that sooner or later, some day our common efforts will bear fruit and our nations will live in a prosperous, democratic society.

CONSIDER THIS:

- How did Mikhail Gorbachev define the concept of *perestroika*? In 1989, Gorbachev described the Communist Party as "society's consolidating and vanguard force." Why did the Communist Party fail? What was Gorbachev's explanation in his resignation speech?
- What had Russians gained from Gorbachev's leadership? Will he be viewed by history as a great leader who, as John Le Carré said, "had the nerve to mount the rostrum and declare he had no clothes?"

Communism: "Far Away from the Mainstream of Civilization" (December 31, 1999)

VLADIMIR PUTIN

On December 31, 1999, Boris Yeltsin resigned as president of the Russian Federation and was replaced by his foreign minister, Vladimir Putin, who became the new elected president in June 2000. Putin was a former KGB officer who brought with him a relentless determination to institute changes in the government that would increase economic production and promote efficiency in the campaign to eliminate organized crime and redefine Russia's international image. In the following speech given as Yeltsin stepped down, Putin sketched the problems facing Russia and some of his proposed solutions.

Russia is completing the first transition stage of economic and political reforms. Despite problems and mistakes, it has entered the highway by which the whole of humanity is traveling. Only this way offers the possibility of dynamic economic growth and higher living standards, as the world experience convincingly shows. There is no alternative to it.

The question for Russia now is what to do next. How can we make the new, market mechanisms work to full capacity? How can we overcome the still deep ideological and political split in society? What strategic goals can consolidate Russian society? What place can Russia occupy in the international community in the 21st century? What economic, social and cultural frontiers do we want to attain in 10–15 years? What are our strong and weak points? And what material and spiritual resources do we have now?

These are the questions put forward by life itself. Unless we find clear answers to them that would be understandable to all the people, we will be unable to move forward at the pace and to the goals that are worthy of our great country.

The Lessons Russia HAS to Learn

The answers to these questions and our very future depend on what lessons we will learn from our past and present. This is a work for society as a whole and for more than one year, but some of these lessons are already clear:

For almost three-fourths of the outgoing century, Russia lived under the sign of the implementation of the communist doctrine. It

"Communism: 'Far Away from the Mainstream of Civilization'" is from Vladimir Putin, speech delivered to the Russian People, The Kremlin, Moscow, Russia, on December 31, 1999. Contained in *Vital Speeches of the Day*, February 1, 2000, pp. 232–236.

would be a mistake not to see and, even more so, to deny the unquestionable achievements of those times. But it would be an even bigger mistake not to realize the outrageous price our country and its people had to pay for that Bolshevik experiment.

What is more, it would be a mistake not to understand its historic futility. Communism and the power of Soviets did not make Russia a prosperous country with a dynamically developing society and free people. Communism vividly demonstrated in inaptitude for sound self-development, dooming our country to a steady lag behind economically advanced countries. It was a road to a blind alley, which is far away from the mainstream of civilization. . . .

Every country, Russia included, has to search for its own way of renewal. We have not been very successful in this respect thus far. Only in the past year or the past two years have we started groping for our road and our model of transformation. We can pin hopes for a worthy future only if we prove capable of combining the universal principles of a market economy and democracy with Russian realities. . . .

A Chance for a Worthy Future

Strong State: We are at a stage where even the most correct economic and social policy starts misfiring while being realized due to the weakness of the state power, of the managerial bodies. A key to Russia's recovery and growth is in the state-policy sphere today.

Russia needs a strong state power and must have it. I am not calling for totalitarianism. History proves all dictatorships, all authoritarian forms of government are transient. Only democratic systems are intransigent. Whatever the shortcomings, mankind has not devised anything superior. A strong state power in Russia is a democratic, law-based, workable federative state. . . .

Efficient Economy: Another important lesson the 1990s is the conclusion that Russia needs to form a wholesome system of state regulation of

FIGURE 14.3 Statues of Lenin, Marx, and other Soviet heroes were destroyed or removed from various cities in Eastern Europe after 1989. Were Marx and Lenin wrong? Were they "Gods who failed history"? (*United Media/United Features Syndicate, Inc.*)

the economy and social sphere. I do not mean to return to a system of planning and managing the economy by fiat, where the all-pervasive state was regulating all aspects of any factory's work from top to bottom. I mean to make the Russian state an efficient coordinator of the country's economic and social forces that balances out their interests, optimizes the aims and parameters of social development and creates conditions and mechanisms of their attainment.

The above naturally exceeds the commonplace formula which limits the state's role in the economy to devising rules of the game and controlling their observance. With time, we are likely to evolve to this formula. But today's situation necessitates deeper state involvement in the social and economic processes. While setting the scale and planning mechanisms for the system of state regulation, we must be guided by the principle: The state must be where it is needed; freedom must be where it is required. . . .

Russia is in the midst of one of the most difficult periods in its history. For the first time in the past 200–300 years, it is facing a real threat of sliding to the second, and possibly even the third, echelon of world states. We are running OUT OF TIME for removing this threat. We must strain all intellectual, physical and moral forces of the nation. We need coordinated creative work. Nobody will do it for us. Everything depends on us, and on us alone—on our ability to see the size of the threat, to pool forces, and set our minds to hard and lengthy work.

CONSIDER THIS:

- According to Vladimir Putin in his address to the Russian people at the outset of 2000, what were some of Russia's most immediate problems and what did Putin propose as necessary solutions?

THE BROADER PERSPECTIVE:

- In this speech, Putin was careful to decry the past mistakes of communist economy and totalitarian rule. Yet he was adamant about the need for a strong and directive government. Why? Is there a precarious balance that must be achieved between personal freedom and political security in order for Russia to maintain its status among the most influential states of the world? Does the United States face the same issue?

The Future of the West (1990–2006)

Political and Economic Initiatives

Few years have seen such fundamental political, social, and economic changes as occurred throughout Eastern Europe in 1989. Poland, Hungary, Czechoslovakia, and East Germany all peacefully established new governments with democratic overtones after more than four decades of Marxist rule. The Soviet Union, continuing to pursue its own liberalization, gave most of its former satellites wide latitude in carrying out reforms in contrast to its earlier suppression of popular movements in Hungary (1956) and Czechoslovakia (1968). Only in Romania was the transition violent, as a swift but bloody revolution toppled the regime of hard-line communist dictator Nicolai Ceausescu in December 1989. He and his wife were charged with genocide and executed.

Perhaps the most symbolic act of freedom occurred on November 9, 1989, when East Germany opened all its borders and allowed its citizens to travel and emigrate freely. The notorious Berlin Wall, constructed in 1961 at the height of the Cold War, was subsequently torn down, and thousands made their way to the West in search of new lives. This act would have important consequences for the future as Germany formally reunited and consolidated its political institutions and economy during the 1990s.

As Europe moved away from the wasteland of World War II and the intellectual confines of the Cold War toward a new era of intranational economic cooperation, its face was radically altered. A tunnel under the English Channel was constructed (dubbed the "Chunnel"), which not only physically links Great Britain and France but threatens, some would way, to meld their cultures as well. Britain lost the island status

FIGURE 14.4 The Berlin Wall begins to fall on the night of November 9–10, 1989, near Bernauer Strasse. (*Corbis/Bettmann*)

that protected it and offered it a unique identity for centuries in exchange for a more intimate link with the economic destiny of continental Europe. So too have the great enemies of the first half of the twentieth century, France and Germany, reconciled past offenses for future gains. With the reunification of Germany and the reintroduction of Eastern countries such as the Czech Republic, Slovakia, Hungary, and Poland into the heart of Europe, there have been great financial opportunities and constant political redefinition. The following speech by French president François Mitterrand in 1990 testifies to the changing nature of Europe and the progress of Western civilization during the last decade of the twentieth century.

The Reconciliation of France and Germany (September 24, 1990)

FRANÇOIS MITTERRAND

Think of the events that have shaken up Europe and the World in 1939, the popular movements that have emerged from the depths which, like the French revolution of two hundred years ago, have triumphed over structures and systems, set ways of thinking and acting, powers and fears, because of the simple, irresistible need to live differently, in accordance with the requirements of the mind. When the walls separating peoples came down, walls built on the foolish assumption that the order they were protecting would never be untouched by the great winds of space, dreams and ideas, I remember saying to my compatriots in France . . . that the end of one order did not necessarily mean that another order would be born immediately thereafter, and that it would be a very difficult process. And I would ask you this: what are we to do with this era we are entering, so promising, so perilous? What shall we make of it?

I think that an era of hope is opening up for mankind, if the peoples of the world accept to overcome what they take to be the fatality of history, and of their own interest. Believe me, such a goal is within our reach. After destroying each other in three wars in less than a century, France and Germany have sealed their reconciliation, a rare occurrence indeed: They belong to the same community, they meet together, they are forging a genuine friendship. While I speak, on the eve of German unity, instead of harping on the tragic events they experienced in the past because of each other, our two peoples are turned toward the same future. And so it is that here in New York, I can send the best wishes of France to the Germans, who are preparing to celebrate a great moment of their history. The deep understanding between France and Germany is a reality. As you know, it makes itself felt in the twelve-nation European Community. Can you imagine the trouble and strife, the conflicts of age-old ambitions that were overcome forty years ago by a bold, almost unbelievable undertaking engaged in first by six, nine, then ten, now twelve countries of Europe?

We Europeans are looking beyond the Community, to the horizon of the continent of Europe, the Europe of geography and history. . . . Where would our old continent be now if audacity had not managed to overthrow well-established patterns of thought? And if peoples and their leaders had not accepted to build a future different from the past? In this Europe these are countries

"The Reconciliation of France and Germany" is from François Mitterrand, speech delivered to the 45th Session of the United Nations General Assembly, New York, New York, on September 24, 1990. Contained in *Vital Speeches of the Day*, October 15, 1990, pp. 5, 7–8.

which yesterday were known as Eastern bloc countries and which belonged to a rival system. Now they control their own destiny, but with what means at their disposal? We must think of them, they are our brethren and we will be by their side, until as I said in France, a more fixed relationship will bring together all the countries of Europe, those of the East, those of the Community, those of the Free Trade Area, those who are part of no system, in what I have called a Confederation. . . . Europe has been the first field of application thereof and a very real one. . . .

At the beginning of this century and at the end of the previous one, our forebears expressed their dreams of peace with these three words: disarmament, arbitration, collective security. Theirs came to be an era of unrest, dictatorship and war. Let us act in such a way, I beseech you, that through the United Nations, law, solidarity and peace may finally rule over a new era.

The Broader Perspective:

- In 1990, François Mitterrand of France offered a philosophical perspective on the unity and progress of Europe. Why was he optimistic? What perspective had been gained over time that justified Mitterrand's belief that "an era of hope is opening up for mankind?"

Monetary Union: Europe's Global Role (1998)

LAWRENCE H. SUMMERS

In the wake of the dramatic political changes from 1989 to 1991 that saw the collapse of the Soviet Union and its control over East European satellite countries, Western leaders were handed new opportunities to redefine borders and to reevaluate goals. This complex process of transition presented many challenges as former Eastern bloc nations rejected the moribund state-directed "command economies," which controlled all production, distribution, and prices, in favor of free-market capitalism. This was a halting process that resulted in great social dislocation. Germany, for example, in its quest for political reunification, had to absorb East German factories that were technological dinosaurs without environmental controls and a population of workers who lacked a competitive wage structure and quality expectation. East Germans initially were viewed as pariahs, second-class citizens who were a threat to the eventual economic success of a united Germany.

As countries like Hungary, Poland, the Czech Republic, and Slovakia opened their borders to the infusion of capital and technological expertise from the West, Europe looked forward to the day when a true European union of nations would present a politically stable and economically vibrant trading bloc to compete with other global alliances.

This ideal of an integrated Europe was not a new concept. In fact, many international organizations were formed after World War II to help rebuild Europe. In 1957, ten years after the launch of the Marshall Plan, the European Economic Community (EEC), known as the Common Market, was created to facilitate trade and economic cooperation. By 1968, internal tariffs were eliminated within Western Europe. Although the Common Market continued to enroll more countries to membership, momentum slowed in the 1970s and 1980s amid sharp disagreements

"Monetary Union: Europe's Global Role" is from Lawrence H. Summers, speech delivered to the Transatlantic Business Dialogue, Charlotte, North Carolina, on November 6, 1998. Contained in *Vital Speeches of the Day*, January 15, 1999.

about the shape of the future. But in 1988, the leaders of the EEC agreed to fashion Europe as a free-trade zone without any restrictive trade barriers or policies among its members. This went into effect in 1992, and by 1993 the Treaty of Maastricht had linked twelve nations into a new confederacy called the European Union (EU). These nations (United Kingdom, France, Germany, Italy, Spain, Portugal, Greece, Denmark, Belgium, Netherlands, Luxembourg, and Ireland) were joined in 1995 by Austria, Finland, and Sweden. In 1999, the Czech Republic, Estonia, Hungary, Poland, and Slovenia were considered for admission. As the economies of the Central European states mature, more continue to apply for membership.

Perhaps the most difficult economic issue facing Europe was the establishment of a single unified currency. Monetary union was a bold but controversial component of European economic integration. A supranational European Central Bank was erected in Frankfurt, Germany, to handle currency exchange and interest rate issues. Finally, on January 4, 1999, the euro was officially adopted for voluntary acceptance by members of the EU. The benefits of the euro are many: lower currency transaction costs, less exchange rate instability, lower interest rates, more investments in Europe, and a currency that now rivals the dollar and the yen.

The transition, however, has been difficult. Because a country's currency is often equated with nationalism and sovereignty, some members of the EU, most notably Britain, Denmark, and Sweden, remain unwilling to relinquish their national currencies in order to adopt the euro. But on January 1, 2002, the euro became legal tender for the great majority of EU members. Much of the future effectiveness of the European Union as a supranational political and economic organization will depend on the continuing success of the euro in international markets.

The following speech, delivered in November 1998 by Lawrence Summers, the U.S. deputy secretary of the treasury, emphasized the international implications of European monetary union and the euro.

I am glad to have this opportunity briefly to address European economic and monetary union and its implications for the United States. Let me state my conclusion at the outset: we have everything to gain and little to lose from the success of this momentous project. Now more than ever, America is well served by having an integrated and prosperous trading partner on the other side of the Atlantic. Europe will benefit greatly from a single currency that supports these ends—and if Europe benefits, this will greatly benefit the United States. . . .

Now more than ever, the effects of the Euro will be extremely complicated and it is difficult to predict with any certainty what the role of the new currency will be. . . . Europe is already an economic superpower. With a successful move to European Monetary Union, and the integrating forces that EMU could unleash, many Europeans look forward to the day when Europe will more fully punch its weight in international policy-making, not merely in economic issues, but in the broader global arena. . . .

European leaders have already committed themselves to working closely with the United States and others. . . . But perhaps the largest contribution that Europeans could make to the continued stability of the global market system today would be to take the structural reform steps needed for a rapid upturn in private investment.

Alone among the major regional economic blocs, Europe has the capacity to increase domestic investment levels substantially. And with the advent of EMU, it has the clear and compelling reasons to do so: namely, reducing unemployment and, more broadly, ensuring that the recent recovery in European growth will be sustained. Truly, by acting to improve Europe's capacity to respond to external shocks on a regional level they would also be taking a major step toward containing them at a global level.

Looking ahead, EMU has of course raised important issues about . . . Europe's participation in organizations such as the International Monetary Fund. We will continue to monitor progress and engage with the EU on these matters as the starting date draws near. In this context the proverbial American question—of which number to call when you want to call Europe—will take on even greater salience as Europe seeks to establish the respective roles of the European Central Bank, European Commission, and various national authorities.

Some have argued that a Europe with a single number in the global directory might ultimately pose a threat to the United States. But in a global economy, the United States has infinitely less to fear from an open and integrated Europe, that continues to take its share in global responsibilities, than a Europe that turns inward and seeks insulation. This has been true since the very start of the European project in the early 1950s and it is true today.

The Untied States has an enormous stake in Europe emerging under EMU with the capacity to play a more active and constructive role on the world state—and with the capacity to be an even stronger economic ally to the United States in the century to come. As ever, Europe is a partner, not a rival. And as our partner succeeds, so will we.

CONSIDER THIS:

- What was Lawrence H. Summers's primary message in this address? Why have some economists seen the move to European monetary union as a threat to the United States? What was Summers's answer to this fear?

THE BROADER PERSPECTIVE:

- Economic integration in Europe mirrors an accelerating trend toward the global integration of economies and markets. Do you foresee the development of European, African, Asian, and American trading blocks with perhaps only four or five different currencies employed throughout the world? Is global integration inevitable or problematical?

Ethnic Strife and Terrorism

One of the most tragic consequences of the collapse of the Soviet Union was the political, social, and economic chaos that accompanied the liberation of Eastern Europe. For nations whose political freedoms and ethnic identities were so long suppressed, the disintegration of Soviet control meant a search for order and equity. This posed new problems that strained domestic relations at a crucial time when stability was most necessary. In the following selection, Austrian ambassador to the United States Helmut Tuerk provided some perspective.

Ethnic Strife in Eastern Europe (April 15, 1994)

HELMUT TUERK

When talking about ethnic strife in Central and Eastern Europe, it must, first of all, be recalled that the continent of Europe has traditionally been a mosaic of peoples with different cultures, languages, traditions, and religions. This diversity has, in the past and present, often been a source of conflict. The tragic events we are witnessing today in parts

"Ethnic Strife in Eastern Europe" is from Helmut Tuerk, speech delivered at the Town Hall of California, Los Angeles, California, on April 15, 1994. Contained in *Vital Speeches of the Day*, June 15, 1994, pp. 517–518, 521.

of the former Yugoslavia are a case in point for the continuing explosiveness of unresolved issues stemming from this diversity.

This very diversity, however, constitutes, at the same time, through a cross-fertilization process, a powerful source of richness of European culture and civilization. If preserved and allowed to flourish everywhere on our continent under conditions of respect for human rights, democracy and the rule of law, this diversity can be a tremendous asset instead of being a source of chaos.

It is obvious that the living together of different ethnic, linguistic and/or religious groups as a rule presupposes that one group forms a majority while one or more other groups constitute minorities. The existence of such minorities is an undeniable feature of almost every European country. With dozens of distinct ethnic groups in Europe alone, the ideas of a separate state for each one of these groups would be totally unrealistic if not altogether absurd. Very often ethnic groups forming a minority in one country are the dominant nationality in another country. On the other hand there are groups which only constitute minorities in a single country or in several countries. . . .

Totalitarian States—as until quite recently was the case in most of Central and all of Eastern Europe—often try to resolve the problem by either denying the very existence of such minorities or by theoretically granting them certain rights which in practice, however, remain largely on paper. When such systems of government collapse, the minorities' aspiration to safeguard and develop their identity may take on a violent form. The comparison has often been made to lifting a lid from a boiling pot. The collapse of communism in Central and Eastern Europe has thus been accompanied by a resurgence of nationalism among peoples and ethnic groups seeking to right the wrongs to which they had been subjected. . . .

Let me now refer to some regions of Europe, formerly under communist domination, where the coexistence of different ethnic groups has either already led to strife, even armed conflict, or is of serious concern for the future. Let me begin with the case of the former Yugoslavia, where conflicting aspirations of various ethnic groups did not only lead to the disintegration of the confederation, but to continuing bloodshed and atrocities of a kind Europe has not experienced since World War II. . . .

The former Soviet Union poses even greater problems. Let me only point to the fact that on the territory of the former Soviet Union there are over 100 different ethnic groups, speaking 130 different languages. The largest groups include Russians, Ukrainians, Uzbeks, Byelorussians, and Azeris.

Tsarist politics aimed at strengthening the empire and at transforming its multi-ethnic character into that of a Russian national State. Under communist rule, the various nationalities at first enjoyed relative autonomy within the Federation and saw their culture and languages promoted. Stalin's policies, however, aimed at putting an end to the various cultural traditions and to forcibly achieve russification of the Soviet Union.

Gorbachev's *Perestroika* finally brought about liberation of the various ethnic groups, however, the Soviet Union fell apart. This development was in no small measure the consequence of decades of oppression. The process of the assertion of rights by certain ethnic groups is still continuing and is threatening peace and stability in some areas of the former Soviet Union.

The problems the former Soviet Republics are facing also stem from the fact that many members of ethnic groups live outside the boundaries of the State where they form the majority, i.e. that State boundaries do not correspond to ethnic boundaries; e.g. out of 145 million Russians, 25 million live outside the Russian Federation; only one fourth of the 6.5 million Tartars live in Tartastan. In the Russian Federation itself, 19 percent of the population is non-Russian. . . .

Looking at today's Europe with its multitude of ethnic groups and the actual and potential conflicts stemming therefrom, the urgency of codifying the rights of these groups on an international level, coupled with an international control mechanism, becomes obvious. Important steps in this direction have already been taken with Austria being at the forefront of these endeavors. We firmly believe that the future of the European continent in no small measure depends on a satisfactory resolution of these issues, the alternative being unending confrontation, strife and even armed conflict.

Ethnic groups should serve as bridges between nations and as an element promoting greater understanding between peoples. This presupposes a democratic political framework based on the rule of law, with a functioning independent judiciary. Such a framework must guarantee full respect for human rights and fundamental freedoms, equal rights and status for all citizens, the free expression of all their legitimate interests and aspirations, political pluralism, social tolerance and the implementation of legal rules that place effective restraints on the abuse of governmental power.

Respect for and promotion of rights of ethnic groups cannot aim at establishing separate states for each and every ethnic group. What we should rather aim for, is to speed up the process of European integration and extend that process as far as possible to Central and Eastern Europe. The importance of the national State will diminish due to the existence of supra-national institutions on the one hand and the increasing role of regions on the other hand. Thus, issues relating to ethnic groups should become less burning, as every individual, no matter to which group he or she belongs, will enjoy the advantage of living in a broader European framework. . . .

In view of the fundamental political changes in Central and Eastern Europe in favor of democracy, the rule of law and a system of market economy there is every reason to believe that the process of European integration can in due course be extended to the east of Vienna. This would be the best guarantee that ethnic strife can be resolved by peaceful means and a new European order will emerge out of ethnic chaos. Austria as a traditional bridge between East and West on the European continent will be happy to make its contribution and will be even more in a position to do so as member of the European Union.

Consider This:

- Helmut Tuerk saw the problems of dealing with ethnic minorities throughout Eastern Europe as one of the most pressing issues facing Europe in the late twentieth century. Why? What solutions did he propose? How have ethnic tensions increased in France and other European countries in the early twenty-first century?

Crimes Against Humanity: "Ethnic Cleansing" (1992)

When Marshal Tito died in 1980, Yugoslavian unity began to break apart. Upon the collapse of the Soviet Union in 1991, there was no longer the fear of a foreign threat to curb domestic bickering. Yugoslavia disintegrated quickly in the face of Serbian aggression to capture and control territory where Bosnians and Croats had formed ethnic majorities. The Serbs justified their aggression on the basis of a need for more "living space," echoing Hitler's demands just before World War II. Under the leadership of Slobodan Milosevic, the Serbs from 1991 to 1993 embarked on a program of "ethnic cleansing" in Croatia and Bosnia. This was a Serbian war aim designed to strike terror into the civilian population by herding men, women, and children from villages into detention centers

"Crimes Against Humanity: Ethnic Cleansing" is from Francis A. Boyle, *The Bosnian People Charge Genocide. Proceedings at the International Court of Justice Concerning Bosnia v. Serbia on the Prevention and Punishment of the Crime of Genocide* (Amherst, Mass.: Aletheia Press, 1996), pp. 18–19, 24–25. Reprinted by permission.

where thousands were tortured and murdered. "Rape camps" were set up so that women could be methodically abused, humiliated, and ultimately impregnated, thus "cleansing" their Croat or Muslim identities and producing a new population of mixed blood. An estimated twenty thousand women were raped by Serb soldiers between 1991 and 1995. Thousands of people were driven from their homes and displaced as refugees.

The International War Crimes Tribunal located in The Hague was established by the UN Security Council in May 1993 to issue indictments against war criminals. For the first time, rape was prosecuted as a "crime against humanity" and several captured Serbs were convicted and sentenced by this international tribunal. The following excerpt is from the trial testimony of two Muslim women who recounted a Serb attack on their village in May 1992.

A Muslim Woman Identified as AD 010 Described an Attack on Her Village by Serbian Forces (Chetniks)

"On the 25th of May, the Chetniks attacked our village, which was a Muslim village. . . . In the first attack they shelled the village. The people out of fear were fleeing their homes. I saw many of them fall, their bodies and limbs flying into the air. Bodies of men, women, children, and all that just because they were Muslims. They killed en masse, pillaged and burnt our houses, detained women, elderly and children and burnt them alive. They took the young men from 20–30 years of age [and] brought them to a school to torture them. . . .

"They have been torturing us all in different manners. Every village had a Chetniks' headquarters where they spent most of the time. They would take our food, our gold and jewelry [and] money. They took [my neighbor's] son away and they threatened to kill him unless she brings some money. She and her husband were collecting money through the village . . . and finally when they brought the money the Chetniks let her son go, but they killed her husband. First they mutilated his body with knives, engraving a cross on his body, [leaving] him to bleed, and finally killing him only at night. In that same manner they killed another of my neighbors—it kept going on; and all this for one simple reason: They wanted to cleanse everything Muslim.

"They raped my neighbor, a 65-year-old woman, and then killed her. They killed her husband as well, who was a totally handicapped and helpless person. When we got the permission to bury them, we found them mutilated. We had to pick up his head and the brain with a shovel."

44E: A Young Muslim Female Identified as JK 001 Reported the Details of Expulsion by Serbian Forces

"Every day they entered houses in which there were only women and children remaining. They plundered, killed and raped even the 5-year-old girls and old women. So our own house was a prison camp to us for they could come in and kill us at any time of day or night. When they were searching my home we were taken into the backyard and made to stand in a row. They threatened to shoot us if they found weapons in the house. There were no weapons; they plundered the house and took the gold and told us they would come back again and kill us because we were Muslims. . . .

"We stayed in the houses that had been plundered and the owners of which had been killed or taken to camps. It was horrible. There were about fifty of us in one house; we slept on top of each other and the odor of the dead bodies, which were in the garages [and] in the gardens, was everywhere. They killed the men and the women had to bury their husband, or son, or father with their own hands and to the best of their abilities. There was blood, blood of an innocent son, child, woman, or man on the walls of the house. . . .

"After a few days, nine trailers and several buses came. . . . We became upset and started to leave, but they made a circle around us and said that we would get what we deserved, and that was death, death to all Muslims or "Bulaks" as they were calling us. They loaded us onto the trailers and we left, not knowing ourselves whether we were going to death or to freedom. . . . When we got out they started to separate girls and women. Fortunately, I had a scarf on my head and my aunt's child in my arms. They set apart about thirty girls. They separated an old woman from her two daughters; she protested, cried, went down on her knees and begged, but there was no mercy—she got a bullet in the head. The girls were taken to an unknown destination and even today it is not known. . . ."

CONSIDER THIS:

- What were the main problems in the Balkan region that resulted in war among the Serbs, Croats, and Bosnians? Why has the United Nations had such difficulty resolving the issues of ethnic strife and freedom in the Balkans?

COMPARE AND CONTRAST:

- Compare the "crimes against humanity" described by the Muslim victims with the crimes perpetrated by the Nazis during World War II. What is genocide? Should acts of rape and murder committed against Muslims, Croats, and Kosovars be considered acts of genocide? What is "ethnic cleansing?"

THE BROADER PERSPECTIVE:

- The Nuremberg Trials conducted by the victorious Allies in 1946 sought to define genocide and punish "crimes against humanity" committed by Nazi functionaries. In subsequent decades, the legitimacy of the Nuremberg tribunals has come under attack by many who believe that crimes against humanity cannot be adequately defined and that punishment by a court under international jurisdiction is not justice but retribution. What do you think of these arguments? Can you define "crimes against humanity?"

- Does the International War Crimes Tribunal in The Hague, which was established under the auspices of the United Nations, have the authority to prosecute war criminals and render justice in an international context? If they do not, then who does?

- As the process of globalization accelerates, why will questions regarding international justice become more important to the integration of the world community?

"We Wage a War to Save Civilization Itself" (2001)

GEORGE W. BUSH

On the morning of September 11, 2001, the United States was stunned when two hijacked commercial jetliners slammed into the twin towers of the World Trade Center in New York City. As the towers burned, another airplane was flown into the Pentagon in Washington, D.C., and still another missed its potential target when the passengers forced a crash landing in the rural fields of Pennsylvania. Thousands of people were killed in the eventual collapse of the towers and in the rescue efforts that ensued. Never before, not even in the Japanese surprise attack on Pearl Harbor, had the United States suffered so aggressive a threat to its citizens and its values as a nation.

"'We Wage a War to Save Civilization Itself'" is from George W. Bush, speeches delivered to the people of the United States and to the General Assembly of the United Nations on September 11, November 8 and 10, 2001. Contained in *Vital Speeches of the Day*, October 1, 2001, p. 738, and December 1, 2001, pp. 98–99;103–104.

The perpetrators of the horror belonged to the al-Qaeda terrorist network, masterminded by Osama bin Laden, a Saudi exile who was also implicated in attacks against American embassies in Tanzania and Kenya, and in the 2000 bombing of the USS *Cole* in Yemen.

In subsequent action, President George W. Bush declared war against terrorism throughout the world with specific orders to hunt down bin Laden and dismantle his terrorist network. Congress passed an antiterrorist law that tightened immigration controls, granted greater latitude to law enforcement officials, and confirmed executive authority to detain foreign nationals and to try and even execute them, if judged guilty of terrorist acts in military tribunals. These controversial measures had precedents during the wartime administrations of Abraham Lincoln and Franklin Roosevelt, but they engendered debate over the potential restriction of civil liberties among U.S. citizens.

Basking in the faint glow of Cold War victory and somewhat adrift in foreign affairs during the 1990s, the United States, its image as a bastion of security and freedom now tarnished, had entered a new era. No longer the invulnerable superpower, the United States once again was given purpose and direction—an evil to confront. The war against terrorism provided a new forum for the confirmation of its values as a nation and for its leadership in the Western world, as these excerpts from President Bush's speeches following the disaster indicate.

FIGURE 14.5 September 11, 2001: "A great people has been moved to defend a great nation. Terrorist attacks can shake the foundations of our greatest buildings, but they cannot touch the foundation of America"—George W. Bush. (*Corbis/Bettmann*)

Address Delivered to the Nation (September 11, 2001)

Today, our fellow citizens, our way of life, our very freedom came under attack in a series of deliberate and deadly terrorist acts. The victims were in airplanes, or in their offices; secretaries, businessmen and women, military and federal workers; moms and dads, friends and neighbors. Thousands of lives were suddenly ended by evil, despicable acts of terror. The pictures of airplanes flying into buildings, fires burning, huge structures collapsing, have filled us with disbelief, terrible sadness and a quiet, unyielding anger. These acts of mass murder were intended to frighten our nation into chaos and retreat. But they have failed; our country is strong.

A great people has been moved to defend a great nation. Terrorist attacks can shake the foundations of our biggest buildings, but they cannot touch the foundation of America. These acts shattered steel, but they cannot dent the steel of American resolve. America was targeted for attack because we're the brightest beacon for freedom and opportunity in the world. And no one will keep that light from shining. . . .

Address to the Nation (November 8, 2001)

We are a different country than we were on September the 10th—sadder and less innocent; stronger and more united; and in the face of ongoing threats, determined and courageous. Our nation faces a threat to our freedoms, and the stakes could not be higher. We are the target of enemies who boast they want to kill—kill all Americans, kill all Jews, and kill all Christians. We've seen that type of hate before—and the only possible response is to confront it, and to defeat it.

This new enemy seeks to destroy our freedom and impose its views. We value life; the terrorists ruthlessly destroy it. We value education; the terrorists do not believe women should be educated or should have health care, or should leave their homes. We value the right to speak our minds; for the terrorists, free expression can be grounds for execution. We respect people of all faiths and welcome the free practice of religion; our enemy wants to dictate how to think and how to worship even to their fellow Muslims.

The enemy tries to hide behind a peaceful faith. But those who celebrate the murder of innocent men, women, and children have no religion, have no conscience, and have no mercy. We wage war to save civilization, itself. We did not seek it, but we must fight it—and we will prevail.

This is a different war from any our nation has ever faced, a war on many fronts, against terrorists who operate in more than 60 different countries. And this is a war that must be fought not only overseas, but also here at home. . . .

Address to the United Nations General Assembly (November 10, 2001)

We're asking for a comprehensive commitment to this fight. We must unite in opposing all terrorists, not just some of them. In this world there are good causes and bad causes, and we may disagree on where the line is drawn. Yet, there is no such thing as a good terrorist. No national aspiration, no remembered wrong can ever justify the deliberate murder of the innocent. Any government that rejects this principle, trying to pick and choose its terrorist friends, will know the consequences.

We must speak the truth about terror. Let us never tolerate outrageous conspiracy theories concerning the attacks of September the 11th; malicious lies that attempt to shift the blame away from the terrorists, themselves, away from the guilty. To inflame ethnic hatred is to advance the cause of terror.

The war against terror must not serve as an excuse to persecute ethnic and religious minorities in any country. Innocent people must be allowed to live their own lives, by their own customs, under their own religion. And every nation must have avenues for the peaceful expression of opinion and dissent.

When these avenues are closed, the temptation to speak through violence grows. . . .

As I've told the American people, freedom and fear are at war. We face enemies that hate not our policies, but our existence; the tolerance of openness and creative culture that defines us. But the outcome of this conflict is certain: There is a current in history and it runs toward freedom. Our enemies resent it and dismiss it, but the dreams of mankind are defined by liberty—the natural right to create and build and worship and live in dignity. When men and women are released from oppression and isolation, they find fulfillment and hope, and they leave poverty by the millions. These aspirations are lifting up the peoples of Europe, Asia, Africa, and the Americas, and they can lift up all of the Islamic world. We stand for the permanent hopes of humanity, and those hopes will not be denied. We're confident, too, that history has an author who fills time and eternity with His purpose. We know that evil is real, but good will prevail against it. This is the teaching of many faiths, and in that assurance we gain strength for a long journey. . . .

We did not ask for this mission, yet there is honor in history's call. We have a chance to write the story of our times, a story of courage defeating cruelty and light overcoming darkness. This calling is worthy of any life, and worthy of every nation. So let us go forward, confident, determined, and unafraid.

CONSIDER THIS:

- What was the primary message that President Bush delivered in the addresses to the American people following the terrorist attacks of September 11, 2001? What does the United States stand for as a nation? What responsibilities do European and other nations have in the war against terrorism?

THE BROADER PERSPECTIVE:

- The attacks of September 11, 2001, caused much debate throughout the world, especially concerning the definition of terrorism. Prime Minister Tony Blair of the United Kingdom in a speech before Parliament on September 14, 2001, argued that the terrorists wore "the ultimate badge of the fanatic; they are prepared to commit suicide in pursuit of their beliefs. Our beliefs are the very opposite of the fanatics. We believe in reason, democracy, and tolerance." How do terrorists differ from "freedom fighters?" Were the American rebels in 1776 guilty of illegitimate terrorist acts?

- What is the difference between "Chechan rebels" and "Chechan terrorists?" Was the crisis in the United States an opportunity for Russian president Putin to legitimize his campaign against Chechan separatists as a war against terror, thereby allying with the United States and gaining moral and perhaps financial support? Will these old enemies be linked through a common goal? Is the goal security or freedom?

Militant Islam and the West

Shortly after the tragic terrorist attack on September 11, 2001, the United States focused its political, economic, and military resources on combating the destabilizing elements that had lent support to the al-Qaeda terrorists. The Bush administration developed an alliance with General Pervez Musharraf's military dictatorship to use Pakistan as a base of operations against the Taliban government in Afghanistan. The Taliban was an extremist Islamic regime that had openly brutalized women and had offered cover and supplies to al-Qaeda. Although the United States was unable to hunt down Osama bin Laden, its invasion of Afghanistan and subsequent overthrow of the Taliban drew general world support as a legitimate response to a vicious terrorist act and a cruel extremist government.

It soon became evident that al-Qaeda was but one of several terrorist organizations that were actively recruiting members and pursuing independent operations against Western governments. In fact, international terrorism had been a product of anger and frustration in the Middle East for decades. But a new era began in 1979 when followers of the exiled Ayatollah Khomeini overthrew the government of the shah of Iran, took hostages at the American embassy, and held them for nearly eighteen months to unify the Iranian revolution and to humiliate the "Great Satan." The next decade saw attacks on the U.S. Marine barracks in Beirut in 1983 and the bombing of Pam Am flight 103 over Lockerbie, Scotland, in December 1988. The World Trade Center was bombed in 1993, followed subsequently by attacks on American embassies in Kenya and Tanzania, and the suicide bombing of the guided missile destroyer, USS *Cole,* in October 2000 as it was harbored in the Yemeni port of Aden.

Although these attacks were sponsored by a variety of terrorist groups or states like Iran, Syria, and Libya, it became apparent that the connecting link was a radical Islamic fundamentalist theology. The attacks were directed against European and American governments, not only for their advocacy of democracy but most importantly for their culture of social permissiveness. Radical Islamic clerics, whose narrow interpretation of Islamic law was absolute in its opposition to Western influences, rejected the corruption of modernity and advocated a doctrinal purity that would redefine the Islamic community spiritually and shape it as a political force. In several Middle Eastern nations, the extreme gulf between rich and poor had limited political and economic opportunities, even for university students, many of whom had attended radical Islamic schools. Militant Islam offered a pathway for the frustrated and empowerment for the devout.

The rise of such fundamentalist devotion stemmed from a complex interaction of social, economic, and cultural factors that increasingly affected European countries after 1945. Many people had migrated after World War II from former colonial holdings to take up residency in the rather homogeneous countries of Britain, France, Germany, the Netherlands, and the Scandinavian region. These nations struggled, especially during the 1980s and 1990s, to provide education, employment, and social services to an increasingly diverse population.

Although Islam remains inherently a moderate religion, nevertheless those fearing change or looking for doctrinal purity have found energy and direction in radical, militant Islam. The first decade of the twenty-first century has witnessed an ongoing debate on cultural integration and tolerance.

"Fanaticism Is Not a State of Religion, But a State of Mind" (July 11, 2005)

TONY BLAIR

On March 11, 2004, a series of coordinated bombings against the commuter train system in Madrid killed 192 people and injured 2,050. Within two days, it was confirmed that the attacks had been perpetrated by a radical Islamic group from Morocco. This had been the largest coordinated attack since the destruction of the

"'Fanaticism Is Not a State of Religion'" is from Tony Blair, a speech delivered to Parliament, London, England on July 11, 2005. Contained in *Vital Speeches of the Day*, July 15, 2005, pp. 578–580.

World Trade Center. But on July 7, 2005, in another example of a large-scale coordinated attack by militant Islam, this time by an indigenous faction of British citizens, three explosions within fifty seconds of each other ripped through London's underground system. An hour later, a fourth bomb destroyed a bus as it was filling with passengers. Over a hundred people were either confirmed dead or injured. Prime Minister Tony Blair's remarks to Parliament four days later demonstrate Britain's commitment to the rule of law without abandoning the values and spirit of moderation that define British society.

The whole Parliament, I know, will want to state our feelings strongly. We express our revulsion at this murderous carnage of the innocent. We send our deep and abiding sympathy and prayers to the victims and their families. We are united in our determination that our country will not be defeated by such terror but will defeat it and emerge from this horror with our values, our way of life, our tolerance and respect for others, undiminished. . . .

It seems probable that the attack was carried out by Islamist extremist terrorists, of the kind who over recent years have been responsible for so many innocent deaths in Madrid, Bali, Saudi Arabia, Russia, Kenya, Tanzania, Pakistan, Yemen, Turkey, Egypt and Morocco, of course in New York on September 11th, but in many other countries too. . . .

Mr. Speaker, the 7th of July will always be remembered as a day of terrible sadness for our country and for London. Yet it is true that just four days later, London's buses, trains, and as much of its underground as is possible, are back on normal schedules; its businesses, shops, and schools are open; its millions of people are coming to work with a steely determination that is genuinely remarkable.

Yesterday, we celebrated the heroism of World War II including the civilian heroes of London's blitz. Today what a different city London is—a city of many cultures, faiths, and races, hardly recognizable from the London of 1945. So different and yet, in the face of this attack, there is something wonderfully familiar in the confident spirit which moves through the city, enabling it to take the blow but still not flinch from reasserting its will to triumph over adversity. Britain may be different today, but the coming together is the same.

And I say to our Muslim community. People know full well that the overwhelming majority of Muslims stand four square with every other community in Britain. We were proud of your contribution to Britain before last Thursday. We remain proud of it today. Fanaticism is not a state of religion, but a state of mind. We will work with you to make the moderate and true voice of Islam heard as it should be.

Together, we will ensure that though terrorists can kill, they will never destroy the way of life we share and which we value, and which we will defend with the strength of belief and conviction so that it is to us and not to the terrorists, that victory will belong.

CONSIDER THIS:

- In his address to Parliament after the London bombings, Prime Minister Tony Blair emphasized the "steely determination" of the British people in confronting adversity and compared it to the heroic attitude that helped Londoners persevere during World War II. How has London changed since 1945? What unites British society in the face of such conflict?

- What did Blair mean by the statement, "Fanaticism is not a state of religion, but a state of mind?" Why has the "true voice of Islam" had difficulty being heard? Is fanatical action more influential than the forces of moderation and tradition that stand in opposition to it?

"This Is Going to Be Freedom's Century" (March 29, 2006)

GEORGE W. BUSH

The United States, after its successful overthrow of the Taliban regime in November 2001, began the difficult process of bringing security and democratic government to Afghanistan. The war on terror, however, lost momentum as Osama bin Laden evaded capture. The Bush administration subsequently focused its efforts on the nation of Iraq, accusing its leader, Saddam Hussein, of harboring nuclear weapons that threatened the United States and its allies. On March 19, 2003, U.S. armed forces invaded Iraq and quickly defeated Saddam's organized resistance. But no weapons of mass destruction were found, and the Bush administration, which had argued there was a direct link between Saddam and Osama bin Laden, was forced to admit that its intelligence was flawed. President Bush's invasion plans were nearly unilateral as he rejected the involvement of the United Nations and only garnered minimal support from other nations beyond the significant commitment of Great Britain.

Although American forces were initially hailed as liberators, it was evident within a matter of weeks that the Bush administration had not prepared adequately for the postinvasion occupation. With the disbanding of the Iraqi army, terrorists throughout the region, most of them advocating radical Islamic doctrine, poured into Iraq, gaining momentum and unity in opposition to Western occupation of the region. Intent on consolidation, the Bush administration changed its invasion justification from defending against Saddam's military threat to defending Iraqi freedom and a nascent democracy as lynchpins in the war against terror.

In the first selection, President Bush explains his policies; in the second, Senator Russ Feingold of Wisconsin argues a different vision of national security. The Western response to militant Islam continues to be a defining component of the global war against terror.

In our history, most democratic progress has come with the end of a war. After the defeat of the Axis powers in World War II and the collapse of communism in the Cold War, scores of nations cleared away the rubble of tyranny and laid the foundations of freedom and democracy.

Today, the situation is very different. Liberty is advancing not in a time of peace, but in the midst of a war, at a moment when a global movement of great brutality and ambition is fighting freedom's progress with all the hateful violence they can muster. In this new century, the advance of freedom is vital element of our strategy to protect the American people, and to secure the peace for generations to come. We're fighting the terrorists across the world because we know that if America were not fighting this enemy in other lands, we'd be facing them here in our own land. . . .

In the wake of recent violence in Iraq, many Americans are asking legitimate questions: Why are Iraqis so divided? And did America cause the instability by removing Saddam Hussein from power? They ask, after three elections, why are the Iraqi people having such a hard time coming together? And can a country with so many divisions ever build a

"This Is Going to Be Freedom's Century" is from George W. Bush, a speech delivered at the Freedom House, Washington, D.C., March 29, 2006. Contained in *Vital Speeches of the Day*, April 1, 2006, pp. 355–358.

stable democracy? They ask why we can't bring our troops home now and let the Iraqis sort out their differences on their own. . . .

The argument that Iraq was stable under Saddam and that stability is now in danger because we removed him is wrong. While liberation has brought its own set of challenges, Saddam Hussein's removal from power was the necessary first step in restoring stability and freedom to the people of Iraq.

Today some Americans are asking why the Iraqi people are having such a hard time building a democracy. The reason is that the terrorists and former regime elements are exploiting the wounds inflicted under Saddam's tyranny. The enemies of a free Iraq are employing the same tactics Saddam used—killing and terrorizing the Iraqi people in an effort to foment sectarian division. For the Saddamists, provoking sectarian strife is business as usual. And we know from the terrorists' own words that they're using the same tactics with the goal of inciting a civil war. . . . Yet, despite massive provocations, Iraq has not descended into civil war. Most Iraqis have not turned to violence.

Finally, some Americans are asking if it's time to pull out our troops and leave the Iraqis to settle their own differences. I know the work in Iraq is really difficult, but I strongly feel it's vital to the security of our country. The terrorists are killing and maiming and fighting desperately to stop the formation of a unity government because they understand when a free Iraq sets root in Iraq, it will be a mortal blow to their aspirations to dominate the region and advance their hateful vision. So they're determined to stop the advance of a free Iraq, and we must be equally determined to stop them. . . . If we leave Iraq before the job is done, the terrorists will move in and fill the vacuum, and they will use that failed state to bring murder and destruction to freedom-loving nations.

I know some in our country disagree with my decision to liberate Iraq. Whatever one thought about the decision to remove Saddam from power, I hope we should all agree that pulling our troops out prematurely would be a disaster. If we were to let the terrorists drive us out of Iraq, we would signal to the world that America cannot be trusted to keep its word. We would undermine the morale of our troops by betraying the cause for which they have sacrificed. We would cause the tyrants in the Middle East to laugh at our failed resolve and tighten their repressive grip. The global terrorist movement would be emboldened and more dangerous than ever. For the security of our citizens and the peace of the world, we will not turn the future of Iraq over to the followers of a failed dictator, or to evil men like Osama bin Laden.

American National Security and the Mission in Iraq (August 23, 2005)

RUSS FEINGOLD

In my view, all Americans. . . must renew a commitment to correcting the mistakes that have been made in American national security priorities by this [Bush] administration. We must speak often, we must speak well, and we must speak with passion about American lives and about protecting our nation from the fanatical persons and organizations that attacked us on September the 11th, 2001 and continue to attack us. . . .

And that threat is presenting itself all over the world. You see it in Indonesia, you see it in the Philippines, and you see it in places like Algeria and Northern Africa, not mention the more obvious examples like Madrid and

"American National Security and the Mission in Iraq" is from Russ Feingold, a speech delivered to Town Hall, Los Angeles, California, on August 23, 2005. Contained in *Vital Speeches of the Day*, September 1, 2005, pp. 678–683.

London. It's good to turn to the definition that the 9/11 Commission report itself gave of what this threat is: "The enemy is not Islam, the great world faith, but a perversion of Islam," the report reads. "The enemy goes beyond al-Qaeda to include the radical ideological movement inspired in part by al-Qaeda that has spawned other terrorist groups and violence. Thus our strategy must match our means to two ends: dismantling the al-Qaeda network and in the long term prevailing over the ideology that contributes to Islamist terrorism."...

In other words, what we need in the fight against terrorism is a major course correction in how we are going about it. The fight against terrorism has to do with the jihadist terrorist threat. And it is my view that the lack of presidential and administration leadership has set up a situation where we are actually feeding the insurgency in Iraq.

Now, I supported the Afghanistan invasion. I thought the Administration did an excellent job post 9/11 of calmly and carefully lining up support for what had to be done to attack the Taliban and bin Laden. And I was therefore awfully puzzled when President Bush shifted the focus to Iraq. . . . The very people who were helping us [root out the terrorists] became less politically able to help us because of the way we went into the Iraq war. So I see it, in many ways, as being a tactical error in the larger war against terrorism. . . .

We must simultaneously and quickly move to the fundamental national security concerns of opposing this international jihadist terrorist network. . . . Let me just list a few ways of trying to oppose this threat. . . . Terrorists find active and passive support among the alienated and disaffected. We need to think about the reasons for that disaffection, and start addressing those problems with our policy and acknowledging those problems with our words. . . . We need to start talking about corruption and empowering those forces to use the rule of law to combat the insidious influence of corruption. . . . Pakistan, Saudi Arabia, and other countries which are symbols among the Islamic people of places where we support regimes that deny the very freedoms that we Americans talk about when we go to war to fight for freedom.

We need to do much more to stop nuclear proliferation and assure that terrorist organizations do not get access to nuclear weapons. . . . And finally, and this goes to the word passion that I used earlier. We need a new massive surge in public and private diplomacy, and a passionate effort to tell the rest of the world who we are, who we really are, and who we want to be with regard to the rest of the people of the world. . . . It is time for a real dialogue, a give and take, and a sustained effort to regain the special American power—our power to lead, persuade, and to inspire that this administration's policies have squandered.

Consider This:

- The Bush Doctrine argues that "preemptive war" is fully legitimate in protecting the interests of the United States. Under this doctrine, the attack or invasion of another sovereign country may be necessary to "root out" and destroy foreign enemies to protect the domestic security of the United States. Do you think this is a legitimate argument and this doctrine is necessary to win the "war on terror?" Did the invasions of Afghanistan and Iraq promote the security of the United States? Was one a war of necessity and the other a war of choice? Or were both necessary?

- According to Senator Russ Feingold, the United States became less secure as a nation after the invasion of Iraq. He argues that terrorism "finds active and passive support among the alienated and disaffected" and that corruption and a disregard for the rule of law are key components in the spread of militant Islam. To what extent do you agree with his vision of national security?

The Broader Perspective:

- How does the "war against terror" differ from previous American military campaigns? Would you describe it as an ideological conflict, a war for "hearts and minds," much like Vietnam during the Cold War era? In the war against terror, how do you identify the enemy?

- How should Western nations defend themselves most effectively against the threat of fanatical terrorists? What is the price that must be paid for greater domestic security? Must personal freedom inevitably be compromised? How much liberty are you willing to lose to be safe?

- Is "defensive imperialism" a valid and necessary security strategy or simply a self-proclaimed justification for invasion that denigrates diplomacy as a tool of foreign policy?

- Do you agree with President Bush that "if America were not fighting the enemy in foreign lands, we'd be facing them here in our own land?" In 1964, President Lyndon Johnson defended the presence of United States troops in Vietnam by arguing that if we did not stop the communists in Southeast Asia, we would be facing them "on the shores of Hawaii." Has the argument changed at all?